PENS AND SWORDS

PENS AND SWORDS

How the American Mainstream Media
Report the Israeli-Palestinian Conflict

Marda Dunsky

COLUMBIA UNIVERSITY PRESS   NEW YORK

Columbia University Press
Publishers Since 1893
New York Chichester, West Sussex
Copyright © 2008 Marda Dunsky

Library of Congress Cataloging-in-Publication Data
Dunsky, Marda.
Pens and swords : how the American mainstream media report the
Israeli-Palestinian conflict / Marda Dunsky.
p. cm.
Includes bibliographical references and index.
ISBN 978-0-231-13348-7 (cloth : alk. paper)
ISBN 978-0-231-13349-4 (pbk. : alk. paper)
ISBN 978-0-231-50826-1 (electronic)
1. Arab-Israeli conflict—Mass media and the conflict.
2. Arab-Israeli conflict—Foreign public opinion, American.
3. Israel—Politics and government—21st century—Public opinion.
4, Middle East—Politics and government— 21st century—Public opinion
5. Palestinian Arabs—Politics and government— 21st century—Public opinion.
6 Public opinion—United States.
I. Title.

DS119.7.D86   2007
956.9405'4—dc22   2007026274

Columbia University Press books are printed on
permanent and durable acid-free paper.

Printed in the United States of America
Designed by Audrey Smith

c 10 9 8 7 6 5 4 3 2 1
p 10 9 8 7 6 5 4 3 2 1

For my father, Fred Dunsky,
who understood the power and beauty of words

CONTENTS

ACKNOWLEDGMENTS

WITHOUT AN EDITOR WHO SHARES HER VISION, A WRITER MAY NEVER realize it. It was my very good fortune to have found such an editor in John Michel of Columbia University Press, who responded immediately and with great enthusiasm when I submitted the initial query for *Pens and Swords* in the spring of 2003.

John recognized that a study of mainstream American reporting of the Israeli-Palestinian conflict could be of interest to a broad audience. His great support—especially the patience and generous amounts of time he extended to me in many phone conversations both before and after this project was under contract—was of immense value to an author undertaking her first scholarly book. I deeply regret that I never had the opportunity to meet John, who passed away in early 2005, and that he did not see this project come to fruition.

I am also indebted to Loren Ghiglione, dean of the Medill School of Journalism at Northwestern University when I wrote and revised the first two drafts of *Pens and Swords* from 2003 to 2005. Loren maintained an unflagging interest in the project and extended to me, as a member of his faculty, the time and other resources needed to complete the project. He read the manuscript from beginning to end and was a continual source of encouragement.

As any reporter knows, cultivating good sources is key to telling the story. Wishing to include the perspectives of correspondents who had reported on the Israeli-Palestinian conflict for major U.S. media outlets, I turned to Stephen Franklin of the *Chicago Tribune*, himself an experienced reporter of that story. A longtime friend and former *Tribune* colleague, Steve was instrumental in identifying and putting me in touch with many of the correspondents whose interviews appear in chapters 5 and 6. Although I will not name them individually here, I am also grateful to each of these fifteen journalists, who agreed to go on record and talk about their experiences and perspectives on reporting the Israeli-Palestinian story from the field. They are identified by name in the chapters in which their interviews appear.

In writing *Pens and Swords*, I had the satisfaction of being able to call on current and former students for assistance. After taking my newspaper-editing course at Medill, Abbas Khan became an invaluable asset to this project as my research assistant and copy editor. His proficiency in database research, intuitive understanding of the topic, and sharp eye in reading two drafts of the manuscript were of immense help. Abbas went on to work as a professional editor in his own right at newspapers in Illinois and Texas.

I also received valuable assistance from Gil Hoffman, another of my former Medill students. Based in Jerusalem as a veteran reporter for the *Jerusalem Post*, Gil conducted database research of Israeli newspapers that facilitated my writing of chapter 4. Medill alums Rebecca Chang and Logan Molyneux also contributed to this project.

The process of manuscript revision and moving the project toward publication was greatly assisted by peer reviewers Robert Jensen of the University of Texas at Austin and Karim H. Karim of Carleton University in Ottawa, Canada. I benefited not only from their knowledge of journalism and mainstream reporting of both the Israeli-Palestinian conflict and, more broadly, the Arab and Muslim worlds, but also from their sense of manuscript organization and the writer's voice.

I am also grateful to Steven Livingston of the George Washington University, who shared his expertise in communications theory and guided me to scholarly sources for the theoretical overview in the introductory chapter.

Juree Sondker of Columbia University Press assumed oversight of *Pens and Swords* in mid-2005 and has seen it through production. I am grateful to Juree for keeping me on track and taking the project from manuscript to publication. I also wish to thank Henry Krawitz and Irene Pavitt for their keen and meticulous editing of the manuscript.

Last—but certainly not least—I wish to thank my husband, Mufid Qassoum. He is my intellectual partner and source of great inspiration.

PENS AND SWORDS

INTRODUCTION

WE LIVE IN A WORLD WHERE GLOBAL PUBLIC OPINION MATTERS. THIS IS NOT to say that Americans should agree with images and interpretations of the United States and its foreign policy as seen in France, China, Nigeria, or anywhere else. Nevertheless, these perceptions form the basis of opinions and actions—however accurate, rational, misguided, or dangerous they may be—that can and do affect the way we live. If the events surrounding September 11, 2001, taught us nothing else, they taught us this.

At the same time, we are living in an age in which American engagement in the Middle East and other regions in the Muslim world has never been greater. In recent years the most visible signs of this engagement have come in the form of U.S. military intervention in Iraq and Afghanistan. However, at the center lies the ongoing American role in the Israeli-Palestinian conflict. On the eve of the American war in Iraq one observer warned: "Those who so vehemently deny any linkage between the Israeli-Palestinian conflict and the broader crisis must pull their heads out of the sand."[1]

Brent Scowcroft, national security adviser in the Ford and George H. W.

Bush administrations, was one of many commentators to link the impending U.S. invasion of Iraq to the Israeli-Palestinian conflict. "The obsession of the region," Scowcroft wrote in the *Wall Street Journal* in August 2002, "is the Is-raeli-Palestinian conflict. If we were seen to be turning our backs on that bitter conflict—which the region, rightly or wrongly, perceives to be clearly within our power to resolve—in order to go after Iraq, there would be an explosion of outrage against us. We would be seen as ignoring a key interest of the Muslim world in order to satisfy what is seen to be a narrow American interest."[2]

In January 2003 Thomas Friedman, foreign affairs columnist for the *New York Times*, paid a prewar listening visit to Cairo to assess the Arab mood. Characterizing the Israeli-Palestinian conflict as the "deepest hurt" of his Egyptian interlocutors, Friedman reported:

> Yes, official Arab newspapers and TV have nourished Arab anger toward America and Israel for decades—and still do. And one regime after an-other has exploited this conflict for political purposes. But when you sit in a room at the U.S. ambassador's house with 30 bright young Egyp-tian entrepreneurs, mostly U.S.-educated, and this issue is practically all they want to talk about—or you meet with American studies students at Cairo University and they tell you that many students in their class refused to play a simulation game of the U.S. Congress for fear of be-ing tainted—you feel that there has to be something authentic in their anger about this open wound. . . . I am not talking about what is right, or what is fair, or even what is rational. I am talking about what is.[3]

More than a year after the war had begun, President George W. Bush was still taking a great deal of diplomatic flak on the issue of the Israeli-Palestin-ian conflict. This was not only because the invasion and occupation of Iraq had failed to stabilize the country and establish a foundation for demo-cratic rule after the capture of Saddam Hussein—which Bush asserted was a prerequisite for resolving the Israeli-Palestinian conflict. It was also because the Bush administration had unilaterally formulated a "Greater Middle East Initiative" aimed at spreading democracy throughout the region beyond Iraq while the peace process had reached a standstill.

At an Arab League summit convened in Tunis in May 2004, Tunisian For-eign Minister Habib Ben Yahia declared, "The issue of the Palestinian people is the first issue and top priority issue."[4] While his words may have seemed both formulaic and predictable, Ben Yahia reiterated what many other Arab leaders were saying in response to Bush's plan for democratization: show us progress on the Israeli-Palestinian issue first and then we'll talk to you about reform. Nail al-Jubeir, spokesman for the Saudi embassy in Washington, told the *San Francisco Chronicle*: "In the Arab world, everything is interconnected. To resolve the Arab-Israeli conflict is a must, to reach justice and equity for the Palestinian people in the territories. Anything without [that] is not going to go anywhere."[5] Nabil Fahmy, Egyptian ambassador to the United States, told NPR: "Calls for reform from abroad will never be given the credibility they need if they don't hold the same standards as responding to the problem that is most difficult for Middle Easterners, which is [the] Arab-Israeli conflict. If you're going to come and say, 'We will help you change your societies, but we won't help you solve the problem greatest on your mind,' people will question your own credibility and sincerity."[6]

It is clear, then, that the American mainstream media have given considerable play to the idea that the Israeli-Palestinian conflict is at the center of U.S. interests and aspirations in the Middle East, and that democratizing the region is tied to resolving the conflict. However, it is also clear, as this study will show, that mainstream reporting of the conflict itself rarely goes much beyond superficial details of failed diplomatic initiatives and intercommunal violence in the field—leaving the American public without important contextual information about why the conflict remains so intractable. The reporting of events takes on a familiar cast: violence begets violence; new diplomatic initiatives are announced; "relative calm" ensues for short periods—and then the pattern inevitably repeats itself.

Clearly something is missing from this picture. How the American mainstream media report and frame key issues of the conflict is the focus of this study. *Pens and Swords* presents evidence of how, time and again, the media bypass important contextual aspects of organic issues, such as the U.S. role in the peace process, the Palestinian refugee question, and Israeli settlements. It examines how superficial, dramatic story arcs of events in the field overshadow and virtually eclipse a number of important questions that go to the root of the conflict and its trajectory—leaving them unasked, unanswered, and virtually absent from public and policy discourses. These include:

- How can the United States claim the role of honest broker in the conflict when it overwhelmingly favors Israel with diplomatic support and economic and military aid? What effect have this support and aid had on the trajectory of the conflict, and how do they currently advance or impede U.S. interests in the region as a whole?

- Of what importance to the peace process are the historical circumstances under which the Palestinian refugee issue originated and the body of international law and consensus on refugee rights? Does a balance exist between recognizing the right of return in principle and the actual return of a significant number of Palestinian refugees to what is now Israel?
- What role has U.S. aid to Israel played in indirectly subsidizing its colonization of the West Bank and Gaza Strip since 1967—and the deep imprint of occupation that has remained in Gaza even after Israel withdrew its settlers and military in 2005? Will realpolitik be the determining factor in the fate of the West Bank settlements, or will international law also play a role?

The patterns of reporting addressed in the chapters that follow suggest that to a significant extent American mainstream journalism on the Israeli-Palestinian conflict toes the line of U.S. Mideast policy. To engage the critical questions just posed would require significant questioning of that policy, something most mainstream reporting of international affairs simply does not do.

The questions left unasked in the reporting of the Israeli-Palestinian conflict have parallels in the reporting of other international conflicts. Whether the dateline is Jerusalem or Bogotá, Belgrade or Karachi, mainstream American foreign correspondence tends toward uncritical reportage of U.S. policy in the international arena while conflicts are in play. Only after tragedies such as the Rwandan genocide are over, costly wars such as the Vietnam War have been fought, and long-running conflicts such as the cold war have ended do the media embark on critical inquiries of American foreign policy. As one media scholar observed, "In each of the historical cases of Kennedy and the Bay of Pigs, Johnson and Vietnam, Nixon and Cambodia, Carter and the hostages in Iran, and Reagan and Lebanon, journalists initially adopted the perspective of the government."[7]

Journalists often see themselves as writing the first draft of history, reporting on events and conflicts as they unfold. However, journalists do much more than that. In framing the issues that underlie those events, they also shape the discourse that can directly or indirectly influence how those events will continue to unfold. Before considering the patterns of American mainstream media reporting of the Israeli-Palestinian conflict, a brief discussion of *why* such patterns in international reporting exist is in order.

A THEORETICAL DIVERSION

Why do American journalism ethics emphasize the concept of balance when in mainstream reporting of certain stories over time some points of view enjoy repeated exposure while others receive next to none? Why is objectivity a cherished precept of American journalism when important contextual aspects of certain stories—particularly those involving international conflict—get little if any media play? The answers to these questions are found not in journalistic codes of ethics but in journalistic phenomenology, not in analyses of what news events themselves mean but in the meanings embedded in the practice of journalism itself. Three key ideas relate to journalism considered as a *social phenomenon* rather than as a practiced profession: journalism is imbued with social values; it constructs social reality; and a process of journalistic framing determines how certain issues are reported.

Considered in this light, journalism does not merely reflect events—despite the old saw that journalists don't create reality but just report it. Understanding the meanings behind journalistic reporting thus requires a bit of theoretical deconstruction. Such a side trip may seem far afield from the empirical "who-what-when-where-why-and-how" terrain inhabited by working journalists and familiar to the news-consuming public. So why leave Kansas for Oz? Why venture into the realm of communications theory when discussing how the American mainstream media report the Israeli-Palestinian conflict?

There are two reasons to consider the theoretical underpinnings of journalism. The first is that a brief theoretical discussion reveals that in some respects mainstream coverage of this particular conflict is not unique, that characteristics of the coverage can be found in reporting of other international conflicts and important social issues. The second is that an exposition of these characteristics in a general theoretical sense provides a framework for understanding the practical evidence that follows, namely, the many examples of reporting on various aspects of the Israeli-Palestinian conflict presented in this study.

A discussion of theory that addresses some of the factors that shape mainstream journalism in general—and mainstream media coverage of the Israeli-Palestinian conflict in particular—first requires a brief explanation of what mainstream media are understood to be, at least for the purpose of the study at hand. The term "mainstream media" is often used as if there is no need to define it, which renders a precise or universal definition elusive.

However, the sense of the term used in a news context frequently links it to public interest, democracy, and/or classical functions of journalism in a free society. As one media observer put it, "A critical aspect of a functioning democracy is to be well informed in order to participate effectively in that democracy. One of the most important ways that many people are informed is through their mainstream media. . . . Most people get their view of the world from mainstream media. It is, therefore, important that mainstream media be objective and present accurate and diverse representations of what goes on around the world."[8]

As to what, exactly, the mainstream media comprise, one definition has it that "technically, 'mainstream media' includes outlets that are in harmony with the prevailing direction of influence in the culture at large."[9] The vehicles of the mainstream news media are commonly identified as daily newspapers, weekly news magazines, broadcast and cable television and radio networks, and news Web sites affiliated with these outlets. Reporting on the Israeli-Palestinian conflict from these types of mainstream news media sources is the basis for the media criticism in this study.

Two characterizations of mainstream media—quite different but not necessarily contradictory—are appropriate. First, phrases that include the word "public" are useful in articulating a characterization of mainstream media that is, in itself, mainstream. Such media produce journalism in the public interest, and that type of journalism is aimed at informing (rather than swaying) public opinion. Mainstream media therefore also serve what Jürgen Habermas has defined as the public sphere, which in its ideal form is "made up of private people gathered together as a public and articulating the needs of society with the state."[10] In contrast to alternative media, which seek to impart distinct personal and/or partisan points of view, the mainstream media in news reporting—as opposed to clearly labeled opinion and analysis pieces such as editorials, commentaries, and columns—seek to report without any identifiable partisan or individual bias for the benefit of an audience that is presumed to be so broadly based that it lacks any single, clear partisan interest or identity.

Given this distinction—and especially in view of the analysis of American mainstream media reporting of the Israeli-Palestinian conflict that follows—it is perhaps advisable to juxtapose an alternative characterization of mainstream media. This view holds that the ultimate product of the system that produces American mainstream journalism—a system that in the twenty-first century is virtually entirely corporate-owned—is not news and information per se but *audiences*, which are sold to the advertisers whose products and services are displayed as part of the news-and-information package. One observer of mainstream media has argued alternatively that, given these circumstances, one could assume that "the product of the media, what appears, what doesn't appear, the way it is slanted, will reflect the interest of the buyers and sellers, the institutions and the power systems that are around them."[11]

Journalistic Values versus Values in Journalism

Any code of journalism ethics, newsroom stylebook, or news organization's credo is bound to contain words that bespeak *professional* values. These values describe the goals of professional journalism, which include accuracy, accountability, balance, diversity, fairness, objectivity, and truth. However, what about the notion that the practice of mainstream journalism is itself infused with *social* values that emphasize various narrative themes and minimize or bypass others—and thus determine, to a significant degree, the nature and message of the product?

Media theorist Herbert Gans has written that journalists do more than observe reality and report events: "The news does not limit itself to reality judgments; it also contains values, or preference statements. This in turn makes it possible to suggest that there is, underlying the news, a picture of nation and society as it ought to be."[12] In deciding what to include and what to omit from their reports, journalists are guided by normative values that they share with their audience. Thus, in journalistic reportage "value exclusion is therefore accompanied by value inclusion, both through story selection and opinions expressed in specific stories."[13] Of the "enduring values in the news" identified by Gans, the most relevant to the present discussion are individualism, social order, altruistic democracy, and ethnocentrism. The media use these and other values to support a shared narrative understanding of the United States and the role it plays in the international community.[14]

Consider, for example, how the Palestinian refugee question and the issue of Israeli settlements are depicted in American mainstream media reporting of the Israeli-Palestinian conflict. What can be understood from reporting that repeatedly and consistently depicts refugees as angry and hostile dreamers and that lacks important contextual references to the historical circumstances that created the refugees' status and their rights as defined by international law and consensus? What can be understood from reporting on Israeli settlements that focuses primarily on the viewpoints of settlers and their supporters or opponents within Israeli society to the virtual exclusion of the status of the settlements according to international law and consensus, as well as their effect on Palestinian lives and the course of the peace process?

According to Gans, such a pattern of reporting could be attributed to a common framework of social values shared by journalists and their audience. In this case, those who hold such values attach minimal importance to the refugees' historical circumstance and recognition of their legal rights while recognizing the historical and moral forces behind the creation of the State of Israel and its geostrategic importance as the United States' primary ally in the Middle East. As Gans has observed, "The values in news are rarely explicit and must be found between the lines—in what actors and activities are reported or ignored, and in how they are described. If a news story deals with activities which are generally undesirable and whose descriptions contain negative connotations, then the story implicitly expresses a value about what is desirable."[15]

The value of individualism that Gans identifies also sheds light on this way of covering Palestinian refugees and Israeli settlements in the sense that the reporting tends to focus on the situations of individuals—be they refugees or settlers—rather than on the social policies, structures, or processes that contextualize their claims vis-à-vis their rights.[16] According to communications theorist W. Lance Bennett, such reporting, whether personalized or individualized, "gives preference to human-interest angles in events while downplaying institutional and political considerations that establish their social contexts."[17]

While journalists depend on this anecdotally based approach as a device to hold the interest of their audiences, such value-infused reporting has political consequences, such as depriving the public of sufficient information with which to challenge government policy. Bennett writes: "Without a grasp of power structures, it is virtually impossible to understand how the political system really works. As a result, the political world becomes a mystical realm populated by actors who either have the political 'force' on their side or do not. The absence of attention to power further encourages the audience to abandon political analysis in favor of casting their political fates with the hero of the moment."[18]

In his study of U.S. television coverage of the Vietnam War, Daniel Hallin found that reporting of the air war during the Vietnam era was based precisely on the value of individualism. The air campaigns involved two controversial political issues, namely, whether the bombing was effective and the moral issues raised by civilian casualties. TV coverage of the air war, however, tended to focus primarily if not exclusively on the pilots' personal experiences and the technology of the aircraft and the bombs, relegating the political issues to the margins. The resulting coverage, Hallin found, was focused squarely "from 'inside' American policy, from the point of view of those carrying it out, with very little critical distance."[19]

Parameters of Discourse

While professional journalism's credos equate informing public opinion with upholding a pillar of democratic society, some scholars and critics view the media as engaging in precisely the opposite: They limit public opinion by adopting assumptions about news values that preserve the social order to which Gans referred or, alternatively, that remain within a field of terms and premises that do not overstep "hegemonic boundaries," as described by media critic Todd Gitlin. Among these assumptions, according to Gitlin, are that "news involves the novel event, not the underlying, enduring condition; the person, not the group; the visible conflict, not the deep consensus; the fact that 'advances the story,' not the one that explains or enlarges it."[20] As such, these assumptions are perfectly compatible with the patterns of reporting on the issues of Palestinian refugees and Israeli settlements characterized earlier.

Using varying schema and terminology, communications scholars have defined parameters of discourse to which the media adhere when reporting on socially or politically sensitive issues, and these parameters reinforce the concept of hegemonic boundaries to which Gitlin referred. Hallin has employed a paradigm illustrated by two concentric circles, with the "sphere of consensus" the smaller, interior circle and the "sphere of legitimate controversy" the larger, outer circle. All else that lies beyond belongs to the "sphere of deviance."

Hallin has characterized the bull's-eye sphere of consensus as the realm where "journalists do not feel compelled either to present opposing views or to remain disinterested observers. On the contrary, the journalist's role is to serve as an advocate or celebrant of consensus values." One step beyond, the sphere of legitimate controversy is the realm where sanctioned opposing voices are heard, permitting "objectivity and balance [to] reign as the supreme journalistic values." The no-man's-land of the sphere of deviance is inhabited by "those political actors and views which journalists and the political mainstream of the society reject as unworthy of being heard." Although Hallin offered a qualifier—namely, that "each sphere has internal gradations, and the boundaries between them are often fuzzy"—he nonetheless concluded that much American television reporting of the Vietnam

War was safely located within the sphere of consensus—despite the lack of military censorship.[21]

In his study of how media tend to use different standards to define violence and terrorism when reporting on Western and Muslim societies, Karim H. Karim used parallel terminology to define these three realms of discourse. *Dominant discourse* provides definitions, frames of reference, and agendas that form the basis for public discussion and tend to reinforce the status quo. *Oppositional discourse* counters the specific viewpoints found in dominant discourse but supports the same basic premises upon which it rests. *Alternative discourse* challenges the very premises of dominant discourse and does not conform to its ideological frameworks.[22] While acknowledging the work of a handful of journalists whose reporting on aspects of the Muslim world exemplified context and nuance found in the realms of oppositional and even alternative discourse, Karim noted that such examples "are drowned out by the constant din of the [dominant] discourses that capitalize on the store of negative images to present 'Islam' as a primary obstacle to global peace."[23]

In international reporting, the boundaries of these realms of discourse become more sharply defined when constituent interest/pressure groups with strengths and weaknesses parallel to those of the parties in conflict abroad—in this instance the pro-Israel and pro-Palestinian advocacy communities in the United States—exist within the journalist's home society. Such a situation can influence reporting of the conflict because the media derive reality judgments and preference statements from themes found in public discourse that such pressure groups generate—the parameters of which are defined by commonly held social values. According to Gans, "Journalists cannot exercise news judgment without a composite of nation, society and national and social institutions in their collective heads, and this picture is an aggregate of reality judgments. . . . Many reality judgments are stereotypes, accurate or inaccurate, which journalists borrow from elsewhere because of their availability and familiarity both to the journalists and the audience."[24]

The task of reporting such international conflicts objectively is further complicated by foreign policy. Foreign policy preferences combine with public discourse from within civil society to set the tone and define the parameters of reporting. The degree of journalistic rigor and challenge that go into monitoring centers of domestic power, whether local or national, is often greatly diminished when it comes to the reporting of international events. The American media, Gans has written, "tend to follow American foreign policy, even if not slavishly, but they hew closer to the State Department line on foreign news than to the White House line on domestic news."[25]

Also relevant are the values of altruistic democracy and ethnocentrism that Gans identifies. For example, can the American mainstream media be expected to question how patterns of U.S. foreign aid—which have greatly favored Israel since 1967—may have negatively affected the chances for a negotiated resolution to the Israeli-Palestinian conflict when that aid is both given by one democratic society to another and assigned a positive social value because it is thought to advance American interests in the region?

When faced with such an apparent contradiction, it is highly unlikely that the media will address such a critical question because the reporting must essentially be self-referential when an ally is the focal point of inquiry. As one media scholar has observed, "When we're talking about ourselves, we tend to tell stories that support official policies and actions and to avoid telling stories that are critical of our military, economic and political institutions."[26] In a similar vein, media critics Edward S. Herman and Noam Chomsky cite patterns of uncritical U.S. media reporting on such American client states as Indonesia—specifically its invasion and former occupation of East Timor—and Chile and Guatemala, whose "basic institutional structures, including the state terror system, were put in place and maintained by, or with crucial assistance from, U.S. power."[27]

Thus, the idea that U.S. aid to Israel has actually helped underwrite the cost of its occupation of the West Bank, Gaza Strip, and East Jerusalem—and has thereby *inhibited if not retarded* the peace process—is not likely to get much if any consideration in the mainstream media, however compelling or relevant the underlying facts may be. Such a notion would implicate U.S. foreign policy as a central driving factor of the Israeli-Palestinian conflict. As such, the idea lies clearly in the sphere of deviance, the realm of alternative discourse—and does not get time on the air or space on the printed page.

Constructing Reality

A foreign correspondent broadcasts a report from a war zone where a battle has just taken place; a metro desk reporter writes an account of an acrimonious city council meeting. In both cases the journalists impart *facts*. Yet they also impart *meaning* in the vocabulary they use, the sources they consult, and the interpretations they ascribe ("this will likely mean that . . ."). Meaning is further ascribed by the length and placement of their reports as determined by producers and editors. While news gathering and production may thus appear to be mere vehicles for conveying "facts" and "reality," a first principle of communications theory posits that the journalistic process also has a theoretical function, namely, to make sense of the world by constructing meanings.[28]

According to media scholar Gaye Tuchman, news does not mirror society but rather helps to constitute society as a shared social phenomenon, "for in the process of describing an event, news defines and shapes that event. . . . Stories actively define both what is deviant and what is normative. . . . By imposing such meanings, news is perpetually defining and redefining, constituting and reconstituting social phenomena."[29] This distinction is drawn more sharply by Gitlin: "The media bring a manufactured public world into private space. From within their private crevices, people find themselves relying on the media for concepts, for images of their heroes, for guiding information, for emotional charges, for recognition of values, for symbols in general. . . . The media specialize in orchestrating everyday consciousness—by virtue of their pervasiveness, their accessibility. . . . They name the world's parts, they certify reality *as* reality."[30]

To help convey reality, journalists rely not only on what they can observe but also on sources who participate in and interpret events. When reporting a dispute or conflict, journalists strive for balance by tapping sources who represent differing or opposing points of view. By balancing "truth-claims," Tuchman writes, "the professional reporter theoretically allows the news consumer to decide who is telling the truth." By doing so reporters "absolve themselves of responsibility by structuring the alternatives."[31] However, such an ideal balancing of sources does not always occur, and in the reporting of the Israeli-Palestinian conflict it routinely does not. One reason for this is that the fundamental imbalance of power between the two sides is reflected in the sourcing.

Several variations on this theme can be seen in the examples of reporting on the conflict that appear in this study: Both parties to the conflict are *not* represented in reporting on an aspect of the conflict that affects them both—or they are, only not in equal proportions. One side is allowed the opportunity to express its concerns directly, whereas the concerns of the other side are parsed and paraphrased by the journalist. The concerns of one side are represented by a mix of authoritative and person-in-the-street or "ordinary" sources, whereas the concerns of the other side are solely represented by the latter. Sources, both ordinary and authoritative, express conflicting claims—but no expert sources are called on to confirm or rebut them. When reporting on the conflict shifts to sources in the United States, representatives of the opposing sides and of equal authority may be afforded equal opportunity to comment. However, more often than not they come from the same closed circle of government and think tanks; alternative viewpoints from the realm of civil society are rarely represented.

Such patterns of sourcing imbalance are rooted in journalists' dependence on institutional or official sources, which, in Tuchman's phrase, makes news an "ally of legitimated institutions."[32] The more reputable the institution, the more reliable the source is deemed to be. Ongoing contact serves not only the reporter but also the source, as reporters "customarily form strong bonds with the sources upon whom they depend for stories. They absorb the worldviews of the powerful."[33] In a situation of conflict where the playing field is not level, reporters *do* seek out sources from the weaker side. However, sourcing imbalances nevertheless persist when one party to the conflict has a functioning government, a strong military, and well-established civil society institutions but the other side does not.

Hegemony, Framing, and the Status Quo

Gitlin calls on the theory of hegemony developed by Antonio Gramsci, the early-twentieth-century Italian Marxist political leader and theoretician, to map the position of journalists and news organizations relative to powerful sources and sources of power. Defined in this context by Gramsci and parsed by Gitlin, hegemony "is the name given to a ruling class's domination through ideology, through the shaping of popular consent." It is a process "in which one picture of the world is systematically preferred over others, usually through practical routines and at times through extraordinary measures."[34]

Gramsci developed his theory of hegemony while in prison, where he contemplated the limited revolutionary capacity of the post–World War I Italian working class. Gitlin used the theory a half century later to study the effect of mass media on the eventual "unmaking" of the American "new left" of the 1960s. The concept of hegemony is relevant to the Israeli-Palestinian conflict, as it is another context of power imbalance in which establishment and revolutionary forces clash. The link between hegemony and mainstream media reporting of the conflict is found in framing, the way in which journalists are prone to see the world, enabled by their social values and the nature of their professional routines.

Media frames, Gitlin has written, are "principles of selection, emphasis and presentation composed of little tacit theories about what exists, what happens, and what matters."[35] Framing enables hegemony through the selection and delivery of preferred images that add up to the composite preferred picture according to which, Tuchman has observed, "all identification of facts is embedded in specific understandings of the everyday world. Those understandings presuppose the legitimacy of existing institutions and are the basis of the news net. . . . News frames strips of everyday occurrences and is not a mere mirror of events."[36]

Gitlin has indicated that media framing of issues is not a conscious act on the part of journalists. Rather, they take dominant news frames for granted, reproducing and defending them without thinking of them as hegemonic: "Hegemony operates effectively . . . yet outside consciousness; it is exercised by self-conceived professionals working with a great deal of autonomy within institutions that proclaim the neutral goal of informing the public. . . . Journalists' ideals are fluid enough to protect them from seeing that their autonomy is bounded: that by going about their business in a professional way, they systematically frame the news to be compatible with the main institutional arrangements of the society. Journalists thus sustain the dominant frames through the banal, everyday momentum of their routines."[37]

According to Gitlin, news organizations "want to honor the political-economic system as a whole; their very power and prestige deeply presuppose that system." Professional journalism ethics, however, compel news organizations to report on oppositional social movements and thus allow them to enter the public ideological space. The strategy for managing contradictory ideologies of radical change versus status quo is for the media "to tame, to contain, the opposition that it dares not ignore" by keeping it within the framework of hegemonic boundaries and by processing social opposition "to control its image and to diffuse it at the same time, to absorb what can be absorbed into the dominant structure of definitions and images and to push the rest to the margins of social life."[38]

Herman and Chomsky have noted a similar threshold for toleration of oppositional discourse, and that media framing promotes hegemony in a largely unconscious way. The U.S. media, they say, "permit—indeed, encourage—spirited debate, criticism and dissent, as long as these remain faithfully within the system of presuppositions and principles that constitute an elite consensus, a system so powerful as to be internalized largely without awareness."[39]

The ultimate result of framing—both generally and as it pertains specifically to reporting of the Israeli-Palestinian conflict—runs counter to the aspirational objective of free media in a democratic society, namely, to enable the public to evaluate and challenge, *on an informed basis*, the policies that are formulated and carried out in its name. Instead, in the view of Herman and Chomsky, the media assume a propaganda function that serves a societal purpose—"but not that of enabling the public to assert meaningful control over the political process by providing them with the information needed for the intelligent discharge of political responsibilities." On the contrary, that societal purpose is to "inculcate and defend the economic, social, and political agenda of privileged groups that dominate the society and the state."[40] "The media are indeed free," they assert, "for those who adopt the principles required for their 'societal purpose.'"[41] At the same time, Herman and Chomsky distinguish clearly between the functions of the U.S. media and propaganda systems of totalitarian states.

. Lest the present analysis appear to suggest media conspiracies or Machiavellianism, it is useful to consider a further articulation of this distinction. Noting the difference between overt agitation propaganda put forth by totalitarian systems and the functions of Western media when reporting conflicts—specifically those that involve Muslims—Karim draws on the concept of *integration propaganda*. There is not, he asserts, "a deliberate plan by the mass media to portray certain issues in particular ways, but a 'naturalized' hegemonic process through which they adhere to a common field of meanings." Accordingly, the resulting integration propaganda "does not involve the aggressive presentation of specific views but a more subtle and ubiquitous mode which operates within dominant discourses. Although mainstream journalists in technological societies do challenge the day-to-day functioning of incumbent governments, they rarely bring into question the fundamental structures of thought or of power. Operating within a particular ideological system . . . mass media workers consciously or unconsciously produce integration propaganda that serves the overall interests of elites."[42]

Thus, by imparting social values, constructing reality, and framing issues, the media are seen to shape ideology that supports the established order and preserves the status quo. Gramsci referred to a "systematic (but not necessarily or even usually deliberate) engineering of mass consent to the established order" as a means to the end of hegemony.[43] Herman and Chomsky have labeled the media's role in the process as one of "manufacturing consent." Tuchman similarly observed the tendency of mainstream journalism to shore up existing processes in existing institutions: "We take for granted the embeddedness of the news net in legitimated institutions and the existence of centralized news gathering . . . and we fail to realize how that embeddedness militates against the emergence of new forms of news."[44]

The patterns of decontextualization and imbalanced sourcing found in American mainstream reporting of the Israeli-Palestinian conflict can be understood—in fact, are clearly illustrated—by these very paradigms of hegemony and news frames. References to international law and consensus are virtually omitted in reporting on Palestinian refugees and Israeli settlements, and neutral, expert sources are not called upon to assess the legitimacy of the parties' competing claims. The impact of U.S. policy on the trajectory of the conflict is rarely if ever examined, and exposition of American geostrategic interests in the region is virtually absent. Instead, the reporting presents empirical details of the conflict that support the hegemonic notions that Israelis and Palestinians alone bear responsibility for the conflict and must negotiate their own way out of it, aided by the good—and neutral—offices of the United States.

Thus, it is not difficult to understand why no "new forms of news"—which would go beyond reporting of the intercommunal violence, political maneuverings, and failed diplomatic initiatives that appear to define Israeli-Palestinian relations—have yet to emerge in U.S. mainstream media reporting of the conflict. In its failure to expose, much less challenge, the underlying status quos of the conflict, the reporting, as we will see, tends to render the conflict as endless and all too often hopeless.

Indexing: A Peg for Media Frames

Although they aspire to monitor centers of power and hold government to account, the American mainstream media nevertheless operate in the same social and economic frameworks as government. This, coupled with the media's reliance on institutional or official sources, results in a degree of interdependence between the two that manifests itself in mainstream reporting. In Bennett's view, evidence of this relationship is found in the media's tendency "to 'index' the range of voices and viewpoints in both news and editorials according to the range of views expressed in mainstream government debate about a given topic."[45] Consistent with the "sphere of consensus" and "dominant discourse" paradigms discussed earlier, indexing—which correlates the parameters of media discourse to the range of viewpoints expressed by official sources—is another device by which news coverage is framed. This tacit media-government relationship is another way in which the parameters of public discourse are limited.

Bennett characterizes indexing as "a quick and ready guide for editors and reporters to use in deciding how to cover a story. It is a rule of thumb that can be defended against questions from uneasy corporate managers and concerned citizens alike." Indexing is thus observable in patterns of journalistic content that point to "the existence of an underlying normative order" (in other words, the status quo, which produces no new forms of news), and is thus typically found in coverage of such topics as military decisions and foreign affairs—"areas of great importance not only to corporate economic interests, but to the advancement of state power as well."[46]

According to Bennett, the range of discourse is not likely to include voices found in government that are isolated or considered to be extreme. Rather, "journalists are more likely to index legitimate voices in the news according to the range of views expressed by prominent officials and members of institutional power blocs likely to influence the outcome of a situation."[47] Furthermore, when voices falling outside this "official range of debate" do find an outlet in the mainstream media, it is usually within negative interpretive contexts that include civil disobedience, protests, or lawless acts[48]—in other words, within the sphere of deviance.

Bennett tested his indexing hypothesis by examining four years' worth of *New York Times* news and editorial coverage of U.S. funding for the Nicaraguan contras, a focal point of the Reagan presidency. Based on constitutional concerns, opinion polls, and a Central American lobbying network, for over two years the House of Representatives rejected allocating any but humanitarian assistance. The turning point came in the spring of 1986, when the House opposition bloc folded and Congress passed a $100 million military aid package for the contras. According to Bennett, the policy shift hinged on "a barrage of intimidating political rhetoric, unleashed against vulnerable House members up for re-election, charging that legislators who opposed administration contra policy were soft on communism."[49]

Before and after this policy shift, Bennett found the *Times'* coverage of the issue to be consistent with the indexing paradigm "at the expense of the democratic ideal." When Congress changed its tune, so did the *Times*.

> News reports from a "watchdog press" might have emphasized more statements by interest groups, played up the outrage expressed by still-committed opponents in Congress or headlined opinion polls showing a strong majority opposed to the policy. . . . As it turned out, following the collapse of official conflict on the issue, not only did nongovernmental opposition voices all but disappear from the *Times*, but a few masthead opinions [editorials] encouraged the once-loathed policy [of U.S. funding for the contras]. . . .
>
> The evidence suggests that *Times* coverage of Nicaragua was cued by Congress, not by the paper's own political agenda or by a sense of "adversarial journalism." . . . The "responsible press" keeps its criticism within the bounds of institutional debate, however narrow or distorted those bounds may become.[50]

The red-baiting tactics as cited by Bennett that the Reagan administration used successfully to win congressional support for the contras were clearly consistent with the social value placed on anticommunist themes during the cold war. Within the brief span of a decade, however, the cold war was succeeded by the "war on terror"—and anticommunist discourse was replaced by the dominant discourse of the post–September 11 era, which cites "radical Islam" as the chief threat to Western freedoms and, by extension, the American way of life.

In contrast to Bennett's findings, a study of U.S. mainstream television reporting on the 1991 Gulf War following Iraq's invasion of Kuwait concluded that while the reporting tended to support the George H. W. Bush administration's strategic reasons for going to war with Iraq, the indexing paradigm did not hold up as clearly as it had in the context of the *Times*' coverage of the contra-funding story. Rather, communications theorist Scott Althaus found a greater degree of journalistic independence from official sources. It is noteworthy that this occurred at the precise juncture in which—the cold war virtually over and the threat of communism greatly diminished—one perception of external threat had all but evaporated and had yet to be replaced by another. Althaus found that television news "did not merely shadow the debate occurring among U.S. officials. Journalists frequently presented competing perspectives and were often the instigators rather than merely gatekeepers of critical viewpoints. . . . Journalists behaved more like dolphins riding the bow wave than mussels stuck to the rudder."[51]

However, it would appear that indexing was back in full force when—during the post-September 11 period of renewed external threat—the U.S. mainstream media lent tacit support to the case for a second war against Iraq. The six-month run-up to the war (September 2002 through March 2003) saw a dearth of vigorous and critical mainstream media reporting on claims by the George W. Bush administration that Saddam Hussein had weapons of mass destruction that posed an immediate danger to the United States. This journalistic lapse would later be acknowledged by some of the most prominent American media outlets. These admissions occurred long after it had become clear that there had been no WMD stockpiles and that the war had taken a difficult and troubling course, contrary to the administration's sanguine prewar predictions. Acknowledging its own failure to report critically on the case for war, in May 2004, the *New York Times* published a statement of "nostra culpa" detailing its reliance on sources within government and others put forward by the administration. In a 1,200-word report labeled "From the editors" that appeared on page A10 of its May 26 edition, the *Times* admitted: "We have found a number of instances of coverage that was not as rigorous as it should have been. In some cases, information that was controversial then, and seems questionable now, was insufficiently qualified or allowed to stand unchallenged. Looking back, we wish we had been more aggressive in re-examining the claims as new evidence emerged—or failed to emerge."[52]

The *Washington Post* was even more forthcoming in detailing its own journalistic shortcomings in its prewar reporting of the administration's WMD claims. In a 3,100-word piece by *Post* media critic Howard Kurtz that ran on page A1 of its August 12, 2004, edition, the *Post* admitted:

An examination of the paper's coverage . . . shows that The Post published a number of pieces challenging the White House, but rarely on the front page. Some reporters who were lobbying for greater prominence for stories that questioned the administration's evidence complained to senior editors who, in the view of those reporters, were unenthusiastic about such pieces. The result was coverage that, despite flashes of groundbreaking reporting, in hindsight looks strikingly one-sided at times.

"The paper was not front-paging stuff," said Pentagon correspondent Thomas Ricks. "Administration assertions were on the front page. Things that challenged the administration were on [page] A18 on Sunday or A24 on Monday. There was an attitude among editors: Look, we're going to war, why do we even worry about all this contrary stuff?"

In retrospect, said Executive Editor Leonard Downie Jr., "We were so focused on trying to figure out what the administration was doing that we were not giving the same play to people who said it wouldn't be a good idea to go to war and were questioning the administration's rationale. Not enough of those stories were put on the front page."

Across the country, "the voices raising questions about the war were lonely ones," Downie said. "We didn't pay enough attention to the minority."[53]

The indexing paradigm is clearly at work in U.S. mainstream reporting of the diplomacy of the Israeli-Palestinian conflict. The range of discourse is exceedingly narrow, and it rarely if ever questions the wisdom or efficacy of U.S. Mideast policy. This is chiefly because the discourse itself emanates from an equally narrow range of sources. Many are or have been affiliated with current or past U.S. administrations or the military. Expert sources from academia appear infrequently, and voices from other quarters of civil society are all but absent. For a number of reasons—including a dominant-discourse view of the U.S. national interest, notions of shared American and

Israeli democratic norms, and pressure from pro-Israel constituent groups—the majority of government-affiliated sources toe the line of the "Washington consensus" on Israeli-Palestinian peace and the American role in achieving it. With few exceptions, the mainstream media index these views and frame the issues of the conflict accordingly.

"Cascading" and Public Opinion

American media take a classical view of the most important of their functions—at least in theory—which is to inform the public so it can judge the performance of elected officials and the policies of government. The indexing paradigm, however, suggests that the media and government are closer to each other than either is to public opinion. Communications scholar Robert Entman has observed that "9/11 revealed yet again that media patrol the boundaries of culture and keep discord within conventional bounds."[54] As the Bush administration "relentlessly pursued its own framing strategy, frequently linking Saddam Hussein with al-Qaeda, 9/11, weapons of mass destruction and a direct terrorist threat on the United States," this frame "cascaded"—in Entman's terms—through the media to the public. Despite the frequent appearance of oppositional discourse in the media—these debates focused primarily on the strategy of waging war sooner rather than later and unilaterally but did not question the underlying value of going to war—the public nonetheless absorbed the administration's message to such a degree that a July 2003 poll found that 72 percent of respondents agreed with the erroneous statement that "Iraq was harboring al-Qaeda terrorists and helping them to develop chemical weapons."[55]

More important, however, were indications that uncritical media coverage also had a reverse cascading effect: it persuaded members of Congress to authorize President Bush to lead the United States into war in Iraq. The reporting "blunted a lot of criticism and cowed a lot of critics. I know it," Senator Dick Durbin told the *Chicago Tribune* in a May 2004 report about the *New York Times* statement of journalistic self-criticism that had been published the day before. "It was too much for some of my colleagues in Congress. The safe vote was the vote for the war," said Durbin, an Illinois Democrat who voted against the October 2002 resolution. The same *Tribune* report quoted former Clinton administration press secretary Joe Lockhart as saying that "when a member of Congress sits down and reads something in the *New York Times*, they believe it's true, and even if they think it's not true, they realize it's on the agenda and has to be dealt with."[56]

The cascade model theorized by Entman is thus bi-directional, with frames flowing not only from the top down—from the administration through other elites to the media and then to the public—but from the bottom up as well. "Framing," he observed, "is just as inevitable going in the other direction, upward from the public's actual sentiments to officials' interpretations of public opinion." The cascade model thus illustrates "the increasingly complicated process of framing foreign affairs," in which "correlations between public opinion and government policy incorporate so many simultaneous interactions among leaders, media and citizens that determining who influences whom remains a large intellectual challenge."[57]

Entman has identified the spark for cascading action as "cultural congruence," which comprises sets of ideas and assumptions based on cultural predispositions that allow a news frame to cascade through different levels and in either direction.[58] As discussed earlier, several factors of cultural affinity or congruence guide American perceptions of the Israeli-Palestinian conflict in different combinations of interaction between government, policy elites, the media, and the public. These include the cold war–era view that support for Israel protects American interests in the Middle East; common American and Israeli democratic norms and practices; and perceptions of what constitutes justified responses to terrorism in the post–September 11 era.

Another point of cultural congruence is the deep symbolic nature that the Holy Land holds not only for the antagonists in the conflict but also for the West. Reporting on the conflict—particularly with reference to Jerusalem—often emphasizes that the Holy Land is sacred to Jews, Muslims, and Christians alike. However, Israeli claims to the land are often juxtaposed with direct or indirect references to the Holocaust, which is of seminal importance not only in Jewish history but also to the modern Western conscience. By comparison, reporting on Palestinian claims to the land—based on historical continuity of physical presence and human rights defined in canons of international law and consensus—often fails to impart the same sense of authority or entitlement.

Furthermore, the post–September 11 era has reintroduced a centuries-old East versus West theme that alludes to the Holy Land, resulting in President Bush's comments about "this crusade, this war on terrorism" in the days after the September 11 attacks.[59] The shared American-Israeli view that suicide terrorism experienced in both countries has but a sole cause—blind hatred of Western, democratic values—and requires reclamation and defense of those societies from this threat has gained significant currency in American mainstream reporting of the conflict, particularly within the year following the September 11 attacks.

More specifically, cultural congruence is relevant to two key political issues of the conflict itself, namely, the Palestinian refugee question and Israeli settlements. U.S. media frame these issues according to American cultural predispositions, which skirt the issue of colonialism due to a lack of direct historical experience with it, on the one hand, and attach a positive value to refugee resettlement rather than return, on the other. "The more congruent the frame is with schemas that dominate the political culture," Entman has observed, "the more success it will enjoy."[60] However, one of the underlying questions that concern this study is to what degree uncritical and decontextualized U.S. mainstream media reporting of the Israeli-Palestinian conflict—and the narrow range of public discourse it engenders—can be considered a success.

THE CONFLICT, THE UNITED STATES,
AND THE ARAB AND MUSLIM WORLDS

The foregoing discussion of theory provides necessary frameworks for understanding patterns of reporting of the Israeli-Palestinian conflict. It also points to several examples of reporting at the intersection of U.S. foreign policy and international conflict that illustrate these patterns of coverage are not unique to the Israeli-Palestinian conflict.

However, it is precisely this conflict—and the role of U.S. policy in it—that remains at the epicenter of American relations with the Muslim world in the post–September 11 era. How Americans understand the conflict through the media therefore requires special consideration. Recent years have seen unprecedented terror attacks against American targets, a preemptive American war in Iraq, and an American initiative to democratize the Middle East. In one way or another all three have been linked to the Israeli-Palestinian conflict. Furthermore, the conflict—which is the hub of a multi-spoked wheel of American interests in the region and beyond—has increasingly been linked to the safety and security of Americans at home and abroad, with Muslim extremists successfully using it as both a rationale and a recruiting tool for targeting Americans.

In a "letter to the American people"—whose full text the *Observer* of London published in November 2002 but which got no apparent play in the American mainstream media[61]—Osama bin Laden opened his purported 4,000-word screed with a statement of outrage over the Israeli-Palestinian-American triangle: "Why are we fighting and opposing you? The answer is very simple: Because you attacked and continue to attack us. You attacked us in Palestine. . . . Of course there is no need to explain and prove the degree of American support for Israel. . . . The blood pouring out of Palestine must be equally revenged. You must know that the Palestinians do not cry alone; their women are not widowed alone; their sons are not orphaned alone."[62]

Bin Laden's line was clearly echoed in June 2004 when an al-Qaeda–affiliated group in Saudi Arabia kidnapped American Paul M. Johnson Jr., an employee of Lockheed Martin, which manufactures Apache attack helicopters. Johnson was beheaded by his captors days after they released a statement, reported by the Associated Press and numerous other American media outlets, claiming "everybody knows that these helicopters are used by the Americans, their Zionist allies and the apostates to kill Muslims, terrorizing them and displacing them in Palestine, Afghanistan and Iraq."[63]

The same week that Johnson was beheaded in Saudi Arabia, the independent U.S. commission investigating the attacks of September 11, 2001, issued a preliminary report that noted linkages between bin Laden—who on two separate occasions pushed to accelerate the date of the attacks—and then Israeli opposition leader Ariel Sharon. The first was prompted by Sharon's visit to the Temple Mount in Jerusalem, which sparked the second Palestinian uprising in the fall of 2000. The second was based on an impending Sharon visit to the White House. The commission text read:

> Bin Laden had been pressuring K.S.M. [Khaled Sheikh Muhammad] for months to advance the attack date. According to K.S.M., bin Laden had even asked that the attacks occur as early as mid-2000, after Israeli opposition party leader Ariel Sharon caused an outcry in the Middle East by visiting a sensitive and contested holy site in Jerusalem that is sacred to both Muslims and Jews.[64] Although bin Laden recognized that [Muhammad] Atta and the other pilots had only just arrived in the United States to begin their flight training, the al-Qaeda leader wanted to punish the United States for supporting Israel. He allegedly told K.S.M. it would be sufficient simply to down the planes and not hit specific targets. K.S.M. withstood this pressure, arguing that the operation would not be successful unless the pilots were fully trained and the hijacking teams were larger.
>
> In 2001, bin Laden apparently pressured K.S.M. twice more for an earlier date. According to K.S.M., bin Laden first requested a date of May 12, 2001, the seven-month anniversary of the Cole bombing. Then, when bin Laden learned from the media that Sharon would be visiting the White House in June or July 2001, he attempted once

more to accelerate the operation. In both instances, K.S.M. insisted that the hijacker teams were not yet ready.[65]

The American mainstream media did not highlight the bin Laden–Sharon linkage in the commission report. By contrast, the American-based weekly *Jewish Daily Forward* reported that the document "shed new light on the role of the Israeli-Palestinian conflict in al-Qaeda's worldview" and noted that its disclosures "seem to weaken Israeli claims that the issue was only a secondary priority for Osama bin Laden, and they could rekindle the debate about whether U.S. support for Israel is hindering national security."[66] An op-ed column in the Israeli daily *Haaretz* took a similar tack, stating that the commission's findings

> do not conform to the initial reasons given by al-Qaeda for its wild attacks, justified as a struggle against the world of secular values represented by American society. . . . The radical Islamic organization that is leaving its mark on the world chooses to grab onto Sharon's provocation to justify its behavior. Through this it intensifies the religious aspect of the Israeli-Palestinian conflict, and of the overall Israeli-Arab confrontation, and grants it enormous resonance: the whole international community, among them about a billion Muslims, learns that harming the holy sites of Islam in Jerusalem was one of the reasons al-Qaeda attacked the U.S.[67]

These security issues are linked to an important aspect of globalization that has facilitated mobility not only of capital and people but also of ideas and images. This mobility of ideas is born of an increasingly free and diverse media around the world, especially in the Middle East. The Internet, global satellite technology, and relaxed governmental control of the media in some Arab countries have brought to Middle Easterners a version of what Americans have long enjoyed: news on demand from an increasing number of independent news sources that feed and shape public opinion. American journalism, with more than two centuries of constitutional freedoms behind it, differs significantly in tone and subtlety from its counterpart in Arab countries with liberalizing media. However, the two media-consuming publics are nevertheless linked. Both now have access to uncensored, twenty-four-hour reporting of events in the region in which the United States is deeply involved.

Simply stated, the Arab public is getting a view of these events—including the Israeli-Palestinian conflict—that doesn't jibe with the official articulation of U.S. foreign policy in the region that Americans are exposed to via uncritical reporting by the U.S. media. *Chicago Tribune* correspondent Stephen Franklin has reported that television in the Arab world

> has become a powerful cheerleader and may be the Palestinians' best mobilizer ever among Arabs sprawled from the gulf to North Africa.
>
> What the Palestinians tried to do for decades and didn't always succeed at, Arab television has achieved with stunning results in a short time.
>
> It has made personal and real the Palestinian issue. It has pumped up the rage toward the Israelis, a fury that was already at boiling levels for many Arabs.
>
> It has stoked the flames of anti-Americanism. Among Arabs who see the U.S. as an accomplice of the Israelis because of its financial and military support, the condemnation of the U.S. is at a fever pitch.
>
> From a loosely organized boycott of American businesses to casual conversations with Americans that almost always explode with heated complaints about the U.S., the anti-American mood today in the Arab world is nearly inescapable.[68]

Understanding the factors that create this mood is vital if the United States is to get beyond the "target or be targeted" mentality that has largely become the paradigm for its relations with the Arab and Muslim worlds. To a great extent, in the United States, as elsewhere, the mainstream media determine the level of understanding that is possible for the public and policy makers alike.

As Israeli-Palestinian violence escalated to unprecedented levels—from the beginning of the second Palestinian uprising in the fall of 2000 through the spring of 2002—the volume of U.S. media coverage of the conflict increased. At the same time, citizen activism across the spectrum of American civil society intensified. From their various platforms and points of view—religious, secular, pro-Israel, pro-Palestinian—these activists have repeatedly taken notice of the role that media coverage of the conflict plays not only in influencing public opinion but also in the formulation of U.S. Mideast policy.

The underlying argument of the present study is that if Americans had a fuller contextual understanding of the key issues of the Israeli-Palestinian conflict via the mainstream media, they would be better equipped to challenge U.S. Mideast policy. It is a policy that in many ways has done more to manage and prolong the conflict rather than resolve it—to the detriment of American as well as Israeli and Palestinian interests alike. There is widespread international consensus that the United States plays a unique and indispensable role in mediating the peace process. The question remains:

Can it do so successfully without the informed consent of the American public? While deficient media coverage is neither to be equated with nor blamed for unwise or ill-informed policy, there is also a need to ask how high the costs ultimately will be for an uninformed public on an issue of such magnitude. In an attempt to answer these questions, this study analyzes past U.S. mainstream media coverage of the Israeli-Palestinian conflict with the hope of sparking a new discourse in American newsrooms and beyond about future coverage.

∾

Pens and Swords examines how the media have framed key issues of the Israeli-Palestinian conflict over a period of four years, from the run-up to the failed Camp David peace negotiations in the summer of 2000 through the Bush-Sharon meeting in the spring of 2004. This period encompassed a hopeful summit as well as an intense cycle of violence and renewed diplomatic movement. As such, the period is representative of a pattern that could, with slight variations, be repeated in the next stage, or stages, of the peace process—relative to events on the ground as well as media reporting of them.

The present study identifies themes and images about the conflict that this reportage has produced and conveyed to the American public *as a body of work over time*. Since what appears in print and on air is a reflection not only of the collaborative news judgment of reporters, editors, and producers but also of a journalistic consensus across media and markets, *Pens and Swords* does not focus on the work of individual reporters or the product of individual news organizations per se. Approximately 350 media reports and transcripts from some 30 major American print and broadcast news outlets constitute the bulk of the media database for this study, which is supplemented by reports from the Israeli press.

The American mainstream media reports and transcripts were selected because they either impart narrative reconstructions of key events and developments between 2000 and 2004 or focus exclusively on key issues of the conflict (e.g., Israeli settlements in the West Bank and the Palestinian refugee question). The number of reports and transcripts cited and the range of mainstream media sources from which they are drawn yield not only an identifiable pattern of coverage but also one that is representative of American mainstream media reporting on the Israeli-Palestinian conflict during the period under review. Given that the United States plays a unique role in the conflict—and that American public opinion has the potential to affect

U.S. Mideast policy—this study is not comparative and focuses solely on American media coverage.

With the exception of the preceding brief theoretical discussion, *Pens and Swords* is not a work of communications theory but rather an examination of journalistic practice. As such, its underlying points of inquiry include the following: How is the reporting under review sourced and how does it convey balance, voice, and point of view? To what extent does the coverage recognize and incorporate critical contextual factors of the history and politics of the conflict, particularly U.S. policy? How do correspondents report the story of this conflict from the field? What effect do interest and pressure groups have on the processing and production of that reporting in newsrooms back home?

To answer these questions, the present study provides qualitative content analysis of print and broadcast news *reporting* on key themes of the conflict. News *commentary* in the form of op-ed pieces, columns, and talk shows—which can offer a broader range of discourse and opinion on the conflict within the mainstream than is often found in news reports—is not included. (Some newspaper editorials are cited, however.) Citations from print reports and broadcast transcripts are provided in sufficient length and number to demonstrate patterns of reporting on key aspects of the conflict that appear in a wide cross-section of media sources and represent a body of journalistic work over time. The number of examples cited and, in some cases, the repetition of detail that volume entails are provided so that readers may judge both the quantity and quality of evidence that is the essence of the media criticism at hand.

The content analysis focuses on four themes. Chapter 1 examines the degree to which media coverage of the conflict reflects the parameters of U.S. Middle East policy. Chapter 2 focuses on media coverage of the Palestinian refugee question. Chapter 3 analyzes reporting on Israeli settlements in the West Bank and Gaza Strip. In addition to content analysis, these three chapters also include contextual background information on various historical and political aspects of the conflict that are frequently either skimmed over or omitted entirely in U.S. mainstream media reporting. Chapter 4 examines reporting on the extraordinary level of violence and suffering inflicted and experienced by Israelis and Palestinians alike during the first half of 2002. It provides examples of reporting that relied heavily, if not exclusively, on official Israeli military and government sources to tell aspects of that story.

These four themes represent two key characteristics of the conflict. Israeli-Palestinian violence and U.S. policy (revolving around aid and diplomatic support for Israel) are crucial *fueling factors* that occur within and outside the physical arena of conflict. These fueling factors, in turn, significantly affect—and arguably retard progress toward resolution of—two of the most difficult *structural* or *underlying factors* of the conflict, namely, Israeli settlements and the Palestinian refugee question. The present study critically assesses reportage of these four themes to demonstrate not only that the Israeli-Palestinian conflict *appears*—through the mainstream media lens—to consist of an unending cycle of failed diplomacy, brutal violence, impervious rhetoric, and dashed hopes for peace but also that many aspects of its organic reality are all but obscured in this refraction. Although the reportage offers no shortage of details and images, its lack of context, coherence, and, ultimately, clarity severely limits the range of American public discourse on the conflict and ultimately stifles public opinion that could effect constructive change.

Chapter 5 examines not only the unprecedented public pressure and criticism that U.S. media outlets faced between 2000 and 2002 for their coverage of the Israeli-Palestinian conflict but also the notion—often alleged by partisan observers—that reporting of the conflict somehow systematically and deliberately projects a pro-Israel or pro-Palestinian bias. By means of original interviews, chapter 6 chronicles how correspondents report the story from the field. Finally, chapter 7 presents an alternative paradigm for reporting the Israeli-Palestinian conflict whose objective is to widen stock frames of reference and broaden the parameters of public discourse.

◦∾

Since 2004 the focus of much U.S. media attention in the region has shifted to the war in Iraq. However, events on the ground in the Israeli-Palestinian arena continue to unfold at great cost but with little if any progress toward peace. The absence of peace has extracted an enormous human toll. According to a report by the Israeli human-rights organization B'Tselem, by the end of 2006 intercommunal violence had claimed the lives of 4,005 Palestinians and 1,017 Israelis since the beginning of the second intifada, or uprising, in September 2000.[69] Consistent with civilian casualty ratios reported for the entire period,[70] B'Tselem reported that in 2006 half of the 660 Palestinians killed by Israeli military forces were civilians, while three-quarters of the 23 Israelis killed by Palestinians were civilians. Also in 2006, according to the report, the Israel Defense Forces demolished 292 Palestinian homes, 95 percent of them in the Gaza Strip, leaving 1,769 homeless; at the end of November, Israel held 9,075 Palestinian prisoners in custody.[71]

Broader regional implications of the Israeli-Palestinian conflict were also manifest in 2006 in the thirty-four-day war between Israel and the Lebanese militia Hezbollah, or Party of God. In July Hezbollah staged a cross-border attack, abducted two Israeli soldiers, and killed three others. Its leader, Hassan Nasrallah, linked the operation not only to the release of three Lebanese prisoners held for years by Israel but also to the release of thousands of Palestinian prisoners. According to the Associated Press, "Nasrallah said the kidnapping of Israeli soldiers had been plotted for the past five months, calling the move 'our natural right and the only logical way . . . to highlight internationally the suffering of thousands of Lebanese, Palestinian and Arab prisoners in Israeli jails.'"[72]

The war between Israel and Hezbollah was remarkable on several counts. Ending as it did in a stalemate and cease-fire, it was the first war in which Israel did not prevail over an Arab adversary—in this case Hezbollah. It was also the first war since 1948 in which Israelis were subject to sustained conventional military attack in their own country. It was the second time in the space of a generation that Israel inflicted devastating destruction on Lebanon's civilian population, infrastructure, and other targets. By holding its own against Israel's military might—and fortified by arms and other assistance from Iran and Syria—Hezbollah and its patrons signaled to Israel and the United States that the regional balance of power was in flux and that the Israeli-Palestinian conflict had broader regional implications that could not be contained in that arena alone.

According to an AP report compiled from various Lebanese and Israeli sources, days after the cease-fire took hold Lebanon numbered its war deaths between 850 and 1,200, all but about 100 civilians and a third reported to be children. Israel reported 157 deaths: 118 soldiers and 39 civilians.[73]

The territorial aspect of the Israeli-Palestinian conflict also saw change in 2005 and 2006, albeit with no appreciable movement toward peace. The withdrawal from Gaza in late summer 2005 emerged as the opening gambit in a strategy—begun by Israeli prime minister Ariel Sharon and carried on in the wake of his debilitating stroke by his successor, Ehud Olmert—of Israeli unilateralism, or so-called disengagement. Even before the democratically elected Hamas-led Palestinian government was formed in March 2006, Israel viewed the unilateral approach as its best option, based on the dual premises that it lacked a partner for peace negotiations and would not be able to maintain control over the Gaza Strip and all of the West Bank while remaining a democracy with a Jewish majority.

Indeed, having pulled its settlers and soldiers out of Gaza, Israel has continued to maintain effective control over the strip's borders, seacoast, and airspace while at the same time consolidating control over areas of the West Bank essential to a viable future Palestinian state. In an op-ed piece published in the *International Herald Tribune*, Manuel Hassassian, the PLO's representative to Britain, argued that this would yield "political geography [that] would concretize the imprisonment of over 2 million Palestinians in a fractured West Bank, just as 1.4 million Palestinians are currently caged up in Gaza. Needless to say, there is no possibility of establishing a Palestinian state under such conditions."[74]

Israeli geography professor Oren Yiftachel of Ben Gurion University came to a strikingly similar conclusion, terming the geographical manifestations of Israeli unilateralism a process of "creeping apartheid":

> The disengagement [from Gaza] should be analyzed not in isolation but as a "package" with parallel Israeli moves to enlarge settlements and construct the wall in the West Bank. . . . Materially, the geography of the West Bank has become increasingly fractured by the growth of the settlement blocs, the checkpoint regime, gerrymandered municipal [boundaries resulting from the] separation wall and a new Israeli strategy of creating "ethnic [bypass] roads." These oppressive measures were coupled with institutional and military impediments to Arab economic development and housing construction. . . .
>
> Israel may well conduct further small "disengagements" by unilaterally evacuating remote settlements. . . . However this is not likely to alter the fundamental obstacles to creating a viable Palestinian state; rather, it will function to ease Israel's problems of managing Palestinian populations. Limited Israeli withdrawals will accelerate a *Bantustanization* process, creating autonomous Palestinian enclaves decorated by state symbols but with little genuine sovereignty free of Israeli control.[75]

This scenario was borne out in February 2006. Olmert, as acting prime minister and candidate of Sharon's Kadima party for the premiership, stated his intention to proceed with further unilateral disengagement in the West Bank aimed at retaining the three major settlement blocs of Ariel, Gush Etzion, and Ma'aleh Adumim, as well as the Jordan Valley, which is the north-south corridor of the eastern West Bank, accounting for some 15 percent of its territory. Approximately 75 percent of Israel's quarter million West Bank settlers live in those four areas;[76] Olmert also announced plans to evacuate smaller settlements and relocate as many as seventy thousand of their residents in the three large blocs[77]—thereby retaining most if not all of the West Bank settler population.

In 2006 that population continued to grow, as did the number and size of settlements. The Jewish settler population grew by 6 percent to reach

268,400 among a Palestinian population in the West Bank exceeding 2.4 million.[78] At year's end, four days after a conciliatory meeting between Olmert and Palestinian president Mahmoud Abbas, Israel gave final approval for the completion of Maskiot, a new West Bank settlement already under construction, which was intended to house former Israeli settlers from the Gaza Strip.[79]

The diplomatic stalemate reflected the intercommunal violence and continuing settlement activity. For its part, the Hamas-led Palestinian Authority remained steadfast in its refusal to recognize the Jewish state but reiterated its willingness to negotiate with Israel under a long-term cease-fire[80]—although without stopping militants from firing rockets from Gaza into southern Israeli towns, which continued to cause upset but few casualties.[81]

Internationally the diplomatic front adhered to a familiar pattern, with the United States casting the sole veto in the UN Security Council twice in the last half of 2006, thereby rejecting resolutions condemning Israel's use of disproportionate force first in the Gaza Strip against the Palestinians and then in Lebanon. Rhetoric espoused in the wake of the Lebanon war indicated that if any lessons had been learned, they pointed to the ongoing disconnect between the United States and Israel, on the one hand, and the international community and Arab and Muslim worlds, on the other, in assessing root causes and solutions. In a speech delivered on the first day of the cease-fire in Lebanon, President Bush placed the blame for Lebanese suffering squarely on the shoulders of Hezbollah and its patrons. Ignoring the punishing nature of Israel's military campaign and the U.S. support of it via diplomacy and weaponry, Bush remarked: "America recognizes that civilians in Lebanon and Israel have suffered from the current violence. And we recognize that responsibility for this suffering lies with Hezbollah. It was an unprovoked attack by Hezbollah on Israel that started this conflict. . . . Responsibility for the suffering of the Lebanese people also lies with Hezbollah's state sponsors, Iran and Syria. The regime in Iran provides Hezbollah with financial support, weapons and training." Without acknowledging U.S. direct as well as indirect opposition to the democratically elected Hamas-led Palestinian government, Bush stated: "The problem in the Middle East today is not that people lack the desire for freedom. The problem is that young democracies that they have established are still vulnerable to terrorists and their sponsors."[82]

In a briefing to the Security Council a week later, however, Nassir al-Nasser, Qatar's ambassador to the UN and the only Arab member of the council, offered a different perspective, asserting that the failure to deal with the Palestinian issue and its root causes "has led to a great deal of turbulence and tension in the region, which manifested itself in the events that took place in Lebanon and those that we are witnessing now in Gaza." Al-Nasser added that Arab states hoped that bringing the Arab-Israeli conflict to the Security Council "would lead to finding a permanent, comprehensive solution on all tracks [that would end] the vicious circle of violence and counter violence" as well as Israel's occupation of Arab territories it captured in 1967.[83]

On the opening day of the annual UN General Assembly ministerial meeting in the autumn of 2006, President Bush gave a speech decrying extremists' use of violence to derail American and indigenous support for democratic reforms in the region. In his speech to the assembly that same day, outgoing UN secretary-general Kofi Annan referred to the Israeli-Palestinian conflict as "the most potent and emotionally charged conflict in the world today." Annan warned that as long as the UN Security Council is unable to end the conflict and, with it, Israel's occupation of Palestinian territory via implementation of UN resolutions, so too "will respect for the United Nations continue to decline. So long, too, will our impartiality be questioned. So long will our best efforts to resolve other conflicts be resisted, including those in Iraq and Afghanistan."[84] Two weeks earlier the Israeli government had issued bids for construction of seven hundred new homes in the West Bank colonies of Ma'aleh Adumim and Betar Illit, the largest settlement construction project since Olmert had taken office.[85]

The link between the Israeli-Palestinian conflict—as well as relations between Israel, Lebanon, and Syria—and stability throughout the region as a whole was again underscored by the the Iraq Study Group Report released in December 2006. The bipartisan panel, convened to analyze the rapidly worsening war conditions facing U.S. forces in Iraq, stated that "the United States will not be able to achieve its goals in the Middle East unless the United States deals directly with the Arab-Israeli conflict." It concluded that "Iraq cannot be addressed effectively in isolation from other major regional issues, interests and unresolved conflicts. To put it simply, all key issues in the Middle East—the Arab-Israeli conflict, Iraq, Iran, the need for political and economic reforms, and extremism and terrorism—are inextricably linked. In addition to supporting stability in Iraq, a comprehensive diplomatic offensive . . . should address these key regional issues. By doing so, it would help marginalize extremists and terrorists, promote U.S. values and interests and improve America's global image."[86]

The report appeared just days after the UN General Assembly had affirmed three resolutions calling for Israel to abide by international law and consensus and withdraw from the West Bank, cease its annexation and other transformational activity in and around Jerusalem, and withdraw from the

Golan Heights. Eighty percent of the 192-member world body supported the first two resolutions, and just over half supported the third. The United States voted against all three.[87]

In its relations with the Palestinians, the Bush administration consistently opposed the democratically elected Hamas-led government, which came to power after a free and fair parliamentary vote held in January 2006. Cutting aid to the Palestinian Authority in the wake of the election, the United States continued to undermine the government of the Islamist Hamas movement, funding the training of rival Fatah fighters to defeat Hamas in its Gaza stronghold in May 2007.[88] On June 17, after Hamas forces won control of the Gaza Strip in a weeklong battle that left dozens of Palestinians dead, Palestinian president and Fatah leader Abbas formed a breakaway government in the West Bank, evicting Hamas ministers and appointing U.S.-backed Salam Fayyad as prime minister.

The next day, Secretary of State Condoleezza Rice announced that the United States would restore aid to Abbas's unelected government (and would provide humanitarian aid for Palestinians, particularly those in Gaza). "The United States supports [Abbas's] legitimate decision to form an emergency government of responsible Palestinians," Rice said, adding that Bush had "pledged the full support of the United States for the new Palestinian government."[89]

I

THE POLICY MIRROR

Let the people know the facts, and the country will be safe.

Abraham Lincoln, 1864

"WHERE IS GOD?" ALI ABED DAOUD JABER, A SEVENTY-SIX-YEAR-OLD
Palestinian resident of the West Bank village of Hares (near Nablus) shouted
in rage after the Israeli army cut down 110 of his olive trees. "They cut down
trees my grandfather tended! . . . What will I eat now? What will I drink?"
Jaber's cries were quoted by Cox News Service reporters in a November 2000
story about the army's clear-cutting of olive tree groves in the West Bank,
where Palestinians reportedly had been taking cover in their battles with
Israeli settlers and soldiers.[1] The *Chicago Tribune* correspondent had also visited Hares and quoted the irate and desolate Jaber: "Do you know God? Do
you know God? You should cut my throat before you cut my trees!"[2]

In November and December 2000, five major American newspapers ran
their own versions of the olive tree story. In addition to the reports in the
Atlanta and Chicago papers, pieces of similar lengths, averaging 1,100 words
each, appeared in the *Baltimore Sun, Christian Science Monitor,* and *Los Angeles Times.*[3] Four out of the five stories ran with a photo; two also had maps.
The *Seattle Times* also ran part of the *Sun* piece with a photo.[4]

The olive tree story had immense media appeal, suffused as it was with drama and graphic symbolism: the chief icon of Palestinian identity and staple of Palestinian agriculture falling victim to the violence of the opening months of the second, or "al-Aqsa," intifada. The story epitomized the colorful but often facile reporting that occasionally supplements the basic U.S. mainstream media menu of coverage of the Israeli-Palestinian conflict: the daily body count from the field; superficial details of the diplomatic story out of Washington; and shuttle diplomacy missions and negotiations aimed at crisis management. However, as important as what is on the menu of coverage is what is missing from it, namely, details regarding how U.S. Mideast policy renders false the claim that United States is an honest broker to the conflict. This, ultimately, keeps the peace process at war with itself.

THE "WASHINGTON CONSENSUS"

The Israeli-Palestinian conflict is not the sole affair of its physical combatants. "The relationship between the United States and Israel has been a curious one in world affairs and in American culture," observed the linguist and political philosopher Noam Chomsky.[5] Although the United States gives Israel diplomatic cover in the United Nations and supplies it with a unique degree of aid and weaponry, American mainstream media rarely acknowledge or analyze this *American* bias. As a result, the U.S. foreign policy tilt is implicitly absorbed into much U.S. media reporting of the conflict.

Time and again, with exceedingly rare exceptions, the media repeat without question and fail to challenge the "Washington consensus"—the official mind-set of U.S. governments on Middle East peacemaking over time. The consensus consists of three basic axioms: Israel and the Palestinians are responsible—each in their own way—for the sustained failure of the peace process; it is up to the parties themselves to reach a comprehensive solution to the conflict; and while the United States has vital interests in Middle East peace, it is not a direct party to the conflict.

According to syndicated columnist William Pfaff, beltway centrism in American mainstream media coverage of foreign affairs is the rule rather than the exception: "Coverage of international affairs in the U.S. is almost entirely Washington-driven. That is, the questions asked about foreign affairs are Washington's questions, framed in terms of domestic politics and established policy positions. This invites uninformative answers and discourages unwanted or unpleasant news."[6]

A clear-cut example of the "Washington-driven" coverage to which Pfaff refers can be seen in the following analysis of U.S. mainstream media coverage of the Mitchell commission report, which was issued in the spring of 2001—nearly eight months after the outbreak of the second intifada.

The Mitchell Commission Report

The al-Aqsa intifada, which began at the end of September 2000, elevated Israeli-Palestinian violence to a new level. In early December 2000 a fact-finding commission led by former U.S. senator George Mitchell went to the region to assess the causes of the violence and to recommend how it could be halted. Although the delegation had international representation, it operated under the aegis of the United States.

By early May 2001 details of the Mitchell commission's findings began to be leaked; by mid-May the Israeli government and the Palestinian Authority were presented with the report, which focused on suggesting possible solutions rather than attributing blame. American news reports made repeated reference to the commission's deliberate evenhandedness, a clear indication of the "respective blame" clause of the Washington consensus. "The carefully balanced report gave both the Israelis and the Palestinians something to like and something to loathe," the *Los Angeles Times* reported.[7] CNN.com quoted an unnamed U.S. official as saying: "It is a balanced report. There is plenty for both sides to be upset with."[8] The key recommendations called for an immediate cease-fire; a cooling-off period of confidence-building measures; a renewal of Israeli-Palestinian security cooperation; and a return to peace negotiations. The focal point of the recommendations was the commission's dual prescription for confidence building: the Palestinian leadership should try to halt the violence—especially shooting—at Israelis in civilian areas; Israel should impose a freeze on settlement expansion.

On May 21 Secretary of State Colin Powell held a news conference to outline the Bush administration's position on the commission's findings. On May 22 U.S. newspapers published extensive front-page coverage of Powell's remarks; many also ran editorials on the topic that day. A survey of news reports and editorials published by four major U.S. newspapers (*New York Times, Washington Post, Los Angeles Times,* and *Chicago Tribune*) illustrates the significant degree to which they adhered to the principles of the Washington consensus—both in the framing of issues and sourcing of stories—in their news and editorial writing. With the Mitchell commission report having established the first axiom of the consensus ("respective blame"), the Powell news conference set forth the second and third axioms. ("It's up to both sides to find a solution" and "The U.S. is not a direct party to the conflict.") While the four newspapers maintained distinctive tones in their news reports and editorials, with one notable exception their overall approach to the topic bore more similarities than differences. Only one paper dared to challenge the postulates of the Washington consensus in its editorial, which clearly provided the basis for the Mitchell commission report and the administration's response, via Powell, to it. An analysis of these news reports and editorials follows.

News Reports

Overall the four news reports offered differing characterizations of the Bush administration's level of involvement in the crisis. However, in reporting the administration's position, namely, that the United States could do little more than guide the parties forward, the papers offered few differing points of view on this issue from sources outside the administration. Although there was consensus among three of the four papers that Powell had stopped short of endorsing the commission's recommendation for a settlement freeze, only one of those three quoted a source outside the administration challenging its position on the freeze issue. Two of the four papers quoted Powell as saying that "there can be no military solution to this conflict" and three of the papers mentioned Israel's use one week earlier of U.S.-supplied F-16 fighter planes to attack Palestinian targets in response to a suicide bombing at an Israeli shopping mall. However, none of the reports linked Powell's "military solution" quote to the issue of the F-16s, either by challenging him directly on the issue or by soliciting quotes from other sources.

Analyzing the papers' news reports individually, the tone of the *New York Times* report was narrative in nature, bordering on omniscient.[9] Unlike the other three papers, the *Times* focused on Powell's announcement that he was dispatching a senior aide on a shuttle mission to meet with the two sides, saying the administration had "stepped into an active role in the Israeli-Palestinian crisis." The report treated Powell's comments on the Mitchell commission report as a secondary issue, quoting him indirectly on the settlement-freeze issue in the third-to-last paragraph: "On the subject of settlements, General Powell said he wanted to bridge the deep differences between the Israelis and the Palestinians." Apart from Powell, the report quoted only an unnamed State Department official. The latter said Powell spoke with Israeli prime minister Ariel Sharon after the news conference and expressed concern that the use of F-16s represented an escalation in the violence but that Washington was "not interested in a public spat with the Israelis."

The *Washington Post* report adopted the most critical tone toward the Bush administration.[10] The paper reported that Powell "offered no new U.S. initiative to resolve the escalating conflict" and that his remarks "sought to raise the profile of U.S. interest in the Middle East without deepening the degree of engagement." The report also noted the administration's "unwillingness to play a more ambitious role in brokering a truce between the sides." The report said Powell "refrained from endorsing" the settlement freeze "because Sharon has made clear he considers it unacceptable" but did not attribute the statement.

The report quoted unnamed administration officials directly and indirectly as saying there were few options beyond the "two sides"/"two parties" putting an end to the violence. It also quoted Martin Indyk, U.S. ambassador to Israel, as attributing blame for the conflict to both the Israelis and the Palestinians. Outside the administration, the *Post* quoted a House Democrat, who called the administration's approach "inadequate"; a Republican senator, who said he was satisfied with Powell's statement ("I don't know if there's much of anything else they could do"); and the chief diplomatic correspondent for the Israeli newspaper *Haaretz,* who remarked: "It looks like a diplomatic initiative but it's nothing. I don't think it's serious."

The tone of the *Los Angeles Times* report occasionally bordered on the sensational in an apparent effort to find fresh angles for a story whose parameters (the Mitchell commission's recommendations) had been known for weeks.[11] The lead paragraph boldly stated that "the Bush administration changed course Monday and plunged into Middle East mediation." In a striking departure from the other three papers' characterization of Powell's position on the settlement freeze, the report stated that the Mitchell commission's conclusions "gave Powell needed political cover to call for a freeze on Israeli settlement activity." The paper also reported that unnamed "U.S. analysts said there was no doubt that the administration adopted the commission's proposals, including the settlement freeze."

The paper quoted Middle East expert Geoffrey Kemp as saying the Bush administration had accepted "the harsh reality" of the need for more active American involvement, warning that without it "America's enemies like [Iraqi president] Saddam Hussein will get stronger." The report also quoted favorable reactions to Powell's comments by Israeli foreign minister Shimon Peres, Israel Television's diplomatic correspondent, and a statement by the Palestinian Authority.

The tone of the *Chicago Tribune* report was straightforward.[12] It said the Bush administration was "stepping up the visibility of its effort" to mediate the conflict, but that "it was not immediately clear what else the Bush administration was prepared to do, beyond urging the parties to consider" the Mitchell commission's recommendation.

The *Tribune* report quoted U.S. representative Henry Hyde, a Republican from Illinois and chairman of the House International Relations Committee, on the need for U.S. mediation of the conflict. It also quoted Shibley Telhami, a University of Maryland professor and Mideast expert, as saying the administration appeared wary of getting too deeply involved and then failing. The report said Powell "leaned strongly toward" the settlement freeze recommendation but that he "chose his words with extreme care" on the question. The report noted that unnamed Mideast experts "pointed out that Powell was careful not to say that the administration endorsed the report's observations" on the settlements.

Most significantly, the *Tribune* was the only paper of the four to offer its readers any insight into Powell's stance, saying his comments "followed intensive behind-the-scenes lobbying by the Israeli government and pro-Israeli groups in the U.S. who support the settlement activity" and attributing this statement to an unnamed "knowledgeable U.S. official." It was also the only paper to offer an opposing point of view on the settlements. James Zogby, president of the Arab American Institute, remarked that Powell "should have said, 'Continued settlement activity is an obstacle to peace and should be suspended.' He should have, but he didn't."

If news reports of the Powell news conference were designed to present an uncritical and/or exclusive platform for the government to voice its position on a sensitive and controversial issue of international import, then the *New York Times* would win hands down, with second place going to the *Los Angeles Times*. If the purpose was to be superficially critical of the administration without challenging the basic assumptions behind its position, then the prize would go to the *Washington Post*. If the purpose was to report the administration's position while offering counterbalancing information and an opposing point of view so readers would have some depth of field with which to assess the issue, then the *Tribune* would take top honors.

Editorials

On the same day that they published news reports of the Powell news conference, all four papers also ran editorials on the topic. The conclusions of the *New York Times* were straight out of the Washington consensus playbook:

- "[T]he Bush administration has wisely decided to play a more active role in trying to restore a semblance of peace."

- "[Powell] should consider a visit to the region to encourage Prime Minister Ariel Sharon of Israel and the Palestinian leader, Yasser Arafat, to still the violence and begin carrying out some of the Mitchell commission's constructive recommendations."
- "Secretary Powell has appropriately defined America's role as bridging the gap between the two sides on this [settlement] issue."[13]

The *Los Angeles Times* was a bit more optimistic and direct, but the paper didn't stray far from the consensus in its conclusions:

- "Palestinians and Israelis are trapped in an increasingly mindless cycle of destruction. . . . The situation cries out for intercession to restore some measure of sanity and proportion. Washington seems ready to answer that cry."
- "Two of the Mitchell panel's proposals loom especially large: The Palestinian Authority must discourage incitements to violence and move decisively to prevent terrorism. At the same time, Israel must freeze all expansion of its settlements in the West Bank and Gaza Strip. These are doable steps."
- "The United States properly is not interested in trying to impose a settlement. Its wholly pragmatic approach is to see the violence controlled as an essential prelude to bringing Israelis and Palestinians back to the negotiating table."[14]

The *Washington Post* came out and called for a settlement freeze, but it stuck to a balancing act and voiced support for American paternalism:

- "The Palestinians are doing nothing to restore security cooperation with Israel. . . . Nor are the Palestinians reducing incitement, re-arresting terrorists or preventing Palestinians from firing guns into Israeli neighborhoods."
- "The Israelis, for their part, should call back the F-16s and accept a key commission recommendation: a freeze on Jewish settlements in the West Bank and Gaza Strip."
- "Only a sustained and serious American push is likely to lead the parties toward acceptance of the Mitchell report. The administration began to acknowledge that yesterday."[15]

The distinctive voice was that of the *Chicago Tribune*. In its editorial, appropriately titled "Breaking Eggshells," the *Tribune* opted for a rare dose of prairie radicalism that left its coastal colleagues looking like poster children for American conservatism:

- "The Bush administration . . . has finally decided to dip its toe in the water. . . . Powell's action is welcome, as far as it goes. But it doesn't go very far. The U.S. is going to have to exert leverage to halt the violence. And like it or not, the leverage it has is with the state of Israel, which gets $3 billion a year in U.S. aid."
- "Is it unfair to single out Israel? Probably. It's the other side, the Palestinian side, that's conducting diplomacy via terrorism. But you use influence where you possess it. And mere words of reproach don't seem likely to head off the escalating violence in the Mideast."
- "Bush needs to make clear he's ready to use the full influence of the U.S. There is little incentive for the Palestinians to return to the table without an Israeli freeze on settlements. Israel does not easily bend to pressure, but it is sensitive to international criticism, especially when it [comes] from its primary benefactor, the U.S."
- "Israel understandably seeks to defend itself. But it won't win this struggle simply by ratcheting up its response. Israelis have to ask themselves why all this is happening."
- "The 1993 Oslo peace accords they signed with Yasser Arafat stipulated they would negotiate the future of the West Bank and Gaza. Since then, both Labor and Likud have expanded Jewish settlements by 40 percent. The settlements, basically colonies on Arab land, are illegal under international law."
- "The U.S. supplied Israel with F-16s. Now it needs to supply Israel with a reality check."[16]

Only the *Post* and the *Tribune* ventured beyond stating the obvious, and only the *Tribune* opted not to fall back on "both sides are to blame" platitudes. Couched amid safe rhetoric, one declarative prescription was forthcoming from the *Post*: Israel should freeze its settlement activity. The *Tribune*, in a dramatic departure from its usually cautious and evenhanded editorial-page approach to the conflict,[17] presented its readers with a provocative tour de force that dared to buck the Washington consensus and, as one reader wrote approvingly in a letter to the editor, took on "the sacred cow of American political and financial support for Israel."[18]

Television Coverage

The focus of broadcast television coverage of the Israeli-Palestinian conflict—and international news in general—is driven by more than just the fact of the medium's visual nature. In the decade between the fall of the Soviet Union in 1991 and the events of September 11, 2001, it was also limited by a combination of factors: a perceived declining interest in international news due to the end of the cold war; rising costs of covering international stories; and increased competition from cable news operations. This led networks to exchange news video and increasingly to rely on television news agency footage, enabling them to provide "worldwide coverage with greater cost efficiency but sacrific[ing] the depth and perspective that an on-the-scene reporter can provide."[19] Nightly network newscast coverage of the conflict during this period was largely reduced to headline summaries and film clips of the violence. Broadcast coverage that blended reporting with some degree of depth and analysis could be found on programs such as *Nightline* (ABC News) and *The NewsHour with Jim Lehrer* (PBS).

Nightline devoted its May 21 broadcast to the Mitchell commission report; *The NewsHour* also had a segment on it that evening. Like most of the previously cited newspaper reports, these broadcasts echoed the Washington consensus and let the honest-broker theme stand virtually unchallenged. Four ABC news correspondents reported the story for *Nightline*. All of them touched on the issue of U.S. involvement in the conflict, but none challenged the tenets of the consensus—either in their own characterization of the situation or in interviews with others—by raising the issue of how the U.S. foreign policy tilt has a pronounced effect on the trajectory of the conflict. A sampling from the broadcast follows.

CHRIS WALLACE (anchor): Secretary of State Powell called for an immediate, unconditional cease-fire. . . . All this is part of the Bush administration's clear effort not to get so engaged in the Israeli conflict, to let the two sides find their own way back to the peace table.

MARTHA RADDATZ (State Department correspondent): Today marked a real change. Instead of saying, "It's up to the parties, it is only up to the parties to work this out, the Palestinians and the Israelis," Secretary Powell said he will send a special assistant over there to try to work this out to try to get to the point where negotiations are possible again.

JOHN DONVAN (Washington-based correspondent): [The] very level of violence is what puts this administration in a delicate position. In one way, U.S. involvement is more needed than ever because things are getting worse there so quickly. But, in another way, the level of violence is so high that it's not really clear what the U.S. can do to stop it.

WALLACE (to Gillian Findlay, correspondent reporting from Jerusalem): [H]ow much effect do you expect this new U.S. initiative to have on the situation on the ground there?

FINDLAY: I think the people on the ground here would argue that it will only have the effect of the strength that the U.S. administration brings to it. If they are expecting to put these recommendations out there and that the two sides will, on their own initiative, pick them up and run with them, I don't think anybody here is terribly hopeful. It really just depends on what the U.S. administration intends to do, how much muscle they intend to back these recommendations up with.[20]

The remainder of the broadcast was devoted to Wallace's interview with Dennis Ross, the Clinton administration's special Middle East envoy. Wallace asked Ross whether the United States needed to "get tougher" with the Israelis and Palestinians. Ross replied: "I think there's a difference between the issue of getting tougher and getting involved at a more intensive level, at a higher level, perhaps, and certainly in a more visible way." Wallace asked whether the United States would "have to put some pressure on, some teeth into it [the Mitchell commission report]." He did not, however, suggest what kind of "pressure" or "teeth" could be brought to bear—and he got no direct response to his question on the subject from Ross.

In the *NewsHour* segment two Mideast think-tank experts from the Reagan and Clinton administrations analyzed the Mitchell report.[21] Perspectives from the right and left got equal time: Geoffrey Kemp, a former Reagan administration staffer and then director of regional strategic programs at the Nixon Center, imparted the right-leaning view; while Robert Malley, a former Clinton staffer and then senior adviser at the Center for Middle East Peace and Cooperation, expressed the left-leaning perspective. Both men, however, voiced themes of the Washington consensus—not surprising from sources whose points of view were informed within the beltway. Kemp characterized the Mitchell report as "very balanced": "That's essentially why the Israeli government endorsed it, with the exception of the call for a freeze on settlements, and why the Palestinians have been overjoyed, I would say, with the report. . . . Now, implementing this, of course, has one prerequisite: The violence has got to stop. So there's no point talking about settlement freezes until there is a cease-fire on the ground."

Malley, however, placed more emphasis on the settlement-freeze aspect. While acknowledging that "the violence has to cease first," he indicated that the Mitchell commission report "allows for the full package and not only a cessation of violence." Nevertheless, toward the end of the segment Malley echoed the consensus line that even with U.S. and international participation, a resolution to the crisis was up to the Israelis and Palestinians themselves:

> I think we're in the right direction in terms of the international environment. Now the job is up to the Palestinians and the Israelis, and the events on the ground are taking a turn for the worse rather than for the better. . . .
>
> [B]oth Chairman Arafat and Prime Minister Sharon would like a way out but neither one has found that way, and neither one wants to blink first. So they'd both like to find a way out, and I think what happened today is a potential ladder for both to climb down from the high tree they've been climbing over the past few months and to get back to what they really want, which is get back to the negotiating table. . . . As I said, it's very difficult because there are people on both sides who are very angry.

NewsHour reporter Ray Suarez posed one direct question on the role of the United States in the conflict. The nonspecific way in which he asked the question and Malley's response to it indicate the unwillingness, implicit in consensus thinking, to acknowledge that the role U.S. Mideast policy plays in the conflict goes much deeper than mainstream media discourse will allow.

> RAY SUAREZ: Now, we've been talking about this reassertion of United States interest in this region as if it is a tangible thing, a meaningful thing. When we talk about something like ending the violence, what is the American role in that, if there is one? Or do we just have to sit to the side and wait until that happens?
>
> ROBERT MALLEY: Well, we can't sit to the side. That's what the past few months have shown. What the U.S. has is credibility with both parties. It has influence with both parties, economic, military and diplomatic with the whole region in fact. And, therefore, when the U.S. speaks, people usually listen. And the Palestinians over the past few months have been saying they need the U.S. back in. The

United States is Israel's strongest ally, a unique ally and, therefore, can play the role of bringing both sides to the table and making them abide by agreements.

Ultimately, however, the results of the Washington consensus approach to Middle East peacemaking—and the mainstream media's virtual wholesale adoption of it—speak for themselves. The Mitchell commission report had virtually no impact on quelling Israeli-Palestinian violence and getting the two parties back on the negotiating track. Rather, the arc of violence continued on its path until it reached the apex in the spring of 2002.

It was not surprising that, being a product of diplomacy, the commission report adopted an evenhanded and nonaccusatory tone. What was questionable, however, was the media's decision to echo that tone to such an extent that they defaulted on their privilege and obligation to ask hard questions of official and nonofficial sources alike. The following questions would have provided a critical perspective to enable the public to evaluate the commission's prescription for ending the violence: Why should Israel freeze its settlement activity if there are no political or economic costs—in the form of the U.S. withholding aid or diplomatic support at the UN—for *not* doing so? How can the Palestinian leadership achieve (rather than merely call for) a halt to violent attacks in the face of continuing and expanding—in the case of Israeli settlement building—occupation?

Not only did the mainstream media fail to seek answers to these hard questions, but they also failed to pursue unambiguous answers to other, perhaps even more difficult, questions: What can and should the United States do to bring the parties closer together and how do U.S. interests complicate—if not preclude—that "can and should do" mission? It is unlikely, however, that those questions could have been asked, given the lack of critical reporting on the factual bases that underlie them: the nuts and bolts of U.S. interest in the Israeli-Palestinian conflict, as evinced by the American formulas for aid, weapons, and diplomacy.

THE TRAJECTORY OF THE CONFLICT:
U.S. AID, WEAPONS TRADE, AND DIPLOMACY

In *Covering Islam,* his classic work of media criticism, Edward Said observed: "What makes . . . knowledge accurate or inaccurate, bad, better, or worse, has to do mainly with the needs of the society in which that knowledge is produced."[22] What, then, does American society need to know about the

Israeli-Palestinian conflict? Their continual playback of the Washington consensus indicates that the American mainstream media seem to regard important factors underlying the trajectory of the conflict—particularly U.S. aid, including weaponry, to Israel—as givens that do not require much if any reporting.

In May 2001, shortly after Ariel Sharon became prime minister, Israel's use of U.S.-supplied F-16 fighter jets against Palestinian targets evoked only brief and limited discussion of U.S. aid to Israel in the American mainstream media. The fuller implications of this aid become apparent only when the issue is addressed in aggregate, but the mainstream media rarely do so. Piecing the picture together requires delving into various academic, U.S. government, and nongovernmental organization sources—and citizens interested in getting beyond the media's frames to test the logic and veracity of the Washington consensus must do the reporting themselves.

U.S. Aid to Israel

Through June 2007, U.S. aid to Israel has totaled an estimated $101.2 billion. According to two Congressional Research Service reports published in 2007, U.S. aid to Israel from 1949 through fiscal year (FY) 2006 totaled approximately $98.7 billion,[23] and the FY2007 allocation totaled $2.5 billion.[24] According to the reports, the $101.2 billion total includes approximately $53.6 billion in military aid and $30.9 billion in economic aid.

Other estimates of U.S. aid to Israel indicate that the total sum could exceed $101.2 billion, however. A report prepared in 2004 by the U.S. embassy in Israel estimated that U.S. aid from 1949 to 2004 alone had totaled $100 billion (compared with a figure of $93.5 billion reported for the same period by the Congressional Research Service), including funds for military development assistance, science and technology cooperation, and interest earned by Israel each year on early, lump-sum transfers of U.S. aid. According to the embassy report, two-thirds of U.S. aid to Israel was in the form of military assistance and one-third was in the form of economic assistance. Approximately 84 percent was in the form of outright grants and other special allocations, while roughly 16 percent was in the form of loans.[25] Economic aid became an all-grant cash transfer in 1981; military aid became all grants in 1985.[26]

Israel has received virtually all U.S. aid—some $100 billion, or nearly 99 percent—since 1967, the year it occupied the West Bank, the Gaza Strip, East Jerusalem, and the Golan Heights.[27] That same year marked what would become the midpoint of the cold war. A 2004 study noted that adjusted for inflation, the $13.3 billion in U.S. funding for the Marshall Plan, which from 1948 to 1952 rebuilt European economies shattered by World War II, equaled approximately $90 billion in 2004 dollars; comparatively, adjusted for inflation, U.S. aid to Israel between 1949 and 2004 equaled approximately $170 billion in 2004 purchasing dollars.[28] Since 1967 Israel's population has averaged 4.7 million, reaching 7.15 million by 2007,[29] which is slightly smaller than the population of Virginia.

The $101.2 billion in regular and supplemental military and economic grants to Israel has included an estimated $1.52 billion in assistance to absorb immigrants to Israel from 1949 to 2007 (not including an additional $9.8 billion in loan guarantees for housing and resettlement of immigrants from the Soviet Union and, after 1991, its successor states);[30] a "Gulf War damages grant" of $650 million in 1991 to compensate Israel for Scud missile attacks by Iraq;[31] and a supplemental $1 billion military grant for Israel's role in the "global war on terrorism" as part of the Iraq emergency supplemental appropriations of FY2003.[32] As part of its regular FY2004 economic grants, Israel received nearly $10 million from U.S. taxpayers for two academic and cultural institutions: $4.97 million for the Yitzhak Rabin Center for Israel Studies in Tel Aviv and $4.97 million for the Center for Human Dignity Museum of Tolerance in Jerusalem.[33]

The $101.2 billion total does not include an additional $24.3 billion in loan guarantees extended to Israel since the 1970s. For these guarantees, the United States did not transfer funds to Israel but instead underwrote loans to Israel from commercial institutions: $600 million for housing for immigrants from the Soviet Union (1972–1990); $5.5 billion in military-debt reduction; $9.2 billion for resettlement of Jews from the former Soviet Union (1993–1997); and $9 billion (allocated in the Iraq supplemental funding bill of FY2003) for economic recovery following the second Palestinian uprising from 2000 to 2003.[34]

A report on U.S. aid to Israel published by the Congressional Research Service in 2005 contextualized the degree of Israel's reliance on U.S. aid and other outside assistance:

> *Israel is not economically self-sufficient*, and relies on foreign assistance and borrowing to maintain its economy. Since 1985, the United States has provided $3 billion in grants annually to Israel. Since 1976, Israel has been the largest annual recipient of U.S. foreign assistance and is the largest cumulative recipient since World War II. In addition to U.S. assistance, it is estimated that Israel receives about $1 billion

annually through philanthropy, an equal amount through short- and long-term commercial loans, and around $1 billion in Israel Bonds proceeds. . . .

U.S. aid to Israel has some unique aspects, such as loans with repayment waived, or a pledge to provide Israel with economic assistance equal to the amount Israel owes the United States for previous loans. Israel also receives special benefits that may not be available to other countries, such as the use of U.S. military assistance for research and development in the United States, the use of U.S. military assistance for military purchases in Israel, or receiving all its assistance in the first 30 days of the fiscal year rather than in three or four installments as other countries do.[35]

In addition to regularly scheduled annual economic and military aid grants, Israel requests and periodically receives special allocations that significantly increase the size of its aid package. The 2005 Congressional Research Service report stated:

In addition to the foreign assistance, the United States has provided Israel with $625 million to develop and deploy the Arrow anti-missile missile (an ongoing project), $1.3 billion to develop the Lavi aircraft (canceled), $200 million to develop the Merkava tank (operative), $130 million to develop the high-energy laser anti-missile system (ongoing) and other military projects. In FY2000 the United States provided Israel an additional $1.2 billion to fund the Wye agreement, and in FY2002 the United States provided an additional $200 million in anti-terror assistance.[36]

The Wye agreement of October 1998 was meant to jump-start the stalled Oslo peace process. The special $1.2 billion grant linked to Wye that Israel received in FY2000 provided $200 million to redeploy Israeli troops and military installations from the West Bank and Gaza; $175 million in "counter-terror" funding that included $90 million for light surveillance aircraft and armored personnel carriers; and $825 million in "strategic" funding that included $100 million for missile-defense research and development, $360 million for Apache helicopters, and $165 million for other "electronic warfare aircraft."[37]

The Palestinian Authority received a special $400 million Wye supplemental grant in addition to its regular annual U.S. aid grants. Unlike the Wye grant to Israel, the bulk of which was allocated for military purposes (including new weapons procurement), the Wye grant to the Palestinian Authority was geared toward infrastructure and development, specifically $200 million earmarked for road and port building; $100 million for community development, including health, education, water, and other infrastructure; and $100 million for rule-of-law programs, industrial-estate development, scholarships, and a contingency fund.[38]

In July 2005, five weeks before it began to withdraw its settlers and soldiers from the Gaza Strip, Israel requested a supplemental $2.2 billion in U.S. aid to help finance the withdrawal and to develop the northern Galilee and southern Negev regions inside Israel proper.[39] The cost of the Gaza withdrawal was reported to total approximately $1.1 billion: $900 million approved by the Knesset to compensate the 8,500 settlers compelled to leave their homes in the Gaza Strip and $223 million for troop redeployment.[40] After receiving a negative response from the United States, Israel dropped its request for $800 million to cover military aspects of the disengagement. Presumably as a result of budgetary pressures from the war in Iraq and Hurricane Katrina, however, U.S. aid linked to the Gaza withdrawal was not appropriated.[41]

A New Formula for Aid to Israel

Enjoying high-tech prowess in the age of the global economy and the peace dividend it had reaped in the mid-1990s during the Oslo process, by the year 2000 Israel had attained a per capita income of approximately $17,000, which was higher than those of Spain, Portugal, and Greece,[42] prompting a shift in the U.S. aid paradigm. In March 2000, the State Department reported a plan to phase out economic aid to Israel by 2008 while incrementally increasing the level of annual military aid (from the starting point of $1.8 billion in 1998) to reach a fixed point of $2.4 billion in 2008[43]—a change that went largely unreported in the U.S. mainstream media.

Beginning in FY1999, Congress reduced the amount of economic aid to Israel by $120 million a year and increased the amount of military aid by $60 million a year.[44] Actual disbursement, however, departed from this plan—in Israel's favor. Through special supplemental grants, the Jewish state received military aid in excess of the planned $60 million annual increase at several junctures between FY2000 and FY2005, while cuts in economic aid progressed closer to plan.

In the summer of 2007, however, shifting regional dynamics effected a change in this new U.S. aid formula. In July the Bush administration announced plans to sell $20 billion in arms to Saudi Arabia and other Persian

Gulf Arab states to counter the influence of Iran; in August, the United States signed a deal with Israel that increased military aid to the Jewish state, guaranteeing it $3 billion a year for ten years beginning in October 2008. The $30 billion package represented a 25 percent, $6 billion increase in the $24 billion that Israel was to have received for that period—and virtually offset completely the elimination of economic aid. The *New York Times* reported that administration officials "insisted the deal was not linked to a simultaneous American plan for $20 billion in sales of sophisticated arms to its Arab allies. . . . But Israeli officials acknowledged that the aid to Israel would make it easier for the Bush administration to win Congressional approval of the arms sales to Arab countries."[45] In July, Israeli prime minister Ehud Olmert had told his cabinet, "We understand the need of the United States to support the Arab moderates, and there is a need for a united front between the U.S. and us regarding Iran."[46]

U.S. Aid to the Palestinians

From 1975 to June 2007, U.S. aid to the Palestinians living in the West Bank and Gaza Strip totaled approximately $1.82 billion, with an estimated additional $3.16 billion in U.S. support for Palestinian refugees living in these territories as well as those living in Lebanon, Syria, and Jordan.[47]

From 1975 to 1993 the United States Agency for International Development made grants to nongovernmental Palestinian organizations (also referred to as PVOs, or private voluntary organizations) in the West Bank and Gaza Strip totaling $173.5 million.[48] According to the 2004 report issued by the U.S. Embassy in Tel Aviv on aid to Israel, from FY1994 to FY2004 the Palestinians living in WBG received $1.27 billion in U.S. aid.[49] (By comparison, from 1948 to 2004 Egypt received $60 billion in U.S. aid, $50 billion of it since 1975, the year Egypt signed a disengagement agreement with Israel following the 1973 war, followed by a peace treaty signed with Israel in 1979.[50] Jordan received $8.4 billion in U.S. aid from 1951 to 2004, with $2.3 billion received in the decade following the peace treaty concluded between Jordan and Israel in 1994.[51])

For FY2005 and FY2006 U.S. aid to the Palestinians in WBG totaled a further $375 million ($75 million in the regular FY2005 grant, $200 million in supplemental FY2005 funds—with $50 million of this sum carved out for high-tech "processing terminals" to control movement of people and goods between Israel and the Palestinian areas—and $150 million requested for FY2006).[52]

The United States reconfigured its aid to the Palestinians immediately following the formation in March 2006 of a democratically elected, Hamas-led government in the West Bank and Gaza Strip. Some $400 million in aid was either suspended or canceled (including: $130 million for infrastructure projects; $45 million in direct aid to the Palestinian Authority; $40 million for political, civil society, and legal programs; $20 million for private-enterprise development, trade, and information technology; $4 million for community policing; and $165 million in ongoing and planned projects subject to further review), while approximately $300 million was allocated for "humanitarian assistance and democracy building" (including $65 million for food programs, $31 million for health programs, $14 million for education programs, $135 million for refugee assistance, and $42 million for programs promoting "moderation and democratic alternatives to Hamas").[53]

Immediately following the Palestinian election in January 2006 (which brought Hamas to power), representatives of the Quartet—comprising the United States, the European Union, the UN, and Russia—made future assistance to the Palestinian Authority conditional on its commitment to nonviolence, recognition of Israel, and acceptance of previous agreements. The U.S. congressional foreign aid bill for FY2007 included no economic support for programs in the West Bank and Gaza.[54]

After cutting aid to the democratically elected Hamas government for a year and a half, the Bush administration announced that it would recognize and support the breakaway West Bank government formed by Palestinian president Mahmoud Abbas in June 2007 after Hamas had defeated his Fatah forces and taken control of the Gaza Strip. The day after Abbas swore in a new prime minister and cabinet, Secretary of State Condoleezza Rice announced that the administration would ask Congress to grant $86 million in aid to his unelected government (and that the United States would contribute an additional $40 million to the United Nations to aid Palestinians, particularly in the Gaza Strip).[55]

Weaponry and Regional Dynamics

According to the U.S. State Department, American military aid to Israel accounts for approximately 20 percent of Israel's defense budget.[56] Just under three-quarters of annual American military aid to Israel is granted in the form of credits that Israel uses to purchase U.S.-made weapons. Israel is allowed to spend the remaining 26.3 percent of the aid on weaponry manufactured domestically—an exception to the general practice that all such military aid, termed Foreign Military Financing (FMF), is spent in the United States.[57]

With regular American military grants to Israel having begun to increase by $60 million a year—beginning at $1.86 billion in 1999 and scheduled to reach a target level of $2.4 billion in 2008—the projected sum of military assistance for this period is $21.3 billion. With a 26.3 percent allowance to buy domestically produced weaponry, Israel would effectively receive a $5.6 billion U.S. subsidy of its weapons industry and economy during this ten-year span, an amount four and a half times greater than the projected $1.2 billion reduction in U.S. economic aid—at a rate of $120 million per year—for the same period. According to the Congressional Research Service, Israel's share of world defense exports is about 10 percent, with its arms sales totaling $4.4 billion in 2006.[58]

American military aid has enabled Israel to achieve the U.S.-stated objective of maintaining the "qualitative edge of the Israeli Defense Forces (IDF) in the regional balance of power" and to protect its own interests and those of the United States in the region.[59] Moreover, the aid has also guaranteed a steady flow of contracts to U.S. weapons manufacturers. Companies whose products Israel used against Palestinian targets to quell the second intifada include Lockheed Martin Corporation, which produces the F-16 fighter jet; the Boeing Company, maker of the F15I fighter jet, the Apache helicopter gunship and Hellfire air-to-ground missiles; Bell Helicopter Textron, manufacturer of the Huey Cobra gunship; and Colt's Manufacturing Company, which produces M-16 machine guns and M203 Grenade launchers.

American military aid to Israel has been characterized as the starting point in a regional arms-race cycle. Estimating that governments in the region spent more than $700 billion on armaments from 1985 to 1995, former Israeli foreign minister Shimon Peres observed: "If they kept the money at home, the entire Middle East would emerge into a different region."[60]

In its request to Congress for foreign operations for FY2008, the State Department designated nine Middle Eastern countries to receive a total of $3.934 billion in FMF: Israel was to receive $2.4 billion (or 61 percent of these allocations); Egypt, $1.3 billion; Jordan, $200 million; Oman, $10.1 million; Lebanon, $9.6 million; Yemen, $4.67 million; Bahrain, $4.3 million; Morocco, $3.65 million; and Tunisia, $2.06 million. These allocations constitute nearly 87 percent of all bilateral FMF requested for FY2008, totaling $4.536 billion—with Israel receiving 53 percent of that total.[61]

Other governments in the region that do not receive American military aid—namely, Saudi Arabia, Kuwait, and Qatar—pay cash for their purchases, leading to the following observation on the spiraling effect of arms procurement by Middle Eastern countries:

> This benefit to American defense contractors is multiplied by the fact that every major arms transfer to Israel creates a new demand by Arab states—most of which can pay hard currency through petrodollars—for additional American weapons to challenge Israel. Indeed, Israel announced its acceptance of a Middle Eastern arms freeze in 1991, but the United States effectively blocked it. . . . In 1993, when 78 senators wrote President Clinton insisting that aid to Israel be continued at the current levels, they justified it on the grounds of massive arms procurement by Arab states, neglecting to note that 80 percent of those arms transfers were of U.S. origin.[62]

The U.S. mainstream media have barely reported on these phenomena, much less addressed why American military aid to Israel should be increased after the cold war has ended. The imperative for increased aid also seems to run counter to the fact that Israel fought its last full-scale war with neighboring Arab states more than thirty years ago and has concluded peace treaties with Egypt and Jordan. In the absence of mainstream media reporting and analysis on these issues, two observations are in order.

First, it seems clear that American taxpayers will continue to increase their subsidy of a military-industrial complex that thrives, to a significant degree, on fueling the Mideast arms race. When a proposed $570 million cut in American military aid to Egypt came before the House of Representatives in July 2004, the *Washington Post* reported that lawmakers were "on notice from arms companies that the shift could result in job losses in home districts," part of a pressure campaign that resulted in the House rejecting the cut.[63]

Second—and perhaps more important for the fate of the peace process—the history of economic and military aid to Israel suggests that the relationship of the United States with the Jewish state is first and foremost geostrategic, its paramount aim being the projection of American power and the preservation of American hegemony in the Middle East—achieved by arming Israel as a proxy regional superpower. According to one commentator, "Immediately following Israel's spectacular victory in the 1967 War, when it demonstrated its military superiority in the region, U.S. aid shot up by 450 percent. . . . The continued high levels of U.S. aid to Israel does [*sic*] not likely spring from concern for Israel's survival. One explanation may come from a desire for Israel to continue its strategic and political dominance over the Palestinians and over the region as a whole."[64]

In 1979, the year of the Islamic Revolution and the taking of American hostages in Iran, Israel received $4 billion in military loans and grants—the largest single-year military appropriation in the history of U.S. aid to Israel.[65] Combined regular annual military and economic aid totaled $3 billion in 1985—this at the height of the Reagan administration's expansion of military spending aimed at bankrupting the Soviet Union and winning the cold war.[66] With the cold war over and the oppositional force of communism seemingly replaced by the phenomenon of militant Islam, military aid to Israel began to *rise* in 1999. Having been fixed at $1.8 billion a year since 1987, the new target for American military aid to Israel was increased and expected to reach $2.4 billion a year by 2008.

Diplomatic Support for Israel

U.S. support for Israel has not been confined to bilateral relations. It also has a distinct history in the international arena, with a clear pattern of U.S. diplomatic and political support for Israel at the United Nations. From 1970—the year the United States cast its first opposing vote in the UN Security Council—through 2006 the United States exercised its veto power eighty-two times, casting forty-one vetoes against resolutions critical of Israel. Of those forty-one vetoes, thirty-one were of resolutions dealing specifically with the Israeli-Palestinian conflict.[67] In casting those thirty-one vetoes, the United States stood alone every time.

The United States cast its first such UN Security Council veto in July 1973. It rejected Resolution S/10974, in which the council expressed regret that six years after it had adopted the hallmark Resolution 242—which emphasized "the inadmissibility of the acquisition of territory by war" and called for Israel to withdraw from territories that it occupied in 1967—those terms had not been met, and that "a just and lasting peace in the Middle East still has not been achieved." The resolution also stated that it deplored Israel's continuing occupation of the territories, declaring that "no changes which may obstruct a peaceful settlement or which may adversely affect the political and other fundamental rights of all the inhabitants in these territories should be introduced or recognized." Thirteen members voted for the resolution, the United States cast its veto, and China abstained from voting.

Over the next thirty years the United States vetoed various UN Security Council resolutions that addressed the following topics: status changes that Israel introduced in occupied East Jerusalem; Israeli violations of Palestinian human rights in the West Bank and Gaza Strip, including deportation and confiscation of land and other property; the demand that Israel abide by the Fourth Geneva Convention; and the deployment of unarmed UN peace-keeping monitors in the territories.

In December 2002 the United States vetoed a draft resolution that condemned Israel both for killing British UNRWA official Iain Hook during a raid in the Jenin refugee camp in the West Bank and for destroying a UN World Food Program warehouse in Gaza. The resultant effect was that "the U.S. veto caused ill feelings at the UN and led to further charges of U.S. bias toward Israel at a time when the U.S. was pressing nations to apply strong pressures on Iraq and its flagrant behavior against international law."[68]

In 2003 the United States vetoed two Security Council resolutions: in September concerning Israel's declaration that it reserved the right to "remove" Palestinian Authority leader Yasser Arafat; and in October concerning the separation barrier Israel was building in the West Bank. (In July 2004 the International Court of Justice, the highest judicial body of the United Nations, declared the barrier illegal according to international humanitarian law. The court ordered that the barrier be dismantled and compensation paid to those Palestinians whose lives and property it had affected. The sole dissenter in the 14-to-1 vote was the American judge.)

In 2004 the United States vetoed another two resolutions concerning the Israeli-Palestinian conflict. The first, in March, condemned Israel's assassination of Hamas leader Ahmad Yassin. The second, in October, enjoined Israel to halt all military operations in the northern Gaza Strip and withdraw from the area. Israel had launched the operation five days earlier after Palestinian rockets killed two children in the southern Israeli town of Sderot. In casting the U.S. veto, Ambassador John Danforth called the resolution "lopsided and unbalanced" and said that it "absolves terrorists in the Middle East."[69] However, neither Danforth nor media reports noted the lopsided nature of the casualty toll and the unbalanced power equation it represented: on the Israeli side two dead; on the Palestinian side, according to the Associated Press, sixty-eight killed (nearly half of them civilians), four hundred wounded (about 60 percent of them civilians), and dozens of homes destroyed, trees uprooted, and roads bulldozed.[70]

On rare occasions the United States has voted in favor of UN Security Council resolutions addressing the Israeli-Palestinian conflict. In recent years these have included Resolution 1397, adopted by the council in March 2002, which affirmed "a vision of a region where two States, Israel and Palestine, live side by side within secure and recognized borders." During the period of heightened Israeli-Palestinian violence in March–

April 2002, the United States voted for two resolutions. One called for a cease-fire by both parties and Israeli withdrawal from Palestinian cities. The other called for access "by medical and humanitarian organizations to the Palestinian civilian population," as well as the deployment of a UN fact-finding team to the Jenin refugee camp, where especially fierce fighting had resulted in scores of Palestinian and Israeli deaths and where Israel had demolished between 100 and 150 Palestinian homes. (The Bush administration, however, subsequently reversed course by supporting Israel in its refusal to grant the UN access to the camp, and the mission was canceled.) In November 2003 the United States voted for a resolution supporting the "road map" peace plan, which it had authored with Russia, the United Nations, and the European Union.

CONNECTING THE DOTS

In January 2001, as the Mitchell commission was at work on its report in response to the outbreak of the second intifada, a delegation from the U.S.-based National Lawyers Guild traveled to Israel, the West Bank, and Gaza Strip to study the link between American military and economic assistance to Israel and Palestinian human rights. The NLG issued its own report, which was radically different in tone and substance from the report of the Mitchell commission and representative of the very type of alternative discourse virtually absent from mainstream media coverage of the conflict. Because the linkages asserted by the NLG shed important critical light on certain dynamics of the conflict—and because the mainstream media virtually ignore them—the following characterizations found in the delegation's seventy-page report are worth noting:

- Virtually all Israel's weapons are provided or financed by the United States.
- The United States, while providing all these weapons, does not appear to have made any effort presently to either control or monitor how these weapons are used. . . . The U.S. Embassy spokesperson pointed out that the United States could monitor weapon sales, could impose conditions on weapon sales, and could delay or cancel the sale of weapons such as the Apache helicopters. None of these actions are being taken.
- The huge number and extensive use of Apache attack helicopters is, at a minimum, a symbol of U.S. foreign policy creating a warlike

atmosphere. . . . Misuse of U.S.-manufactured and financed weapons is also evident in Israel's state assassinations of Palestinians.

- Palestinians view the United States' permissive arms policy toward Israel as a clear sign of U.S. lack of impartiality and support for the belligerent Israeli occupation. A father of a martyred child from the Khan Yunis refugee camp [in the Gaza Strip] articulated this view most succinctly: "One word from the U.S. government would stop all this."

- Continued foreign assistance arguably has made Israel more brazen in its brutal treatment of the Palestinian civilian population. In addition, it creates the impression that the U.S. sanctions and approves of Israel's misuse of U.S. manufactured and financed weapons. Palestinians repeatedly expressed to the delegation that they felt that both the United States and Israel were engaged in a one-sided war against them.[71]

An exceptional instance of the mainstream media shedding light on consequences of U.S.-supplied weapons to Israel appeared on the front page of the *Boston Globe* in May 2001. Charles Sennott reported:

Of the estimated 13,000 Palestinians injured [by Israeli forces] in the seven-month spiral of violence, an estimated 1,500 have suffered disabling wounds, according to the Health, Development, Information and Policy Institute, a Palestinian public health research organization based in the West Bank town of Ramallah. Twenty percent of the 13,000 injured were shot with live ammunition, mostly the high-velocity, full-jacketed bullets from M-16 rifles, which have been criticized internationally because of the extensive injuries they cause. Many will never walk again. The luckier ones will limp.[72]

The story went on to quote Dr. Robert Kirschner, forensic pathologist of the Boston-based Physicians for Human Rights, as saying that the high rate of crippling injuries was partially due to Israel's use of the American-designed M-16 assault rifle. However, the report did not detail how American military aid enabled Israel to acquire these weapons.

The NLG report also addressed legal implications of the weapons issue, contending that "the excessive and indiscriminate force of the IDF and the Israeli police is not necessary to Israel's 'legitimate self-defense' or 'internal security' and thus violates Israel's 1952 mutual defense agreement with the United States and the AECA [Arms Export Control Act of 1976]." The report also concluded that "Israel has demonstrated a 'consistent pattern of gross violations of internationally recognized human rights' which has been well documented by numerous non-governmental organizations. Under these circumstances continued United States funding of military arms and training to Israel is unlawful under the U.S. Foreign Assistance Act of 1961."[73] Although the NLG report recommended that the Bush administration and Congress take up the issue of alleged violations of U.S. law due to Israeli use of American military aid, the call went unheeded.

American journalists have also sought answers regarding the legal implications of Israel's use of U.S.-supplied weaponry. The official transcript of the daily State Department press briefing on August 8, 2001, illustrates such an exchange, which yielded double-talk that is not newsworthy even though the underlying issues are.[74] State Department spokesman Richard Boucher was asked how the U.S. government was responding to Israel's repeated use of U.S.-supplied attack helicopters and F-16 fighter jets against Palestinian targets. The briefing transcript reflects Boucher's nimble and ultimately evasive parrying with journalists:

QUESTION: How does this Department react to the increasing or repeated use of helicopters—US-supplied helicopters, very heavy shelling from helicopters overnight? And I believe that we heard the Secretary say that he didn't think this was going to continue to be a problem. Correct me if I'm wrong, and tell me if it's still a problem.

MR. BOUCHER: I think you are wrong. I think that was F-16s. But in any case, I think I would say that the issue for us is whether the cycle of violence is broken or not. The issue for us is whether the parties take the steps that are necessary to stop the cycle of violence, and to get back to a security that is formed by cooperation, whether they use the opportunities available to stop the violence and to get back to security cooperation.

QUESTION: So you are saying it is not an issue that they are using these helicopters? I know it is. It is discussed frequently, isn't it?

MR. BOUCHER: It is an issue that is raised, but there has been no determination regarding the legal implications of the use of U.S. weaponry.

QUESTION: (Inaudible) said that this afternoon that we don't have any leverage with Israel anymore?

QUESTION: Can I follow up on that one?

MR. BOUCHER: I think we are heavily involved in the process. The parties want us involved in the process. I don't know about leverage, but certainly everybody looks to us and listens to us.

QUESTION: But can I follow up on the use of the American weapons? The Arms Export Control Act would require you to make a finding that [this] U.S.-supplied equipment was being used for non-defensive purposes. You have condemned the targeted killings as excessive force and so forth. And yet, you have said there has been no determination made at this point, and I'm assuming you're referring to the Arms Export Control Act. So I'm just trying to square the circle. If you are condemning the targeted killings—the targeted killings are used—are made with U.S. equipment, then why haven't you made a determination that they are in violation of the Arms Export Control Act?

MR. BOUCHER: Because the two things are not the same. . . . One is a legal determination, and the other is a political judgment. In terms of our political judgment about the situation and how to handle it, in terms of our regret of the loss of life and particularly things like the children who were killed, we do not believe that targeted killings is a good policy. We think it is wrong, and we think it is a terrible tragedy for many of the people that are affected by it. That is not the same as making legal determination.

Boucher was then asked repeatedly about the legal implications of the issue and why it hadn't been raised in Congress. His basic message, laced with doublespeak and capped with a Catch-22, was: Congress hadn't taken up the matter because the administration did not think that a determination that Congress should take up the matter was in order.

QUESTION: Well, just to follow up, then at that point, I mean, is it possible, considering that there hasn't been a legal determination yet, that this building [the State Department] would agree with Vice President Cheney that there are some cases when it is justified, or that there is appropriate use of defense there?

MR. BOUCHER: I am not going to try to expand on that. The White House did that subject thoroughly on Friday, and I thoroughly agree with them.

QUESTION: One more on helicopters, please. Wouldn't this building have the option to write to complain about this? Doesn't it, to Congress to write a report about this behavior, if they think it is a problem? Is there any talk about doing that? And can you also say whether it is being raised regularly with the Israeli Government that the U.S. isn't comfortable with this?

MR. BOUCHER: We have made our position on targeted killings quite clear.

QUESTION: What about the helicopters.

MR. BOUCHER: We have made our position on targeted killings quite clear. You are raising helicopters in that context. Obviously, we are concerned about the violence. We have made our position about the violence, about targeted killings and other things quite clear to the Israeli Government. We do discuss that with them. The report to Congress that you are talking about—I would have to check the law. But I am pretty sure that is a report that is made—if a determination is made. And since we haven't made any kind of determination, that wouldn't kick in.

QUESTION: Is the State Department the lead agency on making that determination?

MR. BOUCHER: Yes, we are the lead agency for the Arms Export Control Act.

QUESTION: Can I just follow up on that? Are you in the process of making a determination? Are you—when would a determination be made?

MR. BOUCHER: We are quite aware of the law. We are quite aware of the events, and a determination would be made when we thought it was necessary to make one based on the events.

QUESTION: Just to follow up on that, can you tell us when the process of making this determination that hasn't yet been made began? Because the question of US—

MR. BOUCHER: No. It began 20 or 50 years ago when the Arms Export Control Act was started. We are cognizant of our responsibilities under the law, and we always evaluate events compared to our law. If we feel that it is necessary to make that determination, we will do so. What I am saying is we have not done that.

QUESTION: The question of Israelis using American-supplied weaponry arose in October, with the first helicopter attacks. Has—was that when this question was first—

MR. BOUCHER: That question has been around for a long time, for decades.

QUESTION: So what is taking so long to make a determination?

MR. BOUCHER: Because we haven't felt it necessary to make that determination based on the facts and the law. We have not made the determination because we don't feel that the facts have yet reached the point where a determination is made under the law.

QUESTION: Well, what are the facts?

QUESTION: I'm sorry if you have already said this, and I just didn't get it, but are you—is there an ongoing investigation at which point you will make the determination?

MR. BOUCHER: No.

QUESTION: Or you just don't feel at this time as if you have to go there?

MR. BOUCHER: We don't feel at this time that the facts have justified a determination under the Arms Export Control Act. We are very aware of our legal responsibility. We follow the events on the ground very closely. But at this point, we haven't made a determination because we don't feel that that portion of our law has kicked in.

Boucher was then asked a question that hinted at the contradiction inherent in the United States supplying arms to Israel, on the one hand, while at the same time being concerned about the flow of weapons to the Palestinians from Arab and Muslim states, on the other. The spokesman quickly sidestepped the issue. He then fielded a question as to what, exactly, it would take for the State Department to make a determination that a congressional investigation of potential Israeli breach of the Arms Export Control Act was warranted. Again, Boucher obfuscated. By the end of the segment of the briefing that was supposed to address Israel's use of U.S.-supplied weaponry, journalists had little if anything at all of substance to report. Rather, their exchange with Boucher more closely resembled the libretto of a comic opera.

QUESTION: A question a little bit different. What about the so-called weaponry that is flowing into West Bank and to Gaza Strip? State Department and Pentagon looked into where this is coming from? Is it coming from rogue states or from Iran or, for that matter, from Iraq?

MR. BOUCHER: I don't think I have any information on that that I can share with you. I will double-check and see if there is anything.

QUESTION: I'm sorry. Could you just tell us what—what would be facts that would justify determination? I mean, I know you don't like to do hypotheticals but what facts would you need? They used weapons, you have . . . criticized the use of those weapons in the targeted killings. What would the facts—what more facts would you need?

MR. BOUCHER: I am not going to get engaged in a process of offering a prescription for what people can do to violate our law. (Laughter.)

QUESTION: I am not asking for a prescription—

MR. BOUCHER: Well, that is what you are asking: List five things the Israelis could do that would violate our law with regard to weapons transfers. I am not going to do that. . . . Read the law. It says what the standards are in the law. If we think those standards are violated, we will make the determinations that are necessary. At this point, we have not done that. That is about as much as I can tell you. I am not going to give you a list of five or 10 things they could do that would violate our law.

U.S. mainstream media reporting of the Israeli-Palestinian conflict thus contributes little to an accounting of the American role in its trajectory. The effects of aid to Israel and U.S. weapons trade in the region go unreported; the effects of U.S. diplomatic and political support for Israel go unanalyzed. Unofficial sources from beyond the beltway—including academics and representatives of secular and faith-based civil-society groups whose research and activism focus on the conflict—could speak to the consequences of these linkages. However, they are not cultivated as sources; their voices are left out of the discourse. The result is that public opinion of U.S. Mideast policy has a very limited spectrum of mainstream perspectives upon which to draw.

Credible data and informed opinions exist outside the mainstream media. The responsibility of piecing the puzzle together, however, seems to have devolved from news providers to highly motivated news consumers, who are not likely to encounter the following type of critical yet evenhanded analysis—the view of a U.S. military officer published by an American military think tank—on *Nightline* or in the *New York Times:*

> Without question the United States has always favored Israel in its relationships with its neighbors. In its early days as a nation, Israel needed help economically and militarily to survive. It was, until 1967, a country under siege. But after the 1967 war, Israel became an occupying power. . . .
>
> Over the subsequent years, Israel lost its memory of what it means to be besieged. It should look to its own history, both ancient and modern. Like others who wielded armed might, Israel's army can go at will into the areas returned to the Palestinians, but its gain is limited to destroying houses and clearing fields of fire by knocking down trees. [Israeli prime minister Ariel] Sharon's policy of strength and determination is being met by a determined spirit of resistance that this time will not be broken, only strengthened, as was Israel's in the first 20 years of its modern existence.

If the violence is to be brought under control, the United States must rethink its current one-dimensional view of the conflict between Israel and the Palestinians. This can be done without detriment to Israel and probably to its long-term benefit.[75]

The Information Deficit

Given the magnitude of importance that the Israeli-Palestinian conflict has for American interests in the Middle East and beyond—and for Palestinians and Israelis themselves—the American mainstream media run a remarkable information deficit on the key issues of the conflict. Reporting the Israeli-Palestinian conflict as they do, mainstream American media break their compact with the American people more often than not by framing coverage of the issues along the lines of the Washington consensus—both in diplomatic coverage originating in the nation's capital as well as in reporting from the field. This flawed approach to reporting the conflict is clearly at odds with the prime journalistic value of "the people's right to know."

Renowned British journalist Robert Fisk, who for decades has covered the Middle East with a unique blend of reportage and commentary for the *Independent*, has been an outspoken critic of U.S. media coverage of the region. Writing from Beirut in 1998, he observed, "Academics may one day decide how deeply the American public has been misled by the persistent bias of the U.S. media, and the degree to which this has led them to support U.S. policies which may destroy America's prestige in the Middle East."[76]

Were American journalists to focus on the impact that U.S. foreign policy has on the conflict, thereby adding much-needed critical depth to their coverage, they would fulfill their own credo: The preamble to the Code of Ethics of the Society of Professional Journalists states that "public enlightenment is the forerunner of justice and the foundation of democracy. The duty of the journalist is to further those ends by seeking truth and providing a fair and comprehensive account of events and issues."[77] In so doing, the media could also advance the cause of a just peace by laying important underlying issues of the Israeli-Palestinian conflict squarely before the American public.

If the media were to connect the dots of U.S. Middle East foreign-policy bias to the trajectory of the conflict, then these issues could become part of public discourse rather than remain relegated to a closed-circuit discussion among elites on op-ed pages and in academic journals. At a minimum, a fuller contextual reporting on these crucial issues would allow for the development of informed public opinion—the way, according to classic American press theory, the fourth estate is supposed to function.

The process could end there—or American public opinion could shift, compelling a change in U.S. Middle East policy. This would not be without precedent. American media eventually came to play a critical role in raising public awareness over U.S. military involvement in Vietnam and economic involvement in apartheid-era South Africa. That awareness gave way to groundswells of public concern over the morality and human cost of those entanglements, driving the policy changes of disengagement and divestment—and spurring an end to the Vietnam War and apartheid in South Africa.

For public opinion to shift, however, it has to be stimulated by something new—and the history of the Israeli-Palestinian conflict holds precedent for this as well. The startling images broadcast on American network television of Israel's military response at the outset of the first intifada in late 1987 and early 1988—in which troops beat unarmed Palestinians and tied them to army jeeps as human shields—contributed to a rethinking of who was who in the David-Goliath metaphor. As the first uprising wore on, the word "Palestinian" entered American popular political discourse on the conflict via the mainstream media. Moreover, when the violence of the second intifada spilled over the Green Line into Israel proper in October 2000, sweeping Arab citizens of Israel into the fray (thirteen unarmed Arab demonstrators were shot dead by Israeli forces), U.S. media began to report on how these Palestinians view their nationality and identity. The coverage posed an alternative discourse to the construct of "Israeli Arabs," a term coined by the Israeli security establishment, promoted by the Israeli academy, and adopted by media around the world to describe this unique Palestinian community.

These adjustments, however, have not significantly altered the American public's big picture of the Israeli-Palestinian conflict—and this will not change as long as media reporting of the conflict is stuck in the mode of merely reacting to the political and military struggles of the combatants themselves. A new way of seeing and reporting is needed—beyond the policy mirror of the Washington consensus and as deep as the roots of the olive trees once tended by Ali Abed Daoud Jaber.

2

REPORTING THE
PALESTINIAN REFUGEE STORY

> Muhammad has never once in his life left the Gaza Strip. Yet when asked where he's from, he'll respond, as many in Gaza do, with the name of a town on the other [Israeli] side of the Green Line. His family left Hamman in 1948, soon after Israel declared its statehood, a period during which tens of thousands of Palestinians relocated to Gaza, which was then under Egyptian control.
>
> *Michael Finkel, "Playing War"*

"MUHAMMAD" IS A RESIDENT OF BEACH CAMP, ONE OF EIGHT PALESTINIAN refugee camps in the Gaza Strip. He, along with a passel of Beach Camp boys in their early teens, was featured in the December 2000 *New York Times Magazine* cover story "Playing War."

The story explored why Palestinian children like Muhammad and his friends were motivated to congregate at the Karni crossing at the northern end of the Gaza Strip in order to hurl stones at Israeli soldiers—despite considerable risk that they would be killed by the soldiers' gunfire in the process. Describing their environment in masterful detail, the piece imparted a sense of compassion bordering on sympathy for its endangered—if not doomed—young subjects. Yet the reporting provided virtually no historical context for the boys' predicament.

Early on the piece reported that half of the Gaza Strip's one million Palestinian residents were refugees, and that the Palestinian population as a whole in Gaza had to make do with 60 percent of the land. The remaining 40 percent of the Gaza Strip at the time was controlled by Israel, the piece reported, and was home to 6,500 Israeli settlers.[1] Having established these facts, reporter Michael Finkel described the Karni crossing as "a place where Arabs are not considered equal citizens," when, in fact, no Palestinian from Gaza, refugee or otherwise, can claim citizenship in any state. Historical context relating to how Gaza became home to half a million refugees was all but absent—the sole exception being a single-sentence explanation that in 1948 Muhammad's family had "relocated" to the Gaza Strip from the village of "Hamman" (referred to in academic literature and henceforth as "Hamama," which is Arabic for "dove").

Indeed, to an American audience the term "relocated" might well imply that Muhammad's family had found opportunities in Gaza that were lacking in their native Hamama—and thus had moved voluntarily in order to take advantage of better employment, housing, and/or schools. However, the historical background of the village—afforded not a single line of consideration by the reporter—indicates otherwise, denoting it as a place lacking neither organization nor opportunity:

> Most of the village residents were Muslims. The village had a mosque and two elementary schools: one for boys, opened in 1921, and another for girls, opened in 1946. In 1946, 338 students were enrolled in the boys' school and 46 in the girls'. A village council administered local affairs. The villagers cultivated a wide variety of crops: grain, citrus, apricots, almonds, figs, olives, watermelons, and cantaloupes. Because of the sand dunes, particularly on the north side, the community planted trees on parts of the land to prevent soil erosion and sand encroachment. In 1944/45, a total of 961 *dunams* [4 *dunams* equal 1 acre] was devoted to citrus and bananas, and 20,990 *dunams* were planted in cereals; 4,325 *dunams* were irrigated or used for orchards. In addition to agriculture, the inhabitants engaged in fishing.[2]

According to the 1944–1945 census of Palestine conducted by the British mandatory authority, Hamama, located fifteen miles northeast of Gaza City, had a population of 5,070 (5,010 Arabs and 60 Jews). Arabs owned 65 percent of the village land, Jews owned 4 percent, and the remaining 31 percent was public land.[3] A detailed description of the circumstances under which the Arab inhabitants of Hamama, and, indeed, most of Palestine, became refugees is provided in the landmark work by Israeli historian Benny Morris entitled *The Birth of the Palestinian Refugee Problem, 1947–49*. According to Morris, by the time Israeli troops conquered Hamama on October 28, 1948—five and a half months after the war between Israel and the Arab states began—it was "reported 'full of refugees' from Isdud [Ashdod] and elsewhere."[4] These localities nearby Hamama on the Mediterranean coast had been under Egyptian military rule since May and were the targets of "bombing and strafing attacks" by the Israel Defense Forces on October 15 and 16.[5]

According to Morris, the causes of the exodus from Hamama were mixed, but they nevertheless occurred under the duress of war. The local and refugee populations "either fled [in panic] southwards after the IDF conquest or were urged or ordered to do so by the troops."[6] In a separate reference Morris attributes the "decisive cause for the abandonment" of Hamama to "military assault on the settlement by Jewish troops,"[7] which he noted as having occurred in dozens of Arab towns and villages across the country. Hamama was but one of 418 Palestinian villages that were depopulated and destroyed by Israel in 1948–1949,[8] and no traces of its houses or landmarks remain.[9]

Why, then, would a story focusing on the behavior of Palestinian refugee children pay no attention to how their refugee status feeds their psychology? Why would such a story, whose cover photo juxtaposed a dramatic image of a youth lobbing a stone with an equally dramatic quote—"I will give all my children if that's what it takes to get our homeland back"[10]—fail to explain any of the factual circumstances under which that homeland was lost?

COVERING THE REFUGEE STORY:
PARADIGMS FOR REPORTING TECHNIQUE

The Palestinian refugee issue is a root cause of the Israeli-Palestinian conflict and remains one of the most difficult to resolve between the two peoples in order to achieve peace. Their living historical attachments to the land will have to be accommodated in the process that will determine borders, capitals, and where Israeli and Palestinian flags will fly.

American mainstream media reporting on the Israeli-Palestinian conflict routinely acknowledges the Palestinian refugee issue, but it is often referred to only in passing as one of the more difficult issues to be resolved. From time to time entire reports are devoted to the issue, and they are usually "pegged" to a news event such as a round of peace talks. The standard reporting technique for this type of story—in which journalists have the opportunity to explore the refugee issue in some degree of depth—is for a journalist to visit a particular refugee camp and interview residents, usually in a single family and/or neighborhood. The journalist then produces a vivid picture of the miseries of camp life and the hopes and dreams that its residents harbor.

Rarely, however, is the history of *how* these people became refugees incorporated into the reporting. Equally infrequently can the reader, listener, or viewer find a discussion of the body of international law and consensus relating to the rights of refugees in general or of Palestinian refugees in particular. American correspondents and their editors and producers often assume that audiences would find such details passé or even irrelevant in light of the current state of the conflict, which produces no shortage of immediate and often palpable drama. However, these contextual details are directly relevant to the Palestinians as well as to many others in the Arab and Muslim worlds. Their notions of how the conflict should be resolved—and their resulting attitudes not only toward Israel but also toward the United States, due to the influence of its policy in the conflict—are based on many of these same details of history and international law and consensus. To omit them, therefore, is to omit an important part of the story, to marginalize important actors, direct and otherwise, in the conflict, and to devalue the meaning of their attitudes and actions. As the following content analysis will show, the majority of American mainstream media reporting on Palestinian refugees does precisely that. It largely omits these contextual background details and employs a point-and-shoot technique that yields evocative images and heated quotes yet sheds little, if any, contextual light.

The scholar Kathleen Christison has noted that the Palestinian refugee issue remains obscure to the American public. In *Perceptions of Palestine* she examined how official and public perceptions of the Israeli-Palestinian conflict, channeled via the media and other conduits, ultimately affect U.S. policy. With regard to the issue of Palestinian refugees in particular, she observed: "The dispossession and dispersal of the Palestinians in 1948 has always been and to a great extent remains 'an unrecognizable episode' even for most informed Americans—unrecognizable in the sense not only that the dispossession has been forgotten but also that it is seldom recognized to be the ultimate cause of the conflict."[11]

A critical analysis of U.S. mainstream reporting on Palestinian refugees, however, is based on three important premises. The first is that all political conflicts, especially those involving territorial disputes, have complex histories with at least two or more competing narratives. Second, as a matter of journalistic practice, it is neither desirable nor possible to reinvent the historical wheel and accommodate all of these competing narratives in every piece of reportage—or even in most of them; the constraints of space (in print media) and time (in broadcast media) simply won't allow for such an accommodation. Third, a basic definition of news is something that is happening, something that has just happened, or something that is about to happen. This renders historical exegesis infrequent in most daily news reporting. But the reporting under review is not, in the main, of the daily-news variety; all the pieces cited are feature stories that focus specifically on Palestinian refugees rather than merely mentioning their disposition in passing as one of the conflict's core issues.

Before embarking on a content analysis, however, a brief review of the historical background of the Palestinian refugee issue and related legal and policy issues is in order. It is precisely this type of important, contextual information that is consistently lacking from the reportage under study.

HISTORICAL ISSUES SURROUNDING THE PALESTINIAN EXODUS: "THEY FLED BECAUSE THEIR LEADERS TOLD THEM TO"

The seminal year of the Israeli-Palestinian conflict was 1948, when the State of Israel was established and the geopolitical entity of Palestine came to an end. Jews the world over had won a sovereign homeland, while Palestinians lost their patrimony and just over half of them became refugees.

Palestine had never been a sovereign Arab state. For four centuries it was part of the Ottoman Empire until the end of World War I. Following a thirty-year period of British control over Palestine, during which Britain had made a series of conflicting promises to the Arab and Jewish populations of the country, the question of Palestine was turned over to the United Nations. On November 29, 1947, the UN General Assembly adopted Resolution 181, which called for the partition of Palestine into a Jewish state and an Arab state. Jews in Palestine owned 6.6 percent of the privately held land in the country and numbered approximately 600,000, or one-third of the population—the majority having immigrated on visas issued by Britain. The indigenous Arab population numbered 1.36 million and owned about 87.5 percent of privately held land.[12] Nevertheless, the partition plan allotted approximately 55 percent of the country's land to the Jewish state and 45 percent to the Arab state.[13] The envisioned Arab state would have a Jewish minority of approximately 1 percent, while the envisioned Jewish state would have an Arab minority of about 42 percent.[14] The Jewish leadership in Palestine accepted the partition plan; the Arab leadership in Palestine and the surrounding countries rejected it.

Thirty-three nations, including the United States, voted in favor of Resolution 181. Thirteen nations—including Afghanistan, Egypt, Iran, Iraq, Lebanon, Pakistan, Saudi Arabia, Syria, Turkey, and Yemen—voted against the partition. Ten nations, including China and Britain, abstained. On May 14,

1948, British mandatory rule in Palestine ended; on May 15 the State of Israel was declared and armed forces from Egypt, Jordan, and Iraq invaded, along with irregular units from Syria and Lebanon.

For the first four decades after 1948, accounts of the Palestinian refugee crisis with which Western publics became familiar through the media were filtered, in the main, through successive Israeli governments and the Israeli academy. In its most basic form, this constructed narrative posited that during the 1948 war Palestinians had been told—via leaflets and radio broadcasts—by their own leaders and those of the surrounding Arab countries to leave their towns and villages. Arab military forces would sweep in, defeat the newborn Jewish state, and pave the way for the status quo ante and beyond. Palestine would be restored to its prewar Arab-majority status and would be delivered to Arab sovereignty. However, just the opposite actually transpired: no such defeat took place, no such return occurred, and no such Palestinian state emerged.

The only trouble with this official Israeli narrative is that it was exaggerated to the point of being false. Palestinian refugees have been quoted in the U.S. media as saying that they had, in specific instances, been evacuated or encouraged by local or outside Arab forces to leave their towns or villages temporarily.[15] However, there is no evidence, either in media or scholarly sources, that Palestinian or other Arab leaders encouraged Palestinians to flee their country in any organized, systematic, or comprehensive fashion. In fact, Israeli historian Morris has documented just the opposite, concluding:

> The Arab leadership inside and outside Palestine probably helped precipitate flight in the sense that, while doctrinally opposed to the exodus, it was disunited and ineffectual, and had decided, from the start, on no fixed, uniform policy and gave the masses no consistent guidelines for behavior, especially during the crucial month of April [1948]. The records are incomplete, but they show overwhelming confusion and disparate purpose, "policy" and implementation changing from week to week and area to area. No guiding hand or central control is evident; no overarching "policy" was manifest. . . .
>
> Regarding April-May and the start of the main stage of the [Palestinian] exodus, I have found no evidence to show that the AHC [Arab Higher Committee in Palestine] or Arab leaders outside Palestine issued blanket instructions, by radio or otherwise, to the inhabitants to flee.[16]

For four decades after 1948, however, the American media reported few if any narratives that contradicted the official Israeli version of events. This can be attributed to two factors. The first was the familiar phenomenon of the victor dominating the vanquished in transmitting the history of a conflict. In the context of the Israeli-Palestinian conflict, this phenomenon has been echoed in the diaspora by the corresponding relative strengths of the Jewish-American and Arab-American communities and their inclinations and abilities to affect media coverage. The second factor was the disparate state of cold war–era relations between the United States and Israel, on the one hand, and the United States and most if not all of the Arab world, on the other, in which allies and foes fit neatly defined, binary classifications and were thus characterized in the mainstream media.

By the mid-1980s, however, a group of Israeli scholars who became known as the "new historians" began to offer a revised narrative based on newly declassified portions of the state archives dealing with the events of 1948. Their work presented a radically different scenario from that of the official Israeli narrative, with the refugee crisis being one very important strand in the skein. Their conclusions have only recently begun to filter into American media reports of the conflict, as will soon become apparent.

One of the best known of this revisionist cadre is Morris, who, working primarily from the archives of the Israel Defense Forces, reconstructed the Palestinian exodus of 1948–1949 in his 1987 landmark study *The Birth of the Palestinian Refugee Problem*. Morris reprised these findings as a contributor to the 2001 book *The War for Palestine: Rewriting the History of 1948*.[17] While laying a share of blame for the refugee crisis at the doorstep of the inept Palestinian leadership as well as other Arab leaders of the day, Morris writes: "Above all, let me reiterate, the refugee problem was caused by attacks by Jewish forces on Arab villages and towns and by the inhabitants' fear of such attacks, compounded by expulsions, atrocities and rumors of atrocities—and by the crucial Israeli Cabinet decision in June 1948 to bar a refugee return."[18]

In this essay Morris also discusses the extent to which the idea of "transfer," or deliberate removal of the indigenous Palestinian Arab population, was part of Zionist thinking. While Morris is careful to note that transfer never became official policy, he documents the fact that Zionist military leaders and development planners from the top down discussed it and wrote about it openly. "Indeed," writes Morris, "the Jewish state faced such a problem in the UN Partition Plan of November 1947: it would have had 55 percent Jews and 40–45 percent Arabs."[19] Morris notes that a decade before the demographic implications of partition became an issue, Zionist leader David Ben Gurion told the 20th Zionist Congress, which convened in Zurich in 1937: "The transfer of population is what makes possible a comprehensive [Jewish] settlement program."[20]

In *The Birth of the Palestinian Refugee Problem* Morris brings to light details of two very important historical aspects of the refugee problem. The first is a chronicling of "Plan Dalet," or "Plan D," which was carried out in March, April, and early May of 1948, before the declaration of the State of Israel on May 14 and the start of the war and invasion by Arab military forces on May 15. From the time the United Nations passed the partition plan the previous November, Arabs and Jews in Palestine had been engaged in a low-level civil war, with both sides suffering casualties. The Jewish community had an organized, relatively well equipped fighting force known as the Haganah. Palestinian fighters were irregulars organized into militias that acted locally with little if any centralized command structure. During the Arab uprising of 1936 to 1939 in Palestine—which was largely aimed at the British mandatory authority over the issues of Jewish immigration to and land purchase in Palestine and their impact on the country's Arab economy—the British succeeded in basically disarming the Palestinian population. By contrast, the British armed and trained Jewish fighting units to help quell the Arab insurrection.[21] Israel also maintained its advantage with respect to troop strength and weaponry during most of the 1948 war with the surrounding Arab states.[22]

In the spring of 1948 the Haganah carried out Plan Dalet, which was designed to thin out the Arab population along border areas of the Jewish and Arab states delineated in the UN partition plan. According to Morris, the magnitude of Plan Dalet's outcome was much greater than anticipated, with 200,000 to 300,000 Palestinians leaving the country in the wake of the Zionist military campaign.[23] In plain terms, this meant that approximately one-third of the 700,000 to 750,000 Palestinians who were to become refugees in 1948–1949[24]—just over half of the total Palestinian Arab population of 1.3 million—became refugees *before* the war between Israel and the surrounding Arab states even began.

In 2004 Morris published *The Birth of the Palestinian Refugee Problem Revisited*, an expanded version of his original 1987 work. Describing his new findings in an interview published in the Israeli daily *Haaretz*, Morris said: "What the new material shows is that there were far more Israeli acts of massacre than I had previously thought. To my surprise, there were also many cases of rape. In the months of April and May 1948, units of the Haganah were given operational orders that stated explicitly that they were to uproot the villagers, expel them and destroy the villages themselves. . . . There was also a great deal of arbitrary killing."[25]

Four months after the war began, Count Folke Bernadotte, the UN mediator on Palestine, issued a report stressing the centrality of the refugee issue in resolving the conflict. He repeatedly emphasized the refugees' right to return to their homes "in Jewish-controlled territory at the earliest possible date." In the report, which was published on September 16, 1948, Bernadotte wrote:

> No settlement can be just and complete if recognition is not accorded to the right of the Arab refugee to return to the home from which he has been dislodged by the hazards and strategy of the armed conflict between Arabs and Jews in Palestine. The majority of these refugees have come from the territory which, under the [UN General] Assembly [partition] resolution of 29 November, was to be included in the Jewish State. The exodus of Palestinian Arabs resulted from panic created by fighting in their communities, by rumours concerning real or alleged acts of terrorism, or explusion. It would be an offence against the principles of elemental justice if these innocent victims of the conflict were denied the right to return to their homes while Jewish immigrants flow into Palestine, and, indeed, at least offer the threat of permanent replacement of the Arab refugees who have been rooted in the land for centuries.[26]

On September 17, 1948, Jewish extremists assassinated Bernadotte in Jerusalem. In December 1948 the UN General Assembly adopted Resolution 194, which recognized the refugees' right of return.

Indeed, according to Morris, the Palestinian refugee issue ultimately precluded a comprehensive Arab-Israeli peace in 1949, with Israel refusing, on security and demographic grounds, to repatriate a significant number of Palestinian refugees. The surrounding Arab states had accepted the formula proposed by the United States in April 1949 that Israel repatriate 250,000 Palestinian refugees.[27] But how could the newly established Jewish state agree to a formula that would have brought the Arab population to some 400,000 alongside a Jewish population of 650,000—with Arabs accounting for more than one-third of the total population? Furthermore, according to Morris, despite calls from the United Nations and the United States for "a substantial repatriation of Palestinian refugees as part of a comprehensive solution to the refugee problem and to the general conflict, allowing back Arab refugees, Israel argued, would commensurately reduce Israel's ability to absorb Jewish refugees from Europe and the Middle East."[28]

Prime Minister Ben Gurion and other Israeli leaders resisted international pressure for significant repatriation, instead offering in July 1949 "to take back 100,000 refugees after there was an overall refugee resettlement plan and after there was 'evidence' of 'real progress' towards a peace settlement."[29] The surrounding Arab states rejected the offer. According to Morris:

The Arab rejection of the "100,000 offer" did not greatly displease Israel. In general, Israel's leaders were not unhappy with the no-war, no-peace situation. Ben Gurion in mid-July [of 1949] quoted [Israel's representative to the United Nations Abba] Eban as thinking: "He sees no need to run after peace—the Arabs will demand of us a price—[in the coin of] borders [i.e., border rectifications], or refugees or both. We will [i.e., can afford to] wait a few years." While ascribing this approach to Eban, Ben Gurion was probably conveying his own thinking as well.[30]

More than fifty years later, Israelis and Palestinians were still waiting. By December 2006 the registered Palestinian refugee population had swelled to 4.448 million, with 1.3 million, or 30 percent, living in fifty-eight UN-recognized camps in Jordan, Lebanon, Syria, the West Bank, and the Gaza Strip administered by the United Nations Relief and Works Agency for Palestine Refugees in the Near East. Originally envisioned as a temporary agency, according to the provisions of UN General Assembly Resolution 194, UNRWA was charged at its inception with the care of Palestinian refugees until they could return to their homes.[31] However, when UNRWA commemorated its fiftieth anniversary in May 2000, CNN broadcast a short feature whose opening implied—as did the *New York Times Magazine* piece "Playing War"—that the Palestinian exodus of 1948 was somehow voluntary or a matter of choice. CNN anchor Asieh Namdar began the report by saying, "It has been 50 years since hundreds of thousands of Palestinian families left their homes to avoid rule by Israel."[32]

LEGAL AND POLICY ISSUES

International Law and Consensus on Refugee Rights

These historical themes depart markedly from the familiar narratives that many Americans encounter in the mainstream media. However, gaps in the reporting do not end there. They continue with the omission—across the board and with few exceptions—of any but the most superficial references to the body of international law and consensus on refugee rights in general, and Palestinian refugee rights in particular, that has been codified and reiterated on numerous occasions in the second half of the twentieth century.

This body of international law and consensus comprises six major identifiable elements, three of which address universal refugee rights and three that specifically address the rights of Palestinian refugees. The first category begins with the primordial Universal Declaration of Human Rights, which the UN General Assembly adopted in December 1948. Often cited in academic writing and discussion of the Palestinian right of return—but rarely in the media—Article 13 of the declaration states:

> 1. Everyone has the right to freedom of movement and residence within the borders of each state.
> 2. Everyone has the right to leave any country, including his own, and to return to his country.[33]

The second iteration of the right of refugee return is found in the Convention Relating to the Status of Refugees, adopted by a UN conference on the status of refugees in July 1951. The convention states:

> International refugee law and international human rights law mutually reinforce each other on the right to return. . . .
> The right of return, as defined in human rights and refugee law, is determined by laws dealing with freedom of movement. While it encompasses the right to enter and settle and leave, it does not include a clear state obligation to bestow nationality. It is possible to hold a different nationality from that of the country to which the person is returning and settling as a resident, although the granting of citizenship to returnees should be encouraged.[34]

The third acknowledgement of the right of return is found in the International Covenant on Civil and Political Rights. The UN General Assembly adopted the ICCPR in December 1966 and it took effect in 1976 in nations that had become parties to the convention. Article 12, Paragraph 4, of the Covenant reiterates the language of the Universal Declaration of Human Rights while also expanding on it: "No one shall be arbitrarily deprived of the right to enter his own country."[35]

In November 1999 the Human Rights Committee, the authoritative UN body for interpreting the ICCPR, produced a comprehensive commentary on Article 12 of the Covenant, known as the "General Comment." It concluded:

> The wording of article 12, paragraph 4, does not distinguish between nationals and aliens ("no one"). Thus, the persons entitled to exercise this right can be identified only by interpreting the meaning of the phrase "his own country." The scope of "his own country" is

broader than the concept of "country of his nationality." It is not limited to nationality in a formal sense, that is, nationality acquired by birth or by conferral; it embraces, at the very least, an individual who, because of his or her special ties to or claims in relation to a given country, cannot be considered to be a mere alien. This would be the case, for example, for nationals of a country who have been stripped of their nationality in violation of international law, *and of individuals whose country of nationality has been incorporated in or transferred to another national entity, whose nationality is being denied them.*[36]

In addition to codifying the rights of all refugees in the Universal Declaration of Human Rights of 1948, the UN General Assembly has adopted three resolutions addressing the rights of Palestinian refugees in particular. The first and most oft-cited of these is Resolution 194, adopted in December 1948, one day after the adoption of the Universal Declaration of Human Rights. The resolution is captioned "194 (III). Palestine—Progress Report of the United Nations Mediator." Article 11 states that the General Assembly

Resolves that the refugees wishing to return to their homes and live at peace with their neighbours should be permitted to do so at the earliest practicable date, and that compensation should be paid for the property of those choosing not to return and for loss of or damage to property which, under principles of international law or in equity, should be made good by the Governments or authorities responsible;

Instructs the Conciliation Commission to facilitate the repatriation, resettlement and economic and social rehabilitation of the refugees and the payment of compensation, and to maintain close relations with the Director of the United Nations Relief for Palestine Refugees [*sic*] and, through him, with the appropriate organs and agencies of the United Nations.[37]

The General Assembly reiterated Resolution 194 in Resolution 2535, adopted in December 1969. The resolution is captioned "2535 (XXIV). United Nations Relief and Works Agency for Palestine Refugees in the Near East." Section B states, in part, that the General Assembly

Recognizing that the problem of the Palestine Arab refugees has arisen from the denial of their inalienable rights under the Charter of the United Nations and the Universal Declaration of Human Rights,

Gravely concerned that the denial of their rights has been aggravated by the reported acts of collective punishment, arbitrary detention, curfews, destruction of homes and property, deportation and other repressive acts against the refugees and other inhabitants of the occupied territories, . . .

Desirous of giving effect to its resolutions for relieving the plight of the displaced persons and the refugees,

1. *Reaffirms* the inalienable rights of the people of Palestine.[38]

The UN explicitly reaffirmed the Palestinian right of return in Resolution 3236, adopted in November 1974, which stated that the General Assembly

2. *Reaffirms* also the inalienable right of the Palestinians to return to their homes and property from which they have been displaced and uprooted, and calls for their return;

3. Emphasizes that full respect for and the realization of these inalienable rights of the Palestinian people are indispensable for the solution of the question of Palestine.[39]

Right-of-Return Counterpoint: Israel's "Law of Return"

In 1950, two years after it was established, the State of Israel legislated the "Law of Return," thereby paving the way for Jewish demographic expansion in the Jewish state. According to the law, "every Jew has the right to come to this country as an *oleh*," or Jewish immigrant to Israel. The right extended to any Jew in the world who was not found to be "engaged in an activity directed against the Jewish people or is likely to endanger public health or the security of the State." In 1954 the "Law of Return" was amended to exclude Jewish immigrants "with a criminal past, likely to endanger public welfare."[40]

In 1970 the law was amended for a second time to extend immigration rights to family members, including "a child and a grandchild of a Jew, the spouse of a Jew, the spouse of a child of a Jew and the spouse of a grandchild of a Jew, except for a person who has been a Jew and has voluntarily changed his religion." The Jewish relation enabling an immigrant's claim to "return" to Israel could be alive or dead, living in Israel or in the diaspora, and need not ever have lived in Israel or Palestine. The amendment defined the term "Jew" to mean "a person who was born of a Jewish mother or has become converted to Judaism and who is not a member of another religion."[41]

The "Law of Return" provided the legal mechanism to enable Israel to maintain a Jewish majority through Jewish immigration; the state's denial of the Palestinian right of return, contradicting international law and consensus, has served as the political means to sustain that majority. U.S. policy has subsidized and supported Israel's means toward this demographic end. From 1949 through mid-2007 U.S. aid to facilitate the immigration of Jews to Israel and their absorption in the Jewish state totaled $1.52 billion.[42] From 1989 to 2005 Israel absorbed approximately 1.19 million immigrants[43] and received $1.072 billion in U.S. aid for immigrant resettlement,[44] which breaks down to approximately $900 per immigrant.

In addition, between 1993 and 1997 the United States guaranteed $9.2 billion in loans to Israel from U.S. financial institutions in order to finance housing, jobs, and infrastructure for the resettlement of approximately three-quarters of a million immigrants from the former Soviet Union.[45] Even as Jewish immigration to Israel plummeted following the boom years of immigration from republics of the former Soviet Union—falling to a total of 27,000 immigrants in 2002–3 and 22,000 in 2003–4,[46] about one-third the rate of a decade earlier—U.S. aid for Jewish immigration to Israel continued apace.[47]

In support of Palestinian refugees, from 1950 to 2007 the United States contributed an estimated $3.16 billion to UNRWA, the UN relief agency for Palestinian refugees.[48] From 1995 to 2005 the Palestinian refugee population averaged 3.78 million a year,[49] during which time U.S. contributions to UNRWA averaged $94.5 million per year,[50] yielding an average of $25 per refugee for each of the eleven years.

In September 2004 at Rosh Hashana, the Jewish new year of 5765, the Israeli press carried its customary reports on vital population statistics of the Jewish state that shed light on the pivotal role that Jewish immigration had played vis-à-vis the country's demographic balance. The country's population was reported at an estimated 6.8 million, 5.5 million of whom were Israeli Jews constituting 81 percent of the population, including the 430,000 settlers living in the West Bank, Gaza Strip, and East Jerusalem; and 1.3 million Arab citizens constituting 19 percent of the population, not including the 3.5 million Palestinians living in the West Bank and Gaza Strip. While the Jewish population had grown by 1.4 percent from 2003 to 2004, the Arab population inside Israel proper had increased by 3 percent.[51] Median ages in the country were reported at 30.4 for Jews and 19.7 for Arabs.[52]

According to one press report, 63 percent of Israel's Jewish population consisted of "native Israelis" born in the country, with the remaining 37 percent having immigrated. The report stated that of the 2.2 million Israeli Jews of European and American origin, 37 percent were immigrants from the former Soviet Union who had arrived in the country after 1990[53]—meaning that some 814,000 such immigrants constituted nearly 15 percent of the country's Jewish population. This 15 percent margin was crucial to the larger regional demographic picture since it enabled a slight Jewish majority among the total population of Israel, the West Bank, and Gaza Strip. By 2007 the ethnic demographic balance between the approximately 11 million Jews and Arabs living between the Mediterranean Sea and the Jordan River was virtually even. In April, Israel's Central Bureau of Statistics reported the Jewish population of Israel at 5.415 million and the Arab population numbering 1.425 million. According to the *CIA World Factbook*, the Palestinian population numbered 2.535 million in the West Bank and 1.482 million in the Gaza Strip.

U.S. Policy Shifts on the Right of Return

The fall of the Soviet Union and end of the cold war in 1991 ushered in a new era for the Middle East peace process. In autumn 1991 multilateral peace talks were convened in Madrid. Though they produced no tangible agreements, the talks were a precursor to direct, back-channel negotiations between Israel and the Palestinians, held under the aegis of the Norwegian government, that led to the signing of the landmark Oslo accords on the White House lawn in September 1993.

Until the year before Oslo, American support for the Palestinian right of return had been consistent. In 1948 the United States had voted to affirm UN General Assembly Resolution 194, which recognized the Palestinian right of return, and had voted in the General Assembly to reaffirm the resolution each year from 1949 to 1991. On the eve of multilateral negotiations on the Palestinian refugee issue, held in May 1992 in Ottawa, Canada, State Department spokeswoman Margaret Tutweiler was reported to have "angered and stunned" Israeli officials when she said: "The U.S. has supported UN General Assembly Resolution 194 since it was adopted [on] December 11, 1948. We continue to support it. I am not going to get into any interpretations of this at this point, of its terms or elements."[54]

The statement prompted Israeli prime minister Yitzhak Shamir to request an immediate clarification of the U.S. position and an unidentified senior Israeli official to remark, "Does the U.S. support the right of 2 million persons who define themselves as refugees to come back to this country?"[55] Seven months later U.S. policy on the refugee issue abruptly veered from the course that Tutweiler had defended. When the annual "Question of Palestine" resolution came up in the General Assembly on December 11, 1992, for the first time since 1949 the United States did not support the resolution, which contained a reaffirmation of Resolution 194—and has continued to vote in the minority against the resolution each year since, through 2006. Typically the United States has cast its "no" vote with other nations including Israel, the Marshall Islands, and Micronesia, occasionally being joined by Nauru, Palau, and Tuvalu.[56]

The U.S. suspension of its support for the principle of the Palestinian refugees' right of return was part of a larger shift in U.S. policy that occurred at the outset of the Oslo peace process, a shift whose implications extended beyond the refugee issue. Before Oslo the United States had recognized UN Security Council and General Assembly resolutions that pertained to the Israeli-Palestinian conflict—and their grounding in international law—as being central to its resolution. After the Oslo accords—of which the United States was a primary architect and broker—the U.S. position assumed that all key issues of the conflict should now be negotiated between the two parties, with prior expressions of international consensus on the conflict relegated to the background. This policy shift was articulated in a letter dated August 8, 1994, written by Madeleine Albright, the Clinton administration's ambassador to the United Nations, to the incoming president of the General Assembly. Outlining U.S. priorities for the coming session, Albright named the Middle East the first "key issue" and advocated "a new realistic approach" in "accord with today's realities." She continued:

> Recently I attended ceremonies in Washington marking the historic agreement between Israel and Jordan, which followed by just ten months the accord between [Israeli] PM Rabin and PLO Chairman Arafat. We need to build on these breakthroughs and make the General Assembly's approach to Arab-Israeli issues accord with today's realities. The UNGA should reinforce the peace process by promoting reconciliation, supporting agreements between the parties, and fostering economic development. Adopting a positive resolution welcoming progress in the peace process, as we did in 1993, will test the UN's new realistic approach. At the same time, contentious resolutions that accentuate political differences without promoting solutions should be consolidated (the various UNRWA resolutions), improved (the Golan resolution) or eliminated (the Israeli nuclear armament resolution and the self-determination resolution).

We also believe that resolution language referring to "final status" issues should be dropped, since these issues are now under negotiation by the parties themselves. These include refugees, settlements, territorial sovereignty and the status of Jerusalem. Finally, we support Palestinian autonomy by redirecting resources from obsolete entities (such as the Special Committee to Investigate Israeli Practices) to UN programs that assist Palestinians to develop the self-governing territories.[57]

The withdrawal of U.S. support for the Palestinian right of return and the general shift in U.S. policy on the Israeli-Palestinian conflict can be understood in the context of changing regional and global paradigms. The synchronicity of the new phase in Israeli-Palestinian peace efforts with the emergence of the United States as the sole superpower at the end of the cold war and the beginning of a new phase of economic globalization was not a coincidence. Just as Israel had served as an American proxy and bulwark against Soviet encroachment in the Middle East during the cold war, so it was seen in the early 1990s as a platform for expanding American economic interests in the Middle East and South Asia in the new era of neoliberal economic globalization, with peace the key ingredient to bring about economic normalization between Israel and its Arab neighbors as well as other developing countries.

Concurrent with the Oslo accords, the United States revoked its recognition of the Palestinian right of return in an apparent bid to guarantee the Jewish demographic majority in Israel, having already bolstered it with the loan guarantees for resettlement of hundreds of thousands of immigrants from the former Soviet Union. Preserving its Jewish majority and outwardly Western orientation was key to Israel serving as a base for American capital expansion in the region. This was apparent in remarks made in July 1994 by John Russell, president of Days Inn, to the Israeli financial newspaper *Globes* concerning why the American hotel chain was expanding its operations to include the Middle East, beginning with Israel: "We wanted to enter [the Israeli market] for a long time. The signing of the peace agreements is an added bonus for us. . . . Israel is a springboard to the whole Middle East. We prefer to enter it first because of its Westernization. It's preferable to take a business risk in a place where we feel comfortable relative to language, culture and mentality. . . . We will start in Israel, and slowly we'll grow: to Jordan, Syria, Lebanon and Greece, maybe even to the countries of the former Soviet Union, Russia. We want to be here, on the map."[58]

The scope of the economic boom that Israel enjoyed in the years immediately after Oslo was characterized as "unprecedented" by Israeli sociologist Uri Ram, who noted that

the two years following the signature of the Oslo accords in 1993 were the peak years of the Israeli economy. Overall economic growth (GDP) had reached 6.8 percent in 1994 and 7.1 percent in 1995. . . . The flow of foreign investment to Israel in the 1990s reached unprecedented magnitude. . . . [I]n 1997 [it] reached an all-time peak of $3.7 billion, which equals 3.8 percent of the GDP. Foreign investment is one-third of all capital import to Israel. . . . The inflow of investment is also evident in the unprecedented presence of giant international or transnational corporations in Israel (in most cases they are in fact American firms).[59]

In October 1998 the *New York Times* reported on a two-day international business conference organized by the Israeli government to commemorate the country's fiftieth anniversary—where Prime Minister Benjamin Netanyahu "handed out etched glass trophies to 53 foreign businessmen whose companies had each sunk $50 million or more into the Israeli economy" in the five years since Oslo. The *Times* reported:

The peace process has already been good for business, Israeli executives say. The Arab boycott of Israel—and of multinationals that did business here—began to fracture after the Oslo accords were signed. Foreign investment climbed dramatically from $400 million yearly before 1993 to a reported $2.4 billion in 1996, as dramatized by last week's parade of CEOs from Boeing, Unilever, Nestle, Cable & Wireless, Johnson & Johnson, Motorola and other multinational heavyweights. Israeli businessmen are penetrating markets in Asia, Africa and the former Soviet bloc, and Japan, long conspicuously absent from the Israeli business scene, opened a trade promotion office here last year.[60]

The Palestinian refugee issue was on the table at the Camp David negotiations in July 2000. However, Israel and the United States asserted that only a very limited number of refugees—to be determined through negotiation—should be allowed to return to the sites of their former homes in what was now Israel—a policy very different from the right of return articulated by the international community in UN General Assembly Resolution 194 in 1948 and reaffirmed for a half century thereafter. Four years later, in April 2004, President George W. Bush would announce an even more stunning U.S. departure from international consensus on the refugee issue. At a White

House meeting with Israeli prime minister Ariel Sharon, Bush declared that "the reality on the ground" had rendered the Palestinian right of return infeasible, thus implying that there was no longer a need to negotiate the refugee issue or, for that matter, the return of West Bank land occupied by Israeli settlements. Under pressure, Bush appeared to back away from his concessions to Sharon on the settlements, but he made no such specific amends regarding the refugee issue.

American media coverage of the Palestinian refugee question in the post-Oslo period framed the right of return issue exclusively in terms of its potential to affect Israel's survival as a demographically Jewish state. The reporting routinely omitted any reference to the historical circumstances under which the Palestinian refugee problem had been created and the means by which international law and consensus sought to redress it. The coverage also appeared oblivious of the larger geopolitical context, specifically the importance that Israeli demographic dominance held for U.S. economic and political interests in the region in the transition from the cold war era to the new age of economic globalization. The next section will identify patterns in U.S. mainstream media coverage of the Palestinian refugee issue, followed by an analysis of the reporting.

Patterns in Media Coverage

Camp David, July 2000

The seven-year trajectory of the Oslo process culminated in two weeks of marathon peace talks at Camp David in July 2000. Israeli prime minister Ehud Barak and Palestinian leader Yasser Arafat arrived at the summit after having staked out their positions on the refugee issue, among others. The Israeli position was that the majority of Palestinian refugees be resettled outside of Israel. In April Barak had asked Canadian prime minister Jean Chrétien to take in 15,000 Palestinian refugees as part of an overall solution. Although an unnamed senior Israeli government official reportedly told Agence France-Presse that "Mr. Chrétien agreed in his meeting with Barak to absorb 15,000 Palestinian refugees," Chrétien flatly denied this, claiming: "We have made no accord with the government of Israel on refugees."[61] Palestinian negotiators went into the summit upholding the principle of right of return, arguing that refugees who had fled or were driven from their homes in what became Israel in 1948 should be granted the right to return to those locales in present-day Israel.

As the summit progressed, Barak and Arafat seemed to agree on the practical necessity of resettling most Palestinian refugees outside Israel's borders, but they reached an impasse over recognizing the refugees' right to return in principle, even if most would eventually end up somewhere else. The Camp David talks ended with neither a resolution of the refugee issue nor other key issues, with Barak reportedly "prepared, as a symbolic gesture, to allow up to 100,000 Palestinians into Israel under a program of family reunification"[62]—the very same number that the Israeli government had proposed in 1949, when the Palestinian refugee population was five times smaller. Barak was also reported to have indicated Israeli "empathy" and financial support for the resettlement of Palestinian refugees without, however, any recognition in principle of their right of return.[63]

In covering the summit, some U.S. media outlets did acknowledge Palestinian rights under UN General Assembly Resolution 194 without explicitly naming or stating it. The *Baltimore Sun* reported that "their demand is based on a United Nations resolution granting Palestinian refugees the right to return to their homes or gain compensation."[64] The *San Diego Union-Tribune* reported that "the United Nations has sanctioned the Palestinian 'right of return'" and quoted Edward Abington, a former U.S. consul in Jerusalem who became a lobbyist for the Palestinians, as saying, "It is extremely important for the Palestinians in the diaspora that the right of return be acknowledged."[65]

With the refugee issue at center stage, several major U.S. media outlets—the *New York Times*, National Public Radio, ABC News, the *Los Angeles Times,* and CNN—ran reports from refugee camps in Lebanon and the West Bank. While the reports may have been intended to illustrate the refugees' situation directly, the characterizations of the historical circumstances that had caused Palestinians to become refugees in the first place were sketchy at best.

New York Times (from the Ein al-Hilweh camp outside Sidon, Lebanon): Most of the families fled from parts of northern Israel in 1948 and are now into their third generation as refugees. Many left in the widespread panic over news of the massacre in the Arab village of Dier [*sic*] Yassin.[66]

NPR (from the Ein al-Hilweh camp): Like most of Lebanon's refugees, Mohammad Haloo's family fled in 1948, from a town inside what is now Israel. . . . Palestinians in Lebanon have had a complicated history. Many Lebanese blame them for fueling the country's long and bloody civil war. The Beirut government has made it clear it will not accept the permanent settlement of Palestinians in Lebanon.[67]

ABC News (airing a BBC tape from the al-Arub refugee camp north of Hebron in the West Bank): Eight thousand people live in al-Arub refugee camp. They came here when they fled their lands in the old Palestine in 1948. Ever since Israel was created, they've had no land of their own.[68]

Los Angeles Times (from the Balata camp southeast of Nablus in the West Bank): Fifty-two years ago, Palestinians fled or were forced from their villages and towns in the fighting that followed Israel's declaration of independence.[69]

CNN (from the Ein al-Hilweh camp): Generations of Palestinian refugees were raised in this camp. They hope to return to the Palestine they left in 1948.[70]

Only two of the five stories mentioned UN recognition of the Palestinian right of return. The *Los Angeles Times* story reported, via a narrative statement, that "under a 1948 United Nations resolution, the refugees are to be allowed to return home or to be compensated for the loss of their property." The CNN report referred to relevant UN resolutions by quoting Mounir Meqdah, commander of a militia in Ein al-Hilweh (as translated by an interpreter): "There won't be stability in the Middle East without solving the issue of the refugees. Europe and all Arab states have to pressure Israeli occupiers to implement UN resolutions calling for our return. There can never be peace if 4 million Palestinians are away from home."

Four of the five pieces provided a stock feature of reporting from Palestinian refugee camps in the form of anecdotal detail of physical remnants of the life in Palestine that the refugees or their elders had left behind. However, the journalism substitutes empirical evidence for historical and political context. These anecdotes—abundant in reports that are devoid of the historical details of the Palestinians' collective exodus and their internationally recognized collective right of return—add texture but little meaning, effectively rendering the artifacts mere souvenirs in the hands of pathetic, wistful dreamers.

New York Times: Ahmed Hajar carefully unfolded the tattered deed, written in Arabic script, dated 1946, and affixed with a double row of green and purple tax stamps from the British Palestine mandate that described the farm his family owned in what is now Israel.

He showed the Government of Palestine identity card, No. 3665, that had belonged to his father, Mahmoud. His elderly uncle,

Muhammad, sitting beside him on a couch in the two rooms where seven people live in this fetid refugee camp, still carries his identity card from the mandate, faded and worn. "Then, we had workers on our land," the uncle remembered about the farm where they grew oranges, bananas and vegetables near the sea in a village then called Smeirya. "Now we must work in other people's lands. It is difficult when you have once been an owner."

NPR: When Isha Ablowe fled her village in Palestine at age 17, all she took with her were three plates and three spoons to serve her young family. Fifty-two years later, seated in her cramped two-room apartment in Lebanon's Ein al-Hilweh refugee camp, she says only one of the plates remains. "This one," she says, holding the scratched porcelain plate. "This one goes back with me to Palestine." Ablowe says she may live in Lebanon but in her heart and mind, she's always in Palestine.

ABC News: Abu Omar used to be a farmer of vast lands. Now this is all he has. He can't even feed himself and his family. . . . Safely stashed away are the keys to the house he left when he was 20. It's only 50 miles away now, but a generation of a world away in Israel. Abu Omar has grown old as a refugee. He's spent two-thirds of his life here. He thinks he'll get home before he dies, but he probably won't.

Los Angeles Times: It is not uncommon for a Palestinian refugee to invite a visitor into his modest home, where he produces an antique key or a raft of decaying papers, the last symbols of a lost land.

Suhaila Abu Hamden was no different. She fetched an old tin cigarette box from its careful storage place in the closet and took out a yellowed, tattered document bearing the lion-and-crown insignia of the British Mandate and the "Government of Palestine."

Dated May 14, 1945, the document registered in faded ink her family's four dunams of land, about an acre, near what is today the Israeli city of Ramat Gan.

The *Los Angeles Times* piece, by far the most balanced and nuanced of the five, reported a dimension of the refugee story that rarely appears in U.S. mainstream media accounts, namely, Palestinian pragmatism. The report, which opened with the anecdote about Suhaila Abu Hamden, indicated not only that many Palestinians consider a mass return to Israel to be impractical but also that there is a basis for political accommodation on the refugee issue if the result recognizes the principle of the refugees' right of return.

Like thousands of Palestinians, Abu Hamden, 52, speaks of returning to a home her family fled when she was just an infant. Some of her 11 children, especially those in high school, also speak with fiery dedication of their desire to return. But others in this family, and in many Palestinian families, have become pragmatic. Nephew Falah, who is 36, has a good job and a pregnant wife, focuses on a strong Palestinian state that he hopes will soon emerge. "I am ready for a normal life," he said. . . .

Despite the rhetoric of their leadership, there is widespread awareness among Palestinians that there will be no collective return home. The faded dream has been replaced increasingly in recent years by the desire for an independent and sovereign state on attainable land, such as the West Bank and Gaza Strip.

"There is a realization that the state is the most important value in terms of national priorities, and that if one is going to sacrifice, it is the state that cannot be sacrificed," said Khalil Shikaki, an expert surveyor of Palestinian public opinion who heads a think tank in the West Bank city of Ramallah.

Shikaki said he first observed the trend about three years ago, when he included a question in one of his regular polls about a proposal . . . [that] called for compensation instead of return, and Shikaki found majority support for it.

Still, recognition of what they see as their entitlement to return home is of utmost psychological importance to many Palestinians, especially members of the older generation such as Abu Hamden, whose lives have passed in squalid camps. They feel that they were done an injustice, and they need vindication.

More typical, however, are reports that overlook such nuances and qualifications in favor of detailed descriptions of the desperate and threatening physical conditions of refugee camps—accompanied by equally desperate or apparently threatening statements uttered by camp inhabitants. The *New York Times* reported from Ein al-Hilweh:

The camp itself is a warren of cinder block houses, built literally on top of each other, because there is no other room but up. Tiny, dark passageways lead to crowded rooms. Children are everywhere.

The streets are so narrow that when two cars try to pass, monumental traffic jams result, resolved only by much patient backing and maneuvering. Walls are decorated with faded paintings of the Palestinian flag, revolutionary slogans and old heroes like Ché Guevara. Clusters of young men stand about with nothing to do. . . .

Some families still have the keys to their old houses, carried with them because they believed the promises of Arab armies that they would be back home in a week. The old people keep alive the memories of more than half century ago. The young make grandiose demands that they return to the old villages.

"My father gave me this before he died," said Ahmed Hajar, a gray-haired man who was born here, smoothing out the torn folds in the old deed. "He told me also, 'The Jews pushed out the Palestinians.' Really, he said, 'They stole your land. Remember this. Don't forget this. This is your country. Your country is very, very beautiful.'"

"What my father taught me, I teach my son," he added, putting his arm around his big-eyed 13-year-old son Mahmoud, adding that he, like many Palestinians here, took his children on Sunday into the area of South Lebanon, occupied by Israel until May, so he could look across the border.

"What is your country?" he asked gently.

"Palestine," the boy replied.

The *New York Times* story is starkly similar in descriptive tone and detail to a *Chicago Tribune* report published two and a half months earlier, in April 2000.[71] The report's news peg was recent talks that Palestinian leader Yasser Arafat had conducted with King Abdullah II of Jordan and President Clinton—in advance of the Camp David summit—on the topic of Palestinian refugees' right of return. The *Tribune* story was also reported from Ein al-Hilweh. Its opening paragraphs painted a dramatic word picture to accompany a photograph of the Hajit family eating by gaslight in their home in the camp:

Inside his family's dim and dilapidated home, Fahdi Hajit can recite the most defiant poetry of the decades-old Palestinian pursuit of a homeland.

For Hajit, just getting home is also difficult. His family has lived in one refugee camp after another since it fled from what is now Israel 52 years ago, and Hajit, disabled since birth, faces a daily struggle to negotiate the shattered concrete and open sewer traps of this camp's filthy passageways.

"If we don't get a solution that allows us to return to our village, then even I am ready to become a suicide bomber," Hajit says with bravado.

Unwanted and unable to envision a better future, Hajit and hundreds of thousands of Palestinian refugees in Lebanon are sensing a new hopelessness, teaching each new generation about a homeland most have never seen.

Fahdi Hajit's comment about becoming a suicide bomber was echoed in the words of militia leader Mounir Meqdah: "When Hezbollah [the Islamic resistance movement battling Israeli occupation troops in south Lebanon] stops, we will start. It's most important that the enemy never rests. If there is one Palestinian refugee left in the region, there won't be peace." The camp itself is described as being "isolated" and "out of sync": "Leaders here still talk about taking Jerusalem by force and rallying the rest of the Arab world to the cause; shopkeepers still display portraits of heroes of causes that are more the stuff of myth than victory—Ché Guevara, Saddam Hussein, condemned Kurdish leader Abdullah Ocalan."

The story paints a portrait of hopelessness and belligerence supported by a carefully yet incompletely arranged narrative. For a "cause" to be "the stuff of myth," it must be part of a conflict that has only vague beginnings and a seemingly endless path of protracted chaos rather than one to which the rationales of international political consensus—much like the ones that cleared the path for the establishment of the State of Israel—may be applied.

The Second Intifada, Autumn 2000

The second Palestinian intifada, or uprising, broke out at the end of September 2000. It was sparked by the visit of Ariel Sharon—then head of the Likud party leading the parliamentary opposition—to the Temple Mount, or "al-Haram al-Sharif" (the noble sanctuary). Hundreds of armed Israeli security forces accompanied Sharon, whose September 28 visit to the heart of Jerusalem's Old City was intended as a show of Israeli sovereignty over a site holy to Jews and Muslims alike. On September 29 Palestinians rioted on the Mount, pelting Jewish worshipers at the Western Wall with stones. Israeli troops answered with gunfire, killing seven Palestinians. The fighting quickly spread to other Palestinian towns in the West Bank.

The conditions leading to the outbreak of the second Palestinian uprising, however, had been simmering for months before Sharon's provocative visit. Palestinians were frustrated by a seven-year "peace process" that saw fortunes recede for most of the population. During the same period the number of Israeli settlers in the West Bank and Gaza Strip had nearly doubled, and the Israeli population as a whole enjoyed the economic and diplomatic benefits that flowed from the Oslo accords. The seven-year Oslo period, capped by the failure at Camp David, also had two other distinguishing characteristics for the Palestinians: widespread dissatisfaction with and distrust of what was perceived to be an increasingly corrupt leadership in the form of the Palestinian Authority; and the formation, arming, and training of thirty thousand to forty thousand Palestinian security and police forces. By the time of Sharon's power play on the Mount, Palestinian frustrations were almost at the boiling point and the stage for armed conflict—albeit a dramatically disproportionate one—had been set.

In October 2000 CNN dispatched reporters to three refugee camps to take the pulse of Palestinian anger against the backdrop of the failed Camp David summit and the raging Israeli-Palestinian violence. The three reports were well suited to the visual nature of television, focusing on heated Palestinian sound bites against backdrops of camp squalor. The historical and contemporary factors contributing to the refugees' rage were glossed over to the point of near exclusion; mention of Palestinian refugee rights was wholly absent.

On October 11 high-profile CNN correspondent Christiane Amanpour filed the first of the three reports from the Qalandia refugee camp, situated between Jerusalem and Ramallah in the West Bank.[72] A paradigm for CNN coverage from Palestinian refugee camps in its focus on the superficial and sensational over the substantive, the transcript of Amanpour's report follows in its entirety:

CHRISTIANE AMANPOUR (voice-over): At the Qalandia Refugee Camp, every day is a day of rage, and the rage is taught at a very early age.

"My family tells us how Israelis kicked us out of our country and they teach us how to get it back," says 10-year-old Mohammed. "We'll kill the Israeli army and get it back."

"Our children are raised to resist the occupation by any means," says Abu Amar. "If the school doesn't teach them how to resist, we do."

AMANPOUR: Mothers may wince at the danger, but for the fathers it's a matter of honor.

"For us, there's no danger because we've lost everything," says Abu Amar. "Today, we're willing to sacrifice our children for Palestine and for the al-Aqsa holy site."

AMANPOUR (on camera): Your father just said that he's willing to sacrifice his children for the struggle.

(voice-over): "I'm not scared," says 12-year-old Suhib. "If I die,
I'll become a martyr."

AMANPOUR (on camera): Wouldn't you rather play football?

(voice-over): "When there are clashes," says Suhib, "I throw stones
to defend my country. When there are no clashes, I play and I study."

AMANPOUR: Mujahed is 16. His name means "fighter."

"I have no dreams," he says. "All I want is weapons to defend
my country."

AMANPOUR: Even 17-year-old Shireen, who wants to be a doctor, is
caught up in these inflamed passions.

"Maybe I have other ambitions," she says, "but I am also willing
to die liberating my country."

Amanpour's only mention of the contextual factors behind her interview
subjects' seemingly sensational statements was brief: "Seven years of peace
efforts appear to be unraveling so quickly because Palestinians, especially
those who live in refugee camps like this one, simply haven't seen the benefits of peace. Once, they say, they had hope, but now they are disenchanted
and, in many cases, destitute."

The camera then reverted to another desperate refugee, whose dramatic
observations were capped by an equally dramatic closing kicker by Amanpour
that foreshadowed more frustration and violence to come rather than making
the frustration and violence already at hand comprehensible to her viewers.

AMANPOUR (voice-over): Hazim is a baker. Like so many people here,
he barely makes a living wage: $250 a month.

"We were optimistic back then, not like now," he says.

AMANPOUR: These men usually work in Israel, but the army has closed
off access since the recent troubles.

"When we work, we eat that day. If not," he says, "there is no
food or drink."

"We don't care about food, we want freedom," yells this man.

AMANPOUR: And for every day that passes without a final peace deal,
there are more youngsters willing to risk life and limb, yet another
generation willing to put its dreams on hold.

On October 14 CNN correspondent Rula Amin reported from the Jabaliya refugee camp in the northern Gaza Strip. Palestinians had demonstrated

there in advance of an Arab summit on the Israeli-Palestinian violence that was scheduled to be held in Egypt in two days. The short report consisted of taped footage of the demonstration, with Amin doing a stand-up from the camp in which she did not interview a single refugee on camera but nevertheless emphasized the potential for violence.

> GENE RANDALL (CNN anchor): For Palestinian reaction to the meeting in Cairo, CNN's Rula Amin is in Gaza—Rula.
>
> RULA AMIN: Gene, we have just [inaudible] Jabaliya refugee camp. This is one of the biggest camps in the Gaza Strip, where there was a major demonstration. This is a replay of the demonstration that took place there.
>
> Hundreds—several hundreds of Palestinians went to the streets. They were protesting this summit, they were saying that they don't want Yasser Arafat to go to the summit. They think he is going to be pressured to compromise and their message was, don't compromise.
>
> They burnt [sic] Israeli flags. They also had caskets wrapped in American flags and Israeli flags. And they really went—there was anger there as they destroyed these caskets. There is outrage on the Palestinian streets. People here are not optimistic.
>
> They think Mr. Arafat will come back empty-handed and he should not go.[73]

CNN correspondent Ben Wedeman filed the third of the three CNN reports from the Beqa'a camp outside Amman, Jordan, on October 30. Like Amanpour's piece, Wedeman's report opened with a sensational sound bite from a seemingly enraged refugee.

> BEN WEDEMAN (voice-over): Ask almost anyone in Jordan's Beqa'a refugee camp, home to more than 100,000 Palestinian refugees, and they'll say the same thing: peace is dead.
>
> "The Israelis can slaughter every one of us," says Abu Khaled. "We won't give up one inch of our land."
>
> WEDEMAN: The talk here is no longer of peace, but of a jihad, a holy war against Israel.
>
> "It's an excellent idea," says Ayman, "so we can fight like the people in Gaza and the West Bank, so we can die like them."
>
> WEDEMAN (on camera): The anger in this refugee camp is echoed across the Arab world, as pressure mounts on Arab leaders to stop talking and do something to act against what is widely seen as Israeli aggression.

(voice-over): But the people here have little faith in those leaders, many of whom are seen as corrupt and weak.

"They're just protecting their throne," says this man. "Here, even the smallest child knows this is true."

"The Arab leaders can do nothing," says another. "Americans control them. So it is up to us, the people, to lead the jihad."

Wedeman included more context in his piece than Amanpour did in hers, but his rendering of the historical aspects of the refugee issue was slight. Moreover, the context of their internationally recognized rights was altogether absent:

> WEDEMAN: The majority of the 4.5 million Jordanians trace their roots back to Palestine, having fled a succession of Arab-Israeli wars since 1948. The ties are still strong, emotions still raw.[74]

The different functions of print and broadcast journalism are widely known and understood. Television can tell a story visually and with great emotional impact, whereas print media can convey important contextual background more easily absorbed by readers than by viewers. Still, contextual reporting by U.S. mainstream print media on the Palestinian refugee question—and many other aspects of the conflict—is rare. In November 2000 the *St. Petersburg Times* published just such a rare example of contextual reporting in a 1,200-word backgrounder on Palestinian refugees.[75] The piece, which was played on page 2 of the front (or "A") section of the paper, bore a Jerusalem dateline and was accompanied by a black-and-white Associated Press photo of a Palestinian man injured in clashes in the al-Arub refugee camp near Hebron. Reporter Susan Taylor Martin, who was virtually alone among her peers in seeking out the perspectives of nonpartisan Mideast experts based in the United States and Canada, filed a report that was remarkable for its thoroughness, balance, and nuance. It began by acknowledging a mainstream American, media-enabled point of view:

> For five weeks now, you've seen them on TV and in the newspapers—Israeli soldiers battling Palestinians, many of them from refugee camps in the West Bank and Gaza Strip.
>
> You've probably seen pictures of the camps, crowded, dirty, dispiriting places.
>
> And you may have wondered:

Why haven't the Palestinian refugees moved to other Arab countries? And why haven't other Arab countries done more to help the refugees?

Jews worldwide often ask those questions, reflecting their frustration, even anger, that a seemingly solvable problem is instead a perennial source of turmoil.

But the issue of Palestinian refugees lies at the emotional and legal nexus of the Mideast conflict. So here's a primer, based on interviews with several experts.

Early on, Martin noted that the 1947 UN partition of Palestine—rejected by Palestinian Arabs and the surrounding Arab states—had allotted just over half of the country's land to the Jewish population of Palestine, even though Jews accounted for only a third of the country's total population. Midway through the piece Martin referred to Jordan, Egypt, and Syria as "poor countries with low standards of living," unable to absorb large numbers of Palestinian refugees "without economic, social and political disruption." The two most contextually informative elements in the piece's Q&A format referred to the enduring nature of the Palestinian refugee problem and UN recognition of the rights of Palestinian refugees. The person supplying the answers was Jon Alterman, a Mideast analyst with the United States Institute of Peace.

Q: Why have the refugees stayed in the camps so long?
A: The Palestinians are from cities in Palestine, so that's where their roots are, that's where they'd like to return. . . . Jews retained an attachment to the land of Israel for 2,000 years and Palestinians retain an attachment to the towns and cities from which they came.
Q: Do the Palestinians have any legal claim to the land they left?
A: Yes, they say, citing two U.N. resolutions.
    Resolution 194, adopted after the 1948 war, says "Refugees wishing to return to their homes and live at peace with their neighbors should be permitted to do so at the earliest practicable date."
    It also says "compensation should be paid for the property of those choosing not to return and for loss of or damage to property."
    Resolution 242, adopted after the 1967 Mideast war, affirms "the necessity for achieving a just settlement of the refugee problem."

Most telling, perhaps, was Martin's ending with a wrap-up quote by John Stigler, a Mideast expert at Carleton University in Canada: "The refugee camp was primarily a Palestinian choice because they were assured by the United Nations that the refugees were going to go home. They didn't want to integrate . . . because the world had promised them the right of return."

The Clinton Plan and the Taba Talks: December 2000–February 2001

After the second intifada had raged for eleven weeks, Israeli and Palestinian negotiators reconvened from December 19 to December 23 for talks at a U.S. Air Force base near Washington, D.C. There President Clinton presented a "bridging plan" that addressed the refugee issue, among others, by endorsing the right of return to a "Palestinian homeland." This was widely interpreted to mean that refugees would return to the Palestinian state that would be established in the West Bank and Gaza Strip, not to the locales they had left in what became Israel. Palestinian negotiators rejected the Clinton proposals overall, finding them too vague and unacceptable because they implied that additional rounds of interim negotiations would be necessary before a Palestinian state might be realized. On the issue of the right of return, Palestinian leaders were inclined "to view strict adherence to UN resolutions as their bottom line," according to a *Baltimore Sun* report quoting Palestinian political analyst Ghassan Khatib. "It's not a bazaar; it's international legality. Either we get it or forget about it."[76] Shortly after the first of the year, Palestinian chief negotiator Yasser Abed Rabbo circulated a memorandum among Jerusalem-based diplomats outlining Palestinian objections to the Clinton plan. A *New York Times* report summarized Palestinian objections on several key issues. Concerning the refugee issue the paper reported:

> The American proposal to recognize the right of Palestinian refugees to return to the Palestinian state, but not to their former homes in Israel, "reflects a wholesale adoption of the Israeli position," the document says.
>
> "The essence of the right of return is choice: Palestinians should be given the option to choose where they wish to settle, including return to the homes from which they were driven," the memorandum adds. "Recognition of the right of return and the provision of choice to refugees is a prerequisite for the closure of the conflict."
>
> At the same time, the document notes that the Palestinians are "prepared to think flexibly and creatively about the mechanisms for implementing the right of return" that would end the refugee problem while accommodating Israeli concerns.[77]

By late January 2001, time was running out for both the Clinton and Barak administrations. Palestinian and Israeli negotiators held a final round of peace talks in Taba, Egypt, from January 21 to January 27, the last such parley before Clinton left office and Sharon was elected prime minister. Although the Taba talks ended with no agreement, reports surfaced in the Israeli and U.S. media over the following months indicating that the two sides had agreed on the parameters of a solution to the refugee issue.[78] A new international body replacing UNRWA would be established to raise funds and administer compensation for property expropriated from the refugees. Each refugee would be offered five options: (1) rehabilitation in the current country of residence, including citizenship; (2) return to the new state of Palestine; (3) resettlement in a designated area in the southern Negev region of Israel; (4) emigration to a third country other than Israel; or (5) return to Israel proper. Refugees would be encouraged, through a package of incentives, to choose to settle outside of Israel. Israel might agree on a quota of forty thousand refugees to return over a five-year period and would retain the "sovereign" right to decide which refugees to readmit. While the Taba talks did achieve a definition of boundaries with respect to the refugee and other key issues, escalating violence between Israelis and Palestinians precluded further negotiations.

Between December 30, 2000, and February 1, 2001, pegged to the Israeli-Palestinian talks held first in Washington, D.C., and then at Taba, eleven major U.S. news organizations carried reports devoted entirely to the Palestinian refugee question: CNN, the *New York Times*, the *Atlanta Journal-Constitution*, NPR, the *Washington Post*, the *Chicago Tribune*, the *Christian Science Monitor*, *Newsweek*, CBS News, NBC News, and *Newsday*. The resulting thirteen pieces—CNN and the *Washington Post* each carried two reports from different refugee camps—focused on two main themes, namely, that the refugee issue posed a "stumbling block" for peace negotiations, and that despite their hopes and dreams, the majority of refugees would likely not return to the lands they left in what became Israel. Five of the thirteen reports made a specific or general reference—albeit in passing and not as a focal point—to one or more UN resolutions recognizing the rights of Palestinian refugees, and two reports referred to refugee rights indirectly. Six of the thirteen reports did not mention these rights at all.

Reporting from the al-Jalazoun refugee camp northeast of Ramallah, CNN correspondent Rula Amin both named and referred to UN General Assembly Resolution 194 in some detail. However, whereas she presented the Palestinian point of view through two unnamed, nonauthoritative sources—an "old man" and a taxi driver—she presented the Israeli point of view through two named, authoritative sources: the current prime minister and a former prime minister. Her piece began:

RULA AMIN (voice-over): Verses of the Koran resonate as people gather at the main square of al-Jalazoun refugee camp waiting for the call to Friday noon prayers. As they flock to the mosque around noon, residents here say, as much faith as they have in God, they have faith that one day they will go back to the homes they left in 1948, when Israel was created.

> This old man says he is sick of being a refugee and named a refugee wherever he goes.

> About 8,000 Palestinians live in this camp. They come from 36 different villages, all now in Israel, most of them destroyed, some turned into Jewish towns. UN Resolution 194 says the refugees have the right to return to their homes, and based on that 52-year-old resolution, Palestinians say Israel must grant the refugees the right to return as a prerequisite to ending the conflict with Israel.

> The prime minister of Israel says, no way.

EHUD BARAK (prime minister of Israel, through translator): The government under my leadership will not accept any agreement under any situation that will recognize the right of return in any shape or form, period.

AMIN: "No way? Then it's no way to make peace," says this taxi driver.

> Israelis say granting 3 million Palestinian refugees the right to return will undermine Israel's Jewish identity.

SHIMON PERES (former prime minister of Israel): The right of return is not negotiable, because this is like committing suicide. It means to convert the Jewish majority into a Jewish minority.

AMIN: Both sides are still looking for a compromise to what is becoming a major stumbling block in the peace process.

However, the CNN report did illustrate an important distinction between theory and practice vis-à-vis the right of return. Quoting Jon Alterman of the United States Institute of Peace, the report stated: "I think there are two separate issues. One is an issue of a right of return, versus the return of Palestinian refugees, and it seems to me that there is a fair bit of play between acknowledging a sort of right on behalf of the Palestinians and also acknowledging that all Palestinians or even most Palestinians won't exercise that right."[79]

The *Atlanta Journal-Constitution* published a report from the al-Amari refugee camp south of Ramallah. Toward the end the story referred to the possibility of a resettlement program "that Palestinians hope will be based on a 1948 U.N. resolution that promised them either return or compensation." More notable, perhaps, was reporter Larry Kaplow's rendering of competing Israeli and Palestinian claims in an exceptionally balanced narrative tone:

> Israel refuses to acknowledge any responsibility for the displacement of the Palestinian refugees. It counters claims that it is to blame by arguing that Arab military attacks on the fledgling state of Israel prompted Palestinians to flee.
>
> But some Israeli historians and many eyewitnesses tell of organized intimidation and killings aimed at driving the Arabs out. In any case, the refugees were not allowed back and the rubble of their bulldozed villages can still be seen on Israeli plains and hillsides. . . .
>
> Israelis say that to allow almost 4 million refugees back would destroy the Jewish nature of Israel, where about 5 million of the 6 million residents are Jewish. They say Palestinians will have to take the compensation and quit fighting history.
>
> Palestinians argue that Israelis should admit that their country was built on a massive displacement of civilians. They note that Israel's demographic mix would not be overturned by a compromise proposal to let some of the refugees back—maybe a few hundred thousand.[80]

The *New York Times* piece was published in its Sunday "Week in Review" section, in which articles often take on an op-ed tone. In an analysis bearing a Jerusalem dateline and not reported from a refugee camp, reporter John Kifner opened with a virtual reprise of the descriptive tack he had taken in his earlier report from Ein al-Hilweh, replete with references to cinder-block houses, keys to houses left behind in Palestine, and replicas of the Palestinian flag. Unlike the earlier piece, explicit mention was made of UN General Assembly Resolution 194. However, there was an erroneous reference to the number of Palestinians who "fled the fighting that commenced with the Arab attack" in May 1948. According to Morris, at that point 200,000 to 300,000 Palestinians had already left the country, with a total of 750,000 having become refugees by war's end.

> They are no longer just refugees, but the children and grandchildren of refugees. Still, in the narrow, muddy streets of Ein al-Hilweh in Lebanon, Balata on the West Bank and the 57 other camps, where cinder

block homes are painted with Palestinian flags and images of rifles, they treasure keys to homes in the Galilee, where they once lived. Old, tattered land deeds with the tax stamps of the British mandate are passed down the generations with equal reverence.

Today, there are today [*sic*] nearly four million Palestinian refugees. For 52 years, since some 750,000 people fled the fighting that commenced with the Arab attack on the newly created state of Israel in 1948, they have cherished the "right of return" enshrined in United Nations Resolution 194, which was adopted that year.

Assuming a condescending tone, the piece mischaracterized the reason behind the longevity of the refugee issue by attributing it to the preferences of Palestinian leaders rather than to the fact that UNRWA was established by the United Nations to administer the camps until a political solution to the refugees' status could be found based on their right of return, sanctioned by Resolution 194. The story then characterized the Palestinian refugees themselves—rather than the unresolved issue of their status—as the key stumbling block in the peace process.

Unlike other refugee groups that eventually dispersed, many of these people, at the direction of the Palestinian leadership, have remained clustered in the camps, which serve as incubators of irredentist nationalism. Here the schools teach about al-Nakba, the disaster, as the Arab world calls Israel's founding, and pass on wondrous tales of the beauty of their former olive groves and orange trees.

It is these people, with their myths and unassuaged grievances, who are emerging, in the wake of President Bill Clinton's last-ditch proposals for a comprehensive settlement, as perhaps the most difficult element in the Middle East peace puzzle.[81]

Near the end of his report from the Dheisheh camp outside Bethlehem, *CBS Evening News* reporter David Hawkins referred to "an existing UN resolution guaranteeing the Palestinian refugees' right of return." However, in the introduction to the piece anchor Russ Mitchell characterized the right of return as a Palestinian rhetorical device that is one of two primary obstacles to peace—sending mixed signals about the validity of Palestinian refugee rights and claims: "And the most stubborn obstacles to peace are the status of Jerusalem and what Palestinians call the right of return. David Hawkins tells us millions of Palestinian refugees will never be content until they can reclaim their homes in Israel."[82]

A *Washington Post* report from the Rashidieh camp in southern Lebanon focused on the "painful reality" that the majority of Palestinian refugees would eventually settle in venues other than Israel "even though rhetoric surrounding the issue remains as absolutist as ever." A third of the way through, the piece asserted that an eventual peace deal would have to be one that "at least appears to redeem the rights of all refugees and complies with U.N. resolutions supporting them." Yet the opening of the piece, which referred to those rights as mere invocations by Palestinian and other Arab leaders and as militant demands by the refugees themselves, once again substituted rhetoric for international recognition of rights as the basis for the Palestinian refugee cause.

> The stamp of militancy is impressed hard on this beachside refugee settlement. Banners back the Palestinian uprising against Israeli occupation in Gaza and the West Bank. Armed guards protect the local leadership. And the 17,000 Palestinians who live here wait impatiently to reclaim homes that they, their parents or grandparents abandoned when Israel was created in 1948.
>
> Along with Palestinian officials from Yasser Arafat on down, and kings and presidents throughout the Arab world, they insist that day will come or Israel will never see peace—language that has elevated the "right of return" to a sacred cause. The long quest for that right was cited as one of Arafat's main objections to proposals put forward by President Clinton last month in a last-ditch effort to shepherd Israel and the Palestinians into a final peace settlement.[83]

A National Public Radio report by Jennifer Ludden from the al-Hussein refugee camp near Amman was one of two reports that made only indirect mention of Palestinian refugee rights. However, the piece offered a nuanced view of the acknowledgement by some Palestinian refugees that returning to what is now Israel would be impractical—and that a compromise would be possible if it included "on principle" an admission by Israel that "it bears some responsibility for the refugees' plight." The NPR report continued: "It is assumed most refugees would not return even if they could, opting instead for compensation or resettlement elsewhere. But there are plenty who say they would go back. In the West Bank city of Nablus, refugee rights activist Hussam Hader says no one can relinquish his internationally sanctioned right to return, not even Yasser Arafat. Hader has no illusions about moving back into his grandmother's house in Jaffa, but he's ready to accept something nearby and become an Israeli citizen."[84]

A *Christian Science Monitor* report from the Beqa'a camp northwest of Amman referred to one camp resident's "idea of a return to his village" as "the leading article of a deeply-held faith," as well as to Clinton's proposal that "Palestinians renounce their long-held insistence on their 'right of return.'" This piece, like others of its type, implied that the right of return was a Palestinian invention. The story mentioned Palestinian refugee rights three other times, but the first two of these references characterized them as demands of Palestinian and other Arab leaders rather than as rights repeatedly recognized by the international community.

> Compounding the difficulty is that these refugees have been nurtured in their waiting by their leaders, who have insisted that their rights would be fulfilled and that the hardships of the present would pay off in the end.
>
> Arab foreign ministers meeting in Cairo with Mr. Arafat yesterday adamantly supported that position. They claimed the Palestinian refugees have a "sacred" right to return to Israel, notwithstanding the fact that most Palestinians say Arab support for their cause has been half-hearted and ineffective.

A refugee made the third reference to Palestinian rights. With international acknowledgement of those rights wholly absent, the piece ended with an implied threat to Israel spoken by another refugee:

> "I am a human being—that much is recognized by the whole world—not some cargo to be sold. [The Israelis] kicked me out of my land, took away my home—how is anyone going to compensate me for that?"
>
> That such a deal might be signed by Arafat is also unconvincing. "He may be our leader but he has no right to sign away our rights."
>
> Mahmoud, Mansour's son, nods in agreement with his father's words, adding that he feels the attachment to the land even more strongly.
>
> A few blocks away, the "daughter of Palestine" indicates what the options are if Palestinians refuse a negotiated settlement. "I'm raising my children to liberate Palestine," she says, tousling the hair of a four-year-old boy clinging to her waist. His pants are camouflage.[85]

A plurality of the reports—six out of thirteen—made no mention of UN resolutions that recognize Palestinian rights. The most dramatic and impressionistic tone was taken by *Newsweek*, an approach common in weekly newsmagazines that seek to summarize and characterize events and trends rather than to report their daily details. Reported principally from the al-Maghazi refugee camp in the central Gaza Strip, the piece resonated with the words "romantic," "odyssey," "fantasy," "myth," "dreams" and "fabled"—all used in reference to Palestinian refugee claims. The refugees' collective future was characterized as "an obstacle, a problem that could prove even more intractable than the division of Jerusalem." The piece was replete with references to unequivocal Israeli rejection of the right of return and "the rusted keys and faded deeds to the property" that Palestinian refugees left behind. However, there was no mention of international recognition of Palestinian refugee rights.

One family's refugee history was rendered in a highly dramatic fashion in the first two and last two paragraphs. This labored description, laced with journalistic interpretation, serves as a recurring trope in such reporting for the expression of Palestinian refugee expectations about their right of return. The resulting portrayal renders the Palestinian subject cartoonish if not foolish and deflates if not negates the Palestinian perspective. At the same time, the journalist's own editorial voice becomes a convenient stand-in for Israeli and American policy consensus on the issue and a substitute for the facts of international law and consensus.

> In the Maghazi refugee camp, where everything is broken and life is wretched, Sami Bin-Said spins romantic tales about the land his grandfather left behind a half-century ago. Someday, he insists, he will reclaim it. At 25, Bin-Said is a third-generation Palestinian refugee. His family's odyssey typifies the plight of many Palestinians—dispossession, wandering, violence and misery. Bin-Said has never been to Beersheba, the town his grandfather fled in the 1948 war. But like other refugees, he can describe his family's life there in rich detail: the fertile soil, the dignity of the land, the tranquility. From his home in Maghazi he points east and says that if the trees were cleared, he could even catch a glimpse of the family plot. With at least 20 miles separating the refugee camp from Beersheba, that's a fantasy. Yet it's also part of a myth that has sustained refugees like Bin-Said through 52 years of camp life: that their land is just over the fence, and their return home inevitable.
>
> The hard truth is, their return is far from likely. In what may be the endgame of Israeli-Palestinian peacemaking, Sami Bin-Said's future and that of 4 million other Palestinian refugees scattered across the Arab world stand as an enormous obstacle, a problem that could prove even more intractable than the division of Jerusalem. The refugees' homes

were seized or destroyed long ago; many of their villages have been razed. Even the most dovish Israelis reject a return of Palestinian refugees as demographic suicide for the Jewish state. Yet no Palestinian, least of all Yasser Arafat, has tried to prepare the refugees for a deal in which their dreams are bargained away. . . .

Refugees have been at the front line of Israeli-Palestinian confrontations, both in politics and on the killing fields. Bin-Said's brother Baha is one of them. An officer in the Palestinian Preventive Security Service, Baha Bin-Said stole into a Jewish settlement not far from Maghazi in late November and killed two Israelis before being shot dead.

Three weeks later his wife gave birth to a boy, a fourth-generation refugee who will know his father only through stories. The boy was given his father's name, Baha Bin-Said, to honor the shahid, Arabic for martyr. If Israelis and Palestinians reach a peace deal, international aid could change the face of Baha's community. If not, he will grow up in the same squalor his parents and grandparents knew. Either way, Maghazi camp will likely remain his home, Arafat may or may not be his leader and his dreams will remain focused on a fabled little plot of land across the fence.[86]

The theme of an *NBC Nightly News* report concerned conflicting claims of what Palestinian refugees "say are their homes" and the disposition of the places they left in what is now Israel. The piece, reported by Martin Fletcher from Tel Aviv, opened with an unidentified man claiming "You will remember, this is our house" and references to keys and title-deed documents retained by the Amara family, now refugees in Jordan. Although Fletcher made no mention of UN recognition of the Palestinian right of return, he did state an apparently erroneous assumption that if given the chance, the majority of Palestinian refugees would return to Israel. Next an Israeli woman presented a counterclaim to the same land that the Amaras left in 1948:

MARTIN FLETCHER: The right of return is the biggest stumbling block in the peace talks. A deal-breaker, says Arafat. But for Israel, that's a problem. Where would this country, with 5 million Jews, put 3.5 million Palestinians? Fifty years ago, the 65 acres of Amara's land was mostly empty land. Today, it's a built-up suburb on the edge of Tel Aviv with hundreds of Israeli families living here. Edna Shaher has never heard of the Amaras.

EDNA SHAHER: (foreign language spoken)

FLETCHER: "One family owns all this?" she asks. "Lucky them! But give them my home?" she says. "Never! I was born here."

Two people, one home, stalemate. Hussein [Amara] did come visit last year. He couldn't find the old family home—it's gone. Hugged a tree where the family cemetery was. Everything's changed except the dream to return to what they say is their home.[87]

A *Newsday* piece reported from the Bourj el-Barajneh camp in Lebanon compared the readiness of younger refugees to resettle in Europe and North America with older refugees' desire to return to the lands they left behind. Palestinian refugee rights were characterized by the reporter as "the dream of return" and "the political wishes of the Palestinians" in a quote by a PLO official. Once again no mention was made of international backing for such rights. The piece ended with a dramatic quote by a fifty-six-year-old refugee whose son had immigrated to Denmark: "The land needs my blood, my brother's blood, all of our blood. If I go to Canada, I will forget my land and I will not do anything to liberate it."[88]

Christiane Amanpour of CNN reported from the Dheisheh camp on the importance that the refugee issue held for upcoming Israeli elections. She took a tack used by many of her colleagues in the U.S. media, omitting any reference to international recognition of the Palestinian right of return. Instead, Amanpour characterized it as a promise made by Palestinian and other Arab leaders to refugees like Fatemeh Odeh of Dheisheh, who in Amanpour's words "has raised her children and grandchildren on a diet of dreams and tales of a beautiful homeland." Amanpour concluded: "Palestinian leaders and Arab leaders throughout the years have always promised their people that they will be able to come back and reclaim homes that they had to leave after the war of 1948, homes here in Israel. And so the ordinary Palestinians continue to live with that hope and tell us that unless they get their homes back, there will be no peace. . . . Palestinian politicians say that their people must have the right to return, even if they never use it."[89]

The *Washington Post* and the *Chicago Tribune* published stories in early January reported from the al-Amari camp outside Ramallah. It is not unusual for foreign correspondents to go out together to report a story, visiting a site such as a refugee camp. The advantages of this practice can include increased safety for the correspondents and savings for their news organizations in the form of shared expenses for transportation and interpreter services. However, the practice can also result in reports that bear striking similarities in content, structure, and interpretive approach, as was evident in the *Post* and *Tribune* pieces. The reporters visited the Nabil café in al-Amari, where they encountered refugee Ayesh Abu Halim.

Post: "I have nine children, five daughters and four sons," said Ayesh Abu Halim, a 64-year-old Palestinian with a red-and-white checked headdress. "And if you ask the youngest one, she will say she is from Lod, where her father is from. . . . I have a house here," Abu Halim said, referring to his dwelling at the camp. "I don't need a house. But I need land; nothing compensates me for my land."[90]

Tribune: "I have nine children, and if you ask the youngest where she comes from, she will say Lod," near what is now Israel's Ben Gurion International Airport, said the retired drywaller [Abu Halim], 64. "I have a house here. I don't need a house. But I need land. There is no land like my land."[91]

Neither story, however, mentioned international recognition of Palestinian refugee rights, for which both reporters used the "dream" and other metaphors. The *Post* characterized the Palestinian national movement as having been "founded on the dream that those who fled were grievously wronged, and, one day, would be allowed to return." The *Tribune* put quotation marks around the phrase "right to return," characterizing it as having been "as much a part of Palestinian identity as Palestinian Authority President Arafat's checkered headscarf, as central to national aspirations as a state itself."

Both the *Post* and the *Tribune*, however, offered a nuanced counterclaim to the traditional Israeli narrative of the refugee problem. In citing the work of Israel's "new historians," the two papers—along with the *Christian Science Monitor* and CNN—indicated that alternative historical narratives about this root-cause issue of the Israeli-Palestinian conflict have, to varying degrees, begun to appear in the U.S. mainstream media.

Post: Israel historically has insisted that most Palestinians who left in 1948 did so voluntarily out of fear, or at the urging of Arab countries that attacked the new Jewish state at its inception. But some instances of forced expulsion have been documented recently. Israeli historian Benny Morris, in his book "The Birth of The Palestinian Refugee Problem, 1947–1949," wrote: "If Jewish attacks directly and indirectly triggered most of the Arab exodus up to June 1948, a small but significant proportion of that flight was due to direct Jewish expulsion orders issued after the conquest of a site, and to Jewish psychological warfare ploys."

In Lod, Morris described how "Arab families were ordered to 'get out' by soldiers who went from house to house."

Tribune: Israel's insistence that most of the refugees left voluntarily has been challenged in recent years by the so-called new Israeli historians, who have questioned Israel's founding notions and uncovered alleged evidence of alleged expulsions.

Christian Science Monitor: Some Palestinian leaders and intellectuals argue that the "right of return" can be satisfied with a more honest accounting of what happened in 1948. In recent decades, some Israeli historians have begun to say that the Arab exodus was not a voluntary exit but the result of deliberate efforts to rid the land of its inhabitants.

CNN: AMANPOUR: Some Israeli academics are beginning to acknowledge that many Palestinians were forced from their homes in '48.
BENNY MORRIS (historian): Until the 1980s, Israelis believed that the Palestinians, the 700,000 who became refugees in '48, left voluntarily. It was a very mixed bag in what happened in '48. Some were expelled, some were, in fact, advised by their leaders to leave; but by and large people left because of the war. There was a war, people were shelled, there was shooting, there were massacres, and people fled.
AMANPOUR: But even doves like Benny Morris believe allowing 4 million Palestinians to come back would be demographic suicide for Israel.
MORRIS: You would have had something like 50–50 Jews and Arabs here, and you wouldn't have had a Jewish state.

Such passages provide an encouraging indication that at least some American journalists are not only aware of the existence of this particular alternative historical narrative—one that addresses a touchstone issue of the conflict and has important implications for one of the key points for its resolution, namely, the Palestinian refugee issue—but are also inclined to include it, even if merely in passing, in their reporting. While this runs counter to the prevailing pattern of ahistorical coverage of the refugee issue (as well as other key issues of the conflict), ironically it is also a further indication of a journalistic tendency whose result is to mute and/or withhold credibility from Palestinian voices. Palestinian refugee claims—and, implicitly, Palestinian refugee rights—are validated via historical fact by Israeli sources representing a minority viewpoint within Israeli society. However, Palestinian sources representing a majority viewpoint within their society are given voice on the refugee issue only within the frame of "myth," expressing their "hopes" and "dreams."

Apex of the Spiral: Autumn 2001–Spring 2002

From the time Ariel Sharon assumed the Israeli premiership in March 2001, Israeli-Palestinian violence escalated—having already claimed scores of lives since the outbreak of the second intifada five months earlier. The Israeli army pursued an accelerated policy of assassinating suspected leaders of Palestinian secular and Islamic militias, using U.S.-supplied helicopters and F-16 fighter jets with unprecedented frequency and often killing Palestinian civilians in the process. The Israeli military escalation was especially apparent in the wake of September 11, 2001. Responding to the terror attacks against U.S. targets that claimed just under three thousand lives, President Bush, adopted a "with us or with the terrorists" dictum—which, intentionally or otherwise, served to give freer rein, if not legitimacy, to Sharon's tactics.

During this period Palestinian suicide bombings continued unabated, with refugees from camps in the West Bank and Gaza playing increasingly prominent roles. The phenomenon can be attributed to two factors. The first was the socioeconomic gap between the top PLO officials who had left Tunisia with Yasser Arafat to establish the Palestinian Authority—many of whom led lives of conspicuous luxury, especially in Gaza—and the refugees, whose worsening economic conditions the PA had done little to alleviate. The second reason was that after seven years of Israeli-Palestinian negotiations under the Oslo framework, the refugees—in the occupied Palestinian territories and beyond—were no closer to achieving their internationally recognized rights.

Wafa Idriss was a divorced and childless twenty-eight-year-old refugee from the al-Amari camp, near Ramallah, who became both famous and infamous in late January 2002 as the first Palestinian female suicide bomber. Detonating a bomb in downtown Jerusalem, Idriss killed herself and an eighty-one-year-old Israeli man and injured dozens of Israeli bystanders, including children. In an evenhanded report from al-Amari, *Washington Post* correspondent Lee Hockstader wrote: "In death she has become her home town's heroine, an object of admiration and amazement to Palestinians—and of deep concern to Israelis. . . . To Palestinians, she has become a symbol of nationalist sacrifice and desperation, a warning of what is to come. To Israelis she is a sign of the conflict's radicalization and a trigger for tough new security measures."

Hockstader reported that Idriss had been traumatized by her work with the Palestinian Red Crescent Society, having two weeks earlier "cradled a 15-year-old boy, Samir Kosbeh, who was hit in the head by a bullet fired by the Israelis" outside Yasser Arafat's Ramallah headquarters. The boy died two days before Idriss blew herself up. Hockstader ended his piece with the suggestion that Idriss's refugee status also may have been a factor in her actions: "A friend of Idriss's family who identified herself as Fadwa grew impatient when asked to explain Idriss's deed. 'Our land has been taken, we've been made refugees, they are demolishing our houses. What can you expect from people like this?' she demanded."[92]

The prominence and motivation of refugees in suicide bombings and militant operations was also noted in an 1,800-word *New York Times* Sunday feature that James Bennet filed in March from the Jabaliya refugee camp in the Gaza Strip.

> The refugee camps have supplied the most fighters, Palestinians say, and the most willing to kill themselves in the cause. It is their vision of earthly paradise lost—not of a heaven full of obliging virgins—that motivates them, said Dr. Nizar Rayan, a leader here of the Islamic group Hamas.
>
> "We are not doing these military operations because of the women," he said, sitting in the study of his comfortable house here. "We are doing them because of my house in Ashkelon. My house is stolen. I want it to go back to my children."
>
> One of Dr. Rayan's sons was shot dead last fall during a suicidal attack on a settlement in the northern Gaza Strip. "No, no, no, it was very easy," he said when asked if it was hard to lose a son. "If we want to get back our land, it seems we have to lose half this generation."

Noting that Israel had begun raiding Palestinian refugee camps in search of "terrorists and their weapons," Bennet opened the piece as follows:

> Now Jabaliya is awaiting its turn to be hit.
>
> Israeli soldiers have torn other camps apart, punching passages through interior walls to ransack house after house, and killing dozens of Palestinians in firefights.
>
> Those raids have set off echoes of past violence among the three generations of refugees who are trapped by poverty, political calculation and their own longing for plots of the land in what is now Israel.

In attacking the camps, Israel is again joining the half-century struggle at the core of the conflict, as the grandsons of the Jews who won the
1948 war square off with the grandsons of the Arabs who lost it.

However, this evenhanded tone was followed by a rendition of historical
and political aspects of the refugee issue that tilted toward official Israeli narratives. "The refugee camps, many Israelis believe, have prevented the Palestinians from moving on," Bennet wrote, observing that the right of return to
lands Palestinians left in 1948 "seems preposterous to most Israelis. Rejecting
that original state [outlined in the UN partition of 1947], Arab nations attacked it, and people . . . fled as the Israelis drove them back and took the
land, in some cases killing Arabs." Making no specific narrative reference
to UN General Assembly Resolution 194 anywhere in the piece, Bennet
construed international consensus as Palestinian claim: "Invoking a United
Nations resolution, Palestinians say they should return to their homes inside
Israel. Israelis fear that a flood of refugees would achieve through demogra-
phy and democracy what the Arabs have failed to do by force of arms—the
erasing of the Jewish character of the state."[93]

At the end of March, Saudi crown prince Abdullah unveiled a Mideast peace proposal that highlighted internationally recognized Palestinian refugee rights. In essence, it offered across-the-board Arab recognition
of Israel, including normalized diplomatic relations, in return for Israeli
withdrawal from the West Bank and Gaza Strip according to UN Resolution 242.

Meeting in Beirut, the Arab League approved the plan. The *Los Angeles
Times* reported that "Abdullah invoked a 1948 UN resolution that proposes
repatriation or compensation for the refugees. Abdullah's proposal said peace
must include 'achievement of a just solution to the Palestinian refugee problem to be agreed upon in accordance with UN General Assembly Resolution 194.'" However, the *Times* story, reported from the Shatila refugee camp
outside Beirut, made no narrative mention of Resolution 194 independent
of Abdullah's reference to it, nor did it mention any other international
recognition of Palestinian refugee rights. Like other U.S. reporting from
refugee camps, the story asserted that the camp itself—not the reasons behind
its existence—"presents a serious hurdle to anyone looking to bring peace to
the region." Headlined "Displaced Palestinians Put Faith in Jihad," the report
focused on the degree of anger among residents of the camp, "scene of a massacre two decades ago by a Lebanese Christian militia allied with Israel," and
the threat implicit in that anger.

Virtually every family here has a rusted key or an old yellowed document proving ownership of a piece of property they were forced to abandon. Everyone has a sense that they are owed something. . . .

Nothing will ever convince Ali of a key element of the Saudi proposal, that Israel has a right to exist—at the expense, as he sees it, of his family.

"It will be very hard to coexist with the Israelis," he said. "Jihad is the only solution."[94]

The *New York Times* also published a story on refugee reaction to the summit from Shatila in which reporter Neil MacFarquhar made an explicit (though erroneous) narrative reference to Resolution 194: "Camp residents had been similarly transfixed by reports from that summit meeting, their mood soured when they learned that Arab leaders were softening the language on the return of refugees. The initiative did mention United Nations Security Council [*sic*] Resolution 194, which states that all refugees who fled in 1948 should be allowed to return or be compensated. But the wording suggested that the return was negotiable."[95]

MacFarquhar's exceptional approach was also evident in a story he reported the following month from the Beqa'a camp in Jordan. Rather than resorting to condescending "dream" or "fantasy" metaphors, he included explicit references to Resolution 194 and other elements of international consensus on Palestinian refugee rights. In a notably balanced 2,100-word story, MacFarquhar wrote that the refugees'

first tents were erected pretty much at the same time the United Nations was founded, on the premise that wars of conquest should become a relic of history.

Various international conventions and at least one specific resolution followed; that resolution promised the Palestinians either a return to their homes or compensation.

The refugees have been clinging to that promise ever since, aided in no small part by the fact that the Arab nations they fled to have largely declined to absorb them. . . .

About 800,000 refugees fled their homes during the first Arab-Israeli war of 1948.

A United Nations resolution, No. 194, passed that year, said they could go home or receive compensation once all area nations were living at peace with their neighbors.[96]

CNN, meanwhile, had sent a correspondent to the Ein al-Hilweh camp to assess the refugees' mood against the backdrop of the Arab summit in Beirut. The report made the requisite references to "aging land documents . . . treasured possessions that help back [refugee Ahmed el-Haj's] claim to property the family abandoned more than 50 years ago during Israel's war of independence." The report, which did not mention Resolution 194 or any other international recognition of the right of return, ended on a wistful and dramatic note: "In Ein al-Hilweh, home of Ahmed el-Haj, there's a new custodian of his land records. Nethu Mahmud inherited the responsibility a year ago when his uncle died. The family takes us to the cemetery where Ahmed is buried. The graves here are filled with refugees. But hopes of a Palestinian return home somehow, sometime, are seemingly undimmed, even as time and life passes away."[97]

The Arab summit was cut short on March 27 when more than two dozen Israelis, while celebrating a Passover seder in a Netanya hotel, were massacred in a Palestinian suicide bombing. Two days later Israeli tanks surrounded Yasser Arafat's Ramallah compound, all but destroying it and beginning a six-week incursion through the West Bank, reoccupying all six major towns and destroying Palestinian government facilities and infrastructure.

The climax of the Israeli incursion was played out in mid-April in the Jenin refugee camp in the northern West Bank, where some 50 Palestinian fighters and civilians and 23 Israeli soldiers were killed in some of the fiercest fighting of the second intifada. Responding to a Palestinian ambush in the heart of the camp, in which 13 soldiers were killed, the Israeli army bulldozed between 100 and 150 of the camp's 1,100 houses, with another 700 made unlivable, according to a report from the camp published in the *Atlanta Journal-Constitution*. The report also cited UN estimates that 2,000 of the camp's 13,979 residents might have been made homeless. Reporter Larry Kaplow painted an evocative word picture of the destruction and its symbolism:

> This week, as residents of the Jenin refugee camp continued sifting through the staggering swath of destruction caused by Israeli troops, their thoughts turned to the familiar cycle of destruction, displacement, militancy and more destruction.
>
> From a plastic chair on her rooftop overlooking the wreckage, Lutfia Abdel Rahman, 65, took in the view. "We have gone back many years," she said.
>
> She came to the camp at age 11 when her family fled the village of Zireen during the war in 1948. Her family home there eventually was destroyed by the Israelis, and her house in the camp just escaped destruction this month.

Below her, on the other side of "Return Street," neighbors poked around in the rubble for lost property or loved ones.

Some half-houses poked up from sand-and-gravel rubble, their upper floors caved in and their walls sheared away, exposing furniture and pictures inside.

The report, however, made no mention of international recognition of Palestinian refugee rights. Of the 1.1 million camp dwellers throughout the region, Kaplow wrote: "They hold on for the unlikely prospect of a 'right of return' to their homelands. The camps also serve as symbols of the Palestinian plight."[98]

CONTENT ANALYSIS

The bulk of U.S. mainstream media coverage of the Palestinian refugee issue consistently and conspicuously omits detailed reference—or reference of any kind—to relevant historical and political aspects of the conflict. In the main, the reporting instead focuses on easily observed anecdotes and easily obtained quotes to the virtual exclusion of the contextual back story. It appears that a media consensus—which has it that the right of return for Palestinian refugees is largely the stuff of "dreams" and "myth," and that the articulation of that right begins and ends with Palestinians and Arab leaders—is often substituted for international consensus, which clearly says otherwise.

Furthermore, much of the reporting on the refugee issue construes the refugees themselves as an obstacle to peace rather than that obstacle being the failure to resolve their status according to the expressly stated international will to do so. It is no wonder, then, that few if any reports in the U.S. mainstream media connect the dots between the palpable sense of oft-reported rage emanating from Palestinian refugee camps and the flouting by Israel of international consensus on the right of return since 1948 and by the United States since the early 1990s.

In August 2002, as part of "a series of occasional articles on obstacles to peace in the Middle East," the *Boston Globe* published a story reported from Taibe, "a vibrant Palestinian neighborhood" in Amman, Jordan. In a piece headlined "Hard-line Refugees Won't Budge on Israel," *Globe* reporter Charles Radin noted the refugees' "fiery passions," and that many in Taibe "say they would leave for Palestine tomorrow if they could. And once there they would do what they could to put an end to the Jewish state." The story made several references to the right of return but failed to link any of them to any international recognition of this right. Instead, the report quoted a refugee as saying, "The right of return will never be implemented," which was followed by Radin's assessment: "On the Palestinian side, any leader who gave up the claim to a right of return would risk his political life, and his physical well-being." In fact, the first mention of a right of return was made in the negative: "Israel is adamant that Palestinians who fled or who were driven from their homes in the war of 1948, when Arab countries and Palestinian irregulars tried to prevent the establishment of the Jewish state, have no right to return. Palestinian negotiators are similarly adamant that without recognition of such a right, there can be no settlement of their struggle with the Israelis." Radin also suggested that Palestinians had languished in refugee camps for more than fifty years due to the manipulation of their leaders. The report did not mention that UNRWA had been established to administer the camps on what was intended to be a temporary basis—until political modalities for implementing the right of return sanctioned by Resolution 194 could be found. Instead, Radin wrote, "Maintaining 'camps' is a way of reinforcing the determination of the refugees to return to territories that have been part of Israel since 1948."[99]

In his report from the Jabaliya camp in Gaza for the *New York Times*, James Bennet gave an accurate rendering of UNRWA's designated role to maintain the camps and not to resettle the refugees—while at the same time invoking an ugly metaphor: "The camps are administered by a United Nations agency created expressly for Palestinian refugees. Unlike the United Nations agency for refugees of other conflicts, this agency was specifically not directed to protect the refugees or to resettle them. It was empowered to house, feed, medicate and educate them, in effect maintaining them as a political running sore."[100]

There are three plausible explanations as to why these trends are so pervasive in much mainstream reporting on the Palestinian refugee issue. The first relates to cultural congruence. American foreign correspondence, like most if not all American journalism and popular culture, is a product of its own social milieu. Within this framework, Americans tend to view displacement and refugee status in a particular and occasionally exceptional manner. While the United States does have a well-documented history of displacing its own Native American population, rarely if ever are members of this community—in narrative accounts of their historical encounters with Americans of white, European extraction—characterized as refugees. Simply put, despite the parallels that exist between Native American and Palestinian displacement, American public discourse does not recognize the former as refugeeism, nor does it empathize with the latter. Americans generally do not see their country as having displaced and relegated its own indigenous population to what arguably could be called internal-refugee status. Rather, they see the United States as offering a haven to refugees who come here from other lands. Furthermore, the use of the word "refugee" to refer to the tens of thousands of Americans in Louisiana and Mississippi who were driven from their homes and communities by Hurricane Katrina in August 2005 aroused considerable objection. Although they are also subject to natural disasters, which make refugees of people the world over, it was argued that Americans should not be referred to as such.

Within this framework, the American (and Western) cultural construction of political refugeeism generally attaches a positive value to resettlement in foreign host countries and integration into their societies—which often have the economic means for absorption that countries in the regions of the refugees' origins do not. In developed host countries refugees are thought of as deserving aid and sympathy on condition that they give up their right or desire to return to their former homes and countries. However, the premise upon which a solution to the Palestinian refugee problem was based from the very beginning—with the United Nations setting the terms of discourse—was exactly the opposite: it envisioned that the Palestinians would eventually return to their homes.

Having supported that notion by voting for UN General Assembly Resolution 194 in 1948 and having reaffirmed it every year from 1949 to 1991, American Mideast policy abruptly changed course. The evolution of this thinking was evident in an op-ed piece published in the *Washington Post* days before the opening of the Camp David summit in July 2000. Its author was Phyllis Oakley, a former U.S. assistant secretary of state for population, refugees, and migration whose work on these issues began in September 1993[101]—the same month and year that the Oslo accords were signed. In her op-ed piece Oakley proposed "an international resettlement program, beginning with [Palestinian] refugees in Lebanon," and suggested that Palestinian refugees now be subject to the same principles of resettlement that apply to other refugees instead of deserving the right of return implicitly accorded Palestinians under UNRWA.[102]

This leads to the second explanation, namely, that consciously or unconsciously U.S. mainstream reporting on the refugee issue largely mirrors U.S. Mideast policy. It is a policy that has been and remains explicitly tilted in favor of Israel in the pursuit of what is officially defined as the U.S. national interest in the region. Mainstream media reporting on many aspects of the conflict can only go so far—that is to say, not very far at all—in challenging the contours of that policy.

Thus, official Israeli narratives regarding the Palestinian refugee question (as well as other aspects of the conflict) get wide media play, and they yield two basic claims. The first is that the surrounding Arab states are to blame for the refugee problem because they encouraged Palestinians to leave their country in 1948 and then refused to make peace with and recognize Israel while simultaneously refusing to absorb the refugees. The second is that Israel cannot and does not recognize the Palestinian right of return for existential reasons. Were Israel to absorb a significant number of Palestinian refugees within its borders, it would struggle to maintain a Jewish majority. Within a relatively short period of time, this would ultimately result in the end of the existence of Israel as the Jewish state. This point of view is routinely conveyed in the American media, as reported in the *Los Angeles Times* during the Camp David summit of 2000:

> Israel says it cannot allow repatriation en masse, because to do so would destroy the Jewish state, undermining its demographics and posing a potential security threat. Further, Prime Minister Ehud Barak has said his country cannot and will not accept responsibility or blame for the refugees' plight because many who fled did so on orders of the Arab leaders of the time. . . .
>
> "We will consider unifying families of Palestinians living in Israel," Haim Ramon, one of Barak's senior ministers, said . . . "not as recognition of the right of return from a legal, political or moral point of view, but as a gesture of mercy."[103]

In addition to incorporating this Israeli view of the refugee issue by quoting Israeli sources directly and paraphrasing their statements, the media often deliver their own journalistic narratives, which take on a similar cast—independent of Israeli sources. This was clearly evident in an April 2002 *Time* magazine report on the "sticking points" of the Israeli-Palestinian conflict. In a three-paragraph summary of the refugee issue, *Time* reported facts about the refugee population and how Israeli and Palestinian negotiators had addressed the issue in 2000. At the same time, the report put forth the following unattributed, declarative assessment: "In 1948 waves of defeated Palestinians fled Israeli territory to find shelter in squalid camps that the years have made permanent. . . . Although Palestinians cling to the UN-endorsed 'right of return,' it's not going to happen. To let hundreds of thousands of Palestinians live inside Israel would be suicide for the Jewish state, destroying it by demographics. Yet the refugees have to find a home somewhere, or succeeding generations will never stop making war on Israel."[104]

The third explanation for why media coverage of the refugee issue is characterized by a paucity of historical and political details supporting Palestinian claims to the right of return is a comparative dearth of official Palestinian response and rebuttal on issues of crucial importance to the peace process. Most of the Palestinian sources quoted in the media reports cited earlier are Palestinian refugees; the rest are political commentators or researchers. Virtually no comment was forthcoming—and it is not possible to know to what degree it was solicited—from Palestinian negotiators, ministers, or other officials of the Palestinian Authority. In existence only since the mid-1990s, the PA has not been in a position to match the resources and precision with which Israeli officials deliver their point of view to the international media. Israeli perspectives are disseminated via multiple institutional channels, including the prime minister's office, the Foreign Ministry, and the army—as well as by individual members of the Knesset, intellectuals, and members of the public.

Palestinians have been slow to marshal an organized media response, and those efforts were no doubt arrested by the PA's state of disarray since the March–April 2002 Israeli military incursion throughout the West Bank, which resulted in the destruction of much of its infrastructure. One Palestinian official likened attempts to put the Palestinian message across in the face of Israeli media penetration to "a baby arm-wrestling a giant."[105] The sentiment that the PA has not adequately represented Palestinian interests found expression in a 2001 *Boston Globe* report in which a Ramallah marketing professional "voiced a cautious criticism of Arafat and the Palestinian leadership. . . . 'We have the most just case in the world, and the worst lawyers representing us.'"[106]

The operative technique, then, in covering the Palestinian refugee issue appears to be for journalists either to report the proceedings of negotiations or to visit a given refugee camp and then relate what can be seen and heard *then and there*, to the virtual exclusion of relevant contextual background.

Two salient trends thus emerge. First, the issue of refugee return—especially in reports emanating from the refugee camps themselves—is usually couched in terms of what Palestinians themselves claim and narrate. These claims are set *in opposition to* the more familiar Israeli claims and narratives rather than being affirmed in any significant detail by historical fact and international consensus or by impartial expert analysis. The implicit right of Jewish refugees to have immigrated to Israel—coming from Europe or elsewhere in the Middle East with or without direct ancestral ties to the land—is often recognized, with the resulting Palestinian displacement seen as a historical inevitability, albeit an unjust one. This theme was illustrated in an exchange between PBS *NewsHour* correspondent Elizabeth Farnsworth and two Israeli women, an excerpt from a balanced report that also took Palestinian perspectives into account.

> ELIZABETH FARNSWORTH: Israeli artist Etti Barchil has been a leader in the effort to protect the old Arab homes. She and her husband restored this 150-year-old house [in Jaffa] themselves. Her family fled anti-Jewish persecution in Iran in 1949. She has little sympathy for the Palestinian refugees' desire to return.
>
> ETTI BARCHIL (through interpreter): The truth is I cannot blame people who fled out of fear, I cannot judge them, but the fact is that a lot of people stayed. Over a million people in Israel today are Palestinian Arabs who chose to stay.[107] I have no problem with that. But we were forced to flee, and that's important to emphasize. We've got a small piece of land. Damn it, let us live!
>
> FARNSWORTH: Gaby Aldor also lives in a restored Arab home. She bought it from the Israeli Housing Authority, which took over abandoned Arab properties after 1948. Some of Aldor's family came from Europe in the early 20th century, some later, fleeing the Holocaust. She's a choreographer/director who has produced a much-awarded theater piece about the overlapping claims in this city.
>
>   How do you justify living in a home that, that perhaps belongs to somebody else?
>
> GABY ALDOR: Well, it's the same as I can't justify or not justify the fact that somebody's living in my father's house in Vienna. I mean this is really the tragedy of history. In this century people have been moved, people move. So what I can do is recognize their pain and say yes, it is painful. . . . [Y]ou can't emotionally say "OK Palestinians, something was done wrong to them" . . . because you can't cut it off from the history of the whole era; and the whole era's history is awful.[108]

Conversely, the Palestinians' right of return to lands that they themselves or their immediate families have inhabited is often cast as opposing these Jewish rights or as being simply passé. In a *Christian Science Monitor* story on the future of separated Palestinian families, Mariam, a Palestinian resident of the village of Masraa in northern Israel and a citizen of the Jewish state, reflects on the possibility of someday being reunited in Israel with her relatives, who live in the Bourj el-Barajneh camp outside Beirut:

"I am an Israeli citizen," says Mariam. But she adds: "All these people should go back to where they're from. The Yemenites, the Russians, they should all go back to their countries or find another country to live in. I don't love them. The Jews are responsible for separating me and my family."

Her children, now in their 30s, shift uncomfortably in their chairs. Many in their generation, aware of what their parents suffered, have moved on to a new coexistence.[109]

The second trend in coverage is that Palestinian refugees are routinely portrayed in mainstream media reporting as a group that is (1) highly emotional, angry over their loss of patrimony and preoccupied with dreams and longing for a homeland many never have seen, and (2) an obstacle to peace in their stubborn and obstinate clinging to those dreams. By and large, Palestinians are *not* portrayed as a group having internationally recognized rights and a tangible, living attachment to the land—the very same land claimed by Israelis for similar reasons.

A sampling of seventeen headlines from reports on Palestinian refugees published and broadcast from 2000 to 2002 bears out these characterizations (emphasis added):

Los Angeles Times: Displaced Palestinians Put Faith in *Jihad*
San Francisco Chronicle: Among Refugees, *Seething Anger*
Boston Globe: Anger Inside Camps, and Out; Plight of Refugees a *Point of Passion* for Arabs, Muslims
CNN: *Anger Mounts* Among Palestinian Refugees in Jordan
CNN: Palestinian Refugee Camp *Outraged* in Response to Mideast Summit
CNN: Crisis in the Middle East: Cultivating *Palestinian Rage* at Qalandia Refugee Camp
Chicago Tribune: Palestinian Exiles' *Hopeless* Life in Lebanon Fuels a *Growing Rage*
New York Times: For Palestinian Refugees, *Dream of Return* Endures
New York Times: In Camps, Arabs Cling to *Dreams of Long Ago*
Chicago Tribune: Arab Refugees Fear *Losing Their Dream*
Washington Post: For Refugees, Hope Is Where the *Dream* Is
New York Times: Out of Place; The Price Will Be *Paid in Dreams*
Lost Angeles Times: Palestinians Divided on *Dreams for a Homeland*
Boston Globe: Hard-line Refugees *Won't Budge* on Israel

NPR: Fate of Palestinian Refugees Remains Key *Stumbling Block* in Efforts to Forge a Final Peace Deal

CNN: Right of Return for Palestinian Refugees Emerges as *Stumbling Block* in Peace Negotiations

CNN: Fate of Palestinian Refugees Remains *Sticking Point* in Israeli-Palestinian Negotiations[110]

On rare occasions, however, nuanced reporting on the Palestinian refugee issue does appear, as exemplified by the following excerpt from an April 2002 report by Neil MacFarquhar of the *New York Times*:

> There is a practical streak among the refugees, a recognition that they are pursuing the unattainable.
>
> For many, any decision will undoubtedly shift from the sentimental to the economic. "They know they are going to have to make a realistic decision one day, but they want to feel they are part of the decision," said Ms. Khader, the lawyer.
>
> She says Palestinians should not be questioned about why they cling to the notion of returning after a mere 50 years when Jews intoned "next year in Jerusalem" as a kind of prayer across the millennia.
>
> "The main point that the Israelis make in justifying their state is its existence 3,000 years ago," she said. "For the Palestinians it is only 50 years. Many of them are still alive, their homes are still there in Jaffa, in Lydda or in Ramleh, all over the place."[111]

Nevertheless, American public opinion is routinely informed not by the nuanced exception but by the stereotypical rule, with coverage excluding much contextual information germane to the refugee issue. It is therefore unlikely that the American public would either understand the importance of the right-of-return issue or question the fairness of U.S. policy regarding it. The question of whether media coverage affects policy or policy determines media coverage thus becomes a chicken-and-egg conundrum. A relationship between the two is clear, however, leading Kathleen Christison to conclude that "the rote assumptions and misperceptions that form much of U.S. public thinking on this issue have always ultimately re-emerged as policy."[112]

In an Independence Day interview with Israel Radio in May 2003, Israeli prime minister Ariel Sharon made an unprecedented declaration, stating that the Palestinians had to renounce their claim to the right of return as a condition for peace talks to continue. A week earlier the United States, in concert with the European Union, Russia, and the United Nations, had presented a peace plan called "the road map," which called for the refugee issue, among others, to be negotiated. In the interview Sharon called the right of return "a recipe for the destruction of Israel" and said Palestinian renunciation of it "is something Israel insists on and sees it as a condition for continuing the peace process."[113]

On April 14, 2004, President Bush issued an unprecedented policy declaration of his own that dovetailed neatly with the one Sharon had made the year before. Meeting the Israeli prime minister at the White House, Bush declared that not only would Israel not have to give up all its West Bank settlements in negotiations but that it also would not have to accept the return of Palestinian refugees to Israeli territory. The move—in which the United States and Israel effectively excluded the Palestinians from negotiating these two most critical issues—stunned observers of the conflict around the world.

Attempting to put a positive spin on the president's statement, two weeks later Secretary of State Colin Powell defended Bush, claiming that the president had merely acknowledged "the reality on the ground." Powell continued: "The president clearly wanted to take account of obvious realities we all recognize with respect to [the] 'right of return' and final borders, [which] have to be aligned in accordance with the reality on the ground."[114]

More backtracking followed. On May 4, the U.S.-EU-UN-Russia "Quartet" that had authored the "road map" plan to revitalize the peace process a year earlier issued a statement that contradicted Bush's apparent fiat, saying "any final settlement on issues such as borders and refugees must be mutually agreed to by Israelis and Palestinians."[115]

In a May 6 news conference with King Abdullah of Jordan and against the backdrop of Arab and European complaints, Bush himself appeared to back away from the concessions he had made to Sharon concerning the settlements, urging Israel to withdraw from territory it captured in 1967 and saying all territorial issues must be negotiated according to UN Resolutions 242 and 338. However, the president made no specific reference to the refugee issue.[116]

If, in this case, international public opinion had triggered a U.S. policy correction, could a more informed American public opinion have an even greater overall effect? If there were to emerge a body of reporting that framed the issue of Palestinian refugee rights differently—if not beginning from the premise of international recognition of those rights, then at least placing that recognition on a par with Israeli counterclaims—could this journalism have a significant impact on U.S. public opinion toward the Israeli-Palestinian conflict and the role of U.S. policy in it?

A policy that recognizes the principle of the Palestinians' right of return is not the same as a policy that advocates the actual return of millions of refugees to present-day Israel. The former would acknowledge a degree of Israeli responsibility for Palestinian flight in 1948 and the ensuing refugee problem, while offering Palestinian refugees a broad range of compensatory options. A 2003 survey conducted by Khalil Shikaki, director of the Palestinian Center for Policy and Survey Research in Ramallah, indicated that the vast majority of Palestinians would not opt to return to what is now Israel.[117]

The survey showed that only 10 percent of 4,500 refugees surveyed in the West Bank, Gaza Strip, Jordan, and Lebanon would choose to rebuild their homes in Israel. A majority 54 percent said they would accept compensation and homes in an independent Palestinian state in the West Bank and Gaza; 17 percent said they would stay where they are; and 2 percent said they would move to a foreign country. When Shikaki attempted to convene a press conference to announce his findings, his office was trashed by dozens of rioters who claimed that he was trying to show that the majority of Palestinians were ready to renounce the right of return.[118]

Whether the result of a misperception or deliberate skewing of Shikaki's findings, the rioters in Ramallah sent a clear signal that the right of return cannot be taken off the table by virtue of fiat—as Sharon had declared in his Independence Day interview in Jerusalem just two months earlier—or reasoned away because of changed realities on the ground, as Bush would indicate in Washington a year later. News reports and editorial comment on the aborted press conference tended to play up the violence, even though Shikaki had been pelted with eggs but not otherwise harmed. The headline on the 1,200-word page 1 story in the *New York Times* the following day read "Palestinian Mob Attacks Pollster," while the *Chicago Tribune* ran an editorial on the subject two days later under the headline "Mob Rule in Ramallah." The context for the passions that fueled the rioters' actions got little if any play.

This is consistent with the overall pattern of U.S. mainstream media coverage of Palestinian refugees. As a body of work over time, the reporting routinely denies its audience the contextual tools with which to assess important historical and political aspects of the issue. It also fails to address important questions, including: Why has U.S. policy shifted from recognition of Palestinian refugee rights during the first four and a half decades of the conflict to withdrawal of that recognition since 1992? Why has the United States concurrently either advocated (or not blocked) the right of refugees to return to their homes in Bosnia, East Timor, Kosovo, and Rwanda? How do this change in policy and apparent double standard serve U.S. interests in the Middle East and beyond?

The prototype for reporting the refugee issue consists of a mixture of dramatic descriptions of angry refugees in squalid refugee camps—holding antique keys and dreaming of perfumed orchards—and summaries of the here-and-now state of negotiations. All of these elements could be found in a July 2000 *Newsweek* piece that assessed Israeli and Palestinian reaction to the Camp David negotiations being held in the United States. Covering the range of issues on the table at the summit, the piece nonetheless began with the refugee question, suffusing it with customarily vivid and combustible imagery and juxtaposing the official and collective Israeli view with the perspectives of two Palestinian refugees.

> Sitting amid the squalor of the Dheisheh refugee camp, Naeem Abu Aker holds up a rusty key. It is, he says, the key to the house near Jerusalem that he fled in 1948—to the 2,000 acres his family lost and their fragrant, never-forgotten apple orchards. It is also the key to Abu Aker's outrage, an all-embracing passion that will brook no excuse or compromise, especially from Yasser Arafat. In the camp, his home for the 52 years since Israel's "War of Liberation," he and his fellow Palestinians live in grim, gray concrete houses piled messily on top of each other like building blocks. Sewage flows down narrow, trash-strewn paths. . . . But last week Abu Aker was concentrating on events at another place half a world away. His mind's eye was trained, as if on the last wisp of a fading dream, on the bucolic mountain retreat where his fate was being decided: Camp David.
>
> In intensive negotiations with Israeli Prime Minister Ehud Barak, Arafat was said to be demanding a "right of return" for millions of Palestinian refugees like Abu Aker. Barak was stoutly refusing to permit most of them to do so; such a vast inflow of Arabs would mean, most Israelis say, the end of the Jewish state. And Abu Aker has begun losing patience with both Israelis and Arafat. "We are at the peak of our worries right now," he said. "If Arafat gives up the right of return then he will go down and the people will rise up against him." His son, Nidal, sitting beside him, said the Palestinian leader is playing with fire by negotiating the issue at all. "Any spark could make things explode."[119]

Having opened with the requisite drama devoid of context, seven long paragraphs later the piece returned to the nuts-and-bolts details of the negotiations on the refugee issue. Details concerning how Abu Aker had become a refugee or what international law and consensus had to say about his fate were absent.

Less typical but observable, however, is reporting that effectively denies the refugees their humanity by adopting odious metaphors that liken them to "a political running sore"—or even to animals. A pattern of unfortunate word choices in the *New York Times Magazine*'s "Playing War" reveals the latter. Seventy-five thousand Palestinian refugees in the Gaza Strip's Beach Camp are described as being "corralled" into a half-square-mile block, while at the funeral of three boys from the camp, the reporter observed "a thousand hands pawing at the graves." Down in the trenches of the Karni crossing, "Muhammad curled himself into an insectlike ball." In a vacant lot at Beach Camp, "small children, many of them barefoot, ran about in hyperkinetic herds."[120]

At worst, reporting on the refugees takes the form of thinly veiled agenda journalism. On April 24, 29, and 30, 2002, in the aftermath of the fierce fighting between Israelis and Palestinians in the Jenin refugee camp, Fox News's *Special Report with Brit Hume* carried three segments on the refugee issue. The message of all three pieces was clear: the Palestinian refugee problem could be blamed on the refugees' own intransigence and the machinations of their leaders, the Arab states, and the United Nations.

Hume set up the April 24 segment, in which he interviewed Marc Ginsberg, former U.S. ambassador to Morocco, by asking:

> Much of the fighting and much of the controversy on Israel's military action in the West Bank has involved refugee camps. But these so-called refugee camps don't look like camps—no tents, no cooking fires. Israelis say these places are breeding grounds of terrorism. A number of them have been there for 50 years or more. How come? Who runs them? Why are they still there?

Ginsberg then gave a brief, factual outline of the refugee problem. When Hume asked him why some residents of Jenin were refugees and others not, Ginsberg replied:

> There are registered refugees. And then there are refugees who are actually registered to live in the camps. And the reason is very simple, economics. Many of these people living in the camps are dependent on [the] . . . UN agency that continues to fund all of their social, educational, and welfare programs.

Hume then asked about the cost of maintaining the camps, to which Ginsberg replied:

> Right now, the rough budget is about $340 million per annum, of which the United States contributes about 30 percent, which is approximately $90 million. The Arab countries collectively . . . are contributing only about five percent—I'm sorry, less than five percent. And that amounts to anywhere between $5 million to $7 million.

Hume did not ask what accounted for the disparity in levels of U.S. and Arab support for the refugees, or whether it was proportionally based on differentials in overall UN dues that member states pay. Instead, he continued to press the funding issue with a leading question, which was followed by an exchange suggesting that the greatest interest Palestinian and other Arab leaders have in the refugees is keeping alive the "myth" of their right of return.

> HUME: We have got a graphic on the screen now that shows the U.S. and the EU are the principal contributors, accounting for more than half. You include the U.K., we're up to about 60 percent. Sweden has a big chunk. And then Saudi Arabia, six-tenths of a percent. Kuwait, less than that. What is that all about? These are the people that would tell that you that they're the ones most concerned about the Palestinians.
>
> GINSBERG: They're least concerned . . . because they don't want to have responsibility for the care and feeding, because they want this issue to remain alive as an issue that they don't want to resolve themselves.
>
> HUME: How is that issue useful to them?
>
> GINSBERG: It's useful because it continues to perpetuate the myth of the right of return, that these people [will] eventually return to what is now Israel. They believe that by keeping the issue alive it deflects attention away from their own preoccupation with other domestic issues.
>
> HUME: In other words, they have got their people worried about the plight of these refugees still stuck in these crowded refugee camps, and therefore they're not thinking about whether Saudi Arabia has a democracy or whether the Saudi royal family are the right people to be governing and that sort of thing.
>
> GINSBERG: And also, Arafat himself, Brit, has continued to perpetuate the myth that these refugees should not be resettled, that they

should not go back to Arab countries and be resettled, largely because he wants to continue the campaign, so to speak, of ensuring
that these people believe that they have a right of return and that
they're his constituency.

Hume returned to the refugee issue in the April 29 broadcast. In his
setup of a report by Fox correspondent Mike Tobin from the al-Amari refugee camp south of Ramallah, Hume reprised his introductory theme of five
days earlier:

When Israeli tanks rolled into Palestinian territories, by and large, they
were entering refugee camps. But these camps don't look anything like
the refugee quarters seen, for example, during the Kosovo conflict or
when Afghans fled the Taliban into neighboring Pakistan. Instead of
being temporary shelters, the refugee camps on the West Bank seemed
to become permanent communities in and of themselves, all on the
United Nations' tab.

Tobin's report focused on Mustafa Abujwila, a fifty-three-year resident
of al-Amari who married in the camp and had nine children and fourteen
grandchildren there. The report characterized Abujwila as prolonging his
refugee status by choice—for political reasons having to do with the destruction of Israel.

MUSTAFA ABUJWILA (through translator): I don't feel this is my home.
    My home is in the village [of] Na'ani.
TOBIN: He says he lived in a farm in Na'ani, in the northern part of
    what is today Israel. When the Jewish state fought its war of inde-
    pendence in 1948, Mustafa was one of many Palestinians forced out
    of their homes into refugee camps in the West Bank, Gaza and the
    neighboring Arab states. Decades later, his family is not trying to get
    permanent housing, not willing to change his refugee status.
ABUJWILA: Because you keep thinking you want to go back to the old
    place.
TOBIN: Israelis say Palestinians are motivated to stay in the camps by
    politics.
SHLOMO BEN AMI (former foreign minister of Israel): Essentially as a
    political springboard in order to continue undermining the legiti-
    macy of the creation of the state of Israel.

Tobin then turned to the cost of maintaining the camps, taking the same tack Hume had in his interview with Ginsberg, namely, accusatory rather than explanatory. Furthermore, he misidentified UNRWA, which stands for United Nations Relief and Works Agency.

> TOBIN (on camera): The camp here was originally a tent city. But over the decades, the tents gave way to bricks, mortar and construction—construction that was paid for by the United Nations with funding that came in no small part from U.S. tax dollars.
>
> (voice-over): Last year, the United States contributed $83.6 million to UNRWA, the United Nations Relief Workers Association [*sic*], 30 percent of its budget. Saudi Arabia contributed $1.8 million, Kuwait, $1.5 million. In the 1980s, all Arab nations combined contributed eight percent of UNRWA's budget. Now, they are down to two percent. . . .
>
> With the funding, the Palestinians lived rent-free in the camps, another reason Mustafa's son Hassan raises his children here.
>
> ABUJWILA: I, of course, cannot allow myself to get out of the refugee camp because I need a lot of money. And I don't have that.

Finally, just as Hume had referred to the refugee camps as "hotbeds of terrorism" in his interview with Ginsberg, Tobin followed suit, offering sound bites from an unidentified child and Abujwila's wife, Zakai, that evoked violence yet to come.

> TOBIN: Living in the camps, each generation learns hatred.
>
> (on camera): Who do you want to fight?
>
> UNIDENTIFIED CHILD (through translator): The one who is killing us, the Jews.
>
> TOBIN: Zakai is not worried that her grandson Mustafa might join up with the militant groups in the camps and die one day. She would be proud.
>
> ZAKAI ABUJWILA (through translator): Everyone knows that he will sacrifice for his homeland.

The third Fox segment on the refugees was broadcast the next day, on April 30. Once again Hume interviewed Ginsberg, who described the health, education, and job-training services UNRWA provides for the refugees. He and Hume discussed the fact that Hamas and Islamic Jihad are active in the camps—because UNRWA has no policing authority—supplementing the refugees' "subsistence rations" from the United Nations and, in Hume's words, "introducing propaganda materials under the guise of education." Ginsberg commented:

> Actually, for all intents and purposes, Brit, the United Nations have [*sic*] to acquiesce in virtually anything that goes on in these camps by the local authorities that represent either the direct Arafat organizations such as Fatah, or by Islamic Jihad or Hamas because there is no real governing authority in each of these camps other than this collective social welfare network that provides support, economic, educational and health and welfare support to the camps.

Despite the fact that UNRWA is not empowered to do more than Ginsberg described, he and Hume wound up the segment conveying the same sense of blame that the other two reports imparted. Fox viewers were once again led to the conclusion that the right of return is not a matter of international law and consensus but rather a fantasy concocted by Arabs in order to threaten Israel and prolong the Israeli-Palestinian conflict indefinitely.

> HUME: Now, has the UN in any sense ever tried to change this? Last question quickly.
> GINSBERG: No. The United Nations has done essentially nothing more than administer the educational, social, and welfare programs to these camps. And Arab states have largely prevented the United Nations from exercising any other authority over the camps.
> HUME: In other words, making them better.
> GINSBERG: Yes. No, they prevented them from doing that. The Arab states will not let these countries—let the United Nations do that.
> HUME: They want them [Palestinians] to yearn for their old homeland.
> GINSBERG: Exactly. They want to preserve the right of return.
> HUME: Got you. Marc Ginsberg, thanks for coming.[121]

3

REPORTING ON
ISRAELI SETTLEMENTS

How can anyone expect peace in the Middle East when Israel continues to create new colonies in Palestine, expands its existing colonies
in Palestine and declares it will maintain its colonies forever? Don't
expect peace from a people whose land is devoured bit by bit by a
neighboring colonial power. And for America, how can we support
this brutal neocolonialism?

Letter to the Editor, Chicago Tribune

THERE IS INTERNATIONAL LAW, THERE IS INTERPRETATION, AND THERE IS
public opinion. And then there are the facts of Israeli settlements in the West
Bank and, prior to Israel's withdrawal in 2005, the Gaza Strip. Article 49 of
the Fourth Geneva Convention states that "the Occupying Power shall not
deport or transfer parts of its own civilian population into the territory it occupies"[1]—and international consensus indicates that lands Israel took over in the
June 1967 Six-Day War constitute occupied territory. The UN Security Council adopted Resolution 242 in November 1967, calling for the "withdrawal of
Israel [*sic*] armed forces from territories occupied in the recent conflict."

Having adopted two condemnatory resolutions in 1968 and 1969 on Israel's annexation of East Jerusalem—which occurred on June 11, 1967, one
day after the Six-Day War had ended— in 1971 the UN Security Council
adopted Resolution 298, which confirmed that "actions taken by Israel to
change the status of the City of Jerusalem, including . . . transfer of populations and legislation aimed at the incorporation of the occupied section, are
totally invalid and cannot change that status."

Between 1977 and 1984—with the Likud party in control of the government for just over six years—Israel established ninety-nine new settlements in the West Bank and Gaza Strip, more than quadrupling the number built in the previous decade.[2] The Security Council responded by adopting Resolutions 446 and 452 in 1979 and Resolution 465 in 1980. All three affirmed the applicability of the Fourth Geneva Convention "to the Arab territories occupied by Israel in 1967, including Jerusalem," and declared the settlements built by Israel on those territories to have "no legal validity."

As recently as December 2006, the UN General Assembly adopted Resolution 61/25, which

> *Demands* that Israel, the occupying Power, comply strictly with its obligations under international law, including international humanitarian law, and that it cease all of its unlawful and unilateral actions in the Occupied Palestinian Territory, including East Jerusalem, that are aimed at altering the character and status of the Territory, including, inter alia, via the de facto annexation of land, and thus at prejudging the final outcome of peace negotiations; . . .
>
> *Reiterates its demand* for the complete cessation of all Israeli settlement activities in the Occupied Palestinian Territory, including East Jerusalem, and in the occupied Syrian Golan, and calls for the full implementation of the relevant Security Council resolutions; . . .
>
> *Stresses* the need for the withdrawal of Israel from the Palestinian Territory occupied since 1967.[3]

Taken together, these articulations of international law and consensus are widely interpreted to mean that Israel's settlement of its citizens in the West Bank, Gaza Strip (until August 2005), and areas of Jerusalem annexed by Israel in 1967 is illegal. By the end of 2006, the number of Israeli settlers in the West Bank and these areas of Jerusalem totaled approximately 452,900[4]—about 6 percent of Israel's total population and 8 percent of its Jewish population.

Since 1967, however, the State of Israel has not considered its hold on these territories to be an occupation. Israeli governments have held that the Fourth Geneva Convention applies only to territory taken from a state that is a signatory to the convention. Because the territories did not belong to such sovereign powers between May 1948 and June 1967—Egypt had administered the Gaza Strip and Jordan had controlled the West Bank—Israel has defined those lands as "disputed" or "administered" territory whose status was to be determined through negotiations.

In 2003 the respected Israeli newspaper *Haaretz* published an in-depth special report on the Israeli settlements in the West Bank and Gaza Strip, noting that such "legal acrobatics have failed to satisfy the international community. . . . To handle the settlement controversy politically, legally and ethically, Israel has developed a unique word-laundering system." Quoting the work of Israeli law professor and constitutional scholar Amnon Rubinstein, *Haaretz* described the relationship between the legal question and the political issue:

> In its policy of establishing settlements in the territories, irrespective of the policy's political wisdom or absence thereof, Israel has clearly violated international law: It has violated the prohibitions concerning an occupying power's transferring nations to the territory it occupies and concerning the expropriation of land for purposes unrelated to the local population's well-being. Regarding these two categories of violation, Israel's High Court of Justice has been unable to restrain the executive branch of Israeli government—perhaps because of the court's awareness of the issue's political nature."

Furthermore, the paper reported, Israel did not sign the statute that established the International Criminal Court in July 1998 "because of Article 8, which includes, in its definition of war crimes, the 'transfer, directly or indirectly, by the Occupying Power of parts of its own civilian population into the territory it occupies.'"[5]

Within Israeli society itself, the Hebrew word *kibush* (occupation) is used widely and daily in mainstream media and public discourse—and U.S. mainstream media reports routinely have made narrative reference to the West Bank and the Gaza Strip as being occupied territories. Occupation, apparently, is defined not only by international law and consensus but also by the practical realities on the ground. Israeli prime minister Ariel Sharon startled his Likud party colleagues—and the nation as a whole—in May 2003 when he stated: "I think the idea that it is possible to continue keeping 3.5 million Palestinians under occupation—yes, it is occupation, you might not like the word, but what is happening is occupation—is bad for Israel, and bad for the Palestinians, and bad for the Israeli economy. Controlling 3.5 million Palestinians cannot go on forever."[6]

Sharon's words caused momentary confusion, with the Foreign Ministry briefly considering whether it should allow its officials to use the word "occupation." Sharon backtracked the next day, telling the Knesset's foreign affairs and defense committee that he had referred to the Palestinian people, not the land on which they live, as being under occupation. "When I used the term 'occupation,'" he explained, "I meant it is undesirable for us to rule over a Palestinian population."[7]

For forty years, however, successive Israeli governments—with little or no concrete opposition from the United States—have radically transformed the Palestinian landscape by establishing "facts on the ground." While demographic considerations have prevented Israel from annexing the West Bank and Gaza Strip, prior to the withdrawal from Gaza in 2005 these territories, along with East Jerusalem, were populated by approximately 8.5 percent of Israel's Jewish population, citizens of the State of Israel subject to Israeli civil law. In matters of Israeli-Palestinian dispute, however, the 3.5 million Palestinians living in the West Bank continue to be subject to laws administered by Israeli military authorities.

To accommodate the building of 143 Israeli settlements in the West Bank and Gaza and the military apparatus that has defended them, Israel confiscated massive amounts of land. Since 1967 this colonization and its defense have compromised many aspects of Palestinian daily life and human rights—chief among them livelihood and mobility.[8] Those Palestinians who have resisted have been subjected to disproportional and often lethal responses by the Israeli army, as well as to torture and expulsion. The Palestinian population as a whole has been subjected to collective punishment in the form of house demolitions, curfews, roadblocks, and closures.

To a lesser degree, Israel has paid the price of occupation in human, financial, and political tender. Its soldiers and civilians have been killed, its economy and system of social safety nets have been eroded, and its international reputation has been tarnished. Consensus worldwide—in all but right-wing religious and nationalist quarters in Israel and among their supporters elsewhere—holds that Israeli settlement beyond the Green Line is illegal, constituting the greatest single obstacle to peace.

U.S. POLICY VIS-À-VIS ISRAELI SETTLEMENTS

The Aid Connection, Inaction, and Acquiescence

The most important aspect of the settlement issue is not the semantic debate over terminology, and it may not be the effects that occupation has had on Israeli and Palestinian societies. The most important aspect could very well be the relationship between U.S. policy toward Israel and Israeli policy vis-à-vis the settlements.

Since 1977, when Israel's first Likud government under Menachem Begin greatly accelerated the process of colonizing the West Bank and Gaza Strip, U.S. administrations have expressed varying degrees of rhetorical opposition to the settlements. Condemnatory statements, however, have had no impact on the aid paradigm. Rather, beginning in 1974 the flow of U.S. aid to Israel increased dramatically against a backdrop of regional and global events, including the aftermath of the 1973 oil crisis, the 1979 Iranian revolution, and what was to be the final phase of the cold war. Of total U.S. aid to Israel since 1948, 99 percent has been disbursed since 1967, the same year Israel occupied the West Bank and Gaza Strip.

Arguably the most direct guarantor of protecting American interests in the region, aid to Israel also has had the effect of strengthening Israel's hand vis-à-vis the Palestinians. This, in turn, has had a significant impact on the trajectory of the peace process. By the time the Clinton administration assumed the role of mediator at the Camp David summit between Israel and the Palestinians in 2000, the aggregate microcosmic effects of the American aid strategy had backfired. While Israel was unquestionably the chief ally of the United States and the strongest power in the region, its colonization of the West Bank and Gaza had nonetheless blocked a negotiated peace to the Israeli-Palestinian conflict.

Without exception, U.S mainstream reporting on Israeli settlements in the West Bank and Gaza Strip has failed to address the key question of how, directly or indirectly, American aid has contributed to Israel's ability to absorb the cost of building, enlarging, and defending the settlements. While Israel is officially prohibited from using U.S. aid in the occupied territories,[9] every dollar of American aid has freed up a corresponding amount in Israeli currency used for Israel's colonization of the West Bank and Gaza. In November 2000 the Israeli organization Peace Now reported that the government of Prime Minister Ehud Barak had earmarked $300 million for the settlements in 2001,[10] a figure that represented 10 percent of Israel's regular foreign-aid package from the United States for fiscal year 2001.[11]

In its special report on the cost of the settlements, published in September 2003, *Haaretz* reported virtually the same percentage of Israeli expenditures on the settlements since 1967 as compared with the aggregate sum of U.S. aid to Israel over the same period. According to the newspaper, between 1967 and 2003 Israeli governments had spent an estimated $10.1 billion on building and defending the settlements, or approximately 11 percent of the $92.3 billion in regular U.S. aid grants for the same period. Annual civilian

expenditures on the settlements had amounted to approximately $555 mil-
lion, *Haaretz* reported, with 36 percent of those funds projected for housing
($111 million) and road construction ($89 million) in 2003. Military expenditures—the cost of defending the settlements—amounted to an additional
$450 million a year, with expenditures nearly doubling to $890 million during each year of the first three years of the second Palestinian uprising from
2000 to 2003.[12]

The *Haaretz* report, unprecedented in its scope and specificity, was the
result of a three-month investigation by a team of fifteen reporters. The introductory piece noted the significant difficulty of reporting the story:

> No government body or agency has ever issued a report or published a
> study on this matter. . . . The deliberate vagueness is founded on bud-
> gets with names that conceal the purpose of the funding, rolling ben-
> efits for settlements into benefits for towns in the Galilee and Negev
> [inside Israel proper], so it is difficult to determine how much money
> is actually flowing beyond the Green Line, or how the money moves
> through indirect channels. . . .
>
> This cover-up contravenes the principle of transparency in proper
> government. It prevents informed decision-making. It denies Israeli
> voters the ability to decide where they want to invest their money as
> taxpayers. It is meant to make sure the money keeps flowing through
> hidden pipelines. . . .
>
> In some cases [*Haaretz* reporters] encountered refusals to deliver
> the information, in the spirit that guides large segments of the regime,
> where the prevailing view is that the information is their property. In
> other cases, even ministry officials had trouble uncovering information
> because it had been so efficiently camouflaged.[13]

Just as *Haaretz* reporters uncovered obfuscatory or nonexistent accounting practices regarding how the Israeli government funds the settlements,
any attempt to trace how U.S. aid to Israel—apart from direct weapons
transfers—is actually spent would be an equally difficult if not even more
daunting task. In its receipt of American aid, Israel enjoys the unique privilege of being the only country that does not have to account for how it
spends U.S. funds. In 2005 the Congressional Research Service reported
that "the United States stipulates that U.S. aid funds cannot be used in the
occupied territories. Over the years, some have suggested that Israel may be
using U.S. assistance to establish Jewish settlements in the occupied territories, but Israel denies the allegation. Because U.S. economic aid is given to

Israel as direct government-to-government budgetary support without any specific project accounting, and money is fungible, there is no way to tell how Israel uses the aid."[14]

A week after *Haaretz* published its report on the settlements in 2003, the Sharon government announced a plan to build six hundred new homes in existing West Bank settlements. American news outlets reported the announcement widely, with some noting the *Haaretz* report's figures on the cost of the settlements. The *New York Times* and *Chicago Tribune* took editorial stands criticizing the Israeli move, and they, too, articulated the *Haaretz* findings. However, none of these news reports or editorials questioned or implied a connection between Israeli settlement building and U.S. aid to Israel.[15]

In February 2006 the independent Israeli Research Institute for Economic and Social Affairs reported that Israel's expenditures on settlements in the West Bank alone topped $14 billion over the four decades since 1967. According to an Associated Press report, the institute based the figure in its eighteen-month study on retroactive cost estimates and aerial photography, a methodology adopted because of lack of cooperation from Israeli government and other official sources during the first six months of the project. The study found the major expenditures for West Bank settlements to be $9 billion for housing; $1.8 billion for schools and public institutions, including government buildings and synagogues; and $1.6 billion for roads. Military, education, welfare, and social-service expenditures were not included in the $14 billion total. Furthermore, as the AP reported, the study "determined that the Israeli government contributes twice as much proportionally to settlement local budgets as it does to local budgets inside Israel." [16]

U.S. Policy from Carter to Bush II

A review of the Carter, Reagan, first Bush, Clinton, and second Bush administrations' positions on the settlements reveals that, to one degree or another, all administrations shared a lack of political will to tackle the issue. High-ranking U.S. officials have sporadically stated that the settlements are illegal, including UN ambassador George H. W. Bush in September 1971, UN ambassador William Scranton in May 1976, and Secretary of State Cyrus Vance in March 1980.[17] Even as various administrations attempted to play direct or indirect roles in mediating a resolution of the Israeli-Palestinian conflict, the U.S. position on the settlements progressively evolved over three decades from briefly considering them to be illegal, to referring to them as "obstacles to peace," to finally acknowledging and implying acceptance of them as a de facto "reality on the ground." In general, the U.S. mainstream media have consistently failed to explore and analyze the apparent contradiction between U.S. peace-making efforts and the evolution of policy on the settlements that hinders rather than advances the peace process.

The following review of official U.S. postures on the settlement issue from the Carter through the Clinton administrations is based on the comprehensive narrative of U.S. policy on the Israeli-Palestinian conflict chronicled by scholar Kathleen Christison in her 1999 work *Perceptions of Palestine*.

The Carter administration adopted the most forceful position vis-à-vis the settlements, terming them illegal under international law. In the end, however, this had little effect. Christison writes:

> [Israeli prime minister Menachem] Begin's determination to build Jewish settlements in the occupied West Bank and Gaza became a particular point of contention between the Carter administration and Israel. . . . Carter and his foreign-policy team regarded the construction of settlements as a kind of "creeping annexation," in the words of [Secretary of State Cyrus] Vance, and Carter made clear to Begin during his initial visit the U.S. belief that settlements violated international law . . . which was to be the consistent U.S. position throughout Carter's administration.[18]

The Camp David accords of 1978 that paved the way for the historic peace treaty between Israel and Egypt in 1979 had among its provisions the establishment of autonomy for Palestinians in the West Bank and Gaza Strip. However, Begin was intransigent on the settlement issue, thereby scuttling any hope that progress on the Israeli-Palestinian track could be derived as a dividend of Israeli-Egyptian peace. Of the Camp David accords, Christison observes:

> Begin won the day on settlements as well. Although the United States understood him to have agreed during the Camp David talks to freezing settlement construction throughout the autonomy negotiations and to ratifying this agreement through a letter to Carter separate from the accords, Begin contended that he agreed only to a three-month freeze, which is all he referred to in the letter to Carter. A month after Camp David he announced that West Bank settlements would be "thickened."[19]

According to Christison, as Carter's term progressed he realized the domestic political difficulties involved in taking a tough stance toward Israel.
Moreover, the hostage crisis in Iran diverted Carter's attention from the Israeli-Palestinian arena during the last year of his presidency. Thus, despite
the administration's initial stance that Israeli settlements were illegal according to international law, the number of Israeli settlements in the West Bank
more than doubled during the first three years of the Begin government,
with the number of Israeli settlers reaching fourteen thousand.[20] "By 1980,"
Christison writes, "Israel had expropriated more than 30 percent of the West
Bank's land area for settlements and military bases and had begun to lay the
foundation for permanent control of the occupied territories by applying
Israeli law to Jewish settlers in these areas."[21]

Ronald Reagan's overriding foreign-policy concern was dealing with the
Soviets in the cold war, Christison writes, "and Israel was regarded as a necessary ally, no matter what its West Bank policies." Influenced by the writings
of neoconservative Eugene Rostow, during his campaign Reagan asserted
that "the settlements were legal, even that Israel had a 'right' to construct
them." According to Christison, once Reagan was in office, the State Department attempted to square the circle and reconcile Reagan's beliefs with
formal U.S. disapproval of the settlements, coming up with the formula
that the settlements were "an obstacle to peace." With that codification of
the American position, "no one in the administration ever again called the
settlements illegal."[22] Following Israel's invasion of Lebanon in the summer of 1982, however, the administration came up with a peace formula
known as the Reagan Plan, which, like the Camp David accords before it,
included autonomy for the Palestinians in the West Bank and Gaza Strip
and an immediate freeze on settlement construction, among other things.
In Christison's account, however, Israeli reaction rendered "this promising
proposal . . . a dead letter. Although the initial Arab reaction to the Reagan
Plan was cautiously favorable, Israel, angered at not having been consulted
in advance, objected to virtually every aspect of the proposal and soundly
rejected it. The Israelis underscored their objections by immediately approving the construction of ten new settlements on the West Bank."[23]

As Carter's attention had been diverted by the Iran hostage crisis, the
Reagan administration soon found itself dealing with the aftermath of the
Israeli invasion of Lebanon, including the massacre of hundreds of Palestinians in the Sabra and Shatila refugee camps by Israel-allied Lebanese Ma-
ronite Christian forces, and the bombing of the U.S. Marine barracks in
Beirut that resulted in the deaths of 241 Marines. Christison writes: "Clearly
disturbed by Israel's continued efforts to expand settlement construction . . .

U.S. signals carried a different message to Israel. . . . U.S. protests were weak, specifically disavowing sanctions, and for all intents and purposes the administration never again mentioned the Reagan initiative to Israel."[24] The quantifiable result of this policy was that

> Without opposing pressure from the United States the number of settlements in the West Bank and Gaza grew exponentially. With yearly increases in the number of settlers in the range of 30 percent and often higher, the Israeli settler population of the territories more than quadrupled during the Reagan administration's first six years. As of mid-1987, a total of almost sixty-eight thousand lived in approximately 140 settlements in the West Bank and Gaza; these figures are for the areas outside the expanded limits of Jerusalem, where another several thousand Israelis lived in urban settlements.[25]

Despite an acrimonious relationship between the administration of George H. W. Bush and the government of Yitzhak Shamir—Bush viewed the settlements as a particular bone of contention—U.S. aid continued unabated, with Israel accelerating settlement construction as a result of the influx of Jewish immigrants from the Soviet Union. "In each of the years 1990 and 1991," Christison writes, "the Jewish population of the occupied territories increased by approximately one-quarter." Housing construction for settlers reached 13,000 units under construction in 1991, compared with 20,000 units in the preceding twenty-five years.[26] "By the end of 1991, over a quarter-million Israeli settlers lived in the West Bank, Gaza, and East Jerusalem. Israel had confiscated 68 percent of the land area of the West Bank."[27]

In an April 1989 meeting in Washington, Bush addressed Shamir "in strong terms" on the settlement issue. At a news conference held in March 1990 the American president announced that the United States did not believe that Israel should build new settlements in the West Bank or East Jerusalem.[28] In September 1991 Bush requested a four-month delay in congressional action on Israel's request for $10 billion in loan guarantees for immigrant-housing construction. Although Christison credits the Bush administration's hardline stance vis-à-vis the loan guarantees as a significant factor in bringing down the Shamir government, she notes that the American administration failed to follow through.

When Yitzhak Rabin visited the United States in August 1992 after being elected Israeli premier, he and Bush arrived at a "loose agreement" to halt construction of new settlements, and the United States soon thereafter granted the delayed loan guarantees. Despite the apparent rapprochement between Bush and Rabin, however, the four years of Labor party rule (1992–1996), which coincided with the first Clinton administration, saw the number of Israeli settlers in the West Bank and Gaza grow by 49 percent, from 101,000 to 150,000.[29]

Benjamin Netanyahu of the Likud party was elected prime minister in 1996. Christison writes that this was followed by "expansion of settlement construction in East Jerusalem and the West Bank, including particularly construction of settlements and takeover of homes in Arab neighborhoods of East Jerusalem in mid-1997." However "Clinton and his team allowed Netanyahu to play a dominating role," avoiding open confrontation and "always taking refuge in the old notion that it was powerless to move until the parties themselves were ready."[30]

Against this backdrop of continuing American passivity, the Israeli settlement population in the West Bank and Gaza doubled during Clinton's two terms, reaching two hundred thousand by the time of the Camp David negotiations in July 2000. This expansion directly contradicted Clinton's consistent efforts to advance the peace process. Christison sheds light on a key factor behind this contradiction, citing a fundamental change introduced into the peace process by Dennis Ross. A member of the Clinton peace team, Ross had formerly been affiliated with the pro-Israel lobby organization American Israel Public Affairs Committee, and the Washington Institute for Near East Policy, a pro-Israel think tank. According to Christison's account, in June 1993—three months before Rabin and Palestinian leader Yasser Arafat signed the Oslo accords on the White House lawn—"Ross authored a statement of principles, released under Secretary of State Warren Christopher's name, that in a key way reframed the objectives of the peace process."[31] In short, the statement abrogated the long-understood basis of UN Security Council Resolution 242, namely, that Israel would relinquish most of the territories it had occupied in 1967, with minor border adjustments, in return for Arab recognition of and peace treaties with Israel. Rather than being assured of eventual sovereignty over most of the West Bank and Gaza, according to the common interpretation of 242, the Palestinians would now have to negotiate for it.

> In Ross' 1993 statement of principles, however, the idea of exchanging territory for peace was not mentioned, and the entire question of the extent of territory to be relinquished by Israel—even the ultimate sovereignty over those territories included during the interim stage in the Palestinian self-governing area—was left to future permanent-status talks. Thus, even in the interim self-governing areas, Palestinian

jurisdiction was not assured and was considered to be temporary and functional rather than territorial.

The United States thereby came to consider the territories to be "disputed"—not, as previously, "occupied." Whereas longstanding U.S. policy had always been that Israel's control of these territories was temporary, it now adopted the Israeli position that Israel had the right to negotiate the retention of some or all of the territory. Under these new terms of reference, what had always previously been understood to mean "full territory for full peace" had become instead, as far as the United States was concerned, "some territory for full peace."[32]

"The Clinton administration," Christison writes, "also changed the language of negotiations and altered the ground rules in other areas. Israeli settlements, for instance, which the Carter administration had called 'illegal' and the Reagan administration had termed 'obstacles to peace,' were labeled mere 'complicating factors' by the Clinton administration."[33]

Preoccupied with the "war on terror" following the September 11, 2001, terror attacks against the United States and the subsequent and impending American wars in Afghanistan and Iraq, the second Bush administration faced international criticism over its failure to intervene as Israeli-Palestinian violence intensified in 2001 and 2002. During this period the administration made few public comments on the subject of Israeli settlements. At the same time young Israeli renegades established some sixty fledgling "outpost" settlements in the West Bank that the Israeli government termed "illegal."

In April 2003 Bush unveiled the "road map" plan that the United States had authored with Russia, the European Union, and the United Nations in an effort to restart the peace process. Much like the Mitchell commission report of 2001, the road map called on Palestinians to "end terror and violence." Israel was enjoined to "immediately dismantle settlement outposts erected since March 2001" and "consistent with the Mitchell Report . . . freeze all settlement activity (including natural growth of settlements)." However, from June through October U.S. news outlets reported continuing Israeli expansion of settlements in the West Bank and Gaza Strip.

In November 2003, as U.S. troops faced a growing insurgency in Iraq, *Haaretz* reported that the U.S. Bureau of Intelligence and Research recommended that the Bush administration "apply 'clear and intentional pressure' on Israel regarding the settlements as part of making headway with the Palestinians, as well as helping to calm the situation in Iraq."[34] The recommendation went unreported in the U.S. mainstream media and apparently was unheeded by the Bush administration.

In April 2004 Bush appeared to contradict decades of U.S. policy on the settlements, telling Sharon in a meeting at the White House that Israel would not have to give up all of its West Bank settlements in negotiations with the Palestinians. At the same time, he endorsed Sharon's plan for unilateral Israeli withdrawal from the Gaza Strip, including evacuation of the settlements there. Israel accomplished the Gaza withdrawal more or less unilaterally, in consultation with the United States but without negotiating with the Palestinians.

In August and September 2005 Israel compelled eighty-five hundred settlers to quit the twenty-one settlements in Gaza and redeployed the IDF from the territory. At the same time, Israel continued to enlarge its existing settlements in the West Bank while simultaneously vacating an additional seven hundred settlers from four small, isolated settlements in the northern end of the territory.

Practically speaking, however, U.S. policy actions already had indicated that American objections to further colonization of the West Bank amounted to little more than posturing, and that U.S. geostrategic interests in the region would accommodate Israel's policy of expansionism at the expense of the peace process. In November 2003 the Bush administration announced that it would reduce by $289.5 million its $9 billion in loan guarantees to Israel in response to plans the Sharon government made public that summer and fall to expand existing settlements in the West Bank and to continue building the separation barrier on Palestinian territory there. The loan guarantees—which provide U.S. government backing for the issue of Israeli bonds—save Israel millions of dollars in interest payments and have been described in a 2004 report by the U.S. embassy in Israel as "a concrete expression of U.S. support for the Israeli economy."[35] The reduction in the loan guarantees—military and economic aid grants were not cut—was estimated to cost Israel some $4 million a year for three years in increased interest costs.[36] As a fraction of the total $2.87 billion in U.S. aid to Israel for fiscal year 2004,[37] the $4 million penalty that year amounted to virtually nothing at .001 percent.

A similar pattern of cat-and-mouse sanctioning had occurred in the mid-1990s, when a $10 billion U.S. loan-guarantee package for resettlement and absorption of immigrants from the former Soviet Union was reduced by $1.35 billion to penalize Israel for its settlement activity in the West Bank and Gaza Strip between 1994 and 1997. However, these reductions were "offset" by funds "reinstated for security interests" totaling $585 million—rendering the net effect of the sanctions a $765 million reduction in available loan guarantees—less than 10 percent of the original package.[38]

With such a negligible sanction—or what might more accurately be termed the appearance of sanction—having been assessed in late 2003, an apparent tongue-in-cheek characterization of U.S. policy vis-à-vis the settlements by *U.S. News & World Report* in January 2004 was thus not surprising. "The United States is insisting that Israel uproot most of the 100-odd makeshift outposts and does not object to—and would no doubt be relieved by—the uprooting of any of the 150 established settlements," the magazine reported.[39]

However, by mid-August 2004 evidence of Israeli settlement-expansion plans surfaced again. The *New York Times* reported that the day before Ariel Sharon was to "face sharp debate about his policies at his Likud Party convention," and in order "to pacify his critics," his government issued tenders for 1,001 new subsidized apartments in West Bank settlements.[40] The construction bids for 604 units in Betar Elite, 214 in Ariel, 141 in Ma'aleh Adumim, and 42 in Karnei Shomron appeared to be in clear violation of the road map, which imposed a freeze on all settlement activity. The same day the *Washington Post* reported that, according to their interpretation of a letter from Bush to Sharon the previous April, "Israeli officials contend that . . . the road map allows the population of settlements to grow, as long as the newcomers remain within existing boundaries." However, according to the newspaper the Bush letter "did not directly address settlement growth, other than reiterating the U.S. commitment to the road map."[41]

Settlement-Policy Thrust and Parry: Journalists and the State Department

On August 17, the same day the Israeli government issued the 1,001 construction bids for settlement expansion, they were the subject of sharp questioning by reporters at the daily State Department briefing. Deputy State spokesman Adam Ereli faced repeated challenges to explain the U.S. position on the new tenders vis-à-vis the terms of the road map as journalists tried to get him to go on the record about the apparent contradiction between the two and what the United States was prepared to do about it. Ereli, however, remained steadfast in his obfuscations despite his interlocutors' insistence.

The exchange was remarkable not only for its tone but also for its content, a clear illustration of the contradictions inherent in stated U.S. policy versus actual U.S. action on the settlement issue. For their part, the journalists appeared unsparing in questioning their official source. That source was unyielding, however, and their persistence failed to produce anything newsworthy—in a frame of newsworthiness delimited by what official sources will actually say. The result was that Americans who tuned in to television and radio news that day and read their newspapers the next would not know that the exchange—on an aspect of U.S. policy crucial to eventual resolution of the Israeli-Palestinian conflict—had even taken place. A portion of the transcript follows.

> QUESTION: The Israeli government invited construction bids for 1,000 new homes in the West Bank. An Israeli official said that it's within the guidelines of the government and the agreements with the Americans. What's your comment on that?
>
> MR. ERELI: Our comment is that we are studying the details regarding the tenders that have been issued by the government of Israel. Our concern is to determine whether these tenders are consistent with the government of Israel's previous commitments on settlements.
>
> As you well know, National Security Council officials were in Israel recently, discussing with Israelis those commitments. I think we made it clear that we expect Israel to fulfill pledges it made to President Bush on the question of settlement outposts and settlement activity. And obviously this is a subject of continuing discussion with the government of Israel.
>
> QUESTION: It seems pretty clear that this is not consistent with the government of Israel's previous statements. There seems to be a fairly obvious case to be made that this is a violation of their road map commitments. Why is it that you can't say that?
>
> MR. ERELI: Because I'm not in a position now to say that any specific action is a violation of commitments. I'm just not—we're not there yet.
>
> QUESTION: Hold on. The road map says freeze all settlement activities. That is what it says, right?
>
> MR. ERELI: Freeze settlement activity, including natural growth.
>
> QUESTION: Okay. This is a tender for a thousand new houses in the West Bank. It seems absurd that that's not a violation or that there's anything to study here.
>
> MR. ERELI: Right. I would say we've got to look at where these tenders are, what previous discussions were, what these tenders are for, what specific commitments were made, and then, based on those discussions, I would perhaps be more comfortable telling you more.
>
> I would also note that there's a technical team that's going out to Israel to work with Israel, to study, you know, some of these specific questions.

QUESTION: I'm sorry. That just does not fly. The commitment that the Israelis made was freeze all settlement activity. This is not freezing all settlement activity. In fact, this is the exact opposite of that.

MR. ERELI: I can't go further than that, Matt. I'm sorry.

QUESTION: You're saying you're studying where these new homes would be. Why would that make any difference? The road map says there cannot be in the occupied areas new settlement activities.

MR. ERELI: Well, let me just leave it where I left it. What I told you is, frankly, what I'm comfortable saying. And I don't want to really—from the podium, at this time, to get into a discussion with you of the specifics of these tenders, because frankly I don't have the exact specifics of the tenders, and pronounce to you at this time whether or not we think it is a violation of commitments.

What I would say to you is: A, we've made clear to Israel what we think it's committed to; B, our view is they should be in no doubt about what our views are; C, that we continue to have discussions with the government of Israel; and finally, at this point I'm not going to tell you that these tenders do or do not violate those commitments.

QUESTION (off mike): Adam, just could you explain under what circumstances the building of 1,000 new houses could be considered not growth in settlements?

MR. ERELI: No. No, I could not do that.

QUESTION: So even in general you can't address this, how it would be possible to build these houses and not be in violation?

MR. ERELI: No, I cannot do that.

QUESTION: Because there aren't any.

. . . QUESTION: Don't you think it's a bit unrealistic to say that the Israeli government should have no doubt about what your position is and on their commitments when you're unable to say right now that this is inconsistent with their commitments? If you're trying to parse the phrase in the road map that says no new settlement activity or a halt to settlement activity, you can't do that. It's black and white. It says it right there. I appreciate that you're on kind of a tight rein on what you can say and what you can't say here and you don't want to go beyond it, but it needs to be pointed out, I think, for the record that you guys are very wishy-washy on this right now.

MR. ERELI: I would point out a couple of things. Number one, not everything we say to the Israelis is on the record.

So we have discussions with the Israelis. As I said, we've had discussions most recently with our ambassador and the senior National Security Council officials about our concerns in this area. We continue to have discussions with the Israelis about our concerns in this area.

Obviously, this issue, these tenders, as well as previous tenders at Ma'aleh Adumim, are subjects of those discussions. And we've been very clear with the Israelis about what our views and what our understandings were—are.

Now just because I'm not in a position to speak to those from the podium right now doesn't mean that it's not something we talk to the Israelis about.

But second of all, I think what's also important is to look at this as part of a bigger picture. We are working on these issues, both with the Israelis and the Palestinians, with a goal in mind. And that goal is to help promote Palestinians and Israelis finding ways to disengage and to promote their own national aspirations.

I urge you to look at this as part of the larger process. And that's the way we're engaging with the Israelis on it, and that's the way we're engaging with the Palestinians.

QUESTION: Well, when you say that not all your conversations with the Israelis are on the record, are you suggesting—because it sure sounds like it—that in a closed-door meeting someplace, someone is saying, "Okay, well, we realize that you signed up for this halting all settlement activity, but wink, wink, nudge, nudge, you can add a few here and there, and we won't say anything."

MR. ERELI: No, I don't mean to suggest that at all.

QUESTION: Well, it certainly sounds like it.

QUESTION: Given that for most people there isn't a gray area here, and this does contradict the formal agreement you have, can you explain what understanding the Israeli housing minister thinks he has with Washington that he said publicly the new settlement activity adheres to understandings he has with Washington?

MR. ERELI: No, I can't speak for the Israeli housing minister.

QUESTION: Well, perhaps you can speak for the United States. What understanding do you have with Israel regarding this? It sounds [like] precisely what I just said: that behind the scenes you guys are saying: Well, you know, we're not really going to hold you to it.

MR. ERELI: We are, I think, very clear, both publicly and with the Israelis, that—

QUESTION: Not today you're not.

MR. ERELI: Let me be clear, if there's any misunderstanding or lack of clarity. We are clear with the public and with the Israelis that they have made a commitment to freeze settlement activity, including natural growth. And that is the position—that is the commitment they have made. That is what we are working with the Israelis to follow through on, both publicly and privately.

QUESTION: Well, if that's the case, then how can you not see this as just a giant slap in the face from Sharon?

MR. ERELI: That's as much as I can do for you. I'm sorry.

QUESTION: How much money does the United States give Israel every year? It's a little over $3 billion. So you're saying that you have zero influence now.

MR. ERELI: No, I'm not saying we have zero influence. I'm saying that we are working with the Israelis to see that they fulfill their commitments that they've made.

QUESTION: Well, does that not necessarily mean that you're telling them to stop, take back these tender offers?

MR. ERELI: I'm not going to get into the details of what we're discussing.[42]

COVERING THE SETTLEMENTS:
PARADIGMS FOR REPORTING TECHNIQUE

With official sources not forthcoming on U.S. policy, much U.S. mainstream media reporting on Israeli settlements is dominated by two salient characteristics. First, it routinely substitutes the descriptive for the analytical, failing as a body of work over time to explore why, in the face of ongoing official U.S. objections, Israel had continued an uninterrupted program of settlement building and colonization in the West Bank and Gaza Strip while at the same time receiving continuous aid and diplomatic support from the United States. The reporting seldom goes beyond a passing reference to U.S. objections to the settlements, as typified in the following excerpt from a *Christian Science Monitor* report that appeared in 2002: "This week, amid renewed U.S. demands that Israel freeze the building of Jewish settlements in the occupied territories, Prime Minister Ariel Sharon resolutely told his cabinet that he would not even discuss the matter until the elections in November 2003. He is not alone in this stand.

Most Israelis, according to recent polls, believe that now is not the time for any such compromise on settlements. Settlers, meanwhile, are busy saying 'we told you so.'"[43]

Second, mainstream reporting on Israeli settlements rarely goes beyond the parameters of the U.S. policy mirror. With American objections to the settlements routinely flouted by Israeli politicians and settlers alike, references to international law and consensus in the reporting—as in official U.S. criticism of the settlements—are few and far between. In some cases coverage can take on a more critical approach, albeit superficially—as in the reporting on the settlements after the release of the Mitchell commission report—but only when official U.S. policy statements provide an opening to do so.

In general, though, U.S. mainstream media reporting on the settlement issue bears a striking similarity to reporting on the Palestinian refugee question. Narrative explanations rely on an "Israelis say . . . Palestinians say" balancing act, with more weight usually given to Israeli claims and little or no reference to international law and consensus. In a CNN background report on the settlement issue during the period of heightened Israeli-Palestinian violence in the spring of 2002, the network's senior political analyst explained:

> After 1967, Jewish settlers began moving into those territories. Some, for religious reasons. They view the West Bank, which they call Judea and Samaria, as part of the biblical land of Israel, given to the Jewish people by God. Some, for security reasons. They see an Israeli presence as essential to protect the center of Israel's population. Some, for economic reasons. The Israeli government gave the settlers subsidies and tax breaks. . . .
>
> Arabs claim that the more than 170,000 Jewish residents of East Jerusalem are settlers as well, although Israel has annexed that territory and considers Jerusalem sovereign and indivisible. . . .
>
> In Israel's view, Jews have a right to live anywhere in historic Palestine. Israeli governments have said they would be willing to compromise that right, but only as part of a peace settlement.[44]

American media coverage of settlements is also characterized by a pronounced imbalance in sourcing. In this way, too, the journalism reflects the tilt of American foreign policy toward Israel. The reporting relies on a formula that places primary emphasis on the viewpoints of Israeli settlers and secondary emphasis on dissenting voices from left-leaning Israelis. Palestinian sources are rarely quoted directly, and when they are, they usually are not individuals in positions of authority. More commonly, American journalists tend to narrate Palestinian concerns in their own words, often characterizing what is supported by international law and consensus as merely a matter of what Palestinians themselves claim or demand. Furthermore, the reporting routinely ignores the detrimental effects that the settlements have on Palestinian lives and fails to attribute those effects as a cause of Palestinian violence.

This approach can be seen in a May 2002 CNN report on two West Bank settlements, in which correspondent Carol Lin interviewed Israeli settlers but no Palestinian residents of nearby villages and towns. From Shilo, populated by ideologically driven, religious Israelis, Lin reported:

> LIN: Lisa Rubin, raised in New York, says there should never be a Palestinian state.
>
> UNIDENTIFIED FEMALE: You want to trust them, and if they were trustworthy, that would be wonderful, but you never know when they will turn around and stab you in the back.
>
> LIN: She then showed us her photo album of newspaper stories about when her husband and baby son were ambushed and wounded near Shilo last year. Shilo settlers insist the violence will not drive them away.

From Alfeh Menashe, whose residents were attracted by subsidized housing, Lin and the settlers imparted their own takes on the Palestinian point of view:

> LIN: Alfeh Menashe's palm trees and swimming pools, indoor and out, are the promised land. The settlement's leaders insist they are not intruding on the Palestinians who live down the hill.
> (on camera): It sounds like it is important to get across that your relation with the Palestinians are [sic] a good one?
>
> UNIDENTIFIED MALE: It's not a slogan; for us, it's a way of living here. At the end of the day, we believe that the only solution is for long-term coexistence. You would never find here so-called extremist people running in the hills with rifles.
>
> LIN: Ruth Gat does not even believe she's in the West Bank.
>
> UNIDENTIFIED FEMALE: I've never ever, ever thought of myself as a settler.

LIN: What does that word mean to you?

UNIDENTIFIED FEMALE: Politics, and I don't get involved with politics, whatsoever. . . . I'm here just for the quality of life.

LIN (voice-over): Here, housing is half the price of neighboring Tel Aviv, due, in part, to cheap government-subsidized loans designed to encourage Jews to move to the West Bank. But they still live on land Palestinians say is theirs.[45]

The sourcing imbalance is reflected not only by the lack of directly expressed Palestinian perspectives. American journalists rarely if ever consult nonpartisan sources from outside the arena of the conflict—such as experts in international law, economics, and development—who could provide a much-needed frame of reference for evaluating Israeli and Palestinian counterclaims vis-à-vis the settlements. Instead, journalists often juxtapose Israeli claims of God-given land or references to the Holocaust against Palestinian threats of jihad until victory. Time and again dramatic description is substituted for thoroughgoing analytical reporting. Reporters arrive on the scene, note the details of the landscape, and collect dramatic quotes. However, rarely do they even scratch the surface to reveal the organic factors underlying the settlement issue.

Patterns in Media Coverage

How the media frame the settlement issue can be seen by examining a body of reporting over three time periods. The first covers the failed Camp David negotiations in July 2000 through the first two months of the second intifada, specifically from late September through early December of that year. The second covers the election of Ariel Sharon as Israeli prime minister in February 2001 through the release of the Mitchell commission report that May. The third covers the heightened period of Israeli-Palestinian violence in March and April 2002 and the building of "outpost" settlements and the enlarging of existing settlements—despite the diplomatic "road map" initiative—in 2003.

The print and broadcast reports culled from these three periods are longer news features that examine the settlement issue specifically rather than address it in passing either as one of the primary issues of the Israeli-Palestinian conflict or in the daily news context of settlers involved in specific incidents of Israeli-Palestinian violence.

From Camp David to Intifada

The first period is characterized by a remarkable lack of contextual and sourcing balance. Consistently omitted from the reporting were contextual references to the legality of the settlements under international law and consensus—and the fact that the increase in settler populations during the Oslo period (1993–2000) violated the spirit of the accords, thus creating further impediments to a final settlement. Furthermore, voices of Palestinians— whose lives the settlements affect on a daily basis—were notably absent.

From July through December 2000 seven major newspapers published nine stories reported from settlements. The *Baltimore Sun, Boston Globe, Chicago Tribune, New York Times, St. Petersburg Times,* and *Washington Post* all ran long "take-out" stories datelined from different West Bank settlements during that period.[46] The *Los Angeles Times* ran two such stories,[47] and the *Chicago Tribune* also published a story from a settlement in the Gaza Strip.[48] In addition, the *New York Times* ran two stories with Jerusalem datelines that analyzed the political implications of the settlements.[49] In general, the eleven pieces got considerable play: they averaged 1,200 words in length; four ran on the front page and eight were illustrated with photos, maps, or both.

Contextually and substantively, however, the stories made little or no reference to international law and consensus or to U.S. aid to Israel. Only three of the eleven stories touched on the legality of the settlements under international law—but only in passing. The *Los Angeles Times* reported that "Palestinians consider the West Bank settlements legitimate targets [of violence] because most were established in violation of international law" and (several paragraphs later) that "the Jewish settlements constructed in the West Bank after the 1967 Middle East War contravene international agreement."

The *St. Petersburg Times* made the most specific reference to international law and offered Israeli counterclaims based on biblical history: "To Palestinians the issue is clear: All Jewish settlements are illegal and should be removed because they are on land Israel captured from Arab countries in 1967. The Geneva Convention bans the movement of civilians into occupied territories. To Jewish settlers the issue is equally clear: They are only reclaiming the ancient Biblical homeland of the Jews, who inhabited the same areas 3,000 years ago."

The *Chicago Tribune* story was ambiguous. Its fifth paragraph reported that many Israelis were asking why "the lives of soldiers [are] being lost protecting settlements that have little connection to Israel, violate international law and would gladly be turned over to the Palestinians by a number of Israelis." However, the story ended with a quote from an Israeli soldier: "By [Israeli] law, the settlers can live here and they have a right to be protected. They know that we are ultimately here for them." None of the three stories that referred to international law called on nonpartisan, expert sources to comment on its relevance to the settlement issue. Instead, the reporting made nonspecific references or played Israeli and Palestinian claims off each other.

Although most of the stories mentioned, directly or otherwise, the housing subsidies that the Israeli government extends to settlers, none reported how much Israel had invested to build and defend the settlements and their supporting infrastructure in the West Bank and Gaza Strip since 1967. Nor did any explore how this investment is likely to affect the determination of final borders in a negotiated settlement. Most of the stories gave a figure for the settler population, but none put that figure into the context of the overall Palestinian-settler population ratio, which was fifteen to one. Furthermore, the settler population was routinely cited as comprising the 200,000 Israelis inhabiting settlements in the West Bank and Gaza Strip. The Jewish population of the dozen so-called neighborhoods built and annexed to Jerusalem on land that Israel occupied in 1967, estimated at an additional 177,000,[50] got virtually no mention in the reporting during this period.

The voices and points of view heard in these eleven pieces virtually all belonged to Israelis. Settlers stated their religious and nationalist claims to the land, recounted how the violence had disrupted their quality of life, and expressed anxiety over what negotiations might bring. The Camp David negotiations and weeks of intifada violence provided news pegs for the two *New York Times* stories reported from Jerusalem and for the *Chicago Tribune* story reported from the Kfar Darom settlement in Gaza. These stories examined how Israeli society as a whole was grappling with the costs of the settlements, measured in terms of the obstacles they presented to a negotiated peace and lost soldiers' lives. In her report published on May 1, 2000, Deborah Sontag of the *New York Times* observed: "The public conversation in Israel reinforced the notion that the Israelis are really negotiating among themselves about what concessions to the Palestinians can be tolerated."

Overall, however, the "reporting conversation" throughout these eleven pieces seemed to suggest—in their consistent omission of Palestinian voices—that the settlements were primarily an Israeli concern, and that Israelis would ultimately determine the outcome of the issue. Only the *Washington Post* stories and one of the two *Los Angeles Times* pieces quoted Palestinians directly on their views of how the settlements affected their lives and the peace process. The *Washington Post* story quoted five Israelis: four settlers and an academic. Its sole Palestinian source was Bethlehem mayor Hanna Nasser, who put the settlements in the context of the one-month anniversary of the outbreak of the second intifada: "We said from the beginning that the settlements are endangering our physical coexistence. They are a time bomb. What we had been expecting is now happening."

The *Los Angeles Times* report published in November was by far the most balanced in its sourcing. Reported from the settlement of Efrat, the piece quoted three Israeli settlers from the colony, located south of Bethlehem. The four Palestinian sources were a resident of East Jerusalem, two Palestinians at work on a construction site where expansion of Efrat was under way, and Khalil Tufakji, one of only two Palestinian Authority planning officials to be quoted in the dozens of U.S. media reports under review. Identified as the director of the Palestinian Department of Maps and "an expert on Jewish settlements," Tufakji said: "The land for Efrat was confiscated from Arab owners in 1980. The people of Efrat may be academic and professional, but that doesn't legalize what they are doing."

More typical of the approach to sourcing apparent in the other nine newspaper reports, however, was the *St. Petersburg Times* story. It focused on the Arad family of Bet Arye, a West Bank settlement with approximately forty-five hundred inhabitants located twenty miles due east of Tel Aviv and about two and a half miles beyond the Green Line. The story discussed in detail the Arads' search for an affordable home to accommodate their growing family, the convenience of the settlement's location ("reached by an Israeli road without going near any large Palestinian towns"), the houses' orange-tiled roofs, and the hot-pink bougainvillea cascading over garden walls. Gilad Arad asked, "'Why should Jews give up their ancient homeland? The Palestinians have enough land and they have another 20 or so [Arab] countries they can go to,' says Arad, echoing a common if controversial settler viewpoint. 'We don't have any place other than Israel. I saw that [in] France the other day they were burning synagogues. Only in Israel can Jews feel secure.'"

While the reporting acknowledged the concerns of Palestinians, it spoke *for* them rather than *with* them. The piece did not quote a single Palestinian, despite two references to a Palestinian village (whose name was not mentioned) near the settlement. Unlike the Arads, their Palestinian neighbors remained nameless, faceless, and voiceless, and not one was given the chance to advocate—as Arad had—for the cause of his people.

> There is a small Palestinian village close by, but relations between it and Bet Arye are friendly enough that many Palestinians work in the settlement as gardeners and builders. . . .

Palestinians charge that the lush attractiveness of the Jewish settlements comes at the expense of their own dusty-looking towns. While water is scarce throughout the entire region, there always seem to be enough to keep the settlers' grass green and the flowers blooming, Palestinians note. . . .

There has been no stone throwing along the road to Tel Aviv, which Arad and his wife still travel daily to get to their jobs. The pistol he keeps for protection remains locked away, as it has for the past five years. Arabs from the nearby Palestinian village still come to work. . . .

While maintaining that all Jewish settlements are illegal, Palestinians seem resigned to the fact many will remain, including Bet Arye and others close to major Israeli cities.

Time magazine published a report in early December 2000 on an apparent Palestinian tactical shift from street demonstrations and shooting into Jerusalem's Jewish "neighborhoods" (primarily Gilo, on the city's southern perimeter, which was built on land occupied by Israel in the Six-Day War of 1967) to taking aim at Jewish settlements in the West Bank and Gaza Strip and at the soldiers protecting them.[51] Although none of the newspaper reports did so, the *Time* story quoted Palestinian leader Yasser Arafat. However, just as most of the newspaper articles failed to provide context, the *Time* piece offered no link between the impact of the Israeli settlements on Palestinian life and their becoming a more frequent target of Palestinian attack, concluding that "eight weeks ago, the Palestinians began the latest protests with old-style demonstrations. Then they started shooting at Israeli towns. Now they are attacking settlements. It's not at all clear what the next step will be, but every step seems to get bloodier."

The notable exception to the general lack of context and virtual absence of Palestinian voices in reporting on the settlements during this time period was a National Public Radio report by correspondent Mike Shuster broadcast in early December on *All Things Considered*. In introducing Shuster's report, host Noah Adams established three important contextual facts: the Jewish population in the "occupied territories" (as Adams referred to them) had increased by 50 percent since the Oslo accords were signed in 1993; nearly all Israeli governments since then had encouraged more Jewish settlement on the West Bank; and while "the Oslo accords made no mention of the settlers' fate . . . the Palestinians believe the agreement implicitly indicated the settlements would be frozen."

Shuster's reporting focused on the debate among Israelis about "whether defending all the settlements is worth the violence and pain." While the report quoted mainly Israelis expressing both pro- and anti-settlement views, it also included two Palestinian voices. One was a woman whose home in Ramallah was near the site of Palestinian shooting into the nearby settlement of Pisagot. The other was Palestinian negotiator and spokeswoman Hanan Ashrawi, who said: "I think the settlements are illegal. They continue to be illegal. There are numerous resolutions about the inadmissibility of the acquisition of territory by war. We are not going to bestow retroactive legality on the settlements." Reiterating the contextual details of the scope of and increase in the settlement population that Adams provided in the setup, Shuster observed: "Israel has been steadily expanding the settlements since the 1970s. There was no real slowdown in that expansion after the signing of the Oslo accords in 1993. Then there were 140,000 settlers in the territories. Now there are nearly 200,000, which does not include large numbers of Israelis who have settled in areas of what was Arab East Jerusalem."[52]

Such contextualized reporting had not been apparent, however, in an NPR *Weekend Sunday Edition* report broadcast two and a half weeks earlier from Ofrah, a settlement of four hundred families in the heart of the West Bank, northeast of Ramallah.[53] To introduce the piece, Liane Hansen, the host of the program, set the scene of ongoing violence, sounding the familiar theme of Palestinian rage: "Israel's settlements in the West Bank and Gaza have long been a focus of Palestinian rage. Now the settlements in the occupied territories are increasingly becoming targets of Palestinian gunmen. The settlers say the government is not doing enough to protect them. Palestinians say the violence will not end as long as the settlers remain."

With no reference to international law prohibiting settlement of foreign populations on occupied territory, reporter Linda Gradstein noted that Ofrah "was established 25 years ago by Israelis staking their claim to sovereignty over what had been Arab territory." She then interviewed settler Anat Baruthi, a mother of five, who expressed her anxiety over a recent killing of another female settler in the area: "I feel helpless. I feel unsecure [*sic*] because I don't think that my government does all that can be done to save us, to help us and to stop what's going on. . . . I believe that the Arabs understand power, and if we don't show that we are strong enough, they will continue. We rule this country. This is our country. You are with us, and you may stay, but we make the rules how to do it. You have to follow it."

Gradstein then interviewed two Palestinian residents of the neighboring village of Silwad, who, she said, "have very different ideas about who this piece of land should belong to." Whereas Baruthi had expressed her claims on the basis of possession, authority, and power, the Palestinians expressed their claims by supporting violent measures to win the land back.

GRADSTEIN: Abdul Kadir Ashayad is pruning the plum trees in his garden. He spent 14 years in Florida, but returned to the West Bank in the mid-1980s as his children grew older. He rejects the claims of his Israeli neighbors across the road that God gave them this land.

MR. ABDUL KADIR ASHAYAD: God gives health, God gives babies, but God don't give land. They have to understand that. God don't give land. You see? This is—my father gave it to me.

GRADSTEIN: Ashayad says he wholeheartedly supports the uprising in the occupied territories even though the Palestinians are paying a heavy price. More than 210 people have been killed in the violence, almost all of them Palestinians. Ashayad's neighbor, Mohamed Hamad, says the intifada must continue despite the casualties.

MR. MOHAMED HAMAD: (foreign language spoken)

GRADSTEIN: "We must make the Jews pay for Palestinian blood," he says. "We care about our children and we cry when they die, but we must have our independent state."

The report made no reference to the rights of occupied populations specified in the Fourth Geneva Convention or to the relevant UN Security Council resolutions proclaiming Israeli settlements to have "no legal validity." Rather, it implied that Palestinians were interpreting matters on their own, noting that "everyone in the village agrees there can be no peace with Israel as long as the settlers in places like Ofrah remain." It then quoted Yossi Sarid, an Israeli Knesset member from the left-wing Meretz party, who said, "We have to do the right thing, and the right thing is to uproot the isolated settlements, which endanger civilians and soldiers as well." The report's sourcing was balanced, giving both Palestinians and Israelis their say and reflecting diversity among Israeli views. Nevertheless this careful balancing offered listeners nothing beyond a "she said, he said, he said" approach to a matter that is addressed by international law and consensus—an approach commonly found in most U.S. mainstream media reporting on Israeli settlements. With no analysis or even mention of that legal context, Gradstein ended her report by seeming to characterize the settlement issue as an ultimately hopeless, deadlocked contest of Israeli and Palestinian wills: "In Ofrah, Anat Baruthi says neither she nor her neighbors are going anywhere. Across the road, Abdul Kadir Ashayad says there can be no peace unless the settlers leave."

The Ascension of Ariel Sharon

The government of Israeli prime minister Ehud Barak collapsed in early December 2000, hobbled by the failed Camp David negotiations and the eruption of the second intifada. Elections were called for February 2001, and Barak's challenger for the premiership was Ariel Sharon, whose candidacy was fueled by increasing violence that had claimed scores of Israeli and Palestinian lives.

Days before the election, the *St. Petersburg Times* reported that settlers were only reluctantly lining up behind Sharon. In a story datelined from the West Bank settlement of Efrat, south of Bethlehem, the *Times* reported: "Unlike Barak, who recently discussed with Palestinian negotiators peace plans under which 40,000 settlers would have to abandon their homes, Sharon has promised repeatedly during the campaign that he would not evacuate a single settlement once elected."[54] Sharon, however, refrained from visiting the settlements during his campaign. Moreover, memories still rankled of the Sharon-ordered evacuation of the Yamit settlement in Sinai two decades earlier, as a result of the Israeli-Egyptian peace treaty. Efrat resident Nadia Matar warned: "We'll make sure that any wrong move toward the left will bring down the government. I'm not loyal to a person," she said. "I'm loyal to ideas."

With settlers increasingly targeted by Palestinian militants, however, the feeling that Barak had not done enough to ensure the settlers' safety seemed to be decisive in many of their minds, the *Times* reported: "Since the new intifada started in September, residents of Efrat, a settlement of about 1,400 families that acts as a southern suburb of Jerusalem, have felt threatened daily. The 10-mile road between Efrat and Jerusalem has repeatedly come under showers of stones and occasionally gunfire from Palestinians."

According to a *Washington Post* report two days after Sharon's February 6 landslide victory, the settlers' caution appeared to give way to "cause for celebration." Two dozen settlers had been killed in recent Palestinian attacks and children riding in school buses had been maimed. "'We're very relieved," said Benny Kashriel, mayor of the largest settlement, Ma'aleh Adumim, just east of Jerusalem. "We were really in danger. Our people were [living] under terrorism without any reprieve." Said David Wilder, the American-born spokesman for the 450 Israeli settlers living in the center of Hebron, with a Palestinian population of 120,000: "We hope that he [Sharon] will take off the handcuffs. He knows how to deal with terrorism."

The *Post* described Sharon as the architect of settlement building in the occupied territories. That narrative, however, focused on Sharon's vision and sheer force of will, with no mention of how U.S. aid and diplomatic support enabled that vision to be realized and that will to be enacted—despite international law and consensus.

> Sharon is seen as more than just a protector of the settlements; they are, in fact, largely his brainchild and his creation, a reflection of his grand vision of a Greater Israel encompassing land captured in the 1967 Middle East war. After retiring from the army following the Arab-Israeli war of 1973, Sharon entered politics, and in 1977 he became agriculture minister under Prime Minister Menachem Begin. It was a job that allowed him to oversee the rapid creation of dozens of settlements in the West Bank and Gaza.
>
> Whenever Sharon changed cabinet posts, Jewish settlements remained one of his top priorities—as Begin's defense minister and later as industry minister and housing minister. With his political history so intertwined with the expansion of the settlements, the settlers now are counting on Sharon's continued patronage.
>
> "He built a lot of the settlements in Judea and Samaria," said Kashriel. "Once he built these settlements, he will not destroy them."[55]

The force of Jewish nationalism, coupled with Sharon's will, were themes echoed in an Associated Press report carried in the *St. Louis Post-Dispatch* a few days later. "As a Jew, I don't think anyone has a right to tell me that I don't belong here," said Israel Medad, a leader in the Shilo settlement, located between Nablus and Ramallah. Observed Peace Now spokesman Didi Remez: "It's pretty obvious that unless there is a dramatic change in Sharon, as a person and in his policy, this is a good time for settlers." Israeli and Palestinian claims were presented in narrative opposition, with no reference to international law and consensus. Israeli claims were given direct voice and historical authority, wherereas Palestinian claims, linked to violence, were not.

> Some 200,000 settlers live in 144 settlements in the West Bank and Gaza Strip. Some came because of a belief that Jews have a right to reclaim their historical homeland, and they see the West Bank as the heart of ancient Israel.
>
> Shilo, for example, is mentioned in the Old Testament as a settlement of the ancient Israelites.

"We believe we have a right to our heritage, a right to Jerusalem and a right to live in the biblical heartland," said Yehudit Tayar, spokeswoman of the Settlers' Council.

Other settlers were attracted by government-subsidized housing.

The Palestinians claim the West Bank and Gaza for a future state. Palestinian gunmen have targeted settlers in their uprising against Israel, with militia leaders saying such attacks were aimed at driving the settlers out.[56]

Soon after it was established, the Sharon government announced plans to expand existing settlements. In April NPR broadcast a report on *All Things Considered* that opened by noting mounting "international criticism" over the fact that "the presence of some 200,000 Jewish settlers in the West Bank and Gaza Strip is considered one of the greatest obstacles to a peace deal."[57] The report by correspondent Jennifer Ludden was carefully balanced, quoting the mayor of Efrat as well as a shopkeeper from the neighboring Palestinian village of al-Hadder. Israeli government claims that it would not build new settlements but instead expand existing ones to accommodate "natural growth" were offset by the counterclaims of Israeli peace activists and a minister in the Palestinian Authority.

In hinting at the underlying context of the settlement issue, its inherent contradictions vis-à-vis U.S. policy and the inevitable result, the piece was ahead of others of its type—yet it stopped short of full-blown analysis: "The Housing Ministry says there are plans for a huge new settlement of 6,000 units. All will come with generous government subsidies." This was followed, later in the piece, by: "The U.S. State Department has called the expansion plans provocative and inflammatory." Most telling, perhaps, was the reaction of one of Efrat's Palestinian neighbors.

LUDDEN: The Palestinian village of al-Hadder, near Efrat, is one of those sandwiched amidst the expanding network of settlements and bypass roads. Shopkeeper Esa Nagee says it all makes negotiating a peace deal pointless.

MR. ESA NAGEE (shopkeeper): (foreign language spoken)

LUDDEN: "How can there be a Palestinian state like this?" he asks. "It would be just a bunch of separate places cut off from each other."

The Mitchell Commission Report: In the Wake and Beyond

The Mitchell commission report was released on May 21. It recommended an Israeli settlement freeze and a halt to Palestinian attacks on Israeli civilian targets. In the days leading up to and following the release of the report, four newspapers published stories from various West Bank settlements and CNN broadcast a segment from one. This reporting—informed as it was by the implicit criticism of Israeli settlement policy in the Mitchell commission report—reflected a marked change in contextual and sourcing balance. The tone of pieces published in the *Atlanta Journal-Constitution, Chicago Tribune, Christian Science Monitor,* and *Washington Post* and broadcast on CNN was both more analytical and indirectly critical of the settlements—as if the Mitchell report had empowered the media to approach the subject more aggressively. Still, no mention was made of the connection between U.S. aid and Israel's ability to absorb the cost of settlement building and defense.

On May 9 two teenage boys from the Tekoa settlement, south of Bethlehem, were stoned to death by Palestinians in a nearby cave. On May 18, about two weeks after the contents of the Mitchell commission report began to be leaked, the *Christian Science Monitor* published an interview with Tekoa's chief rabbi, Menachem Frohman, who argued that new settlements should be built in response to the killings. Frohman's sentiments were juxtaposed with reporter Cameron Barr's observations:

> That these lands have been inhabited by Palestinians or their forebears for millennia is of no major consequence for Frohman. He sees a future in which the Jews and Arabs can live among each other in peace, and in his own way actively works to achieve this end.
>
> But in the meantime, Frohman's inclination to turn Jewish grief into more Jewish settlements can only illustrate how hard it will be to halt the action and reaction of the Israeli-Palestinian conflict.
>
> Violence doesn't just beget violence. It begets more settlements, and that, so far, has begotten more violence.[58]

On May 21 the *Washington Post* published a 900-word, staff-written story based on a Peace Now report that fifteen new settlements had been built in the West Bank since January. The play given the story is significant in that most major U.S. newspapers usually cover reports on settlements by Peace Now and human-rights organizations as a secondary angle, devoting to them a couple of paragraphs inserted into stories that focus on other related news developments, or covering them with short wire briefs. Noting the impending official publication of the Mitchell commission report, the story also took an aggressive tone in putting the settlement question in context: "More than any other issue, the construction of Jewish settlements in Israeli-occupied territories has infuriated the Palestinians and convinced them that

Israel is not serious about a negotiated peace deal. But in Israel, the construction has been pursued vigorously by left- and right-leaning governments for 30 years. It is widely viewed as an attempt to cement Israel's physical control over the West Bank, which it has occupied since the 1967 Middle East war. Some 200,000 Israelis live in about 150 West Bank settlements."[59]

On May 22 CNN broadcast a segment from Ofra in the West Bank on the settlements, which it termed the "one big sticking point" in U.S.-Israeli relations. Against the backdrop of "dozens of new homes" being built at the settlement, reporter Sheila MacVicar offered a critical view of the Israeli government's claims that such building did not constitute settlement expansion but instead answered a legitimate need for housing based on "natural growth."

> MACVICAR: In Ofra, they say there are many new families waiting to come and live here.
>
> ISRAEL HAREL (Ofra settler): Everything is sold. Some families will come in the summer because of the time when the children finish school or kindergarten.
>
> MACVICAR: But Israeli peace activists who closely monitor the settlements say there are now more than enough finished houses in all the settlements to meet all the needs for at least another four years.
>
> GILAD BEN-NUN (director of research, Peace Now): There is construction that is going on all the time, and basically the Israeli government is building vacant apartments for nobody to live in for political reasons.
>
> MACVICAR: Daniel Ben-Simon writes about the settlements for an Israeli newspaper.
>
> DANIEL BEN-SIMON (Israeli journalist): Natural growth is a myth, an Israeli myth that is fading away day by day. It doesn't work anymore the way it used to.
>
> MACVICAR: And they say it doesn't work anymore largely because of this. In the eight months since the Palestinian uprising began, vacancies, which were already on the rise before the uprising, have increased. . . . Life in many of the settlements has now become so uncomfortable, so dangerous that Israeli analysts say many of the families are leaving. They say that up and down the West Bank and the Gaza Strip there are now thousands of vacant apartments.[60]

The May 23 *Atlanta Journal-Constitution* report opened by batting back and forth the notion of whether Givat Ze'ev, a community north of Jerusalem, is a settlement or a neighborhood: "To many Israelis, this cozy neighborhood is a benign suburb of Jerusalem, part of the natural growth of the Jewish state. But to much of the rest of the world, Givat Ze'ev and communities like it are obstacles to peace between Israelis and Palestinians." The story quoted an Israeli real estate dealer as saying: "This is not a settlement here. . . . Yes, it is over the Green Line, but there are 10,000 people here." Three paragraphs later came the following assessment in reporter Larry Kaplow's own words: "Givat Ze'ev is a settlement, meaning it was built on Arab land captured by Israel in the 1967 Middle East war." And two paragraphs later: "An American-backed commission this week suggested that the growing settlements are 'provocations' that hinder peace." The report continued to maintain an aggressive yet balanced tone throughout:

> The Oslo peace accords, signed in 1993, say the status of the settlements should be left up to negotiations between the two sides. But in the intervening eight years, Israel has boosted the settlement population more than 40 percent.
>
> This growth infuriates Palestinians, who see it as a land grab meant to pre-empt negotiations. Every U.S. administration for the past 25 years has considered the settlements an obstacle to a peace deal. . . .
>
> But Israeli leaders downplay settlement construction as "natural growth."
>
> "If a child is born, if you have to build a kindergarten, it is very difficult to stop it," [Israeli foreign minister Shimon] Peres said recently.
>
> But the growth far outstrips the natural rise in population. Many moving to the settlements relocate from homes within Israel's borders or from overseas, including America. . . .
>
> "Natural growth is a false argument," says Israeli Gilad Ben-Nun, director of research for the anti-settlement group Peace Now. "It's a political statement. They are trying to make facts on the ground that give them an advantage."[61]

On May 24, in a report from the West Bank settlement of Alon Shevut, located between Bethlehem and Hebron in the southern West Bank, the *Chicago Tribune* also focused on the issue of "natural growth." In its opening paragraphs the story quoted settler Ruthie Lieberman, a Cleveland-born Israeli immigrant: "We hope to keep growing. It would be very painful if my children couldn't live next door to me when they grow up." In the next paragraph, however, reporter Hugh Dellios challenged Lieberman's assertion with this characterization: "But the Liebermans and their neighbors live on occupied Palestinian land, and their desire to expand has become the latest obstacle to ending the violent Mideast crisis in the wake of the Mitchell Commission report released this week." At its midpoint the story stepped up the degree of contextual analysis even further: "Despite the Israeli government's long-running policy of expanding the settlements, their presence is a violation of United Nations resolutions and other international laws calling for the lands to be returned as part of the final negotiations under the 1993 Oslo peace accords." The story then cited Prime Minister Sharon's linking of settlement expansion to Israeli security. It quoted Sharon as defending settlement growth in order to accommodate natural growth of settler families. These characterizations were immediately rebutted by Nabil Shaath, the Palestinian Authority's minister for planning, who said: "The idea of natural growth is a lie. The idea is simply to . . . deepen occupation and to create facts on the ground to pre-empt the outcome of permanent negotiations."[62]

Once the news peg of the Mitchell commission report had faded, however, three U.S. mainstream media reports devoted entirely to the settlement issue reverted to a familiar pattern of sourcing imbalance by favoring Israeli settlers over Palestinians whose lives were affected by the settlements—if the latter were quoted at all—and with no reference to the legal status of the settlements.

The first of the three reports, a July feature in *Newsweek,* focused on the ideologically driven, religious Israeli settlers who populate seven West Bank settlements dubbed "'The Wild East' because of their history of illegal construction and clashes with Palestinians."[63] Reported from Bracha, the piece noted that a total of nearly eighty settlers had been killed in nine months of intifada violence, but it did not mention the number of Palestinian lives lost in clashes with settlers. The piece opened with a vivid description of the settlers' surroundings and gave voice to Bracha settler Jackie Behar, who cast her Palestinian neighbors as murderers and barbarians:

> Even inside her guarded enclave in the heart of the West Bank, the intifada is never far from Jackie Behar's view. On a torpid summer afternoon, Behar is leading a visitor through the Jewish settlement of Bracha, perched high in the arid hills near Nablus. Neat rows of red-roofed stucco houses stand like sentries along the ridge line; far below, a tarmac road built just for the settlers twists past olive groves and the Palestinian village of Huwarah before it disappears behind a hill. "See that curve in the highway?" Behar asks, gesturing across the dusty landscape. "That's where the Arabs murdered Gilad Zar."
>
> Zar, 41, head of security for the nearby settlement of Itamar, was struck by a barrage of bullets [and] then finished off at point-blank

range five weeks ago, a killing that sent a spasm of rage through his community. Hundreds of angry settlers converged on Prime Minister Ariel Sharon's Jerusalem office to protest the killing, carrying Zar's bullet-riddled corpse. "A lot of us get frustrated," Behar says, as a hot wind whips across the mountaintop. "We'd love to go to Huwarah and shoot at a few cars, but then we'd stoop to their level, and that would be barbaric."

Reporter Joshua Hammer observed of the settlers that "most Israelis have little sympathy for them, and many Palestinians regard them as land grabbers who deserve to be killed." However, the report itself was suffused with apparent sympathy for Behar and her fellow settlers, offering insight into their humanity, motivations, hospitality, and personal security:

Behar's religious fervor is typical. A dark-haired, pleasant-looking woman in her late thirties, she was born into a secular Jewish family in Canada, and became a *ba'alat tshuva*—a returning Jew—while in her teens. In the mid 1980s she enrolled in an orthodox yeshiva in Jerusalem, where she met her future husband, Jonathan, a U.S.-born Zionist. The couple lived first in the settlement of Bar El; three years later friends invited them to join them in Bracha, then a tiny outpost of caravan homes. "We came up during the Sukkos holiday," she says. "There were six families living here. Jonathan took one look and fell in love with the place. He said, 'this is it.'" . . .

The past few months [of violence] have felt "like a lifetime," Behar admits, pouring a visitor a glass of orange juice in her tidy home as two of her five children play in their bedroom. . . . "I've had stones thrown at my car several times," Behar says. . . . Behar rarely leaves the confines of the gated and guarded settlement; her husband, a technical-book translator who works in Jerusalem, usually commutes by armored bus. When he travels by private car, he brings along his M-16 semiautomatic rifle and a handgun.

The Palestinian point of view was conveyed in the last three paragraphs of the 1,700-word report, almost an afterthought that mentioned attacks on Palestinians by armed settlers, with one such incident claiming the life of a local seven-year-old boy. Asfad al-Kuffash, a resident of a nearby Palestinian village, was the sole Palestinian quoted. "It's our livelihood," said al-Kuffash of the olive trees chopped down by settlers. "It's almost like losing your children." About the intercommunal violence he observed, "This situation will only end when the settlers leave our land." To which Hammer observed: "That's unlikely to happen soon." The last word was had by the settlers. The piece ended with an evocation of the landscape, the settlers' determination to control it, and the prospect of eternal conflict: "Walking along the top of Mount Bracha, Behar extends her hands toward the bare brown hills that surround the settlement—a vast expanse of emptiness just waiting to be built on. 'All this is ours,' she says exultantly. Arabs and Jews have been fighting over that claim for decades—and the resolution still seems nowhere in sight."

In August CNN broadcast a segment on settlers in the Gaza Strip. Mike Hanna, CNN Jerusalem bureau chief, opened his dispatch from the same point of view that the *Newsweek* report had: a settler pointing to places where Palestinians had attacked Israelis.

MIKE HANNA (voice-over): Missubim, the point at which the settlers cross from Israel into Gaza, ahead, a 20-minute drive through hostile Palestinian territory. Layser Amitay has driven this road for 13 years and in the last 11 months have [*sic*] seen it get more and more deadly.

LAYSER AMITAY (Kfar Darom resident, through translator): Here at this intersection, a suicide bomber blew himself up against the concrete blocks. Here there were two grenade attacks.

HANNA: And a little further on . . .

AMITAY (through translator): We're getting to the place where my wife, Mary, was murdered. The murder took place here next to these palm trees. They used the palm trees as a marker. When the bus got between the two trees, they joined the wires and the bus exploded.

HANNA: Layser Amitay's wife was one of two Israelis killed by that Palestinian bomb last November. Nine people were injured.

AMITAY (through translator): If I was once connected to this place because I was building in it, now I'm connected by blood. To go past the place where Mary was murdered hurts me, but it has bound me to the land even tighter.

The report made no reference to Palestinian deaths in clashes with Gaza settlers. Hanna interviewed seven Israeli residents of four Gaza settlements but failed to interview a single Palestinian. The sole references to the Palestinian point of view were conveyed through the reporter's own narrative and a quote by an Israeli settler.

HANNA: In the Palestinian view, the settlement is a visible sign of an illegal policy of occupation, a symbol of Israeli oppression and defiance of international law. For settlers, the Palestinians who live all around are enemies. The Palestinian goal is far greater than just the destruction of the settlements.

DR. SODY NAIMER (Neveh Dekalim resident): [Palestinians] actually want one thing . . . to destroy the Jewish nation and to see an end of the state of Israel. So we're back to square one where there's no other side to discuss and agree on anything. It's just a matter of your existence or your disappearance.

The report closed much the same way the *Newsweek* piece had, with another evocation of the landscape, further expression of the settlers' determination and, once again, the prospect of protracted conflict.

(*Music playing*)

HANNA: It's a balmy night, a group of settlers relax next to the beach, a light wind blows in off the sea, all apparently tranquil.

EITAN MATZLIAH (Netzer Hazzani resident, through translator): I don't sleep at night. At this time, I used to be asleep, now I can't sleep at night. So I sleep during the day and I am awake during the night. The whole night, I live in fear but my life has to go on.

HANNA: And life does go on. The daily routine, children gather to play, morning prayers at the synagogue, the belief routine itself is an act of defiance. The conviction of all that by their very presence they protect and preserve the state of Israel and that they do so with pride and with dignity.

AMITAY (through translator): We know that it is possible to absorb the blows and not lose our humanity, to look the whole world in the eye and say that we will act as human beings in the shadow of God. We will soak up this conflict and the strength of ourselves and we will get through it.

RACHEL ASSRAF (Kfar Darom resident): I understand today that the Arabs want us out of here, and we're not going to give them that. We're going to stay on because we feel we're on a mission here. And I believe we're going to see better times. I don't—I hope they're not far away.

HANNA: But as each day passes, that hope fades along with the sun setting on the settlements.[64]

In November the *New York Times* published a 1,200-word report from the Netzarim settlement in Gaza. It opened with the observation, that "this community is either one of the safest and most pleasant spots for Israelis to live or one of the most dangerous and damaging to any hopes for peace." The latter characterization was based on a statement that week by Secretary of State Colin Powell that "the building of settlements for Israelis in the West Bank and Gaza Strip 'has severely undermined Palestinian trust and hope' and 'cripples chances for real peace and security.'"

Instead of using Powell's statement as a news peg to address U.S. and Israeli policies on the settlements, the piece let a settler answer Powell herself. Reporter James Bennet observed: "Like others in Netzarim, Orit Litov wondered how Secretary Powell could make sweeping pronouncements about her life without having seen how she lived." Asked about Secretary Powell's remarks, Mrs. Litov said, "I respect him, but I really don't think he knows reality as it is. If the settlements are torn up," she continued, "in the end, it doesn't matter to his life. It won't affect his kids. We have to listen to the U.S.A., and respect what they tell us, but in the end it's our life, and the life of our nation."

The story was full of details about life in the settlement, with Bennet—as had Hammer and Hanna—observing the settlers' milieu from within: "Never typical, life here has become very strange. Netzarim is a fenced and patrolled island encircled by the larger fenced and patrolled island of the Gaza Strip. Children ride their bicycles through streets empty of cars, but at the margin of their community, where the brick walkways and emerald grass stop and the dunes begin, a sign warns: 'You Are Exposed to Shooting.'"

In addition to Litov, twenty-eight, described as a "thoughtful, confident woman" and an expectant mother of three, the story quoted three other sources, all of them Israeli. Comments on the settlers' safety came from Benny Cohen, the town manager of Netzarim, and Itzhik Levy, the driver of an armored bus that ferried the settlers to and from Netzarim, escorted by army jeeps. Benny Elon, "a right-wing minister" in the Sharon government, observed of the recent Bush administration signal to restart the peace process: "I don't think that's a real thing. Ariel Sharon will not accept it now. I don't think that America will really push it."

The story did not quote a single Palestinian, however, on intercommunal violence, Bush administration pronouncements, or any other matter related to the settlements. Instead, it related Palestinian concerns via the reporter's own narrative, which parsed Palestinian demands but failed to mention their basis in international law and consensus. Having noted that between six thousand and seventy-five hundred settlers living in twenty-two settlements controlled "20 percent of Gaza's land and 42 percent of its coastline," Bennet reported:

Gaza's 1.2 million Palestinians live on the remaining land. Most say the Gaza settlements steal their water, land, and liberty, and provoke the clashes and bombings that kill their children. For the Palestinians, the settlers and the soldiers who stand guard over them—people they glimpse these days through bulletproof glass or beyond the barrel of a gun—are the embodiment of occupation. As part of any peace deal, Palestinians demand that soldiers and settlers withdraw completely from the Gaza Strip and West Bank, territories Israel occupied in the 1967 war. The community that became Netzarim had its start in 1972.

Israeli claims to the land, however, were given Israeli voice:

Settlers contend that in staying, they are acting on behalf of fellow citizens. If Israel gives up Gaza, they say, the Palestinians will only demand more land. "There's no end to it," said Mr. Cohen, when asked about the argument that there were relatively few Jews in Gaza. "They will say only Tel Aviv has a large concentration of Jews." The problem, he said, "is not the settlements. The problem is Israel as a state."

The solution, he said, was "to figure out how to live together."[65]

Violent Spring 2002

In March 2002 more than one hundred Israelis were killed in a devastating series of nine Palestinian suicide bombings. The deadliest of these attacks, which claimed thirty lives, occurred during a Passover seder at a Netanya hotel. From March 29 through the third week of April the Israeli army reoccupied the six major West Bank towns, causing massive damage to the physical infrastructure of the Palestinian Authority, Palestinian NGOs, and private property.

In the months immediately preceding this escalation, amid reports of steady Israeli settlement expansion, some U.S. media reporting on the settlements took on a critical tone. In a Fox News segment broadcast on January 23, correspondent Jennifer Griffin countered Israeli claims of "natural growth within existing settlements."

[A]n investigation by Fox News found [that] vigorous settlement expansion outside the boundaries of the existing communities continues with government support. When U.S. ambassador Dan Kurtzer recently suggested Israel spend more of the $800 million the U.S. gives it in civilian aid on the disabled and less on subsidizing these settlements, he was described in anti-Semitic terms by an Israeli Knesset member.

A few weeks ago, the U.S. ambassador confronted Israeli officials about their claims that no new building was taking place. He provided them with satellite images that proved the contrary. Those high-tech methods may have been overkill. We simply brought our cameras here to Betar, an Israeli settlement just 10 miles west of Bethlehem.

The settlers place mobile homes like these near Efrat, another settlement on the outskirts of Bethlehem. These trailers are set up on hills, sometimes up to a mile from the existing settlement, and create what settlers call "facts on the ground." The mobile homes are then replaced with new houses, and the settlement expands.[66]

On February 18 the *Rocky Mountain News,* a Denver-based paper with no foreign bureaus, published a 1,300-word bylined report headlined "Settlements Take Toll on Rights." Reported from the West Bank town of Hebron and its environs and illustrated with three photos, the story focused on the ongoing tensions between the 500 Jewish settlers and 130,000 Palestinians inhabiting the town, as well as Israeli demolition of Palestinian homes in the surrounding area to make way for the expansion of the nearby Jewish settlements of Kiryat Arba and Harsina. The story attributed to a Christian Peacemaker Team composed of American and Canadian volunteers the characterization that "the land grabs . . . have escalated to the point where Israel has confiscated more than a third of the Hebron district."[67]

On March 19 the *New York Times* published a news brief reporting that, according to a survey by Peace Now, thirty-four new, smaller "outpost" settlements had been built in the West Bank since Ariel Sharon had been elected prime minister thirteen months earlier, in February 2001. While the brief quoted the survey as saying that "the new sites were spotted at distances ranging from a few hundred yards to nearly two miles from existing settlements," it also quoted Sharon spokesman Ra'anan Gissin as saying that many of the sites had been approved by the previous government of Ehud Barak, and that the Sharon government "has given no approvals for new settlements."[68]

The tone of reporting on the settlements, however, appeared to shift in the wake of the escalation. The Sharon government's claim that it was "rooting out the terrorist infrastructure" in the West Bank in the same way that the United States had gone to war in Afghanistan was designed to resonate with the American public just six months after September 11—and it got wide play in the American media. In the weeks during and after Israeli military operations in the West Bank, five major pieces on the settlement issue appeared in the *Boston Globe, Chicago Tribune, Christian Science Monitor, New York Times,* and the *St. Louis Post-Dispatch.* Overall, the coverage tended to be uncritical and was based on the settlers' points of view.

The stories in the *Post-Dispatch, Times, Christian Science Monitor,* and *Tribune* all averaged 1,200 words and took a similar tack. Their common theme was that despite the escalation of Palestinian violence aimed at settlers as well as civilians inside Israel proper, most settlers were determined to stay put based on an unshakable conviction that the land was theirs. Not one of the four stories, however, referred to the status of the settlements under international law and consensus. The *Tribune* and the *Times* quoted Israeli sources critical of the settlements, but none of the four stories quoted any Palestinian sources. Once again the Palestinian point of view was conveyed in single-sentence characterizations parsed by the reporters themselves.

"The Palestinians believe this land is theirs, and they want any peace agreement to include the return of settlement lands," the *Post-Dispatch* reported.[69] "Israelis are just as militant in the belief that they have a historic right to be here, and the Fredmans [settlers originally from the St. Louis area] and their neighbors have no intention of leaving." The Palestinians, treated collectively in the *Dispatch* story as wanting their land back, remained nameless and faceless. Israeli settlers' view of the imperative of holding on to the land, however, was given voice through immigrants Lisa and Michael Fredman, former St. Louis–area residents whose current home in Efrat gave the *Post-Dispatch* report a local-angle focus. Celebrating Israeli independence day with a cookout in their backyard, the Fredmans "chose this community in part because of its suburban appeal . . . [with] grocery stores and video rental shops, good schools and like-minded neighbors, including many Americans who, like the Fredmans, immigrated here to be in what they view as their true homeland."

Apparently focused to give local *Post-Dispatch* readers characters and metaphors with which they could relate, the report lacked any directly articulated Palestinian point of view or reference to international law and consensus. Instead, it focused on the Fredmans' reaction to the fact that more than a year's worth of intercommunal violence had turned their "West Bank suburban community into a fortress," driving its families into isolation. The Fredmans expressed a sense of loss, having exchanged their easy American lifestyle for more existential concerns.

[Lisa Fredman] and others dismissed criticism that Palestinians are living in fear in their houses, locked down under a 24-hour curfew. Or that even before the war, being stopped at checkpoints to get to their own homes subjected Palestinians to daily humiliation.

"It must be belittling," Michael Fredman said. "But we didn't bring them to that situation." They brought it on themselves, he said, with suicide bombings. . . .

Reflecting on the celebration of Independence Day at a time of such strife, she added: "In America on the Fourth of July, you don't think about losing your independence. It's just a day to have a barbecue. In Israel, we're still fighting for independence and existence."

In its report on settler sentiment amid the violence, the *New York Times* introduced a note of lyricism by quoting Dov Weinstock, a resident of the West Bank settlement of Mitzpeh Michvar:

As a dry wind whipped orange sparks from a flickering charcoal fire, Mr. Weinstock, a patient man in a patient cause, explained the settlers' dogged approach.

"Catch the land, live on the land, work the land—and no matter how many people are killed, it is yours," he said. "The main idea of the Jewish communities in Samaria [the northern West Bank] is, we don't fight, we build. We just build. Another hill—they kill us. Another hill. We go on."

The story balanced Weinstock's poetic musings with a mention of the Peace Now report citing the thirty-four new settlements, as well as the reporter's characterization of Palestinian discontent. However, once again Palestinians were denied the opportunity to speak for themselves. The legal status of the settlements was posited as an issue of Palestinian interpretation rather than one related to international law and consensus, and the resulting Palestinian claims were linked to violence: "To Palestinians, settlers are the embodiment of illegal occupation. With startling red-tile roofs, fences topped with barbed wire and patrols of Israeli soldiers, the settlements stand on the hilltops where the Palestinians' grandfathers' olive trees once did, a daily reminder, they say, of their freedom denied. Settlers, they say, are fair game for resistance fighters."

The report included an oppositional Israeli point of view by quoting Dror Etkes, coordinator of the settlement watch team for Peace Now: "I don't see how occupation of millions of people, and establishing an apartheid system in the West Bank, is going to contribute to a constructive solution." A Haifa University political scientist was quoted on the theory behind popular Israeli support for the settlements, saying: "For many Zionists, the notion of resettlement is a fundamental tenet of ideology." The settlers got the last word, however, as their point of view was the focus of the piece. "I personally don't think that God brought us back here to throw us out again, either from Hebron or from the land of Israel," said David Wilder, spokesman for the Hebron settlers. "The land of Israel belongs to us." [70]

Similar sentiments were reinforced from the religious and secular points of view held by two Israeli settlers profiled in the *Christian Science Monitor* piece, which similarly did not include any directly articulated Palestinian point of view or reference to international law. It opened with the forceful statements of a settler, followed by a sympathetic, flesh-and-blood rendering of his background and motivations:

> "The only way to have security is through force," says Michael Bukchin, a resident of the Jewish settlement Yitzhar, three miles from Nablus. "Force and facts on the ground. It has taken a long time to convince the people of Israel of this. Luckily [Palestinian Authority president Yasser] Arafat helped us get that message across."
>
> The son of a Holocaust survivor, Mr. Bukchin was born in Tel Aviv and became Orthodox later in life. He has a master's degree in human resource management from Columbia University in New York, six young children, a long gray beard, and a love of fast motorcycles. He moved to the West Bank 11 years ago because, he says, he was "sick of hectic modern society" and looking for "some clean country living." Ideology, of course, also played a part. "This is my land. Why shouldn't I live here?" he asks. The last vacation he took was to the Gaza Strip. "I like the beach there," he says and grins.

The report acknowledged that settlement in "the occupied territories" had been "either encouraged or tolerated by every Israeli government since 1967," and that in creating these "facts on the ground [the settlers had] succeeded in becoming a serious obstacle to creating a geographically contiguous future Palestinian state." This brief narrative parsing of Palestinian concerns was juxtaposed with an emotional quote from Bukchin that evoked biblical prophecy and, once again, the Holocaust.

> "The Bible says this is our homeland. This is my birthright. If not here, where else can I live?" asks Bukchin. "I have no other place. Every other place I go, you kill me, you murder me, you burn me. We have to do what we have to do. We have to stay here, and we have to fight for what we believe in. Especially when we know it's right."

Several paragraphs later, Bukchin evoked September 11—and Hitler.

> "We need to be strong and make sure they know they will pay dearly for Jewish blood." The U.S., he notes, already knows this rule. "That's the only way the U.S. responded to the twin towers attack. That is the natural way," he says. The recent incursions into the West Bank, says Bukchin, were "not enough. We needed to stay there. Get everybody. Get all the weapons."
>
> Bukchin says he knows the time could come when settlement evacuations will return to the government's agenda—but he believes that moment recedes with every passing day of violence. "Things will get worse before they get better," he says. "Dictators," he explains, referring to Mr. Arafat, "never have enough. Look at Hitler."

The piece then profiled settler Ahuva Shilo, a resident of Ma'aleh Shomron, located just inside the West Bank near the Palestinian town of Qalqilya. Describing Shilo as "a secular woman with spiky red hair and shiny gray nail polish," the article reported that she "grew up in the left-wing movement." Her humanity, like that of Bukchin, was rendered three-dimensionally.

> In her 20s, partly as a consequence of meeting her husband, a right-winger, she became convinced that it was her duty to help settle the "Greater Land of Israel." She soon moved from Tel Aviv to a small outpost in the West Bank. She lived in a trailer home and packed a gun. Otherwise, she maintains, her lifestyle remained much the same— with frequent trips into nearby Tel Aviv to go to the movies, shop, or meet up with friends in cafes. Those friends would not come to the settlement to see her. "I would not apologize or feel embarrassed," she says. "But it was hard."

The only other hint in the piece that Palestinians were afoot in the land inhabited by Bukchin and Shilo occurred in another narrative reference that referred to Palestinians generically as "Arabs." "A month ago, Ma'aleh Shomron, like many Jewish settlements, decided not to let in any Arabs. Shilo says her Arab gardener, who had been working for her for 18 years, cried. 'He asked me how he was going to support his family,' she says. 'I cried too, but I told him he needed to ask Arafat about that.'"[71]

A clue as to why these stories conveyed such unabashed sympathy for settler points of view can be found in the *Chicago Tribune* piece. Like the *Chris-*

tian Science Monitor, Post-Dispatch, and *Times* reports, the *Tribune* story neither referred to international law and consensus nor quoted any Palestinian
sources. However, referring as the *Times* piece did to the Peace Now report
on the thirty-four new outpost settlements, *Tribune* correspondents Stephen
Franklin and Christine Spolar offered a fresh insight.

> Not long ago U.S. officials, armed with aerial photos of the growth
> taking place at various settlements, reportedly complained to Israeli
> officials.
>
> The Israelis first denied there had been growth. Faced with addi-
> tional evidence, Israel "clarified its position" to acknowledge some
> growth but rebuffed any attempt by the U.S. government to address
> the issues, sources said.
>
> The Americans have backed off on the issue because of the attacks
> on Israeli civilians, sources said.[72]

That U.S. officials would back off from challenging the Israeli government
on settlement expansion due to the political capital that Israel gained from
Palestinian violence against Israeli civilian targets is a notable piece of reporting. It would have been much stronger, however, had the sources been named
or identified in some way and the point been more central or perhaps the
focus of the story itself. Yet it is remarkable that just as the U.S. government
would back off from the settlement issue during a period of Palestinian violence against Israeli civilians, so, too, would the American media.

The most distinctive of the five newspaper reports on the settlements was
published in the *Boston Globe*, a piece of nearly 2,400 words presented as
the "first in a series of occasional articles on obstacles to peace in the Middle
East." *Globe* reporter Charles Radin provided a detailed history of the Israeli
settlement movement and government settlement policy since 1967. The
story succeeded in introducing the international law issue in the opening
paragraphs, presenting both the Palestinian and Israeli points of view without, however, soliciting nonpartisan, expert interpretation or comment on
their relative merits.

> Jad Ishaq, a member of the Palestinian negotiating team at Camp Da-
> vid, says the settlements are illegal; the Palestinians argue that Article
> 49 of the Fourth Geneva Convention bars an occupying power from
> transferring part of its population to occupied land.
>
> Even Israelis who would vacate the settlements in return for a reso-
> lution of the struggle with the Palestinians reject that view.

Israel's belief, according to Foreign Ministry legal adviser Alan Baker, is that the territories were illegally occupied by other countries—Jordan and Egypt—before the Six-Day War, that there was never a Palestinian state that was conquered, and so there is no occupation in the Geneva Conventions meaning of the term.

The story did not make a connection between U.S. aid to and diplomatic support of Israel, on the one hand, and the continued presence of the settlements in defiance of international consensus and international law, on the other. It did, however, succeed in clearly articulating the connection between the settlements and the future of the peace process, from Palestinian and Israeli sources alike.

The settlements, the bypass roads that serve them, and the buffer zones between Israelis and Palestinians that the Sharon government recently began creating all are part of "a plan to cut the West Bank into parcels" so that there cannot be a viable Palestinian state, says [Jad] Ishaq, the Palestinian expert on settlements. Unless the settlements are removed, "there will be no cease-fire, and continued intifada," he adds. "There is no hope."

Retired general Shlomo Gazit, who was the first director of government activities in the territories, agrees.

The settlements "have become a clear message to the local population that Israel is planning to turn this area into greater Israel, and that they should not even dream about having a Palestinian state," he says. "If we don't do something" to signal a willingness to change this policy, "there is no hope for any future agreement."[73]

The Acceleration of Outpost Settlements

Despite the Bush administration's repeated calls in March and April for a halt to the Israeli army siege of Palestinian towns in the West Bank, Ariel Sharon remained defiant. That summer Sharon continued to flout U.S. admonitions—this time over settlement building. As the Israeli government continued to enlarge existing settlements and to take no action against the establishment of dozens of new, smaller outposts by renegade settlers, the U.S. media took note. From May through August 2002 the *New York Times*, *Washington Post*, and *Newsweek* published reports on the increase in settlement activity. The *CBS Evening News* broadcast one segment devoted to the settlements, while NPR's *All Things Considered* ran two such reports.

Two years after the collapse of the Camp David talks and more than a year and a half after the start of the second intifada, media outlets seemed to realize a newfound sense of urgency in reporting on Israeli settlements. This may have been the result of several factors: More than a thousand Israelis and Palestinians—in an approximate 1 to 3 ratio—had been killed in intercommunal violence that increasingly targeted Israeli settlers. Sharon continued to defy the stated will of the Bush administration. The latter continued to do little more than pay lip service to the issue, voicing periodic objections backed by neither policy initiatives nor punitive sanctions.

However, despite the significant time and space they devoted to the readily observable and easily reportable aspects of the settlements, it appeared that the U.S. media could not get—or would not move—beyond the policy mirror. Instead, the reporting followed a familiar pattern, falling back on several stock themes. The settlements constituted an obstacle to peace. Successive Labor and Likud governments built the settlements apace, offering significant financial incentives to lure non-ideologically driven Israelis to take advantage of real-estate bargains beyond the Green Line. Ideologically driven settlers believed they had a God-given right to occupy the land. Many of the reports noted that the most singular factor in three and a half decades of Israeli colonization of the West Bank and Gaza Strip was the sheer force of Sharon's political will—which effectively rendered moot the position of the U.S. government. With few exceptions, little was heard directly from Palestinians themselves, and only one of the six reports referred to international law and consensus. The *CBS Evening News* segment typified the paradigm.

> DAN RATHER (anchor): One major obstacle to peace between Israel and the Palestinians is the presence of scores of Jewish settlements in the West Bank and Gaza, but an Israeli peace group released a poll today showing that two-thirds of the settlers polled would leave to bring peace, and only 2 percent would violently resist leaving. CBS' David Hawkins has more on these key settlements and the settlers.
>
> DAVID HAWKINS reporting: The West Bank of the Jordan River is one of the most disputed pieces of real estate on Earth. Most Palestinians consider it occupied territory, the land on which they hope to establish a state. For many Israelis, though, especially the settlers that live here, the land belongs to the Jews.
>
> MS. HALLIE KON (settler): This is Israel. It is our home. It is our country.

HAWKINS: Steve Braun, from Skokie, Illinois, moved to the West Bank 12 years ago.

MR. STEVE BRAUN (settler): The land was given to us in the Bible from God. . . .

HAWKINS: Not all the settlers are here for religious reasons. Most came because of the generous grants and tax breaks designed to encourage Jews to move into the area. . . .

Kobi Friedman moved to a settlement to build his dream house. The intifada, however, has turned his dream into a nightmare.

MR. FRIEDMAN: At one point I was offered more than a million dollar [*sic*].

HAWKINS: And how much is it worth now?

MR. FRIEDMAN: Less than $1.

HAWKINS: Friedman says 70 percent of the settlers, himself included, would leave in a minute if it would bring peace to the region. . . .

Despite the fact that a majority of Israelis are in favor of abandoning the settlements, Prime Minister Ariel Sharon won't even talk about it, especially while Palestinian violence continues. He says as long as he's in charge not a single settlement will be evacuated.[74]

The NPR piece was reported by Anne Garrels from "the unauthorized outpost of Nefain ne Himya," near "the mother settlement of Rehelim," midway between Nablus and Ramallah in the central West Bank. Garrels quoted three Israeli sources—two opposing the settlements and one in favor—but no Palestinians. Although she referred to a statement by Defense Minister Benjamin Ben-Eliezer that he would dismantle a number of the new outposts, she ended the report by indicating that both Ben-Eliezer's statements and protestations from the Bush administration were little more than posturing.

GARRELS: But Ezra Rosenfeld, the settlers' spokesman, is happy to say he's seen nothing more than words so far.

MR. ROSENFELD: If [Ben-Eliezer] felt that it was beneficial to his political career to talk about the fact that these were outposts which he evacuated, then I have no difficulty with him doing so.

GARRELS: In other words, there were no outposts that were removed.

MR. ROSENFELD: I don't know of any people who are now homeless as a result.

GARRELS: As the U.S. seeks to revive peace negotiations and help formulate boundaries for an eventual Palestinian state, American officials say the Israeli settlement machine stands as one of their most formidable obstacles.[75]

The detailed *New York Times* report, which was filed from the outpost of Givat Eshkodesh, near Nablus and the established settlement of Shilo a bit farther south, ran just under 2,200 words and was accompanied by three photographs, charts and graphs tracking settlement growth from 1970 to 2000, and a West Bank map delineating municipal boundaries of Israeli settlements and areas of formal Palestinian authority.[76] The text opened by juxtaposing expressions of theocratic zeal with the specter of eventual Armageddon.

> GIVAT ESHKODESH, West Bank—There is no discernible charm to this barren hilltop, but the young, Israeli settlers who have occupied it say they will do whatever they must to defend it.
>
> "If you have faith, there is no force that can move you," one 24-year-old settler, Shalom Israeli, said, smiling as he clutched the grip of his M-16 assault rifle on a recent day. "This is just one hill, but it points straight up to God."
>
> Palestinians in the village of Singil can see the outpost from their terraces. To them, it makes no difference that such settlements are not officially sanctioned by the Israeli government. Their land is disappearing, the villagers say, and only the settlers have the army on their side.
>
> "The Jews here believe they have been chosen by God and that we are animals," said Khaled Hussein, 35, a stonecutter in Singil. "They are coming closer all the time. Now, I think, there are only two possibilities: either Israel will destroy us, or we will destroy Israel."

The report referred to "sporadic appeals from the United States" for a cessation of settlement activity. It cited a speech ten days earlier in which President Bush "echoed the familiar American appeal, saying 'Israeli settlement activity in the occupied territories must stop.'" Not only did the piece go so far as to suggest that Israeli settlement building through the 1990s violated the Oslo accords, but it also used the exact wording NPR had in quoting American officials: "As the United States seeks to revive the peace negotiations and help formulate boundaries for an eventual Palestinian state, American officials say that Israel's *settlement machine stands as one of their most formidable obstacles* [emphasis added]. The sharp rise of the settler population over the last decade has come despite Israel's vow, under the Oslo peace negotiations, not to 'change the status' of the occupied territories pending final negotiations."

Despite its apparently critical tone, however, the piece did not link U.S. aid to Israel with the amount of money needed to keep the settlement enterprise running—even as it reported these financial aspects in detail.

> How much Israel spends to sustain and defend the settlements remains a closely held secret. Estimates run upward of $1 billion a year, including security costs, even as the country struggles with its most severe economic crisis in decades.
>
> A former finance minister, Avraham Shochat, calculated the cost of the government's incentive system at perhaps $400 million. Based on supplemental defense appropriations since the Palestinian uprising, or intifada, began in September 2000, he estimated that the security forces are also spending more than $1 billion in additional funds each year, part of it to protect the settlements.

Newsweek also reported detailed financial aspects of the settlements. It described the incentives for settlers, the perks they enjoyed—including, in the settlement of Ariel, "wireless broadband in homes and offices, computers in the pre-schools, and elementary schools that teach Web design and robotics"—and what the general costs of the Israeli settlement enterprise were thought to be.

> Lisa Nahmani would have preferred to stay in Jerusalem but she couldn't afford to buy a house for her family of five. The four-bedroom homes she was seeing ran about $250,000, much more than the Nahmanis could manage. She began looking at neighborhoods beyond the Green Line. . . . The differences were astonishing. In a town like Ma'aleh Adumim, the largest settlement in the West Bank, the schools and health services were better (funded more generously by the government), and the houses were cheaper, in part because the government subsidizes construction. As a bonus, she discovered, Israelis who moved to the West Bank got a 7 percent reduction in income tax. Just because they were settlers. . . . "It was a financial issue. We paid $100,000 less and we got a house that's big enough for our family," she says, sitting in the Ma'aleh Adumim home she purchased last summer. . . .
>
> [Avraham] Shochat, the former finance minister, estimates government subsidies to settlers at $300 million a year, about 10 percent of the amount Israel wants to slash from its deficit. Instead of eliminating the incentives, the government has proposed deep cuts in Israel's social programs and a re-evaluation of the deficit target. But economists say

the $300 million is only a fraction of what the settlements really cost. Israel has raised its defense spending by $1.5 billion in the past year, in part to defend the outposts in the territories.

Despite the abundance of dollar figures, the report stopped short of raising the issue of how Israel could afford the cost of the settlements. The story's lead-in acknowledged that "Israel's economy is a shambles. But the perks to people willing to settle in the occupied territories keep coming." However, the text acknowledged the link between U.S. policy and the settlements only in passing: "Even Washington, Israel's closest ally, regards the settlements as a growing problem. Just last month President George W. Bush said, 'Israeli settlement activity must stop.' Yet thousands of new housing units are under construction in the West Bank, and Jewish ideologues have thrown up 40 new outposts since Ariel Sharon was elected last year."

Critical in tone if not substance, the piece relied exclusively on Israeli sources. It quoted five settlers, an economist, and a former finance minister—but no Palestinians. Instead, the Palestinian point of view and the Palestinians' very existence in the settlement tableau were intimated through the reporter/writer narrative. Two passing references buried in the story's 1,469-word text read: "Although Sharon would rather focus on Yasser Arafat's peace-deal breaches, Palestinians argue that settlement expansion fuels popular rage toward Israel and Israelis, hindering negotiations and making a final peace deal increasingly remote" and "The 25 families that live in Neguhot, at the end of a narrow dusty road, are surrounded by Palestinian villages and guarded round the clock by a platoon of soldiers."[77]

The *Washington Post* report, at 2,415 words, was the longest of the six pieces and ran on the front page. However, it also exhibited a similar imbalance in sourcing. The story quoted eight Israeli sources with various perspectives on the settlements: four settlers; a researcher from the human-rights organization B'Tselem; and one spokesman each from the Sharon government, the Civil Administration, and the Ministry of Defense. Conversely, the Palestinian point of view was conveyed via the reporter's narrative, which was succinct and accurate, rather than through authoritative Palestinian voices belonging to academics, political commentators, or Palestinian Authority officials.

Such settlement activity is one of the roots of Palestinian frustration with the peace talks that followed the Oslo accords, Palestinian analysts say. The creation of settlements required the confiscation of private and communal land and a permanent stationing of Israeli troops to protect settlers from hostile Palestinians, which in turn led to check-points and more friction with the Palestinians.

Bypass roads built to segregate Palestinian and Israeli travelers also have meant more confiscations and further division of territory set aside for Palestinian rule under the Oslo agreements. This has helped turn Palestinian-run areas into an archipelago of unconnected islands. In the Arab view, the settlements and the Israeli army activities they bring nourish the rage that has fueled the bloodshed of the last 20 months.

The only Palestinian individual to appear in the *Post* piece was shepherd Mahmoud Hamamdi, whose life was being complicated by two of the new settlement outposts. He turned up in the final three paragraphs of the story and was given voice in an eleven-word direct quote:

Concurrently, the government pressured a clan of Palestinian shep-herds to abandon their traditional cave dwellings and tents in a valley below Maon. The Israelis said the Palestinians were squatting on state land. Settlers from the Dribben camp came and cut down scattered fields of wheat. Regional officials ordered the dismantling of a tent-mosque.

Mahmoud Hamamdi, clan head and father of 11 children, has asked an Israeli court to block eviction. "I am not new here. I was born in these caves," Hamamdi said.

The *Post* story was distinctive in that it was the only piece among the six to discuss U.S. policy toward the settlements within the context of interna-tional law. However, the piece did not address the apparent contradiction between the two.

B'Tselem, in line with international rights organizations, the Inter-national Committee of the Red Cross and most world governments, regards settlement development as a breach of war rules in the Geneva Conventions. The conventions forbid a country to transfer "parts of its own civilian population into the territory it occupies."

Successive Israeli governments have contended that the Geneva Conventions do not apply because the world did not recognize the rule of Jordan and Egypt in the West Bank and Gaza. The land is not occupied, they have argued.

The Carter administration was the last U.S. government to label the settlements illegal. The Bush administration has criticized settlement expansion as unhelpful to renewing peace talks but has not dealt with their legality. In doing so, President Bush has followed a pattern established under Presidents Ronald Reagan, George H. W. Bush and Bill Clinton, whose administrations referred to the settlements as an obstacle to peace but not illegal.[78]

The other five reports exhibited the typical approach. When Palestinian sources were consulted at all, their claims were juxtaposed with Israeli claims to suggest a symmetry completely divorced from other relevant factors— international law and consensus regarding the settlements and how U.S. support for Israel has facilitated their existence at the heart of the conflict. Outside expert sources who could provide a context for evaluating these competing claims were not consulted. The *New York Times* reported that settler Pinchas Wallerstein, described as a "political operative" and an "old-guard veteran of the militant settler movement Gush Emunim,"

> makes no secret, for example, of his dream to use outposts like Givat Esh-kodesh to link isolated settlements in the Jordan Valley all the way across the West Bank to Ariel, the settlement city that is a gateway to Tel Aviv.
> "In a few years, all of this area will be covered by Jewish population," he said as he stood on a hilltop near the settlement of Shiloh. "I can show you how you can connect this area to Tel Aviv without any major Arab population inside."

Shifting to the Palestinian point of view, the report noted that

> Palestinians look out on the same landscape, but see it more darkly.
> In Singil, a contractor traced a map of what had been lost: Palestinian farms swallowed by a settlement over there, Palestinian lands taken for an outpost, Palestinian olive groves that had been placed off-limits by the military to safeguard the transit of the settlers.
> "Every day that the occupation continues, we lose more of our land," the contractor, Fathi Shabaneh, said. "Every day that the occupation goes on, more of the hope that we have for a just peace evaporates."[79]

A similar balancing technique was apparent in the NPR report by Peter Kenyon, which juxtaposed Israeli and Palestinian counterclaims while providing no context with which to evaluate them. Familiar themes were evoked: Israelis taking a wasteland and making it bloom; Palestinians inevitably resorting to jihad.

KENYON: Some modern Israeli historians say one of the myths of the pioneer settlers was that they turned an Arab wasteland into productive ground. Standing just outside the old Jordanian police station that now serves as his office, Elkana Mayor Maurice Ganz says the settlers today are still performing feats of alchemy.

MAYOR MAURICE GANZ: Want to know how Elkana was before we came here, you look at that hill, this hill on the other side. You'll see it's wasteland, nothing on it. Now I take you far around and you can see what you can make out of it. . . .

It doesn't depend [on] who is in the government, it's left or right. The area of Elkana up to Ariel, it's all understood that it will forever belong to Israel.

KENYON: Ganz says before he ordered the fence put up a couple of years ago, settlers and Arabs mixed freely and were good neighbors. But once again, just down the road, the neighbors have another view altogether.

Walking along the edge of a field in the village of Mossah, less than a hundred yards from the fence that marks the beginning of the Elkana settlement, Palestinian farmer Juma Amir points to the fields that have been in his family for generations. This, he says, is what's left of a 50-acre parcel.

MR. JUMA AMIR (farmer, through translator): In 1979, the military governor decided to confiscate the land for military purposes, and after they confiscated the land, they used it for building a settlement.

KENYON: Like many Palestinians, Amir has no written title to the land, only old tax receipts to show his family's claim. But Deputy Mayor Ahmed Amir says everyone in Mossah over the age of 25 can refute the settlers' claim that the land Elkana sits on was undeveloped state property or a wasteland. He says it only became a wasteland when the Israeli bulldozers moved in and made it one. . . .

Shop owner Abdel Amir . . . has a 1933 map of the village, surveyed when Palestine was run by the British under a League of Nations mandate. In those days, Mossah covered a lot more ground. When asked what happened, Amir smiles and grabs for a reporter's microphone. "Just like that," he says. "They wanted it and they took it." . . .

These men relate all this matter-of-factly and then, just as calmly, they explain that the only solution is to drive the Jews from Palestinian land, no matter how long it takes.[80]

The Settlements and the "Road Map"

In an effort to restart the peace process, in 2003 the Bush administration joined forces with the European Union, the United Nations, and Russia. Together the "Quartet" produced the "road map" plan to get Israel and the Palestinians back on track. Announced on April 30, the road map required the Palestinian Authority to rein in violence by militants. It required Israel to "immediately dismantle settlement outposts erected since March 2001" and "consistent with the Mitchell Report . . . freeze all settlement activity (including natural growth of settlements)." The plan's ultimate stated objective was "Israeli-Palestinian negotiations aimed at a permanent status agreement in 2005."

The *Chicago Tribune* reported that sixty-two of the one hundred unauthorized outposts had been established since Ariel Sharon became prime minister in February 2001. About half were uninhabited, with the rest populated by about a thousand settlers.[81] The *New York Times* quoted a settler as saying that the uninhabited sites were meant to be "a kind of ruse . . . thrown up precisely so the army can dismantle them and the government can respond to international pressure by announcing it has eliminated some settlements."[82]

Apparently it worked. The announcement by Sharon on June 9 that Israel had begun to dismantle fifteen "illegal" settlement outposts in the West Bank got widespread play in the American media. While NPR reported that day that only four of the fifteen outposts were populated, ABC News reported that in demolishing three uninhabited trailer homes and an unmanned watchtower, "Israeli Prime Minister Ariel Sharon today had enough power to confront the settlers he once championed."[83] The *New York Times* and *Chicago Tribune* both ran front-page stories about the outposts the following day; the *Los Angeles Times* ran an 1,100-word story on page 12.[84] The *Washington Post* described the dismantling of the outposts as "a limited action" and limited its coverage to 250 words at the end of a report on page 14 that focused on Palestinian prime minister Mahmoud Abbas condemning the killing of five Israeli soldiers by militants two days earlier.[85]

Throughout June, media outlets focused on settlers' dramatic expressions of having been betrayed by Sharon's acceptance of the road map and the dismantling of the outposts. "We saw him as our partner," veteran West Bank settler Pinchas Wallerstein told *U.S. News & World Report*. "There's hardly a single settlement that Sharon didn't . . . have some part in building." At a rally of angry settlers in Jerusalem, a teenager shouted, "We want to tell Ariel

Sharon that whoever surrenders the land of Israel and agrees to a Palestinian state will not go on being prime minister!"[86] Gaza settler Rifka Goldschmidt of the Gannei Tal settlement told NPR: "They'll have to fight me. I'm not packing up and going; they'll have to fight me. Because it's mine, and nobody in the world will tell us, the Jews, not to settle the land of Israel. It's not the State of Israel; it's the land of Israel." Said settler Rahael Sepperstein of Neveh Dekalim, also in Gaza: "Strategically, it's very important for us to be here, a Jewish presence here that must remain here in Gaza. There is no way the Arabs can live in Gaza without Jewish supervision."[87]

With most reports focusing on settler anger and fear, analysis of the settlements' legal disposition according to international law and consensus was all but absent. On June 19 Fox News pegged a report about the settlements to "an explosive situation on the West Bank. . . . [H]undreds of angry, screaming Jewish settlers are squaring off in a volatile scuffle with Israeli troops." Interviewer Greta Van Susteren raised the legality question with former presidential adviser David Gergen of Harvard University's Kennedy School of Government. The exchange began with dramatic descriptions but ultimately proved short on facts since neither Van Susteren nor Gergen made reference to the Fourth Geneva Convention or the relevant UN resolutions. Furthermore, Gergen seemed to lend legitimacy to the permanent settlements, characterizing them as "authorized" small villages.

> VAN SUSTEREN: David, Jews against Jews, the settlers against the army and the police.
>
> GERGEN: We've seen this before with [the] assassination of Rabin in Israel. There are factions in Israel who are deeply, deeply opposed to giving back any land—as they see it, it's their land—to the Palestinians. And Sharon now has a very active militant group on his right, just as Abbas has on—that's the Palestinian leader—on his left. And that's why the politics of the Middle East are so murderous. This settlement where they've been demonstrating here in the last 24 hours is just a year old. It is an unauthorized settlement.
>
> VAN SUSTEREN: What's an outpost versus a settlement? And what's an illegal one? . . . Or unauthorized one?
>
> GERGEN: They're small, in effect, villages which have been authorized by the Israeli government for people to move in. There are a lot of incentives to move into those places. And those are called the authorized settlements, and they're all over the West Bank.
>
> But after those go in, some really hard-line folks will move in with tents between settlements, the authorized settlements, and

they'll line a hilltop, and you'll see a dozen tents out there where people are just living off the land, in effect, and arguing that that's theirs. And the Palestinians, of course, find it totally unacceptable, find all the settlements unacceptable. But because these are unauthorized, it's a lot easier for Sharon to say—Well, we'll get rid of those first.[88]

On June 3, five weeks after the Quartet announced the road map, Bush told a summit of Arab leaders convened in Sharm el-Sheikh, Egypt, that "Israel must deal with the settlements." On June 4 Bush met with Sharon and Abbas in Aqaba, Jordan, and the road map was formally launched. Nevertheless, as *Newsweek* reported on June 9, the Sharon government was continuing to expand its permanent settlements: "In recent weeks, Israeli Minister of Housing Effi Eitam has quietly initiated construction of 11,000 additional units in four major settlements in the West Bank. Last week Sharon assured the Jewish settlers, 'there is no restriction here, and you can build for your children and grandchildren, and I hope for your great-grandchildren as well.'"[89]

On July 31 the *Christian Science Monitor* reported that although Sharon had met Bush two days earlier in Washington and had told him that progress was being made on dismantling outposts, facts on the ground indicated otherwise.

In Washington, Sharon pledged to remove 12 "illegal" outposts from Palestinian land and told Bush he had removed 22 others.

Dror Etkes, settlement watch director for the Israeli group Peace Now, says 22 outposts have been evacuated in the past year, but others have been built. That dynamic has continued so that since the road map was launched on June 4, outpost numbers haven't changed at all, says Mr. Etkes.

"Serious infrastructure works are going on in some outposts so that altogether, we are in a worse place than we were before [June 4]," says Etkes. "We have the same amount of outposts—but now they have more houses, electricity, roads, more of everything that makes an outpost."[90]

On July 31, two days after Sharon had met with Bush, the Israeli Lands Authority opened bidding for contracts to build 22 new homes in Neveh Dekalim, the largest Jewish settlement in the Gaza Strip. The move was reported on August 1 by various media outlets, including the *Atlanta Journal-Constitution*, New York *Daily News*, *Chicago Tribune*, *Los Angeles Times*,

New York Times, and *Newsday.* On August 2 Agence France-Presse reported that the Israeli army had confiscated seven and a half acres of land near Neveh Dekalim.[91]

On August 7 the Associated Press reported that the Israeli Hebrew-language daily *Maariv* had reported that Sharon was backing a $95 million plan to attract more settlers to the Jordan Valley in the West Bank. Not yet approved by the cabinet, the plan "would provide free housing to young couples promising to live in the Jordan Valley for at least four years . . . underwrite their college educations and provide one-time grants of $2,700 if they found employment in the area."[92]

On October 2 the Israeli Housing Ministry began advertising for bids to build 604 new homes in three West Bank settlements—Ariel, Betar Illit, and Ma'aleh Adumim—on the northern, southern, and eastern perimeters of Jerusalem. Sharon adviser Zalman Shoval justified the settlement expansion by saying Israel did not have to meet its obligations under the road map as long as attacks by Palestinian militants continued. He told the Associated Press: "The road map is stalled as long as there is no action taken by the Palestinians to dismantle the terrorist infrastructure."[93]

The road map, however, had done little to quell Israeli-Palestinian violence from the outset. By June 14, ten days after the plan was officially launched, sixty-two Israelis and Palestinians had been killed in intercommunal violence.[94] The spiraling violence included the killing of nine Palestinian civilians by Israel and its failed attempt to assassinate a Hamas leader, as well as a Palestinian suicide bombing of an Israeli bus in Jerusalem that killed seventeen. The violence was interrupted for five weeks after three Palestinian militant groups unilaterally agreed to a cease-fire at the end of June. However, with individual Palestinian attacks continuing and the Israeli army targeting and killing two Palestinians in Nablus and Hebron, by early August, the violence had resumed, replete with Palestinian suicide bombings and Israeli rocket attacks.

In announcing the merger of the Preventive Security Service in the West Bank and Gaza Strip under a unified command, Palestinian security chief Muhammad Dahlan said on August 9 that it would take $250 million and three years to rebuild Palestinian police posts in the territories. In its report of the announcement, the Associated Press noted that Israel had destroyed the facilities shortly after the second uprising broke out in September 2000, "arguing that the Palestinian police forces were involved in some attacks on Israelis and doing nothing to stop them." Palestinians, the AP reported, "have refused to confront militants, like the powerful Islamic groups Hamas and Islamic Jihad, arguing that their police forces are too weak and that such a showdown could spark a civil war."[95] Despite the AP dispatch, major U.S. mainstream media outlets did not report Dahlan's announcement.

By contrast, Israel's insistence that its obligations to freeze settlement building according to the road map were nullified by Palestinian violence did get significant media play. In early October the *New York Times* reported that "while the administration has backed Israel in charging that Palestinian failure to crack down on terrorism is the main cause of the peace plan's breakdown, U.S. officials appear to be increasingly impatient with Israeli steps" to expand existing settlements.[96] The long-term, passive acceptance by the United States of Israel's use of the settlements as political bargaining chips had become self-defeating.

On October 23—three weeks after announcing its plan to enlarge three West Bank settlements by building 600 new homes—the Israeli government announced plans to build another 333 homes in two other existing settlements: 153 in Karnei Shomron, southwest of Nablus, and 180 in Givat Ze'ev, near Jerusalem.

CONTENT ANALYSIS

Although there has been no dearth in the quantity of column inches and airtime the U.S. mainstream media have devoted to the issue of Israeli settlements in the West Bank and Gaza Strip, the coverage has been short on quality. In their consistent reliance on Israeli rather than Palestinian sources, the media have omitted the important context of how the settlements have affected Palestinian life and, in turn, the trajectory of the peace process. In their consistent omission of the link between U.S. policy and the Israeli settlement enterprise, the media have conveyed a distorted picture of Israeli-Palestinian violence to the American public, giving the impression of a senseless and unstoppable spiral. Reflecting the ethos of their own culture, moreover, the American mainstream media do not equate Israeli settlement with colonialism—although it is often seen that way by peoples who have had direct experience either as colonizers or as colonized, particularly in Europe and the Arab and Muslim worlds. As one *Chicago Tribune* columnist observed:

> American publications rarely make serious efforts to get beyond the formulaic coverage that portrays Israel as a beleaguered democracy valiantly fighting off evil, anti-Semitic terrorists. There is another perspective of the struggle that casts Palestinians as valiant anticolonialists

fighting a legitimate struggle against illegal occupation of their land by imperialist forces.

This latter view calls into question the priorities of U.S. foreign policy, however, and is seldom highlighted in American media. Publications from other, particularly European, countries provide coverage that is more textured and contextual—often portraying Palestinians as anticolonialists.[97]

An apt metaphor for the reporting under review is a string of dots waiting to be connected. Throughout the collective text are scattered references to Palestinian areas of the West Bank as "a bunch of separate places cut off from each other" and "an archipelago of unconnected islands." The Israeli settlement scheme itself is variously seen as "a plan to cut the West Bank into parcels so that there cannot be a viable Palestinian state" and "a serious obstacle to creating a geographically contiguous future Palestinian state." However, these textual references are few and far between.

The body of reporting on settlements during and immediately after Camp David, as well as in subsequent years, has essentially missed the story of the degree to which the settlements have inhibited prospects for peace—and the role that American compliance has played in the process. Instead, the journalism under review has offered an abundance of description and anecdote, heavily weighted with a back-and-forth dialogue between settlement proponents and their left-wing Israeli opponents, with only a smattering of Palestinian voices. Rarely if ever has the reporting reached the stage of critical analysis that would link the "cycle of violence" and "Palestinian terrorism" to the Palestinian population being gradually but continuously stripped of its primary natural resource—land—and the ability to maintain productive capacity on it.

Instead, the media have tended to report without challenge Israeli and American assertions that Palestinian violence must be halted before negotiations can resume—with little acknowledgement that ongoing Israeli settlement activity and its attendant military defense have been a root cause of that violence. U.S. policy will not publicly link the settlements to Palestinian resistance and the resulting spiral of intercommunal violence, and the media have complied. Rarely if ever does American journalism question why U.S. policy has confronted the settlement issue with little more than diplomatic wrist-slapping.

The reason for this flawed reporting paradigm is clear. Once again the media have willingly opted to limit their discourse to the confines of the policy mirror and the Washington consensus. This has precluded journalistic examination of how Israeli settlement policy and de facto American acceptance of it are linked to Palestinian violence and disruption of the peace process.

The Settlements, the Peace Process, and the Camp David Summit

That geopolitical analysis is absent in coverage of the settlements is exemplified by U.S. mainstream media reporting on the failed Israeli-Palestinian negotiations held at Camp David in July 2000. The coverage was characterized by the remarkable absence of a basic and essential element, namely, maps. Palestinian scholar Edward Said, writing six weeks after the second intifada erupted in the wake of the failed Camp David summit, observed this "absence of geography in this most geographical of conflicts."[98]

Indeed, American news consumers in search of maps depicting the territorial issues at the heart of the Camp David talks would have searched in vain. In the absence of such graphic illustrations, however, the texts of news reports were rife with references to a potential Israeli concession of 90–95 percent of West Bank territory. This, along with the possibility of limited joint sovereignty over Jerusalem, was repeatedly characterized in the U.S. mainstream media as constituting the "generous offer" made to the Palestinians by Israeli prime minister Ehud Barak.

The widespread Israeli claim that the Palestinians had walked away from a great deal at Camp David in July 2000 was prevalent not only in American coverage of the failed summit but has prevailed and been perpetuated in the U.S. mainstream media in subsequent years as well. A *Newsweek* report in May 2002 noted: "Many Israelis argue that Palestinian violence, not Israeli settlement activity, is the real problem with the peace process. As proof, they point to Israel's offer two years ago to dismantle many settlements and consolidate the rest."[99] Ra'anan Gissin, a senior adviser to Prime Minister Ariel Sharon, told the *New York Times* in February 2003: "You wouldn't see these [West Bank settlement] outposts if the Palestinians hadn't rejected the chance to negotiate in 2000. Until there is an agreement, Jews have as much a right to settle in their ancestral homeland and live unrestricted as Palestinians do."[100]

Did the Palestinians really pass up "a generous offer" or was this oft-repeated characterization—which went virtually unchallenged in the American mainstream media for a full year after Camp David—yet another indication of the policy mirror in play? In attributing the failed summit to Palestinian intransigence, the mainstream media reporting coming out of Washington put a decidedly American spin on the matter, softening President Clinton's failed attempt to link his presidential legacy to Middle East peace in place of domestic scandal. Mainstream U.S. reporting coming out of Israel and the West Bank did little to contradict this spin despite the fact that evidence contradicting the "generous offer" notion was readily accessible from local Israeli and Palestinian sources. Although American correspondents were working in close physical proximity to these sources, they apparently were operating in a different orbit.

Yediot Aharonot is Israel's largest mass-circulation Hebrew-language newspaper. On May 19, 2000—some seven weeks before the start of negotiations at Camp David—the newspaper published a multipage spread in its Friday supplement bearing the sub-headline: "final-status map presented by Israel to the Palestinian Authority."[101] The full-color map accompanying the story showed the West Bank divided into three areas of future Palestinian sovereignty that would be cut off from each other by territory containing settlements to be annexed to Israel, 80 percent of whose residents would remain. Moreover, the map showed each of the three Palestinian areas as being crisscrossed by a spaghetti network of bypass roads built around Arab towns and villages to ensure settlers safe passage, effectively subdividing the three areas into dozens of smaller fragments.

Just as American foreign correspondents had overlooked the Israeli media as an important source, they bypassed Israeli and Palestinian academics who had formed their own conclusions about the impact of West Bank settlements on the peace process. Zuhair Sabbagh, a sociologist at Birzeit University in the West Bank, concluded that

> Israeli negotiation positions do not indicate that Israel desires a permanent solution to the Palestinian problem, but a transitional one based on the colonial "facts" that were established in the last 33 years of colonization. . . . One could conclude that the hidden functions of these [settlement] clusters are to destroy the territorial contiguity of the West Bank and subvert the development of any meaningful sovereignty that could be exercised by the Palestinians, prevent the national unity of the Palestinian people, perpetuate the dependency of the Palestinian economy, and provide more efficient control of the indigenous population.[102]

Jeff Halper, an anthropologist at Ben-Gurion University in the Negev region of Israel, wrote that settlements in the West Bank constituted a "matrix of control" that enabled Israel, somewhat deceptively, to offer a "94 percent solution" at Camp David.

> Sovereign and contiguous territory is, of course, a prerequisite for a viable Palestinian state, and those within the Palestinian Authority who measure successful negotiations in terms of territory might be inclined to accept the Camp David proposal. But the question should be who will actually control the PA lands after the 94 percent solution floated at Camp David. (Some reports even pegged the figure at 95 percent.) Since 1967 Israel has laid a matrix of control over the West Bank, East Jerusalem and Gaza. Because the matrix operates by control and not by conquest, it enables Israel to offer a generous 94 percent of the West Bank, creating the illusion of a just and viable settlement. Understanding how the matrix works is critical for comprehending the Oslo process as a whole. Focusing on the political process while ignoring the emerging realities on the ground is a sure recipe for a Palestinian bantustan.
>
> What is the matrix of control? It is an interlocking series of mechanisms, only a few of which require physical occupation of territory, that allow Israel to control every aspect of Palestinian life in the Occupied Territories. The matrix works like the Japanese game of Go. Instead of defeating your opponent as in chess, in Go you win by immobilizing your opponent, by gaining control of key points of a matrix so that every time s/he moves s/he encounters an obstacle of some kind.[103]

U.S. mainstream media reporting on the territorial issues at Camp David was not only graphically inadequate but mathematically lax as well. The operative question, as Halper intimated, was: 95 percent of what? A reporting methodology that favored anecdote and facile observation to the virtual exclusion of interpretation and analysis had failed to put before the American public one of the most important organic reasons for the failure of the summit. What had been billed as a historic opportunity for Middle East peace may in reality have been a nonstarter from the get-go.

A careful analysis of the *Yediot Aharonot* map revealed that the U.S.-backed Israeli offer to relinquish between 90 and 95 percent of the West Bank was questionable. It showed that Israel intended to retain control over three key areas: the Shomron settlement cluster, which separates the northern region of the West Bank from the central region; the Jerusalem settlement cluster, which separates the central region of the West Bank from the southern region; and, on a "temporary" basis, the Jordan Valley settlement cluster along the eastern edge of the territory.

Collectively these areas account for at least 25 percent of the West Bank. According to the map, the bypass roads for the settlements that would remain within the areas to be ceded to the Palestinians amount to approximately another 5 percent. Thus, Israel's starting point for relinquishing West Bank territory was 90 to 95 percent of the remaining 70 percent—and the Palestinians would have ended up with chunks of territory totaling not more than 65 percent of the entire West Bank land area.

The mainstream media, however, did not begin to carry substantial or nuanced analyses of why the summit failed until a full year later, when a trend of Camp David revisionism began to appear. Perhaps the first indication that mainstream media characterizations of Camp David to date had been less than accurate came in an op-ed piece published in the *New York Times* in July 2001. Robert Malley, a special assistant for Arab-Israeli affairs in the second Clinton administration who had been present at the summit, analyzed the "fictions" behind its failure. While citing Barak's "uncommon political courage," Malley argued that "the measure of Israel's concessions ought not to be how far it has moved from its own starting point; it must be how far it has moved toward a fair solution." In his opinion, Israel's stance at Camp David vis-à-vis territory and the settlements, among several other key factors, did not presage such a fair solution: "To accommodate the settlers, Israel was to annex 9 percent of the West Bank; in exchange, the new Palestinian state would be granted sovereignty over parts of Israel proper, equivalent to one-ninth of the annexed land. A Palestinian state covering 91 percent of the West Bank and Gaza was more than most Americans or Israelis had thought possible, but how would Mr. Arafat explain the unfavorable 9-to-1 ratio in land swaps to his people?"[104]

In an essay published that August in the *New York Review of Books,* co-authored with Hussein Agha, a Palestinian academic in Britain long active in Israeli-Palestinian relations, Malley offered a fuller analysis of the failed Camp David negotiations. In a detailed narrative of the nature and substance of the summit, the authors asked: "Was there a generous Israeli offer, and if so, was it peremptorily rejected by Arafat?" While acknowledging that "Barak broke every conceivable taboo and went as far as any Israeli prime minister had gone or would go," Agha and Malley emphasized shortcomings not only in the summit's substance but also in its modalities. These, they maintained, were controlled to a great extent by Israel—which, in their view, had actually not made an offer at all.

The final and largely unnoticed consequence of Barak's approach is that, strictly speaking, there never was an Israeli offer. Determined to preserve Israel's position in the event of failure, and resolved not to let the Palestinians take advantage of one-sided compromises, the Israelis always stopped one, if not several, steps short of a proposal. The ideas put forward at Camp David were never stated in writing, but orally conveyed. They generally were presented as U.S. concepts, not Israeli ones; indeed, despite having demanded the opportunity to negotiate face to face with Arafat, Barak refused to hold any substantive meeting with him at Camp David out of fear that the Palestinian leader would seek to put Israeli concessions on the record. Nor were the proposals detailed. If written down, the American ideas at Camp David would have covered no more than a few pages. Barak and the Americans insisted that Arafat accept them as general "bases for negotiations" before launching into more rigorous negotiations.

According to those "bases," Palestine would have sovereignty over 91 percent of the West Bank; Israel would annex 9 percent of the West Bank and, in exchange, Palestine would have sovereignty over parts of pre-1967 Israel equivalent to 1 percent of the West Bank, but with no indication of where either would be.[105]

The definitive account of Camp David revisionism reported by an American journalist based in Jerusalem at the time of the summit was written by Deborah Sontag of the *New York Times*. In a 5,000-word exposition of the summit's many flaws and foibles of its Israeli, Palestinian, and American participants alike, Sontag offered a painstakingly balanced analysis that began with the characterization that

Mr. Barak did not offer Mr. Arafat the moon at Camp David. He broke Israeli taboos against any discussion of dividing Jerusalem, and he sketched out an offer that was politically courageous, especially for an Israeli leader with a faltering coalition. But it was a proposal that the Palestinians did not believe would leave them with a viable state. . . .

"It is a terrible myth that Arafat and only Arafat caused this catastrophic failure," Terje Roed-Larsen, the United Nations special envoy here, said in an interview. "All three parties made mistakes, and in such complex negotiations, everyone is bound to. But no one is solely to blame."

With regard to the territorial aspects of the negotiations, Sontag reported that Palestinian negotiator Ahmed Qurei, known as Abu Ala', told his Israeli counterpart, Shlomo Ben-Ami, that "'I cannot look at the maps. Close them.' . . . [Abu Ala'] declared that he would discuss only the 1967 borders. 'Clinton was angry at me and told me I was personally responsible for the failure of the summit. I told him even if occupation continues for 500 years, we will not change.'"[106]

Qurei's insistence at Camp David on the 1967 borders was well justified from the Palestinian point of view. When Yasser Arafat signed the Oslo accords in 1993, the Palestine Liberation Organization recognized the State of Israel.[107] To Palestinians this meant that the PLO had made an implicit and historic statement of territorial compromise.[108] It would concede to Israel the 78 percent of mandatory Palestine that lay within the pre-1967 borders known as the Green Line, allowing for minor border adjustments. Israel would then cede to the Palestinians the remaining 22 percent, comprising the West Bank and Gaza Strip. The settlements would be dismantled, and an independent Palestinian state would be established. Not only did the Palestinians fail to get this written into the accords' Declaration of Principles, but they also failed to convey to the media, throughout the seven-year course of the Oslo peace process, their position of having made a significant territorial compromise—one that has been gravely weakened by the continuing presence and enlargement of West Bank settlements.

A year after Camp David, in late July 2001, Qurei held a press conference in Ramallah to explain that the summit negotiations had not provided the basis for a viable Palestinian state. At the same time, the Israeli newspaper *Haaretz* reported that Palestinian experts who had worked alongside the Palestinian negotiating team at Camp David were engaged in public relations, making "a round of appearances throughout Israel. They lecture at living room meetings in Herzliya and meet with forums of confused intellectuals in Jerusalem." *Haaretz* reported that in making their rounds, the experts presented Hebrew- and English-language versions of an 11-point document explaining the Palestinian view of Camp David—including the claim that Israel's territorial overtures would serve only to legitimize and expand "illegal Israeli colonies in Palestinian territory."[109]

However, this rebuttal to the widespread notion that Palestinian rejectionism lay at the root of the failed Camp David negotiations was too little, too late—and went largely unnoticed by the American mainstream media.

Reporting on the Settlements After Camp David

By late 2002 the Israeli settlement enterprise had achieved such proportions that it was doubtful whether a negotiated two-state solution was still possible. From the viewpoint of the Negotiations Affairs Department of the PLO,

> Israel's ongoing colony construction and other unilateral measures in the Occupied Palestinian Territories are effectively pre-empting the possibility of a two-state solution of a viable Palestinian state alongside Israel. If the international community continues to remain unwilling to rein in Israeli colony construction and expansion, irreversible "facts on the ground" and the de facto apartheid system such facts create will force Palestinian policy makers to re-evaluate the plausibility of a two-state solution.[110]

Alternative perspectives should be considered—for example, that Israel is indeed interested in the establishment of a viable Palestinian state, albeit one that would pose no security threat. However, this Palestinian viewpoint—which insists on "the rights guaranteed to [Palestinians] under UN resolutions, the Fourth Geneva Convention, and other international treaties"[111]—places a key aspect of the conflict in sharp focus: without a change in Israeli and U.S. policies on the settlements, a negotiated resolution to the conflict as a whole that answers both Israel's security concerns and Palestinian national aspirations is unlikely to be achieved.

Mention of international law and consensus was virtually absent from two U.S. mainstream media reports on the settlements in late 2002 and early 2003, both of which were notable for their length and detailed description. These reports corroborated the idea that without a dramatic shift in political and diplomatic events—which was nowhere apparent on the horizon—the settlement enterprise could have reached the point of no return.

In December 2002 the *Washington Post* published a 2,900-word, front-page story chronicling the fact that the number of settlement outposts in the West Bank had "exploded" in the two years since the outbreak of the second

Palestinian uprising and the election of Israeli prime minister Ariel Sharon: "At least 66 new Jewish outposts, or fledgling settlements, have sprouted across the ridgelines and hilltops in those two years, compared with the 44 outposts started over the previous five years combined, according to Peace Now."[112] In February 2003 the *New York Times Magazine* published a 5,420-word piece, illustrated with several color photos, on the so-called hilltop youth populating these outposts increasingly dotting the West Bank landscape. "About 70 of these small encampments, known in Israel as outposts, have been built in the last two years," the piece reported. "Together they represent a movement that intends to transform the West Bank, and the conflict in the Middle East, from the ground up." The story noted that the total number of inhabitants populating these new outposts—most of which had yet to receive permanent housing structures—was small, estimated at five hundred to a thousand, and that the outposts seemed to be of an ad hoc nature unauthorized by the government. It nevertheless added: "It's clear that they have some contact with the government—who else sends the soldiers [to defend them] and the garbage trucks?—but it is a relationship that for the most part is invisible."[113]

Also invisible in both the *Washington Post* and *New York Times Magazine* pieces was any mention of the underlying relationship between U.S. policy and Israeli settlement policy. True to the form of their type, both pieces provided extensive description but little analysis, with primarily Israeli sourcing. The *Post* piece quoted a total of eleven sources—four settlers, three Israelis opposed to the settlements, three Israelis with ties to the Sharon government, and one Israeli soldier—with not a single Palestinian among them. The *Times Magazine* piece quoted twenty sources—eighteen Israelis (thirteen of whom were inhabitants of the fledgling outposts) and two Palestinians.

Speaking at the World Economic Forum in Davos, Switzerland, in January 2003, Secretary of State Colin Powell foreshadowed the road map plan to come, saying a "viable, democratic" Palestinian state could emerge by 2005 if both sides would do their part. While admonishing Israel to stop building settlements, Powell said the Palestinians must "clamp down on terrorism." However, according to Associated Press and Reuters reports, the secretary added, "A Palestinian state, when it's created, must be a real state, not a phony state that's diced into a thousand different pieces."[114] Reuters added that "Israeli Foreign Ministry spokesman Ron Pros-Or responded that Powell's statement was 'very important' and Israel 'would take it into consideration.'"

Such consideration may already have been under way. In February 2004 Sharon told leaders of his Likud party that he planned to dismantle all the settlements in the Gaza Strip. By the time Sharon met with Bush at the White House in April, the plan had taken shape as Israeli "unilateral disengagement" from all of Gaza and four outlying West Bank settlements by the end of 2005. A *U.S. News & World Report* piece noted Sharon's strategy: "After failing to end the intifada uprising militarily or diplomatically, Sharon has decided to seek security for Israelis by clearing out settlers and soldiers from the heart of the Palestinian areas, leaving nearly all 3.5 million Palestinians enclosed inside fortified barriers and thereby separating the two warring sides. His plan would dismantle many tiny outposts . . . and even some permanent, suburban-style settlements."[115]

Sharon's plan, in effect, was to clear out all of the settlers in Gaza while keeping in place the vast majority of those in the West Bank—who numbered at least twenty-five times as many—and then enlarging existing settlements there. This approach represented the same formula Israel had proposed at Camp David. In June 2004 the *Christian Science Monitor* and the *New York Times* cited a report in the Israeli newspaper *Maariv* noting that Sharon would seek to expand a large settlement bloc near Jerusalem in order to absorb the evacuated Gaza settlers. "But such plans would contradict the road map to Middle East peace," the *Monitor* observed, "which calls on Israel to halt settlement growth." An unidentified U.S. official added, "Philosophically, we don't want to see settlers leave Gaza so they can move to the West Bank."[116]

In the months leading up to Israel's withdrawal from the Gaza Strip in August 2005, the stock dynamics of the settlement issue and American mainstream reporting of it proceeded apace. For its part, Israel persisted in its intention to expand West Bank settlements. As *Haaretz* reported, in September 2004 the agriculture minister announced a plan to expropriate 31,000 *dunams* (7,750 acres) in the Jordan Valley "to hold [the land] and designate it for Jewish settlements . . . and to prevent the possibility of [it] being taken over by hostile elements." [117] In October Dov Weisglass, one of Sharon's closest advisers, told the newspaper: "The meaning of the disengagement plan is a freeze to the diplomatic process . . . [and] when you freeze the political process, you prevent the establishment of a Palestinian state and you prevent a discussion on the subject of refugees, borders and Jerusalem. This whole package called 'the Palestinian state' has been removed from the daily agenda for an unlimited period of time."[118]

For their part, American officials continued to make firm-sounding pronouncements about the settlements that contradicted actual developments on the ground. In a February 2005 speech in Brussels, Bush articulated a checklist for peace, insisting that the Palestinians get contiguous land in the West Bank and that "a [Palestinian] state on scattered territories will not work."[119] At a White House news conference in May—after receiving Mahmoud Abbas, who had been elected Palestinian president in January—Bush declared: "Israel should not undertake any activity that contravenes road-map obligations or prejudices final-status negotiations with regard to Gaza, the West Bank and Jerusalem. Therefore, Israel must remove unauthorized outposts and stop settlement expansion."[120] On August 17, as Israel began to withdraw from the Gaza Strip, compelling eighty-five hundred settlers to vacate the twenty-one colonies that had been established there, Secretary of State Condoleezza Rice told the *New York Times*: "Everyone empathizes with what the Israelis are facing" in terms of those forced to leave their homes. However, she added, "It cannot be Gaza only."[121]

Ten days later, however, the Associated Press put the Gaza withdrawal in context—which the majority of the mainstream media had failed to do, focusing instead on the drama of Jewish soldiers evicting Jewish settlers. According to the AP:

> As Israel basked in world admiration for pulling out of the Gaza Strip, new official figures released Friday showed the Jewish population of the West Bank is expanding rapidly, growing by more than 12,000 in the past year alone.
>
> Prime Minister Ariel Sharon made no secret of his desire to expand large West Bank settlement blocs even while withdrawing from areas he says became untenable for Israel to hold.
>
> According to Interior Ministry figures, the Jewish population of the West Bank in June stood at 246,000, an increase of 12,800, or 5 percent, in one year.[122]

Further contextualization of the bigger picture of the Gaza withdrawal, beyond its superficial drama, would have revealed that the 246,000 West Bank settlers, amid a Palestinian population of approximately 2.2 million,[123] represented 11 percent of the territory's population. Sharon, in effect, had conceded relatively little to gain significantly more, namely, the removal of approximately 9,000 settlers (those from Gaza as well as several hundred others from four small, isolated West Bank settlements) so that at least twenty-five times that number could remain in the West Bank. Moreover, by relinquishing direct control over Gaza's Palestinian population, Israel was able to extract a slight demographic advantage in addition to bolstering its image. The withdrawal had the effect of beefing up the Jewish-Arab population ratio under Israeli control—in Israel proper and the West Bank—to 1.47 Jews for every Arab following the withdrawal, as opposed to 1.08 Jews for every Arab prior to it.[124]

Unable and/or unwilling to venture beyond the parameters of official discourse on the contradictory if not hypocritical nature of U.S. policy on the settlements, the American mainstream media continued to serve up reporting no more enlightening, exploratory, or critical about the issue than that policy itself. This tendency was exemplified by a 625-word feature on a housing boom for Israelis settling east of the Green Line published in the *New York Times*'s Sunday "Week in Review" section in June 2004 and headlined "The Suburban Lure of the West Bank." Reported from a housing fair at a Jerusalem hotel, the story noted that the West Bank settler population was growing by about ten thousand a year, "lured by advertising, low prices and, curiously, a promise of relative security."

The report, however, made no reference to international law and consensus on the legality of the settlements, nor did it note how the West Bank settlement boom might affect chances for a negotiated peace. Rather, the story was accompanied by three photographs, one showing a buyer and another a salesman at a real estate fair. The third showed a billboard near a construction site in the Gush Etzion settlement bloc south of Jerusalem. The ad depicted an Israeli commuter, dressed in jacket and tie, gripping the steering wheel and slapping his forehead in apparent frustration over traffic. "You could have been at work a long time ago!" the billboard read. The *New York Times*, it appeared, had published an illustrated press release promoting settlement on occupied territory:

> Salesmen at the housing fair said Prime Minister Ariel Sharon's plan to pull out of Gaza by the end of 2005 has not kept home buyers from looking at the large West Bank settlements near Jerusalem and Tel Aviv where most settlers live.
>
> Indeed, it may be bringing in more customers. Mr. Sharon has stressed that he is working to consolidate Israel's hold on most West Bank settlements.
>
> "Ma'aleh Adumim is a city, it's not a little settlement," [prospective buyer Arieh] Weinstein said. "I can't see a situation where Israel will give it back." . . .

"We've broken ground on two big projects" in the West Bank, said Aliza Weizman, a vice president for the Tivuch Shelly real estate firm.

The threat of violence has not slowed projects, she said. Perhaps the biggest challenge is finding enough construction workers now that builders face Israeli restrictions on using Palestinian labor.[125]

4

APEX OF THE SPIRAL

Reporting the Violent Spring of 2002

The impact of what we managed to do in North America has been
huge. Within a four-week period, all polls showing that people who
believed Arafat to be a terrorist and unreliable went way up.

Colonel Miri Eisen, head of doctrine,
Israel Defense Forces Combat Intelligence Corps

ON MARCH 27, 2002, ABDEL BASSET ODEH, A MEMBER OF THE IZZEDIN
al-Qassam Brigades of Hamas from the West Bank town of Tulkarm, entered the dining room of the Park Hotel, located in the Israeli coastal town
of Netanya, where 250 Israelis were in the midst of a Passover seder. In an
instant the room was transformed from a scene of celebration to one of
carnage when Odeh detonated an explosive device. More than 12 Israelis
died on the spot; in the days and weeks that followed, the final toll of the
suicide bombing would rise to 30 Israelis killed and 140 injured, 20 of
them seriously.[1]

On March 24, three days before the Netanya bombing, the death toll in the
second intifada had surpassed the 1,500 mark, with 1,198 Palestinians and 355
Israelis killed in eighteen months of violence.[2] The Israeli government acted
quickly and decisively in the days following the Passover attack. It was not,
however, responding to the Netanya bombing alone. According to a report
published by the Israeli daily *Haaretz* that chronicled suicide bombings, in
the four months prior to that attack—from December 1, 2001, to March 26,

2002—suicide bombers had struck inside Israel fifteen times and in the West Bank three times.[3] The fifteen bombings inside Israel—seven of them in Jerusalem—had killed 61 people and injured 543. The three attacks in the West Bank had killed 2 Israelis and injured 46.[4]

On March 29, two days after the suicide attack in Netanya, Israeli tanks and bulldozers moved against the Ramallah compound of Yasser Arafat, all but destroying it and isolating the Palestinian leader in the few rooms left standing. Over the next month, the Israeli army reoccupied all six West Bank towns, devastating their infrastructure in the process. During this period President George W. Bush publicly declared Israeli prime minister Ariel Sharon to be a "man of peace." At the same time, Bush asked Arab governments in the region to condemn suicide bombings while also imploring Sharon on several occasions to pull Israeli forces back. Secretary of State Colin Powell was dispatched to the region to get Sharon to desist, but the mission failed. Sharon persisted with the campaign. At the end, approximately $360 million in Palestinian infrastructure lay in ruins.[5]

This massive show of Israeli force failed to prevent further suicide bombings, however, both during the incursion itself and in its wake. According to the *Haaretz* report, during the incursion, which lasted from March 29 to April 30, suicide bombers struck inside Israel six times—three times in Jerusalem, once in Tel Aviv, once in Haifa, and once near Haifa—killing 32 Israelis and injuring 210. A seventh bombing in the West Bank settlement of Efrat injured 4 Israelis. In the three months following the incursion, from May 7 to August 4, suicide bombers struck inside Israel thirteen times, killing 90 people (including 3 foreign workers in an attack in Tel Aviv) and injuring 538. A fourteenth attack on a bus traveling between two West Bank settlements killed 9 Israelis and injured 20.[6]

In sum, according to the *Haaretz* chronology, during the four-month pre-incursion period, eighteen suicide bombings killed 63 people and injured 589. The four-month incursion/post-incursion period, by contrast, saw an increase in frequency, magnitude, and impact: twenty-one suicide bombings killed 131 people and injured 772.

The Passover bombing evoked a distinct brand of horror and condemnation around the world. It was neither the first nor would it be the last in the long string of Palestinian suicide attacks that began in the mid-1990s. However, this particular attack seemed especially loathsome, striking as it did at civilians celebrating a religious holiday.

As the spiral of Israeli-Palestinian violence reached its apex in the spring of 2002, the American mainstream media channeled a steady stream of images of Israeli and Palestinian suffering alike, expressed primarily by "ordinary" men and women in the street. Reporting on the suicide bombings detailed Israeli loss of life and limb, utter fear, depression, and despair; reporting on the incursion and its aftermath chronicled Palestinian deaths, humiliation, confinement under extended curfews, and the destruction of national infrastructure and personal property. Throughout that violent spring, all such events were reported on an almost daily basis, both in print and on the air, in copious, vivid, and wrenching detail.

Despite this apparent balance in chronicling Israeli and Palestinian suffering, American mainstream media revealed yet another salient and noteworthy tendency in reporting the events surrounding the bloody spring of 2002. Unfolding as it did just six months after the September 11 terror attacks in the United States, this phase of the second Palestinian uprising seemed to represent a period of congruence for the United States and Israel. Both targets of suicide attacks perpetrated by Muslims, Americans and Israelis perceived—and were told on numerous occasions by their leaders—that they had become targets because of who they were and the freedoms their societies represented. With citizens in both countries so caught up in the pain and suffering that these attacks caused, political discourse focused entirely on themes that were emotional, moral, and patriotic.

In times of national calamity, that is not surprising. What is questionable, however, is how closely free mainstream media in democratic societies followed suit. During those particular periods of national trauma in the United States and Israel, more often than not mainstream American journalism tended to assume a "circle-the-wagons" cast. While understandable if not preferable in the American context—after all, American journalists are members of the culture and society about which and for which they report—in the context of reporting the Israeli-Palestinian conflict it is curious that such a paradigm continued to hold.

Why did so many American journalists during this period seem to take at face value information provided by official Israeli sources—in many cases, sources from the Israel Defense Forces—without seeking balance from Palestinian sources? Why, in several notable instances, did American reporters ride along with IDF patrols on the trail of Palestinian suspects? Why did the American media report, with little or no questioning, allegations put forth by the Sharon government that documents the IDF had seized during the reoccupation of the West Bank revealed that Palestinian leader Yasser Arafat was directly linked to acts of terrorism—and should therefore be excluded from the peace process?

In hindsight, these reporting modalities bear a striking similarity to the manner in which American mainstream media reported the Bush administration's case for war in Iraq in the fall of 2002 and winter of 2003, linked as it was to the terror attacks of September 11 and the need to depose Saddam Hussein based on erroneous claims involving weapons of mass destruction. Patterns of reporting evident in coverage of the Israeli-Palestinian spring of 2002 illustrate a deeply etched sense of cultural congruence leading to a skewed framing of events. The following content analysis of American reportage from this period demonstrates such a framing, which, despite a superficial sense of balance, stifled the best practices of journalistic skepticism and investigation and, in many cases, sacrificed context and obscured the bigger picture.

REPORTING THE SUICIDE BOMBINGS: A CHRONICLE OF SUFFERING

American news coverage of the Netanya attack was immediate and graphic, consistent with reporting on suicide bombings both before and after the beginning of the second intifada. On March 27, the evening of the attack, *NBC Nightly News* correspondent Keith Miller reported that

> the bomber entered the hotel through the front door, walked through the lobby and blew himself up in the dining room. . . . The devastation was enormous. It's clear where the suicide bomber detonated. Just over my shoulder here, the entire facade of the dining room has been blown away. Inside were hundreds of people having their Passover dinner. Inside, the force of the explosion blew out windows, caused the ceiling to collapse, leaving nothing untouched. The hotel had been on alert.[7]

The next morning Netanya mayor Miriam Fireberg spoke to anchor Jane Clayson on the CBS News program *The Early Show* via satellite, describing for American viewers the physical and psychological terror of the Passover attack.

> I—I was here a few minutes after it happened. I was here. And it was—it's difficult to describe because human being [*sic*] can't understand and can't imagine—imagine what we saw here. Bodies, parts of bodies, little children, people took the children in their hands and they die on their hands [*sic*] and they get—and they were in shock as they shout. And people looked to the family, everyone look [*sic*] to the children and to the parents, and I know about whole families which were all killed here.

And you can im—you know, in the world sometimes, it happen accidents and you have citizens—innocent citizens, but here, it's not like this. People came and they knew from the beginning they're coming to kill innocent people who are celebrating the holy day for them, Passover. It's something that only people like Palestinian [*sic*] can do. . . . It's not the resistance. . . . It's a terror. They're murderers.[8]

On the same day, Cox News Service correspondent Larry Kaplow interviewed a survivor of the attack, seventy-three-year-old Isaac Atsits. The report ran the next day in the March 29 edition of the *Atlanta Journal-Constitution*.

Atsits, a combat veteran of four Israeli wars, barely survived the suicide bombing being called the Passover Massacre. . . . As Atsits recovered from an eye injury Thursday in a hospital bed in Kfar Sava, about 10 miles from Netanya, he talked about the impact of the bombing.

As a religious Jew who immigrated [*sic*] from Syria when he was a child, Atsits holds Passover dear. He shares the outrage of other Israelis at what was one of the deadliest attacks in 18 months of fighting.

"We've gotten used to these attacks daily. The attack last night was especially painful, though," he said. "I could describe it as 10 attacks. Like the 10 plagues." . . .

He remembers entering the hotel dining room and settling down into his seat with others in a group of former court employees who take trips together and share dinners. The room was decorated with colored lights and flowers.

Atsits was seated and people were still filing into the banquet hall when the bomb exploded. He said the room went dark and he struggled with others to find a way out to the rainy street. He doesn't know where the others in his group ended up; they were whisked off to different hospitals.

"There was one couple I felt badly about," Atsits said. "He was bent over with a cane and she was using a walker. I don't know what happened to them. What is the fault of these old people to have this happen to them?"[9]

The record of U.S. mainstream media reporting on the deaths, fear, and anguish that Israelis suffered as a result of the continuing string of suicide bombings belies a salient argument in the bias charges that supporters of Israel leveled against the U.S. media during the spring of 2002. Many such readers, viewers, and listeners claimed that coverage during this period glossed over Israeli suffering in favor of reports sympathetic to Palestinians, including those that highlighted the backgrounds and motivations of suicide bombers. However, a pattern of coverage exists to prove quite the contrary.

On April 9 *The NewsHour with Jim Lehrer* on PBS broadcast a segment reported from Jerusalem by Martin Himel, entitled "Living in Fear." The piece evoked the existential fear these suicide bombings wrought on Israelis and echoed the unshakable belief—like that expressed by Mayor Fireberg—that the actions of the suicide bombers were not linked to occupation or resistance but instead stemmed from sheer blood lust that sought to eradicate the Jewish presence in their midst.

MARTIN HIMEL: Like many Israeli teenagers, Marva Marom's life has been transformed by the suicide bombing. She's just 14 years old. Marva is not allowed to go to the movies. She's forbidden to go downtown. Concerts are out of the question. Her parents are afraid a suicide bomber could kill her. . . . A suicide bomber destroyed the popular Moment cafe in March. He killed ten customers.

MARVA MAROM: I used to walk inside there. . . . The people who got killed, who got injured, everybody knew. I try not to think about it, because when I live in such a place, you learn to develop this universe of your own. I always think about what will happen in the future, who I'm going to be, what I'm going to become. And then I see I didn't consider the fact that there might be no future.

MARTIN HIMEL: Eyal Meged, Marva's stepfather, is more comfortable with Marva in the house. . . . His grandmother became a widow in 1951 when an Arab stabbed her husband in his orchard. Meged says little has changed since then. He believes the Palestinian goal is still the destruction of the Jewish state.

EYAL MEGED: The Arabs didn't want us here at all, and it's the same story all over again all the time, and we have to realize it. Nothing to do with . . . nothing to do with the occupied territories we are talking about now, nothing to do with Judea and Samaria or Gaza. It's about living here and leading normal lives in the land of Israel. . . .

DANIEL MAROM (Marva's father): Here, at night, fears tend to come out before the children go to sleep, and they'll say, "Could you promise me, could you give me a guarantee that tomorrow will be safe, or that in a year from now, it will be safe?" Or, "when is this going to change?" "I'm afraid; is the door locked?" "How do you know that someone couldn't get in from the roof and do violence to us?" "Could you take me in the car tomorrow instead of in the bus, because who knows what could be in the bus?"[10]

On April 19 a front-page *New York Times* story reported the sentiments of members of five families who had lost relatives in suicide attacks. Correspondent Joel Brinkley clearly described the profound emotional and psychological toll the bombings had on victims' kin. "I don't go anywhere anymore," said a mother whose son had been killed in a bombing on the streets of downtown Jerusalem the previous December. "Now I'm afraid of my own shadow," said another mother whose daughter had died the preceding August in the bombing of the Sbarro pizzeria in Jerusalem. Reporting the Israeli government's efforts to comfort the bereaved, the *Times* story also spoke to the sense of national resolve the bombings evoked.

> On Memorial Day on Tuesday, the government held a special service for relatives of people who have died in terror attacks, on Mount Herzl, the nation's graveyard for the honored dead, akin to Arlington [National] Cemetery in Washington.
>
> President Moshe Katsav spoke from a podium set in the angle between bleached stone walls bearing stark, black plaques. They are inscribed with the names of Jews killed here by terrorists starting in 1860.
>
> The plaques for the period from 2000 to today already appear to hold more names than those from any previous decade.
>
> "Here on the hill of remembrance," President Katsav proclaimed, "lie the buried heroes of Israel, the great ones of Israel, and it is here that the government decided to put up a memorial to the victims of enmity and terror."[11]

The *San Francisco Chronicle* published a similar front-page story on April 29. Staff writer Anna Badkhen opened with the graphic details of a mother's agony. Two of the woman's daughters had fallen victim to the Sbarro pizzeria bombing in Jerusalem eight months earlier; one had died and a second remained hospitalized. Badkhen closed her report with the lament of a father whose son had been maimed in the bombing of a Jerusalem outdoor market just two and a half weeks earlier. The story evoked not only the physical destruction wrought by this Israeli-Palestinian war but also its dehumanizing effects.

> Yokheved Shushan was like a flower, her mother said, a beautiful, wonderful child with long blond hair like intricate curls of gold. . . . She always kept her room clean and did her homework on time.

On August 9, 2001, a suicide bomber walked into the Sbarro pizzeria in downtown Jerusalem with a 20-pound explosive device packed with nails, screws and bolts and blew the girl's 10-year-old body to bits. . . . The same bomb drove dozens of minuscule particles of shrapnel into the body of Yokheved's sister, Miriam, 16, who remains confined to a hospital bed. Pieces of burning furniture broke Miriam's hips and ankles and burned her stomach. The blow from the explosion ruptured her spleen.

It also ruptured forever the life of Ester Shushan, the single mother of Yokheved, Miriam and their six siblings. Shushan says she can barely look after the house anymore. She has stopped leaving her apartment, even to go shopping; she cannot cook, cannot eat. She keeps a photograph of her slain daughter in the living room: an oily trace of Shushan's lipstick clouds the glass on the picture frame over the girl's smiling face. . . .

"We must do to the Palestinians what Americans did in Afghanistan," said Shimon Marian, father of Yudah, 13, one of the survivors of the April 12 suicide bombing attack outside the Mahane Yehuda food market in Jerusalem that killed six people.

Yudah, whose body is black from shrapnel bits that penetrated his skin during the blast, has spent the last three weeks moaning in agony at Jerusalem's Shaare Tzedek Medical Center. A piece of shrapnel buried itself in his left eye; Yudah will never be able to see with it again. His left ear is also damaged.

"They ruined the child," said his father, tenderly pulling a hospital blanket over the boy's wounded legs. "My child is a wreck."

Then, his face became hard. "We treat them [Palestinians] with silk gloves, and they retaliate with bombs," he said. "These people are not human."[12]

The *Chicago Tribune* conveyed the horror of suicide-bombing survivors in a front-page report, published on May 9, whose graphic descriptions of the physical and psychic traumas suffered by the victims rendered those traumas almost surreal. The story cited a statistic from Israel's National Insurance Institute that more than thirty-three hundred Israelis had been wounded in suicide attacks since September 2000. However, it made no parallel reference to the number of Palestinians wounded in clashes with the Israel Defense Forces during the same period.[13] Correspondent Uli Schmetzer reported:

Daniel Turjeman picked up his severed arm and carried it to the ambulance, already crowded with victims from a suicide bombing at the Moment cafe in Jerusalem.

"Take the next one," the paramedic told Turjeman.

Still cradling his arm, Turjeman staggered to another ambulance. This time he was lucky. There was room.

Two months later, the feeling has yet to come back in Turjeman's surgically reconnected arm. His nightmares have yet to go away.

Turjeman, 27, is one of more than 3,300 Israelis wounded in Palestinian attacks since the uprising began in September 2000, according to figures compiled by the National Insurance Institute. That toll grew by at least 56 Tuesday night when a suicide bomber blew up a pool and gambling hall in the city of Rishon Letzion south of Tel Aviv.

Unlike the dead, many of the wounded are quickly forgotten, even though for some the real ordeal has just begun. They remain in trauma wards, in rehabilitation centers or under psychiatric treatment, some physically maimed or mentally crippled, perhaps permanently.[14]

REPORTING THE INCURSION

Throughout Israel's monthlong incursion in the West Bank, Sharon and other government and military officials repeatedly stated that the goal of the campaign was to root out the terrorist infrastructure in the West Bank. The phrasing appeared to be deliberate. It was a precise echo of the language President Bush had used to describe U.S. military and intelligence campaigns intended to eradicate Taliban bases in Afghanistan and dismantle al-Qaeda's network in the wake of the September 11 terror attacks. When the Israeli incursion got under way some seven and a half months later, the psychic wounds of the September 11 attacks—which had killed nearly three thousand people in the United States—had barely begun to heal. The idea that Israel was fighting a mirror-image "war on terror" parallel to that being waged by the United States was expressed repeatedly by Israelis—both in official statements and by people in the street. It was an oft-repeated theme in U.S. media reports, one that resonated with many Americans. However, the disruption and damage to everyday life experienced by the Palestinian population as a whole as a consequence of Israel's "war on terror"—beyond its destruction of ministries and other facilities of the Palestinian Authority—had been slower to emerge via the media. A 2004 Congressional Research Service report stated: "In its search for terrorist infrastructure, the IDF has destroyed much of the water, electrical, telephone and transportation systems in Ramallah, Nablus, Jenin and other West Bank cities."[15]

Israel's Public Relations Campaign

On March 29—the same day that the Israeli army began its campaign in the West Bank—the Israeli public relations machine shifted into high gear, a phenomenon that was duly noted by U.S. mainstream media outlets. According to a *New York Times* report, "Even as the tanks rumbled into Ramallah this morning, Gideon Meir, Israel's deputy foreign minister for public affairs, was setting up a huge government information office in Jerusalem's Convention Center to provide daily briefings for the international press corps pouring in here. It was, he said, part of an emergency plan that had been developed over the past two months." *Times* correspondent John Kifner elaborated:

> This is a country obsessed with its image abroad, and public relations is regarded as a vital—and sometimes losing—part of the battle. The Hebrew word is *hasbara*, which literally means "explanation," but carries the connotation here of something like "information offensive."
>
> All of the Israeli embassies and other offices abroad, normally closed for the weeklong Passover holiday, have been ordered reopened, Mr. Meir said today, and all Foreign Ministry personnel have been recalled to duty, many of them reassigned from their usual jobs to the public relations effort.
>
> "We will fight the Palestinian incitement and propaganda campaign," he said. "It will take some time, it will take a lot of patience."
>
> Workers bustled about today, setting up tables, computers and telephone lines. On a long row of tables, there were handouts ranging from maps and pamphlets with basic facts on population to piles of CD-ROMs.
>
> The discs included "Surviving Terrorists" ("The gripping stories of six Israelis whose lives were turned upside down by terrorist attacks. Their will to live represents the courage and hope for peace that every Israeli represents."), and "Seeds of Hatred" ("Today, the Palestinian Authority is methodically and systematically indoctrinating a new generation of children with dangerous and irrevocable messages.").[16]

The following day the *Times* published a 2,500-word, front-page story from Jerusalem outlining the diplomatic difficulty that the renewed Israeli-Palestinian violence posed to the Bush administration and its envoy to the region,

General Anthony Zinni. For the second time in as many days, the newspaper referred to the importance that Israel attached to public relations, this time noting the upper hand it enjoyed over the Palestinians in the spin game:

> Interviews with Israelis, Palestinians and diplomats here and in Washington provide a picture of a sophisticated Israeli government campaign to influence General Zinni to view the conflict through their eyes.
>
> "They were very clever, very persuasive," said a senior diplomat here involved in the talks. By all accounts, Palestinians officials were ineffectual, even ham-handed at presenting their case, and anything they had to say was loudly overridden by the bombings and attacks by their followers.[17]

During the first week of April, the *Jerusalem Post* published two reports stating that Sharon and Foreign Minister Shimon Peres had approached former Israeli prime ministers Benjamin Netanyahu and Ehud Barak—neither one a member of the coalition government—to help with Israel's "information efforts." On April 2 the *Post* quoted Sharon as saying: "Netanyahu can help a great deal in explaining Israeli policies to the world at a time when the State of Israel is conducting a military campaign to eradicate the terror infrastructure."[18] After meeting Sharon on April 4, Netanyahu told reporters that while he would not join the government, he would lend his support to the propaganda campaign: "We talked about aiding the PR of the state, not the government. The State of Israel needs help in revealing to the world the murderous terror of Yasser Arafat," the *Post* reported.[19] Barak, meanwhile, was "glad to agree to Sharon's request," according to the report.

Within the first twenty-four hours of the incursion, however, the Israeli government began to limit reporters' physical access to the story while continuing to spin it. First Ramallah was declared a closed military zone, and then several days later Bethlehem was declared off-limits to reporters, prompting the Jerusalem-based Foreign Press Association to lodge a protest. A *Boston Globe* report quoted an official of the New York–based Committee to Protect Journalists: "Here's a case of a very important military operation that the press should be able to cover, but it's being restricted. . . . Some journalists feel there is an attempt to intimidate those still covering events." The *Globe* elaborated:

> The last few days have proved harrowing for reporters trying to chronicle the confrontation in the West Bank. Several CBS employees were escorted out of Ramallah by Israeli forces, prompting the network to

file a protest with the Israeli Consulate in New York. More ominously, NBC says correspondent Dana Lewis and his crew were shot at by Israeli forces while traveling in Ramallah in a clearly marked vehicle on Monday. And on Sunday, Boston Globe reporter Anthony Shadid was shot and wounded by what he believes was an Israeli soldier while in an area near Arafat's compound. [Boston Israeli Consul Hillel] Newman said . . . "as far as we can tell, [Lewis] was not shot at by Israeli forces." . . .

Bob Zelnick, a former ABC correspondent who was stationed in Tel Aviv for two years, said, "The Israelis realize they are in an extremely delicate public relations situation as well as an extremely delicate military situation. . . . They realize the vast majority of the world is sympathetic to the Palestinians in this situation" and that pressure on Washington to crack down on the West Bank operation could soon get "acute."[20]

Israel's Public Relations Challenge

Despite the strength of its public relations capabilities, however, Israel was not immune to the setback its image suffered as foreign journalists began to report on the physical devastation left in the wake of the IDF incursion. Just as they had duly reported the horrific and dramatic details of Israeli suffering at the hands of Palestinian suicide bombers, the U.S. mainstream media carried dozens of detailed reports on the extent of the destruction in the West Bank as well as the emotional and material devastation it caused tens of thousands of Palestinians.

The reporting also highlighted what many observers, both Palestinian and international, viewed as the Sharon government's political motivation, namely, to smash the Palestinian Authority, isolate Yasser Arafat, and end the peace process. Israel was on the defensive to explain and justify its show of force in the West Bank, which had been given the name Operation Defensive Shield. The *Philadelphia Inquirer* reported that the IDF had caused $5,000 worth of damage to a Palestinian cultural center in the West Bank and quoted its director as follows: "This was not a security operation. It was just vandalism, part of a conscious desire to ruin everything Palestinian." This prompted Giora Becher, the Israeli consul general in Philadelphia, to register a complaint with the newspaper's ombudsman: "There is war taking place, and $5,000 worth of damage is worth a front-page article?"[21]

Beginning in mid-April, after two weeks of continual military closure throughout much of the West Bank, journalists were permitted an initial look at the damage. Print and broadcast reports began to appear detailing the systematic destruction of Palestinian ministries, many of which were located in Ramallah, less than ten miles north of Jerusalem. Reporters from several news organizations focused on the remains of what had been the Palestinian Ministry of Education, among others. When the Israeli army lifted the curfew in Ramallah for five hours on April 15, *New York Times* correspondent Serge Schmemann was one of the journalists to survey the damage.

In one room of the Palestinian Ministry of Education, the litter of papers, glass, paper clips and periodicals was ankle-deep. The filing cabinets had been ransacked, and some toppled. Personal computers sat on the desks, their hard drives ripped out.

In another room, the Israeli soldiers had blasted open the safe. The explosion brought down the suspended ceiling there and in adjoining rooms, leaving a mess. Dr. Naim Abu Hommos, the deputy minister of education, said the safe had been used to keep all school test records since 1960. All were gone, he said, along with 40,000 shekels—about $8,500—that had been kept there for petty cash.

That was the Ministry of Education. The neighboring Palestinian Legislative Council meeting hall was torn apart, and officials said the video archives of its sessions were gone. At the Ministry of Agriculture, the door had been blasted open by an explosion that also took out all the windows, and a neighbor said Israeli soldiers had filled two armored personnel carriers with boxes, presumably of records. It was the same at the Ministry of Industry. . . .

Similar reports came from all across Ramallah—offices in ruins, files and hard drives gone. The Ministry of Civil Affairs, the Central Bureau of Statistics, the Ministry of Finance, the Land Registry, the municipal administration buildings of Ramallah and neighboring Al-Bireh, including its library, had all been raided.

"What they are doing . . . is that they are destroying all the records, all the archives, all the files, of the Palestinian Authority," said Yasser Abed Rabbo, the Palestinian minister of information. "This is an administrative massacre, and this will lead to chaos."

An Israeli military officer said the reason for seizing documents from the ministries was the same as for seizing them from Yasser Arafat's compound in Ramallah, namely, "to see what's going on there. . . . A lot of these places turn up unexpected things, by accident. Documents have a very important value."[22]

The *Times* story quoted the Israeli officer as saying that Israel did not seek the collapse of the Palestinian Authority. Asked what interest Israel had in Palestinian education records, Sharon adviser Dore Gold told ABC News that "the ministry of education has been used in part for the programmatic incitement of the Palestinian population," adding that it may have been a front for terrorist organizations.[23] In a *World News Tonight* segment broadcast on April 17, Gold did not offer, nor was he asked for, evidence to back up his allegations. However, the report by correspondent Gillian Findlay appeared to question the defensive nature of Operation Defensive Shield and indicated that its target was much broader than specific alleged pockets of terror.

> GILLIAN FINDLAY (voice-over): Amid all the damage—smashed buildings, torn-up roads, power and water systems that no longer work—there has been another casualty here: the Palestinian Authority itself. This is the Ministry of Education: doors blown in, offices trashed, employees who say they were forced at gunpoint to lead soldiers from room to room.
>
> MR. SALAH SOUBANI (Palestinian Ministry of Education): They told us that they are looking for weapons. We told them this is an educational institution. . . .
>
> FINDLAY (off camera): Palestinians say what happened here was not only systematic; it was vengeful. Israel, they believe, is trying to destroy the Palestinian Authority and every single vestige of a Palestinian state.
>
> MR. SAEB EREKAT (chief Palestinian negotiator): Everything of the civilian infrastructure and security infrastructure have [sic] been destroyed.[24]

An April 20 *Washington Post* report offered a balanced Israeli-Palestinian back-and-forth over the rationale behind the Israeli raid on the Ministry of Education:

> Israeli officials said they could not confirm what data were seized by troops who entered Palestinian Authority ministries in Ramallah. But "in general, we are looking for documents that show a connection between the Palestinian Authority and terrorists," said Lt. Col. Adir

Haruvi, a spokesman for the Israeli army. Israeli technicians spent nine hours removing the data storage units from more than 40 computers in the Education Ministry, according to two ministry workers forced at gunpoint to open the offices. . . .

"The only conclusion I can make is they don't want to see any Palestinian institution able to work again," said Naim Abu Hommos, acting education minister, as he surveyed the damage during a brief break in the curfew that has locked down this town on the northern outskirts of Jerusalem.

Asked why troops would seize education records of students, Haruvi replied, "What we cannot understand is why they are educating 6-, 7-, 8-year-old students to say that 'I want to be a martyr.' You go in these schools and you see pictures of martyrs and students saying they want to grow up to be a martyr and explode [themselves] in the middle of Jerusalem."

"That turns the truth totally on its head," said Hommos. "The pictures you see in the classrooms are of children killed by the Israelis. There have been 172 students killed" since the current Palestinian uprising began in September 2000, he said.[25]

On April 19 the *Christian Science Monitor* reported varied Israeli assessments of the military operation while, the paper noted, "the West Bank continues to smolder . . . amid continued international condemnation."

Israeli officials acknowledge the idea was to show the Palestinians that not only does Israel have the military might to fight back against terror—it also has the political will to do so.

"We have a right to self-defense, and no one has a right to condemn us because we want to defend our citizens," says Israeli President Moshe Katzav. . . .

Critics say the ruin leveled at the Palestinians, and the personal grief caused millions of Palestinian civilians, many of whom have been under curfew for more than two weeks and have seen family and friends arrested or killed, will only strengthen the motivation to lash back.

Each escalation of violence fuels the next, says Yossi Beilin, a left-wing member of Israel's Parliament. "This battle against the terrorist infrastructure will give birth to more terrorists because the terrorist infrastructure lies within people's hearts," he says. "It can be uprooted only if there is hope for a different kind of life—not by force."[26]

On April 21 the Israeli army began to pull back from some West Bank towns, allowing journalists increased access to report on the scope and magnitude of destruction the incursion had caused. In a dispatch, published April 23, headlined "West Bank Wasteland," *Newsday* correspondent Edward Gargan rendered a stark picture of the devastation:

> After a three-week military campaign designed to fight terrorism, according to Israeli Prime Minister Ariel Sharon, Israel has essentially destroyed the ability of the Palestinians to run their own affairs. Across the West Bank, not only have schools been wrecked, but so have banks, postal services, hospitals, transportation, law enforcement and basic commerce.
>
> As they continue their slow withdrawal from Palestinian cities and towns, Israeli troops leave in their wake devastation of such magnitude that they have eviscerated Palestinian civilian institutions. Even homes have been demolished wholesale.
>
> From Jenin to Nablus, Ramallah to Bethlehem, everywhere water and sewage pipes have been damaged.
>
> Banks have been shelled by tanks.[27]

The incursion also targeted the Protective Services Compound, the Palestinian police complex located in Beitunia, next to Ramallah. In a report published on April 22, *Chicago Tribune* correspondent Christine Spolar vividly described the degree and intensity of destruction that Operation Defensive Shield had wrought on the facility. "Hit hard by Israeli helicopters," Spolar reported, "the facility . . . was a ruin, scarred with black smoke and pocked with huge rocket holes."

> Not one room escaped damage. Concrete-block walls were knocked from their foundation in some places. Images of Arafat, in photos or tapestries, were smashed or sliced with knives. The office of West Bank security chief Jibril Rajoub, who reveled in the 2-year-old, multimillion-dollar complex built with U.S. funds, was a particular mess.
>
> Every drawer and file in Rajoub's suite was thrown to the ground. Leather sofas were slit open. Glass fragments glittered across rugs and floors. Ten bullet holes penetrated the thick safety glass behind his desk.
>
> Another office was shattered by an explosion that had darkened the walls and turned the windows into shards. The room was left ankle deep in papers that had incinerated instantly, still in their stacks. When touched, the papers crumbled into powder.[28]

Palestinian schools escaped neither destruction nor defacement, *Newsday*'s Gargan reported, noting Palestinian bitterness over such targeting:

> On the first day of school yesterday, Miriam Masharkah, the principal of the Azia Shaheen School [in Ramallah], said hello and goodbye to the 400 girls from grades 7 to 12. "I had to send them home," she said. "The school was too damaged."
>
> As she talked, she strolled through the school pointing to the damage. "When I came in, for me it wasn't a school, it was a military post," she said. "They went through all our files. They tried to destroy the books. They threw the Holy Koran into the toilet. They wrote obscenities. They smashed our musical instruments."[29]

Nongovernmental organizations were also targeted in the Israeli sweep. *Washington Post* and *Baltimore Sun* correspondents visited the Ramallah offices of the Palestinian human-rights organization Mattin. Reports published in both papers on April 22 noted obscene graffiti scrawled on the walls of the trashed office of Salwa Diabis, which the *Post* reported had been vacated by Israeli soldiers just hours earlier—compelling many Palestinians to want to avenge their individual and collective humiliation as a result of such tactics.

> The furnishings had been heaped in a pile littered with garbage. The fax machine had been thrown onto a ledge. Photos of Diabis's family had been stripped from the wall. A reporter saw that in their place was a message written in English with a marker, starting with an obscenity and adding: "Arabs, never mess with us again."[30]

> [Diabis] found a cash box but said $1,000 was missing. And she was furious. In her office, someone had left a handwritten note in English that began with an obscenity, was signed in the name of the Israeli army and read, "Never mess with us again."
>
> "I am going to chase everyone who was here," she said of the soldiers. "This is the only mission left in my life. I will use the law. Too many Palestinians have the same feeling. My whole life is damaged."[31]

The incursion also targeted privately held Palestinian businesses, large and small, with no ties to or funding from the Palestinian Authority. Several media outlets reported the ransacking of the privately owned Palestine International Bank. In an April 22 *NewsNight with Aaron Brown* segment, CNN correspondent Christiane Amanpour reported that the Israeli army had interrogated Palestinian detainees: "In the process, the main automated teller machine was destroyed in an apparent attempt to get the cash inside. It failed, and so did this effort to bust a safe with a drill and hammer. And downstairs, at the bank's main vault, General Manager Osama Khader says this vault contained millions of Israeli shekels, and strongboxes with customers' tools and valuables. Here in this bank, records, computers, hard disks and data were removed, even customers' checks."[32] The *Baltimore Sun* report also described conditions at the bank: "'This is professional looting,' said Amar Khudiry, a technology manager trying to put back together a computer system in which hard drives were taken from the mainframe and individual work stations, leaving the bank without records. 'They know what they're doing.'"[33]

National Public Radio and the *New York Times* both carried reports on April 22 that bore a common theme: Palestinian shop owners surveying the damage in Ramallah's central business district, their trauma and outrage, like that of Salwa Diabis, clearly apparent. On NPR's *Morning Edition* Linda Gradstein reported:

> GRADSTEIN: In the center of Ramallah, in Manara Square, the Israeli tanks have pulled out, leaving behind coils of barbed wire, uprooted electricity poles and smashed shop fronts. Yesterday business owners came back to their shops and began to assess the damage. The seven-story Arian Building on the square had been taken over by Israeli soldiers, and just about every store here has been broken into. Twenty-four-year-old Faris Gosha walks into his computer game store, shaking his head in shock. At least half of his computers have been trashed, with many of the components—the hard disks and special 3D screen cards—gone. All that's left of half-a-dozen Sony PlayStation2s are empty boxes. Gosha is shaking with anger.
>
> MR. FARIS GOSHA (shop owner): I don't think that there is any terrorist here. I don't think that there's anything in the mind of these soldiers, except destruction—and destruction, that's all.
>
> GRADSTEIN: Gosha says all Israel has managed to accomplish is encouraging Palestinian extremism.
>
> MR. GOSHA: If we have got nothing to lose, we will be desperate, and we'll do everything desperate. Desperate things will be our solutions, even though they'll call it suicide bombing or they'll call it anything they want. But, I mean, I've got nothing to lose.[34]

The *New York Times* report began: "Instead of taking to the streets in celebration after Israeli tanks withdrew today from much of this city, Palestinians took to the streets seething."

> Palestinians see the goal of the operation as humiliation. Aymen Al-Khatib, an engineer at the Palestinian Petroleum Corporation, whose offices he said were also ransacked, saw the incursion as a blunt message. The message of the Israeli leaders, he said, was: "You as a people have to accept what we give you. If you start to feel strong, I will show you there is no one stronger than us. I will stomp on you." . . .
>
> Palestinians predicted a continuation of the cycle of retaliation and retribution of the last 18 months.
>
> "There is a wound that we managed to cure," said Wael Abdullah, a 30-year-old policeman. "But unfortunately it was opened again."[35]

Most of the reports included balancing comment and reaction from official Israeli sources, who offered rationales for the army's targeting of Palestinian businesses and civilian institutions. Captain Jacob Dallal, identified as an Israeli army spokesman, was quoted in the *New York Times* and the *Baltimore Sun*. "The searches are very thorough because the terrorist infrastructure has sunken [sic] deep into the civilian arms of the Palestinian Authority," Dallal told the *Times*. "Acts of vandalism and looting are not acceptable, and if there is credible evidence, the military police is ready to carry out an investigation."[36] Dallal expressed a similar disclaimer to the *Sun*, which quoted him as saying the army did not seek to "undermine or to destroy the civilian infrastructure of the Palestinian Authority."

> "Overall, there were a lot of offices and in some cases residential buildings searched," [Dallal] said. "That was part of what we felt was needed in an attempt to uproot and get to the bottom of the network of the various organizations involved in terror. And unfortunately it is a testimony of how deep-rooted this whole thing was and is that these were things not done in previous incursions." . . .
>
> "A bank obviously serves clients but it is also used to transfer funds and to get a handle on the movement of finances is also something important. That is not to say that the bank should be destroyed either."[37]

Another military spokesman, Lieutenant Colonel Olivier Rafowicz, told the *Washington Post* that soldiers found "not operating by the rules would be punished." However, according to the report, Rafowicz denounced what he called "a huge campaign of lies" by Palestinians. "These false allegations have the clear intention by the Palestinians to shift from the real problem of terrorism and mislead public opinion," Rafowicz said.

"We condemn looting. But how do you know these things were stolen? How can you see something stolen if it's not there? It's really easy for them [Palestinians] to blame us for all the problems. That's the easiest way to avoid facing the truth of the reality, that the Palestinian leadership has led the Palestinian people on a totally irresponsible policy of supporting terrorism."[38]

THE IDF AND THE BATTLE FOR HEARTS AND MINDS

U.S. mainstream media reporting of the effects of suicide bombings and the Israeli incursion balanced Israeli and Palestinian suffering and emotion as expressed mainly by nonofficial sources. By its very nature, however, the incursion engendered reporting that relied to a much greater degree on official military and diplomatic sources. Israel was able to tap the strength of its multifaceted institutional public relations apparatus served by the IDF intelligence and officer corps, the Ministry of Foreign Affairs, and the Government Press Office. Its media skills rudimentary and unorganized and its infrastructure in ruins, the Palestinian Authority was no match for Israel on the propaganda battlefield. Patterns of U.S. mainstream media reporting on the incursion and its aftermath, from the West Bank to Washington, indicate that when opportunities arose for official sources to spin the story, Israeli PR efforts often had a distinct influence on the direction of the reporting irrespective of whether it referred to the Palestinian point of view or contained a Palestinian rebuttal.

The Fire at the Church of the Nativity

After major operations of the incursion ended in late April, a standoff developed between the IDF and Palestinian fighters holed up in the Church of the Nativity in Bethlehem. On May 1 television broadcasts around the world carried live coverage of a fire burning on the upper floor of one building in the church compound. Although the church itself was not affected, the parish hall and offices of the Franciscan monastery were destroyed.

Ted Koppel, anchor of the ABC News program *Nightline* and one of the most recognizable faces in American news broadcasting, was in the region to report on the effects of the incursion. Koppel got the first television interview with Palestinian leader Yasser Arafat since the siege began. On the May 1 *Nightline* broadcast a visibly shaken Arafat spoke to Koppel about events at the church compound, including the fire. Before beginning his interview with Arafat, Koppel noted "an exchange of heavy gunfire at the Church of the Nativity in Bethlehem. And there were fires there, caused by the Israelis, say the Palestinians, set by the Palestinians, the Israelis insist."

MR. ARAFAT: I am very nervous because what is going on in the Nativity Church is very difficult, not for me only, for all the Christians, for all the Muslims, for all the whole world. Unbelievable.

KOPPEL: But should we—should we not wait until we know what has happened there?

MR. ARAFAT: Just now I was in contact with them. They were . . . firing with all kinds of fires, including this (foreign language spoken)— burning bullets.

KOPPEL: You were—you were in touch with the [Palestinian] men inside . . .

MR. ARAFAT: Yes.

Koppel did not ask Arafat to clarify what he or his interpreter meant by "burning bullets" or who was firing them. Later in the interview Koppel returned to the topic of the fire. When he tested the Israeli theory that Palestinians had deliberately set the blaze in order to thwart an anticipated attack by the IDF, Arafat became angry:

KOPPEL: The Israelis are saying that the men inside the church thought that the IDF was going to attack and they began to set fires inside the building.

MR. ARAFAT: Can you believe that?

KOPPEL: I'm telling you what they are saying.

MR. ARAFAT: Big lies. . . . Can anyone burn himself? His house? The place where he is sleeping? The church where he is praying?

KOPPEL: If they thought they were under attack by the Israelis, maybe.

MR. ARAFAT: Maybe? How? I am a general. You are—you are speaking with Yasser Arafat. Can you believe that I would make a fire here when you are attacking me?

KOPPEL: You are telling me no?
MR. ARAFAT: Definitely not. You are speaking to General Arafat.
KOPPEL: I understand. I understand.
MR. ARAFAt: What is going [*sic*] is a big crime. A big crime! And I am
    asking for the whole to move quickly to stop this crime . . .
    against this holy, sacred place.[39]

The May 2 *Nightline* broadcast focused on efforts by Israelis and Palestinians to spin perceptions of unfolding events to their own advantage. At the
top of the broadcast Koppel remarked:

There are at least two wars being waged here, and the military one
may be the less important of the two. This is primarily a war of images and perceptions. The participants themselves are glued to their
television sets, acutely aware of how everything is playing, not just in
the living rooms of America, but in the foreign ministries of Europe
and on the Arab street. The soldiers fight the first battles and then the
public affairs specialists and the intelligence officers put their spin on
what has happened and how they feel the media should report it.

Koppel then focused on the fire, showing a snippet of his interview with
Arafat the day before. "The event, as the Palestinians quickly realized, had
the makings of a genuine and serious public relations disaster for the Israeli
government," Koppel told his audience, adding, "Arafat, not surprisingly,
was unprepared to accept even the possibility that the fire had been started
by the Palestinians themselves." After showing another snippet containing
Arafat's angry response the night before to the suggestion that Palestinians
had set the fire, Koppel shifted to a full-blown explanation of that very
claim, as asserted by three Israeli officials: the IDF commander of the battalion at the church, a press official with the Israeli Foreign Ministry, and an
unidentified Israeli army intelligence officer. Arafat's denial notwithstanding, Koppel did not interview a single Palestinian source who actually had
been at the church about the fire.

KOPPEL (voice-over): This afternoon, we returned to Bethlehem and
    talked with Colonel Ronnie Numa, the commander of the Israeli
    paratroop battalion laying siege to the church compound.
COLONEL RONNIE NUMA: We didn't shoot anything that's by the
    church. We are not stupid. We know exactly what we are doing
    here. We know this is the most sensitive place for the Christians.

KOPPEL (voice-over): It had been Colonel Numa, early this week, who had taken us to one of his battalion's sniper positions. Colonel Numa who had shown us that next to each sniper is a video cameraman, recording precisely what the marksman at his side is shooting. As we were also shown, what happens at the site of the siege is videotaped from the underside of a blimp that flies overhead, from a camera attached to the top of a tall crane. All of this is monitored from at least two locations, where other soldiers sit in front of television screens showing images fed from those overhead cameras. The Israelis certainly don't share everything recorded by all of their cameras, but they can and do when they need to, as now. . . .

Amir Otek, a press official with the Israeli Foreign Ministry, was conveniently available in Bethlehem this afternoon. What he shows us, he contends, demonstrates that the fire was started by those inside the burned room. The windows, he points out, were broken from the inside out, not from something fired from the outside in.

AMIR OTEK: If, at all, something from outside caused the fire, so definitely we should have find [sic] the piece of the windows, the glasses [sic] inside the room.

KOPPEL (voice-over): An Israeli army intelligence officer, a colonel, whose face cannot be shown, was on site when the shooting began last night.

UNIDENTIFIED MAN: They [the Palestinians] will stop the Israelis from getting inside because it was immediately covered worldwide and immediately the pressure came. And this is their weapon to stop any Israeli attempt to get inside. I am not for sure [sic] that yesterday wasn't such an attempt.

After a brief discussion of what it would take for Palestinian fighters to leave the church or Israeli soldiers to enter it, Koppel ended this segment of the broadcast with his own deduction that it was most likely Palestinians who had started the fire at the compound. His evidence, both forensic and testimonial, came from three Israeli military and diplomatic sources on hand at the scene but no Palestinians who had been there. In entering the church, Koppel suggested, the IDF "might destroy one of Christianity's holiest sites, which, for reasons of world opinion, they simply cannot do. And that, in the final analysis, is probably also the strongest reason for believing that they did not set the fire to the church last night. The Israelis still feel that they can win this confrontation by waiting. The Palestinian gunmen inside may not."[40]

Koppel's colleagues in the U.S. mainstream media, however, did not reach similar conclusions. Fox News took a more balanced approach, even though it, too, quoted no Palestinian sources.

> BRIT HUME (anchor): Last night's fire at Bethlehem's Church of the Nativity compound destroyed the offices of a Franciscan monastery. In a statement, the Roman Catholic Franciscans blame the Israelis and the Palestinians equally for the blaze and called the situation, quote, "intolerable and increasingly dangerous." . . .
>
> MIKE TOBIN (correspondent): One fire broke out in the Franciscan monastery. Another burned out in the Greek Orthodox monastery. Palestinians say the Israeli flares caused the fires when they landed in the compound. The Israeli Defense Force held a press conference and said Palestinians deliberately set the fires where the press could see them burn . . . and started the battle just in time for the prime news hours in the U.S.
>
> LT. COL. OLIVIER RAFOWICZ (IDF): Who is responsible for this crisis? Who is actually using weapons in the church? Who is controlling the violence in the church? . . . It is Arafat. It is the Palestinian side.
>
> TOBIN: Late in the day, the IDF softened its position. An intelligence officer, Miri Eisen, looked at the footage of the battle and said there is a chance flares caused the fires. The IDF will now investigate.[41]

On May 2—the same day as the *Nightline* broadcast in which Koppel implied that Palestinian fighters had set the fire—NPR and ABC News on *World News Tonight* also reported that an IDF representative had acknowledged that the fire could have been started by one or more of its own flares[42]—perhaps one of the same "burning bullets" that Arafat had mentioned to Koppel the day before. The *Los Angeles Times* and CNN reported on May 2 that the cause of the fire remained unclear, with both sides blaming each other.[43] On May 3 both the *Los Angeles Times* and the *Atlanta Journal-Constitution* reported that Miri Eisen, the Israeli military intelligence officer, said the IDF was investigating the possibility that Israeli flares had started the fire;[44] the *New York Times* reported that the cause of the fires remained uncertain.[45] As had Koppel, the *Washington Post* reported on the high-tech gear Israel used at the church to assert Palestinian culpability for the fire. However, where Koppel had not been skeptical, the *Post* was:

> The Israeli army today showed reporters photographs apparently taken by an observation balloon or a crane-mounted camera above the com-

pound. Army Maj. Hertzel Makov said the pictures showed broken window glass lying outside the church. He said that proved the fire began with an explosion from inside the church.

The photographs were grainy, however, and Makov said he might have been confused about precisely what location they showed.[46]

Such balanced and cautious references to the cause of the fire typically amounted to one or two paragraphs in long reports on related events. They did not receive the spotlight that the *Nightline* report, led by Israeli military and diplomatic sources, had given to Israeli claims—ironically in a report on how both parties to the conflict were attempting to spin perception of events in their favor. In the end, the cause of the fire apparently remained undetermined and the story faded from view in the U.S. media after May 3.

Embedded with the IDF

On May 12 the cover story of the *New York Times Magazine* opened with a description of IDF sniper Yigal Kelman taking shots near—but being careful to avoid hitting—a family of unarmed Palestinians who had violated curfew regulations and remained on their rooftop terrace in the village of Atil, in the northern West Bank. The strange game of cat and mouse—during which Kelman continued to shoot at the building while the Palestinians held their ground on its roof—vividly illustrated the story's headline, namely, that Israel had become bogged down in "an impossible occupation."[47]

"You see how it is?" the Israeli sharpshooter told the American reporter observing him and his elite reserve unit for the *Times*. "They could have left after the first or second shot. But no, they had to stay until I did something to them. So now they have a punctured [water] tank and a damaged satellite dish. That's how they want it."

In his 7,400-word piece on the Palsars, Kelman's paratroop unit, reporter Scott Anderson did not confirm with Palestinians in Atil whether they wanted it that way. Rather, the magazine's centerpiece that Sunday—told through the sharp and detailed observations of Anderson, a freelancer embedded for several days and nights with the Palsars during the second week of Operation Defensive Shield, as well as through quotes from members of the platoon—clearly conveyed the idea that the Israeli occupation had become something of a losing battle in both the short and long terms, but that it was nevertheless being fought by men acting humanely and with restraint.

Reporters for at least two other American mainstream media outlets rode along on two similar IDF missions. On June 2 ABC News on *World News Tonight* broadcast a report by Dan Harris on patrol with an IDF unit in Bethlehem. The lead-in to the report explained that "ABC was granted special permission to accompany the Israel Defense Forces on their mission." The patrol was seeking "one to four" Palestinian suspects, Harris reported, but "after an eight-hour operation, the Israelis did not succeed in finding their man."[48]

In its July 15 edition *Newsweek* featured a 2,275-word report by correspondent Joshua Hammer on Palnat Company, another elite IDF reserve unit tracking seven wanted Palestinian men in the northern West Bank. The suspects were alluded to as stealthy predators in the story's headline, "A Shark Hunt in the Night." Of his insider's access Hammer wrote, "Last week *Newsweek* spent three days and nights with these soldiers in their camps at the edge of hostile territory, and on patrol through the heart of it."[49] Like the *New York Times Magazine* and *World News Tonight* reports, Hammer's piece conveyed the insights of Israeli soldiers on a mission they found regrettable but necessary. However, in none of the three missions reported by these major American news outlets were Palestinian suspects apprehended.

Anderson's *New York Times Magazine* report did not refer to how he had gained access to the Palsars—but his bird's-eye view of their mission in Atil—like those of the other American reporters on the road with the IDF—most likely would have required special army clearance. "Given the extreme danger of their operations," he wrote, "the Palsars maintain a secretive guerrilla-like cell structure." According to Anderson, the commandos "wear no distinguishing insignia upon their regular-issue olive uniforms, and this is clearly their preference; when, at a back-base refueling center, a senior army officer asked a young Palsar for his unit affiliation, the soldier simply refused to answer. 'The culture of silence is so ingrained that it becomes automatic,' one member explains. 'There are some guys here who haven't even told their wives they're Palsar.'" However, this didn't prevent the Palsars from talking openly with Anderson; his report quoted seven members of the unit by their full names as well as ages, places of residence, and professions. Furthermore, the piece indicated that Anderson's observations of the unit appeared to be unrestricted as he accompanied it on a nighttime raid of a Palestinian home in which guns were drawn.

The Palsars were frustrated that the incursion had yielded relatively few meaningful arrests, Anderson wrote, adding that they found it "increasingly difficult to ascertain whether they are winning—or even to calculate what victory would mean." Yaniv Sagee, a thirty-eight-year-old kibbutznik and leader of a leftist youth movement, asked: "The government talks about how many guns and bomb factories and suicide belts it's capturing in the offensive, of how we are going to break the terrorist infrastructure. But what infrastructure? I think the most terrifying thing here—and maybe it's something that a lot of people don't want to see—is that there's very little of an infrastructure to break." To which Kelman added: "The problem with an operation like this is that it is like shaking a tree. Maybe the people you're looking for fall out, but so do a lot of innocent people. By shaking them, by disrupting their lives, you're creating the next set of problems."

The men of Palsar articulated for Anderson a range of political sentiments about the occupation. "I've spent 20 years of my life fighting the Arabs," said Ofir Dvir, 37, identified as a commercial lawyer from Tel Aviv, "and what I've learned from this is that force is the only thing they understand, the only way to get their respect. First, we have to defeat them, and maybe then they will want peace."

From the other end of the spectrum, Sagee attributed international criticism aimed at Israel to the occupation itself. "We can give all kinds of reasons for why we are occupiers, and some of them you can argue are quite legitimate in the current situation—but that doesn't change the basic point that this is Palestine and we should not be here," he told Anderson. "This is exactly what I'm struggling with myself, because as much as I'm trying to be moral, as humanely as I try to treat the Palestinians, I've put myself here to do something that is basically immoral."

Sagee's view about the immorality of occupation notwithstanding, throughout the piece Anderson interwove detailed characterizations of the Palsars as sensitive, if reluctant, occupiers—which is noteworthy since it was published at the precise juncture that Israel's image was in need of just such a boost. International media reports had shown evidence of what was seen around the world as the IDF's heavy-handed and disproportionate tactics against Palestinian civilians and nonmilitary targets—including schools, community centers, medical clinics, banks, and ministries of the Palestinian Authority. These image problems were further compounded in the wake of the fiercest Israeli-Palestinian fighting of the incursion, which had occurred over a week's time at the Jenin refugee camp and had resulted in a stream of images depicting houses in the camp left in ruins by IDF tanks and bulldozers.

In several places, however, the *New York Times Magazine* piece pointed to specific justifications of Israeli military tactics during the incursion, in both the paratroopers' own words and Anderson's characterizations. The Palsars, Anderson wrote, harbored "deep resentment at how their actions in the West Bank are being represented—deliberately misrepresented, in their view."

Amichai Burstein, a twenty-eight-year-old reservist and mathematics student, insisted: "In everything we do here, there is a sound military reason for it. And if we didn't use these tactics, more of them [Palestinians] and more of us would get killed." To this Anderson added his own observation:

The list of tactics that they believe are necessary but misunderstood is long. Temporarily taking over Palestinian homes, men like Burstein argue, is the only way to place soldiers in a relatively secure environment to watch what goes on in towns and villages. The blanket curfews allow them to search for suspects in a way that minimizes civilian casualties. The new policy of having Palestinian men raise their shirts and lower their trousers at checkpoints is the only way to determine if someone is a suicide bomber. And the detention and searching of ambulances, which has been much criticized, is necessary because Palestinians have used ambulances to transport guns and bombs in the past.

This was followed by another Burstein quote: "But everyone refuses to see this. Instead, they talk of 'collective punishment' and 'tactics of humiliation.' So from this, I think you can understand why we feel most of the rest of the world is biased against us."

Anderson also described at length the unease of the Palsars over the decision to evict a Palestinian family from their home in Atil in order to use it as a command post. "To a man," Anderson wrote,

the soldiers profess to be extremely uncomfortable with this house-seizure policy, and that unease is evident as they gingerly explore their new surroundings. . . . They take a certain quirky pride in trying to minimize the effects of their presence. Within minutes of their arrival, they roll up the family's better carpets, moving them, along with various breakable objects, to one corner of the upstairs sitting room. There are chickens in the small backyard, and one soldier is given the task of making sure that they are regularly fed and watered. By long-standing policy, nothing of the family's is to be used—not the onions sitting on the kitchen sill or the soap in the bathroom—and on the day the Palsars leave, a cleanup crew will give the house a quick scrubbing, perhaps even leave behind a bit of money to compensate the family for its inconvenience. Such are the tactics and considerations of this peculiar war.[50]

However, Anderson's detailed description of the "tactics and considerations" he observed among Palsars, such as taking care not to disturb the contents of one Palestinian home in Atil—which he then generalized as representing the mores of Israel's greater "peculiar war" with the Palestinians—differed significantly from American and Israeli media reports about the conduct of other IDF soldiers who had been in Palestinian homes, shops, and offices during the incursion.

On May 6—about a month after Anderson's embedding with the Palsars and six days before his story was published (but with the May 12 issue of the magazine likely already in print)—the Israeli daily *Haaretz* published a report on its English-language Web site detailing how IDF soldiers had vandalized the Palestinian Ministry of Culture in Ramallah. Amira Hass, the paper's Palestinian affairs correspondent, reported that even after Isr⸱⸱li forces had withdrawn from the area on April 21, it was kept under
c⸱   Ministry officials and employees of local Palestinian
r   stations with offices in the same building who went
                           hat evening "did not expect to find the building the
                           ' Hass reported. "But what awaited them was beyond
                           also shocked representatives and cultural attachés of
                           who toured the site the next day." According to the
                           :es

                           and electronic equipment had been wrecked or had
)uters, photocopiers, cameras, scanners, hard disks,
                           :nt worth thousands of dollars, television sets. The
                           na on top of the building was destroyed.
                           :ts vanished. A collection of Palestinian art objects
                           :mbroideries) disappeared. Perhaps it was buried un-
                           documents and furniture, perhaps it had been spirited
                           e was dragged from place to place, broken by soldiers,
                           toves for heating were overturned and thrown on heaps
                           apers, discarded books, broken diskettes and discs and
                           lowpanes.
                           om of the various departments—literature, film, culture
                           ₍nd youth—books, discs, pamphlets and documents were
                           led with urine and excrement.

....: two toilets on every floor, but the soldiers urinated and defecated everywhere else in the building, in several rooms of which they had lived for about a month. They did their business on the floors, in emptied flowerpots, even in drawers they had pulled out of desks.

They defecated into plastic bags, and these were scattered in several places. Some of them had burst. Someone even managed to defecate into a photocopier. . . .

Now the Palestinian Ministry of Culture is considering leaving the building the way it is. A memorial.

No response was available from the IDF by press time.[51]

On May 8 the Associated Press reported that the IDF had issued indictments against six soldiers suspected of looting Palestinian homes, businesses, and ministries during the incursion. Citing the indictments, the AP reported that one of the soldiers "was accused of breaking into homes in the West Bank town of Ramallah when his unit took up positions there during the fighting. He allegedly stole a silver sword with a golden scabbard, two wooden pipes, fifteen computer parts including a number of hard disks, four mobile telephones and seven batteries."[52]

On May 27 the AP reported that five Israeli soldiers had been sent to prison for up to five months and demoted to the rank of private for looting and vandalizing Palestinian property.[53] According to the report, another twenty soldiers were being investigated on similar charges, including a platoon commander accused of abusing a Palestinian while searching his home.

Reports of looting by IDF soldiers in March continued throughout the summer. In an Israel Radio broadcast on August 25, a former soldier detailed how he and members of his unit had looted Palestinian property during the incursion. According to a Reuters report carried on the *Haaretz* English-language Web site, the IDF said it was investigating thirty-five such cases. The report continued:

> The recently discharged soldier, interviewed under the assumed name "Danny," told Israel Radio that troops stole from Palestinian homes during the six-week-long sweep for militants launched after suicide bombings killed scores of Israelis.
>
> "During each search, the head of the family was meant to accompany the soldiers to every room. What we would do is take the man to one room as the soldiers searched other rooms, and they would pocket things while out of his sight," [the soldier] said.
>
> "When it came to commanding officers, some know about it and some were involved. When it came to squad leaders, all of them know and were involved," Danny said.

Israel Radio said Danny was among several soldiers to come forward. Another man who was not named told the radio he saw troops ransack a shopping mall in Ramallah and make off with electronic appliances, water pipes and other "souvenirs."[54]

Anderson's report on the Palsar commandos drew "many letters praising their restraint" from readers of the *New York Times Magazine*, according to an editor's note and several readers' responses published on the "Letters" page of the May 26 issue. One such reader who found Anderson's report "fascinating" observed:

> The soldiers in this intimate portrait, while not eager for war, operate with professionalism, caution and a strong awareness of the limits of military force.
> By allowing their voices to be heard and their actions to be seen, the soldiers are replacing much of the distorting rhetoric that engulfs discussions of the conflict with the voices of those who are responsible for doing what they must do to stop terrorism. At the same time, they are also concerned with the long-term implications of their actions for peace between two peoples.[55]

Another reader, however, responded with skepticism—perhaps informed by reporting that did not bear the imprint of the IDF's PR apparatus:

> Does Anderson seriously believe that under his watchful eyes—one of the rare times when a journalist has been allowed to accompany Israelis during their reoccupation of many West Bank cities—soldiers would actually behave as they normally do in the latest siege? . . . It certainly appears that the apologists for the latest phase of Israel's war have scored an overwhelming public-relations victory.[56]

THE DIPLOMATIC CAMPAIGN:
"ARAFAT SUPPORTED TERROR"

By isolating Palestinian leader Yasser Arafat, destroying Palestinian Authority ministries, and reoccupying the West Bank, Operation Defensive Shield went far beyond a sweep of specific "terrorist network" targets and apprehending Palestinians suspected of engaging in suicide-bombing operations. As a member of the parliamentary opposition, Ariel Sharon had opposed the Oslo peace process. As prime minister he had declared that it was over, invalidated by the second Palestinian uprising. By the time the incursion began on March 29, two days after the Passover bombing, the uprising had just passed the eighteen-month mark.

The strategy of the Sharon government was to isolate Arafat and cripple the Palestinian Authority. According to an April 5 *Washington Post* report, the PA's ministerial apparatus had been reduced to "vestiges" within the first week of the incursion. Saeb Erekat, Palestinian minister of local government, concluded: "There is no Palestinian Authority. Anyone who has an IQ of 14 can see that the goal of this operation has been to make sure that there is no government for the Palestinians."[57]

Physically incapacitating the Palestinian political apparatus, however, was but one objective of Operation Defensive Shield; incapacitating it politically was another. Convincing the world—particularly Washington and American public opinion—that Arafat was personally responsible for the terror and that the PA had been the mechanism for its implementation would lead to the conclusion that Israel should no longer be obligated to deal with Arafat in the peace process.

From a journalistic point of view, such assertions by Israeli officials constituted bona fide news. However, in reporting them American media outlets displayed a variety of journalistic approaches, ranging from careful contextualization and guarded skepticism to accepting the Israeli claims at face value. Irrespective of the presentation, the coverage had PR value: Israel's claims that Arafat and the PA were linked to terror were repeatedly impressed on U.S. government officials and the American public through the media. An exchange between correspondent Christiane Amanpour and anchor Aaron Brown on the April 22 broadcast of CNN's *NewsNight* illustrated that while the claims appeared porous, the media nonetheless continued to cover them.

> AMANPOUR: When we ask about ministries and the like, [Israeli sources] say they're unlikely to find terrorists there, but these ministries are involved in incitement and others even in perhaps financing. So that, they say, is one of the reasons why they've been going through the ministries.
> BROWN: Christiane, I want to be clear on this, I guess. The Israelis don't deny, is this correct? They do not deny that they went into these places, the Ministry of Education, for example, and tore up the place pretty good?
> AMANPOUR: That's correct.

BROWN: And—

AMANPOUR: They don't deny it.

BROWN: And they say, well that's just—we were looking for important stuff and that's just what happens, the whole building gets destroyed?

AMANPOUR: Basically, yes, and when you press them, they talk about
the whole sort of infrastructure. You know, they've used this word,
the infrastructure of terrorism, and it turns out that that is being
used as a very big catch-all phrase, and a big catch-all method for
what they've been doing.

And basically, what we've seen, certainly in these ministries—and
there are others that we didn't go to but we'd heard about—there has
been a great deal of damage done in the process of what they say has
been trying to find any kind of reference to terrorism or incitement
or the kind of things that they say that they're after.[58]

On April 2, four days into the incursion, the IDF announced that it had
seized documents directly linking Arafat and the Palestinian Authority to terrorism. The Sharon government began distributing to the international and
Israeli media copies of Arabic-language documents said to have been seized
from Arafat's compound and various ministries and offices of the PA. Journalists were given copies of selected documents, along with Hebrew- and Arabic-
language translations, but there was no independent verification of the documents' authenticity or explanation of how they had been discovered.

The documents were the focus of that evening's edition of *Hardball with
Chris Matthews* on CNBC.[59] In an interview with PLO legal adviser Michael
Tarazi, Matthews assumed a prosecutorial tone, for the most part appearing
to accept the documents as evidence that needed to be disproved rather than
proved, even as he acknowledged the PR implications of the story surrounding them.

MATTHEWS: One document's an invoice from the Al-Aqsa Martyrs
Brigade found inside Arafat's compound itself. It requests money
for suicide bombings. Quote—this is from the document—"The
cost of supplying electronic and chemical components for explosive
devices and bombs—this was our largest expense. The cost of pre-
paring a bomb is at least 700 units. We need to equip five to nine
bombs each week for our cells in various locations."

This has the look of an invoice that apparently was found in the
possession of the finance minister for Mr. Yasser Arafat. [To Tarazi:]

What do you make of that, that Yasser Arafat's apparently paying the bills for these suicide bombers?

MR. TARAZI: I think we have to stop being so naive. I mean, there was an article in the [Israeli newspaper] *Haaretz* today that talked very expressly about the fact that in times of crisis, in times of war, the Israeli government is notorious for leaking out documents that miraculously and coincidentally bolster its case.

MATTHEWS: So you're saying that these are fraud? That these are bogus documents, you're saying?

MR. TARAZI: Well, absolutely. I mean, are we so naive to think that . . .

MATTHEWS: How do you know this? How do you say absolutely? Do you know for a fact that these were forged by the Israelis?

MR. TARAZI: Well, let's think about this logically. Are we so naive as to think that all of a sudden Israel has found a document that proves its case in a very timely manner and just coincidentally comes out at a time it's trying to sell the war to its people?

MATTHEWS: Well, they've just gone through the compound, pulling all the documents from the Palestinian Authority. They are in possession now of the Palestinian Authority's records.

MR. TARAZI: Right. Right.

MATTHEWS: Let me just ask you a question of PR here. How can you deny the authenticity of a document without being told that it was unauthentic by someone in the Palestinian Authority? Has someone told you that these documents are not genuine?

MR. TARAZI: Look, I'll turn it around on you. And I'll say, "How can you just assume that it's authentic because people in the government tell you it's authentic?"

With the PLO adviser holding his ground, Matthews next appeared to put him on the stand as a proxy for Arafat, starting with a patronizing compliment paid to the American-born Tarazi:

MATTHEWS: Well, Michael, it's great to talk to somebody—you have a very clear American accent. You have the same language we have. You speak in our idiom, obviously. I want to ask you in clear idiomatic American, forget the Arabic, is it wrong to commit suicide in the killing of civilians for a political purpose?

MR. TARAZI: Absolutely. And it is also wrong to kill civilians, whether they're being done by F-16s or by suicide bombers. . . . Killing civilians for political purposes is wrong.

MATTHEWS: When is the man you speak for, Yasser Arafat, going to speak as clearly as you just did? When is he going to go on and speak in Arabic to the people of Palestine and say, "Stop sending your daughters to me, stop sending your kids to me to commit suicide. I'll have nothing to do with it"?

MR. TARAZI: He said it very clearly—Chris, he said it very clearly in Arabic and he said it very clearly in English on February 3 in The New York Times in black and white for the entire world to see.

MATTHEWS: Has he said it in Arabic?

MR. TARAZI: It was in The New York Times, was published in Arabic and printed in the Arabic press as well.

MATTHEWS: OK. I'm not sure that was well understood to be the case. No one, I think, in the Palestinian Authority area believes that Yasser Arafat is opposed to these suicide bombings.

To get the Israeli perspective, Matthews then interviewed Alon Pinkas, Israel's consul general in New York. Rather than ask Pinkas to explain how the documents proved Israeli claims, Matthews referred to those claims as fact, proceeding to give the Israeli diplomat advice on how to conduct a public relations campaign.

MATTHEWS: Mr. Ambassador, simple question: Do you stand behind the fact that these documents, discovered by the Israeli defense force today, do, in fact, represent evidence that Yasser Arafat's chief financial officer has been signing checks for the Palestine [sic] suicide bombers?

AMBASSADOR ALON PINKAS: Absolutely, Chris. I'll tell you more than that. There are other documents that will be divulged in time. These documents have been submitted by Israel to various American, British, French and German intelligence services for their review in the last several months; leaders of various countries, President Bush, Tony Blair, Britain, President Chirac of France. . . .

MATTHEWS: So you've got the smoking gun. I assume we don't have a notary public approving this, but you've got the smoking gun, in terms of your government has proof now that Yasser Arafat is not an unwitting accomplice, but he, in fact, is paying the cost of these bullets and all the other crap that goes along with killing yourself.

AMBASSADOR PINKAS: Oh, absolutely. We had the proof all along. We just thought it was time to share it with you.

MATTHEWS: Well, I'd say. Why did you hold it back?

AMBASSADOR PINKAS: Because some of it was obtained in ways that we could have compromised had we . . . provided you with it earlier. I was listening to Mr. Tarazi, you know, about—about his conviction about the lack of authenticity. I was expecting him to say that he saw Elvis Presley in Ramallah. I mean, several weeks ago they said that the [*Karine A*] ship [allegedly smuggling weapons to the PA] was bogus. Then they said that there's no such thing as the Al-Aqsa Brigades. Next thing, they're going to see Elvis in Ramallah. They're going to deny that there ever were suicides.

MATTHEWS: Well, you don't have to get clever.

AMBASSADOR PINKAS: I'm not.

MATTHEWS: Let me give you some public-relations advice. When you got the guy caught red-handed, you don't have to be clever about it.

On April 4, with the incursion a week old, President Bush delivered an eighteen-minute speech in the White House Rose Garden calling on both sides to end the violence and announcing that he would dispatch Secretary of State Colin Powell to the region the following week to restart peace efforts. Urging the Palestinian Authority and Arab governments in the region "to do everything in their power to stop terrorist activities, to disrupt terrorist financing and to stop inciting violence by glorifying terror in state-owned media or telling suicide bombers they are martyrs," Bush also called on Israel "to halt incursions into Palestinian-controlled areas and begin the withdrawal from those cities it has already occupied," while adding that "America recognizes Israel's right to defend itself from terror."[60] Arafat's cabinet released a statement saying the Palestinian leader had accepted Bush's remarks and renewed peace efforts "without conditions."[61] While not referring to Bush's remarks, a statement by Sharon said the incursion would continue, with no indication for how long, and that "giving in to terror will lead to it spreading to other places in the world. Thus it is necessary to act."[62]

On the same day that Bush delivered his speech in Washington, Israeli officials held a news conference in Jerusalem during which they distributed copies of documents said to have been seized by the IDF from Arafat's compound in Ramallah. The documents were part of a two-truckload haul, according to the *New York Times*, which ran a 775-word report on the news conference that began:

Israel made public several documents today that it says prove that Yasser Arafat, the Palestinian leader, authorized cash payments as recently as January to members of his Fatah faction accused of terrorist acts against Israeli civilians.

The documents were copies of facsimiles bearing what appeared to be Mr. Arafat's signature. They approved payments, ranging from $350 to $600 each, to 15 men identified by Israel as terrorists, including a leader of a Palestinian militant group who was killed by the Israelis with a concealed bomb on Jan. 14.

The *Times* report characterized the release of the documents as "part of a long-running Israeli campaign to tie Mr. Arafat personally to suicide bombings and other attacks on civilians and to increase international pressure on him." It quoted cabinet member Dan Meridor's charge against Arafat made at the news conference: "He personally finances the terror. He pays the people who do it." The report then balanced and qualified such claims, stating that "Palestinian officials dismissed the significance of the records and questioned their authenticity," and that PA official Erekat said he expected, sight unseen, that the documents were fabricated. The *Times* also noted that "despite the vehement Israeli claims that the documents amounted to proof of Mr. Arafat's direct involvement in financing terrorism, there was no evidence tying the payments to specific attacks."[63]

The *Washington Post* reported the release of the documents in a passing reference contained in a single paragraph of a story that focused on the day's developments in the West Bank incursion.

So far, tangible results of the offensive seem modest. Some caches of weapons, ammunition, explosives and bomb-making equipment have been seized and a few score suspected terrorists are among more than 1,000 Palestinian detainees. Israel also has scored some public relations coups. On Thursday, for instance, it revealed two seized documents, signed by Arafat, authorizing payment to militants wanted by Israel for shooting and bombing attacks. When similar documents were made public on Tuesday, Palestinian officials dismissed them as frauds.[64]

Other media reports, however, appeared to take Israeli claims at face value. A Cox News Service report published in the *Atlanta Journal-Constitution* focused on the day's battlefield events but included five paragraphs on the release of the documents. The story conflated facts from the documents with the Israeli interpretation and juxtaposed that interpretation with further Israeli spin.

Israeli officials gave journalists copies of documents they said proved Arafat has served as a terrorist paymaster, even after Sept. 11.

Two documents seized from Arafat's headquarters were requests for payment for particular individuals. In each case, Israeli officials said, Arafat had written his approval in the margin and signed his name.

In one case, on Sept. 19, Arafat authorized the payment of $600 to each of three men, all of whom were on a list of wanted people the Israeli government had given to Arafat. On Jan. 7, 2002, he authorized the payment of $350 each to 12 men who were all "active terrorists . . . every single one of them on our wanted lists," said Israeli Col. Miri Eisen, a military intelligence officer.

Cabinet minister Dan Meridor said the documents meant Arafat no longer could claim he did not know the details of what his own activists were doing.

"Mr. Arafat is the head of a terrorist organization," Meridor said. "This is why we are treating him in this way."[65]

Two weeks later Israeli claims about what the seized documents revealed were still making headlines. On April 19 anchor Tom Brokaw introduced an *NBC Nightly News* report billed as an in-depth investigation into the funding of Palestinian terrorism, telling viewers that correspondent Martin Fletcher had "studied those documents for himself." In addition to quoting one such document at length, he interviewed both an Israeli and a Palestinian source. Nevertheless, he provided no glue to cement the contents of the documents into coherent proof of Israeli claims. Instead, the report relied on specious logic: the material contained in the documents proved the Israeli case because Israel said it needed no further proof—the Palestinian rebuttal notwithstanding.

> FLETCHER: NBC News spent hours poring over the documents and followed a money trail, a trail the Israelis say leads from Arafat's signature to a mass murder at a bat mitzvah hall. To Israeli Army Colonel Miri Eisen, the papers are a smoking gun.
>
> COLONEL MIRI EISEN (Israeli Army Intelligence): You have to find the money, and if you follow the money, you'll find the terrorist.
>
> FLETCHER: And the money comes from Arafat?
>
> COLONEL EISEN: The money comes from the treasury, but the person who tells the treasury to pay these terrorists is Arafat personally.
>
> FLETCHER: The Israelis claim the trail starts here with this document dated Sept. 19, 2001. It's from Hussein al Sheik, an Arafat aide, ad-

dressed to, quote, "the fighting president, Yasser Arafat." It requests $2,500 each to be paid to three, quote, "brethren." But Arafat keeps a tight grip on the bottom line, knocking it down to $600. The Israelis say this is Arafat's signature.

Among his recipients, Ra'ed Karmi. Karmi was the notorious commander here in Tulkarem of the Tanzim, Arafat's militia. He's a local hero, but Israeli intelligence accuses him of numerous attacks against Israelis and of heading a local terror network that killed dozens. The Israelis say [in] this document, dated Jan. 7 this year, Karmi himself requested money for 12 of his men. Here's Arafat's signature okaying the request.

One of the men who received $350 is Mansur Saleh Sharim, who Israel claims had the job of planning suicide attacks. [On] Jan. 18, Sharim sends a gunman to this bat mitzvah party in Hadera. The shooter whipped out an automatic rifle, shot the guard, barged in and killed six guests. Case closed for Israel.

COLONEL EISEN: I think what we've shown is the direct connection of Arafat personally with his own signature, funding terrorists—and funding terrorists is part of terrorism.

MR. MICHAEL TARAZI (PLO legal adviser): Stop. Where is the evidence?

FLETCHER: Legal advisers to the Palestinian Authority object. First, they say Israel may have forged the documents. And second, they ask, "What do they really prove?"

MR. TARAZI: All we know is that they received money. Where is the link to terrorism? Where is the link to terrorism?

FLETCHER: Except that these people are terrorists?

MR. TARAZI: But where is the proof of that?

FLETCHER: Israel says it doesn't need more proof. Arafat is now under virtual house arrest in Ramallah. And Ra'ed el Karmi? Israel assassinated him in mid-January.[66]

Sharon Goes to Washington

On May 5 Sharon and other Israeli officials traveled to Washington for a meeting with Bush two days later. On May 6 the American media were full of reports about the meeting and the set of documents Sharon had brought with him to further press the Israeli case linking Arafat to terrorist activities. In a front-page story the *Washington Post* reported:

As Prime Minister Ariel Sharon arrived in Washington for his fifth Oval Office meeting with President Bush, the Israeli government released a thick report today detailing what it calls the personal support Palestinian leader Yasser Arafat has given to terrorism.

The 103-page report, based partly on documents captured by Israeli forces in Palestinian cities and offices last month, is the most painstaking effort yet by Sharon's government to lay out such a case against Arafat. The Israeli leader has often called Arafat a "terrorist" and his Palestinian Authority a "coalition of terror."[67]

However, since the documents and Israeli claims about them were no longer "new news," reports throughout the mainstream media tended to be more balanced and reserved about the claims than in previous weeks. The *New York Times* reported that the documents "do not appear to show definitively that the Palestinian leader ordered terror attacks. In some documents, Mr. Arafat criticizes certain suicide bombings and the distribution of money from Saudi Arabia to Islamic Jihad and Hamas."[68] The New York *Daily News* reported that the documents Sharon brought with him "do not show a direct link between Arafat and specific acts of violence. Instead, they show Arafat signing off on payments for things like weddings, college tuition, construction costs and family aid to men wanted in Israel for terrorism."[69] The *Washington Post* piece went on to state: "The [Israeli] report features original and translated documents, some of them seized from Palestinian computer disks, along with a great many assertions and allegations for which no documentary proof is offered. Throughout the report, Israel identifies individuals as 'terrorists' without providing evidence to substantiate the characterization."[70]

On CNN's May 6 prime-time broadcast of *Wolf Blitzer Reports*, Sharon foreign policy adviser Daniel Ayalon and PLO legal adviser Tarazi had equal chances to address the documents and the issue of whether Israel should continue to deal with Arafat in the peace process.

> BLITZER (to Ayalon): Are you ready to listen to the president and accept his appeal to you to give Yasser Arafat in effect one last chance?
> DANIEL AYALON: Well, we always listen to the president. As you mentioned quite well, he is our best friend. And we look forward very much to the meeting tomorrow. It's going to be a meeting between friends and allies.
>
> Right now, we have a problem. We deal not only with the man, Arafat, which is a terrorist, but also with the system he created. A

system which is bent on terrorism, on corruption and on tyranny. And this cannot be. There is no coexistence with terror.

BLITZER: Is it too late, though, for him to change? Can he change from your vantage point and still negotiate some sort of settlement with your government?

AYALON: Well he had more than three strikes, so he is definitely out. But we see even today that not only he is not abiding by the commitment to stop terror, but he himself inspires and directs and finances terror. This is not going to change, and it's not changing right now.

In an earlier taped interview Tarazi had told Blitzer:

I've looked at a few of the documents. I know, for example, the 100-page report only has about five documents in it. The rest of it is all Israeli rhetoric. But I have looked at some of the documents that are very similar to the documents that Israel released a few weeks back, and there's nothing new here, Wolf.

There is no link to terrorism. This is simply Yasser Arafat approving funds to go to members of his political party. And it could very well be sustenance payments because of the destroyed economy or salary payments. We're not talking about large numbers here, $300, $600, something to that effect.

The bottom line is Israel doesn't really have any legal case here. But they're not fighting this in the court of law, they're fighting this in the court of public opinion. And Israel, throughout its history, has learned that to win in the court of public opinion you don't need to actually have any evidence, you just need to act as if you do.

We haven't had a chance to sit down and investigate all of these things. You have to remember Israel never likes it when independent third parties come in and actually investigate. You saw that with respect to the Jenin refugee camp and the atrocities committed there.

And you have the same situation here with these alleged documents. We have no idea where these documents came from, how they were discovered. They could very well be forgeries. But frankly, Wolf, even if they're not, they don't prove anything.[71]

The same evening ABC News on *World News Tonight* also broadcast a "curtain-raiser" report intended to preview the Bush-Sharon meeting by providing relevant background. "The documents that Mr. Sharon has brought with him to Washington are part of a larger campaign by this Israeli government to undermine or discredit the Palestinian president," anchor Peter Jennings told viewers. Although similar in format to Fletcher's report on NBC two and a half weeks earlier—Jennings noted that correspondent Gillian Findlay had studied the documents, just as Brokaw said Fletcher had done, and both reports referred to some of the same documents—the ABC report exhibited a much more noticeable degree of journalistic skepticism.

GILLIAN FINDLAY: Israel says it seized the documents in dozens of raids on Palestinian Authority offices. Three of them appear to carry Yasser Arafat's signature. In this one, dated last September, Arafat authorized the payment of $600 each for three members of his Fatah political party. One of them was Ra'ed Karmi, who in an interview with ABC News a month earlier had admitted killing Israeli civilians. Israel says a second man on the list later masterminded this attack in which six Israelis died.

MR. DANI NAVEH (Israeli cabinet minister): He knew for sure that these people are involved in terrorist attacks.

FINDLAY: But did Arafat know? According to the document, the request was simply for "financial aid."

MR. MICHAEL TARAZI (Palestinian Authority legal adviser): All they show is that President Arafat allowed financial transfers to members of his Fatah party, and that is a perfectly normal thing for him to do.

FINDLAY: The report is even more damning in what it says about some of Mr. Arafat's closest aides, including one of the Palestinian Authority's top financial advisers. This is a letter Israel says that the Al-Aqsa Martyrs Brigades wrote to him asking for money to carry out attacks against Israelis.

The "greatest expense" the letter says is for materials to make explosive charges and bombs. "One charge costs 700 shekels. We need five to nine every week." A second letter asked for construction materials, "$25,000 for a lathe, $40,000 for milling machines."

MR. NAVEH: What is the purpose of these materials if not for explosives?

FINDLAY: Israel insists the group was building a heavy-weapons factory. But nothing in the document proves that. Nor is there anything to show that Mr. Arafat or the financial adviser approved either request.

MR. TARAZI: I'm an American attorney. If I went into a court of law right now and made the arguments that Israel is making, I would be laughed out of court.

FINDLAY: The difference is this battle is being fought in the court of public opinion.[72]

The documents Sharon brought with him also alleged a Saudi connection to Palestinian suicide bombings. On May 6 the Associated Press reported that "Israel accused Saudi Arabia of encouraging Palestinian bomb attacks against Israeli civilians, including one that also killed a U.S. citizen in 1985."[73] CNN Jerusalem correspondent Mike Hanna also reported the Saudi angle that day, observing that the Israeli documents sought not only to impugn and discredit Arafat but also to challenge the very assumptions underlying U.S. peacemaking policy, which viewed the Saudis as playing a key role in leading the Arab world to comprehensive peace with Israel.

Despite the ongoing argument between Israelis and Palestinians about the documents, the critical issue ultimately is what the U.S. president thinks of them and what course of action he takes, if any at all, based on them. And it's not just the rocky U.S. relationship with Yasser Arafat that is at stake.

The two constants of recent U.S. policy have been, firstly, that Yasser Arafat is a man with whom negotiations take place. And, secondly, that Saudi Arabia has a critical role to play in any negotiation process. But on page 67 of this briefing paper, the Israeli allegation [is] that Saudi Arabia is financially supporting families of suicide bombers, and that it is directly funding Hamas and Islamic Jihad, two extremist groups that the U.S. has labeled terrorist organizations.

In short, this document questions the very assumptions on which U.S. involvement in the Middle East is based.[74]

Two days later Eisen, the Israeli intelligence officer, told CNN that the Palestinians "are getting prize money. They are getting prize money from the Saudis, and the Saudis know it."[75]

Two months later the Israeli Hebrew-language daily *Yediot Aharonot* published a 4,800-word report on the confiscated Palestinian documents, which, according to the paper, totaled half a million. Reporter Ronen Bergman wrote that he had been given special access by IDF intelligence to examine a handful of the documents and that the contents of most he referred to in the report were being published for the first time. One such document was a daily Arab media briefing provided to Arafat detailing a report by the London-based, Saudi-owned MBC network on Saudi donations to families of suicide bombers. Arafat, the Israeli newspaper reported, made a note next to the item "to immediately check with the Saudis why this money was going directly to the families and not passing through the PA's coffers. From this point starts a wearisome correspondence between the Palestinian ambassador to Riyadh and the kingdom's authorities. The documents show that the Saudis, politely but firmly, did not agree to transfer the money via the PA, and they kept their reasons to themselves."[76]

Bush and Sharon met on May 7 but were unable to agree on the U.S. position that peace talks should result in an eventual Palestinian state. As the two leaders were meeting, a suicide bomber killed sixteen people and wounded fifty-five in a pool hall in the town of Rishon Letzion, near Tel Aviv. Sharon cut short his visit to the United States and returned to Israel.

For Want of a Smoking Gun

On May 8 CNN correspondent David Ensor reported that "just minutes before the blast, Israeli officials in Washington were showing a mock-up of the terrorists' favorite weapon, a vest filled with homemade explosives costing, they said, only about $200." Israeli officials, Ensor said, hoped to use the intelligence to convince the Bush administration that Sharon "should not have to sit down and negotiate with a government headed by Yasser Arafat." However, he also added that "U.S. officials say from what they have seen so far of the documents, they don't see smoking-gun evidence of Arafat ordering terrorism."[77]

In the same CNN report Eisen had said: "Everybody is ready for me to bring out the documents in which it says that Arafat writes, 'please do a suicide bombing on the 17th of March somewhere.' We are not going to find that. He is paying the terrorists. He knows very well what they are doing." Reports in the Israeli press indicated that, lacking that smoking gun—to which CNBC's Chris Matthews and NBC's Fletcher had so definitively referred in their April reports—the IDF's challenge was to be able to make a convincing case that what it claimed Arafat knew, thought, and acted on was what the Palestinian leader actually did know, think, and act on. *Haaretz* observed: "The Arafat file does not provide proof that Arafat gave direct orders for terror attacks. In some documents he authorizes payments for operatives defined as 'brother warriors.' . . . The most incriminating part of the Arafat file would appear to be documents bearing the PA chairman's signature, which authorize payments to people Israel regards as Fatah terrorists."[78]

The *Yediot Aharonot* piece noted: "It seems that no one today, with the exception of perhaps the PA, disputes the authenticity of the documents. The problem of the IDF's credibility is in its analysis of them. Until now, for example, there hasn't been found even one document in which Arafat has signed an order to carry out an attack or a statement that he knows that someone or other will carry out an attack; neither do intelligence branch personnel expect to find something like this."[79]

On May 17 the *New York Times* reported that a State Department report sent to Congress the same week of the Bush-Sharon meeting "found 'no conclusive evidence' that Yasser Arafat or other senior Palestinian leaders planned or approved specific terrorist attacks on Israel in the six months that ended in December, an assertion sharply at odds with recent Israeli claims." According to the *Times*, the State Department report, which got limited play in the U.S. mainstream media, also said "'the weight of evidence' suggests that Palestinian leaders knew their subordinates were involved in violence and 'did little to rein them in' or punish them."[80] Two months later, the *Yediot Aharonot* report on the documents cache said much the same thing. Referring to the "hundreds of thousands of documents" that were seized during the incursion, Bergman wrote that "only a small part . . . have been translated and studied as of today." The report continued: "Beginning in 1997, Arafat and his cohorts began to willfully and systematically create, in gross violation of the agreements they signed with Israel, a series of militias, shadow armies that are seemingly unconnected to the Palestinian Authority. . . . From the documents, it arises in an unequivocal fashion that even when it was clear to senior PA officials that members of their security services were involved in terror, not only did they take no action against them, but they continued to finance them."[81]

According to a report in the *Jerusalem Post*, while addressing a meeting of an international Zionist organization in Jerusalem on June 19, Eisen had trumpeted the PR successes associated with the incursion. "The impact of what we managed to do in North America has been huge," she said. "Within a four-week period, all polls showing that people who believed Arafat to be a terrorist and unreliable went way up."[82]

Five days later, on June 24, in Washington, President Bush gave a signature speech on U.S. Mideast policy that appeared to deliver to Israel its objective of American approval to exclude Yasser Arafat—until then the United States had recognized him as the legitimate, if somewhat unsavory, leader of the Palestinians—from the peace process. Without referring to Arafat by name, Bush said: "I call on the Palestinian people to elect new leaders not compromised by terror. Today, Palestinian authorities are encouraging, not opposing, terrorism. This is unacceptable."

Bush urged the Palestinians to adopt democratic reforms, including legislative elections and the drafting of a constitution, that could lead to an independent state by 2005. "When the Palestinian people have new leaders, new institutions and new security arrangements with their neighbors," Bush said, "the United States of America will support the creation of a Palestinian state."

Bush called on Israel, for its part, to withdraw to positions it held in the West Bank before the beginning of the intifada and to stop enlarging settlements in the West Bank and Gaza Strip. Bush said he envisioned that the borders and certain aspects of Palestinian sovereignty would be "provisional until resolved as part of a final settlement in the Middle East." Ultimately, he said, Israel would end the occupation through a negotiated settlement based on UN resolutions calling on the Jewish state to withdraw to "secure and recognized borders."[83]

A Case Study in IDF Propaganda: "The Arafat Papers" on *60 Minutes*

Like Michael Tarazi, the American-born lawyer serving as a legal adviser to the PLO, the IDF's Colonel Eisen was born in the United States and spoke to the international press in clear, American-accented English. "Eisen is part of Israel's new pre-emptive offensive," the *Jerusalem Post* reported in June 2002 of the chief media spokeswoman for Israeli army intelligence. "Instead of responding to Palestinian allegations against Israel, she brings up Israel's issues, stating what terrorism is and citing collaborative facts."[84] The next day *Post* readers learned more about Eisen in the paper's weekly gossip column:

> How long does it take to become an international television star? Would you believe less than three months? That's certainly the case with Col. Miri Eisen, the San Francisco-born IDF intelligence officer, who as a 9-year-old child came with her parents to live in Israel in 1971. . . . Eisen, who has the distinction of being the first Israeli intelligence officer to be exposed to television cameras, has been speaking on Israel's behalf for several years, but only since the end of March this year has she been a special spokeswoman for the IDF, featured on television screens around the world.[85]

On September 29 Eisen appeared on American television screens from coast to coast when she was featured as the centerpiece of a report broadcast on the CBS News program *60 Minutes.* Entitled "The Arafat Papers," it was reported from Israel by correspondent Lesley Stahl. In the segment Eisen presented Israeli allegations that widened the scope of Arab and Muslim complicity in terror operations against Israel beyond Arafat and the Saudi regime. Assisted by Stahl, Eisen asserted that the document cache that the IDF had seized in March and April contained newly mined proof that Iran and Iraq had also been collaborating with the Palestinians to foment suicide bombings and other acts of terror.

Notable for its imbalanced sourcing and Stahl's presentation of Israeli claims virtually unchallenged, "The Arafat Papers" represented a stunning if exceptional example of an American mainstream media outlet disseminating Israeli propaganda with implications beyond the realm of the Israeli-Palestinian conflict, and as such merits a detailed content analysis. Reminiscent of the exaggerated claims and false characterizations about Saddam Hussein's Iraq made by Iraqi exiles and reported largely uninvestigated by top American mainstream media outlets, the IDF claims reported by *60 Minutes* amounted to transparent Israeli advocacy for a U.S. war in Iraq.

The report consisted of six short segments in which Stahl interviewed four sources, three of them from the IDF: Eisen, another senior Israeli intelligence officer, and the IDF major general who headed Israel's northern command. Stahl interviewed her fourth source, a Palestinian prisoner in the custody of the IDF, through an interpreter. At no point in the piece did Stahl consult any other Palestinian source to comment on or rebut the IDF's claims.

Stahl introduced the first segment—an exchange with Eisen—by saying that among the seized Palestinian documents, Israel had found "a paper trail of terror leading from both Iran and Iraq." This, Stahl said, led the Israelis to conclude that the intifada "is neither an uprising, nor homegrown. It is, they claim, violence planned, funded and directed largely from Iran and Iraq." Stahl referred to the Israeli discoveries in the documents as "smoking guns"—a term that her IDF sources did not use on camera—and she equated the IDF's interpretations of the documents with proof of IDF claims about what they revealed. The first exchange between Eisen and Stahl established a pattern for the report as a whole. Stahl would state a specific assertion, with or without attribution to the IDF. Then an IDF source would add general or vague statements that were related to the assertions but did not prove them.

EISEN: We went into what is the equivalent of the Palestinian CIA, the Palestinian FBI, the Palestinian Bureau of Education and the Palestinian Treasury.

STAHL: And you're going through these methodically looking for what? Acts of terrorism, bank accounts, weapons, that kind of thing?

EISEN: Anything we can find. It can be files about terrorism, it can be descriptions of terrorist acts. . . . We've taken their mind, to a certain degree. We took their database.

STAHL: And in it, she said, they were surprised to find connections between Arafat and a terrorist in Iraq. The database, she said, is filled with smoking guns. Smoking gun number one: That Iraq has infiltrated teams of operatives and weapons into Israel for what Israeli intelligence considers megaterrorism. This puts Iraq in the terror business to a far greater degree than the Israelis had realized.

Stahl then interviewed Ido Hecht, a senior intelligence official who, according to her, "told us that the Israelis have caught and interrogated members of a Palestinian terrorist cell who admitted they were trained in Iraq by Iraqis this past June." However, Stahl did not ask Hecht how it would have been possible for a Palestinian terror cell to cross the Israeli border into Jordan from the West Bank en route to Iraq and then to return across the Israeli border with Jordan undetected by military border patrols.

HECHT: They were trained in an Iraqi base near Tikrit, Saddam's hometown and a Republican Guard installation. They were trained by people from the Iraqi intelligence. So this was an operation that had full Iraqi backing.

STAHL: What were they trained specifically to do?

HECHT: Firearms of various types, RPG, anti-tank rockets, how to manufacture explosives, how to make those explosives into actual bombs.

STAHL: And most alarmingly, he said, they were taught how to shoot down an airliner.

HECHT: The training included use of shoulder-launched anti-aircraft missiles, equivalent to the American Stinger, SA-18.

STAHL: Were they given specific instructions, to shoot down—what— a civilian aircraft, a military aircraft?

HECHT: We don't know about the specific instructions, but they were operating in the area of Ramallah. They had information about Ben Gurion Airport. Ben Gurion Airport is a civilian airport. Ra-

mallah is next to Ben Gurion Airport, so the obvious target would
be a civilian airliner.

Stahl did not ask Hecht why, having extracted considerable detail on the
training the cell had allegedly received in Iraq, IDF interrogators were unable
to learn the specific instructions the Palestinians had purportedly been given
about targets. Furthermore, she let pass the questionable logic that because
Ramallah is near Ben Gurion Airport, it was obvious the target would have
been a civilian airliner. She then informed her viewers of an astonishing Israeli
claim, saying: "Saddam Hussein has been using the Palestinian Authority as
a middleman in his illegal selling of oil." Stahl did not ask Hecht or Eisen
for supporting details, such as how Arafat would have arranged for transport
of the contraband oil, who bought it, or where the money trail led. Instead,
Eisen made more vague and unsubstantiated statements.

STAHL: So Saddam Hussein was using the Palestinian Authority—Arafat—to smuggle oil, and giving them what? Kickbacks, is that what
you'd say?

EISEN: That would be the term, that's true. It's kickback money.

STAHL: Do you know how much money the Palestinian Authority
made that way?

EISEN: We don't know exact sums, but it's certainly in [the] millions
and probably in double-digit numbers.

The third segment began with footage of Stahl and Eisen looking at various
weapons—seized not during the incursion in March and April but from a
cargo ship in January—everything, Stahl said, "from rockets to land mines;
machine guns and guided missiles run remotely with a joystick. Just as troubling were the tons of explosives." Eisen then demonstrated how suicide
bombers load their explosive belts by motioning around her own waist with
sticks of the plastic explosive C-4 and cautioning Stahl not to touch it. After
more footage of the weapons, the visuals then shifted to images of an unidentified Iranian city, with a voice-over of Stahl sharing with her viewers the
conjecture that "the weapons may have been paid for by Iraqi oil money, but
they came from Iran, another country in President Bush's axis of evil. Iraq is a
threat, but Israel considers Iran an even bigger and more immediate threat."

To illustrate the alleged Iranian connection, the fourth segment showed
Stahl on the Israeli side of the border with Lebanon. Looking at the camera,
Stahl said that Israel considers Iran a bigger and more immediate threat than
Iraq, "because of its links to various terrorist organizations like Hezbollah.

We're on an Israeli army post in the north, only a stone's throw from positions manned by Hezbollah guerrillas." After repeated references to the proximity between Israel and Hezbollah—to whose lookouts Stahl waved and said hello, telling viewers that "they won't talk to us"—she then interviewed Major General Benny Gantz, head of Israel's northern command. Once again Stahl spoke for one of her IDF sources, saying that according to Gantz "Iran funds, equips and trains Hezbollah and tells it what to do. He says Iranians are even operating here." Gantz's own on-camera comments were of a vague and general nature, however.

GANTZ: A few weeks ago, we had Iranian patrols, you know, like supervisors or experts that came with Hezbollah and patrolled the entire area from the mountain to the ocean, along the border.
STAHL: Right here?
GANTZ: Absolutely, ma'am.
STAHL: Iranians themselves here?
GANTZ: Iranians with Hezbollah all along this area.

The discussion of Iran then shifted back to Eisen, with Stahl herself continuing to articulate IDF assertions. Eisen claimed, somewhat evasively, that Iran had also been training Palestinians for terror operations against Israelis. Once again Stahl failed to ask how that would have been logistically possible.

STAHL: But what they're doing along the border is only part of the picture. Iran supports other militant organizations inside Israel and the territories. The captured documents spell out how much money Iran spends to do that.
EISEN: $400,000, $700,000. These are huge sums of money to buy weapons, to train, to fund, to educate.
STAHL: Are the Iranians doing training themselves?
EISEN: We have been interrogating hundreds, thousands of Palestinians from April of this year, and talking to them, we have found some that have been trained in Iran.
STAHL: Trained for what? For suicide?
EISEN: Let's put it this way, they weren't taught how to—you know, Chemistry 101.
STAHL: No, but for what? Bomb making? What?
EISEN: Explosives—we've had divers in the Gaza Strip trying to get into Israel proper through the sea—taught their diving capability in Iran.

In the fifth segment, Stahl interviewed Palestinian prisoner Haj Ali Safuri. Referring to a set of seized Palestinian Authority documents in her lap, Stahl began to interrogate Safuri through an interpreter, first telling her viewers— and without attribution to an IDF source—that "Iran provides training and funding to the terrorist organization this man belongs to. Haj Ali Safuri, now in Israeli custody, admitted that he helped plan suicide attacks." It was Stahl herself who intimated a connection between Iran and Safuri. Not asked about it, Safuri made no mention of ever having been in contact with Iranians. More- over, so completely did Stahl appear to identify with her Israeli sources that she characterized the Palestinian Authority documents as describing Safuri "as a prominent terrorist leader." While it is more than likely that Israeli intelligence sources would use such a description, it is also a virtual certainty that the PA would not refer to Safuri or any other Palestinian involved in acts of resistance to the occupation—violent or otherwise—as a terrorist.

> SAFURI (through interpreter): I did arrange martyrdom operations in-
> side the territory of Palestine. I don't dispute any of that.
> STAHL: Haj Ali is a leader of the Palestinian Islamic Jihad, another
> Iranian proxy. [To Safuri:] I have some documents from the Pales-
> tinian Authority.
>
>   (voice-over): I read to him his description in the document as
> a prominent terrorist leader. . . . The Israelis say the man you're
> looking at masterminded and set in motion at least 10 suicide at-
> tacks. I quoted to him from one of the documents taken from
> Arafat's compound, which says . . . [to Safuri]: You played an im-
> portant role in preparing explosive belts and explosive charges.
> You made them. This true?
> SAFURI: I would defend my people in every manner at my disposal,
> whether by explosive belts, explosive charges or by opening fire.
> STAHL: Did you?
> SAFURI: I did. I did prepare them.

In the final segment Stahl had another exchange with Eisen. Stahl articu- lated an IDF claim that, "according to the documents, Haj Ali's group and other militant organizations funded by Iran were instructed by Iran to com- mit their terrorist attacks at critical junctures." The *60 Minutes* report itself seemed to come at a critical juncture as well, just two and a half weeks after President Bush had delivered a speech at the United Nations in which he said that, in the wake of the September 11 attacks, the United States would go to war against Iraq unilaterally if need be in order to protect Americans from terrorist dangers emanating from Saddam Hussein's regime. Stahl ended her piece by claiming that a link existed between alleged Iraqi and Iranian complicity in Palestinian terror attacks in Israel and the terror attacks of 9/11. Eisen provided no context for the bloodshed occurring on the ground between Israelis and Palestinians at the time of the terrorist attacks in the United States when, she alleged, Iran had directed Palestinians to maintain the pace of suicide bombings. Having offered no concrete proof of the alleged Iraqi and Iranian ties to Palestinian attacks, Eisen substituted her own interpretation of what the Iraqis and Iranians must have been thinking—which conveniently echoed the Bush administration's claim that potential terror threats emanating from Iraq constituted a casus belli.

> STAHL (voice-over): Colonel Eisen showed us a document from Arafat's files about meetings of terrorist groups in late October 2001, just six weeks after 9/11. Iran sent a message telling the groups, "You must not allow a calming down at this period. Carry out suicide attacks against Israeli targets in Gaza, in the West Bank and inside Israel." [To Eisen]: What do you think [was] Iran's main motive in asking that they increase the violence here after 9/11?
>
> EISEN: 9/11 is a watershed day in the world, certainly for those who are for violence, because for them, they're now the ones who are in the focus of the axis of evil.
>
> STAHL: What we certainly have seen is a diversion from what happened at the World Trade Center and at the Pentagon to the violence in Israel.
>
> EISEN: What we have here is a document which says, for the Iranians, "Let's divert the attention from us, the Iranians." I think the Iraqi documents say, "From us, the Iraqis, to the Palestinian issue." Sadly, I can say that they've almost made it work. I think that the world's attention has been that the Palestinian issue is the problem, and everybody has sort of forgotten that the Iranians fund it, that the Iraqis fund it, that they send in these terrorists and that they train them from afar."

In the closing minutes of the interview, Stahl introduced the sole hint of journalistic skepticism, asking Eisen about the timing of Israeli allegations about Iran and Iraq.

> STAHL: People in the States are going to want to know why you're putting this information out now, and a question will come to mind whether this is meant as ammunition for President Bush to go after Iraq.

EISEN: The Iraqi documents we've only had for around six weeks. So
for us, it's a question of bringing them out as we study them and
understand them.
STAHL: But you know that people are going to think that.
EISEN: Should we, because of that, keep it under wraps, when at the
end, for us, it's important to show the whole picture of what's going
on here in the Palestinian Authority areas?[86]

The sensational spin that the CBS newsmagazine had put on the allegations made by Eisen and her colleagues notwithstanding, neither the Israeli nor the American media picked up the story put forth by *60 Minutes* in
any significant way, either in the six months from the time the IDF seized
the documents to the time of the CBS broadcast or in the months that followed.[87] References to the Palestinian-Iraqi connections that the seized documents allegedly showed and that the *60 Minutes* segment highlighted had
surfaced previously in Israeli press reports. However, they either tended to be
passing or vague references that did not link such contacts and associations to
the actual attempt or commission of terror acts by Palestinians against Israeli
targets or they were unsubstantiated IDF claims asserting that such contacts
constituted proof of Iraqi collusion in Palestinian terror.[88]

The single exception appeared to be the reference in Stahl's piece to the
attempt by a Palestinian cell trained in Iraq to infiltrate Israel and shoot
down planes over Ben Gurion Airport. At the time of the CBS broadcast,
however, this was apparently old news. An Associated Press advance story
on the *60 Minutes* segment reported: "In November 2001, Israeli officials
said they had arrested a group linked to [the Iraq-based Palestinian guerrilla Mohammed] Abbas which had planned attacks on targets including
Ben Gurion airport and some in Jerusalem."[89] The *60 Minutes* presentation of the IDF allegations seemed to confirm an observation in a *Haaretz*
analysis published in May 2002, about a month after the documents were
seized: "It appears that the uncovering of various documents during [Op-
eration] Defensive Shield furnished Israeli spokesmen with materials to
substantiate charges that had previously been based on classified intelligence information."[90]

The Israeli daily *Maariv* published an advance story on the *60 Minutes*
piece and the IDF claims it contained, while *Haaretz* published advance and
follow-up stories. However, both papers reiterated the claims made on the
broadcast without confirming them—and *Maariv*, unlike CBS, went to the
trouble of getting a response from the Palestinian Authority. The Israeli paper quoted a PA official's denial: "Just as the U.S. tries to find a connection

between al-Qaʿeda and Saddam, Israel is trying to find a connection between Arafat and the Iraqi ruler."[91]

The media silence in both countries on the revolutionary intifada theory put forth by Stahl—namely, that Israel's trouble with the Palestinians was not the result of a homegrown, popular uprising in response to a failed peace process and an ongoing thirty-five-year military occupation but rather an Iranian-Iraqi export—cast a shadow of doubt if not on the credibility of the IDF's claims, then on the overreliance by *60 Minutes* on Israeli military sources in reporting them. In her report Stahl appeared to be delivering breaking news courtesy of the IDF—an impression articulated by members of the Washington press corps at a routine State Department briefing the next day but dismissed by spokesman Richard Boucher in the following exchange:

> QUESTION: Did you get a chance to see the *60 Minutes* piece on Sunday that disclosed what looked like new information from the Israelis showing that there was not only a financial link between Iraq and some of the terrorists in the West Bank, but there was also a significant amount of training? And I was wondering . . .—I understand that there was an Israeli delegation that may have presented some of this information last week to State Department—what you thought of some of these things that were put out on *60 Minutes*.
>
> BOUCHER: Frankly, I didn't see the show. I'm not sure if others did, but I don't have any particular comment on somebody else's television show.
>
> QUESTION: Is there anything you can say on the record about something more than financial links between Iraq and some of the terror groups operating in the West Bank?
>
> BOUCHER: We've talked about that on various occasions in the past, but I don't have anything new right now.
>
> QUESTION: It's in the terror book?[92]
>
> BOUCHER: Yeah.
>
> QUESTION: On the training?
>
> QUESTION: It's not in the terror report! This is training. It's a totally new thing.
>
> QUESTION: Okay, sorry.
>
> QUESTION: It's a totally new thing. It's not in the terror report.[93]

The only American media outlet that appeared to pick up on the *60 Minutes* piece was Fox News,[94] where the IDF claims transmitted by CBS enjoyed a ripple effect in a conservative media pond and venue for advocating a U.S. war in Iraq. With no further reporting on or validation of the claims in Stahl's piece, Fox News commentator Bill O'Reilly reiterated the alleged ties between Saddam Hussein and Palestinian terrorists four times in the eleven days following the CBS broadcast.[95] O'Reilly made each of the four references to the *60 Minutes* piece in the context of arguing for the necessity of war. He would refer to the alleged Iraqi-Palestinian terror connection, independent of the *60 Minutes* report, another three times before the start of the war in March 2003.[96]

On the October 3, 2002, edition of his show *The O'Reilly Factor*, O'Reilly told viewers that the *60 Minutes* report had showed "captured Palestinian documents that say flat out Saddam is training and paying for bombers that kill innocent Jewish women and children." On the October 7 show, during an interview with former U.S. labor secretary Robert Reich, O'Reilly said: "You don't really want this guy [Saddam Hussein] to stay there. You know that he's training terrorists to blow up Jewish babies in Israel. You know what he's doing. You don't really want him to stay there." Later in the same broadcast, O'Reilly opined: "*60 Minutes* a couple of weeks ago gets all these Palestinian-captured [*sic*] documents that show Saddam Hussein is training and funding Palestinian suicide bombers. I don't think containment has worked. I think the guy is sending out people to commit terrorism all over the world, and the proof was right there in those documents."

REPORTING THE APEX THROUGH A FRAME

In reporting the deaths and trauma suffered by Israeli and Palestinian civilians during the violent spring of 2002, the U.S. media exhibited balance as well as an appetite for excruciating emotional detail. In reporting the larger, organic political framework underlying the deaths and trauma, however, the media fell critically short.

It does not necessary follow—and it would be simplistic to conclude—that, through Operation Defensive Shield, Israel achieved its ultimate political objective of sidelining Yasser Arafat from the peace process—with a nod of approval from the White House—as a result of having won the PR battle that it had staged through the media. Several factors independent of the media converged to produce that result, perhaps the most significant being the impact of continued Palestinian suicide bombings in Israel in the months following the terror attacks of September 11, 2001, in the United States. The killing of civilians in these two circumstances, no matter how distinct their origins, had similar effects on the American and Israeli publics. Furthermore, the declaration by President Bush of a "war on terrorism" lent credence if not justification to the Sharon government's tactic of dealing with suicide bombings through harsh and accelerated military means.

Given those similarities—and with the Bush administration having already installed one leader in Afghanistan while making plans for the "regime change" that would soon follow in Iraq—it is not surprising that the administration would likewise view the marginalization of Yasser Arafat as being of a piece with broader policy. The notion that the United States could and should, directly or indirectly, implant a new breed of leaders throughout the Arab and Muslim worlds in order to bring peace and stability to the region emerged as a staple of Bush policy in the aftermath of September 11—a policy that, as so often in the history of the American-Israeli alliance, dovetailed the interests and objectives of the two countries in a near-seamless fashion.

So seamless, in fact, that the discourse emanating from the White House and Israeli sources was often virtually identical, their common conduit being an uncritical media. Just as Bush had declared in June 2002 that "today, Palestinian authorities are encouraging, not opposing, terrorism," so an Israeli military official told the *New York Times* in September 2003, "You'll never find Arafat giving a direct order for terror. That's not his method. What we have are a series of clear signs that he supports, and does not prevent, terrorism."[97]

Politics and policy aside, however, patterns of coverage in U.S. mainstream reporting of the Israeli-Palestinian conflict in the spring of 2002 raise several questions. The first is why American journalists reported many aspects of the story from perspectives favoring—if not parroting—IDF claims. The answer would appear to be that rather than seeing the events of that bloody spring as the apex of the spiral of occupation, the media accepted the Sharon government's frame that Israel was waging a war on terror. Furthermore, media framing followed but did not overstep the bounds of the political discourse emanating from the White House. In the first week of the Israeli incursion into the West Bank, with images of destruction and devastation on television screens around the world serving as an irritant to the administration's plans to go to war in Iraq, Bush had at first asked and then almost demanded of his ally Sharon to pull back. The implicit criticism of Israeli actions embedded in those requests gave the U.S. media an opening to report in great detail on the physical devastation of Palestinian ministries and the anger and humiliation felt by Palestinians.

However, the larger framing of the incursion—as articulated by Sharon, backed by Bush, and accepted by the media—was that Israel had the right to take up arms to "root out the terrorist infrastructure" in order to protect its citizens from suicide bombings. This frame allowed no room for the Palestinians to take up arms through the mechanism of the Palestinian Authority, or to be seen as fighting the ever-increasing military force employed by Sharon, with the IDF often using high-powered American weaponry and killing scores if not hundreds of Palestinian civilians in much greater numbers than the Israelis who had been killed by suicide bombers.

The frequency with which the IDF used Apache helicopters and F-16 fighter jets against Palestinian targets escalated sharply after Sharon became prime minister in February 2001, yet these tactics drew a muted public rebuke from the Bush administration. By contrast, in the months prior to the incursion, the administration had become visibly and vocally angry with Arafat over the *Karine A* affair, in which Israel intercepted a ship carrying high-powered weapons apparently intended for the Palestinians. With Arafat denying knowledge of or connection to the affair, in February 2002 Secretary of State Colin Powell told a congressional committee: "He should have known, and may well have known. I just can't prove that he did know or had direct control over the operation. But it's close enough that the [Palestinian] Authority has to take responsibility for it."[98] Bush's speech that June, in which the president signaled that the United States would no longer deal with Arafat, indicated that similar logic was in play.

A second question is why American correspondents, purporting to report objectively on a conflict in which the U.S. was not a physical participant, would themselves physically participate in ride-along missions with the IDF—a foreshadowing in miniature of the embedding of American reporters with U.S. troops during the war in Iraq. In the latter case, American journalists were riding along with their countrymen to report a war that their own country was fighting. The same could not be said of American journalists riding in Israeli patrols through the streets of Bethlehem and the countryside of the northern West Bank.

A third question is why high-profile American broadcast journalists, such as Ted Koppel and Lesley Stahl, would rely primarily or exclusively on IDF sources in reporting stories in which Israel stood to gain a clear PR advantage—while at the same time, with a wink and a nod, acknowledging to their viewers an awareness of the PR game being played.

The answers to these questions would appear to be that in being led by—if not riding along with—the IDF, American journalists were operating within the sphere of cultural congruence—a comfort zone where journalistic skepticism and balance were often overshadowed or displaced by the political discourse of the Bush administration, in which a "war on terror" could be prosecuted by the United States and, by extension, its closest ally.

The implicit framing of a one-sided, Israeli-Palestinian war found in U.S.

mainstream media reporting during the bloody spring of 2002 contrasts sharply with other Western journalistic coverage of the same events. One such example, a one-hour BBC report entitled "Battle for the Holy Land," aired in the United States on the PBS documentary series *Frontline* in April 2002. Unlike American coverage, the BBC report represented an in-depth examination of—and gave equal time to—Israeli military pursuit of Palestinian suicide bombers as well as Palestinians who had taken up arms, including suicide bombs, to fight the Israeli occupation. The report portrayed the conflict as a two-sided war and allowed combatants on both sides to express the rationales for their actions and their causes. Thus, viewers could judge for themselves the value of these conflicting arguments rather than have the debate framed for them. The report began:

> Five times during Holy Week [Easter and Passover 2002], Palestinian suicide bombers attacked Israeli civilians. The Israeli army counterattacked, isolating Yasser Arafat inside his compound. There were mass arrests and deaths.
>
> Full-scale war is in the air. How did events in the Middle East spin so dramatically out of control? . . .
>
> Last December, two BBC film teams achieved remarkable access to the fighters from both sides for a one-month period. What they found shows how this war plays itself out on the battlefields.[99]

The American media's tendency to frame such issues differently was observed by a reader of the *Chicago Tribune* in a May 2002 letter to the editor that noted this difference as well as the effects of such U.S. reporting on American public opinion, Mideast policy, and chances for peace. Responding to an op-ed column that had attributed a higher level of sympathy for Palestinians among Europeans than Americans to "fundamentally opposing worldviews," the letter writer argued that those sympathies were instead the result of "a simpler reason"—differing media coverage.

> Having traveled to Great Britain, the Netherlands, Ireland and Germany in the past year, I can identify a simpler reason: European media offer a considerably more balanced viewpoint of the conflict and show, in particular, much more of the devastating effects of Israel's policies on the Palestinian population.
>
> Each time I watch European television, I am reminded of how barren the information is that we receive.

Here in the United States, most newspapers and television stations follow the narrative and "terms of debate" put out by the Sharon government. Many articles, in fact, seem to have been lifted directly from Israel Defense Forces press statements. In Europe, one is much more likely to see journalists greet the IDF spin with skepticism.

I personally believe that if more Americans, and more American Jews, were able to see and hear what the Israeli military does to ordinary Palestinians, we would be less likely to support these actions and more likely to call on President Bush to compel Ariel Sharon to end his attacks on an entire people. And if that would happen, terror attacks against Israelis would stop. Then with neither Israelis nor Palestinians living in terror, they could pursue a lasting peace.[100]

5

THE WAR AT HOME

Tell the story of the diversity and magnitude of the human experience
boldly, even when it is unpopular to do so.

Code of Ethics, Society of Professional Journalists

The truth does not change according to our ability to stomach it.

Flannery O'Connor

THE EVENTS OF 2000 TO 2002 MARKED NOT ONLY AN APEX OF VIOLENCE
between Israelis and Palestinians in the century-long history of their conflict. The turmoil and bloodletting on Israeli and Palestinian soil also evoked
reaction worldwide. In the United States partisan constituent groups—pro-
Israel and pro-Palestinian alike—brought an unprecedented level of pressure
to bear on American mainstream news organizations concerning their coverage of the conflict. The media, however, felt the impact from the two sides to
significantly different degrees.

Claims of media bias—and recognition that media coverage of the conflict plays a key role in public opinion vis-à-vis the images of Israelis and
Palestinians and has the potential to affect policy—did not begin with the
start of the second Palestinian intifada in late September 2000. Organized
campaigns to protest American media reporting of the conflict were apparent as early as 1982, when Israel, with Ariel Sharon at the helm as minister of
defense, invaded Lebanon with the goal of driving Yasser Arafat and the Palestine Liberation Organization from Lebanese soil. For the first time since

1948—fueled by media-borne images of the bombing and battering of an already civil war–torn Beirut by Israeli jets—Israel's military actions were perceived to be as much if not more aggressive than defensive. This tarnishing of Israel's image, in turn, generated palpable unease among Israel's supporters in the diaspora.

One local Jewish community's displeasure with Israel's image as reflected in media coverage of the Lebanon war was articulated in a seventy-three-page booklet that critiqued seven weeks of war reporting by the *Washington Post* in June and July 1982. Written by a member of the community and published in 1983 by a regional branch of the Zionist Organization of America, the analysis concluded that the paper's coverage had been "dismaying."

> The *Post*'s presentation of the events of the war, week in and week out, was flawed by bias and distortion, with the cumulative effect of favoring the PLO and its supporters and of presenting a negative image of Israel. *Post* readers—from Capitol Hill staffs to government officials and concerned citizens—had a right to expect objectivity, fairness and balance. Instead, readers were victimized, time and again, by reports which carried an editorial message in the very selection of the news, as well as in the words by which it was conveyed. The nation's capital—and *Post* readers far beyond the Washington area—surely deserved better.

An internal *Post* memo written in February 1984 reported that the critique had raised some valid points, including: inconsistent reporting of Lebanese casualty figures; stories that dealt with "Palestinian people, their life and their leaders" with no parallel "people coverage" of Israelis in the context of the war story; and a failure to label clearly some analytical articles as news analyses. However, the memo also noted that the critique

> contains not a single finding favorable to the *Post*. . . . Time and again, the *Post* is faulted for accepting at face value—or accepting critically but not knocking down—statements by Arabs. Time and again, the *Post* is faulted for failing to accept at face value statements by Jews and Israelis. . . . On using the news columns for image-building, [the author's] main point . . . is that she doesn't want the PLO presented as anything but murders [*sic*] terrorists and thugs, and wants the Palestinian cause presented in nothing but a bloodthirsty light.[1]

Two decades later, American mainstream media reporting of the events of 2000 to 2002 would evoke a thrust and parry between constituent groups and news organizations that had evolved considerably. This evolution was marked by three notable characteristics. First, there was a change on the ground in the United States: pro-Palestinian media-watch and Arab/Muslim advocacy groups had emerged as counterpoints to such long-established pro-Israel groups. While less well funded and with memberships not as efficiently mobilized as their pro-Israel counterparts,[2] these Arab/Muslim/pro-Palestinian groups nonetheless succeeded in projecting—via op-ed pages and in broadcast forums—their views of media coverage of the conflict. Members of a first generation of Arab Americans and American Muslims born and educated in the United States and cognizant of the nexus between media and politics began to make their voices heard on topics of concern to their communities—chief among them being media portrayals of Palestinians and other Arabs and Muslims—and they did so not only as individuals but also through organizations, just as American Jews had long done.

Two other factors contributed to a shift in the intensity and magnitude of U.S.-based constituent groups' outcry over American mainstream media coverage of the conflict in 2000 to 2002, both of which reflected two significant changes in the arena of conflict itself. The first was the emergence of the Palestinians as legitimate actors in the conflict, a direct result of the Oslo peace process, which was officially launched in 1993 with a handshake, brokered by President Bill Clinton, between Israeli prime minister Yitzhak Rabin and Palestinian leader Yasser Arafat. Not only was Arafat to become a frequent visitor at the Clinton White House, but also for the first time since 1948 an internationally recognized Palestinian leader led an internationally accepted Palestinian governing authority—the newly minted Palestinian Authority—operating on Palestinian soil. Virtually overnight the Palestinians' image had been broadened for the better, far beyond the decades-old media stereotypes of refugees and terrorists.

The second factor affecting the correlation between U.S. mainstream media coverage of the conflict and public reaction to it—and perhaps most significant in terms of the sheer intensity of that reaction—was the horrific level of bloodshed between Israelis and Palestinians, beginning with the outbreak of the second Palestinian intifada on September 29, 2000. With emotions running high over mounting casualties among Palestinians and Israelis on Middle Eastern soil, their partisans in the United States responded with unprecedented vehemence to American media organizations as the conduits of this news.

For both sides, the issues of violence, agency, and victimization formed a triangle of urgent concern. From the pro-Palestinian point of view, the media failed to grasp that Israeli occupation was itself a many-faceted source of daily violence against Palestinians, which, except in cases of dramatic or multiple deaths, was reported only selectively and with a paucity of detail. From the pro-Israel point of view, media reporting of the motivations and contexts behind acts of Palestinian violence toward Israelis—reporting on the backgrounds of suicide bombers that went beyond the often shocking outcomes of the violence itself in an attempt to explain its genesis—appeared to lend some kind of moral justification to that violence.

This chapter will address the perception of bias in American mainstream media reporting of the Israeli-Palestinian conflict from a number of perspectives. From the vantage point of newsrooms, it will demonstrate that charges of bias from pro-Israel and pro-Palestinian constituents alike proved to be a powerful force in 2000 to 2002, although pressure was exerted in much greater proportion from the former than the latter. Furthermore, during this period news organizations paid serious attention to their critics and attempted to respond to audience concerns, all the while maintaining that journalistic integrity—not caving in to pressure groups—was of paramount importance.

The perspectives of correspondents who reported the story from the field over a decade and a half—including during the second intifada—corroborate the imbalance in partisan reaction to the coverage and the need to heed audience reaction while maintaining journalistic integrity based on professional standards. Furthermore, several correspondents indicated that pro-Israel media critics perceive the balance of power in the conflict in a way that does not match the reality of Israel's superior strengths on the ground. An examination of four academic studies of media coverage of the conflict—particularly in the period from 2000 to 2002—reveals that when bias in coverage is detected, patterns of news reporting and presentation tend to favor Israel over the Palestinians.

These perspectives demonstrate that journalistic practice and product debunk many common charges of pro-Israel or pro-Palestinian media bias. More important, the concluding analysis of media coverage of a controversial academic paper on the Israel lobby published in 2006 demonstrates that mainstream news organizations persist in presenting a limited range of discourse on the key factor of how U.S. policy affects the trajectory of the Israeli-Palestinian conflict. Although more subtle, this is arguably a far more significant indication of bias in reporting of the conflict—bias in what is *omitted* from the coverage, rather than what is there—than the time-worn and less credible charges from opposing partisan camps that the mainstream media deliberately and systematically tilt their coverage toward Israel or the Palestinians.

THE WAR AT HOME: NEWSROOMS BESIEGED

In the spring of 2002, the level of bloodshed between Israelis and Palestinians commanded an abundance of daily media coverage. However, charges leveled by pro-Israel and pro-Palestinian groups that this coverage was biased also became a story in and of itself—one that the media reported as well. Such reports shared a common theme: while charges of bias were heard from partisans of both sides of the conflict, the accusations were coming primarily—in some cases overwhelmingly—from supporters of Israel.

On April 28 the *Los Angeles Times* ran a 1,900-word report in the front section of the paper headlined "The Middle East: From Jewish Outlook, Media Are Another Enemy." The story began: "Major Jewish organizations and other supporters of Israel in this country have increasingly bombarded newspapers in recent weeks with charges of biased reporting on hostilities in the Mideast." The piece reported that supporters of Israel had targeted the *Los Angeles Times, New York Times,* Minneapolis *Star Tribune, Washington Post,* and *Philadelphia Inquirer* using various forms of protest against the papers' coverage, including calls for a boycott, taking out a full-page ad, and hundreds of calls and e-mails—with the *Times* itself having experienced a protest by almost a thousand subscribers who suspended home delivery of the paper for one day. The *Times* report quoted *Post* ombudsman Michael Getler as stating that "the overwhelming majority [of calls and e-mails are] saying our coverage is pro-Palestinian, anti-Israel." Ned Warwick, foreign editor of the *Inquirer,* said his paper was subjected to "an intense barrage of criticism" from the local Jewish community—"100, 120 e-mails a day, a very sophisticated, ongoing campaign."

Timothy McNulty, associate managing editor for foreign news at the *Chicago Tribune,* told the *Times:* "We're fallible, but we're not biased. A newspaper, as a human institution, can make mistakes. . . . But the mistakes are honest mistakes, not a product of bias in any fashion." The sub-headline to the *Times* story acknowledged that some of the criticism was indeed warranted; the story reported that mistakes in coverage had, in fact, been made, such as both the *Times* and the *San Francisco Chronicle* having "failed to cover major Jewish rallies in their respective cities."

The *Times* story devoted three paragraphs to the charges of bias that were also being made by Arab Americans and other supporters of the Palestinians. It quoted Ahmed Bouzid, president of the Philadelphia-based Palestine Media Watch, as saying, "It's misleading, sloppy coverage that does not relate the true suffering of the Palestinian people." All but these three paragraphs of the story, however, focused on the criticisms and pressure tactics of supporters of Israel. While most of the *Times* report quoted newspaper editors' reactions to the bias charges, it did quote two members of the local Jewish community. John Fishel, president of the Jewish Federation of Greater Los Angeles, said the paper's failure to cover the pro-Israel rally was an indication of "increasing negative bias against Israel . . . that makes more and more people question if there is a conscious decision at the Times to portray Israel in a negative light."[3]

On May 23, the *New York Times* ran a 1,200-word piece in its front section under the headline "Some U.S. Backers of Israel Boycott Dailies Over Mideast Coverage They Deplore." The story's lead paragraph reported that "intense public reaction to coverage of the violence of the Middle East conflict has prompted unusually harsh attacks on several news media outlets and has led to boycotts of The New York Times, The Los Angeles Times and The Washington Post." The second paragraph of the story noted that "the criticism has come largely from supporters of Israel." While reporting that protests had targeted other news outlets, the *Times* story focused on criticisms about its own coverage, quoting three members of the local New York Jewish community. The last three paragraphs of the story reflected pro-Palestinian groups' criticism of overall media coverage of the conflict, quoting two advocates on that side of the controversy.[4]

The *Chicago Tribune* published a 1,900-word report on page 1 of its May 26 edition under the headline "Pro-Israel Groups Take Aim at U.S. News Media." Only two paragraphs in the story reflected pro-Palestinian criticism of reporting of the conflict, with the single quote about that criticism coming from Phil Bronstein, executive editor of the *San Francisco Chronicle*. Elsewhere in the report four prominent American Jews were quoted about pro-Israel criticism of the coverage. Moreover, the opening paragraphs of the *Tribune* piece situated the locus of the controversy squarely in the pro-Israel camp: "The contentious issues of the Middle East have spilled over into the U.S. media as pro-Israel organizations are pressuring news outlets, through boycotts and other measures, to change the way they report on the Israeli-Palestinian conflict. . . . News executives accused of having a pro-Palestinian bias respond that the critics are not seeking evenhanded reporting but advocacy on behalf of Israel."[5]

At Issue: Specific Charges of Bias

Palestinian supporters' specific criticisms of coverage of the conflict appeared in media reports of bias charges leveled by both sides, albeit in a somewhat fleeting way. By contrast, the nature of criticisms about the reporting by supporters of Israel was characterized in a much more detailed and systematic fashion in news reports about the controversy and in letters to the editor published in newspapers and newsmagazines. This disparity was consistent with the imbalance in the abilities of the two sides to marshal both resources and responses in support of their claims.

Pro-Palestinian critics of media coverage tended to focus on the overall narrative of the conflict vis-à-vis the broad issues of occupation, terrorism, and the nature of Zionism itself. Bouzid, who was frequently quoted to represent the Palestinian view, told *Newsday* that "the basic narrative [of the conflict] is not challenged, it has not changed. Why always say the Palestinians are initiating the terrorism?"[6] Quoted in the *New York Times*, Bouzid observed that the media frequently used the word "retaliation" to characterize Israeli attacks on Palestinian targets, which "frames it as a reaction to something, not an action initiated by Israelis."[7]

Ibrahim Hooper, communications director of the Washington-based Council on American-Islamic Relations, observed on the PBS *NewsHour* program that "we're seeing increasing stories about Palestinian humanity, the suffering they go through, the hardship of occupation, but I think the problem is [that] the spectrum of debate needs to be widened. . . . There's still self-censorship in the American media that prevents overt criticism of the basis of the Israeli policies, the occupation, and even Zionism itself."[8]

Pro-Israel critics of media coverage tended to focus on two specific, narrower points. The first was the perception—often not expressly stated by supporters of Israel themselves but characterized as such in media reports—that Israel's image was being tarnished by media characterizations of Israel as the aggressor in the conflict. The second consisted of direct and repeated claims that reporting on Palestinian suicide bombers not only served to legitimize their actions but also conveyed an unjust and unacceptable sense of moral equivalence between the bombers and their victims.

The concerns of Israel's supporters over image were noted in the May 2002 *Chicago Tribune* report about charges of media bias: "The campaigns are motivated by the desire in Jewish communities that the United States maintain its traditional support of Israel and by a concern that media coverage of the Mideast, especially articles deemed sympathetic to Palestinians, could weaken public backing for Israel and ultimately alter U.S. policy."[9] In August 2002 Nathan Gutman, the Washington-based correspondent for the Israeli daily *Haaretz*, reported that American Jews had been "losing sleep" over Israel's public image as reflected in the American media, a fear reinforced by a poll sponsored by the American Jewish Committee showing some erosion in support for Israel and an increase in those taking a neutral position on the conflict. Gutman observed:

> This subject surfaces again and again at Jewish gatherings, in synagogues and in private conversations, and the overall sense is that more can be done to improve Israel's image.
>
> Over the past year, American Jews have tried almost everything in an effort to influence public opinion—from organized boycotts of media outlets . . . and public demonstrations of solidarity to a concerted effort to influence decision makers in the American administration and on Capitol Hill. Still, Jewish activists are frustrated and fear they have not succeeded in the battle over public opinion.[10]

These concerns led to the first-ever television ad campaign aimed at bolstering Israel's image, which debuted in October 2002. Sponsored by the American Jewish Committee and Israel 21C, a pro-Israel consortium based in Silicon Valley, the million-dollar ad campaign ran on cable outlets, including Fox News and MSNBC, as well as on local cable channels.[11]

Concerns about Israel's image were sparked, at least in part, by media coverage resulting from the surge in Israeli-Palestinian bloodletting that began in late summer 2001. The reporting detailed not only the daily violence visited upon Israeli and Palestinian victims alike but also focused on the hardships of Palestinian daily life under occupation. In an August 2001 interview with the online *Palestine Report*, Edward Said, a Columbia University professor and advocate for the Palestinian cause, offered a sharp assessment of why the Palestinian perspective was coming through in the media more clearly than it had previously: "I think the perception has improved largely because the Israeli behavior has become more outrageous. If you watch tanks and helicopters and M-16s—all American—mowing people down and assassinating and killing and blockading, it is very hard to have anything but a negative perception about it. So in a sense, we have benefited negatively."[12]

In the three weeks from August 15 to September 7 four major newspapers ran five stories reported primarily or exclusively from the Palestinian point of view.[13] Four appeared on page 1, with the pieces ranging in length from 1,200 to 2,000 words. Headlines and subheads for the stories denoted the human—or, in some cases, dehumanizing—aspects of Palestinian life under occupation:

Washington Post: Conflict Deepens Despair for Palestinians in Gaza

Los Angeles Times: Israel Boosts Its Policy of Retaliation: Palestinians Are Unfazed; The Strategy Merely Strengthens Their Resolve to Attack

Los Angeles Times: Another Kind of Intifada: When Their Uprising Began, Palestinians Put Off Weddings and Other Celebrations; Now They Are Trying to Lead Normal Lives and to Fend Off Despair

New York Times: For Palestinians, a Daily, Dirty Obstacle Course

Christian Science Monitor: Palestinian Morale Rises with Death Toll

During the same three-week period the *Post* ran a page 1 story headlined "Reports of Torture by Israelis Emerge" (with the subhead "Rights Groups Document Frequent Police Abuses Against Palestinians"), and two other front-page stories, one each giving equal weight to the violence perpetrated by both sides and to suffering experienced by Israelis and Palestinians alike.[14] In addition, the *New York Times* published an op-ed piece by Amira Hass, Israeli journalist and Palestinian affairs correspondent for *Haaretz*, headlined "Separate and Unequal on the West Bank."[15]

No single topic reported against the backdrop of the escalating violence between Israelis and Palestinians appeared to draw more visceral responses of protest from supporters of Israel than the backgrounds and motivations of Palestinian suicide bombers. In July and August 2001 a spate of such Palestinian attacks carried out in Jerusalem, Tel Aviv, and Haifa killed at least fifty-eight Israelis. In August five major U.S. newspapers published seven feature stories on Palestinian suicide bombers, which ranged in length from 900 to 3,600 words.[16] Five ran on the front pages of the various newspapers; all seven quoted Palestinian sources over Israeli sources in ratios ranging from 2 to 1 to 5 to 1. Threaded throughout the stories were common themes: why the young Palestinian perpetrators had become suicide bombers; the strategy and tactics they used for the deadly attacks; their families' expressions of regret, sorrow, and admiration for the bombers; and growing popular support among Palestinians for the militant group Hamas. Once again headlines and subheads evoked vivid images and stirred emotions:

Washington Post: Palestinians Find Heroes in Hamas: Popularity Surges for Once-Marginal Sponsor of Suicide Bombings

Washington Post: Where Palestinian Martyrs Are Groomed: West Bank City of Jenin Emerges as Suicide Bomb Capital

New York Times: City Israel Raided Is Oddly Jubilant

Newsday: Dying for a Cause: West Bank Town Sees Sons Become Suicide Bombers

Chicago Tribune: "No Room for Mistakes": Radicals Lament Rash of Thwarted Suicide Bombings

Los Angeles Times: Anguish, Not Pride, Fills Parents of Suicide Bomber: Palestinian Couple Reject the Idea that They Should Rejoice in Their Son's Deadly Decision

Chicago Tribune: His Father's Son: The Making of a Bomber

That August the *Washington Post* also published a 1,750-word cover story in *Outlook*, its Sunday analysis and commentary section, that was reported from the sole perspective of one Israeli family whose teenage daughter had been killed in the suicide bombing of a Jerusalem pizzeria ten days earlier.[17]

Pro-Israel readers took editors and reporters to task for their news judgment in devoting full-length features to the suicide bombers and their motivations based on the assessment that, no matter how heinous their actions, the bombers themselves were a key part of an ongoing news story and thus a legitimate focus of journalistic inquiry. By and large the feature stories on the bombers did not repeat the previously reported horrific details of the bombings, instead focusing on Palestinian perspectives of what led up to them. Moreover, the pieces omitted the details of the victims' suffering in favor of reporting them elsewhere. However, protesters of the coverage in these stories saw them as deliberate attempts by the media to justify—and even glorify—the actions of suicide bombers. The *Chicago Tribune* carried several letters to the editor written in response to two stories about suicide bombers that the paper had published on August 24 and 27. The letters conveyed anguish, indignation, and outrage, as the following excerpts show:

> I was appalled by the tone of the front-page article regarding suicide bombings in the Middle East. In the article, the subject of failed terrorist attacks was presented in a format usually reserved for tragedies: It featured an interview with a grieving parent whose son was arrested

before he could detonate himself, and comments by a political leader distressed by the situation because failed attempts made it harder to recruit new suicide bombers. . . . In a satirical publication, this article might have been appropriate as dark humor. . . . As serious news in a serious newspaper, it shows an astonishing lack of sensitivity.[18]

Change the nationality of the targets of these suicide bombers to American. How does your story glamorizing the exploits of killers come off now? Still like it? Perhaps a committed suicide bomber or bioterrorist running amok in Chicago might change your opinion.[19]

The anti-Israel bias of the Chicago Tribune has hit a new low with your front-page photo of a mournful, somber Palestinian father holding the photo of his 19-year-old son, a suicide bomber, who was captured by the Israelis before he could detonate his bomb and kill more innocent women and children. . . . One would think the Palestinian father's photo would have appeared in a Palestinian newspaper, not a newspaper in the United States, a country which extols liberty and freedom and decries terrorism. . . . This has all been done under the guise of front-page human-interest stories. . . . It is pathetic and shameful. You should be embarrassed.[20]

On September 11, in a special extra evening edition published to cover the terror attacks against the United States, one reader wrote: "Still want to write one-sided Mideast stories aggrandizing suicide bombers? . . . Your reporting of Mideast events has contributed to legitimization of what happened today."[21]

The controversy generated by such reporting on suicide bombers continued in 2002 and 2003. In late March 2002 Ayat al-Akhras, an eighteen-year-old Palestinian woman from a West Bank refugee camp, walked into a Jerusalem neighborhood supermarket and detonated the bomb she was carrying, killing two Israelis—a security guard and seventeen-year-old Rachel Levy—and herself. On April 5 the New York Times reported on page 1 that "the suicide bomber and her victim look strikingly similar. . . . The vastly different trajectories of their lives intersected for one deadly moment, mirroring the intimate conflict of their two peoples."[22] On April 15 Newsweek took the same tack in reporting the story, running it on the cover, which was illustrated with juxtaposed full-color photographs of Akhras and Levy—looking nearly identical with their dark eyes, delicately arched eyebrows, and center-parted, long, dark hair—and the headline "Suicide Mission: A Human Bomb and Her Victim; How Two Teens Lived—and Died." Inside the magazine, the headline above the center-spread story declared: "How Two Lives Met in Death."[23]

Some readers of both publications found the parallel narrative treatment, in text and image, of the two young women and their family backgrounds to be intolerable—as if the reporting had conferred a moral equivalence between bomber and victim. Two weeks after it published the story, *Newsweek* ran several letters to the editor indicating a range of positive and negative reader responses, excerpts of which follow.

Placing the murderer and the victim side by side and equating their deaths is the height of perversity.

Ayat al-Akhras, a Palestinian teenage girl, straps a bomb to her body and kills Rachel Levy, an Israeli teenage girl, and a security guard in Jerusalem, and Newsweek reports that there are now "three more victims of the madness of martyrdom." Al-Akhras was a murderer, plain and simple. She was no more a "victim" than were the 19 terrorists who attacked the United States on September 11, and any attempt to suggest a moral equivalency between suicide murderers and their innocent victims is outrageous and absolutely indefensible.

Israelis have tanks and airplanes. Palestinians have suicide bombers. In war, you fight with what you've got.

I very much liked your article . . . and was glad the story was not told from only one point of view. It was intriguing to hear from both families. I assumed that Ayat al-Akhras' Palestinian family would have shared her radical beliefs and was surprised to learn that they did not exactly approve of her suicide-bomber mission.[24]

In a July 2002 column detailing reader criticism of her paper's reporting of the conflict, Lillian Swanson, readers' advocate for the *Philadelphia Inquirer*, reported that a demonstration staged by more than one hundred pro-Israel protesters outside the paper's main office had coincided with a boycott "by some pro-Israeli groups, led by the 2,000-member Philadelphia district of the Zionist Organization of America," in which 360 subscribers had either dropped the paper for the month or canceled their subscriptions. "The biggest recent flashpoint," Swanson wrote, "was a front-page article describing the Israeli practice of holding on to the remains of suicide bombers. The story . . . and the headline 'Palestinians' remains fuel a bitterness,' prompted dozens of responses from furious readers who saw the piece as sympathetic to bombers' families."[25]

In October 2003 the *New York Times* published a 1,400-word news feature by reporter John F. Burns headlined "The Attacker: Bomber Left Her Family with a Smile and a Lie," about a Palestinian suicide bomber who had killed nineteen Israelis and herself in an attack carried out the week before in a Haifa restaurant.[26] Five days later, in another *Times* piece, Burns recounted how a reader, in a letter to the editor, had accused the paper of encouraging future suicide bombings by publishing the original story: "What this brutal, barbaric human being wanted, you have given her. She wanted notoriety, and your actions not only aided her in her quest but by featuring her life and family you are an active participant in encouraging more barbaric men to send more young people to slaughter innocent civilians."[27]

Media Response Case Study: The CNN Factor

Across the American mainstream media spectrum, news outlets did not take lightly charges that their reporting of the conflict was biased. Many news organizations made significant and repeated efforts to respond to such criticism while standing their ground on journalistic principle. From July 2001 to July 2003, *Washington Post* ombudsman Michael Getler—like many of his counterparts across the country—devoted six entire weekly columns to readers' concerns about the paper's coverage of the conflict and referred to it in five others.[28] In November 2001 and February 2002 four *Chicago Tribune* executives and top journalists—the foreign editor, Middle East editorial writer, ombudsman, and corporate counsel—appeared together at two suburban synagogues to answer readers' concerns about the *Tribune*'s reporting of the conflict.

In 2002 and 2003 National Public Radio, a frequent target of bias charges by pro-Israel and pro-Palestinian partisans—but in much greater proportion by supporters of Israel—posted statements on its Web site about its reporting of the conflict and responses to criticism of its coverage. Signed by NPR ombudsman Jeffrey Dvorkin and CEO and president Kevin Klose, the statements encouraged listeners to voice their concerns. Included were detailed self-evaluations, conducted by the NPR news division, of the network's reporting of the conflict based on criteria of accuracy, fairness, and balance in sourcing; story selection; choice of language; and depth and context. In a 2002 statement entitled "NPR's Middle East 'Problem'" that was posted on the network's Web site, Dvorkin wrote: "NPR is an organization that depends on public largesse, and [critics] know that NPR may be more vulnerable to financial pressure than other media. . . . It may be that at the end of the day, once a reasonable and detailed discussion with its critics has taken place, NPR may lose some of its longtime supporters. But that may be the price it must pay for not losing its journalistic soul."

Such was the case in 2001 and 2002, when Boston-based NPR affiliate WBUR participated in an extensive dialogue, via meetings and letters, with pro-Israel corporate donors who alleged a consistent anti-Israel bent in the station's programming. Despite efforts that included statements expressing sensitivity to critics' concerns but that also stressed a paramount concern for journalistic integrity, WBUR failed to appease these critics, who withdrew between $1 million and $2 million of their support in 2001 and 2002.[29]

However, no American media outlet appeared to respond to pressure over allegations of biased coverage like CNN, the cable news giant with a combined U.S. and international audience larger than most, if not all, other major U.S. news organizations combined—a reported one billion viewers in 212 nations and territories worldwide.[30]

In the summer of 2002 CNN did not respond directly to the charge supporters of Israel had been making for years: that its coverage of the conflict had been consistently pro-Palestinian. Instead, controversy surrounding an inadvertent comment made by CNN founder Ted Turner in an interview with a British newspaper had the apparent effect that the network was ready to pay major heed to such criticism.

On June 18, 2002, the *Guardian* published a 2,500-word profile of Turner. One of the story's twenty-five paragraphs attracted international attention when Turner, in a passing comment about the "war on terrorism," opined about the Israeli-Palestinian conflict: "Right now, aren't the Israelis and the Palestinians terrorizing each other? It looks to me like they're both doing it. . . . The rich and powerful, they don't need to resort to terrorism. . . . The Palestinians are fighting with human suicide bombers; that's all they have. The Israelis . . . they've got one of the most powerful military machines in the world. The Palestinians have nothing. So who are the terrorists? I would make a case that both sides are involved in terrorism."[31] The next day Turner, who at the time was not involved in CNN's day-to-day operations, issued a statement of apology, saying: "I regret any implication that I believe the actions taken by Israel to protect its people are equal to terrorism. . . . My view was and is that there is a fundamental distinction between the acts of the Israeli government and the Palestinians. I believe the Israeli government has used excessive force to defend itself, but that is not the same as intentionally targeting and killing civilians with suicide bombers."[32]

In its own statement CNN declared: "Mr. Turner's comments are his own and definitely do not reflect the views of CNN in any way."[33] Against the backdrop of the uproar generated by Turner's comments in the *Guardian*—published the same day that a suicide bomber killed nineteen people in Jerusalem—the network took additional steps. On June 21 CNN chief news executive Eason Jordan traveled to Israel to meet with Communications Minister Reuven Rivlin, who, Reuters reported, "has been unhappy with CNN coverage, which some Israelis believe is tilted toward the Palestinians. CNN denies any such basis."[34] The next week, six days after the publication of the *Guardian* profile of Turner, CNN began to broadcast a five-part series on Israeli victims of terror, first on *CNN Wolf Blitzer Reports* and continuing throughout the week on *CNN Live Today*.[35] During that week the CNN.com Web site also carried a series of stories on Israeli victims of terror.[36] At the top of his June 24 broadcast, Blitzer told his audience: "CNN does not wish to minimize the political elements involved or the suffering of the Palestinian people. That suffering, of course, is very real, but we've covered that. We'll continue to cover that. This week, we're focusing in on the victims of terror."[37]

On July 1 the *New York Times* ran a 1,350-word feature on the front page of its business section headlined "CNN Navigates Raw Emotions in Its Coverage from Israel." Recounting the events of the previous month—including a videotaped statement by CNN chairman Walter Isaacson to a media program on Israeli television disavowing Turner's comments, and the network's announcement that it would no longer broadcast statements of suicide bombers or their relatives except "in extreme circumstances"—the *Times* story noted that, "taken together, the moves were interpreted by Israeli and Palestinian officials, media critics and reporters covering the conflict as an appeasement of CNN's critics in Israel and the United States." Furthermore, according to the *Times*, the events "have led to bad feelings among some inside CNN." Said one CNN staff member in Jerusalem: "It appears as if we're in an unseemly rush to try to fix things, and I think we're going to dig ourselves into a deeper hole if we continue this course." The same staffer also said that complaints from Israelis to the office there were coming through loudest and with the most ferocity.[38]

Two months later, it appeared that CNN was continuing to follow the course lamented by the Jerusalem-based CNN staffer in the *Times* report. The network instructed its journalists to stop referring to Gilo—built and incorporated into Jerusalem by Israel on land it had occupied as a result of the 1967 war, in contravention of international law—as a "Jewish settlement" and instead refer to it as a "Jewish neighborhood." On September 3 Robert Fisk reported in the British newspaper the *Independent*:

Many journalists at CNN are angered by the new instruction. "There's a feeling by some people here that what we are doing is searching for euphemisms for what is really happening," one of them told the Independent yesterday. "We've managed to eliminate the word 'terrorism'—we now talk about 'militants'—because we know that the word 'terrorist' is used by one side or another to damage the other side. But now there's pressure on us not to use the word 'settler' in any context—but just to refer to the settlers as 'Israelis.'"[39]

FROM THE FIELD:
CORRESPONDENTS ON THEIR AUDIENCE

Interviews with correspondents who reported the Israeli-Palestinian conflict from the field in Jerusalem-based postings from 1985 to 2002 reflect the fact that Americans relate to this conflict with an intensity that has no parallel within the milieu of international news.[40] It is not surprising, therefore, that American mainstream media reporting of the conflict—especially during periods of heightened violence, such as the second intifada—would elicit audience reaction that was both sharp and voluminous. According to the correspondents, no other story of international conflict arouses the same degree of passionate interest in and deconstruction of media coverage as the Israeli-Palestinian conflict—and they, along with their editors and producers in newsrooms back home, are acutely aware of this audience attention.

Before he assumed his five-year posting in Jerusalem for the *Baltimore Sun* in 1987, Robert Ruby had been based in Paris. "The most immediate difference in Jerusalem was that readers were paying very close attention to what I was writing," he recalled. "Within my first month in the Middle East, I had more complaints, compliments and queries from readers than I had in any given year in Western Europe." George Moffett, Jerusalem-based correspondent for the *Christian Science Monitor* from 1987 to 1991, observed:

People have an intense curiosity about the Middle East. Every place name on the map has been known to most people since childhood, from Sunday school, and so we all feel, and have, a very special interest in the Middle East. So when you write about this particular story you have sense that more people are scrutinizing your copy more deeply. They feel that they have standing to criticize in a way that they probably wouldn't if you were writing a story from the Balkans or from Africa or from Azerbaijan. That may or may not be true, but that's the perception.

David Shipler of the *New York Times* wrote once of Jerusalem that it's an arena for the conflict of certainties. That's what gives this story such emotion. Everyone feels so emotional about it for deeply felt personal and historic and religious reasons. It has no equal anywhere else in the world.

According to Ethan Bronner, who was based in Jerusalem for the *Boston Globe* for six years beginning in 1991, the extent to which U.S. policy is enmeshed in the conflict and the interest and influence of the American Jewish community are other factors that contribute to unparalleled reader interest.

The conflict involves the state of the Jews, Israel. Given the size of the population of the United States, the number of Jews is not that great. But their influence and their interest in foreign affairs and public affairs is greater than their population. They are very avid and careful readers of papers like the *Boston Globe* and the *New York Times*. So you're writing for an audience that has a great interest and emotional investment in what you're writing. There is also an unusual American governmental interest and involvement in the conflict. Israel receives more [U.S.] foreign aid than any country in the world. So there's a great deal of interest at the policy-making level as well.

Barton Gellman, Jerusalem-based correspondent for the *Washington Post* from 1994 to 1997, attributed the unique degree of attention paid to the conflict—not only in the United States but also around the world—to the fact that "it has constituencies everywhere."

There are groups that are invested in a belief about the justice of the cause. There are organizations devoted to deconstructing your work. You don't tend to see the same intensity in the other big stories. Perhaps they don't have as much domestic constituency in this country; perhaps they just don't have quite the same resonance around the world. If you look at Rwanda, the Balkan conflict or what was for many years the No. 1 bureau with the most postings from news organizations around the world, Moscow, you seldom saw this kind of intense, partisan ideological deconstruction of the coverage itself. Certainly not to the same degree.

Audience Response: Partisan Proportions

The disparity in the relative strengths of Israeli and Palestinian societies in the conflict is mirrored in the two sides' constituent groups in the United States relative to media advocacy. The correspondents noted that the pro-Israel media audience tends to be organized, well-funded, collective, and strategic in its responses to coverage, while the pro-Palestinian media audience tends to be less organized, individual, and random in its responses. Furthermore, in recounting their own experiences with reader and viewer responses, the correspondents noted that the overwhelming majority of reaction—most of it critical rather than congratulatory—came from supporters of Israel. However, several also noted a gradual trend in recent years toward a more coordinated pro-Palestinian response in the United States.

Tim Phelps reported from Jerusalem for *Newsday* from 1987 to 1991. "Reader reaction was 99-to-1 pro-Israel to pro-Palestinian," he recalled of his tenure. "That has changed somewhat over time, but when I started doing this, no pro-Palestinian lobby existed in this country, and people were afraid to speak up on behalf of the Palestinians. That has changed fairly dramatically, but at that time, it was all one-sided." Ruby of the *Baltimore Sun*, whose posting covered the same period, said: "I heard more from people concerned that Israel's actions or policies were not being presented or understood properly or fairly described than I heard from people concerned about the Palestinians. Reactions ranged from 'you have this factually wrong' to 'you're a born anti-Semite' with many gradations in between."

Carol Morello, Jerusalem-based correspondent for the *Philadelphia Inquirer* from 1990 to 1994, also said that the reader reaction she experienced came overwhelmingly from the pro-Israel camp: "Ninety-five percent of the criticism, maybe more, came from supporters of Israel. That didn't mean people sympathetic to the Palestinians didn't have criticism, but they were not as well organized. Once in a while Arabs would contact us about the news coverage, but their criticisms were of a more general nature than those of pro-Israel readers." Storer Rowley, Middle East correspondent for the *Chicago Tribune* from 1994 to 1998, recalled a similar pattern of reader response:

I heard from many more pro-Israel folks than I heard from pro-Palestinian folks. It was usually supporters of Israel—Jewish readers in Chicago—who would write or contact my desk. And more often than not, people like to criticize more than to compliment; they tend to be more motivated when they're angry than when they're happy. I rarely heard from many Palestinians or pro-Palestinians complaining about our coverage. I found that Palestinians or their supporters tended to be grateful when they felt you were covering them fairly.

Reporting in the mid-1990s for the *Washington Post*, the major paper in the nation's capital, Gellman said he received much reader response from both sides "but in an 8:1 ratio from Israel sympathizers to pro-Palestinian readers. I got phone calls. I got letters. I got faxes. My editors had a steady stream of phone calls and faxes complaining about the coverage. There was a growth of press-criticism publications, newsletters and, toward the end of my time over there, Web sites that tried to influence public opinion about how we were doing our job." Dan Klaidman, based in Jerusalem for *Newsweek* in 1999 and 2000, also recalled significant response from both sides, albeit with a greater proportion coming from supporters of Israel.

I got much, much more response from both sides on this story than on any other story I've ever covered, but it wasn't on the level that some other news organizations got. I heard more from the pro-Israel side, probably because they're better organized.

Certain news organizations got bombarded with e-mails, largely from some pro-Israel groups, such as CAMERA and other organizations. There were campaigns against individual reporters and news organizations that were perceived to be more pro-Palestinian—I think for the most part unfairly. NPR was always targeted. A good [journalist] friend of mine was a target of one of these campaigns; she got bombarded.

Deborah Horan, who reported for the *Houston Chronicle* from 1997 to 2001, said—as did several other correspondents—that her paper didn't forward readers' letters to her in order to shield her from the pressure.

They decided that I was under enough strain just trying to work. They dealt with the criticism. They had meetings with the Israeli consulate in Houston, for instance, and whatever Palestinians were writing to them. I didn't get e-mails, but I know the newspaper got so many e-mails that somebody in tech support put up a firewall, because they were clogging the system. One British journalist I knew got 25,000 e-mails from BIPAC, the British version of AIPAC. I don't know how many she got from Palestinians, but it was nowhere near 25,000.

The source and proportion of reader response, Horan observed, is "a matter of organization and resources."

> People sit in their living rooms and think, why bother writing a letter? It has to do with thinking that your voice matters. It has to do with knowing where to send it, whom to send it to, knowing how a newspaper functions. Do I write the letter to the writer? Do I write the letter to her boss, or do I write to her boss's boss?
>
> American Jews think their voice makes a difference. It's a reflection of voting patterns and other things. A lot of Arab Americans aren't registered to vote, but that's changing with the generation of Arabs who were born in America. Their parents say, "No, don't write a letter, don't make waves." But the young generation is saying, "I can make a difference."

The Substance of the Criticisms

Correspondents recall being challenged—mainly by supporters of Israel—about various aspects of coverage of the conflict, ranging from their understanding of specific factual issues to their perceptions of Israel's image, particularly when the reporting focused on Palestinian life under occupation. Klaidman of *Newsweek* said readers who support Israel "would say the history was not presented properly. A lot of the criticism focused heavily on the long sweep of the narrative itself, going back to who started various wars, who was responsible for the refugee problem, why didn't Palestinians accept the 1947 UN partition [of Palestine]." Rowley of the *Tribune* recalled: "The biggest complaint would be about accuracy and fairness as they [readers] saw and interpreted it. For example, if I wrote a story about Palestinian refugees suffering in Jabaliya [a camp in Gaza], there would be complaints: Why aren't you covering the other side enough? Or you're giving too much attention to their pain. What about ours?" Bronner of the *Globe* pointed out that partisans of both sides of the conflict tend to believe the solution to unsatisfactory reporting of it lies in better PR.

> American Jews and Israelis tend to take the view that Israel's problem is that it has a primitive public-relations mechanism or superstructure. That what they really need to do is let Ogilvy & Mather or the best organization out there take it over and make it work. If I'm right, then they are barking up the wrong tree that it's just a question of getting the message out there in a more sophisticated way.

Both sides are convinced that the other side totally dominates the media. The Israelis think that we just write the "poor Ahmed" stories, as they're called. And the Palestinian side is convinced that we are in the tanks with the Israeli government line, and that they can't get through, they can't pierce the armor. So the Palestinians argue the same thing: If only they had a more sophisticated way of dealing with press relations, their story would get out.

Several correspondents, however, indicated that the concerns of pro-Israel readers went far beyond issues of fact, balance, or media relations—reflecting their own personal knowledge of Israel and their perception of its strength relative to the Palestinians. Noted Morello of the *Inquirer:*

The criticism of supporters of Israel is not hard to understand. We are writing about a country that many have visited. When they go, they are generally exposed to a point of view from one side—the segment of society that believes Palestinians are only out to push Israelis into the sea. Israel is engaged and has been engaged in an existential battle.

These readers walk in the shoes of the Israelis, not the Palestinians, and they come back to the U.S. with an idea of what the story is. When they don't see that view buttressed [in the paper], they think the coverage is a fraud.

Any criticism of the press is a good thing. But their view is different from [that of] those of us who see it more on the level. They see it differently because they have different exposure when they are over there. They don't understand that reporters go to different places and see different people. You need to be sure your stories have diversity. You need to be fair and to cover all the bases over time.

Phelps of *Newsday* offered a similar observation based on his experience reporting Palestinian life under occupation in the months before the first intifada broke out in December 1987. For his readers "it wasn't a matter of balance. For them, it was a matter of what they perceived to be untrue. They thought it was a lie, and you can't balance a lie."

Initially [the criticism] was about stories I wrote about the occupation, stories that seemed modest and not so controversial to me. Very, very few journalists at that time had been writing about the occupation. So [readers] refused to believe that some of these things were true. People were genuinely shocked to the point where they didn't believe it.

They'd never heard it from anywhere else before. It wasn't just readers who reacted to the coverage. It was extremely controversial for some editors within the paper as well.

We all grew up, myself as much as anybody, with the lore of Israel surviving, this tiny state in the Arab world. It was a very idealistic view of the country, so this other view was a different vision of Israel. When I did a series about the occupation before the intifada started, the idea of a brutal and inhumane Israeli military was just beyond the pale to most readers. The intifada changed that, because of television. People saw this brutality with their own eyes.

The "truth" factor, observed the *Post*'s Gellman, has led many pro-Israel readers to believe that "there is essentially one correct narrative of this conflict." Moreover, said Gellman, they also perceive that Israel's position on the ground vis-à-vis the Palestinians is much weaker than it actually is.

The general indictment of those who felt we were too hard on Israel was that there is essentially one correct narrative of this conflict, which is a historical narrative of suffering and victimhood—and that if you don't repeat that narrative at every opportunity, and if you focus on stories that don't fit easily within that narrative, then you are against us. You are grossly distorting reality because the reality is that narrative.

Because Israel has the power is one of many explanations why the intensity of criticism from pro-Israel readers was greater. It is very hard for some American Jews to reconcile themselves to the image of a dominant, powerful Israel. The storyline of the Jewish people, for very good reasons, is one of suffering, victimhood, powerlessness, minority. But that just isn't what's happening in Israel. Israel has the GDP of all its neighbors combined and then some. It has the military capability to defeat all its neighbors combined and then some.

For all those fears of an existential threat, there is not now an existential threat to Israel, and there has not been one from not long after the 1973 war to the present. All the trends since then have been in favor of Israeli power and against Arab power in that conflict. There is one potential existential threat, and that is the nuclear one.

According to Gellman, reader criticism of coverage perceived to be biased against Israel also stemmed from a greater "disparity between the self-image of pro-Israeli readers and facts on the ground" than exists among supporters of the Palestinians.

American Jews don't see Israel as powerful. They see Israel as belea-
guered, both in international forums, which is true, and on the ground
in the Holy Land, which is not true. It has certainly suffered greatly
from terrorism and from other forms of violence that I would not define as terrorism but as violent resistance to occupation. They [Israelis]
suffer. But they are not in danger of losing.

So there is a greater disparity between the self-image of pro-Israeli
readers and facts on the ground than there is on the Palestinian side.
But there is a very great disparity on the Palestinian side because of
conspiratorial, false beliefs and an unwillingness to take on the implications of attacking civilians, suicide bombings and terrorism as
almost anyone would define it.

No one's self-image is perfectly accurate. But if you speak in terms
of dispossession and victimhood and loss of one's share of power and
privilege and ownership, then the Palestinians' sense of victimhood
is more accurate than Israel's, in the current context, simply because
Israel is winning. I'm not making any comment on the justice of the
relative causes. Then there's a much larger and much more powerful
American Jewish constituency than Arab-American constituency, even
though gradually Arab Americans are becoming more numerous and
more organized. But they don't have anything like the same impact in
American politics.

Ann LoLordo reported from Jerusalem for the *Baltimore Sun* from 1996
to 1999; the fiftieth anniversary of the conflict occurred during her posting
in 1998. She recalls that "the biggest criticism I got, and the one that was
most troubling to me," involved a package of stories the *Sun* ran about
the anniversary:

We published a special supplement, and the *Sun* sent a second reporter
over to help. We wrote 14 or 15 stories for this special section that was
marketed to the Jewish community. I wrote one long Palestinian story
that I believed was supposed to go into that supplement. It was about
the 50th anniversary of the *nakba* [Arabic for "disaster"], the Palestinian view of Israel's independence.

The story didn't run in the package. It ran a week later on a Sunday,
on the front page of the paper. I got a scathing letter from someone in
Baltimore who said that I was an advocate for the Palestinians, that the
people I interviewed had lied. That one of the villages I had focused
on hadn't been overrun by Jewish soldiers at the time. He claimed that

he had been part of a Jewish unit during the War of Independence that went into this village and that they didn't kick anybody out. And he wouldn't let it go. He wrote several letters and called for a retraction. But I hadn't just interviewed these people. I had looked at other primary and secondary sources about the West Bank villages and what happened to them.

Nothing was ever retracted. But I had wanted an editor's note that said this story wasn't based only on one person's remembrance of what happened fifty-some-odd years ago. Other sources had been consulted. But that's not the policy of the paper because we weren't correcting anything.

Afterward, I came home to give a speech when I was being honored at a college in Maryland for my coverage. When I opened it up to questions, the guy who wrote that letter was in the audience and took me on right there. I engaged with him and I tried to explain myself, but this was long after my story had been published.

Effects on Coverage

Correspondents agreed that audience criticism of their work deserves attention, especially when that criticism has journalistic merit. They stressed the importance of attention to fairness and balance, especially when it comes to phrasing and terminology, and observed that balance over time—not necessarily in every reported story—is key. Several correspondents said they considered even-handedness and open-mindedness to be part of their job.

Although mindful of these factors, some correspondents nonetheless said that reader reaction had little if any effect on how they went about reporting the story, which was guided by their sense of professional experience and obligation. Ruby of the *Sun* was straightforward: "I don't think reader reaction had an effect on my reporting. You cover the news, period. Whether a reader liked or disliked what you did the day before should not enter into the calculation." Phelps of *Newsday* agreed but qualified his view based on the realities of constituent-group pressure:

I was determined to do what I was going to do, so the bravado answer is that [reader reaction] didn't affect me at all. But there's also no question that for all of us [journalists], there was more attention paid to this story because the supporters of Israel in this country were more vocal. There was more attention paid to fairness on their behalf than on anyone else's behalf. Certainly any reporter in that situation would be mindful of that. As a reporter you cannot argue with fairness, so I'm not being critical of it. You just cannot argue with editors who are insisting that you get the other side of the story.

Recalled Morello of the *Inquirer:* "I was aware that there were complaints about me, my reporting [from readers back home]. Every adjective needed to stand up to scrutiny. I liked and had empathy for both sides. Not every story was 50/50, but over time the reporting was balanced."

LoLordo of the *Sun* said the local Jewish community made clear to her its interest in her reporting of the story:

I knew going into the job that I was going to be watched. It was brought home very clearly to me when my appointment hadn't even been announced in the paper and I was getting calls from the Jewish community. I got a call of congratulations from the head of the Baltimore Jewish Council, and that brought home to me that they were interested in me and they were interested in how I was going to go about my job. But I never was lobbied.

When I was over there, the Baltimore Jewish Council brought people over, and I always spoke to them. Some colleagues might say that they would have no interest in speaking to members of the local Jewish community when they come to Israel. That's fine. But I saw no reason not to. Some of those relationships turned me on to this story, helped me do my job better, and that's what my interest was. It's important to hear everybody's point of view whether you agree with it or not. I tried to be as open-minded and even-handed about the place as I could, because I thought that was my job.

Rowley of the *Tribune* echoed the sentiment: "Journalists who cover that region know intuitively that you have to be open to points of views on all sides, and you have to report them fairly. I gave the feedback consideration, but it never affected what I did or how I covered the story, despite what some critics of the media say." He continued:

Those of us who have done this for a long time take very seriously that you don't set out to report a biased story. You set out to report an accurate story that reflects what you see on the ground. But in places like Bosnia and Croatia, in a place like the Holy Land, where there is a lot of death and destruction and dispute, you are even more careful about reporting every story accurately because you know it's going to be examined under a microscope by the constituents of those two sides at home. But that doesn't affect or change how you cover a story.

When [Israeli settler] Baruch Goldstein goes into a mosque and kills people praying, that's a story, and you run out the door to cover it. When a [Palestinian suicide] bomb goes off in the Ben Yehuda mall, that's the story, and you run out to cover it. Over time it swings back and forth. One side suffers; the other side suffers. But over a period of four years you'd hope that your work, taken in totality, shows that you reported the triumphs and tragedies on both sides fairly.

Gellman of the *Post* said he would have considered certain kinds of reader criticism to be constructive, but he rarely received them. Nonetheless, readers' critiques did compel him to scrutinize certain aspects of his work more closely.

I was doing it story by story as I went along, but I felt that the picture would have been susceptible to smart, fair criticism, in which you could say I've understated or undercovered this dimension of these societies and overcovered that dimension or missed some important things. Or even got some important things wrong. I would be susceptible to that as I think almost anyone would be. But I almost never got that kind of sophisticated criticism. I actually thought I would have liked it. It was almost all so tendentious and so uni-dimensional that I just couldn't take it very seriously.

I'm not a proponent of the view that because everyone's criticizing us we must be right. It's not true. If everyone's criticizing you, you may be wrong. Just because you get it from both sides doesn't mean you're doing it right. I'm simply saying that if whole categories of stories are impermissible because they don't fit the wide explication of victimhood, then I just don't take this criticism seriously.

But the one impact that all this had on me is that I got in the habit in Israel—and it's a habit I've kept to varying degrees since—of reading my stories with extreme care to look for unintended double meanings or words or phrases that were sufficiently vague so that they would be susceptible to either deliberate or innocent misreading. I was very careful to say, well, someone could read this sentence and say: "See, he's doing X, see, he's taking a side, see he's ignoring that other thing." And I would rephrase it. I would never soften my story selection or the sharpness of my observation about what was happening. But I was very careful to avoid unnecessary conflict by removing ambiguities or language that could have double meanings.

Horan of the *Chronicle* observed, "Editors read the letters. They're not thrown in the wastepaper basket. They read as many as they can, and they consider them. They don't want to make a mistake, to offend the readers. They're trying to bring people the news, but they try to be sensitive. They take this issue seriously and try to evaluate whether a reader has a valid complaint or is just really angry. This conflict touches so close to home. It's about narrative, it's about identity, it's a conflict on so many levels that are so personal." However, she added that reporters covering the story in the field are compelled to do well not only for the sake of the people about whom and for whom they are reporting but for themselves as well.

For journalists, being in Jerusalem is part of their career. For most people it's a three- or four-year stop in a career that is going to take them to a lot of different countries or to a foreign-editor position. So they're just trying to do a good job.

They're trying to do a job that impresses people in the industry. They're trying to write well. They're trying to report well.

They're motivated by things that people who write letters to the editor don't realize.

VIEWS FROM ACADEME:
THE REPORTING UNDER SCHOLARLY SCRUTINY

The intense level of engagement between partisan constituent groups and news organizations over claims of bias in reporting of the Israeli-Palestinian conflict has spurred scholarly examination of the question. Four such academic studies indicate that, contrary to claims that media coverage has tended to be biased against Israel in favor of the Palestinians, reporting produced by specific media outlets either exhibited various types of biases favoring Israel or achieved an overall balance between representing Israeli and Palestinian points of view, claims, and interpretations of events. None of the four studies found patterns of coverage indicating a pro-Palestinian bias.

Two of these studies focused on content analyses of four American newspapers—the *New York Times, Washington Post, Chicago Tribune,* and *San Jose Mercury News*—during the period of heightened intercommunal violence, from the beginning of the second intifada in September 2000 through the violent spring of 2002. A third study focused on content analysis of the *Philadelphia Inquirer* in 1998, while a fourth study focused on content analysis of and audience response to British television coverage of the conflict by the BBC and ITV networks during 2000 to 2002.

The *New York Times, Washington Post,* and *Chicago Tribune*

In 2001 the Jewish Federation of Metropolitan Chicago commissioned an academic study of reporting of the conflict by the *Chicago Tribune* for perceived anti-Israel bias. A trio of scholars from the Annenberg School for Communication at the University of Pennsylvania and the University of Illinois at Chicago examined thirty days of coverage of events that occurred between September 2000 and June 2001—as reported not only in the *Tribune* but also, comparatively, in the *New York Times* and the *Washington Post.* While the federation itself declined to make public the results of the report, which was completed in October 2001, they were published at the end of 2002 in an academic journal, with the authors acknowledging that the study had been derived from "the findings of an internal report commissioned" by the federation.[41]

The study examined news reports—including headlines, photographs, and graphics—for criteria that included, among other factors, story structure, length, play, sourcing, language, and tone. It also examined editorials, columns, and cartoons for these criteria. The authors found the reporting in all three newspapers to be "remarkably similar" in many respects, noting that they "displayed a form of coverage that communicated a certain shared perspective."

With regard to language, although the study acknowledged the "impossibility" of escaping word choice that exhibited bias, given the nature of the conflict, it also noted that the three papers "used similar words to describe the conflict, liberally using terminology that was problematic to at least one side of the conflict without acknowledging sensitivities surrounding its usage." Finding a tendency among the *Times, Tribune,* and *Post* to use language "aligned with an Israeli perspective on events," the authors observed:

> All three newspapers chose similar labels when describing those engaged in violent acts against Israeli citizens, calling such individuals "terrorists" or "suicide bombers" rather than the "martyrs" preferred by the Palestinians. Phrases describing victims who were "caught in the crossfire"—a phrase said to denote yet soften Israeli culpability—appeared

intermittently. Contested terms like "occupation" disappeared from all three newspapers, "occupied lands" became "disputed lands" and "Israeli settlements" were often labeled "Israeli neighborhoods." . . . Civilian Israelis were sometimes called "dovish" or "peaceniks," but these terms were almost never applied to Palestinians. Such word choices suggest a consonance with the Israeli way of framing events.[42]

The study also noted a "geographic bias" in the coverage of all three papers in that "the largest percentage" of intifada stories were reported from within Israel proper, whereas "a substantially smaller percentage" were reported from territory controlled by the Palestinian Authority. Here the authors noted: "Such a slant persisted despite the fact that the events provoking the most intense reactions occurred inside or alongside the borders of the Palestinian Authority. This discrepancy, a common result of reporting from the place of the reporter rather than the place of the event, in itself set in place a prism for reporting—and understanding—events in ways that undercut the supposed neutrality of the coverage."[43]

Other similarities in coverage, according to the study, included: reporting of body counts in a way that "tended to list at length Israelis who died while not always according the same treatment to Palestinians"; sourcing patterns that were more or less equal and balanced; and editorial columns that criticized the Palestinians—"and Arafat in particular"—more than they criticized Israel.

The study also reported a number of respects in which coverage by the *Times* differed markedly from that of the *Post* and the *Tribune*, whose coverage the authors found to be more similar to each other than to that of the *Times*. "In this regard," the authors noted, "the *Times* displayed more consonance with the claims of a pro-Israel slant that have been leveled against the American press," as well as a "reflection of an Israeli perspective on events that was not always matched by the newspaper's attitude toward the Palestinians."

The study cited specifics vis-à-vis headlines, lead paragraphs, and photos. With regard to headlines, it noted:

The *Times* tended to portray the Israelis as victims and the Palestinians as aggressors in its headlines. It was two and a half times more likely to position Palestinians as aggressors and Israelis as victims in its headlines than to do the opposite. This was revealing, for the headlines of the *Tribune* and the *Post* displayed a different pattern, positioning Israelis and Palestinians as aggressors in a roughly equivalent number of headlines. . . . This difference in headline use offered a clear reading of the story of events to follow. The tendency of the *Times* to portray the Israelis as victims and the Palestinians as aggressors persisted across events.[44]

Regarding the lead paragraphs of stories in all three papers, the study cited a single instance of coverage tilting toward the Palestinians. While lead paragraphs in the *Times* highlighted Palestinian-instigated violence twice as often as they focused on Israeli-instigated violence, according to the study both the *Post* and the *Tribune* "were more prone to highlight Israeli-instigated violence over Palestinian" violence in lead paragraphs. The study also found a tendency in the coverage by the *Times* "to portray a middle ground, by which both Israelis and Palestinians were held accountable for the violence." The authors found that, according to the *Times*, "violence was more likely to originate with either the Palestinians or with both parties, but rarely with the Israelis alone. By contrast, both the *Post* and the *Tribune* entertained the possibility that for at least some of the events that occurred, Israel bore independent responsibility for the ensuing violence."[45]

Similarly, the study noted that in its use of photos the *Times* "more often displayed photos suggesting Palestinian culpability than Israeli. . . . Aggression on the part of the Israelis was not depicted by the *Times*." By contrast, the *Tribune* and the *Post* "depicted the culpability of both groups in similar percentages of photos," and both papers "depicted Israeli soldiers in aggressive acts." Moreover, similar to the middle-ground tendency observed with regard to the lead paragraphs in the *Times*, the study noted that during the first twelve days of the conflict (from late September through early October 2000), "the visuals in the *Times* seemed to show either Palestinian culpability or both sides clashing with each other, rather than one-sided Israeli-instigated violence." This visual middle ground, however, appeared at odds with reporting elsewhere, which included "a number of events for which Israel was roundly criticized by the international press," according to the authors, leading them to assert that "the newspaper's decision, then, to portray violence and aggression as either a Palestinian action or a shared attribute of both Israelis and Palestinians, rather than hold Israel independently responsible for some of the aggression and violence, constituted an outlying use of visuals that established a perspective on the conflict more favorable to Israel."[46]

The study concluded by noting the broader implications of the "distinctiveness" of coverage by the *Times* and its "often pro-Israeli slant," compared with the *Tribune* and the *Post*. The authors wondered whether the *Times*, considered to be the "gold standard" of American journalism, had "helped mobilize discussions of a pro-Israeli slant more generally in American coverage of the Middle East."

Israeli and Palestinian Deaths in the *San Jose Mercury News*

How the *San Jose Mercury News* reported the Israeli-Palestinian conflict from April through September 2002 was the focus of a study published online in December 2003 by the Grade the News media research project at Stanford University.[47] Affiliated with Stanford's graduate program in journalism, GTN publishes online critiques and in-depth analyses of print and broadcast news outlets in the San Francisco Bay Area. GTN undertook its study of Mideast coverage by the *Mercury News* as a follow-up to a study published by If Americans Knew, an independent Bay Area group focusing on media coverage of the Israeli-Palestinian conflict that had found the paper's front-page-headline treatment of the conflict to be significantly biased in favor of Israel. The GTN study reported similar results, finding that in 140 *Mercury News* stories published during the time period under review, "an Israeli death was 11 times more likely to make a front-page headline in San Jose than a Palestinian fatality."

GTN qualified these findings, stating that beyond front-page headlines, the text of stories about the conflict that started on the front page and continued inside, as well as accompanying sidebar pieces, "came closer to balance." It also cited "obvious instances on inside pages where editors struggled to match accounts in which each side described its victimization." While falling outside the scope of the study, editorials "also appeared to treat both Israelis and Palestinians with respect." Moreover, photos of Israeli and Palestinian grief "were often paired." Nevertheless, GTN reported, "To the editors at the *Mercury News*, the story was much more about Israeli deaths than Palestinian, even though during those six months 499 Palestinians and 192 Israelis died in the conflict. Over the period, *Mercury News* page-one headlines reported 147 Israeli fatalities and 35 Palestinian, 77 percent and 7 percent, respectively." Language issues followed a similar pattern, according to the study, with Palestinian forces "consistently labeled as 'gunmen' and 'militants'—terms with negative connotations in our culture—but rarely as 'fighters' and never as 'resistance forces.'"

Furthermore, GTN cited a statistic by the Israeli human-rights group B'Tselem that 247 Palestinians had been killed by Israeli troops in April 2002, including 26 under the age of eighteen. However, the study found that "not one was mentioned in a *Mercury News* front-page headline in April, but three headlines described Israeli fatalities."

The GTN report also found that "the priority given to Israelis suffering in front-page headlines was reinforced throughout the stories by the order in which casualties were described, and first-person accounts of Israeli deaths contrasted with second-hand and approximate estimates of Palestinian fatalities." The report further noted that "front-page text in the *Mercury News* expanded the percent of Israeli deaths mentioned slightly to 88 percent, and Palestinians more substantially, to 54 percent. But a single story, of the 140 analyzed, accounted for more than half the mentions of Palestinian deaths. Absent that article, fewer than one in four Palestinian deaths were mentioned in front-page text."

The study quoted three academic sources who acknowledged the importance of headlines in setting the tone of coverage. William Woo, a journalism professor at Stanford and former newspaper editor, told GTN: "If all I'm seeing are Israelis being killed by Palestinians, I'd be likely to conclude that the Israelis are the predominant victims of violence." The GTN study also sought the perspective of the newspaper. It reported that Daniel Sneider, who had been foreign and national desk editor at the *Mercury News* during the time frame of the study, said he did not agree that the paper's coverage had been biased but would not say why on the record. According to the study, two other top editors at the paper contacted by GTN researchers declined to comment, deferring to Sneider.

Because the *Mercury News* ran Associated Press reports in addition to copy filed by its own reporter during the period under study, and because AP serves so many American newspapers, GTN also analyzed every story it found to have been reported by the news agency on the Israeli-Palestinian conflict during that time frame—a total of seventy-seven—by using the LexisNexis database. While the GTN analysis of AP's coverage "could not distinguish between front page and inside stories, since those choices are made by editors at each paper using the service," the study found that in AP headlines Israeli deaths were twice as likely to be mentioned as Palestinian deaths. When the focus was broadened to include the first five paragraphs of each article, where fatalities were most likely to be mentioned, the ratio narrowed but the overall pattern remained the same, with Israeli deaths 37 percent more likely to be reported than Palestinian deaths.

The GTN study also explored several "possible sources of bias" that would account for the pattern of front-page headline treatment. These included the perception that most Israelis killed in the conflict are civilians and therefore "predominantly innocent," as opposed to the perception that the majority of Palestinians killed are combatants. Another possible source of bias was journalists having greater access to Israeli sources than Palestinian sources and encountering barriers imposed by the Israeli military to sites of news events. Other possible factors suggested included greater cultural and political affinity for Israelis over Palestinians by many Americans, including reporters and editors; and pressure from partisan community groups, with pro-Israel supporters being better funded and organized than their pro-Palestinian counterparts. Also cited was the nature of American journalism as being event-driven rather than issue-driven. Thus, suicide bombings, which have often resulted in a large number of Israelis being killed at once, get greater news play than do killings of Palestinians, including civilians, by Israeli military forces in smaller numbers per event but in greater numbers over time.

Balance in the *Philadelphia Inquirer*

Years before the period of intense Israeli-Palestinian violence during the second intifada, claims of media bias in the reporting of the conflict persisted. According to a study that analyzed reporting of the conflict by the *Philadelphia Inquirer* in 1998, the paper "faced intense criticism in the 1990s from two mutually antagonistic sources. Active, highly vocal Jewish and Palestinian groups holding opposing views were intensely unhappy with [the paper's] news coverage of the Mideast."[48] Editors at the paper commissioned a study of its coverage of the conflict, to be conducted by three professors from the Manship School of Mass Communication at Louisiana State University who, according to the report of their findings, were given "free rein to design, implement and publish the study."

The researchers examined 387 news stories, news briefs, photos, and graphics published from January to October 1998. In a summary of its overall findings, the study reported that the *Inquirer* had "provided its readers with ample information about the Israeli-Palestinian conflict, continuously reporting major developments in the peace process and providing rich background on the U.S. role." Furthermore, the study found that "the portrayal of the two political entities was balanced overall as both parties had a roughly equal percentage of positive, neutral or negative coverage in the time period studied. Weakness of the coverage lay in heavy reliance on Israeli sources and viewpoints compared with those of the Palestinians."[49]

Each article in the study was read and categorized as "positive, neutral, negative or mixed for each political entity involved in the story," a coding system meant to capture "the overall impression of the event that an average, impartial reader would form." For example, a story about a leader calling for peace negotiations would be coded positive, whereas a story about a setback in such talks would be coded negative. Accordingly, the study found that "nearly the same percentage of stories on Israel and the Palestinians were considered negative."

The study found bias in sourcing patterns, however, noting "heavy use of Israeli sources in the *Inquirer* stories," with 677 Israeli sources compared with 360 Palestinian sources. Furthermore, only 20 percent of the stories did not quote Israeli sources, while twice as many did not quote Palestinian sources.

The *Inquirer*'s use of photographs seemed to correlate with these tendencies. According to the study, "overall, when the headline, photo and caption were considered together, the Palestinians' image was slightly more negative than that of the Israeli counterpart, while Israel received more neutral photos."

Similar to the study of *New York Times, Chicago Tribune,* and *Washington Post* coverage, the *Inquirer* study noted an element of geographical bias. Specifically, it found that "most of the news stories had datelines from inside Israel (excluding disputed territories), with the greatest percentage in Jerusalem," accounting for 49 percent of all news stories analyzed.

Furthermore, the *Inquirer* study noted that Associated Press reports accounted for 30 percent of the stories analyzed, and that "about 44 percent" of both the AP stories and those written by *Inquirer* reporters or reporters for other Knight-Ridder newspapers had Jerusalem datelines. "Both entities relied more on Israeli than Palestinian sources," according to the report, "although this tendency was more pronounced with *Inquirer*/Knight-Ridder staff." A further comparison of AP and *Inquirer* coverage noted that "AP stories were slightly more negative toward Israel and a little more neutral toward Palestinians than was the *Inquirer* coverage overall. The result was that the two entities canceled each other out, making overall coverage equally positive and negative for both Israelis and Palestinians."[50]

A Cross-Cultural Comparison: British Television Coverage

British television coverage of the Israeli-Palestinian conflict by the BBC and ITV networks from September 2000 through April 2002 was the focus of a major study produced by the University of Glasgow Media Group in 2004 entitled *Bad News from Israel.*[51] The study undertook a content analysis of 189 television reports broadcast during September–October 2000, October–December 2001, and March–April 2002. It also included audience studies in which more than eight hundred male and female respondents of diverse ages and incomes were surveyed by questionnaire and interviewed in focus groups.

The authors concluded that "our study does not support the view that Israel is portrayed unfairly" and that overall "the results suggest that it was Israeli perspectives which predominated in TV news."[52] One of the study's citations indicating "areas where the news was apparently partisan" echoed the findings found in the American studies referred to earlier: "Through the period of our work, Palestinians consistently incurred the highest number of casualties. The number killed was greater than that of Israelis by a ratio of 2–3:1. But on the news there was an emphasis on Israeli casualties both in the amount of coverage they received and in the language used to describe them."[53]

Three factors make the study relevant to a discussion of media bias in U.S. mainstream reporting of the Israeli-Palestinian conflict—in addition to the fact that the conclusions of the Glasgow researchers corroborate the findings of their American counterparts. First, in interviews with working British broadcast journalists, the authors highlight work practices and audience/market perceptions similar if not identical to those found in American broadcast journalism. The former include the mode and structure of television news reporting of conflict within strict time constraints and via a medium that stresses visual imagery. The latter comprise determinations made by reporters and/or producers that audiences prefer action-oriented narratives supported by strong visuals to the virtual exclusion of explanatory and contextual background information.

Second, citing "the very close political and communication links which exist between the U.S. and Britain" as a key factor affecting British media coverage, the authors reported:

> Our content analysis showed that speakers from the U.S. were frequently featured on TV news and that they commonly endorsed or supported Israeli positions. There was no comparable referencing of the governments of other nations who were more critical of Israel. Given the significance of the U.S. as the world's sole remaining superpower and its relationship with Britain, it is not surprising that the views of its politicians would be featured, but nonetheless it had a significant effect on the balance of TV news coverage. There is some evidence to suggest that the perspectives on the Middle East adopted by U.S. politicians are strongly influenced by pro-Israel lobbies.[54]

The study also made comparative references to pro-Israel lobby and pressure groups in Britain and the United States, citing in the British context a report in the London *Observer* that pointed to "the influence of lobby groups such as the conservative Friends of Israel, which invites senior journalists to lunches at the House of Commons."[55] In the authors' observation, "the level of pressure, lobbying and public relations which exists in this area is likely to affect the media climate in both Britain and the U.S. This has important implications for the clarity and impartiality of the information which is received by mass publics."[56]

The third factor common to American mainstream media coverage of the Israeli-Palestinian conflict and the results of the Glasgow group study is the tendency of mainstream media in the United States and Britain to frame certain key issues of the conflict as revolving around Palestinian terrorism and the resulting need for Israel to defend itself—while at the same time excluding frames that the study referred to as "key elements of Palestinian history" and "the fact of military occupation and its consequences." The authors asserted that "television news has largely denied its audiences an account of these relationships and their origins, and in doing so has both confused viewers and reduced the understanding of the actions of those involved."[57] The Glasgow group's audience studies revealed prevalent themes in public perceptions of the conflict—themes familiar in American mainstream media reporting of it as well.

> Many in our audience samples did not even understand that there was a military occupation or that it was widely seen as illegal. There was very little knowledge of the conditions of the occupation or its effects on the Palestinian economy. . . . The absence of the Palestinian rationale also meant that on the news they were frequently presented as "starting" the trouble while the Israelis "retaliated."
>
> In contrast, Israeli views, such as their need to defend themselves against terrorism, were very well represented on the news. Israeli perspectives were more frequently featured in headlines and were often highlighted to the exclusion of alternatives. A frequency count of the coverage given to interviews and reported statements also showed the Israeli dominance.
>
> Journalists sometimes adopted the language of Israeli statements and used it as their own direct speech in news reports. On controversial issues such as the Israeli settlements in occupied territory, there was a tendency to present these as "vulnerable" and under attack without indicating that many are heavily fortified and play a key military and strategic role.[58]

THE WAR AT HOME REDUX: "THE ISRAEL LOBBY"
AND U.S. FOREIGN POLICY

In March 2006 two prominent American political scientists published a highly critical analysis of what they termed "the Israel Lobby" and its influence on American policy in the Middle East. More than two years after the intense violence of the second intifada had waned and media attention in the region had largely shifted to the war in Iraq, once again a spotlight shone on an aspect of the Israeli-Palestinian conflict, evoking a furious response. Even though the genesis of the controversy now came from within academe and not the media, mainstream coverage of "the Israel Lobby" once again underscored the inability and/or unwillingness of American news organizations to report—or report critically—on events and topics that cast Israel, its supporters, and U.S. Mideast policy in a less than favorable light. It also proved that critical voices and ideas are much more readily accessible in friendly international venues, including Britain and Israel, than they are at home.

In their eighty-two-page working paper entitled "The Israel Lobby and U.S. Foreign Policy," authors John Mearsheimer of the University of Chicago and Stephen Walt of Harvard University argued that the "combination of unwavering U.S. support for Israel and the related effort to spread democracy throughout the region has inflamed Arab and Islamic opinion and jeopardized U.S. security," a phenomenon they linked to the assertion that "the overall thrust of U.S. policy in the region is due almost entirely to U.S. domestic politics, and especially to the activities of the 'Israel Lobby.'"[59]

The authors defined the lobby as "the loose coalition of individuals and organizations who actively work to shape U.S. foreign policy in a pro-Israel direction," at whose core are those "American Jews who make a significant effort in their daily lives to bend U.S. foreign policy so that it advances Israel's interests."[60] That core, the authors contended, is dominated by AIPAC, the American Israel Public Affairs Committee; however, the lobby's membership also includes "prominent Christian evangelicals" and "neoconservative gentiles," among them prominent media commentators.[61]

Reading the Text: Provocative Arguments, Explicit Qualifications

Mearsheimer and Walt laced their argument with bold and provocative assertions in support of their thesis, perhaps the boldest being that Israel has become a strategic liability to the United States vis-à-vis terrorism. They wrote: "Saying that Israel and the United States are united by a shared terrorist threat has the causal relationship backwards: rather, the United States has a terrorism problem in good part because it is so closely allied with Israel, not the other way around. U.S. support for Israel is not the only source of anti-American terrorism, but it is an important one, and it makes winning the war on terror more difficult."[62]

The authors also asserted that a further reason for questioning Israel's strategic value is that "it does not act like a loyal ally," citing as examples that Israel has spied on the United States more aggressively than any other ally; that it has made transfers of sensitive U.S. military technology to China; and that it has frequently ignored U.S. requests and reneged on promises made to the United States to halt settlement construction and refrain from targeted assassinations of Palestinians.[63]

With regard to AIPAC, Mearsheimer and Walt characterized the pro-Israel lobby organization as "a *de facto* agent for a foreign government [that] has a stranglehold on the U.S. Congress."[64] The political scientists further argued that "the Lobby" as a whole not only has unduly influenced the legislative and executive branches of the government with respect to its Middle East policy but also routinely attempts to stifle debate and discourse within American civil society—specifically in the media and academe—on matters pertaining to Israel.

"It does not want an open debate on issues involving Israel," the authors wrote of the lobby, "because an open debate might cause Americans to question the level of support that they currently provide. . . . The goal is to prevent critical commentary about Israel from getting a fair hearing in the political arena. Controlling the debate is essential to guaranteeing U.S. support, because a candid discussion of U.S.-Israeli relations might lead Americans to favor a different policy."[65] Regarding the media, the authors asserted that in order to "discourage unfavorable reporting on Israel, the Lobby organizes letter writing campaigns, demonstrations, and boycotts against news outlets whose content it considers anti-Israel."[66]

Mearsheimer and Walt focused the last quarter of their analysis on the assertion that the war in Iraq, which the United States commenced in 2003, "was motivated in good part by a desire to make Israel more secure."[67] They contended that members of the lobby—some within the Bush administration itself—have strenuously promoted the notion of extending the policy of regime change beyond Iraq to Iran and Syria.

The authors made an apparent effort to balance their provocative arguments and unflaggingly critical tone regarding U.S. policy and the lobby with several plainly stated qualifications and disclaimers. They acknowledged

Israel's right to exist, the noxious nature of anti-Semitism, and the right of American Jews and other supporters of Israel to lobby on its behalf. They also qualified the role of American Jewish influence in the Bush administration's decision to go to war in Iraq.

Early on in their paper Mearsheimer and Walt twice asserted that the history of Jewish suffering and "the despicable legacy of anti-Semitism . . . provides a strong moral case for supporting Israel's existence," and that "Europe's crimes against the Jews provide a clear moral justification for Israel's right to exist."[68] However, the authors also asserted that "the tragic history of the Jewish people does not obligate the United States to help Israel no matter what it does today."[69]

The authors also acknowledged wrongs perpetrated by Israel and the Palestinians alike against each other. Arguing at one point that "the creation of Israel involved additional crimes against a largely innocent third party: the Palestinians," Mearsheimer and Walt also plainly stated their view that "Palestinians have used terrorism against their Israeli occupiers, and their willingness to attack innocent civilians is wrong."[70]

The authors were also careful to qualify their characterizations of the role of American Jews in the lobby and to acknowledge the legitimate existence and functions of the lobby itself. "Not all Jewish Americans are part of the Lobby because Israel is not a salient issue for many of them," the authors observed, citing a 2004 survey sponsored by the Jewish Agency for Israel in which 36 percent of American Jews polled said they were not emotionally attached to Israel to one degree or another.[71] Furthermore, Mearsheimer and Walt asserted,

> In its basic operations [the Lobby] is no different from interest groups like the Farm Lobby, steel and textile workers and other ethnic lobbies. What sets the Israel Lobby apart is its extraordinary effectiveness. But there is nothing improper about American Jews and their Christian allies attempting to sway U.S. policy toward Israel. The Lobby's activities are not the sort of conspiracy depicted in anti-Semitic tracts like the *Protocols of the Elders of Zion*. For the most part, the individuals and groups that comprise the Lobby are doing what other special interest groups do, just much better.[72]

The authors appeared to strive for a similarly balanced approach with respect to other aspects of their argument. Concerning anti-Semitism, they wrote that "anyone who criticizes Israeli actions or says that pro-Israel groups have significant influence over U.S. Middle East policy—an influence that

AIPAC celebrates—stands a good chance of getting labeled an anti-Semite. . . . In effect, the Lobby boasts of its own power and then attacks anyone who calls attention to it." However, this assertion was immediately followed by the statement: "This tactic is very effective, because anti-Semitism is loathsome and no responsible person wants to be accused of it."[73] Relating the role of Jews within the lobby to the Bush administration's decision to go to war in Iraq, Mearsheimer and Walt wrote: "It would be wrong to blame the war in Iraq on 'Jewish influence.' Rather, the war was due in large part to the Lobby's influence, especially the neoconservatives within it."[74]

The authors concluded their paper with an appeal for greater transparency in public discourse about the lobby and its relationship to U.S. national interests in the Middle East.

> Although the Lobby remains a powerful force, the adverse effects of its influence are increasingly difficult to hide. . . . What is needed, therefore, is a candid discussion of the Lobby's influence and a more open debate about U.S. interests in this vital region. Israel's well-being is one of those vital interests, but not its continued occupation of the West Bank or its broader regional agenda. Open debate will expose the limits of the strategic and moral case for one-sided U.S. support and could move the United States to a position more consistent with its own national interest, with the interests of other states in the region, and with Israel's long-term interests as well.[75]

Media Coverage of "The Israel Lobby"

On its face, Mearsheimer and Walt's monograph exhibits both strengths and weaknesses. Concerning the latter, from a methodological point of view the authors rely almost exclusively on secondary sources—in the form of previously published media and scholarly articles and other tracts cited in forty pages of endnotes in the eighty-two-page document—as a substitute for carrying out original research to support their argument.

Perhaps more significant is the authors' tendency to make their case by substituting broad brush strokes for subtle delineation. Their tract is imbued with a polemical tone that gives virtually all the credit to the power of the lobby as the principal force driving U.S. Mideast policy, to the exclusion of other important economic and political factors. These were cited by critics of U.S. Mideast policy and the U.S.-Israel relationship who nevertheless found the argument in "The Israel Lobby" to be lacking. Within the first two weeks of its publication they offered reasoned critiques of the monograph's substance.

Writing in the alternative online media venue *ZNet*, MIT linguist Noam Chomsky asserted that U.S. Mideast policy is derived not from the lobby but from "strategic-economic interests of concentrations of domestic power in the tight state-corporate linkage." Asserting that Mearsheimer and Walt "tend to conflate the alleged failures of U.S. Mideast policy [with] the role of the lobby in bringing about these consequences," Chomsky also argued that the tract failed to address the "far more powerful interests that have a [greater] stake in what happens in the Persian Gulf region than does AIPAC (or the lobby generally), such as the oil companies, the arms industry and other special interests whose lobbying influences and campaign contributions far surpass that of the much-vaunted Zionist lobby and its allied donors to congressional races."[76]

Writing in the English-language Egyptian newspaper *Al-Ahram Weekly*, Joseph Massad, a professor of modern Arab politics at Columbia University, found fault with the logic of "The Israel Lobby," according to which, he wrote, "it is not the United States that should be held directly responsible for all its imperial policies in the Arab world and the Middle East at large since World War II; rather it is Israel and its lobby who have pushed it to launch policies that are detrimental to its own national interest and are only beneficial to Israel." Instead, Massad argued, a half century of U.S. policy has aimed at defeating third world national liberation movements around the world, including but not limited to those in the Middle East, giving the lobby power because its interests dovetail with those of the United States and not the other way around. According to Massad, "The fact that it is more powerful than any other foreign lobby on Capitol Hill testifies to the importance of Israel in U.S. strategy, and not to some fantastical power that the lobby commands independent of and extraneous to the U.S. 'national interest.'"[77]

From within the mainstream the *Washington Post* published a 7,700-word Sunday magazine piece the following July about the history and influence of the Israel lobby, presumably inspired by the controversy surrounding "The Israel Lobby" four months earlier. The piece also critiqued the substance of Mearsheimer and Walt's argument, finding little merit in it not only via Israeli voices but also via the voice of the reporter himself.

> Listening to Walt, you get the sense that he believes there is one correct and objective foreign policy that an enlightened elite would be able to agree upon if only those grubby ethnic interest groups were not out there playing politics. . . . He doesn't allow for the possibility that

foreign policy in a pluralistic democracy is inevitably the product of a noisy clash of interests, or that the success of Israel's supporters may stem from the country's popularity here or from American revulsion over Palestinian suicide bombings. Or for that matter that American opposition to the prospect of Iran achieving a nuclear bomb has little to do with Israel and more to do with American fears of ayatollahs with nukes.[78]

The significance of Mearsheimer and Walt's work, however, lies not in the data it presents or in the strength of its overall thesis. Rather, the unambiguous nature of that thesis clearly raises discrete questions of value concerning a topic of crucial importance vis-à-vis U.S. foreign policy and the standing of the United States in the Arab and Muslim worlds—especially at a time when U.S. policy sought democratization via public diplomacy in those societies. Furthermore, in view of the fact that the topics of U.S. policy toward Israel and the influence of the Israel lobby are rarely if ever broached in American mainstream political and media discourse, the authors' determination to bring these issues to light under their own names and those of their highly respected academic institutions—while almost certainly anticipating the visceral, negative responses their paper would evoke—is a further indication of the strength of their piece.

Not surprisingly, such controversy did materialize in the United States and abroad. The monograph was variously described as having set off "a firestorm in intellectual and political circles," "ignited a furious debate," "stirred a tempest," and evoked "a furious outcry from prominent American Jews."[79] Despite the paper's subject matter having wide impact for Americans and the event of its publication being rife with conflict and drama—three traditional values that inform news judgment—the American mainstream media were remarkably silent when it came to reporting on the monograph as a bona fide news story in the wake of its publication, about which readers and viewers could form their own conclusions concerning the merits of the authors' argument.

In the three weeks following the publication of "The Israel Lobby," the only three mainstream major U.S. dailies that saw fit to devote space to the story on their news pages were the *Boston Globe,* the *Washington Post,* and the *Chicago Tribune*—while at the same time newspapers in London, Jerusalem, Sydney, Hong Kong, and Kuala Lumpur were running news and feature reports on the monograph.[80] Most major U.S. papers, including the *New York Times* and the *Los Angeles Times,* opted not to report the story in the weeks immediately after it broke; similarly mute were *Time, Newsweek,*

U.S. News & World Report, and ABC, CBS, NBC, PBS, and NPR. CNN ran a thirty-second brief on the monograph. In its usual fashion, Fox News ran a segment that was all editorializing and no reporting.

Several other U.S. media outlets did carry word of "The Israel Lobby" without actually reporting on it by either running editorials or signed commentary pieces that were largely condemnatory, or by publishing blocks of mainly negative quotes from opposing scholars, pundits and other supporters of Israel. Some newspapers, such as *Newsday*, the *San Francisco Chronicle*, and the *Houston Chronicle*, posted an Associated Press report about the monograph on their Web sites—leaving readers to search and find it for themselves.[81]

News Coverage: Scant and Skewed

Mearsheimer and Walt's working paper first appeared on the Web site of the John F. Kennedy School of Government of Harvard University on March 13. The first American media outlet to report on the paper was CNN, which on the March 20 edition of *Lou Dobbs Tonight* wedged a thirty-second brief on the monograph between a video report on the North Korean nuclear debate and teasers to other stories that were to follow. Regarding "The Israel Lobby," Dobbs reported:

> There are new charges tonight that the United States for decades has put the interests of Israel ahead of the U.S. national interest. These charges are in a new study of the U.S.' relationship by two of the country's leading geopolitical academics.
>   Stephen Walt of Harvard University and John Mearsheimer of the University of Chicago in their study says [*sic*] U.S. policy in the Middle East is driven almost entirely by domestic politics and the so-called Israel lobby. Critics call these charges baseless.[82]

The identities of those critics and the substance of their opposition remained unclear, however. CNN did not return to report the story in greater detail as the controversy surrounding it began to heat up in the days that followed—especially after the *London Review of Books* published an edited, unannotated version of "The Israel Lobby" on March 23.[83]

Print media news reporting was more detailed with respect to the central arguments of "The Israel Lobby" and tended to present some balance in terms of reaction to it. However, all three reports carried by the *Boston Globe*, *Washington Post*, and *Chicago Tribune* tended to emphasize reaction that was negative rather than positive and none looked beyond the heat of the controversy itself to shed light on the substantive issues that Mearsheimer and Walt had raised. These tendencies toward scant news reporting on the monograph, coupled with the preponderance of editorials and signed columns that other U.S. mainstream papers ran in opposition to it, prompted the *Financial Times* of London to editorialize: "Judgment of the precise value of the Walt-Mearsheimer paper has been swept aside by a wave of condemnation. Their scholarship has been derided and their motives impugned. . . . On various counts, this is a shame and a self-inflicted wound no society built around freedom should allow."[84]

For the *Boston Globe* "The Israel Lobby" was first and foremost a local story, with Walt a Harvard University faculty member. As the controversy spread, the newspaper reported that the university's Kennedy School of Government took a series of steps to distance itself from the monograph. First it removed its logo from the paper and added a disclaimer stating that it did not represent or reflect the "official position" of either Harvard or the University of Chicago. Second, it opened faculty working papers to rebuttal by other Harvard professors. The *Globe* ran several news articles on the unfolding events, initially reporting the flap as a front-page story on March 29.

Although the 1,000-word report offered a detailed summary of the authors' assertions, the journalistic framing of reaction to it clearly cast the scholars as being on the wrong side of hegemonic discourse. Outside of Harvard, no credible, nonpartisan supporters were heard from, with the *Globe* report characterizing reaction to the monograph as having "received attention far beyond academia, drawing praise from former Ku Klux Klan leader David Duke and Arab world media, and condemnation from many intellectuals and Israel advocacy groups." The report next quoted at length from an Internet radio broadcast endorsement for the piece by Duke, which was followed by yet another summary of reaction: "The paper is also getting heavy play on websites operated by the Arab satellite television network Al Jazeera, the Islamic extremist group Hamas, and the Palestine Liberation Organization."

The piece went on to quote Walt as saying: "My coauthor and I stand behind our paper, and we welcome serious scholarly discussion of its arguments and evidence. Period." It also quoted a Kennedy School representative as saying the school was firmly committed to academic freedom and supportive of "scholars introducing ideas into the public arena where they can be discussed and debated." It then quoted three local sources at length about their opposition to the monograph, including two Harvard professors and the associate director of a Boston-based pro-Israel media watchdog group.[85]

The *Washington Post* was the second paper to report on the controversy. On April 3 it published a 950-word report on page three that was more balanced in its sourcing than the *Globe's* page-one report but still tilted toward the naysayers. Two Harvard professors were quoted, one calling the monograph "paranoid and conspiratorial" and the other saying that it played "into the terrible argument that Jewish no-goodniks control the media and our foreign policy." These outright negative assessments were followed by two benignly negative quotes at the end of the piece in which two other academics did not deride the authors' conclusions but disagreed with the substance of some of their arguments.

In between these four reactions, which were negative in varying degrees, was a supportive comment from Juan Cole, a Middle East scholar at the University of Michigan, who was quoted as saying: "There's nothing intellectually wrong with arguing that U.S. policy in the Middle East is dislodged from its natural moorings by the power of a domestic constituency. But most people are timid—they don't want to be smeared and risk having their lives ruined." Walt himself was also quoted in the *Post* report as reiterating a central thesis of the monograph: "We knew that some of the responses would not be gentle or fair."[86]

The *Chicago Tribune* was the third of the three papers to report the story. Given the local angle of Mearsheimer being on the faculty at the University of Chicago, the piece got prominent play on page three of the paper's April 6 edition. While focusing to a significant extent on Mearsheimer's past statements about Israel and the Iraq war, the 1,100-word piece, like the *Globe* and *Post* reports, gave greater weight to critics of "The Israel Lobby" than to its proponents, citing five negative reviews and two positive notices. The *Tribune* also reported that "a piece [by Mearsheimer and Walt] on Israel and the U.S. national interest originally was commissioned by The Atlantic Monthly, but when editors saw it, they declined to run it. Some of Mearsheimer and Walt's supporters take that as further proof of the Israel lobby thesis, saying such is the power of the Jewish state's supporters that dissenting views can't get published in the U.S."[87]

This echoed what Mearsheimer had told the *Jewish Daily Forward*, a weekly journal of Jewish affairs, in a report it published on March 24. "I do not believe that we could have gotten it published in the United States," Mearsheimer said, adding that the paper was originally commissioned in the fall of 2002 by one of America's leading magazines, "but the publishers told us that it was virtually impossible to get the piece published in the United States. . . . Publishers understand that if they publish a piece like ours it would cause them all sorts of problems."[88]

Opinion Coverage: More Plentiful but Still Skewed

Whereas four U.S. mainstream media outlets reported on "The Israel Lobby" as news, nine news organizations covered it within the realm of commentary: Fox News, the *Boston Globe*, *Washington Post*, *Los Angeles Times*, *Christian Science Monitor*, *Boston Herald*, *Chicago Sun-Times*, *Newsday*, and *U.S. News & World Report*. These outlets ran a total of thirteen pieces, of which ten were negative assessments of "The Israel Lobby," two were neutral and one was positive. According to type, the thirteen pieces comprised five guest commentaries or op-ed pieces (three negative, one neutral, and one positive), three roundup pieces of reaction to the monograph (two negative and one neutral), three signed columns (all negative), and two editorials (both negative).

In a format similar to a broadcast version of an op-ed piece, Fox News addressed "The Israel Lobby" on the March 25 edition of its *WSJ Editorial Report*. Editorial board members Paul Gigot, Dan Henninger, Rob Pollock, and Bret Stephens discussed the Mearsheimer-Walt paper from a defensive and oppositional posture. The conservatism of Fox News and the *Wall Street Journal* dovetailed seamlessly in the segment, which, as Fox's sole coverage of the story, amounted to a discussion that ultimately focused more on allegations that the monograph was anti-Semitic than on a balanced and substantive assessment of its thesis.

> GIGOT: Rob, let's get to this issue of the Israel lobby, because it's really an accusation of dual loyalties. It's not anti-Semitic, but it's basically saying that to those of us who support Israel are as loyal to Israel as we are to the United States. This argument has always existed, sort of on the fringes of the Right and Left . . . but usually it's been on the fringes. Why is it suddenly coming to the mainstream in these two very prominent academics making the case?
>
> POLLOCK: I think it has a lot to do with frustration over the Iraq war. I know the people's sense of vulnerability, and they're [the authors] trying to exploit that. What's particularly offensive about this paper . . . it does verge on anti-Semitism. And the reason I think that is because it rests entirely on a largely unargued assertion, which is that support for Israel is indefensible on the merits, and of course that's absurd. Israel is a democracy. In fact, until the Iraq war Arab votes counted more in Israel than they did in any Arab country.

GIGOT: But I think you can make a case, Rob, that you can criticize American strategic interests dealing with Israel and not be anti-Semitic. But I do think it is a smear . . .

POLLOCK: And they need to argue that case. They don't argue it.

STEPHENS: But absolutely you can criticize Israel and Israeli policy and not be an anti-Semite, but what's strange about this argument is to say the reason Americans have supported Israel by broad majorities for decades, 59 percent to 50 percent, is that there is a kind of conspiracy of editorialists and lobbyists and other sorts of nefarious players who are pulling the strings in Washington, so the small state, Israel, actually becomes the patron of the large state, the United States. And that's a classic anti-Semitic trope.[89]

Apart from its news coverage of the controversy, the *Boston Globe* devoted considerable space to opinions on the matter, with staff columnist Jeff Jacoby weighing in against "The Israel Lobby" on March 29. Jacoby argued that the truth of the matter, vis-à-vis the authors' thesis, was "precisely the reverse": "America's loyalty to Israel isn't engineered by a Zionist cabal that dupes American citizens and hijacks their government. U.S. policy tends to align closely with Israel's because Americans like Israel. . . . If public opinion weren't robustly pro-Israel in the first place, the White House and Congress would be far less inclined to give Israel's advocates the time of day. There's a name for that phenomenon. It's called democracy."[90]

In the "Ideas" section of its April 2 Sunday edition the paper published two pieces on the Mearsheimer-Walt monograph. The longer of the two was a favorable 2,000-word critique written by British journalist and author Geoffrey Wheatcroft—the only apparent evidence of an unequivocally positive critique of "The Israel Lobby" to run in the American mainstream media. Noting that the "ferocious response" to the monograph "suggests a taboo being broken," and that "there is always a danger when something is willfully ignored," Wheatcroft went beyond Mearsheimer and Walt's pointed critique of the lobby itself to observe: "It has been plausibly argued that no 'Israel lobby' is needed to sway the American people, who are bound to Israel by deeper ties of sentiment. That may be so, but it may also be that the really sensitive nerve that Mearsheimer and Walt have touched isn't 'the lobby' as such. They have raised a graver question: Is unconditional American support for Israel—whatever its motives or origins—actually in the truest interests of both countries?"[91]

In an apparent attempt to balance Wheatcroft's probing assessment, the second piece was a "sampling of reaction" roundup consisting of quotes from seven observers—six of them American and all writing in American media outlets—all of whom opposed the monograph.[92]

In addition to its news coverage of the monograph, the *Washington Post* published two commentary pieces. The first ran in its Sunday "Outlook" section on March 26, with about half devoted to citations from the monograph and the other half a roundup of previously published reactions to it—six of which were negative and two positive, including one from former Klan leader Duke.[93] On April 5 the *Post* published an opposing op-ed piece by Eliot A. Cohen, a professor at Johns Hopkins University, under the headline "Yes, It's Anti-Semitic"—a paraphrase of Cohen's ultimate characterization of the monograph.

> Inept, even kooky academic work, then, but is it ["The Israel Lobby"] anti-Semitic? If by anti-Semitism one means obsessive and irrationally hostile beliefs about Jews; if one accuses them of disloyalty, subversion or treachery, of having occult powers and of participating in secret combinations that manipulate institutions and governments; if one systematically selects everything unfair, ugly or wrong about Jews as individuals or a group and equally systematically suppresses any exculpatory information—why yes, this paper is anti-Semitic.[94]

In the absence of news reporting, the *Los Angeles Times* ran two commentary pieces, the first a neutral if somewhat hedging piece that appeared in the paper's March 26 Sunday "Current" section. Written by Nicholas Goldberg, editor of the paper's op-ed page, it favored description over analysis, leaving readers to reach their own conclusions: "So what are we to make of all this? Is it anti-Semitism or honesty? Propaganda cloaked in academic respectability—or a courageous willingness to identify the elephant in the room? . . . It seems silly to deny that a powerful lobby on behalf of Israel exists. The real question is how pernicious it is. Does it, in fact, persuade us to act counter to our national interest—or is it a positive thing? . . . My advice is to judge for yourself."[95]

On March 29 the *Los Angeles Times* published a negative assessment of "The Israel Lobby" by Max Boot, a former *Wall Street Journal* editor and fellow at the New York–based Council on Foreign Relations, who sarcastically concluded:

> After finishing [Mearsheimer and Walt's] magnum opus, I was left with just one question: Why would the omnipotent Israel lobby (which, they claim, works so successfully "to stifle criticism of Israel")

allow such a scurrilous piece of pseudo-scholarship to be published? Then I noticed that Walt occupies a professorship endowed by Robert and Renee Belfer, Jewish philanthropists who are also supporters of Israel. The only explanation, I surmise, is that Walt must himself be an agent of those crafty Israelites, employed to make the anti-Israel case so unconvincingly that he discredits it. "The Lobby" works in mysterious ways.[96]

Of the three reaction roundup pieces, only that of the *Christian Science Monitor*—published April 5 on its Web site but not in its print edition—offered a balanced mix of perspectives.[97] Both the *Boston Herald* and *Chicago Sun-Times* saw fit to editorialize against "The Israel Lobby." On March 26 the *Herald* declared: "We can't recall an academic document as misleading as an anti-Israel tract turned out this month by a Harvard dean and a University of Chicago professor." On March 27 the *Sun-Times* called the monograph "a shameful and irresponsible article . . . [that] reflects the hate-distorted things [former Klan leader David] Duke believes about Jews and Israel: that there is a Jewish cabal that controls the media and the U.S. government on behalf of Israel."[98]

In addition to Jacoby of the *Boston Globe*, two other columnists came out in opposition to "The Israel Lobby." In an April 3 *U.S. News & World Report* column, David Gergen devoted a good deal of his critique of Mearsheimer and Walt's "nerve-jangling essay" to a defense of the loyalty of American Jews. "As a Christian," he wrote, "let me add that it is wrong and unfair to call into question the loyalty of millions of American Jews who have faithfully supported Israel while also working tirelessly and generously to advance America's cause, both at home and abroad. They are among our finest citizens and should be praised, not pilloried." Gergen bypassed the substance of the monograph's analysis of how the lobby exerts its influence, focusing instead on his own empirical observations as an adviser to several presidential administrations: "Over the course of four tours at the White House, I never once saw a decision in the Oval Office to tilt U.S. foreign policy in favor of Israel at the expense of America's interest. . . . I can't remember any president even talking about an Israeli lobby."[99]

In a piece published on April 7, *Newsday* columnist James Klurfeld found "at least two major problems" with "The Israel Lobby": the equivalence it attributed to Israeli and Palestinian actions and its contention that "the neoconservative Israeli lobby" forced the Bush administration into war in Iraq in order to help Israel. "Has the United States made mistakes?" Klurfeld asked. "Obviously. Washington [has] failed to adequately oppose Israel's settlement policy, a 40-year mistake. But it has been the Palestinians' failure to meet the Israelis even halfway—and their use of terrorism—that has caused the U.S. tilt toward Israel."[100]

Views from Abroad and the Upshot at Home

An explanation as to why "The Israel Lobby" received little news coverage in the U.S. mainstream media could be found in the *Forward*, which reported the media story behind the monograph story on March 24. In a piece headlined "Scholars' Attack on Pro-Israel Lobby Met with Silence," the *Forward* reported that in the ten days since the monograph had been posted on the Kennedy School's Web site, "most major print outlets had ignored it."

> Despite their anger, Jewish organizations are avoiding a frontal debate with the two scholars, while at the same time seeking indirect ways to rebut and discredit the scholars' arguments. Officials with pro-Israel organizations say that given the limited public attention generated by the new study . . . they prefer not to draw attention to the paper by taking issue with it head on. As of Wednesday morning [March 22], none of the largest Jewish organizations had issued a press release on the report.
>
> "The key here is not to do what they probably want, which is to have this become a battle between us and them, or for them to say that they are being silenced," said Malcolm Hoenlein, executive vice chairman of the Conference of Presidents of Major American Jewish Organizations. "It's much better to let others respond."[101]

That pro-Israel organizations had made a clear strategic calculus about the dynamics of media coverage was further echoed by Ken Jacobson, associate director of the Anti-Defamation League, who told the *Forward*, "In these kinds of things you're always trying to debate how important will it be in terms of the impact, if you give it more attention. The amount of attention we will give it will depend on how it plays out."

The *Forward* report also suggested that editors in the mainstream press were clearly taking a cautious approach to reporting on "The Israel Lobby"—further evidence that a cat-and-mouse game, deliberate or otherwise, was being played out between the media and those who would likely protest coverage of the story. The report noted that "several editors, foreign affairs reporters and columnists for major American newspapers contacted by the

Forward did not know about the study. They didn't sound especially interested when told of the report's findings. . . . A senior editor with one of America's largest daily newspapers, who asked not to be quoted by name, said: "We don't get excited about academic papers unless they tell us something new, and this one doesn't."[102]

Many news organizations outside the United States, however, had a very different sense of news judgment about "The Israel Lobby," which got substantial press in Britain, arguably the most stalwart ally of the United States with respect to official policy toward Israel and the war in Iraq. Following the publication of an edited version of the monograph in the *London Review of Books*, no fewer than four British newspapers reported on the ensuing controversy. The *Observer* headlined its April 2 story "Israel Row Spreads to Britain: London Review of Books Stands Its Ground After Being Accused of Anti-Semitism in an Article Attacking Pro-Israeli Influence on U.S. Policy." The liberal *Guardian* and *Independent* also reported the story, with the latter running a feature on April 7 headlined "At Last, a Debate on America's Support of Israel."

In addition to editorializing favorably about "The Israel Lobby," on April 4 the *Financial Times* published a 1,200-word commentary by Mark Mazower, a history professor at Columbia University—who, apparently like Mearsheimer and Walt, was compelled to seek publication in Britain of sentiments that had little if any chance of being published in the United States. "What is striking is less the substance of their argument," Mazower wrote of Mearsheimer and Walt, "than the outraged reaction: to all intents and purposes, discussing the U.S.-Israel special relationship still remains taboo in the U.S. media mainstream." Noting that leading American newspapers "have remained silent" on the monograph and its ensuing controversy, Mazower observed, "Whatever one thinks of the merits of the piece itself, it would seem all but impossible to have a sensible public discussion in the U.S. today about the country's relationship with Israel. . . . There is no reason why the partnership between the U.S. and Israel should not be susceptible to the same kind of cost-benefit analysis as any other area of policy."[103]

Quoted in international press reports, the monograph's authors tended to sound notably less defensive than they had in the American press. In a piece reported from Washington that appeared under the headline "U.S. Professors Accused of Being Liars and Bigots over Essay on Pro-Israel Lobby," Mearsheimer told the *Guardian*: "We argued in the piece that the lobby goes to great lengths to silence criticism of Israeli policy as well as the U.S.-Israeli relationship and that its most effective weapon is the charge of anti-Semitism. Thus, we expected to be called anti-Semites, even though both of us are philo-Semites and strongly support the existence of Israel. Huge numbers of people know this story to be true but are afraid to say it because they would [be] punished by pro-Israel forces."[104] Walt told the *South China Morning Post*: "We wrote the article in part to encourage a broader discussion of the forces shaping U.S. foreign policy in the Middle East at a time when U.S. policy is of great importance."[105]

Moreover, international reporting on "The Israel Lobby" also tended to cast the "now it can be told" aspect of the controversy in a positive light. Despite running the sensational headline "Harvard Disowns Anti-Jew Report" and noting that the monograph had caused "a furious outcry from American Jews," the *Weekend Australian* nevertheless observed that "no one disputes that the Jewish lobby is an influential force in U.S. politics and that the American Israel Public Affairs Committee is one of the most powerful organisations in Washington."[106] In a piece headlined "Looking Anew at Israel Through Clear Lenses," Malaysia's *New Straits Times* referred to "The Israel Lobby" as an "extraordinary monograph" and observed of the authors: "They have introduced not a single new fact, but in assembling the known data and by asking the right questions, they have suddenly transformed the permitted dialogue in the United States on relations with Israel. Maybe we should say they have made it possible now to have a dialogue. What is important about the essay is not what they say but who is saying it."[107]

Given that the American mainstream media apparently could not find and/or would not publish any wholly positive assessment of "The Israel Lobby" by American sources or commentators; that the overwhelmingly negative press the monograph received in the United States was shot through with direct and indirect charges of anti-Semitism; and that the majority of the negative reaction was more prone to attack the authors than the merits of the case they had laid out—perhaps the most remarkable notice given to "The Israel Lobby" from abroad was published in Israel.

In an op-ed piece in the liberal daily *Haaretz*, Daniel Levy, a former adviser to the prime minister's office and a member of official Israeli teams that had negotiated with the Palestinians, offered a qualified but nonetheless sober assessment of "The Israel Lobby." He wrote:

> The tone of the report is harsh. It is jarring for a self-critical Israeli. It lacks finesse and . . . it sometimes takes AIPAC omnipotence too much at face value. Yet [the authors'] case is a potent one: that identification of American with Israeli interests can be principally explained via the impact of the Lobby in Washington, and in limiting the parameters of public debate, rather than by virtue of Israel being a vital

strategic asset or having a uniquely compelling moral case for support (beyond, as the authors point out, the right to exist, which is anyway not in jeopardy). The study is at its most devastating when it describes how the Lobby "stifles debate by intimidation" and at its most current when it details how America's interests (and ultimately Israel's, too) are ill-served by following the Lobby's agenda.

The bottom line might read as follows: that defending the occupation has done to the American pro-Israel community what living as an occupier has done to Israel—muddied both its moral compass and its rational self-interest compass.[108]

That such candid assessments were wholly missing from American mainstream reporting on "The Israel Lobby"—and the effects of that lacuna—were duly noted by the *Financial Times*. In a lead editorial published on April 1, the British paper pinpointed that which apparently lies beyond the American mainstream media's ability to grasp and report on regarding the interconnectedness of U.S. policy on Israel, the trajectory of the Israeli-Palestinian conflict, the influence of pro-Israel forces in the United States, and American interests and standing in the Arab and Muslim worlds.

Honest and informed debate is the foundation of freedom and progress and a precondition of sound policy. It is, to say the least, odd when dissent in such a central area of policy is forced offshore or reduced to the status of samizdat. . . .

Nothing is more damaging to U.S. interests than the inability to have a proper debate about the Israeli-Palestinian conflict, how Washington should use its influence to resolve it, and how best America can advance freedom and stability in the region as a whole. Bullying Americans into a consensus on Israeli policy is bad for Israel and it makes it impossible for America to articulate its own national interest.[109]

6

IN THE FIELD

HOW DO AMERICAN FOREIGN CORRESPONDENTS REPORT THE STORY OF the Israeli-Palestinian conflict in the field? How do they gain access to official and unofficial Israeli and Palestinian sources and process "spin" from both sides? How do they perceive the reporting field as they try to cover a story marked by intercommunal violence, one that requires them to navigate simultaneously through two distinct cultural milieus?

A work investigating American mainstream media reporting of the Israeli-Palestinian conflict would not be complete without the observations and insights of those who actually have done the job. It is one thing to consume the coverage, evaluating its merits and flaws. It is quite another to produce it.

The following interviews with fifteen correspondents who have covered the story for thirteen major American news organizations address the journalistic practice and ethos at work in reporting the Israeli-Palestinian conflict from the field. The interviews were conducted on the record and for attribution, twelve in person and three by telephone, from November 2003 to March 2004.[1] At the time they sat for the interviews, none of the journalists was reporting the Israeli-Palestinian story. All had moved on to other assignments, some to other news organizations. Their postings in the Middle East spanned seventeen years, from 1985 to 2002. The majority of the correspondents interviewed—twelve of the fifteen—averaged three and a half years in the field; three averaged eight years in the field.

At the time of their postings, the correspondents worked for ABC News, the *Baltimore Sun, Boston Globe, Chicago Tribune, Christian Science Monitor, Dallas Morning News, Houston Chronicle, New York Times, Newsday, Newsweek, Philadelphia Inquirer, Time,* and *Washington Post.*

The interviews make clear that while the Israeli-Palestinian conflict is neither the most physically dangerous nor inaccessible of international conflicts to cover, for the American audience it may be the longest-running conflict with the most familiar themes. This, however, has not necessarily facilitated deeper journalistic exploration either of historical and political root-cause issues relating to claims made by Israelis and Palestinians themselves or of the impact that U.S. policy has had—and continues to have—on the conflict. Such critical reporting may actually be impeded, at least in part, precisely because the reporting field is characterized by a ready supply of easily accessible official and nonofficial sources, combined with a constant dramatic arc occurring against a familiar backdrop and within a relatively small geographical expanse. Understanding these factors from the correspondents' points of view—coupled with the audience's familiarity with the conflict and its expectations for and responses to the reporting (see chapter 5)—sheds further light on the nature of the journalism produced in terms of what it covers and what it omits.

Furthermore, the interviews indicate that despite the conflict's accessibility, journalistic standards require that correspondents not only constantly balance competing claims but also frequently test those claims by gathering information that can be empirically verified at the scene or through eyewitness accounts—especially when it comes to reporting on acts of intercommunal violence that so often mark the trajectory of the daily story. Reliance on empiricism as a tool to reconstruct events—coupled with the acute awareness on the part of both Palestinians and Israelis of the American media's importance as a conduit for their claims to perhaps the most important of international audiences *and* the fact that their respective mechanisms for conveying those claims on an official level are not equal—make reporting the Israeli-Palestinian conflict from the field a multidimensional journalistic challenge. It is within this context that the results must be evaluated by lay and academic audiences alike.

During the interviews correspondents responded to questions specifically geared toward issues of work process based on their own experiences in the field. However, from their responses also flowed anecdotes and narrative analyses of how the conflict evolved during the periods of their postings and, in some cases, how it has evolved since then. The interview responses that follow are grouped thematically. However, the correspondents' words and ideas have not been parsed or synthesized. Although the interview transcripts have been edited for conciseness and narrative flow, the correspondents' words stand unfiltered, with the ideas of each journalist presented individually to allow for the most direct and accurate reflection of how each has viewed his or her work of reporting the conflict.

The interviews corroborated two main themes, with response patterns indicating that these phenomena have continued to characterize the process of reporting the Israeli-Palestinian conflict from the field over time. The first theme involves access to sources. The correspondents noted the ease and eagerness with which Israelis and Palestinians—official and unofficial sources alike—engage with American journalists, so much so that two correspondents characterized reporting the story as a reporter's "dream." Another observed wryly: "This is a country of six million or seven million people, and probably all of them have been interviewed more than once." According to the correspondents, Palestinians and Israelis themselves are acutely aware of the importance of image and of conveying their sides of the story via the media, especially to the American audience.

The second theme involves how Israeli and Palestinian media relations compare and how the two sides process spin. The correspondents acknowledged that the imbalance of power and disparity in societal development between the two sides affect how they relate to journalists. Correspondents all agreed that Israel's system of media relations is far ahead of its Palestinian counterpart in terms of sophistication, organization, and access generally, although some observed a Palestinian learning curve in recent years.

Several correspondents noted that this discrepancy in the ability of both sides to deal with the media is entirely logical, given the fact that for more than half a century Israel has been a sovereign state with democratic mechanisms, including a free press. Palestinian society, conversely, has been under occupation for four decades and has been unable to develop similar systems of governance and media. These differences also manifest themselves in the presence of a broader range of opinion about the conflict existing within Israeli society than within Palestinian society.

The correspondents also concurred that these disparities and other factors—including the fact that most American and other Western correspondents choose to live among Israelis in West Jerusalem because of its higher standard of living rather than residing among Palestinians in East Jerusalem or other locales—have had little or no effect on their actual work product, that is, on the coverage itself. Several correspondents stated that despite their sophistication, Israeli media relations don't necessarily work to Israel's benefit, just as the Palestinians' relative lack of facility with the media doesn't necessarily work to their disadvantage. As one correspondent noted, "Journalists have the good sense not to judge a people's cause on the basis of their organizational skills and media relations."

The highly familiar and dramatic arcs of the conflict and its accessibility to those reporting it yield encounters with people and events—many of the latter violent in nature—that evoke subjective awareness on the part of the correspondents. Nevertheless, they concurred on the primary importance of achieving balance and fairness in their reporting. To that end, the section of interview excerpts captioned "Vignettes" reflects how correspondents attempt to balance these sensibilities with professional standards. A subtext of compassion for Israelis and Palestinians alike could be discerned in the reminiscences of many of the correspondents about the time they spent covering the conflict. Several expressed the notion that Israelis and Palestinians are in many ways similar and that they share a common destiny. Three of the correspondents used the word "heartbreaking" to describe what has transpired between the two peoples since late 2000: the deterioration of the situation on the ground, marked by a spiral of violence and death; and the rollback of political progress toward a resolution of the conflict.

The final section of this chapter is devoted to the perspectives of four correspondents who reflect at length on their reporting of the Israeli-Palestinian conflict. In the course of this reflection, they offer not only critical views of the subjective factors that drive the reporting process—both in the field and from audiences and newsrooms back home—but also insight with respect to how these factors can shape and/or limit the parameters of journalistic discourse on key aspects of the conflict. The correspondents' observations include the following: the sheer volume of U.S. mainstream media coverage of the conflict may actually mitigate against prospects for its resolution; a preoccupation with that which can be encapsulated in a headline or broadcast image diverts attention across time and media from deeper yet vital aspects of the conflict, frequently rendering the reporting repetitive and unilluminating; to attempt unfiltered reporting on aspects of the Palestinian experience under occupation and Palestinian historical claims not only is often discouraged by newsroom culture but can also result in swift and unstinting audience censure; and there is a proportional relationship between the level of violence at any given stage in the conflict and media attention afforded it.

❧

The major theme of the analysis of American mainstream media reporting of the Israeli-Palestinian conflict presented in this study is that the coverage routinely omits two key underlying contexts: the impact of U.S. policy on the trajectory of the conflict; and the importance of international law and consensus regarding the key issues of Israeli settlement and annexation policies and the right of return of Palestinian refugees. However, it should be noted that these contextual issues were not addressed in the questions put to the correspondents; the interviews focused on their work process of reporting the story from the field. Nevertheless, these issues appeared to be absent from the majority of correspondents' frames of reference in the answers and observations they provided. Two correspondents mentioned international law but did so only in passing. Only one correspondent—a citizen of Canada—found it germane to comment on U.S. policy.

This explains two important phenomena. First, as was indicated earlier, the dynamics of the story in the arena of conflict itself, namely, in the field, are so suffused with drama and relatively easy access to Israeli and Palestinian sources that crucial contextual elements originating elsewhere—for example, in Washington and at the United Nations—are overshadowed to the extent that more often than not they are omitted from the reporting. Second, for this and other reasons—including the tendency of U.S. policy action (as opposed to policy rhetoric) to minimize or even bypass international law and consensus on key issues of the conflict—the journalistic product, as demonstrated in the reporting patterns presented in the preceding chapters, frames media discourse on the conflict in a way that reinforces and supports rather than scrutinizes and challenges U.S. policy that in many ways undergirds it. Despite the fact that for the past forty years American foreign policy has had a profound influence on the Israeli-Palestinian conflict, that reality seems largely detached from and even irrelevant to how the story is reported in the field.

IN THE FIELD

Access to Sources

Robert Ruby, Baltimore Sun, *June 1987–September 1992*

It was a very turbulent time; a lot of things were changing for the worse for everyone concerned. The first Palestinian intifada began. When everyone realized that it would be going on for a while, that it was more than a three- or four-day event, for the first time reporters were perceived as part of the problem. Israel's self-image was at issue. There was so much criticism of Israel's military tactics and the conduct of some of its soldiers that many Israelis got angry at the messengers. It was only the second time—the first time was the Lebanon war—that Israelis had to deal with a tremendous amount of internal dissent.

So the status of the foreign press changed dramatically—not with official Israeli sources, but in interactions with members of the Israeli public. Going to communities to interview people, you'd get many more harangues about your own failings or failings of the American government than in the past. But this had no concrete effect on reporting the story, though.

The Palestinian leadership was in Tunis. There were ancillary figures, such as Faisal Husseini in East Jerusalem and other notables, who clearly spoke for more than just themselves. It was neither legal nor safe for them to talk about their relations with the PLO, which was banned at the time. Their positions were veiled, but you could figure out that they did have some authority and leadership roles. There was Palestinian spin. Each side had its cause, and each side was invested in making its cause seem like the central concern of the time. It was a contest of righteousness: who was suffering more.

George Moffett, Christian Science Monitor, *October 1987–January 1991*

I had excellent access to everyone on the Israeli side I needed to see. The press people were very generous with their bosses' time. The difference between the Israelis and the Palestinians is that with the Israelis you have a central source from which information is disseminated. There was coordination in their responses. So even though you have a range of opinions within Israel extending all the way from right-wing Jewish settlers, on [the] one hand, to Peace Now, on the other, when it came to the official line, it was always easier to discern exactly where the government was, issue by issue. With the Palestinians it was different. There you have a range of opinions, and there was no central authority to fill that gap because the people who ran the operation were far from Jerusalem, in Tunis. That's not to say Palestinian sources weren't also very forthcoming. But you had to do a little more piecing together of the story to ensure getting the real drift of where the Palestinians were on any given issue.

In terms of unofficial sources, people were only too happy to talk. You couldn't walk into a Palestinian refugee camp without running into people eager to talk, and they all said essentially the same thing. We used to refer to them as "cassettes" because they imparted the same general message about the brutality of the occupation and the need for a Palestinian state and their rights being taken away.

In Israel it was the same thing. People were utterly willing to talk, and you had then a very significant division of opinion. Half of the Israelis—and I'm using these percentages loosely—looked at the intifada and said it was a reason to get out of the West Bank and Gaza Strip. The other half looked at the intifada and said it was a reason to stay there because security was threatened.

The sense I got from people on both sides was one of victimization. It was a prevalent theme. At the root here you're dealing with two peoples, neither of which have a secure sense of national identity, and for perfectly understandable reasons. The Jews had been without a homeland for two thousand years. They've been persecuted. They've been killed. They've been tortured. Is it any wonder that they want a secure state? The Palestinians have never had a state. And a good portion of the real estate that would make up that state has been seized in violation of international law. And so they feel like victims, too.

With respect to official Arab sources, there were some interesting complications. For example, whenever I went to Tunis [where the PLO was headquartered], there was always this polite fiction maintained. They would never ask—and you would never disclose—that you were based in Jerusalem. Not because there was anything to hide, but because there was always concern on the part of the reporters that our Arab sources would assume that we would bring with us a pro-Israel bias instead of the neutrality that characterizes good journalism.

Carol Morello, Philadelphia Inquirer, *January 1990–February 1994;*
return reporting trip November 1995

Before Oslo you could go to Tunis and interview PLO officials. But they weren't inside, they were detached from what was happening on the ground. You got a line; there was no diversity of opinion.

[In the West Bank] you could also interview Hanan Ashrawi, Sari Nusseibeh, Faisal Husseini. You could go to Gaza and see Haider Abdel Shafi. These were people who were the de facto leaders, not officials but notables who had power and influence within Palestinian society. You could go to their homes, see them without much advance notice. Unofficial sources also were accessible. You could interview members of the Fatah Hawks or Islamic leaders, but you'd need a fixer and it might take two or three days to arrange.

The Israelis make it very easy for you. The IDF has a spokesman; every ministry has a spokesman. You can get officials; you can get the story. The sources are right out there waiting to be picked. If you don't get it, then you're not doing your job.

Every government has its take, depending on who is in power. Rabin told AIPAC, "You don't speak for the government of Israel; we do." [Beyond government] there is a diversity of opinion that reflects the society. There are three broad categories: a third of the population that wants peace at any cost; a third that values the land more than peace; and a third that falls somewhere in between.

Palestinian society is more communal, so there is less diversity of opinion. Dissent is not as tolerated and respected. Generally when you go out and talk to Palestinians in villages, towns, and cities, they tell you what they think you want to hear, what will advance the cause, not necessarily what is true. How do we keep from getting played? We use more than one source and double- and triple-check certain statements.

Ethan Bronner, Boston Globe, *August 1991–July 1997*

[When covering violent events] on the Israeli side, physical access was easier. First of all, because [Western journalists] tend to live in Israel, and there aren't military checkpoints stopping you from getting there. And then, once you get there, you have a whole range of people who will give you witness accounts, and then you will very easily get to a hospital and get survivors to talk to you. And usually within a few hours, depending on the scale of the atrocity or of the attack, the prime minister or the police minister comes to the scene and gives an impromptu press conference, usually in both Hebrew and English. On the Israeli side, when something like a suicide bombing happens, you really get a whole notebook full of stuff, and then the problem is to pare it down.

On the Palestinian side, it's less easy to get to the spot because the Israeli military is likely to close the area off. Assuming you get through, you tend to have a less educated population to interview. So their descriptions may be somewhat less detailed or sophisticated. There is an incredible sense of victimhood in Palestine—understandably—and so there's not a lot of "let's step back and analyze what happened." There's a lot of "look how they're killing us" talk. When you get to the hospital, it's more chaotic, it's less clear and you tend to be less sure of the details.

Once at a hospital in Beit Jala [in the West Bank] I recall seeing three guys on IVs. At some point I understood that the IVs were not needed, but the doctor had taped them to [the] arms [of the wounded] so that if [Israeli] soldiers came in, they would not take [the wounded] away. The doctors exaggerated the injuries in order to prevent Israelis from removing these guys. A doctor told me that. There was a communal effort to protect people.

Storer H. Rowley, Chicago Tribune, *August 1994–September 1998*

This is a country of six million or seven million people, and probably all of them have been interviewed more than once. I studied Arabic for a couple of months before I went there. It's a very difficult language, and you can't learn it in a couple of months. I could understand a few phrases of Arabic and a few phrases of Hebrew, but I couldn't conduct interviews in them. On the Israeli side, most people speak English. In the Palestinian territories, far fewer people do. But it was never an issue that prevented me from writing a story. The few times I had to go off on my own when I didn't have time to find a guide or an interpreter, I made my way. I found that just a little bit of Arabic could get you to the point where you found someone who spoke English. As long as you can get into a place, you can find whomever you need, whether it's people in the Jabaliya refugee camp [in the Gaza Strip] or the psychologist at the institute in Gaza or a professor at Tel Aviv University. It's a country where access to unofficial sources is in general pretty easy.

Regarding official sources, it was an uneven playing field in the years I was there. The Israelis had a government, a long-established relationship with the media, and a very efficient operation for getting their message out and trying to shape the message that is reported there. They understand the value of getting the correspondents the interviews they want and need for stories and were very good at facilitating when they could.

The Palestinians were starting a new government. The PLO had a history of being an underground guerrilla group in many ways. Learning how to operate efficiently in the glare of international media publicity is not something they did well. But they were learning in the years I was there. They would have news conferences. They built a government. They had ministers and press officers in those ministries. President Arafat had press officers who would contact us when news conferences and events would happen. They were reachable on their cell phones when there was an incident or breaking news story that required comment. Certain people who were closer to Arafat were often better [sources] than the Palestinian public affairs office. Arafat would often make people wait. He could never seem to get anywhere on time. You'd have a room full of press people waiting for him, sometimes for long periods.

But the Palestinians were learning, and they were getting cooperation from Israel where they could. And they were getting help from the U.S. government.

Edward Abington, who was the consul general in Jerusalem, was instrumental in trying to advise and help the Palestinians. Ed was the unofficial ambassador to the Palestinian Authority. When major events would happen, Arafat got a lot of advice from [Abington's] senior people and sometimes from U.S. government officials on how to deal with things. The U.S. was the mediator: the embassy in Tel Aviv was dealing with the Israeli government, and the consul general in Jerusalem was dealing with the Palestinian government.

The day Rabin was killed, Abington was with Arafat shortly thereafter. He advised him to be in touch with the Israeli government, to express condolences and to make a statement about how damaging this could be for the peace process and how committed he was to it. The United States was doing all it could to keep the process going over every bump in the road and every disaster along the way, right down to trying to let the Palestinians know what would be expected of them in terms of how to deal with the media.

Barton Gellman, Washington Post, *October 1994–December 1997*

The general level of politicization and media awareness among the [Israeli and Palestinian] populations is stunning. It's simply remarkable the degree to which consciousness of international media and one's role in the struggle—in talking to the media and the appropriate storyline to take—have penetrated to the very grass roots of both populations.

You can't walk into a town or a village or a home and find someone who doesn't get the idea of a foreign correspondent interested in the conflict, doesn't get what they're supposed to say and who doesn't tend to say it at least the first few times you ask the question. And then you have to look for ways of getting beneath the surface position, the history of injustice. They all know all the lines, and they all know they're supposed to talk to you.

There's almost no overt hostility toward the press, very small pockets of it. I felt quite comfortable talking to Hamas, Islamic Jihad, the Palestinian Authority, Fatah loyalists, and the whole spectrum of Israeli society save, occasionally, elements of the hard-line settlement movement. They tended to feel that the press was against them and occasionally they were hostile. But even they would tend to want to talk to you and to convince you—or at least get their quotes in the story. Even if they didn't appreciate what I or we [journalists] were doing, they recognized it as a vital battleground for the rival claims to a certain historical argument, to persuading the world of the justice of their cause. Both sides clearly saw world opinion—and U.S. opinion in particular—as vital to the success of their national mission.

Deborah Horan, Houston Chronicle, *January 1997–August 2001*

People on both sides are so used to the press asking for quotes that most people whom you stop have some comment. During elections I went to a working-class Israeli neighborhood and asked, "Why do you want to vote for Ariel Sharon?" And everybody was willing to talk.

In the West Bank people are willing to talk as long as you can get there. When you're stuck at a checkpoint, you can call up the army spokesman's office in Jerusalem and say, "Hey, these guys [soldiers] won't let me in. Is this a closed military area?" And they say, "No, it's not a closed military area." And I say, "Why won't your soldier let us pass?" So I hand him my cell phone, and eventually he would say, "Okay, you can go in."

Everybody has something to say and everybody knows exactly the issue at hand and exactly what's going on. It's not like here, where there's voter apathy, people are busy with their lives, doing other things. People there know exactly what every politician said, and they know exactly what's at stake.

Lisa Beyer, Time, *September 1991–August 2000*

I was astonished to go into a refugee camp in Gaza and talk to the most ordinary of individuals—a cobbler—and he knew how to give you a sound bite.

People are familiar with being covered, for the most part, and that makes your job easier. You don't have to explain to people what *Time* magazine is. Most people were very happy to have you cover them, whether it's the director-general of the Israeli prime minister's office or some member of the military wing of Hamas. They understood and were happy to facilitate.

This is a conflict in which you are able, more so than a lot of other conflict stories, to find out what really happened [in a breaking news event]. There is a certain truth that comes out because these are societies that are accustomed to talking to journalists. In part this is because Israel is a working democracy, and democracies tend to tell truth better than nondemocracies. Israeli officials or individuals have at least one part of the picture that they can share with you, and they often will—even if it doesn't reflect well on Israel. Both of these societies are very intimate, very small. People know each other. There are a lot of eyewitnesses to things that happen. If something happens on a street in Hebron to an individual, pretty soon that individual's cousins know it.

So you have a way to find things out. It's not like being dropped suddenly into Somalia or Liberia. In Liberia there was this terrible conflict that resulted in the ousting of the president. Nobody could figure out what it was about. What were the two sides fighting for? Part of that is because you don't have three hundred foreign journalists based in Liberia as you do in Jerusalem. That's one of the ways in which this conflict is unique.

Dan Klaidman, Newsweek, June 1999–October 2000

One of the interesting things about Israeli and Palestinian societies is despite the fact that they've been at war for so long, they have been intertwined for a long period of time. Some of the characteristics and attributes of one side rubs off on the other side. Israelis tend to be pretty accessible. It's a small country. Not to engage in stereotypes, but Israelis are talkative and they're also pretty vehement about getting their story out. As a result, it's a foreign correspondent's dream to be in Israel because you can literally get the cell-phone numbers of just about every member of the cabinet.

To a lesser extent, that has rubbed off on the Palestinians, probably because they know that they are not just in a military and political struggle, but they're in a PR struggle as well. Although their message may not be as sophisticated [as the Israelis'], they're still pretty accessible. Part of it is that people want to reach American audiences, and they know that a weekly newsmagazine reaches a large audience in the United States. And so everyone is always looking for a way to get the message out. I don't know that I had to try much harder with Palestinians than with the Israelis. They were about equally accessible. It's just that the Israelis had a machinery of public relations and press information that the Palestinians didn't have.

The diversity of opinion in Israel was pretty impressive. You would have people, average Israelis, who were very hard-line and believed in a lot of the mythology that had been part of Israeli education since the beginning of the state. And then you had people who had very different views and a more nuanced sense of the issues. So there's a very broad spectrum of [understanding of] what the history was and what had to be done about it. You could pick up the phone and talk to one of these revisionist historians, Israeli historians who had a very different picture of the history than you might get from the average Israeli on the street.

Palestinian opinions were more limited because of the kind of press they had and the history books that they read in their schools. If you went to refugee camps, for example, I'm not sure you would get the same kind of diversity of views as you would get talking to average Israelis. That stems largely from the fact that we're talking about a democracy, on the one hand, and a regime that is much more authoritarian and where the media are much more controlled by the government.

On the other hand, I would hear from the Palestinian intelligentsia and some members of the Palestinian Authority during Camp David that the right of return was not going to be a sticking point. They said, "We recognize that ultimately there can't be an absolute right of return because we understand that that would mean the end of Israel and a two-state solution." But then I would go and talk to people in a refugee camp in Gaza who said they couldn't compromise on the right of return, and that if Arafat compromised on this, there would be a civil war.

Toward the end of Camp David, I was quoting Israeli and Palestinian officials as saying that if it didn't work—and they were speaking with almost utter certainty—there would be a violent reaction. The Israelis were saying that they would have to prepare for guerrilla warfare. I thought that to some extent this was hyperbole on the part of Israeli officials. How could they know this? But we reported it because it was such a widespread view among Israelis and also among Palestinians. Two things happened the closer Israeli and Palestinians got to a settlement. It brought into focus all of the disputes on the key issues. But it also got Palestinians thinking about their own plight and the fact that despite years of the Oslo process, their conditions hadn't improved as much as they had been led to believe by both their own leaders and by the Israelis as well.

We had beepers. We'd get beeped constantly, we'd get e-mails, we'd get telephone calls from the IDF, and they were constantly briefing us and providing very senior people like the deputy chief of staff and intelligence officers. With the Palestinians you had to be more proactive. You could get to sources, but it was harder—you had to rely on your own initiative as opposed to them coming to you, which the Israelis did on a regular basis. Ultimately, even though the Israelis made it easier, I don't think it had much effect on the coverage.

We constantly tried to get interviews with Arafat and were always unsuccessful. It was a period when he simply wasn't talking, before he was isolated by the Israelis. I don't think he felt that he necessarily needed to get his message out to the American press.

Processing Spin

George Moffett

It felt as if both sides were desperately eager for Western journalists to understand their viewpoint. I'm going to make an aside here that will put the time during which I was reporting in a somewhat better perspective. After the Holocaust, after the exodus of Jewish immigrants to Israel at the end of World War II, after struggling against the British Mandate before 1948, and after being the victim of a number of coordinated Arab attacks, suddenly, for the first time in its history [during the first intifada], Israel was no longer in the role of underdog.

That was huge at the time. There was a sense that the Israelis lost some of their innocence during the intifada. Suddenly they were the Goliath and not the David. The sense of the plucky little state surviving against all odds—the public perception of that began to change. It changed because so much light was suddenly thrown on conditions in the territories and because the Israelis resorted to such harsh measures to quell the intifada. I guess the symbol of that was Yitzhak Rabin's "break their [Palestinian] bones" policy. You had human-rights workers looking under every rock in the territories, in the West Bank and Gaza, and suddenly, in every newspaper around the world, a different sense of Israel was being conveyed.

I remember that shortly after the intifada began, Zbigniew Brzezinski, Jimmy Carter's national security adviser, gave a talk in Jerusalem. It was a pointed reminder to the Israelis that the indispensable link in the U.S.-Israeli relationship was not political or strategic but moral, and that if that link were weakened, it could have significant effects on relations between Washington and Jerusalem. So that's why this whole issue had enormous resonance with both sides. The Israeli side wanted to get out from underneath this changing sense of Israel, and the Palestinians were eager to capitalize on it by putting themselves in the position of the new underdogs.

Initially, in some government quarters, there was a tendency to respond [to international press coverage] with charges of anti-Semitism. This was not prevalent, but I do recall one day receiving a call, fairly early on after the start of the intifada, from an official in the prime minister's office. He said, "We want you to be aware that we believe that the *Monitor*'s coverage has been anti-Semitic." I thanked this official and told him that my newspaper would certainly want to know if its coverage appeared to be biased. I said it would help me to explain to my editors if [he] could give me an example of something that would fall into the category of anti-Semitism. There was a long pause; there was no specific example. But the call was a measure of the raw nerve that was hit by all of the coverage. Some of my colleagues also received calls.

It was a passing phase, but, I thought, an illustrative moment. I never really heard that from government officials after that. But when I would go to the settlements, I would hear lots of charges of anti-Semitism, lots of references to the fact that Israel had a right to take control of the West Bank and Gaza, partly for historical reasons. Those references came freely from a certain segment of the Israeli population. And the farther out into the West Bank they were from Jerusalem, the more pronounced those perceptions were. The farther out you got the more crucial it was to have a rationale for why you would implant yourself in the middle of the Palestinian population in the West Bank.

The Palestinians were acutely aware that, for the first time, they had the attention of the world. With an equal measure of intensity, they were eager to capitalize on this moment by portraying themselves as helpless victims. It was not a difficult case to portray given that, at that point at least, they were throwing stones and the Israelis were shooting guns, sometimes with live ammunition.

Tim Phelps, Newsday, *January 1987–April 1991*

Israel had a very efficient and effective system for dealing with the press, and it was extremely good at making key officials available to the press. You could always get a spokesman from whatever relevant branch of the government, whether it was the prime minister's office or the army, to comment on whatever was needed twenty-four hours a day or close to it.

The complete opposite was true of the Palestinians. There were no official spokesmen, there was no official government. It was a matter of reporters having to track down people who were deemed to be in a position to speak on behalf of the Palestinians, and it was difficult.

The Israelis understood the culture of the press. The Palestinians, as well as most Arab countries, generally did not, and so that often made for a somewhat lopsided presence in our stories of Israeli spokesmen. Arab governments generally didn't do a much better job than the Palestinians in most cases of getting their point across. Gradually the Palestinians are learning something about press relations, but they're light-years behind the Israelis. If you don't have a free press in your own country or your own culture, it's hard to understand what it is that we are up to and what we need—and that we don't just take our information from official sources and [write] what we're told.

I suspect that it goes deeper than that in Arab culture. It's much more closed and private. Arabs are extremely friendly in terms of hospitality. But it's not polite to go into somebody's house and ask them questions about their lives or their political beliefs. There's also a cultural difference. The Israelis don't care so much about politeness. They're very direct. With an Israeli, whether an official source or not, I would blurt out exactly what I wanted to know from them, and they would be impatient if I didn't. What I learned to do in the West Bank was to sit for hours, drink tea and coffee and wait. Most journalists either don't have that kind of time or aren't willing to invest that amount of time.

The Israelis had a very organized spin. In a crisis or on a big issue, they would have a coherent story line and talking points about what happened and why. It would be something that was agreed upon ahead of time, and all the official people would be pretty much saying the same thing, and it might or might not reflect reality. With the Israelis, there was usually a reflection of reality, but certainly not the whole truth all the time. The Palestinians had no mechanism to agree on a message. You would get hearsay, stories, and rumors. There was a very limited Palestinian press at that time, so you would find different stories about what had happened if there was a big event.

In October 1990, during the first intifada, there was a massacre on the Temple Mount. The Israelis went in and shot nineteen Palestinians [who had been throwing stones at Jewish worshipers at the Western Wall]. I got there within a few minutes after it happened; there was blood everywhere. The initial Israeli version of it was far-fetched and essentially dishonest, as later Israeli commissions eventually bore out. From the Palestinians you could hear all sorts of wild things far beyond reality.

The trick was to find individuals who actually saw what happened. I found that if I disregarded all of what people who hadn't seen it told me and limited it to people who had seen it, there was a certain amount of consistency. I came to believe that the Israeli account of it was wrong, and I wrote it that way—of course including the Israeli account.

On the Israeli side you have this very sophisticated propaganda that tended to be much more believable than what you got from the Palestinians. They would tell you anything that popped into their heads—unless you found people who had actually seen the event and you were very careful to press them for specific details at each step along the way: Did you see that? Or did you see that?

Ethan Bronner

There's a big difference between the way the two sides dealt with the press. The Israelis had a much more sophisticated structure for press relations. When you arrive in Israel as a correspondent, whether you're a visiting correspondent or coming to stay for several years, the government press office will give you a list of all members of parliament, their press spokespeople, their phone numbers and now their cell-phone numbers. Israel has a very active academic commentary community and a very active press filled with people used to talking to outsiders. So getting people to talk to you in Israel about the conflict is very easy.

On the Palestinian side, it's more complicated. They're better than other Arab governments, but they're still not great at it. The classic example [was] trying to get an interview with Yasser Arafat. You had to go hang out for night after night after night. You wouldn't be given an appointment to see him.

If you want to see a particular Israeli cabinet minister, you make an appointment. Basically it works like it works here. That's a big distinction. They understand how the press works and how we function. The terms "off the record," "background," "on the record" are more clearly understood by the Israelis than the Palestinians.

The Israelis are good at issuing statements in good English. I remember when Shimon Peres, who was the foreign minister of Israel in 1994, went to Jordan for a meeting with Jordanian prime minister Abdel Salam Majali. It was on the Jordanian side of the Dead Sea. It was a moment of reckoning; there was going to be a peace treaty. Peres spoke, and after it was over, we got his speech in Hebrew, English, and Arabic, stapled and ready. Then the Jordanian spoke, and [the text] wasn't available in print in any language. That's fairly typical of the difference in press relations.

There's no question that this affects the coverage. But it's a very complex impact, because journalists as a group tend to be sensitive to the needs and stories of the underdog in any conflict. So while there is a slick, professional press relations operation in Israel, that is sometimes seen as something to pierce through, not to accept at face value. Israel might be subject to greater scrutiny by journalists, in fact, than the Palestinians are. It works as you'd expect, which is to say that the Israeli side gets its story out better and faster. But it also has this paradoxical or counterintuitive effect of pushing journalists to sometimes write off the Israeli side as just a PR machine and to try to go seek the real story—not to get manipulated by the great military machine that is the Israeli occupation. So I don't know that it's necessarily all to Israel's good, frankly.

One of the hardest things about reporting on Arab society, not just Palestinian society, is the fact that there is not a very broad spectrum of thought about the conflict. There is a certain uniformity, a certain conformity of thought that seems to be endemic. In Israel, if you want to talk to someone who believes that Zionism is illegitimate, or to someone who believes that Zionism is the word of God, you just open your Rolodex. You'll have no problem getting from one end all the way to the other, with many stops in between. If you want to find a Palestinian who will say to you: "Listen, the Jews have a historic right to be here. These are two just conflicts, two just causes," you'll have a great deal of trouble. There are very, very few Palestinians who will say that. In fact, I'm not sure I know of any.

[Why that is so] is a very, very complicated question. It's very difficult to spin out a full theory about it, to try to theorize. I do think it has to do with culture, but I don't fully understand why. Israelis do a better job of talking the language and concepts that are closer to the way we deal here. The Palestinians tend to speak in terms of conspiracies, the Israelis less so. I tend to not place much stock in conspiracy theories. In that sense the Israelis typically will have a more pragmatic, realpolitik explanation for something. The Palestinians might have a slightly more mystical, ideological explanation.

The trouble is, when you're abroad, you have these two instincts as a foreign correspondent that are propelling you, and you get whip-sawed between them. One is to say: "These people are just like you. These people that I'm reporting on, they eat, they have children, they care about their children, they want a good future, just like you." That's one view. The other view is: "These people are so different from you that if you think that by knowing that they have children, that they eat and that they care about their land that you can understand them—forget it. They are a completely different culture."

Storer H. Rowley

Everyone in the Holy Land interprets history to promote their view of things. There's so much history there that it's possible to see why both sides can take the same set of facts and come up with completely different narratives. Wading through that is a daily challenge. There are specific events, the 1947 UN resolution calling for the creation of two states, one Jewish and one Arab, in Palestine, for example, whose facts are indisputable. But what has happened since—and why it happened—can be in dispute. And the solution can be in dispute.

The language in the Oslo accords was very specific about what they were going to do and what they were trying to accomplish. The Israelis saw it as a gradual approach: "If we go on to the next step, if everyone complies with the details of this step, then we'll move farther along; we'll see." They interpreted Oslo very literally.

A lot of the Palestinians I interviewed saw Oslo as the beginning of their deliverance and their liberation. There was an expectation that, "Yes, we're taking small steps, but soon our land will be ours again," they would say. When the process dragged on, and when Rabin's assassination or suicide bombings happened and it would be delayed, the official Palestinian spin was that their government was doing all it could to comply with everything it had to, the setbacks notwithstanding, the occasional violence notwithstanding. "We're still waiting for our state," they would say, "with complete autonomy and the land, the dignity, the respect"—all the things that they'd waited all these years to have.

Both sides spun it the way they saw it going, and within each side there was an incredible amount of division about what was enough and what wasn't. There was a multiplicity of viewpoints, not just Palestinian versus Israeli narratives, but right-wing, left-wing inside Israel, Labor versus Likud. Inside the Palestinian territories there was Arafat's government, more moderate, pro-Oslo. Then there were the militant groups—Hamas, Islamic Jihad, and others—who were completely rejecting Oslo and saying this is half a loaf. They wanted all or nothing.

Barton Gellman

Israel has one of the most advanced PR operations on the planet, and it is exceptionally effective because it accommodates enormous diversity and very little effort to discipline a message the way that you have in Washington. One of my first interviews was with Yossi Beilin. He was deputy foreign minister to Shimon Peres at the time. He said X, and I said I thought Foreign Minister Peres had said the opposite the week before. And Beilin said—in fact he said it in Hebrew—*"Az mah?* So what? That's him, this is me." It's stunning the degree to which everyone freelances there. Yet on the core message they'll agree.

[The official Palestinian message] wasn't as universal. You had inside and outside Palestinians. The ones who stayed all through the intifada and all through the Israeli domination of the West Bank and Gaza, and the ones who were in Tripoli and Beirut and Tunisia. They didn't have the same exposure to a vibrant debate and to the role of the press. So some of them were much less inclined to talk or to talk at length, or they were less sophisticated in their spin. Spin is effective as long as it stays reasonably close to verifiable facts. If it can be easily disproved, then it's not effective.

There's enormous Israeli accessibility. The foreign minister, the defense minister, the prime minister—you can get direct home phone numbers for almost anybody: Here's the car phone, the home phone, the bathtub phone, my mistress's phone. You can find almost all of them all the time, and this was before cell phones and e-mail had penetrated quite as much as they have now.

The night that Rabin was shot, before he was dead, I'm frantically calling around and I get the health minister on his cell phone in his car. And he says, "Here's a report I have from the hospital." It's that kind of accessibility you really miss when you leave Israel. You can talk to everybody. They will speak their minds in a diverse way, and yet on the core message about the cause and the nation and the national interest, they overlap very significantly and therefore are very effective.

On the Palestinian side, you can't get them on the phone. You can't get them to call back. You can't make appointments very easily. You had to work in the way that you tend to work most places in the world except in the very developed world, which is you simply have to go find them. Even if they wanted to, they can't always keep appointments because their travels are interfered with [due to Israeli-imposed checkpoints and roadblocks]. You don't have as many English speakers among Palestinians, so phone work is automatically much more difficult. It's harder to have an interpreter on the telephone. To the discredit of the foreign correspondent corps, there are not very many fluent speakers of Hebrew or Arabic, and I confess the same for myself.

Even though the Israelis are so much more sophisticated in dealing with the press, I don't know that it makes their message much more effective. A very important dimension of covering any institution or conflict is holding people of power accountable for their use of power, and so there is a strong tendency in the press corps to examine the actions of the victor very closely. It is no secret to correspondents—it's just as obvious it can be—that the Israelis are better at PR than Palestinians are. And you correct for that.

You know what you have to do to penetrate it if you're doing your job seriously. You know you need to look for motives on both sides. You need to look for hidden machinations. You have to relentlessly make yourself get in the car—it's a small country, small territory—and drive there and look at it and talk to witnesses and look for physical evidence. Because for different reasons you're going to get different distortions on each side.

I don't think that having a much more sophisticated PR establishment did Israel much good relative to the Palestinians' incompetence in this area because the press had strong incentive to probe beneath it. We recognized that there were different forms of spin or falsity in the arguments of each side as well as truth, and that we had to find ways of compensating for that. I didn't see many correspondents who sat in their offices and gathered quotes and put that stuff in the paper. You saw people in the field all the time.

There was quite a lot of dishonesty among Israeli officials, but it was most often Washington-style, such as: "We're not destroying homes for retribution. We're doing it for security reasons." They would cover motivations with plausible reasons that were not actual reasons and did not reflect actual policy decisions. Whereas you'd get a much more naked sort of dishonesty from Palestinians. I'm not universalizing, but they would say, for example, that there was no one with a gun in the crowd. And you would review the footage, and there was plenty of firing from the crowd. Just black-and-white kinds of false statements. And they'd stick to them.

Ann LoLordo, Baltimore Sun, June 1996–September 1999;
return reporting trip October 2000

Israel's press relations were much better than the Palestinians', light-years ahead. Accessibility was equal on each side. But the big difference was that on the Israeli side people were speaking for the government. There was a legitimate, working government in place that had a mission, an agenda. Everybody was pretty much on the same map. I never felt that [to be true] on the Palestinian side. Yes, there was a president. Yes, there was a parliament. But never the twain shall meet. When we spoke to Arafat's spokesman, I was never confident that I had the sense that this is what Arafat really thought. Even when you could get [Palestinian spokesman and negotiator] Saeb Erekat, I didn't feel confident that he was meeting every morning with Arafat, and that this was what the Palestinian line was. The Palestinians seemed to be making policy by the seat of their pants.

It [had] a lot to do with the way Arafat operate[d]. He [held] everything in the pocket of his coat. He had people who were close to him, but they weren't functioning as a cabinet. After Ed Abington, the American consul [in East Jerusalem] who handled most of the Palestinian affairs, came back here, he was hired by the Palestinian Authority to be their spokesman in Washington. They needed an Ed Abington when we were there.

In some ways, though, the Israeli government had a harder time of spin because the government is functioning in a democratic society. There was plenty of opposition within government and outside of government and within the public at large that could deflate the spin factor. That helped you as a journalist. For example, every time the government would say, "We're taking down settlement outposts," there was someone who would come back and tell you about all the ones that they've put up since. Every time [Prime Minister Benjamin] Netanyahu would talk about making a stride forward, the Labor party would talk about how he was foot dragging, or how it really wasn't so much of a step forward.

On the Palestinian side, there was only one spin, which was that the Israelis weren't doing what they were supposed to be doing under Oslo. That they kept delaying and delaying. That all they were interested in was keeping as much of the West Bank as they could and keeping the Palestinians in cantons. That was their line. The difficulty in getting through their spin concerned the militant groups. It was very difficult to get access to the Palestinian Authority or to Arafat if you were trying to make a connection between what Israel was arguing about Arafat controlling terror. It was very difficult to make that connection.

The Palestinians would tell you: "Arafat doesn't control terror. These are independent groups; Hamas has its own governing body. We don't have any connection with them. They run their own shop." And Hamas wouldn't admit whether there was a connection between the two and whether they were taking orders from Arafat. You couldn't really make the connection definitively or show it. We wrote about a connection, but none of us ever proved it. It was clear from the Israeli perspective that Arafat controlled the terror.

Deborah Horan

When Israelis first started targeted killings or assassinations—depending on what you wanted to call them—of Palestinian militants, journalists were calling them assassinations. We were printing "assassination." The Israelis had a big campaign to get journalists to say targeted killings. And they wrote letters to editors saying these aren't assassinations. They're targeted killings. Other newspapers continued to use the word assassination. AP started using targeted killings. So we started using targeted killings because we follow AP style.

Palestinians consider the neighborhoods in Jerusalem that were built after 1967 to be settlements, and the Israelis consider them neighborhoods. But you don't have time to explain in every story why the Palestinians consider them settlements. Journalists try to be fair. You want to get both sides of the story even if it comes down to what something is called. You're trying to make sure that you're not favoring one side or you're not using language that only describes one side's worldview of something.

The Israelis are better funded and better organized. They are media-savvy and very accessible. They give you their cell-phone numbers. You can call them at night. I had the numbers of people in the government, people in the Knesset, and they called you back. The army would work with you. You could call them up and ask for a response to an incident and you would get a quote from them.

The Palestinians are not very well organized. They're not as well funded; they have too many other problems. But they are very accessible, and some are very media-savvy, like Saeb Erekat and Hanan Ashrawi. Some official sources tend to have trouble verbalizing their position—sometimes they think it just stands on merit, that they don't really need to explain. Some are not so good at describing what it is that they want or why they're doing what they're doing. A lot of times they answer questions with questions. I ask the question, and the answer is: "What would you do?" They don't understand why I'm asking the question. But you can get around it. You can put in a paragraph that sums up what you have seen or what somebody on the ground has said to you.

Lisa Beyer

The Israeli press offices are exceptionally well organized from my perspective as a representative of a major American news organization. If I wanted to see a minister, I saw a minister. If I wanted to see the prime minister, chances are I'd see the prime minister.

In my nine years of reporting on the conflict, I must have asked to see Arafat fifteen times. And the only reason I saw him the one time I did is because we made him person of the year along with Yitzhak Rabin in 1993, the year of the Oslo accords. The Palestinians are not necessarily going to be very helpful in telling you what it is you need to know, in being able to field very simple questions. Often when you speak to government officials, what you want to know is the inside story of how the government is thinking about something. That's very hard to get.

Even in '98, '99, 2000, when the PA had been established for four, five, six years, it didn't improve much. In six years I remember being invited to one Palestinian press conference. There were joint press conferences from time to time with the Israelis and the Palestinians, when Arafat would meet with Peres at the Erez checkpoint [at the north end of the Gaza Strip]. I remember one solo Palestinian press conference. It was to meet one of the Palestinian intelligence chiefs. It was in a fancy hotel in Ramallah, and they served us an exquisite, many-course lunch. Then he came out, and we were able to ask him questions.

In those same six years, there were probably about three hundred Israeli press conferences. The vast majority I wouldn't have gone to because I didn't need to, reporting for a weekly magazine. In the six years that I was covering the Palestinians, I probably met three or four Cabinet ministers. For the Israelis, about twenty.

The availability of information or propaganda is different on the two sides. The Israelis offer a lot more information, or propaganda, than the Palestinians do. But as a group, American and western European reporters were at least as sympathetic to the Palestinian Authority as they were to the Israeli authority—probably more. The American journalists tended to be more sympathetic toward the Israelis than western Europeans. The western Europeans tended to be more sympathetic to the Palestinians than the Americans were.

I would not say that the Americans tended to be more pro-Israel and anti-Palestinian. You can be sympathetic toward the Israelis and sympathetic toward the Palestinians. There's a difference between being sympathetic to a side and being pro that side—because if you're pro one side, you're anti the other side.

Palestinians get a lot of sympathy from both American and European journalists, despite the fact that their press organization was so screwed up. Journalists have the good sense not to judge a people's cause or a people's situation on the basis of their organizational skills and media relations. But it's also because the Palestinians are the underdogs. In this conflict the Israelis are the ones who have their rights. They have their state. They have their independence. They have their sovereignty. They have their national institutions. They have their international recognition. And the Palestinians are without those rights. The Palestinians are the group that is without.

Israelis always complain that the Western media cover Israel like a Western country. And the Israeli media cover every wart you could imagine on the State of Israel. But there's a double standard, people will say: They cover Israel as if it's America. They'll write about every political scandal, cover every terrible thing that the Israeli army does, every atrocity, every scandalous remark made. Whereas the Arab countries, the Arab governments—and this is certainly true of the Palestinian government—aren't covered so well, even though the atrocities were much worse, and the instances of government corruption clearly much worse than they are in Israel. It is, after all—aside from its treatment of the Palestinians—a functional democracy.

It was very hard to write about the underside of Palestinian governance even once there was a Palestinian government because no one would tell you the truth. It was very hard to find out the truth. There were muckraking prosecutors among the Palestinians who would be sources of information, or muckraking journalists who would turn up the first tip, or human-rights groups. But they're limited in what they can do and say. And so it's very difficult to cover the Palestinians. It used to be deadly business to talk about PLO finances. It was made very clear by the PLO in the early days that talking about what Arafat [did] with the PLO money was extremely dangerous. People were very scared to give information, and they were quick to warn you that publication of any damaging information about PLO finances could result in their death and your death. I experienced that.

That has started to change. You started to see articles written first in the Palestinian press starting in 1998 and 1999 about corruption. It began to be pretty openly reported—even names named. It became an open issue. But the level of public or media scrutiny in the Palestinian territories is still not what it is in Israel, where you have a very active press. Israel gets a tougher time in the media because Israel is an open society. The Palestinian Authority got more of a ride from the [Western] media in part because they cannot be covered like an open society.

When the Palestinian Authority came to power, foreign journalists wanted them to succeed. They wanted it to work. They wanted to see Palestinians get their rights. Probably there were quite a few moments when journalists chose not to look under the rock, especially in those early days. Whereas with Israel, people were looking under rocks every chance they got.

Interactions

Lisa Beyer

Most [Western journalists] lived among Israelis, and they got to know Israelis pretty well. Israelis are tough people. They're brusque and they're very straightforward. They're aggressive verbally. They're aggressive generally. After living there for nine years, I deprogrammed myself when I got back [to the United States]. I was so accustomed to saying exactly what was on my mind.

A big fear among people in Israel is to be caught as a *frier*, as they say, a sucker. Which means that nobody yields in traffic. You don't stand in a line, you jump ahead of people. It's just a really tough, unforgiving culture. You can understand all the reasons why that's true—and why it's an asset, actually, to the Israelis in the situation that they're in. God knows, [with] the history of the Jewish people, you'd be the same way. But it's tough to live with sometimes.

Hardly any [journalists] live among the Palestinians. It's very difficult to live among Palestinians. If you live in the West Bank, or even in East Jerusalem, you don't get garbage picked up, your electricity's not regular. You'll end up getting stuck behind checkpoints. And the nicer housing tends to be among the Israelis.

But, on the other hand, when you're visiting that culture, which is what everybody was doing as a foreign journalist, Palestinians are extremely hospitable. You go into someone's house, and they bring you a nice cup of sweet tea and make sure that you have the most comfortable chair in the house. If you compliment someone's rose garden, they'll cut every rose in their garden and send you home with them. They're very gentle and polite. I think that a lot of journalists make grander assumptions based on the manner of people, because in some ways it was more pleasant to be among Palestinians as a visitor.

Deborah Horan

Where [correspondents] live probably influences their perspective. I lived for four years in East Jerusalem and four years in West Jerusalem. When I was living in East Jerusalem, I saw [Israeli] soldiers in the Old City overturning Palestinians' carts. You see the daily friction, people getting carded, having to lift shirts or take off shoes. When I first moved into the Old City, there were Palestinian women [sitting] on the ground selling goods without permits. The city would come and confiscate their stuff twice a week, so little boys would look out for the municipal vans and they would go running through the market when they saw them.

The way these people are living is in your face. When I moved out of the Old City, I didn't see any of that every day anymore. But when I moved to West Jerusalem, I still went to the Palestinian side of the city and to the West Bank to work. I would still see both sides. When I lived in East Jerusalem, I went to West Jerusalem all the time. It's not as if living on one side you don't have any contact with the other side.

Where you live has some effect on your perspective because of what you're looking at when you walk out the door, how you know your neighbors and what they're thinking. When I lived in West Jerusalem, there were some Moroccan Jews living next door who were very right-wing, very pro-Netanyahu. The woman living on the other side of me was a potter, extremely left-wing. She went to city hall and complained because someone stuck a Netanyahu sticker on her pottery. She wanted the city to pay to have it removed. You get to see people on a very personal level, get to know people on a personal level when you see how they live.

Most of the journalists live in West Jerusalem because it has a higher standard of living. When I moved to West Jerusalem, suddenly I had cable. I could get mail at my house. I could wear what I wanted. I didn't have to worry about wearing long sleeves and having my miniskirt underneath a long skirt. But journalists go to restaurants in East Jerusalem, to the money changers. So it's not an either/or thing.

Storer H. Rowley

We lived in West Jerusalem for various reasons. One is we had two young daughters who were going to go to school, and the best school available to them, we decided, was in West Jerusalem. The standard of living is better there, and it approximates more what we're used to. I don't think living in West Jerusalem colored what we [journalists] reported, because we also spent a lot of our time reporting in East Jerusalem, the West Bank, and Gaza. That's where news was.

The incredible thing about covering this particular conflict is that it's in an area in which you can reach any place in four hours. It's a country of journalistic nonstop shopping because you can cover almost anything there in a day and be home. You can go to the Golan Heights in the morning and be back [in Jerusalem] and file your story at night. You can be on the border with Lebanon or the border with Egypt and be back and file that same night. It's always easier to be home with your family than it is to stay out. But where you live doesn't color what you write. The story dictates what you cover on a daily basis.

Tim Phelps

I lived in a lot of different places. I lived in the American Colony Hotel. Then I moved to West Jerusalem for a while. I had two different places in West Jerusalem. Then for a year we lived in Beit Jala [near Bethlehem in the West Bank]. I still had a place in West Jerusalem because of the curfews.

My familiarity with the West Bank made me much more relaxed, not just from living there but from speaking the language to some extent and spending a lot of time there. I generally felt I could go anywhere and do anything anytime, and I could tell through my fingertips that something bad was going to happen. When most journalists went into the West Bank during the intifada, they would roll up all their windows and drive as fast as they could. I would roll down all the windows and drive as slowly as I could. And I got attacked a lot less than anybody else. My impression was that those people who were most afraid were the ones who got attacked the most, because if you act like you're afraid, then people think you must have something to be afraid of.

VIGNETTES

George Moffett

I remember being in France in the lobby of a hotel and running into a man who was one of the original founders of the PLO back in the 1950s. I interviewed him every time I went to Tunis. He was an excellent source, and the subject of where I was based never came up. This was a spontaneous meeting; we were both waiting to see Arafat, who had gone to France to give a speech to the European Parliament. And so we ended up just sitting there for about forty-five minutes, and for the first time he looked me in the eye and asked, "Where are you based?"

I had to make a quick decision whether I wanted to be honest with him. I decided to be honest, and I told him I was based in Jerusalem. There was a very pregnant pause, and my immediate thought was that I had probably lost a source. Without saying a word, he reached down into his briefcase and pulled out a legal pad. He drew a line down the left-hand side and said, "You know the road that goes from Tel Aviv up to Haifa?" I said, "Yes, I know that road very well." He said, "You know where it gets wedged in between the bluffs and the railroad tracks?" I said, "I know that." He said, "You know where the road makes a right turn just after you pass the bluffs?"

And so on a piece of paper he drew the road, leading to a circle, and he drew little houses all around the circle. Then he circled one and he said, "That was my house." He said, "My family was driven out of that house by the Israelis in 1948. I've spent a lifetime dreaming that I would see that house again, and now my dream is that my children and my grandchildren will see it." He said, "If you ever go back there, will you take a picture of that house and bring it back to me?" It was a very interesting moment and a real insight into why the Palestinians feel what they do.

Not more than two weeks later I was at a dinner party with an Israeli journalist. She told her story about being raised in France, where at age twelve she was seized by the [Nazi] S.S., put in a boxcar, and sent to Auschwitz. Miraculously she survived.

Those two stories epitomize the utter difficulty of this issue, because you have two peoples, both of whom for very legitimate reasons have a desperate need for a clear and permanent sense of identity—and to a large degree identity is linked to geography.

One of the privileges of being a reporter in the area is the freedom to go back and forth all the time across the Green Line. But it was disheartening to hear Palestinians talk about the Israelis and Israelis talk about the Palestinians, because the Green Line is, metaphorically, a thousand-foot-high wall that is a barrier to mutual understanding. Anybody who crossed the line back and forth, day in and day out, knew that there was potentially such a coincidence of interests between the two peoples. We [journalists] had close friends on both sides, and it was always a tragedy to hear them talk about each other. Absolutely heartbreaking.

Storer H. Rowley

The Israelis and the Palestinians share so much of the same history but look at it so differently. I was there at a very good time, if you consider the history of the last fifty years. Arafat had just returned in 1994, and the 1993 Oslo peace process had started to be implemented. They started with Gaza and Jericho first, gradually trying to move toward giving the Palestinians more autonomy in the West Bank and Gaza.

It was a renaissance in some ways, the beginning of openness. It came after a six-year intifada from '87 to '93, and all of a sudden things were beginning to happen that had never happened before. The two sides were beginning to communicate with each other more, to understand each other more. Impossible things were happening: Arafat was back in the Holy Land, the Israelis and Palestinians were speaking to each other officially, and the Palestinians were trying to create a government. There was a lot of really good and happy coverage to do on both sides as the possibilities opened up.

But then various things started to happen that took you back to the conflict that wouldn't go away. Rejectionist Palestinians began suicide bombings. Israeli religious groups were opposed to the peace process, the most terrible result of which was the killing of Yitzhak Rabin. He was an inspiring leader.

It differed on a case-by-case basis, but in general when suicide bombs would go off in Israel proper, it was easy to cover them. Everyone jumped in their car and went to the scene. There might be security around the immediate area to deal with the death and destruction and the wounded, but we found access generally easy, and people gathering around were easy to talk to. If officials at the scene were busy, the Israeli government press operation was always very quick to explain what had happened, to notify the press. It was a very efficient operation.

The only bomb I actually ever heard go off was the triple bombing in 1997 in the Ben Yehuda mall, which is not far from Beit Agron, the building where a lot of foreign correspondents have their offices. I was in the building when the bombs went off. There was a distinctive double boom and then a pause and a third boom. It was immediately clear to me what I was hearing from the way it echoed through the city. I ran through the streets immediately to the scene; several people had been killed. The café had been blown up. The bodies of the bombers were still strewn around. At that point there had been enough suicide bombings so that people always were nervous that one bomb could be a deliberate effort to draw rescue workers and police so that another bomb could be set off to kill more people. So it was a very frightening scene to go to in that sense as well. But it was very easy to get access. I was there within minutes before even some of the rescue workers.

Getting into and out of the West Bank and Gaza was controlled by Israeli checkpoints. In the good days of Oslo, you could pretty much just drive through the checkpoints in the West Bank. In times of heightened security—suicide bombings or other violence—the checkpoints tended to be more securely armed, the cars more rigorously screened. Sometimes areas were closed off for security reasons, and there were many times I had to wait to get into Gaza. But because of the efficiency of Israeli press operations and their understanding of the media, I could get on the phone immediately with someone at the IDF, the foreign ministry, or at the government press office and say: "I and other journalists are being held up at this checkpoint. We need access." Most of the time we got it.

If you couldn't get through, there were ways to get around the checkpoints. You'd go to another road, you'd park your car and you'd walk. You would get in however you could because the story wasn't going to wait and your deadline wasn't going to wait. But most of the time you could get to where you needed to go.

Things started to go south in 1996. The Israelis had assassinated Yehia Ayyash with a cell phone that exploded. He was called "the engineer" because he was the primary Hamas bombmaker at the time. The extremist or guerrilla groups—the militants of Hamas and Islamic Jihad—made it absolutely clear that they would retaliate for that. And it was generally thought that the four bombs that went off in rapid succession in February and March of 1996 were in retaliation for the killing of Ayyash. That was the most serious spate of bombings while I was there. Dozens of people were killed in eight days.

In general, journalists go out and cover the most compelling stories. Compelling in this case means human drama and, often, human suffering. The story of the daughter of a Jewish family in Jerusalem who died in a suicide bombing, or someone who was badly wounded and still believed in the peace process, would be a compelling story. In my mind I never consciously said, "If I've done a story about Israelis killed and wounded in a suicide bombing, next week I have to go out and do a story about Palestinians who just lost their olive groves because the Israelis put in a new bypass road to a settlement and destroyed a hundred-year-old olive grove that this family depended on."

Subconsciously or not, though, you always tried to make sure that you were telling the best and the worst about both sides, because that was a reflection of the facts on the ground. If there was a story one week about a Palestinian family suffering in a refugee camp, the next week you might find yourself reporting an equally sad story on the side of Israel.

You would also look for stories of hope. One of the most interesting stories I reported was about the creation of the first *Sesame Street* program in Israel. It was a cooperative effort with the Palestinians, and it was so intriguing to see how putting this children's program together was a microcosm of the conflict. The Palestinians didn't want to just show up on the street. They wanted to be included, and if they were going to be in a segment, there had to be a reason for them to be there. When a bomb would go off, and the territories would be closed, some of the Palestinians couldn't get to the studio. For them to physically get to their jobs to do this show, which was intended to show peace and hope, they had to fight their way through the morass of closures and checkpoints.

Barton Gellman

I'm deeply uninterested in he said/she said stories. I really want to know what happened. I really want to try to establish fact, even with the usual imperfections of newspapering, and especially daily newspapering. I recall an incident in which there were two explosions in Gaza that Israel said were suicide bombings. Later that day Arafat said they were spontaneous firings by Israeli soldiers, that there were no Palestinians involved—no bombs at all. I talked to one of Arafat's senior security officials. He said, yes, there was a suicide bombing. He had been on the scene and didn't know yet that Arafat's line was going to be something different. So I wrote Arafat said this, but his own security guy said that, and here's what witnesses said, and there was a big hole in the ground, and bullets can't make that kind of big hole in the ground. So I showed that on that particular day the truth was on the Israeli side.

There were certainly times when the opposite proved true. The Israelis would say: "We're just doing normal searches with a minimum of disruption. We're not interested in harming civilians. We're only interested in getting the bad guys." And then you go to the place and you see holes in all the walls and damage that's hard to relate to their statements. Then you have a basis for showing otherwise. We juxtaposed statements with observable facts. There were flat lies from Israelis, too.

Israel has this dual identity as Middle Eastern and also Western. It wants to see itself as—and in many very important ways it is—a Western-style democracy with vigorous debate and some respect for empirical facts. It has a very vigorous and oppositional press itself, which will create domestic consequences for outright lying. You don't have that kind of free and vigorous Palestinian press. You don't have the same democratic traditions, although Palestinians have much more democratic and vigorous public debates than almost anywhere—if not anywhere else—in the Arab world. Some Palestinians have said to me quite forthrightly that they owe a lot of that to watching Israel and participating in the Israeli conversation. There are lots of Israeli reporters who will talk to Palestinians, and they've learned it's good for them to talk to Israeli reporters.

There's a cultural, social difference. It's different to be the loser in a hundred-year conflict than it is to be the winner. The loser feels humiliated and looks for explanations, and the explanations tend toward conspiracy. So there is a greater tendency among Palestinians—and maybe among Arabs more broadly—to search for some explanation because they feel themselves to be the losers—basically they are the losers—in this long conflict with Israel.

My highest calling is to identify trends or dimensions of a story that no one's talking about. I really want to surprise people. I want to surprise myself. If you walk into a house of mourning in Hebron and the mother says, "I'm so glad that my son Muhammad was killed. I'm proud of him because he's advanced our cause and he's getting his reward in heaven," you can be pretty sure that that's not what she really thinks. There are not very many mothers who are glad their sons were killed in a conflict. You can probe, and you can spend some time on that, and after a while you'll find other dimensions of a story that you can report and verify. Sometimes I found people who had begged their sons: "Stay out of politics. Stay out of the conflict. Go to school." Sometimes I found people who believed they had been pressured to conform.

Tim Phelps

During the [first] intifada, the great mystery for the Israelis as well as everybody else was how the Palestinians were running the intifada. Whoever it was in the early days, they were communicating and they were issuing leaflets—but even the Israelis, with their incredible intelligence network in the West Bank, were having a hard time tracking down who was passing out these leaflets. I spent a lot of time in the West Bank in Palestinian villages, getting to know people, going out there, even when I didn't have a particular question to ask. I just had a hunch that a friend of mine in Dura, south of Hebron, might be able to tell me something.

So I drove all the way down there. It was not an easy drive. I sat with him and spent several hours talking, and I wanted to ask him this question about who's distributing the leaflets. But I sensed that perhaps it wasn't a question I could ask because of the sensitivity of information. That kind of information obviously was of great interest to Israeli intelligence, and when a Western journalist asks those questions, people are going to think, "Who are you working for?" There were some questions like that that you can't ask. So I'm with my friend for several hours, and he says, "Come on, I have an errand to do. Come ride with me." And he takes me in the car, and he starts handing out leaflets.

I hadn't asked the question, and because I didn't ask the question I got the answer. But the investment in time was enormous, and most journalists are under too much pressure either from their bosses or from their internal clocks to take the kind of time that it requires in the Arab world to get to know people. You cannot march up to strangers in Palestinian society and just start firing off questions. It's too rude, too much a violation of their culture. When it comes to sensitive questions, there are at least two distinctions: one is the cultural thing, privacy; the other is that there are spies everywhere. So the more you ask, the less you're going to hear.

Carol Morello

The Israeli-Palestinian story is a reporter's dream. There is never a shortage of stories. There is the story of the conflict, how Israeli society is changing. Israel has a freewheeling press and an active democracy. There are politicians, academics, analysts—no shortage of people among Israelis ready and willing to talk. It is unbelievably easy to find stories and to reach people.

With the Palestinians it's a bit harder. There is not as much diversity of opinion, but you can find it. The society is not as freewheeling. There is a language barrier, and often you need an interpreter. Some villages are not so easy to reach, and you need somebody local to take you in.

The story of what's going on over there is more than just the conflict. Israel is deciding what kind of country it wants to be. It can be consuming to find time to cover these other things, but that's one of the challenges.

On the surface, the conflict is between Arabs and Jews. On a deeper level, though, it is a conflict between those on both sides who would compromise for peace and those who would not. Oslo seemed like magic: anything seemed possible. People were ready to deal with each other as human beings, as neighbors, to make peace and to live with each other.

The story is unique. It's a story that combines passion and emotion, on the one hand, and intellectual challenge, on the other: history, geography, politics, religion. You're not locked into doing dry, analytical stories but ones fraught with emotion: suicide bombings, collective punishment. On both sides of the street, it's a heartbreaking story.

Ann LoLordo

I thoroughly enjoyed my time there because I wasn't just writing about the conflict. That was the beauty of the job when I was there. I wrote as much about

Israeli and Palestinian life as I did about the conflict. The peace process was moving along, so I was writing about the societies. I thought it was probably the best job I had in journalism, and I think I was successful at what I did because both sides made themselves accessible to me—they wanted to share what their lives were about. That was the best way to humanize the conflict, to make the two sides seem human.

Early on when I got there, I went to an Orthodox Israeli wedding and I went to a Muslim wedding. They were like bookends, and the similarities in those two family events really showed me the similarities of these two peoples. Both stories came out of interviews that I was doing on another story where the two sides said, "Wouldn't you like to see how real people live?"

The Israeli wedding was the daughter of an American Jew that had lived there many years, an Orthodox rabbi who was running a yeshiva. He invited my husband and me to come to the wedding to see what life was like. On the Palestinian side, the sister of one of my Palestinian translators was getting married and he invited us. Those were the things that I remember about the place and what makes what's happening now so heartbreaking. I really got to know people. It wasn't as though they were just faces on a poster.

Deborah Horan

A lot of the reporting is driven by the violence. You wake up and something has exploded, so you're running out to cover it. But you also look for slices of life to show what's it like to be there. After there were a lot of bombings, I went to a mall in an Israeli town near the West Bank and I talked to people about what it's like to avoid going to certain places. A lot of times Israelis don't want to say that they alter their lives because of these things. But I altered my life, so I assumed that they altered their lives, too. A woman told me that she was going down side streets, trying to avoid major streets, trying not to go near the central bus station. So a lot of the reporting is people-driven. You're trying to find real people who illustrate an issue on a grassroots level.

As the second intifada went on, it got more and more stressful to be there. When the intifada first started, I worked something like forty-eight days in a row. It just exploded, and nobody really knew what it was. I was physically exhausted. I got up at seven in the morning and listened to the English-language news, and then I would start running around to whatever happened that day.

My editor called me on a Wednesday night at two o'clock in the morning my time, and I'm in bed, in my pajamas. The light is off and I've got the phone by my ear so that if he had a question about a story I'd written I could answer it. The phone rings, and he starts asking me these questions, reading back something he edited. And he said, "Does that sound good?" I was so tired that I didn't know what he had just read. I said, "I cannot do this again tomorrow." He was very cool about it. He said, "Take four days and I'll talk to you on Monday." So I slept for four days. And I went to the Dead Sea and relaxed and put mud on my face. The place is burning and I'm at the Dead Sea putting mud on my face.

You see some gory stuff. If a bomb hit a car in Ramallah, you get there and stare at pieces of flesh on the ground and know these were people. It's very gory. People think that the more you see things like that, the more emotional you're going to get, but it actually has the opposite effect on journalists. The first time you see something is the most shocking. By the time you've seen or heard it the tenth time, you start thinking, "Is this new? Can I find a new angle?" I don't mean to sound callous. But you're not thinking: "Oh, I'm talking to a mom who just lost her son." You're thinking: "Did I spell the son's name correctly, and how many brothers and sisters did he have? And who is that over there? Was that the dad or the uncle?" And you're thinking, "What's my first paragraph? Do I need to talk to some more people, or do I have enough stuff in my notebook?"

You're driven by the story. You're driven by not making a mistake, by having your colleagues get online and read your stuff and think it's good. I don't think people realize that's something that drives you. But you want people in the business to think, "Hey, that was really well done." And so you're thinking about your editors, thinking, is everything in this story correct?

Dan Klaidman

Reporting for a weekly magazine, we don't do the daily stories. We look for themes, not just the story of the day. We'll take that story and whatever else is going on and try to weave it together in a piece about the larger picture. Sometimes that vehicle may be a profile of someone who embodies some of the issues. It may be a narrative story that allows you to shed light on what various conflicts and controversies are. We want to be fresh when the magazine comes out, so we can't simply rehash what the daily newspapers have been doing. So there's an emphasis on enterprise reporting, looking for things that no one else has reported.

In the summer of 2000 Camp David began. That was a huge political and diplomatic story, and there was a moment where at least some people thought that there actually could be a peace settlement. It was being covered extensively by newspapers, by television, by the wire services. We tried not to get too caught up in the ins and outs of the negotiations because it was such a fluid story that what you ended up writing one week would be very different from the next. So we tried to step back and look at some of the big issues.

Clearly Jerusalem was one of the final-settlement issues and clearly it was going to be one of the most contentious ones. We decided to put a spotlight on this city that was held so sacred by so many people around the world but at the same time was a microcosm in some ways of all the disagreements over the future of Israel and Palestine. We did two things with that story: We did a biography of the city and we also wrote in great detail about the disagreements and the possible solutions for solving this riddle. That was a way to make our coverage of Camp David distinctive and at the same time be able to write about the summit itself.

Fairly soon after the summit ended, I started talking to participants on both sides to get the different perspectives on what happened and why it broke down. It was a classic newsmagazine technique, a reconstruction of the summit itself and the breakdown. It was called "Walking Off a Cliff: The Inside Story of How the Mideast Peace Process Unraveled." I spent weeks talking to participants on both sides. They were quite accessible. It was a difficult process to sort out the different views of how it fell apart because you had the same dueling narratives that you did for the entire Israeli-Palestinian conflict. People see these stories through very different prisms, and over time the facts can be twisted and can change. To some extent you're [writing] the first rough draft of history, so you're not sure that you're going to get everything a hundred percent right. You have to depend on what you hear from your sources. Sometimes you'll take one fact that seems objective, and you'll get very different interpretations from both sides about what actually happened and what it meant.

With the uprising and people getting killed every day, that became the only story. So there just wasn't the time or the interest in writing about other issues. When I first came to Israel, it was a fairly peaceful period. It was a time when you had the luxury of going out and writing about all sorts of things—Israel's own social problems, for example. But every story was connected in some way to the Israeli-Palestinian conflict. You couldn't do a story in Israel without connecting it in some way to the conflict—partly because it was relevant and there were true connections but also because American readers accustomed to reading about Israel expect to read about the conflict because that's the context that they understand.

For example, I wrote a story about the ecstasy craze in Israel. Israeli kids were very heavily into the whole rave culture, and a lot were taking ecstasy. I remember sending the story in and getting a note from an editor saying: "Well, isn't part of the reason that Israeli kids are doing this is because they spend all this time in the army and now feel that they are in a peaceful period—so they are able to indulge in this kind of behavior? That they do it because Israel is such a tense society because of the conflict with the Palestinians and conflicts between Sephardic Jews and Ashkenazi Jews, between religious and secular Jews?" But after Sept. 28 [2000], the day that Sharon went up to the Temple Mount—and the intifada began—we just didn't have the luxury of doing that kind of story.

I spent most of the next two months in Gaza and West Bank. You tend to go where the action is—that's as true for a newsmagazine as it is for a daily newspaper or television. People were getting killed, and that was an incredibly important story. But a newsmagazine is not going to report that there were flashpoints in Netzarim [an Israeli settlement in Gaza] and in Hebron yesterday, and twelve Palestinians were killed and two Israeli soldiers were killed. We look for stories where we can step back and say this is what it means, or here's a narrative story about the violence that sheds light on where this [larger] story is going.

Lisa Beyer

In 1993 we named four persons of the year: [F. W.] De Klerk, [Nelson] Mandela, Rabin, and Arafat. Arafat was in Tunis. Four of us went, two correspondents and two editors. We arrived in the afternoon. The appointment was that night. So we checked into the hotel and we were told, "Wait for the call." We knew from experience that it wasn't going to be ten o'clock or eleven o'clock or probably not even twelve o'clock. We all had dinner, wrote out some questions, and then sat in our hotel rooms and waited. And waited. At two o'clock in the morning Arafat's office called and said, "The chairman will see you now."

They sent a car to the hotel and sped us through the streets of Tunis to his compound. We got out of the car, and they searched us like I've never been searched before. Then we went into the compound and we waited and waited. Around three-thirty Arafat came in, so charming and so personable, and he had obviously been briefed on who each one of us was. He must have known—although I wasn't introduced that way—that I was based in Jerusalem because every time he talked about Jerusalem he would gesture to me. We asked him questions; he gave us answers. He didn't answer the question that you asked him necessarily. He was a real politician in that respect. But he had us—especially the two senior colleagues of mine who had less experience in this part of the world—in the palm of his hand. After an hour and a half we were told that's it. Then he posed for our photographer. Afterward we went back and interviewed Arafat for another hour or so because we decided we didn't have enough material. And that was that.

I knew Rabin very well, going back to when he was in the [parliamentary] opposition, when I first arrived in Israel. I had interviewed him probably a half dozen times. When we decided to name him person of the year, I went to his house to tell him personally. We had that sort of institutional relationship. But every time I met him—and I met him several times after we named him person of the year, including about a month before he died—he always acted as if he didn't know who I was, which was classic Rabin. The guy never offered you a drink or made a personal comment. No chitchat.

We went to see Rabin, which was very easy to set up. I called his spokesman and said, "The editor [of *Time*] is going to be here on this date. What time can we come?" It was very straightforward. We showed up. We were whisked in. We went through some metal detectors and they X-rayed our bags. When you get inside the building, they ask if you have any weapons. We saw him. Rabin sat down with us in a little receiving area in his office. We asked our questions; he answered our questions very directly. Very charmless as he always was. It's what the Israelis call *doughri*—perfectly straight, which was his asset. But he didn't have a lot of charisma.

The editors loved the whole rigamarole with Arafat. They insisted that we write it into the story because they thought it was part of the lore of Arafat, romantic. It only added to his aura. But in the end it came down to what both [Arafat and Rabin] had to say.

TALES FROM THE FRONT

Clyde Haberman, New York Times, *July 1991–August 1995;*
return reporting trips 2001

What made coverage of the conflict distinct when I was there was not the nature of the conflict but the unusual and bizarre intensity of the coverage and the interest in it by the home office. Covering Israel and the Palestinians for the *New York Times* is unlike anything else—one of the hardest jobs at the paper. It's like being on a jackhammer: the intensity of the scrutiny and the inevitable criticism; and the fact that I would not have quite the freedom that a foreign correspondent normally would to get up in the morning and say, "Well, what do I feel like doing today?" There are passion and intelligence on both sides of the Green Line. But it was not an assignment that I leaped to get because I knew being the *New York Times* guy is different from being the *Boston Globe* guy or the *Washington Post* guy. It's not because I'm a better newsman; it's my audience.

The *Times* covers Israel more intensely than we cover large portions of New York City. [A large part of] our readership has a deeper interest in that particular story than any ethnic group does for any conflict going on in the world—be it the India-Pakistan conflict over Kashmir, be it China and Tibet, or be it Serbs and Croats. Those ethnic groups are only recently here in large enough numbers to make their impact felt as readers. They're still not nearly in the large numbers that Jewish readers are, particularly in a city like New York.

Because there's a heavy concentration of Jews in and around New York City, they are natural *New York Times* readers and, to a large degree by extension, natural *New*

York Times critics. What has changed in the last couple of years is that there has been a sufficient growth in the number of Arab Americans—with Palestinians being a special subset—to make themselves heard. So what exists now that did not exist when I was a correspondent are various groups willing to present the Palestinian perspective on this issue and the Arab perspective in general, and to take on what they consider to be unfair coverage. I heard very little from Arabs when I was there from '91 to '95, maybe 5 percent [of reader feedback]. I heard more when I went back for two months in the summer of 2001.

Is [the process of] covering the story itself that unusual? No. Israel and the Palestinian areas are not more dangerous than many other places, such as the Balkans. The suicide bombings started on my watch, back in April of '94. When I went back for two months in 2001, it was a hard story, much harder than when I was there before. What makes it different is not the inherent danger, although there is an element of that with all the violence in recent years, but the nature of who's reading you. Because in the end it's a tiny little piece of real estate that gets an unbelievable amount of ink for all sorts of historical and religious and cultural and social imperatives. That was the difficult part of it.

I've been a professional journalist for thirty-eight years. I have been the *Times* correspondent and bureau chief in Tokyo and in Rome; I covered many countries while based there. I've been our city hall bureau chief. I've written a people column. My experience has long been that I get a decent mix of praising and critical letters. In Israel it [reader reaction] was all intensely negative. There were orchestrated campaigns by CAMERA and other groups. For a while I answered the letters if they were rational, but I realized that it was self-defeating because people weren't interested in dialogue. What struck me was not that I'd get irrational, negative reaction. It was the virtually complete absence of positive comments—that's not an exaggeration—that ran counter to my experience in any other assignment. So either I was uniquely incompetent in Israel or the people who would write me praising letters [about my coverage] on Japan, on Korea, on Italy, on Turkey, on my column in New York were completely misguided.

The specific complaints were that the *New York Times* was trying to delegitimize Israel. This was a constant sort of attack. Forget the topic with the Palestinians. This was if you wrote on any social issues, which often were cast in religious terms there, [such as] the power of the Orthodox branch of the religion over marriage, divorce, death; or the question of lingering tensions between Ashkenazim and Sephardim, Jews of European origin versus Middle Eastern or North African; or basic poverty questions. Or whether there was a rise in domestic violence as a result of the first Gulf War. Israel absorbed thirty-nine scud missiles from Iraq at U.S. insistence that it sit on its hands and not respond, and [the issue was] whether in a society not used to sitting on its hands that led to a pent-up aggression among a lot of men. For a disturbing number of readers—at least those who made themselves heard—these themes were all seen as delegitimizing Israel as a state by showing that it is—well, I would argue, normal. It is the nature of journalism to write about conflict.

Did this affect my coverage? Terminology was also a big issue, often a reader complaint. I rejected a lot of the complaints as being politically motivated and not journalistically fair-minded, like: "Why do you call it the West Bank instead of Judea and Samaria?" Some would even question the use of the word "Palestinian" as being imprecise, [saying] they're the Arabs of Palestine. But some of it made sense. There are loaded terms, and I would rethink some of them, such as "terrorist." I made clear to my Palestinian stringer, who would talk about "activists," that I'm not calling [just] anybody an activist. Some guy who blows himself up in a pizza shop is not an activist to me. I called him a terrorist. Now, do I apply the same thing to a guy who blows himself up and gets two Israeli soldiers at a checkpoint right outside Beit Sahur [in the West Bank]? It gets a little dicey.

Reader reaction had a positive effect on me in that regard. I would probably be lying if I didn't admit that some of the more strident letters did not make me want to dig in a little bit and in my own stubborn way think, "You're not going to push me around." But I listened and I participated. Groups [of Jewish leaders] would come over [to Israel] and I would agree to see them. I felt I am a quasi-public figure in this regard; [my work] does have an effect on people. So I would make myself available to these groups and often have people scream at me left and right. I got pretty good at deflecting it.

There is an outsized identification with the *New York Times* on the part of Jewish readers, who see it as being "our" newspaper. There are a lot of historical reasons for this: the demographics of the city for a long time; the fact that we have had a Jewish ownership [of the newspaper] for a long time; and the unbelievably abysmal coverage of the Holocaust, on the part of the American media in general and the *New York Times* in specific.

If arguably the best paper in the country were the *St. Louis Post-Dispatch* or some other paper in a city without the enormous Jewish population that New York has, then maybe Israel wouldn't loom so large, because the *St. Louis Post-Dispatch* likely would not have covered Israel and its Arab neighbors quite as intensely as the *New York Times* clearly has. We set the agenda for a lot of people on covering that conflict. A lot of American media coverage to some degree follows the lead of the big newspapers, and you don't get bigger than us in many respects. When the *New York Times* puts something on the front page—let alone repeatedly—people pay attention. They follow that lead. I'm not saying that everyone goes in lockstep with us, but you can't ignore us.

I have always felt that nothing would serve both the Israelis and Palestinians better than a certain measure of what in another context Daniel Patrick Moynihan referred to as benign neglect. They are over-covered [by the media]; they each have an outsized, oversized sense of their importance. Yes, the centrality of this conflict looms larger than ever in the Middle East. But to the degree that we can make them Cyprus would probably serve the cause of world peace. It might even push them closer [to a resolution]. I don't literally mean let's cover them the way we do occasional stuff on the Tamil uprising in Sri Lanka or the Cyprus issue, which has been going on for thirty years. It can't happen, it won't happen, but it should happen.

The old notion that the very act of observing something changes it is true. The intense observation that is given to this conflict and to the individual sides may actually push them further apart because they take themselves more seriously than perhaps they have a right to. Which is not to say they're unimportant.

I understand the difficulty in what I'm saying. But I do believe—and I did believe when I was the correspondent there—that the intense coverage ill serves the cause of peace and the development of each society. To some degree we in the international news media—and their own domestic media as well—make matters worse. This is because people behave differently when they're under the intense gaze that the world media puts on them than they would otherwise. One might argue that the political leaders on either side would be more willing to compromise if every word, every nuance, and every raised eyebrow were not noodled over endlessly.

Gillian Findlay, ABC News, September 1997–June 2002

In my tenure as a correspondent working for an American network,[2] it was very difficult to break away from the headlines of this story. When there was a bus bombing, or if the Israeli army went into a Palestinian refugee camp and a number of Palestinians were killed—and increasingly it had to be significant numbers of Palestinians killed—then I could get onto a newscast. There wasn't, in my opinion, enough appetite for context. There certainly wasn't an appetite for history. Not all of that is different in Canada. The CBC [Canadian Broadcasting Company] is under many of the same kinds of pressures. But for all kinds of reasons—including that Canada doesn't play the same kind of role in the Middle East that the United States does—there is a greater willingness to try to give this [story] a broader context.

Having said that, I think ABC did better than any of the others [American networks] because there were people within the organization who had a real interest in the Middle East, who had worked previously in the Middle East, who understood the story very well. Nevertheless, we all didn't do a very good job—and I would say we continue to not do a very good job—of providing context to the story. For anybody reporting the Palestinian-Israeli conflict to have spent five years in the region as I did and to never have gotten a story on *World News Tonight* about the settlement issue has got to tell you something.

It's not as if anybody ever said to me, "No, we don't want to do that." It was just one of those things that never happened. We would report things that happened in settlements, such as settlers being killed. There was a period of time where there was a lot of shootings on roads that settlers would use in the West Bank. Sometimes there might be a paragraph in the middle of one of those stories that talked about the number of settlers who live on disputed land, but really very little beyond that. Somewhere there should have been an opportunity to take a broader look: What are the settlements? Why are those people here? Why do they justify their presence there? How do the Palestinians view them? That never happened. I honestly can't remember that we ever went out to do a piece specifically about settlements.

Probably the most controversial story that I did in the time I was there was broadly about the right of return [of Palestinian refugees] but specifically about an elderly Palestinian man who was living in a refugee camp in the West Bank. We went with him back to the town of his birth, which is now in Israel and populated by Israelis. That was extremely controversial. It was seen as violently pro-Palestinian. It was the only piece that we'd ever done that said, "Okay, what is this right of return? Why do the Palestinians feel strongly about it?"

So either there was no context given or when we did try to provide context, it became such a controversial thing, not only among viewers but also within the news organization. A lot of people wondered why we had done the story at all—and if we were going to do it, why we didn't do another story about the way Jewish immigrants to Israel had been treated [in Europe during World War II]. They argued that there was a lack of context within the story.[3] So if you were to get that kind of reporting on the air, you were sticking your neck out a lot of the time. That's okay; that's part of your job. But it wasn't a very welcoming environment.

Because it was told from the perspective of a Palestinian refugee, we got a lot of positive reaction from Palestinians and Palestinian groups. They said things like: "Finally somebody is showing this conflict through our eyes. This is something that we don't expect to see, especially on American television." I remember getting a flood of e-mails. Word of the story got out there, and so it was clear I was getting e-mails from Palestinians associated with different groups because I would get ten or twenty that all came from the same address with very similar messages. It became clear that many of the people had never seen the piece but had been told about it and were just writing to say thank you for doing it.

I heard from the other side mostly when we failed to do stories. Things would happen that for whatever reason we didn't report on, or, as often happens on TV news, they got turned into fifteen seconds of voice-over. Two young boys went missing from a West Bank settlement, and eventually their bodies were found in a cave. That night on *World News Tonight* we didn't do a story. It was reduced to fifteen seconds of voice-over. I remember getting a lot of flak from people who said how could we have done that? Surely the lives of these two boys warranted better coverage than that on ABC.

History is everything in this conflict. You can't talk about the conflict without examining the history. Television is not a historical medium in that sense. It doesn't cherish history in the same way that you sometimes see in print. I remember having a conversation once with an editor who said: "Tell me what happened today. I don't want to hear about '67; I don't want to hear about '48. That's ancient history and that's boring to our viewers."

That may be the case, but if your purpose is to provide a context for people to understand the events of today—in that part of the world in particular—then you can't ignore that kind of history. You can't ignore what came before. This was a bit of a surprise to me, how little our audience understood about the roots of the conflict. I'd get that through some of the viewer comments, or what people would tell me anecdotally. Sometimes even in conversations with editors and writers it struck me as surprising how people weren't that well versed in a lot of that history. There wasn't a willingness to say: "This is something that the audience needs to know, and if they're not well versed, then it's our obligation to provide that sort of education to them."

What international treaties and UN resolutions say is interpreted in different ways by the parties, and the fact of the matter is that those words are interpreted differently on both sides. So there is the sense that the Israelis will tell you this and the Palestinians will tell you that—and who's right? You get back to the same old argument, and so therefore why go there.

Again, television news, almost by definition, doesn't deal with history. It deals with what's happening now. This is all caught up in the whole twenty-four-hour phenomenon and the need for the latest information live, live, live. That doesn't lend itself to a discussion of how we got to this point. That lends itself to telling what's happening now and what's likely to happen in the future as a result of this. That's where so much of our reporting was.

There were so many times I did stories late at night. At midnight local time you'd start getting reports that there were Israeli helicopters over Gaza and that bombing was about to begin. So many stories became almost formulaic: this happened today, and now there are reports that Israeli helicopters are over Gaza, so everybody understands what's going to happen next. There's this sense always of looking forward and not wanting to look back because that's what the medium lends itself to. That's what the twenty-four-hour networks are doing, and that's the competition. We're not going to do a thumb-sucker about what is the right interpretation of UN Resolution 242 when, in fact, everybody else is talking about whether the Israelis are going to bomb Gaza City tonight. What would you prefer to watch?

U.S. [Mideast] policy is something that people need to ask questions about. In the reporting generally that I saw, and in the reporting that we did as well, we gave the administration a very easy ride in terms of what they were doing and what they weren't doing.

I remember being on *Nightline*, and there was a [studio] roundtable of various ABC correspondents talking about events that had happened. There was a reporter who had been covering the State Department at that particular time, and the anchor turned to this person and said, "Well, what should America be doing? What can America do?" And the correspondent said, "Well, the truth is there's very little that America can do." And then it ended. I was sitting there [in Jerusalem] fighting to get on to say, "Well, what about the $3 billion that the American government gives to the State of Israel each year? That's not a lever?" That's what I wanted to say.

There's a sense that the Israelis and Palestinians have been warring forever, and they will forever, and there's really nothing the American administration can do. That's a cop-out in reporting. The Palestinians were saying there's plenty that the Americans can do to force Israel kicking and screaming to the negotiating table. And frankly there's plenty the Americans can do to bring the Palestinians to the table as well. But it almost got to the point where if you were to raise that, to suggest that, then you were seen to be buying into the Palestinian agenda, becoming a mouthpiece for the Palestinians. I'm not saying that was universal, that it was ever said at any point, or that it was overt. But there wasn't very rigorous reporting and analysis of what the Americans were doing.

From my observations as a viewer, before I worked at ABC I had the impression that the press generally in Washington—specifically at the State Department, people who would cover foreign policy—were much more rigorous in terms of questioning whether this was the right foreign policy or not, or reporting on alternative policies that others had argued might be better. Why that is not the case now I don't know.

I don't want to put the blame for everything on television news and twenty-four-hour networks. But when you see live briefings all the time from the Pentagon or the State Department, the correspondents say, for example, the secretary [of state] did this and this and this today. That's what people in our newsroom watch all the time. There's not the sense that we have to do more than just re-report everything that's been going on throughout the day; that we should be analyzing it. It has definitely gotten worse since 9/11. I was in Israel on 9/11, and I know that it got worse after that. But it wasn't great before that either.

When Clinton was in office, there was a process under way that culminated at Camp David. It appeared that it might actually bear some fruit. Maybe there was a sense that there was not a lot to criticize, that the administration is doing something that might actually work—and therefore who are we to say that it's not the right way, or to suggest that's it not the right way. But when Camp David collapsed, I didn't see a lot of reporting that analyzed why that happened from any other perspective other than the Palestinians once again had missed an opportunity. It took about a year for people to analyze what actually happened there. But that was not the kind of reporting that we were doing at the time. We weren't doing that kind of analysis. You could argue that we should have, and if we weren't doing it from Israel or from the West Bank, somebody in Washington should have been doing it.

One of the great ironies is that as a reporter there you always fought to elevate the story beyond things that people didn't already know. That was always the biggest battle. The challenge was to elevate it beyond Palestinians hate Israelis and Israelis hate Palestinians and this conflict has gone on forever and will go on forever.

But the reality is that the way the conflict has been reported—and I include myself in this—has contributed to an even greater apathy about it, because it is so much tit for tat. Today there was a bus bomb and X number of Israelis died. Then that was followed by an Israeli raid on a Palestinian refugee camp, and X people died. And on and on it goes. Back and forth. Tit for tat. If we don't elevate it beyond that, why should anybody watching or reading have any interest to think that there might be solutions? Or to educate themselves to understand why this is happening and bring themselves to a point where they might be active participants in a debate about how you end this?

I watch television as much as anybody. But I find it very hard to watch coverage of the Middle East because, like the average viewer, I find it so repetitive. I'm not engaged by it. I don't see that there's anybody really prepared to say, "Well, hang on, this isn't always tit for tat. Sometimes one side or the other has legitimate grievances." It all gets reduced to this happened and this happened; they did this and they did that. You never really get a discussion of what actually has some legitimacy and what doesn't.

I don't know how you break out of that. One way might be not to talk so much about what happened this day and that day. Not that you can ignore it, but also to provide some sort of a context that tells you something more. The lack of context applies to so much reporting these days. It's not just this issue.

Chris Hedges, New York Times, *January 1991–June 1995 (based in Cairo);*
return reporting trips 2000, 2001, 2003;
Dallas Morning News, *January 1988–May 1990*

Most people walk into the Israeli-Palestinian conflict with an assumption that the Israelis are the victims. That has historical precedent, but it's not borne out on the ground. The Palestinians' ability to deal with the press is dismal. It's extremely difficult to work in the West Bank and Gaza. Most reporters rely on translators, who have pretty clear political agendas. I think most reporters are uncomfortable working in the Palestinian areas, so they will drive down from Jerusalem to Gaza with a precooked story, stay two or three hours, get the few requisite quotes, and leave. They don't understand the nuances of Palestinian society at all, or the factual disputes. Papers like the *New York Times* do a very good job of covering the nuances within Israeli society and a very poor job of covering the Palestinian nuances because we don't understand them. So Palestinians are painted as a monolith.

[There are] all these clichés about how [Palestinian] families are so happy that their children are martyred. Having spent a lot of time with families over a period of days, I have seen that the grief that these mothers feel over the loss of their sons is as strong, as palpable, as the grief that Israeli mothers feel over the loss of their children. But funerals, both in Israel but especially in the occupied territories, are political events. They're taken over by groups like Hamas. You get to a house within an hour or two after the young man has been killed or committed a suicide attack. All the plastic chairs are out in the street, and the banners are up, and the Hamas people are everywhere. It's extremely difficult for the family to speak openly about the grief. They know the line that they're supposed to parrot back, especially to the international press. This is an example of how we lap up these kinds of clichés and leave without ever exploring the reality of what's going on.

A lot of it is due to the fact that we're uncomfortable. Arab culture is incomprehensible to us because we've never taken the time to understand it. It's the great failing of the press that when something is incomprehensible to us, we certify it as incomprehensible to everyone. That's very much what's happening in the coverage of the Israeli-Palestinian conflict. Look, for instance, at the coverage in El Salvador, or the coverage of the Balkans. The press spent far more time with the victims, those who were suffering the brunt of oppression. Here we spend most of our time with the victimizers.

We see the results of oppression—the suicide bombings, for instance—but we don't understand the long, slow drip of oppression that has created suicide bombers. It's as if the Palestinians are walled in behind this huge glass enclosure, and for years they have been trying to scream through this glass to us, but we can't hear them. They are made mute. Between 1967 and the first intifada [which began in 1987] there was no big eruption. Because the press tends to be crisis-driven, these long historical precedents end up distorting and deforming. We finally only see the convulsions. We see [the Palestinians] when they break through the glass bloodied and angry and furious and enraged and fanatic. We think they come from another moral universe. They don't, of course. But we don't understand that because we've never taken the time to understand them. And that is the fundamental failure of the coverage of the Palestinians.

The situation in Israel is analogous to what happened under the apartheid regime in South Africa. The notion that we would ever give as much credence or as much space to the leaders of the apartheid regime as we do to the Israeli government is staggering. Part of that is due to the absolute ineptitude of the Palestinian leadership. They bear some responsibility. They never developed the sophistication that the ANC developed in South Africa or the FMLN developed in El Salvador or the Muslim-led government developed in Sarajevo.

At the same time, it is easy [for correspondents] to sit in Jerusalem. Israelis are accessible, especially if you work for the *New York Times*. You can get through to almost any government official with a phone call. They understand the press. They understand the need for speedy responses. I won't say accurate [responses] because they will give their version of an event. The way they spin it is often very far from the truth, but they know very well that in this kind of journalistic world, where it becomes he said, she said—this is the Israeli version, this is the Palestinian version—it's a way to cancel things out. Because most reporters don't actually go and witness these events, do the hard reporting on the ground—partly because they often don't have time—it has a way of neutralizing a lot of the atrocities that the Israelis are committing against the Palestinians.

It's appalling the brutality that's exercised by the IDF, which does not practice even minimal forms of crowd control. This has been true since the first intifada. They will fire live rounds into crowds of unarmed civilians that include large numbers of children. It just amazes me that they can do this for so long and get away with it.

I think it's partly because reporters are not out in the territories in the way that they should be and because of the effectiveness of Israeli press relations. Ultimately most Western reporters feel far more comfortable with English-speaking Israelis than they do with Palestinians, very few of whom speak English. There's a kind of racism to that.

Reporters have a critical eye, and those who have been in Jerusalem long enough understand what's going on. But there's logistical difficulty, a cultural divide. I was in the West Bank in the summer of 2003. Going in and out, I could waste four hours trying to get through a checkpoint. I think most reporters have a pretty dark view of how the Israelis handle the Palestinians, but I don't think that's reflected in the reporting.

If you, as I have, try to write about the destruction, about the disintegration of the very moral fabric of Israeli society and treatment of Palestinians, there is a very organized campaign against you. After I wrote the piece "Gaza Diary" [published in *Harper's* magazine in October 2001]—where I went and lived in Khan Yunis and wrote day by day, without interviewing Palestinian officials or Israeli officials, about what it was like to be a Palestinian in a refugee camp—there was a concerted campaign against me. There was a letter-writing campaign to the *New York Times*, although I didn't publish it in the *New York Times*. There were many, many angry phone calls to *Harper's*; I believe they shut the phone lines down for the first day. There were visits by Israeli officials to the editors of *Harper's*. [There were also] organized demonstrations when I spoke at college campuses. At Dartmouth they had to bring in uniformed security guards. I was picketed out front. Nobody was allowed to get up or leave while I spoke. No electronic devices were allowed in the hall.

That piece would not have raised many eyebrows if it had been published in France or Britain, but here we are just not used to hearing voices from the other side. That is the terrible failing of the American press. It has less to do with sympathy toward the Israelis. The press that is based in Jerusalem realizes pretty quickly that there's no pressure or incentive to give voice to the Palestinians. In fact, when you make that effort, you're often punished for it—and that cuts down on a lot of reporters' willingness to do it. They're not going to win any brownie points by moving to Gaza and doing good, detailed reporting on the Palestinians. In fact, you're probably just going to create a huge headache for yourself and the news organization you work for.

I have had complaints from Palestinians, who can be just as unreasonable as Israelis, but they're not organized. Palestinians are very quick to see an Israeli bias even if it's not there. No side likes to see the truth. Each side has a very idealized version of their own truth and cause. So any time there's a tainting of that, whether it's Palestinian or Israeli, you get a response. The difference is that the Palestinians don't begin to have the clout or lobby that the Israelis have here, either in terms of money or sophistication or organization. So Palestinian responses tend to be individual responses, and they tend to be not strategic. The Israeli lobby groups know very well whom they want to go gunning for and why. They'll use form letters. It's clear that it's concerted.

Israel is different from other conflicts in that editors who have never been to Israel still think they understand it. They don't, of course. But there's a feeling that they do. So you have a lot more people in newsrooms who are self-appointed experts on the conflict—even though they've never covered it—than you did with the Balkans, for instance. You would not have editors who have strong opinions about the Serbs or the Croats or the Muslims in Bosnia because [that conflict was] relatively new to them. That's not true with Israel. There are all sorts of assumptions carried into this conflict that are not carried into other conflicts.

People who rise within big bureaucracies are very careful not to cause controversy of any kind, and that includes [about] Israel. They are driven by personal ambition and have very little moral sense. That's true of every institution. People who run institutions just don't want the headache. It's not conducive to their own personal advancement.

Not all foreign reporting is stenographic. The coverage that we had in El Salvador during the war was not stenographic. But there are land mine fields that reporters don't want to walk into. This is the big elephant in the garden nobody wants to touch. It could be touched if there were better editorial direction, but those [in the] hierarchies don't ask those questions, and they don't want those questions to be asked.

How did "Gaza Diary" end up in print? I was extremely frustrated with the coverage and how we never saw what life was like for Palestinians in these refugee camps. It is horrendous. I wanted to write a piece that did that without any rhetoric. Straight reporting on a day-by-day basis about what it was like to live there. I knew I would have to do this on my vacation time—and I did.

I picked the worst camp, Khan Yunis. I knew where I was going, and I knew the *New York Times* would never print it. So I went to Edward Said and asked him, "Who do you think would have the guts to run a tough piece?"[4] He said *Harper's*. They're immune from advertising pressure because Rick MacArthur, the publisher, uses the money from the MacArthur Foundation to run the magazine. It's the same reason that publications like the *Christian Science Monitor* can be more objective on the Middle East—because they are not subject to that kind of pressure.

If my objective is to paint a scene of a corner of life in Gaza, and I choose a Palestinian refugee camp, why would I drive to Jerusalem to ask the IDF spokesman for comments? I didn't drive to Gaza City to ask the Palestinian Authority for comments. That wasn't the point of this piece. The point was to show what it was like to be a Palestinian in Khan Yunis on a daily basis. I wrote almost nothing that I didn't see. The Israelis claimed that kids weren't taunted [by IDF soldiers]. But I had not only the names of the kids, I also had the days they were shot, where they were wounded. I went to the hospitals and saw them after they were shot. I went to the funerals. I heard these taunts [from the soldiers] in Arabic on the first day. They would beckon like this: *"ta'al, ta'al"* [come on, come on]. I speak Arabic, and I was listening to these words coming out of a megaphone.

Sitting around a refugee camp in Gaza, as sympathetic as I am to the plight of the Palestinians, as soon as we get to the point of Israel, there's this deadly silence. This huge chasm that opens up between me and the Palestinians because I don't support the eradication of Israel.

Khan Yunis takes a full day to get to from Jerusalem because of roadblocks. If any [reporters] go there, they're not going to spend eight days there. That's the whole point; we don't do that. Israelis [journalists] do a much better job of covering the Palestinians. They speak Arabic. They get it. We have not come close to the level of sophistication within the Israeli press. There is far more understanding in Israel of what's going on than there is here.

Dean Reynolds, ABC News, November 1986–May 1995;
return reporting trips 1995, 1996, 2002, 2003

In television first you need pictures. Action helps, although it's not a necessity for every story. Occasionally you can go back to a place where there were no cameras and tell the story through the eyes of witnesses, which is not very active. But by and large you need pictures—good pictures, active action pictures that will arrest the viewer.

In many respects the first intifada was a tailor-made television story because we had tremendous action from both sides. And we had history at the same time, because the first intifada came after a long period of nothing on that score, no pitched battles. Israelis were still shopping in Nablus and Ramallah. So you had history and you had pictures to tell the story. Now you have pictures, but you don't have history anymore, because it's always the same story—more murderous stuff—but it's the same.

Back then it was news, and that was the most important thing that was driving it. It was a tectonic shift in the viewers' perspective of the conflict. Suddenly the terrorists and the plane hijackers were David, and our erstwhile allies and good buddies were Goliath. This was new *within* the new. It was history that the Palestinians were rising up—and the way in which they were rising up made a lot of American viewers scratch their heads and wonder what the hell was going on.

At the same time, the Israelis were saying, "Why are you criticizing us?" [Yitzhak] Shamir was prime minister, and the Israeli reaction was a story in and of itself. It was a very arched reaction, a "how dare you" reaction to the media and to the Bush administration. They were still in the victim mode, and they didn't accept being the aggressor that the pictures depicted them as. They still will argue that the pictures don't tell the story.

Things have changed dramatically. When I was there, every network went and shot its own version of an event. A riot in Nablus was shot by ABC, CBS, NBC, CNN,

CTV, the CBC. Competition was crazy; it was vicious. And to my undying regret one of the most vivid pictures of the first intifada was shot by CBS: Israeli soldiers hitting a young Palestinian guy with rocks. There were a million different kinds of angles [being covered] that don't exist today. Today, if there's a helicopter attack on Gaza, the same picture will be on CBS that's on ABC. It's [news] agency footage.

One of the things about the story at the time was that it seemed to be going in a direction, and that's always compelling. There were perceptible changes within the body politic of both sides, changes that would to Westerners be seen as positive. We always run the risk of applying our logic to that part of the world, which is a huge mistake. But to my audience it looked like the Palestinians were doing something that was effective, and the Israelis were not matching it; they were almost making a case for the Palestinians in the way they responded to them.

The Palestinians were arguing that the occupation was unlivable and racist, and there you had prima facie evidence that bore it out in the way that the army was reacting. The metaphor I always use is pushing the stone up the hill. It was a very heavy stone and got heavier the higher it went, but nonetheless it was being pushed up in a positive direction. George Shultz—secretary of state to Ronald Reagan, who had been the staunchest ally Israel had ever had in the White House if you don't count Harry Truman—recognized the PLO. Many of us on the ground got the feeling from our reporting that the PLO had to be brought into the process. Tunis had too much control over things, not the homegrown leaders. So Shultz bought into the idea after Arafat recognized Israel in 1988.

The sense was that the Americans were on board now, and the Palestinians had pushed the rock up the hill. Then the first Bush was elected, and instead of furthering Reagan's comfy-cozy policy with the Israelis, he unleashed James Baker on both sides. Baker played tough with them, and the Israelis could no longer get away with the argument that for forty years we've extended our hand, but no one is there. The last thing they wanted the Palestinians to say was yes. And Arafat said yes.

Then the first Gulf War happened, and Shamir followed Bush's advice not to retaliate [for Iraqi scud-missile attacks on Tel Aviv]. But again Shamir overplayed his hand. He thought that by cooperating he would then be allowed to settle a million Russian immigrants on the West Bank. Bush said, "You can get the loan guarantees, but you can't settle them on the West Bank," and Shamir said, "If this comes down to a fight between us and the White House and Congress, we will win." And I reported it that way, thanks to a leak by Shamir's spokesman. This pissed off the Americans tremendously, and about the same time Bush said, "I'm just poor little me, and they have a thousand lobbyists up on the Hill." Next thing you know, Labor comes to its senses and nominates Rabin over Peres, and Rabin beats Shamir. And immediately the Oslo process begins.

In the beginning the two sides were hopelessly ignorant of each other. The intifada showed the Israelis a different side of the Palestinians that the rest of the world was beginning to pick up on too—that they had grievances, that the army was treating them harshly. There was a sense that as the Israelis got to know the Palestinians, they began to think, "Maybe there's a way that we can talk to these people, because God knows we're getting sick of this conflict." That was reflected in my reporting. We would talk to Israelis, not just left-wingers but right-wingers, too, soft Likudniks. Arafat said the Palestinians would negotiate. Maybe he decided that the intifada had done its job. It had put the Israelis in a position of weakness on an international stage, and the time was right.

The pace of the story was never-ending. When you have a running story like that, you keep your foot on the pedal. My network was always looking in my direction for something, anything. So, if it was a particularly slow week [on the political front], I would do something about all the Russian immigrant musicians playing for a shekel or two on the sidewalk; or how the Israelis lent their expertise in prosthetics to the Armenian earthquake victims, because the Israelis were among the very best at that sort of thing; or a school for the deaf in Gaza. I happened on it in the midst of a riot, when we took cover behind big, heavy iron gates in this courtyard that just happened to belong to the school. We just walked into this scene where all of these deaf kids were walking around, but they didn't know what was going on. We did a story that said imagine living in Gaza. Now imagine you're deaf.

You could do that in the midst of the hot conflict. New York would say, "We've seen that; it looks like the piece you did on Wednesday. How about something else for Thursday?" It was a great story. You're answering the alarm bell; you're a fireman. We were on every night because we were having a big effect. People were tracking us. It all had to do with this new narrative.

We got reaction from various pro-Israel media monitors—super-overheated, histrionic criticism, vague suggestions of anti-Semitism. New York was getting pressured too from various interest groups, especially after there was a riot on the Temple Mount in 1990. The interest groups were demanding "tick-tocks"—[asking] "Where were you, when did you see this, give us your notes"—as if I were being subpoenaed. This was dutifully passed along to me by some executives at ABC, but I politely declined. I said, "You can get somebody else here, but I'm not going to supply my modus operandi to interest groups." A lot of the criticism came to New York and died there. Aside from that one incident and from expected pressure groups, I got very little mail from people who were upset.

I remember there were Palestinian Americans who came to Jerusalem for a convention two years into the intifada, and I was like Brad Pitt. They all came up and wanted to introduce themselves to me and said what a great job I was doing. That gave me pause right there.

The other side of that coin is that if you don't have a running story you're dead. You can't even get a nice human-interest story on because nobody's looking in your direction anymore. That's what's happening now, why you very seldom see stories from Israel. There is no running story that's going somewhere—with a beginning, middle, and end—as opposed to just running in place.

The first intifada started with most Americans knowing about the Middle East vaguely, believing that Israel was on our side and the Palestinians vice versa. That changed. In the second intifada, the Palestinians have done immeasurable harm to their cause in terms of public opinion by dovetailing with 9/11. Americans who may have followed the first intifada and thought the Israelis really needed to do something for the Palestinians now believe that the Palestinians have brought this on themselves. So in many respects it's back to the way it was.

Once the assault on [the] Jenin [refugee camp] took place [in April 2002], everybody wanted to know what was going on there. Half of that was because you couldn't get in, and journalists—being journalists—want to know. And it was fed in no small part by the sentiment, "Why won't they let us in there? They must be hiding something." Even the pictures of the fighting were from a distance: bursts of gunfire heard from another village way off in the distance. You could not get a camera crew in.

We began telling the Israelis: "You are hurting yourselves, because whether or not this happened, it's now there. It's implanted. It's up to you to show us that it didn't happen. The Palestinians are claiming that there are mass graves, five hundred dead." Saeb Erekat, to his everlasting shame, spread that around. It showed up in print, and *Good Morning America* wanted a piece on that.

I had done stories to the effect that people were suspicious of the Israelis because they wouldn't let anybody in. But even after that wave of stories, and after there had been escorted tours permitted by the Israelis—and even interviews with Palestinian doctors—there was still pressure to keep it going. The audience had been conditioned to believe that it was possibly true, whether or not it was true.

GMA wanted another story on Jenin. I thought this was ironic because they almost never want hard news. They don't want real blood and guts. I gave them a different story that said Israeli intelligence had detected a plot to attack mourners at Israeli funerals. This was a fresh story that had not been reported on American television. It resonated with me because I remembered how outrageous the behavior of the Serbs was when they would shell Bosnian Muslim mourners during funerals. It struck me as bloodthirsty.

They did not air that piece. I was told: "We don't have time for that story, but give us one on Jenin." I finally said to the senior producer: "If you want me to report that the Israeli army was bulldozing bodies into mass graves in Jenin, you've come to the wrong place. I can tell you from nine years in this place that they may be hard, they may be brutal, but they are not going to be bulldozing bodies into mass graves. Not Jewish soldiers knowing what they have seen in films from [Nazi] Germany."

I had to draw on experience. I had to bring to bear what I knew to be the facts about how the Israeli military operates. I was under no illusions. I'm sure that the Shabak [Israel's domestic intelligence agency] was involved [in the Jenin operation], too, and they can be very nasty. But you can't report something that you don't know.

7

TOWARD A NEW WAY OF REPORTING
THE ISRAELI-PALESTINIAN CONFLICT

To the press alone, checkered as it is with abuses, the world is indebted for all the triumphs which have been gained by reason and
humanity over error and oppression.

The right of freely examining public characters and measures, and
of free communication among the people thereon . . . has ever been
justly deemed the only effectual guardian of every other right.

James Madison, 1798

THE CRITIQUE OF AMERICAN MAINSTREAM MEDIA REPORTING OF THE
Israeli-Palestinian conflict presented in this study repeatedly points to the
missing context of the impact that U.S. Mideast policy has on the trajectory
of the conflict. This is not to imply conspiracy theory. The Israeli-Palestinian
conflict is not the result of American foreign policy. Two peoples claim the
same land as their own based on history, nationalism, religion, and culture.
Nor can American policy be ascribed as the sole factor that drives Israeli and
Palestinian actions, whether they are undertaken by governments, political
and social groups, or individuals. Indeed, the direct parties to the conflict
themselves have agency.

However, to ignore or minimize the profound impact that U.S. Mideast
policy has had—and continues to have—on the trajectory of the conflict
is to adopt and promote a tunnel vision that does more to discourage the
prospects for peace than to encourage them. This, unfortunately, is an apt
characterization of American mainstream media reporting of the Israeli-
Palestinian conflict. The omission of the policy factor—in particular how

U.S. policy on the conflict relates, or chooses not to relate, to international law and consensus—is the single most significant flaw, over time and across media, in shaping and defining the coverage.

Variables relevant to the work process of reporting the story in the field—for example, the unequal strengths of official Israeli and Palestinian channels to convey their points of view to the media—can affect the tone and/or balance of coverage in some instances. The same is true of the pressures exerted in the United States by pro-Israel and pro-Palestinian groups, which in significantly different measures have had periodic short-term effects on coverage, as the events of 2001 and 2002 demonstrated. Yet the credo and methods of professional journalism appear to allow it to adjust for such imbalances and to keep such pressures at bay over time.

However, the same cannot be said when it comes to the deep imprint that U.S. Mideast policy leaves on mainstream reporting of the Israeli-Palestinian conflict. As the evidence presented in this study has demonstrated, the media do not begin to examine, much less question, the impact of U.S. policy on the trajectory of the conflict as a whole or on its key issues, particularly Israeli settlements and the Palestinian refugee question. This has had the dual effect of both polarizing and dulling American public opinion by limiting the scope of public discourse and thus inhibiting the potential of public opinion to constructively affect U.S. Mideast policy, which in its decades-long failure to be a constructive force in resolving the conflict has been detrimental to Israelis and Palestinians alike. As one scholar of U.S. Mideast policy observed, "If public discourse had not been warped, policy may have been quite different."[1] In plain terms, it is not the media's role to deliver Mideast peace. However, it is nonetheless the media's responsibility to do no harm in this regard either.

Like American mainstream journalism in general, coverage of the Israeli-Palestinian conflict relies on the traditional news values of conflict, drama, impact, magnitude, and timeliness, among others. These values provide journalists with a useful set of formulaic guidelines for shaping daily news in a format that the public can easily recognize and digest. At the same time, these news values fit the media's need to impart information within limited constraints of space and time. To accommodate the needs of both news consumers and producers, the reporting focuses mainly if not exclusively on the empirical, producing dramatic yet superficial snapshots of that which can be easily observed, quantified, and commented on.

In essence, the Israeli-Palestinian conflict—with its recurring dramas, cycles of violence, and repackaged formulas for peace—is much more than a daily story. However, U.S. mainstream media reporting routinely fails to get beyond the parameters of daily coverage. The current stage of the conflict, with roots in the events of 1948, has been most broadly marked by events since 1967. That year marked two seminal phenomena: the Israeli occupation of the West Bank, the Gaza Strip, East Jerusalem, and the Golan Heights as a result of the Six-Day War; and the beginning of accelerated U.S. economic, military, and diplomatic support for Israel during the height of the cold war. While any formula for peace will have to recognize the consequences of 1948 as they relate to the Palestinian refugee question, the essence of that formula—assuming it is to be based on a two-state solution—will have to focus on returning to a reasonable and mutually acceptable version of the status quo ante of 1967 to determine future borders and sovereignties that guarantee the safety and prosperity of Israelis and Palestinians alike.

Taken together, the Israeli occupation and U.S. Mideast policy constitute the organic and systematic underpinnings of the current state of the conflict. Some would argue that Palestinian violence is yet another factor. Whether that violence is more effect than cause is open to varying interpretations. However, the fact remains that, unlike the fundamental and structural aspects of the Israeli occupation and their relation to U.S. policy, Palestinian violence does not fail to attract a significant share of media attention. The challenge before the American mainstream media, then, is how, over time, to report the conflict in this broader organic context—in addition to requisite coverage of daily developments—in an age when satellite broadcasting and the Internet, coupled with the economic imperatives of corporate-owned media, discourage deeper contextual thinking and reporting.

The American public, which depends on the mainstream media as a vital source for news and information on international affairs, faces a challenge of its own. That challenge is how to obtain sufficient contextual information to be able to understand the emergence of a critical triangular relationship: the impact that U.S. policy has on the trajectory of the Israeli-Palestinian conflict; the impact that the conflict has not only on the attitudes of the majority of the world's Arabs and Muslims toward the United States but also on the actions of a minute minority among them who seek out American targets; and how these two factors have begun to dramatically and negatively affect the safety of individual Americans and American interests as a whole in the twenty-first century.

It is time for a new approach to reporting that, over time and across media, investigates and illuminates the organic essence of the conflict as a much-needed complement to the easily obtained snapshots of the daily drama unfolding between Israelis and Palestinians in the field. The four elements of this new paradigm are:

1. Reframing the frame used to define the conflict by acknowledging and analyzing the impact that U.S. policy has on its trajectory
2. Broadening the parameters of mainstream media discourse by expanding the pool of sources who can contribute broader and deeper interpretations and analyses of key elements of the conflict
3. Reconsidering the role of audience reaction to critical coverage of the conflict
4. Rethinking the concept of journalistic objectivity as it relates to reporting the conflict

REFRAME THE FRAME

It is clear that U.S. policy—via economic and military aid and diplomatic support for Israel—continues to affect the trajectory of the Israeli-Palestinian conflict profoundly. It is equally clear that in their reporting of the conflict the American mainstream media do not explain, expose, or analyze the impact of this policy.

The last decade and a half of active if not vigorous American mediation in the Israeli-Palestinian conflict—from the Madrid conference in 1991, through the Oslo process from 1993 to 2000, to the road map plan of 2003—has failed to produce a solution. This is so primarily because U.S. Mideast policy continues to work toward conflicting ends. At its center is the objective of maintaining Israel's military and economic superiority so the Jewish state can continue to promote American dominance in the strategic, oil-rich region. At the same time, the policy has relatively recently recognized and articulated Palestinian aspirations and the need for an independent state.

However, since 1967—through military and economic aid and diplomatic support—U.S. policy has accommodated if not enabled Israel's colonization and annexation of territories that it occupied during the Six-Day War. Initiated during the cold war as a hedge against Soviet encroachment in the region, this de facto U.S. policy, with its inherent acceptance of these Israeli measures, has continued for a decade and a half since the cold war ended. The result has impeded the peace process and contributed significantly to the impairment of American relations with Arab and Muslim countries.

The Palestinians themselves have not been passive actors in this scenario. However, the illusion of the Oslo process was to elevate the Palestinian leadership to apparent equal-partner status without affording it the equal power or preference Israel enjoyed as a result of its long-standing alliance with the United States. Furthermore, Oslo failed to guarantee the Palestinians that the peace process would be based on the four and a half decades of international law and consensus that had addressed the conflict—vis-à-vis the Israeli occupation and the Palestinian refugee question—rather than on the realpolitik of "realities on the ground." When the process broke down, the Palestinian leadership, while not blameless, was credited with a disproportionately equal if not the greater share of blame by the Clinton and Bush administrations—a perspective that has flowed, largely unfiltered, through the American mainstream media since the outbreak of the second Palestinian uprising in late 2000.

For its part, the international community—through dozens of UN Security Council and General Assembly resolutions affirmed over a period of several decades—has consistently condemned Israeli annexation and occupation of Palestinian land as violations of international law and has deemed reversal of these violations a necessary condition for achieving a just and lasting peace between Israel and the Palestinians.

However, U.S. opposition to these articulations of international consensus on the Israeli-Palestinian conflict—and passive acceptance of Israeli violations of them on the ground—has rendered them largely inert. This, however, is no reason to cease reporting on them. There nevertheless appears to be a direct correlation between the virtual absence of reporting on international law and consensus in American mainstream media coverage of the conflict and the routine manner in which U.S. Mideast policy and politics have flouted them in a continual demonstration of American unilateralism long before it became a signature of U.S. foreign policy under the administration of George W. Bush.

In July 2004 the International Court of Justice in The Hague issued a nonbinding, advisory ruling that the separation barrier being built by Israel on Palestinian land in the West Bank violated international law. The opinion rejected Israel's claim that the barrier was a legitimate action of self-defense meant to thwart Palestinian terror attacks. The court ruled that Israel must cease construction of the barrier, dismantle it, and pay reparations to Palestinians who had suffered damages, including land confiscation and severely limited physical access to their sources of livelihood, medical clinics, and schools. However, the sole dissenter on the fifteen-member panel of international jurists was the American justice, and both houses of Congress introduced legislation to condemn the ruling soon after it was issued.

Two weeks after the ICJ ruled, the UN General Assembly affirmed—by a 150 to 6 vote, with 10 abstentions—a resolution demanding that the barrier be demolished in accordance with the court's opinion. The United States voted against the resolution, along with Israel, Australia, the Marshall Islands, Micronesia, and Palau. The twenty-five-member European Union voted to affirm the measure after language reaffirming Israel's right to self-defense was included.[2] That same day Israeli bulldozers and backhoes continued the work of building the barrier.[3]

American mainstream print and broadcast media had chronicled the building of the barrier and the controversy surrounding it—including the Israeli self-defense argument and the ample evidence of Palestinian suffering caused by the barrier—from the time Israel began construction in June 2002 up to the ICJ ruling in July 2004. However, despite this extensive, detailed coverage, reporting of the ICJ ruling and the UN General Assembly resolution failed to analyze the significance of the American stand in these forums.

The media failed to investigate and explain how the world court applied principles of international law to arrive at its ruling, or how the American vote on the UN resolution seemed to contradict the U.S. public-diplomacy campaign in the Arab and Muslim worlds at the height of the Iraq war. These omissions exemplified a clear pattern of coverage. Since the outbreak of the second Palestinian uprising in September 2000, U.S. mainstream media reporting had, to one degree or another, reflected the hardships of Palestinian life under occupation—both the suffering and the violent response it has engendered. At the same time, the coverage failed to connect the dots concerning how U.S. policy, in bypassing international law and consensus, has given Israel the latitude it needs to establish facts on the ground that make chances for a peaceful negotiated resolution of the conflict even more distant.

In February 2005 the Israeli cabinet approved the modified, final route of the separation barrier, bringing it closer to the Green Line than the original route. The amended route, however, effectively annexed 7 percent of West Bank territory to Israel and left four Palestinian villages with a total population of some ten thousand on the Israeli side. Taken the same day as the vote to approve the withdrawal from Gaza, the move was characterized by the Associated Press thus: "With Sunday's twin votes, Sharon's government began charting Israel's final borders unilaterally, something none of his predecessors have attempted since Israel captured the West Bank, Gaza and east Jerusalem in the 1967 Mideast war."[4] The Israeli daily *Haaretz* reported:

Sharon said . . . that the new fence route combines Israel's security needs with its judicial decisions.

"The amended route provides an answer to Israel's security issue and is compatible with the decisions of Israel's High Court of Justice," he said.

Government sources said the U.S. administration has accepted the new route of the separation fence.[5]

Interviews conducted for the present study with American correspondents about the work process of reporting the Israeli-Palestinian conflict from the field yield clues regarding why analytical coverage of American unilateralism and Israeli exceptionalism vis-à-vis international law and consensus has been absent. Speaking in general terms, one correspondent who had reported from Jerusalem for six years for a major American newspaper observed:

> Journalists are skeptical of the importance of international law because they see a kind of might-makes-right rule of law out there. Like it was OK to film Saddam Hussein when we captured him. We captured him. We're showing it. Whoever wants to see it, fine. Don't talk hoity-toity. In [the Israeli-Palestinian] conflict there's a sense that there is going to have to be a realpolitik settlement.
>
> The layers of law are so many and messy about Palestine that you just get lost in it. The whole business of what the Ottoman, British, Jordanian or Israeli law was at any given moment is such a nightmare. It becomes very, very messy.[6]

A correspondent who had reported the conflict for another major paper for three years said he believed that "it's not my job to put things in a moral or legal framework for the readers," noting:

> One of the major aspects of my job is to measure people's words, either about their actions or their analysis of facts on the ground, against what I can observe, and what I believe to be true. Whether it was Palestinian policies and claims, Israeli policies and claims or American ones, I spent a lot of time measuring things against what I could observe. The official lines that you get either from the outside or the inside are so often clueless or unilluminating. You'd have political statements about what's happening in the West Bank and what American policy's going to try to do to change it that simply didn't resemble what I was seeing. I'm not going to let them decide what the story is.[7]

However, the perceived absence in U.S. Mideast policy of a moral framework, or one that is consistent with international law, is precisely what has helped to fuel the deterioration of attitudes toward the United States in Arab and Muslim countries, where it is commonly thought that the United States applies a double standard to its friends and foes.

In autumn 2002, during the run-up to the U.S. war in Iraq, the Bush administration repeatedly justified its intention to depose Saddam Hussein based on the Iraqi leader's violation since 1990 of twelve UN Security Council resolutions requiring Iraq to submit to UN arms inspections and to destroy its chemical and biological weapons. A study by University of San Francisco political scientist Stephen Zunes published in October 2002 showed that American allies had surpassed Iraq when it came to Security Council violations. Israel led the list, having failed to comply with thirty-two such resolutions since 1968; Turkey claimed the number two spot by violating twenty-four resolutions since 1974.[8] The mainstream media paid relatively scant attention to the study, however, and failed to produce similar independent analyses.[9]

By 2004 the decline in the relationship between the United States and the Muslim world was frequently linked to U.S. foreign policy with respect to both the Israeli-Palestinian conflict and the war in Iraq. The mainstream media's tendency to focus on effect rather than cause in reporting the conflict was illustrated by the fairly wide play given to a poll on Arab attitudes toward the United States released in July by Washington, D.C.–based pollster Zogby International. The survey of 3,300 people in Egypt, Jordan, Lebanon, Morocco, Saudi Arabia, and the United Arab Emirates showed that Arab attitudes toward the United States had taken sharply negative turns in all of these countries except the UAE since 2002—declines attributed in large part to U.S. policies on the Israeli-Palestinian conflict and Iraq.[10] The same week that the poll was released, the 9/11 Commission Report noted in passing that "it is simply a fact that American policy regarding the Israeli-Palestinian conflict and American actions in Iraq are dominant staples of popular commentary across the Arab and Muslim world." The commission, however, made no concrete policy recommendations on either issue.[11]

Also in July 2004 the *Daily Star,* a Lebanese newspaper, noted a U.S. policy link between Israel and Iraq to which the American mainstream media had paid scant attention following the visit to Beirut of Iraqi interim prime minister Iyad Allawi. A commentary in the paper asserted:

There is an unreal, almost fantastic, dimension to official American engagement with the governments and peoples of the Middle East. Washington feels it pursues a noble mission to bring peace, prosperity and democracy to the region; yet the vast majority of the people of this region vehemently reject and shun Washington's policies.

A dramatic example of this was the statement by Iraqi interim Prime Minister Iyad Allawi—hand-picked and installed by the U.S.—a few days ago here in Beirut that Iraq would not normalize relations with Israel before the other Arab states did so. Allawi rejects the American and Israeli desire for Iraq to unilaterally establish normal working relations with Israel, presumably because he understands that the majority of Iraqis and other Arabs strongly oppose current American and Israeli policy toward the Palestinians. America has no dearer Arab "friend" than Allawi—and yet even he cannot go along with America's preferred policy options for Iraq's ties with Israel.[12]

Events in Washington, Algeria, and Israel that played out over a ten-day period in March 2005 further illustrated the futility of U.S. policy trying to square the circle of its tolerance of Israeli settlement expansion, on the one hand, with its goal of improving relations with the Arab and Muslim worlds, on the other. On March 16 President Bush held a news conference during which he addressed the renewal of his administration's public diplomacy campaign to improve the image of the United States abroad with the naming of Karen Hughes as ambassador charged with the task. When asked by a reporter what it would take to address "the question of antipathy to America around the world," Bush included a reference to Israel and the Palestinians that stressed alliances and beliefs while ignoring policy. He stated:

It is very important for us to have a message that counteracts some of the messages coming out of some of the Arab media, some of it coming out partly because of our strong and unwavering friendship with Israel. Israel is an easy target for some of the media in the Middle East, and if you're a friend of Israel, you become a target.

And since we're not going to abandon our alliance with Israel, you know—there was some churning in the press and there were some unhelpful things being said. And so part of that is to make sure people understand the truth, and that is on this particular issue you bet we're going to stand by Israel.

We also believe the Palestinians have the capability of self-governance in a truly democratic state that will live side by side with the Israelis in peace.[13]

On March 18 the Associated Press reported that the Arab League summit set to convene in Algiers three days later had on its agenda a proposal by King Abdullah II of Jordan that called on Arab leaders to normalize relations with Israel while "omitting long-held demands on the Jewish state to return land seized from Arabs during the 1967 Six-Day War." The AP reported that although the proposal mentioned "international resolutions, the principle of land for peace and the (1991) Madrid peace conference," it omitted direct reference to UN Security Council resolutions 242 and 338, suggesting that "the king, whose country signed a 1994 peace deal with Israel, wants the Arabs to accept the geographical changes Israel has made in the territories since 1967. This would mark a major shift in Arab strategy, which has called for a full normalization of relations with Israel only after a complete peace, with the return of all Arab territories under Israeli occupation."[14]

The AP also reported that on March 19 Jordan had accepted amendments to its "contentious" proposal that reaffirmed "the Arab commitment to peace with Israel in return for the land Arabs lost to the Jewish state" in 1967.[15] However, on March 20 the Arab summit formally rejected the Jordanian proposal, with the AP quoting Arab League secretary-general Amr Moussa as saying, "If Israel implements all its commitments, all the Arab countries will be ready to normalize relations with Israel. We are not going to move even 1 millimeter away from this."[16]

According to the AP, on the very same day that the Arab summit rejected the Jordanian proposal, Israel Radio reported that Israeli defense minister Shaul Mofaz had approved construction of 3,500 homes to enlarge the West Bank settlement of Ma'aleh Adumim, located east of Jerusalem. The AP characterized the move as "an apparent violation of Israeli obligations" under the U.S.-backed road map peace plan.[17] In the days that followed, a familiar pattern of U.S. response played out. The AP reported that on March 23 two senior U.S. envoys from the National Security Council and the State Department met with Prime Minister Sharon in Jerusalem "to ask pointed questions about plans to expand the West Bank's largest Jewish settlement in violation of a peace plan . . . 3,500 new housing units around the settlement to encircle Arab east Jerusalem with Jewish neighborhoods."[18] On March 25 the *Los Angeles Times* reported that Secretary of State Condoleezza Rice warned Israel "in unusually sharp terms" that the settlement-expansion plans were "at odds with American policy" and that the explanations proffered by Israel were "not really a satisfactory response."[19]

A statement from the Arab summit concerning normalization of relations with Israel carried a much clearer public message to Rice and her colleagues in Washington than she would muster toward Israel. On March 22 the AP reported that Arab League leader Moussa addressed the settlement issue directly, asserting that "Israel is pressing to gain concessions without anything in return. It imagines that our rights will be forgotten and that the support and immunity it enjoys [from the United States] will allow it to continue building settlements and erecting the imperialist wall [separation barrier] and keeping the occupied territories—or most of them."[20]

On March 24 Hussein Hassouna, the Arab League's chief envoy to Washington, reiterated the Arab League's message to the Bush administration during an interview with the AP's diplomatic correspondent: "You cannot give everything to Israel with nothing in return. There is no free lunch. . . . If Israel wants peace it has to recognize it has to give up the [occupied] territories." Criticizing Israel for its move to expand Ma'aleh Adumim, Hassouna added, "If you create a climate of defiance, you cannot expect the Arab world to accept recognition [of Israel]. It is impossible." About a possible link between U.S. policy and the Jordanian proposal that the Arab summit had rejected earlier that week in Algiers, the AP report noted that "although the proposal was put forward after King Abdullah met in Washington with President Bush, U.S. officials said there was no connection. However, the State Department did call on Arab countries to establish relations with Israel without preconditions."[21]

Given these patterns and tendencies in U.S. policy and related events—and in media coverage of them—it is clear that American mainstream reporting of the Israeli-Palestinian conflict is imbued with the assumptions of the Washington consensus, chief among them being that the United States is not a party to the conflict but merely plays the role of honest broker. The deeply flawed notion implicit in the Washington consensus and adhered to by the media—namely, that the United States assumes an objective role in the conflict—dovetails seamlessly with the approach of American journalists, who see their role as reporting "objectively" on what Israelis and Palestinians do and say. If true objectivity were indeed possible, it would require acknowledgement that the conflict is not binary, that is, between Israelis and Palestinians alone, but tripartite, involving the United States as well.

Thus, the mainstream media's first and perhaps primary task in formulating a new way of reporting the Israeli-Palestinian conflict is to reframe the conceptualization, as it presently exists, to include U.S. policy as a major factor in the conflict's trajectory. The media must also investigate how the United States continues to maintain its own geopolitical interests in the outcome of the conflict, allowing it to proceed along a course that contradicts stated U.S. policy. Furthermore, the media must challenge the inherent falsity of the postulates of the Washington consensus that address Israel and the Palestinians as if they were of equal standing (versus having equal rights and obligations) in the power equation of the conflict.

The death of Palestinian leader Yasser Arafat in November 2004 provided yet another opportunity for the mainstream media to rely on the frame of the Washington consensus in order to analyze the state of relations between Israel and the Palestinians at this particular turning point, as well as the particular challenges faced by Mahmoud Abbas, Arafat's successor. In February 2005 the *New Yorker* magazine devoted thirteen pages to such an assessment. The headline, "Checkpoint: A New Palestinian Leader Confronts Ariel Sharon," was telling in that it established the binary frame from the start, setting forth an implicit context of a contest of coequals. The piece provided a detailed exposition not only of the foibles of both leaders but also of various viewpoints of extremists in both the Israeli and Palestinian camps who would seek to derail Sharon and Abbas—in particular over the issues of the future of Israeli settlements and Palestinian violence. However, mention of U.S. policy in the conflict was absent from the piece, as if to suggest that it played no role in the actions that the two leaders would take or how their constituents were likely to respond.[22]

In March 2005 the *New York Times Magazine* published an 8,200-word profile of the new Palestinian leader with the headline "The Navigator: Where Can Mahmoud Abbas Take the Palestinians?" superimposed over a photo of Abbas on the magazine's cover. Unlike the *New Yorker* piece, which was reported in nearly equal measure based on Israeli and Palestinian sources, the *New York Times* piece focused squarely on Abbas and the Palestinians themselves. "Where Are They Going, and How Far Can Mahmoud Abbas Take Them?" read the subhead above the article's first paragraph. Similar to the *New Yorker*'s approach, however, the *Times* piece never suggested that the answers to those questions depended as much on Israel and the United States as they did on Abbas and the Palestinians. Instead, the piece relied more on the writer's impressions than it did on the sober analysis it would take to answer the questions posed by its headlines.

Although a range of Palestinian sources were consulted as the reporter traveled through the West Bank and Gaza Strip, their input seemed to serve as a descriptive backdrop for his own characterizations. Describing the Israeli-Palestinian conflict as "a narcissistic face-off that pays little notice to the world around it," the piece contended that

to the outside world Abbas may look like the one-eyed man in the land of the blind. He is trying to persuade Palestinians of things that seem obvious: that firing crude rockets into Israeli fields harms Palestinians more than Israelis, by summoning overwhelming Israeli retaliation; that dispatching the young to blow themselves up among Israelis is also a form of national suicide. Yet seen from inside Palestine, the violence has developed a logic of its own. Militants in Gaza and on the West Bank believe that it is they who see the world as it is.

Rana El Farra, of Khan Yunis in the Gaza Strip, who was both a supporter of Hamas and a professor of cell biology, was quoted as saying: "We just need a break. I know the war between the Israelis and the Palestinians will be there until God stops the whole system. But we just need a break of five years. We got used to this system, of taking this break for some time, probably 10 years, and then, when things reach a point where no one can deal with them anymore, then war will be for some time."

Mahmoud Hawashin, a resident of the Jenin refugee camp in the West Bank, was described as "not a militant leader or a politician, though he functions as a liaison between them. . . . He leads a considered life. He trimmed his ambitions to fit his unyielding environment rather than conserve them as dreams." Alternating between the voices of the reporter and Hawashin, the piece concluded:

> Like other Palestinians, Hawashin is already anticipating the fire next time. "There will be another intifada, of course," he told me. The Palestinians will once again be ruled by their hearts, not their heads, he said, and in their hearts they will never surrender.
> "I don't consider myself a defeated person," Hawashin said. "I consider myself a weak person."[23]

Framed by a construct that gives agency in the conflict to Israel and the Palestinians but none to the United States through its policy, the piece never gave Hawashin the chance to explain why.

BROADEN THE PARAMETERS OF MEDIA DISCOURSE

American mainstream media reporting of the Israeli-Palestinian conflict presents a conundrum. On the one hand, American media freedoms are rooted in the idea that the public's interest is served when journalists act to report, explain, and expose the workings of the government and the effects of its policies. The classic theory of a free press holds that unfettered, uncensored reporting on important issues—especially of political import—will empower the public to have a say in policy formulated and carried out in its name. That is to say, public knowledge of these issues will result in the election of leaders who, short of carrying out policy in accordance with the public's will, at the very least would pay it heed.

On the other hand, even though U.S. Mideast policy has for decades revolved around Israel, the mainstream media seldom examine that policy in a critical light. As a result, alternative and oppositional discourse are effectively stifled, with public challenge to that policy unable to accumulate a critical mass.

An ironic result is that the range of public discourse on the Israeli-Palestinian conflict, as it emerges via mainstream media reporting, is broader and deeper in Israel than it is in the United States. When Israelis are critical of the policies of their own government, however, the American media are not slow to report that discontent. In December 2003 *Nightline* reported on decorated Israeli air force pilots who had refused to carry out assassinations of Palestinians in the West Bank and Gaza Strip. Introducing the piece, anchor Ted Koppel observed:

American politicians have always found it difficult to criticize Israel publicly. And the Israeli government has done a particularly skillful job of tapping into this country's post-9/11 psyche. . . . American policy toward the Palestinians, therefore, has rarely been tougher. Prime Minister Sharon has pointedly echoed some of President Bush's toughest rhetoric in the war against terrorism. And the White House has been mostly silent as the Israelis and Palestinians have drifted further and further away from the much-touted road map to peace.

Far from dismantling settlements on the West Bank, the Israelis have actually begun constructing more. One only yesterday in East Jerusalem. In the face of continued suicide attacks by militant Palestinians, the Israelis have launched targeted assassinations, often killing innocent bystanders in the process. Washington has been largely mute.

The criticism, paradoxically, has come from the most unexpected quarter. Israel's army chief, Lieutenant General Moshe Ya'alon, has called his own government's policies counterproductive. That was in late October. Four former chiefs of Shin Bet, the Israeli equivalent of the FBI, denounced the Israeli government's treatment of Palestinians as immoral and disgraceful. That was in mid-November. But it was in late September that a group of 27 Israeli air force pilots denounced the practice of targeted killings as illegal, immoral, and corrupting to Israeli society as a whole. The pilots drafted a petition to their own air force commanders calling for an end to the policy.[24]

In March 2005 the *New York Times* devoted 1,000 words to a "damning" Israeli report by a government-commissioned investigator that condemned "illegal financing of settlement outposts" and recommended criminal investigations of some officials involved.

> In a scathing report commissioned, under pressure from Washington, by Prime Minister Ariel Sharon, Ms. [Talia] Sasson said she had uncovered a pattern of law-breaking that presented a threat to Israeli democracy, and she demanded action to change the "continual, blunt and institutional breach of law, executed by the institutions of the state themselves."
>
> ... She found at least 105 outposts built illegally without government authorization since the mid-1990s but said she was convinced there were more. Of those 105, at least 15 were built entirely on land privately owned by Palestinians and "are totally illegal and must be removed," she said. At least 7 outposts are on disputed land, 26 are on land in the West Bank claimed by the Israeli state and 39 are on parcels that include private Palestinian property.
>
> There are at least 6 illegal outposts where all legal appeals were exhausted months ago, she said, but which have not been dismantled because the Ministry of Defense has not issued an order to do so.
>
> ... Ms. Sasson's report is limited to outposts, and it is full of detail. For example, the Housing Ministry established a new budget line in 2001 called "miscellaneous general development" that was used to finance outposts. The budget line doubled from 2001 to 2003, and from 2000 to 2004 the ministry gave more than $16.7 million to illegal outposts, according to her report.[25]

Lacking Israeli sources, however, critical analysis of American and Israeli policies in American mainstream media news reporting is often presented elliptically, relying heavily on fleeting descriptions and "he said–he said" exchanges rather than in-depth investigation of the policies themselves. In December 2003 *60 Minutes* presented a full-length report on Israel's rationale for constructing the separation barrier in the West Bank and its effects on Palestinians there. Correspondent Bob Simon ended the segment by noting

> During his state visit to London, President Bush called on Israel to end what he characterized as "the daily humiliation of Palestinians" and to not prejudice final negotiations with the placement of walls and fences. Israeli Prime Minister Ariel Sharon responded defiantly, saying,

"We're accelerating the fence and we won't stop it because it's essential to the security of the state."

In turn, the Bush administration has decided to impose an economic sanction which will cost Israel about $4 million next year. Israel gets $2.6 billion in aid from the United States every year.[26]

The rare instances in which tension in the American-Israeli relationship surfaces publicly allow for direct yet fleeting media criticism of Israeli policies. In August 2004 reports surfaced about allegations that a Pentagon analyst had mishandled classified U.S. intelligence documents on Iran that were thought to have been received by AIPAC, the pro-Israel lobby. On August 28 ABC News reported on the complexities of U.S.-Israeli relations in which correspondent Dean Reynolds noted areas of policy disagreement between the two countries:

Israel continues to build [Jewish settlements] on occupied Palestinian land and claims it has a right to do so, even though seven American administrations have asked them to stop. Israel has tried to enrich its defense industries with foreign sales, sometimes involving U.S.-made technology, even though Washington objects. The two countries shared information during the first Gulf War when Iraq attacked the Jewish state.

Israel and its supporters here say Washington has not always been so forthcoming. That's what motivated Jonathan Pollard, the U.S. Navy intelligence officer who sold classified material to Israel in the 1980s, and who was imprisoned for life because of it. And, almost 40 years later, there is lingering U.S. suspicion that the Israeli air force attack on the USS *Liberty* off Gaza was not the mistake the Israelis have always said it was but a deliberate attempt to shield Israeli secrets at the height of the Six-Day War.[27]

Since September 11, 2001, American mainstream media have increasingly noted widespread discontent in Arab and Muslim countries over U.S. policy toward the Israeli-Palestinian conflict while at the same time failing to examine the reasons behind that sentiment. Reports on American relations in the Middle East and South Asia and the U.S. "war on terror" now routinely quote leaders and intellectuals in Arab and Muslim countries to this effect, as was the case when *World News Tonight* anchor Peter Jennings interviewed Pakistani leader Pervez Musharraf in September 2004.

JENNINGS: You have said many times that you believe the root causes of terror are poverty, lack of education. Do you believe that the United States is ignoring those root causes in its campaign against terrorism?

MUSHARRAF: I think they are. They are only—we are only—involved at the moment in fighting terrorism frontally, the military perspective. So I think those root causes are not being addressed. And I hope they are; otherwise we are not going to succeed. We may be winning battles but we'll lose the war.

JENNINGS: Do you mean to say, seriously, that the United States could lose the war on terrorism?

MUSHARRAF: Well, if you don't go addressing political disputes, yes. That is a possibility.

JENNINGS: And what do you think is the principal political dispute that must be addressed?

MUSHARRAF: First of all, Palestine. Because I think that has the maximum negative perspective all around, all around the Muslim world. And the United States is seen or perceived as an Israeli supporter and totally against Muslims. So I think this is the one which needs to be resolved immediately.[28]

Also that September the *Los Angeles Times*, in a 5,000-word, front-page report headlined "The New Face of al-Qaeda," observed that "the al-Qaeda movement now appears to be more of an ideology than an organization," with adherents sharing basic principles that include "a profound sense of indignation over the deaths of Muslims in Palestinian territories and Iraq." The report further noted that "Moroccans and officials of other Islamic countries agree that anger over U.S. policies in the Israeli-Palestinian conflict provides much of the motivation for [terror] attacks. 'If the Palestinian issue were settled, if Iraq were stable, 70 percent of the threats would disappear,' said [Mohammed] Bouzoubaa, the justice minister."[29]

In October 2004, as part of an NPR series examining attitudes toward the United States emanating from Arab countries surrounding Iraq, correspondent Deborah Amos reported on the largely pro-American sentiments among Kuwaitis, while also making the following point:

AMOS: The battle of ideas can be lost not over Iraq but over U.S. failures to address the Israeli-Palestinian conflict, says Saba Jamai. This former government official believes that as long as the Bush administration seems to say Israel is always right [and] the Palestinians

[are] always wrong, transforming the region to democracy and human rights will stall.

JAMAI: I think the United States have [*sic*] actually saved Muslims
in this country. They have saved Muslims in Iraq and in Afghanistan and in Bosnia. But they're not doing their homework when it
comes to the Arab-Israeli conflict, the Palestinian issue. They are
not at all. Look at the current administration. They're just sitting
idle while people are being killed, and I'm talking about innocent
people killed on both sides.

AMOS: Even in Kuwait, he says, it is the issue that allows the radicals
to win recruits.[30]

Repeated reporting of such assertions that U.S. policy bias toward Israel is
a key factor in Arab and Muslim hostility toward the United States—while
further journalistic exposition and analysis of the substance of those assertions is lacking—makes it easy to dismiss statements like the one issued by
Ayman al-Zawahri in October 2004 as one-dimensional sloganeering. The
deputy of al-Qaeda leader Osama bin Laden, Zawahri released an audiotape
calling for attacks against American and British interests in the form of a
resistance that would "stand up to the crusader campaign like the holy warriors organized their affairs in Afghanistan, Chechnya or Palestine."[31] Three
weeks later, just days before the U.S. presidential election, bin Laden himself
released a videotape in which he purported to speak to the American public,
linking the September 11 attacks on the World Trade Center to Israel's 1982
invasion of Lebanon and tacit U.S. backing of it.

I will tell you about the reasons behind these attacks and will tell you
the truth about the moments during which the decision was made for
you to contemplate.

God knows that it had not occurred to our mind to attack the towers, but after our patience ran out and we saw the injustice and inflex-
ibility of the American-Israeli alliance toward our people in Palestine
and Lebanon, this came to my mind. The incidents that affected me
directly go back to 1982 and afterward, when America allowed Israelis
to invade Lebanon, with the help of the American Sixth Fleet.

In these tough moments, many things raged inside me that are hard
to describe, but they resulted in a strong feeling against injustice and a
strong determination to punish the unjust.

While I was looking at those destroyed towers in Lebanon, it sparked
in my mind that the tyrant should be punished with the same, and that

we should destroy towers in America, so that it tastes what we taste and would be deterred from killing our children and women.[32]

To argue that the media should broaden the parameters of mainstream discourse on the Israeli-Palestinian conflict by enlarging the pool of sources from which perspectives on it are reported is not necessarily to advocate giving equal time or prominent space to pronouncements from al-Qaeda. However, in order to inject critical reporting of the conflict squarely into mainstream discourse—that is, beyond the editorial and op-ed pages and into the news columns and on news broadcasts not dominated by partisan shout-downs—the media will have to rely less on facile, contrapuntal use of Israeli, Palestinian, and official U.S. sources. They will have to do more investigative reporting that cultivates a much broader range of live sources, including nonpartisan experts, and documentary evidence.

It is abundantly clear that Israelis and Palestinians view their histories and rights differently. What is not clear is why so much American mainstream media reporting on the conflict is limited to a superficial balancing of these beliefs and claims. As one former Jerusalem-based correspondent put it: "I find it very hard to watch coverage of the Middle East because, like the average viewer, I find it so repetitive. I'm not engaged by it. I don't see that there's anybody really prepared to say, well, hang on, this isn't always tit for tat. Sometimes one side or the other has legitimate grievances. It all gets reduced to this happened and this happened; they did this and they did that. You never really get a discussion of what actually has some legitimacy and what doesn't."[33]

Testing the legitimacy of historical claims and interpretations of rights and obligations according to international law and consensus can indeed be done. However, such reporting must be invested with two critical elements. The first is time, the precious resource that would allow correspondents to do their own basic research on important historical issues, points of international law and consensus, and U.S. policy, and then to seek out nonpartisan experts—at least some of whom should be far removed from the arena of physical conflict and/or the United States—to help explain and interpret the issues in these fields as well as others, including development, economics, and foreign policy.

In conducting their research, journalists could tap a cache of documentary sources in order to measure not only Israeli and Palestinian claims against international articulations of their rights and obligations according to international law and consensus but also—and equally important—to measure stated U.S. policy on the conflict against the actual record of U.S. action on the conflict. Such documentary sources include the State Department's annual budget request to Congress, which provides precise details of U.S. aid to Israel (both military and economic) and to the Palestinians; UN voting records on resolutions pertaining to the conflict adopted by the Security Council and General Assembly; and periodic reports on U.S. policy toward Israel and the Palestinians issued by the Congressional Research Service. In addition, if journalists were to review a critical mass of State Department briefing transcripts that reflect exchanges on key issues of the conflict, such as the U.S. response to Israeli settlement expansion, they might conclude that consistent official obfuscation doesn't mean that there is no story, and that the refusal of the U.S. government to be forthcoming about these issues with the media—and, by extension, the American public—is a story in and of itself.

The second critical element with which such reporting must be invested is a dedication to serving the public's right to understand these issues more broadly and deeply than what point-and-shoot journalism ("Israelis say, Palestinians say") will allow. Realizing that critical coverage of the issues is bound to elicit objections from domestic pro-Israel and pro-Palestinian constituent groups, news organizations must have the vision and fortitude to absorb negative reaction as a natural part of reporting the story and not view it as a reason to limit the depth and parameters of the reporting process itself.

The willingness—indeed, the obligation—to exercise independent judgment is one of the cornerstones of free media, in which reporting of such complex and controversial issues as the Israeli-Palestinian conflict can be done not only critically but also with depth *and* balance. Credible voices that reflect complexity, balance, and a critical approach do exist; the question is whether the mainstream media will permit themselves to hear these voices and, in so doing, allow the American public to hear them as well. Alternatively, the question is whether such voices will be relegated to the realm of pure opinion (as distinct from fact-based reporting) within the mainstream or be heard only via alternative media, which by definition command narrower audiences. The following critical yet evenhanded articulation on the conflict, published in the *New York Review of Books* in December 2004, would most likely not have been given space in the *New York Times* or *Newsweek* or time on Fox News.

Clearly, nothing has played more directly into Sharon's determination to avoid a political process than Palestinian terrorism directed at Israeli civilians. Terrorism and Arafat's disastrous failures at Palestinian institution building have been exploited by Sharon to discredit the entire

Palestinian national enterprise and to undermine those in Israel and in the international community who have sought to help it succeed. But Palestinian failures do not begin to legitimize Sharon's policies, or those of the Bush administration, for that matter. Palestinians have the right to a state in the West Bank and Gaza not because they meet certain standards set by Sharon, the man who aspires to acquiring much of their land, or because Bush has a "vision" of two states living side by side, but because of universally recognized principles of national self-determination.[34]

In addition to nonpartisan American and international expert sources who either currently hold or have previously held positions in government, academia, NGOs, or the military, there exists in the United States a host of civil-society groups devoted to Middle East peace. Their points of view, while often representing distinctive religious and/or ethnic identities, are rarely represented in media discussions of prospects for peace. Such discussions are primarily dominated, both on the air and in print, by those who have formerly served in various U.S. administrations or who currently hold positions in partisan think tanks.

This relatively narrow range of sourcing, informed as it is by variations of beltway logic and the Washington consensus, leaves the American public with little indication of the diversity of its own range of opinions on the conflict. Contrary to the media's tendency to allow voices that represent the official U.S. line and Israeli interpretations, both official and nonofficial, to dominate mainstream discourse in reporting on the conflict from the Middle East and Washington alike, there is evidence that the range of American public opinion on the conflict is wider and more diverse than the discourse that is found on the air and in print.

RECONSIDER AUDIENCE REACTION

Many Americans reacted with disdain to the bin Laden video preceding the 2004 election, seeing in his message reason for reinvigorated national unity and resolve to fight terrorism. Such sentiments were echoed on the editorial pages of several prominent American newspapers. The *Chicago Tribune* opined that bin Laden had "tried to intimidate U.S. citizens into changing their government's policy of relentlessly pursuing al-Qaeda. . . . In short, you can avoid more days like Sept. 11, 2001, if you stop menacing us."[35] The *Christian Science Monitor* took a similar tack, asserting that bin Laden's "attempt to divide Americans helps unite them." If the al-Qaeda leader's videotaped message was an October surprise, the paper reasoned, then perhaps "a 'November surprise' could be that Americans reunite against terrorist intimidation."[36]

USA Today took a more nuanced approach, stating that while bin Laden "has a very poor understanding of Americans and American government," his understanding of his own base was more to the point. The editorial continued:

> But he certainly understands how to play to angry Muslims. And for that reason, bin Laden's message deserves the closest scrutiny because it suggests he may be recasting himself for another role—one that puts the U.S. at a disadvantage. . . .
>
> The new image and message may be aimed elsewhere, and as improbable as it sounds, at putting bin Laden on a trajectory from terrorist to political leader.
>
> Bin Laden's appeal to alienated Arabs rests in his ability to blame the U.S. for all they see wrong with their lives. To their ears, he might sound like a champion of freedom and of removing the corrupt dictatorships from throughout the Middle East.
>
> The long-term challenge for the U.S. is to convince that audience that the U.S. vision of freedom is superior; that, in the end, the U.S. values of democracy and human rights are the path to real freedom; and that the "freedom" bin Laden offers is fundamentalist repression.[37]

If, as USA Today suggested, there is any hope that the United States will be able to convince the Arab and Muslim audience that the U.S. vision of freedom is indeed superior—and that American values of democracy and human rights apply to all—then there is no doubt that U.S. policy on the Israeli-Palestinian conflict will have to change. In order for that to happen, the American public must have a more complete, detailed, and contextual picture not only of what that policy entails but also of the effects it has had on the peace process and how it has helped to inspire those who would join the jihad against the United States. Furthermore, if Americans had a detailed and contextual understanding of how U.S. policy undermines international law and consensus on key issues of the conflict—particularly Israeli colonization of the West Bank and the rights of Palestinian refugees—it is questionable whether the majority of Americans would support such a policy even passively.

The American mainstream media have the potential—and the power—to facilitate such understanding. However, in order to do so they must be guided by journalistic ethics and best practices, which would permit them to adopt a critical approach to reporting the underlying issues of the conflict. In addition, they must resist the apparent tendency to calculate potential audience response that such critical reporting may elicit and then opt not to undertake it if the "cost" is deemed to be too great.

Despite the facts that U.S. policy tilts heavily toward Israel, and that the organized pro-Israel camp in the United States is far stronger than its emerging pro-Palestinian counterpart, there are credible indications that sentiment already exists among the American public that U.S. Mideast policy should be evenhanded. A study of U.S. public opinion on a host of international issues released by the Chicago Council on Foreign Relations in October 2004 found that three-quarters of Americans think the United States should not take sides in the Israeli-Palestinian conflict. However, the study also found the perceptions of those in leadership positions to be "far off" regarding actual public sentiment on the issue.

> Only 17 percent of the public and 15 percent of leaders favor taking Israel's side in the Israel-Palestine conflict, with 10 percent of administration officials, 21 percent of Democratic staffers and 44 percent of Republican staffers taking this position. Instead, 74 percent of the public and 77 percent of the leaders favor taking neither side.
>
> But here again, leaders' estimates of the public are far off. Only 32 percent of leaders correctly guess that a majority of Americans favor not taking either side, and only 13 percent assume that this would be a large majority. Administration officials do slightly better, with 42 percent correctly estimating the view of the majority, though only 10 percent correctly estimate the magnitude. Among Congressional staffers, 21 percent of Republican staffers and 30 percent of Democratic staffers correctly assess majority sentiment.[38]

Letters-to-the-editor pages of newspapers also reveal a broad range of public sentiment. While there is significant American sympathy for Israel's right to defend itself against terrorism, there is also widespread understanding that the Israeli-Palestinian conflict and the U.S. role in it cannot and should not be viewed within the narrow parameters of the terrorism issue alone. These sentiments were expressed by readers of the *Milwaukee Journal Sentinel* in mid-April 2002 at the height of Israel's incursion into the West Bank and following a string of Palestinian suicide bombings in Israel. Reacting to the call by President Bush for Israeli prime minister Ariel Sharon to pull back Israeli forces, one reader wrote:

By insisting that Israel leave the Palestinian terrorist network alone and that it withdraw its military forces from the West Bank, Bush and Secretary of State Colin Powell have legitimized terrorists with the message to the Palestinian bombers that terrorism against the Jewish state bears no negative consequences. . . .

It seems that the current administration has learned nothing from the sad events of Sept. 11. Notwithstanding the utter immorality of selling out Israel, Washington, in its frantic search for a quick political fix in the Middle East, has forgotten its own national-security interests.

If Palestinian terror gangs are to be rewarded with their own state, that state will be run by al-Qaeda or its local equivalent, Hamas. How many suicide squads will this terrorist state be sending here to the U.S.?[39]

In the same issue another reader wrote

Instead of weeding out terrorism, Sharon is laying out fertile ground for increased terrorism and worldwide hate against Jews and against all of us in the United States, regardless of what ethnic or religious groups we might belong to. He is increasing risks for innocent Americans here and abroad to be harmed or even killed.

And when all the destruction is done—by the mighty Israel[i] military, built up and paid for by innocent American taxpayers—we, the American taxpayers, will have to foot the bill for rebuilding.

The terrorism in the Middle East is terrible. But this is not the way to settle the trouble. Especially when the undisputed fact is that Israel has taken other people's land. That is the way the rest of the world sees it, regardless of any fancy political excuses and religious explanations.[40]

Readers of the *St. Petersburg Times* came to similar conclusions that April. One asked:

Why should Israel not have the same right to eradicate terrorism within miles of its borders in order to protect its citizens? Why should Israel give Yasser Arafat yet another chance? It should be remembered that Arafat supports, finances and encourages terror and in doing so has violated all the promises he made to Israel and the United States.

If the Israeli army is forced to withdraw, it will only allow terrorists to retake Israeli streets and murder innocent men, women and children. Should Israel not be permitted to finish its war on terrorism, Israel might not survive as a nation, and as it goes with Israel, so it will go with all of us.[41]

However, on the matter of Palestinian suicide bombings another reader asserted:

> Why is it that no one is asking, "Why do these people feel so desperate as to blow themselves up and take as many people with them as they can?" Why is our government only scolding Yasser Arafat? Why is our government supporting Ariel Sharon in the genocide of the Palestinian people? Why do we question why other nations hate Americans?
>
> Why are the Israeli Defense Forces not equivalent to the Taliban? Why does the United States support such horror?
>
> I'm sure the Palestinian suicide bombings will stop when Israel withdraws and gives the Palestinian people back their land and their dignity.[42]

Operating free of government censorship, the media must not submit to pressure from other quarters and opt to censor themselves when it comes to reporting sensitive political topics, including aspects of the Israeli-Palestinian conflict. Rather, the media must be guided by their own sense of journalistic ethos and ethics. This approach to reporting was embodied by Peter Jennings, to whom ABC News paid tribute upon his death in August 2005. In a documentary report on his career, Jennings's colleagues recalled his determination to ask tough questions about important issues on behalf of his audience without pandering to it. ABC News senior producer Terence Wrong said of Jennings: "He covered the world the way he thought was important, and [he] respected the audience enough that they'd watch and process the information, make their own decision about what we had said. But he had enormous respect [for the audience], and I think he didn't realize how much respect the audience had for him or the connection he had to his audience until he got sick."

The report intercut clips of Jennings's reporting from various venues in the Middle East with commentary from his colleagues about Jennings having been perceived as pro-Arab or pro-Palestinian in his coverage. Nonetheless, Jennings appeared to have stuck to his journalistic instincts and principles when reporting the story.

JENNINGS: Until the Palestinians have some measure of self-determination, America's efforts in the Middle East will ultimately flounder.

TERENCE WRONG (producer): But the Middle East and the controversy that surrounded his reporting of the Arab-Israeli conflict followed him to the end.

JENNINGS: There was supposed to be a cease-fire today between Israelis and the Palestinians, but passions are clearly too inflamed. Many walls are covered with pictures of the [Palestinian] boy who was shot on Saturday. His mother said that if President Clinton is moved by the death of her son, he should stop the Israelis from doing what they're doing.

MIKE LEE (reporter): Peter became a target for his coverage of the Middle East. Many people felt he was anti-Israeli or pro-Palestinian. I don't think he was that way. I think that he felt he was trying to redress balances in what he felt was an under-covered Palestinian story, under-exposed in a way.

CHARLIE GLASS (reporter): He was both pro-Arab and pro-Israeli. He loved Arabs and Israelis and had close friends in the Arab world and in Israel... .

JENNINGS: The damage has been extensive. This has been the biggest [Israeli] attack on Lebanon ever, and the local officials say hundreds of houses have been destroyed and hundreds of Lebanese left homeless. The Israelis say they were used by the commandos. The Lebanese say by innocent villagers. Israeli jets make a final pass over the valley. The villagers remark bitterly that the planes were a gift from America.

BARRIE DUNSMORE (reporter): I think that the early accusations that Peter was pro-Palestinian came at a time when there was very, very little attention being paid to the Arab side generally, and certainly to the Palestinians. And that anyone who was willing to talk about them and to try to explain their position and so on was seen as carrying their baggage, as it were.

JENNINGS: Debamusa knows nothing of Geneva Conventions. She knows she's afraid of the Israelis. That when the first bombs fell, her daughter ran, was hit, and not seen again.

HANNAN ASHRAWI (Palestinian legislator): The fact that Peter dared to go beyond the cliché and the label and seek the truth made many people label him as being pro-Palestinian or pro-Arab.

YAEL LAVIE (producer): As a colleague and ABC producer, and as an Israeli, I admired Peter's reporting of the Middle East. But as an Israeli, I can also tell you that there were people that felt that Peter was not even-handed, which comes from when you live in that country as an Israeli. A country that in the 50 years of its life span has seen terror attack after terror attack on a daily basis.[43]

RETHINK JOURNALISTIC "OBJECTIVITY"

Given the virtual absence of reporting on the impact of U.S. policy on the trajectory of the Israeli-Palestinian conflict, and the media's self-acknowledged failure to report the run-up to the war in Iraq critically, is it not reasonable to argue that the time-honored, almost mythic concept of journalistic objectivity may have outlived its usefulness?

A critical essay entitled "Re-thinking Objectivity," published in the *Columbia Journalism Review* in 2003, argued that the principle of objectivity had served—in prewar mainstream reporting of the Bush administration's eve-of-war linking of al-Qaeda and the September 11 attacks to Saddam Hussein's Iraq and other topics—to make journalists "passive recipients of news, rather than aggressive analyzers and explainers of it." The media have become hypersensitive to charges of bias and do not want to risk losing access to official sources by seeming to argue with or contradict them. To quote a *Washington Post* economics reporter, "If you are perceived as having a political bias, or a slant, you're screwed." The *CJR* piece nevertheless cautioned: "Our pursuit of objectivity can trip us up on the way to the 'truth.' Objectivity excuses lazy reporting. If you're on deadline and all you have is 'both sides of the story,' that's often good enough. It's not that such stories laying out the parameters of a debate have no value for readers, but too often, in our obsession with . . . 'the latest,' we fail to push the story, incrementally, toward a deeper understanding of what is true and what is false."[44]

Rather than focus on the amorphous if not impossible standard of objectivity, to what sources can journalists turn in order to find values and guidance not only for their work in general but also to formulate a new way of reporting the Israeli-Palestinian conflict? One source is academe. Working journalists do not make a habit of consulting media theorists about how to do their jobs or the consequences of their method. However, journalists who report, edit, and produce news of the conflict—both from the field in the Middle East and in newsrooms back home—might do well to understand that scholarly ideas can transcend the realm of theory. As one media scholar noted, "If the press cannot independently hold officials to account, if it is unable to constitute a critical forum for the exchange of ideas about what the government should or should not be doing, then it becomes difficult to imagine how the people at large can exercise popular sovereignty over their institutions of government."[45] Without a "return to an independent press willing to exercise independent judgment," another mass communications theorist asserted, "we will continue to live with news that subverts its own historic ideas." By doing so, the media "have helped create a political world that is, culturally speaking, upside-down. It is a world in which governments are able to define their own publics and where 'democracy' becomes whatever the government ends up doing."[46]

In plain terms, one team of media scholars argues, "one has to work hard, to produce evidence that is credible, to construct serious arguments, to present extensive documentation—all tasks that are superfluous as long as one remains within the presuppositional framework of the doctrinal consensus. It is small wonder that few are willing to undertake the effort, quite apart from the rewards that accrue to conformity and the costs of honest dissidence."[47]

At its very essence, the paradigm for a new way of reporting the conflict can be shaped through an understanding of critical theory, which goes beyond a problem-solving approach to superficial issues to actively examine the organic systems that underlie them. As Canadian political scientist Robert Cox has written, "Critical theory does not take institutions and social and power relations for granted but calls them into question by concerning itself with their origins and how and whether they might be in the process of changing." As such, critical theory may be applicable to journalistic investigation of U.S. Mideast policy and could perhaps serve as the basis of a new "critical journalism" approach to American mainstream media reporting of international affairs, particularly in the Arab and Muslim worlds. Such an approach would be as grounded in the reality of interests and power relations as it would be in questioning them. According to Cox, "Critical theory is, of course, not unconcerned with the problems of the real world. . . . [It] allows for a normative choice in favor of a social and political order different from the prevailing order, but it limits the range of choice to alternative orders which are feasible transformations of the existing world. A principal objective of critical theory, therefore, is to clarify this range of possible alternatives."[48]

The foregoing are not obscure constructs but rather compatible theoretical equivalents of best-practice measures that journalists themselves have recognized and codified in a second source to which they can turn for guidance in formulating a new paradigm for reporting the conflict, namely, their own Code of Ethics of the Society of Professional Journalists. The code, which dropped the word "objectivity" in 1996,[49] advises journalists—under the rubric of "seek truth and report it"—to "tell the story of the diversity and magnitude of the human experience boldly, even when it is unpopular to do so." Journalists are encouraged to "give voice to the voiceless; official and unofficial sources of information can be equally valid." The code advises that reporters "support the open exchange of views, even views they find repugnant." Perhaps most important of all, according to the code journalists should "examine their own cultural values and avoid imposing those values on others."[50]

While a code of ethics can provide inspiration and aspirational values, working journalists have still other practical and immediate channels through which they can ponder and formulate a new paradigm for reporting not only the Israeli-Palestinian conflict but also related matters of international import. There are hard questions to be asked, but there are also venues in which to ask them.

Professional conferences and established institutions devoted to media ethics and practice can serve as natural venues in which editors, producers, and reporters can engage in constructive discussions and healthy self-criticism on these topics. In the words of one American media observer, "Getting outside one's own value system takes a great deal of self-questioning."[51] A voice from outside that value system belonging to an Arab journalist implored: "It is time for the American media to seriously examine its coverage of this decades-long conflict . . . [to] question U.S. policy. American editors and reporters need to take a step back and examine their one-sidedness and self-censorship, especially at a time when Americans would like to project themselves as believers in [the] free flow of information and exporters of democracy."[52]

Institutions that devote themselves to media ethics and practice—among them the Poynter Institute, the Pew Research Center for the People and the Press, and the Joan Shorenstein Center on the Press, Politics and Public Policy, Harvard University—should assume leadership roles in facilitating an examination of American mainstream reporting of the Israeli-Palestinian conflict. This could be undertaken as a case study in a series of broader discussions of American mainstream media reporting—or the lack thereof—on the practical and immediate effects of U.S. policy in the Arab and Muslim worlds. Such an examination should begin with a discussion of the value of applying the same standards of journalistic scrutiny and rigor when reporting on U.S. foreign policy as those used when reporting on policies of local and state governments as well as federal domestic policy.

Such discussions among professional journalists should question the logic of reporting, at face value, American plans to democratize the Middle East when U.S. policy encourages and often underwrites antidemocratic trends and practices—including breaches of international law and consensus—that Americans would not tolerate on their own soil.

The discussions should examine whether Arab societies being exposed to freer and democratizing media that have explicitly Arab points of view are receiving only propaganda or whether at least some of that reporting has factual bases worthy of American journalistic investigation.

The discussions should also consider whether points of view and biases in Arab media have identifiable parallels within the American media landscape—not by virtue of what is reported but by virtue of what is omitted from the coverage, especially with respect to U.S. Mideast policy.

Finally, journalists should consider how superficial coverage of the Israeli-Palestinian conflict may actually serve not to inform and facilitate constructive change but rather to reinforce repeating patterns of heightened expectations and, ultimately, dashed hopes for peace.

෴

The numbing, senseless, and seemingly endless harm inflicted by Israelis and Palestinians on each other has caused one American correspondent to lament: "Whether the casualties on any given day are on one side or the other or both, there is also, in a dark space, somewhere, a reality. There is a dead child; there is an exit wound. How many dead children is too many is a question often asked by Palestinians and Israelis, but it shows no hint of being resolved."[53]

Beyond pathos and poetics, the true work of reporting the conflict remains to be carried out by asking and investigating the difficult question: Why is this so? To understand why there is no hint of a resolution in sight requires getting beyond vivid and artfully crafted word pictures based on empirical observation and superficial balancing of adversarial perspectives. To accomplish this would be to realize what American journalism has for so long aspired and claimed to be, as well as to fulfill the promise of what it can, indeed, still do: contribute truths, clarity, and hope toward the resolution of a conflict that in its continuum of tragedy has all but ceased to produce news, despite the illusion of it.

NOTES

INTRODUCTION

1. John Waterbury, "Hate Your Policies, Love Your Institutions," *Foreign Affairs* 82, no. 1 (January–February 2003): 59.

2. Brent Scowcroft, "Don't Attack Saddam," *Wall Street Journal*, August 15, 2002.

3. Thomas Friedman, "Sealing the Well," *New York Times*, January 12, 2003.

4. "Arab Leaders Pledge Reform on Their Terms," CNN.com, May 23, 2004.

5. Robert Collier, "Arab Summit Blow-up Appears Bad for Bush: U.S. Plan for Reform Resented as Meddling," *San Francisco Chronicle*, March 30, 2004.

6. Vicky O'Hara, "Reaction to the Greater Middle East Initiative Which Encourages Democracy in Arab Countries," NPR/*Morning Edition*, March 23, 2004.

7. Philo C. Wasburn, *The Social Construction of International News: We're Talking About Them, They're Talking About Us* (Westport, Conn.: Praeger, 2002), p. 21.

8. Anup Shah, "Mainstream Media Introduction," December 2005, www.globalissues.org.

9. "Mass media," Wikipedia, http://en.wikipedia.org.

10. Jürgen Habermas, *The Structural Transformation of the Public Sphere: An Inquiry into a Category of Bourgeois Society*, trans. Thomas Burger with Frederick Lawrence (Cambridge, Mass.: MIT Press, 1989), p. 176.

11. Noam Chomsky, "What Makes Mainstream Media Mainstream," *Z Magazine*, October 1997 (from a lecture presented at Z Media Institute in June 1997).

12. Herbert J. Gans, *Deciding What's News: A Study of* CBS Evening News, NBC Nightly News, Newsweek, *and* Time (New York: Pantheon, 1979), p. 39.

13. Gans, *Deciding What's News*, p. 182.

14. Wasburn, *Social Construction*, p. 12.

15. Gans, *Deciding What's News*, pp. 39–40.

16. Wasburn, *Social Construction*, p. 16.

17. W. Lance Bennett, *News: The Politics of Illusion*, 3rd ed. (White Plains, N.Y.: Longman, 1996, cited in Wasburn, p. 16.

18. Ibid., p. 17.

19. Daniel C. Hallin, *The "Uncensored War": The Media and Vietnam* (New York: Oxford University Press, 1986), pp. 135–36.

20. Todd Gitlin, *The Whole World Is Watching: Mass Media in the Making and Unmaking of the New Left* (Berkeley: University of California Press, 1980), p. 263.

21. Hallin, *"Uncensored War,"* pp. 116–17.

22. Karim H. Karim, *Islamic Peril: Media and Global Violence* (Montreal: Black Rose, 2000), p. 5.

23. Ibid., p. 14.

24. Gans, *Deciding What's News*, p. 201.

25. Ibid., pp. 37–38.

26. Wasburn, *Social Construction*, p. 12.

27. Edward S. Herman and Noam Chomsky, *Manufacturing Consent: The Political Economy of the Mass Media* (New York: Pantheon, 2002), p. 33.

28. Gaye Tuchman, *Making News: A Study in the Construction of Reality* (New York: Free Press, 1978), p. 87.

29. Ibid., pp. 183–84.

30. Gitlin, *Whole World Is Watching*, pp. 1–2.

31. Tuchman, *Making News*, pp. 90–91.

32. Ibid., p. 4.

33. Gitlin, *Whole World Is Watching*, p. 263.

34. Ibid., pp. 9, 257.

35. Ibid., p. 6.

36. Tuchman, *Making News*, p. 99.

37. Gitlin, *Whole World Is Watching*, pp. 257–58, 269.

38. Ibid., pp. 258–59, 5.

39. Herman and Chomsky, *Manufacturing Consent*, p. 302.

40. Ibid., p. 298.

41. Ibid., p. 304.

42. Karim, *Islamic Peril*, pp. 5, 23.

43. Quoted in Gitlin, *Whole World Is Watching*, p. 253.

44. Tuchman, *Making News*, p. 196.

45. W. Lance Bennett, "Toward a Theory of Press-State Relations in the United States," *Journal of Communication* 40, no. 2 (spring 1990): 106.

46. Ibid., pp. 108–9, 111, 122.

47. Ibid., pp. 106–7.

48. Ibid., p. 107, citing Gitlin, *Whole World Is Watching*.

49. Ibid., p. 113.

50. Ibid., pp. 113–14, 121.

51. Scott C. Althaus, "When News Norms Collide, Follow the Lead: New

Evidence for Press Independence," *Political Communication* 20, no. 4 (October 2003): 402.

52. "The *Times* and Iraq," *New York Times*, May 26, 2004.

53. Howard Kurtz, "The Post on WMDs: An Inside Story," *Washington Post*, August 12, 2004.

54. Robert Entman, "Contesting the White House's Frame After 9/11," *Political Communication* 20, no. 4 (October 2003): 428–29.

55. Robert Entman, *Projections of Power: Framing News, Public Opinion, and U.S. Foreign Policy* (Chicago: University of Chicago Press, 2004), p. 112.

56. Leon Lazaroff and Mike Dorning, "Rare Admission, Then Tough Scrutiny: *Times* Apology Puts Focus on News Media's Prewar Role," *Chicago Tribune*, May 27, 2004.

57. Entman, *Projections of Power*, pp. 125, 147, 156.

58. Ibid., p. 14.

59. Tom Raum, "Bush Pledges Crusade to 'Rid World of Evil-Doers,' Says 'No Question' Bin Laden Is Prime Suspect," Associated Press, September 16, 2001.

60. Entman, *Projections of Power*, p. 14.

61. "Full text: bin Laden's 'Letter to America,'" *Observer* (London), November 24, 2002. In an editor's note the *Observer* explained that the bin Laden letter "first appeared on the Internet in Arabic and has since been translated and circulated by Islamists in Britain." A LexisNexis search for other publications of the letter turned up a single source: a 392-word excerpt published in the *Daily Telegraph* (Sydney) on November 26, 2002.

62. As to the authenticity of the bin Laden letter, in a companion news article published the same day the *Observer* reported that "the letter was originally posted in Arabic on a Saudi Arabian Web site previously used by al-Qaeda to disseminate messages. . . . Although there is no way to confirm the letter's authenticity, senior Arab journalists in the Middle East believe it is from bin Laden. 'It is an extraordinary glimpse into his mind,' one told The Observer" (Jason Burke, "Al-Qaeda in New Threat as Martyrs Prepare for War," *Observer*, November 24, 2002).

63. Donna Abu Nasr, "Authorities Search for American Abducted in Saudi Arabia: Al-Qaida Threatens Abuse, Claims Killing of Second American," Associated Press, June 13, 2004.

64. The reference linking bin Laden's plan for an advanced attack date in mid-2000 to Sharon's visit to the Jerusalem holy site appears to be in error. It is likely a reference to mid-2001. Sharon visited the Temple Mount on September 28, 2000.

65. "Excerpts from Statement by Sept. 11 Commission Staff," *New York Times*, June 17, 2004.

66. Marc Perelman, "Bin Laden Aimed to Link Plot to Israel," *Jewish Daily Forward* (online), June 25, 2004.

67. Uzi Benziman, "Twin Towers and Temple Mount," *Haaretz*, June 20, 2004.

68. Stephen Franklin, "Arab Media: A New Force in the Mideast," *Chicago Tribune*, December 22, 2002.

69. "B'Tselem: Israeli Security Forces Killed 660 Palestinians During 2006," *Haaretz*, December 28, 2006.

70. These civilian casualty ratios also appeared in the article by Steven Erlanger, "Intifada's Legacy at Year 4: A Morass of Faded Hopes," *New York Times*, October 3, 2004.

71. "B'Tselem."

72. Zeina Karam, "Hezbollah Raid Boosts Group's Image," Associated Press, July 12, 2006.

73. "Mideast War, by the Numbers," Associated Press, August 17, 2006.

74. Ibid.

75. Oren Yiftachel, "Neither Two States Nor One: The Disengagement and 'Creeping Apartheid' in Israel/Palestine," *Arab World Geographer* (Toronto) 8, no. 3 (2005): 126–27.

76. Laurie Copans, "Olmert Wants to Hold On to Three Major Settlement Blocs, Jordan Valley: Report," Associated Press, February 7, 2006.

77. Laurie Copans, "Israel Beefs Up Settlements Even While It Talks of West Bank Withdrawal," Associated Press, June 2, 2006.

78. Shahar Ilan, "Population Administration: West Bank Settlements Grew by 6 Percent Last Year," *Haaretz*, January 10, 2007.

79. Ravi Nessman, "Israel Settlement Breaks Promise to U.S.," Associated Press, December 27, 2006.

80. On September 21, 2006, Palestinian president Mahmoud Abbas told the United Nations General Assembly that a Palestinian unity government comprising his Fatah party and Hamas would recognize Israel. On September 22 Palestinian prime minister Ismail Haniyeh of Hamas, based in Gaza, rejected Abbas's claim, leaving ambiguous whether Hamas might eventually recognize the Jewish state after the establishment of a Palestinian state. Haniyeh told the Associated Press: "We support establishing a Palestinian state in the land [occupied by Israel in] 1967 at this stage, but in return for a cease-fire, not recognition" (quoted in Diaa Hadid, "Palestinian Prime Minister Says He Won't Head a Government That Recognizes Israel," Associated Press, September 22, 2006).

81. In August 2006 the *Washington Post* reported: "The Palestinians launch an average of about six crude Qassam rockets a week into Israel, causing minimal damage, no fatalities and about a dozen injuries since June 28, an army spokesman said. 'Any Qassam fired toward Israel is too many,' said Maj. Tal Lev-Ram, a spokesman for the Israeli army's Southern Command. 'Every act of terrorism against Israel will be dealt with severely from our side'" (quoted in Doug Struck, "Israeli Siege Leaves Gaza Isolated and Desperate," *Washington Post*, August 28, 2006).

82. "Text of President Bush's statement on the Mideast," Associated Press, August 14, 2006.

83. Edith M. Lederer, "U.N. Political Chief Calls for New International Effort to Settle Arab-Israeli Conflicts with the Palestinians, Syrians and Lebanese," Associated Press, August 23, 2006.

84. Nick Wadhams, "Annan Opens General Assembly Debate Decrying Unjust World Economy, Global Disorder and Contempt for Human Rights," Associated Press, September 19, 2006.

85. Amy Teibel, "Olmert Government Issues Its Biggest Bids Yet for West Bank Settlement Construction," Associated Press, September 4, 2006.

86. The Iraq Study Group Report, James A. Baker III and Lee H. Hamilton, co-chairs, published by the United States Institute of Peace, December 6, 2006, www.usip.org/isg/iraq_study_group_report/report/1206/, pp. 39, 33.

87. UN General Assembly Resolution 61/25 (December 1, 2006), "Peaceful Settlement of the Question of Palestine": 157 nations voting in favor, 7 against (Australia, Israel, Marshall Islands, Micronesia, Nauru, Palau, United States), 10 abstentions, 18 absent.

UN General Assembly Resolution 61/26 (December 1, 2006), "Jerusalem": 157 nations voting in favor, 6 against (Israel, Marshall Islands, Micronesia, Nauru, Palau, and United States), 10 abstentions, 19 absent.

UN General Assembly Resolution 61/27 (December 1, 2006), "The Syrian Golan": 107 nations voting in favor, 6 against (Canada, Israel, Marshall Islands, Micronesia, Palau, United States), 60 abstentions, 19 absent.

88. Scott Wilson, "Fatah Troops Enter Gaza with Israeli Assent: Hundreds Were Trained in Egypt Under U.S.-Backed Program to Counter Hamas," Washington Post, May 18, 2007.

89. U.S. Department of State, "Special Briefing by Secretary of State Condoleezza Rice," June 18, 2007.

1. THE POLICY MIRROR

1. Michael Browning and Larry Kaplow, "Wielding the Ax of Bitterness / Israelis Chop Down Palestinians' Precious Olive Trees, Insisting It's Retaliation for Rocks Being Hurled at Settlers," Cox News Service, published in the Atlanta Journal-Constitution, November 29, 2000.

2. Hugh Dellios, "Knotty Olive Tree Symbolizes Israeli-Palestinian Conflict," Chicago Tribune, December 13, 2000.

3. Mark Matthews, "Palestinians Reaping the Bitter Harvest as Israelis Clear West Bank Olive Trees," Baltimore Sun, November 8, 2000; Ben Lynfield, "Another Casualty of War: Trees," Christian Science Monitor, December 8, 2000; Mary Curtius, "Olive Harvest Becomes a Palestinian Casualty," Los Angeles Times, November 25, 2000.

4. Mark Matthews, "A Life's Work Uprooted in Minutes: Israel Bulldozes Old Woman's Olive Trees for Soldiers' Security," Seattle Times, November 13, 2000 (identical with Baltimore Sun article in note 3).

5. Noam Chomsky, Fateful Triangle: The United States, Israel, and the Palestinians, 2nd ed. (Cambridge, Mass.: South End Press, 1999), p. 1.

6. William Pfaff, "Grasping the Nature of Anti-Americanism," *Chicago Tribune*, April 3, 2001.

7. Norman Kempster and Robin Wright, "White House, in an About-Face, Tackles Mideast," *Los Angeles Times*, May 22, 2001.

8. "Source: Mideast Report Offers 'Plenty' to Upset Both Sides," CNN.com, May 4, 2001.

9. Jane Perlez, "U.S. Widens Role in Mideast Crisis, Sending an Envoy," *New York Times*, May 22, 2001.

10. Alan Sipress, "Powell Urges Halt to Mideast Violence: No New Plan to End Conflict Is Offered," *Washington Post*, May 22, 2001.

11. Kempster and Wright, "White House."

12. John Diamond, "Mideast Report Stirs Powell Call for Truce: Violence Continues as U.S. Raises Role in Israel-Arab Fray," *Chicago Tribune*, May 22, 2001.

13. "The American Mideast Initiative," *New York Times*, May 22, 2001.

14. "Summon the Courage to Act," *Los Angeles Times*, May 22, 2001.

15. "Heeding the Mitchell Report," *Washington Post*, May 22, 2001.

16. "Breaking Eggshells," *Chicago Tribune*, May 22, 2001.

17. In a May 11, 2000, editorial titled "Five Hundred and Counting," which noted the five hundredth death in the al-Aqsa intifada, the *Tribune*'s typically balanced approach was evident: "Yet neither Israelis nor Palestinians seem capable of pulling back from their deadly minuet of violence and retaliation." The editorial then batted back and forth the transgressions of both sides, concluding: "Five hundred dead. There's no argument about this: Everyone has blood on his hands."

18. John Bentley of Chicago, letter to the editor, *Chicago Tribune*, May 26, 2001.

19. Garrick Utley, "The Shrinking of Foreign News: From Broadcast to Narrowcast," *Foreign Affairs* 76, no. 2 (March–April 1997): 6–7.

20. Chris Wallace, "Can the U.S. Put the Middle East Peace Process Back Together?" ABC News/*Nightline*, May 21, 2001.

21. Ray Suarez, "New Peace Effort," PBS/*The NewsHour with Jim Lehrer*, May 21, 2001.

22. Edward Said, *Covering Islam: How the Media and the Experts Determine How We See the Rest of the World* (New York: Random House, Vintage Books, 1997), p. 168.

23. Jeremy Sharp, "U.S. Foreign Aid to Israel," Congressional Research Service, April 25, 2007, p. 17.

24. Carol Migdalovitz, "Israel: Background and Relations with the United States," Congressional Research Service, July 6, 2007, p. 22.

25. U.S. Embassy in Israel (U.S. State Department), "U.S. Assistance to Israel: 1949–2004 Total," Economics Section, 2004, pp. 1, 12–14. The $100 billion estimate included annual budgeted economic and military aid as well as special supplemental appropriations. The latter included special allocations tied to regional events, such as the Wye Agreement of 1998 (part of the Oslo peace process) and the U.S. war in Iraq in 1993; absorption and resettlement of immigrants; and research and develop-

ment (primarily for weapons systems). Loan guarantees were not included in the $100 billion estimate.

26. Clyde Mark, "Israel: U.S. Foreign Assistance," Congressional Research Service, April 26, 2005, p. 1.

27. According to Sharp, "U.S. Foreign Aid to Israel," U.S. aid to Israel from 1949 to 1966 totaled $1.2 billion. This is the sum of military and economic grants and loans listed on a year-by-year basis on the table appearing on page 18 of the report.

28. Bernhard May, "The Marshall Plan: Historical Lessons and Current Challenges in the Balkans" (updated version of paper presented at a conference organized by the Institute for EastWest Studies [New York] and the Foreign Economic Relations Board [DEIK; Istanbul], May 1999). The figures also appear in Tom Hundley, "Marshall Plan Still at Work in Germany," *Chicago Tribune*, October 12, 2004.

Using the Consumer Price Index calculator of the U.S. Federal Reserve (http://minneapolisfed.org/Research/data/us/calc/index.cfm), the total of U.S. aid to Israel from 1949 to 2004—adjusted for inflation and converted to 2004 purchasing dollars—equaled approximately $170.692 billion.

29. Israel Central Bureau of Statistics, archived population statistics, http://www.cbs.gov.il; Shelley Paz and Haviv Rettig, "Israel's Population Reaches 7,150,000," *Jerusalem Post*, April 23, 2007, citing Israel's Central Bureau of Statistics.

30. Mark, "Israel: U.S. Foreign Assistance," pp. 11–12.

31. U.S. Embassy in Israel, "U.S. Assistance to Israel: 1949–2004 Total," p. 14.

32. Ibid., p. 4. These grants were part of the $78 billion emergency supplemental allocation to fund the U.S. war in Iraq and related costs. Of the total $78 billion, $4.52 billion was appropriated for international assistance to twenty-two countries identified as "coalition partners and cooperating states in the war on terrorism." Israel received a $1 billion military grant and an additional $9 billion in loan guarantees (the latter not calculated as part of the $4.52 billion in international assistance); Jordan received $1.1 billion; Turkey, $1 billion; Afghanistan, $325 million; Egypt, $300 million; and Pakistan, $200 million. See Amy Belasco and Larry Nowels, "Supplemental Appropriations FY 2003: Iraq Conflict, Afghanistan, Global War on Terrorism, and Homeland Security," Congressional Research Service, April 18, 2003, pp. 31–36.

33. Mark, "Israel: U.S. Foreign Assistance," p. 11.

34. Ibid., pp. 4, 10, 12.

35. Ibid., unnumbered "Summary" page at beginning of document; emphasis added.

36. Ibid., unnumbered "Summary" page.

37. Ibid., p. 2.

38. Clyde Mark, "Palestinians and Middle East Peace: Issues for the United States," Congressional Research Service, December 5, 2001, p. 4.

39. Barry Schweid, "White House Takes U.S. Request for New Aid Under Consideration," Associated Press, July 12, 2005; "U.S. Demands Aid Be Used to Boost Bedouin and Druze," *Haaretz*, July 15, 2005.

40. Steven Erlanger, "Sharon Wins Another Crucial Vote on Gaza Withdrawal Plan," *International Herald Tribune* (rpt. from *New York Times*), November 4, 2004; Ramit Plushnick-Masti, "Israel Plans Remote-Control Border After a Withdrawal from Gaza Strip," Associated Press, June 18, 2004.

41. Carol Migdalovitz, "Israel: Background and Relations with the United States," Congressional Research Service, July 26, 2006, p. 18.

42. See World Bank Web site: http://www.worldbank.org.

43. U.S. Department of State, "Congressional Budget Justification of Foreign Operations, Fiscal Year 2001/Near East," March 15, 2000, pp. 8–9.

44. Mark, "Israel: U.S. Foreign Assistance," p. 3.

45. Steven Erlanger, "Israel to Get $30 Billion in Military Aid from U.S.," *New York Times*, August 17, 2007.

46. Steve Weizman, "Israel Agrees with the U.S.: Iran Threat Justifies Upgrading Saudi Military," Associated Press, July 30, 2007.

47. The $1.82 billion figure applies to aid for Palestinians residing in the West Bank and Gaza Strip, but it does not include U.S. allocations to the United Nations Relief and Works Agency (UNRWA), which aids the Palestinian refugee populations in the West Bank, Gaza, Jordan, Lebanon, and Syria. U.S. contributions to UNRWA from 1950 to 2007 have been estimated at approximately $3.16 billion. See Mark, "Palestinians and Middle East Peace, April 26, 2005, p. 15; and Paul Morro, "The Palestinian Territories: Background and U.S. Relations," Congressional Research Service, July 5, 2007, p. 13. For a discussion of U.S. aid to UNRWA, see chapter 2.

48. Sara Roy, "U.S. Economic Aid to the West Bank and Gaza Strip: The Politics of Peace," *Middle East Policy* 4, no. 4 (October 1996): 58.

49. U.S. Embassy in Israel, "U.S. Assistance to Israel: 1949–2004 Total," p. 19.

50. Ibid. See also Charles Levinson, "$50 Billion Later, Taking Stock of U.S. Aid to Egypt," *Christian Science Monitor*, April 12, 2004.

51. U.S. Embassy in Israel, "U.S. Assistance to Israel: 1949–2004 Total," p. 19; "U.S. Never Threatened to Cut Aid to Jordan—Muasher," *Jordan Times*, August 5, 2004. Marwan Muasher was the Jordanian foreign minister at the time of the report.

52. Mark, "Palestinians and Middle East Peace, April 26, 2005, p. 5.

53. U.S. Department of State, "Palestinian Assistance."

54. Jeremy M. Sharp and Christopher M. Blanchard, "U.S. Foreign Aid to the Palestinians," Congressional Research Service, Library of Congress, June 27, 2006, pp. 1–2.

55. Anne Gearan, "U.S. Ends Economic, Political Embargo on Palestinian Government," Associated Press, June 18, 2007.

56. U.S. State Department, "Congressional Budget Justification of Foreign Operations, Fiscal Year 2006," p. 450, www.state.gov/documents/organization/42258.pdf.

57. Mark, "Israel: U.S. Foreign Assistance," p. 3. See also Rachel Stohl, "Middle East Remains Attractive Market for U.S. Arms," *Weekly Defense Monitor*, Center for Defense Information, Washington, D.C., February 17, 2000. According to the Defense Security Cooperation Agency, Foreign Military Financing (FMF) is defined as

"the U.S. government program for financing through grants or loans the acquisition of U.S. military articles, services, and training [that] supports U.S. regional stability goals and enables friends and allies to improve their defense capabilities" (www.dsca.osd.mil).

58. Migdalovitz, "Israel: Background and Relations with the United States," July 6, 2007, p. 25, and "Israel: Background and Relations," July 26, 2006, p. 19.

59. U.S. State Department, "Congressional Budget Justification of Foreign Operations, Fiscal Year 2001/Near East," March 15, 2000, p. 8.

60. Shimon Peres, "A Better World" (text of speech), *International Law and Politics* 27, no. 2 (winter 1995): 287.

61. U.S. Department of State, "Summary and Highlights/International Affairs (Function 150)/Fiscal Year 2008 Budget Request."

62. Stephen Zunes, "The Strategic Functions of U.S. Aid to Israel," *Middle East Policy* 4, no. 4 (October 1996): 96.

63. Dan Morgan, "House Rejects Cut in Military Aid to Egypt," *Washington Post*, July 16, 2004.

64. Zunes, "Strategic Functions of U.S. Aid," p. 92.

65. "Israel: U.S. Foreign Assistance," Congressional Research Service Issue Brief for Congress, August 28, 2003, p. CRS-13: "Table 3. U.S. Assistance to Israel, FY 1949–FY 1996."

66. Ibid.

67. Saliba Sarsar, "The Question of Palestine and United States Behavior at the United Nations," *International Journal of Politics, Culture and Society* 17, no. 3 (spring 2004): 466; "Changing Patterns in the Use of the Veto in the Security Council," Global Policy Forum, http://www.globalpolicy.org/security/data/vetotab.htm.

68. Quoted in Sarsar, "Question of Palestine," p. 465.

69. Gerald Nadler, "U.S. Vetoes Resolution Calling for Halt to Israeli Military Operations in Gaza," Associated Press, October 5, 2004.

70. Ibrahim Barzak, "Israeli Military Official Says Low-Level Cease-Fire Talks Have Begun," Associated Press, October 5, 2004.

71. National Lawyers Guild, "The Al Aqsa Intifada and Israel's Apartheid: The U.S. Military and Economic Role in the Violation of Palestinian Human Rights; Report of the National Lawyers Guild Delegation to the Occupied Palestinian Territories and Israel, January 2001," New York, pp. 40–44, 65–67.

72. Charles Sennott, "Intifada Toll: Disabilities at Alarming Rate: Blindness, Paralysis the Cost of 'Eye for Eye,'" *Boston Globe*, May 3, 2001.

73. National Lawyers Guild, "Al Aqsa Intifada and Israel's Apartheid," p. 67.

74. U.S. State Department Daily Press Briefing, August 8, 2001, Richard Boucher, spokesman, http://www.state.gov/r/pa/prs/dpb/2001/4481.htm.

75. Col. Daniel Smith, "Sorting Out Interests and Responsibilities—An Opinion," *Weekly Defense Monitor*, Center for Defense Information, Washington D.C., April 19, 2001.

76. Robert Fisk, "U.S. Media Mirror Distorts Middle East," *Independent*, June 10, 1998.

77. Society of Professional Journalists, Preamble, Code of Ethics, www.spj.org/ethics_code.asp.

2. REPORTING THE PALESTINIAN REFUGEE STORY

Epigraph. Michael Finkel, "Playing War," *New York Times Magazine*, December 24, 2000. The village is identified as "Hamama," not "Hamman," in two definitive sources on the Palestinian refugee issue: Benny Morris, *The Birth of the Palestinian Refugee Problem, 1947–49* (Cambridge: Cambridge University Press, 1987); and Walid Khalidi, ed., *All That Remains: The Palestinian Villages Occupied and Depopulated by Israel in 1948* (Washington, D.C.: Institute for Palestine Studies, 1992).

1. Finkel, "Playing War."
2. "Hamama," in Khalidi, ed., *All That Remains*, pp. 98–99.
3. Ibid., p. 97.
4. Morris, *Birth of the Palestinian Refugee Problem*, p. 223.
5. Ibid., pp. 219–20.
6. Ibid., pp. 223–24.
7. Ibid., pp. xiv, xvii.
8. Khalidi, ed., *All That Remains*, pp. xxxi, xxxii.
9. "Hamama," in Khalidi, ed., *All That Remains*, p. 100.
10. Comment by Afaf Abutayeh, mother of Ahmed, a slain fifteen-year-old Palestinian youth. The cover photo appeared in the *New York Times Magazine* on December 24, 2000.
11. Kathleen Christison, *Perceptions of Palestine: Their Influence on U.S. Middle East Policy* (Berkeley: University of California Press, 1999), p. 2.
12. Population figures from the mid-1940s British census of Palestine, cited in a UN subcommittee report dated November 1947, appear in Walid Khalidi, "Revisiting the UNGA Partition Resolution," *Journal of Palestine Studies*, 27, no. 1 (autumn 1997): 11. Citing a March 1948 Jewish National Fund document, Khalidi notes the Jewish land-ownership figure as "less than 7 percent of the total land area of the country" (p. 13). According to "Palestine Facts/Land & Settlements" (Jerusalem: Palestinian Academic Society for the Study of International Affairs [PASSIA], http://www.passia.org/palestine_facts/pdf/pdf2006/6-Land-Settlments.pdf): "Before the war of 1948, Palestinians owned about 87.5% of the total area of Palestine, while Jews owned 6.6% of the total lands. The remaining 5.9% was 'state land' as classified by the British Mandate. (British Government, *A Survey of Palestine*, 1945–1946)" (p. 297). The 6.6 percent figure is also found in *The Palestine Question in Maps, 1978–2002* (Jerusalem: PASSIA, 2002), p. 26.
13. According to Khalidi, the partition resolution awarded 55.5 percent of the total land area of Palestine to the Jews and 45.5 percent to the Palestinians ("Revisiting the UNGA Partition Resolution," p. 11). The approximate 55 percent figure for land allotted for the Jewish state is also found in the following sources: J. C. Hurewitz,

The Struggle for Palestine (New York: Norton, 1950), p. 302; and Don Peretz, *The Arab-Israel Dispute* (New York: Facts on File, 1996), p. 36. Slightly different figures are found in PASSIA's study, which states that the partition "granted the Zionists a state in 56.47% of Palestine, leaving the Palestinians with 42.88% and creating an international zone [in and around Jerusalem] of around 0.65%" (*Palestine Question in Maps*, p. 24). Khalidi confirms that the land designated as the international enclave of Jerusalem was less than 1 percent of the total land area of Palestine, stating that the zone would contain 187,000 *dunams* (p. 13) out of a total Palestinian landmass of 27 million *dunams* (p. 11).

14. Howard M. Sachar, *A History of Israel from the Rise of Zionism to Our Time* (New York: Knopf, 1989), p. 292. See also Benny Morris, *Righteous Victims: A History of the Zionist-Arab Conflict, 1881–1999* (New York: Knopf, 1999), pp. 184–86.

15. Interviewed in the Bourj el-Barajneh camp south of Beirut, Lebanon, a Palestinian refugee recounted his family's exodus from the village of "Quikat" in early July 1948: "We didn't have any weapons, and they [local leaders] told us that the Arab armies want us to leave, that they're coming to defend us, and we could go back to our homes in two weeks" (quoted in Ilene R. Prusher, "Of War and Peace and a Family," *Christian Science Monitor*, August 16, 2000). The bracketed insertion appears in the original article.

However, Morris chronicles the exodus from the village differently: "Dov Yirmiya, a company commander in the 21st Battalion, recalled the attack on Kuweikat thus: 'I don't know whether the artillery softening up of the village caused casualties but the psychological effect was achieved and the village's non-combatant inhabitants fled before we began the assault.'" Furthermore, Morris wrote that officers of the Arab Liberation Army (comprising irregulars from Lebanon and Syria) "apparently told the villagers during the First Truce to prepare defences and not to send away their women, children and old; it was probably felt that leaving them in the village would bolster the militiamen's morale" (*Birth of the Palestinian Refugee Problem*, pp. 198–99).

The *San Diego Union-Tribune* reported that the Jordanian government "hired buses and trucks to evacuate" the unnamed village of a refugee interviewed in the al-Wahdat camp outside Amman, who stated: "They picked us up and told us to come with them and we'd be back to Palestine in just two or three weeks. That was 50 years ago" (quoted in Dean Calbreath, "Longing for Homeland: Many Of Jordan's Palestinian Refugees Vow to Return, But Place Little Faith in Peace Plans," *San Diego Union-Tribune*, November 20, 2001).

16. Benny Morris, *The Birth of the Palestinian Refugee Problem Revisited* (Cambridge: Cambridge University Press, 2004), pp. 593–94. Morris wrote: "The Arab states, apart from appealing to the British to halt the Haganah [Jewish military forces in Palestine] offensives and charging that the Jews were expelling Palestine's Arabs . . . did not appeal to the Palestinian masses to leave, but neither, in April [1948] did they publicly enjoin the Palestinians to stay put. . . . During the summer [of 1948], the Arab governments intermittently tried to bar the entry of new

[Palestinian] refugees into their territory. The Palestinians were encouraged to stay in Palestine or to return to their homes" (pp. 594, 597). These conclusions also appear in Morris's original 1987 work on pp. 289–92.

17. Benny Morris, "Revisiting the Palestinian Exodus of 1948," in Eugene L. Rogan and Avi Shlaim, eds., *The War for Palestine: Rewriting the History of 1948* (Cambridge: Cambridge University Press, 2001), pp. 37–59.

18. Ibid., p. 38.

19. Ibid., p. 40. In a 2004 newspaper interview prior to the publication of his expanded work, *The Birth of the Palestinian Problem Revisited*, Morris observed: "Ben Gurion was right. If he had not done what he did, a state would not have come into being. That has to be clear. It is impossible to evade it. Without the uprooting of the Palestinians, a Jewish state would not have arisen here." Later in the same interview Morris expressed the opinion that Ben Gurion had not gone far enough in expelling the Palestinian population: "If he was already engaged in expulsion, maybe he should have done a complete job. . . . This place would be quieter and know less suffering if the matter had been resolved once and for all" (quoted in Ari Shavit, "Survival of the Fittest," *Haaretz*, January 9, 2004).

20. Morris, "Revisiting the Palestinian Exodus of 1948," p. 43.

21. Rashid Khalidi, "The Palestinians in 1948: The Underlying Causes of Failure," in Rogan and Shlaim, eds., *War for Palestine*, pp. 12–36.

22. Avi Shlaim, "Israel and the Arab coalition in 1948," in Rogan and Shlaim, eds., *War for Palestine*, pp. 79–103. About the specifics of troop strength and weaponry, Shlaim wrote: "In mid-May 1948 the total number of Arab troops, both regular and irregular, operating in the Palestine theater was under 25,000, whereas the Israel Defense Forces (IDF) fielded over 35,000 troops. By mid-July the IDF mobilized 65,000 men under arms, and by December its numbers had reached a peak of 96,441. The Arab states also reinforced their armies, but they could not match this rate of increase. Thus, at each stage of the war, the IDF outnumbered all the Arab forces arrayed against it, and after the first round of fighting, it outgunned them too. The final outcome of the war was therefore not a miracle but a faithful reflection of the underlying military balance in the Palestine theater. In this war, as in most wars, the stronger side prevailed" (p. 81).

23. Morris, *Birth of the Palestinian Refugee Problem*, p. 128.

24. Estimates of the number of Palestinians who became refugees in 1948–1949 vary widely, from a low estimate of 520,000 according to Israeli sources to as high as 1 million according to Arab sources. The most widely cited estimates range from 700,000 to 750,000. Morris states that "it is impossible to arrive at a definite, persuasive estimate." He cites a British analysis of September 1949 estimating 711,000 refugees and makes his own estimate of "between 600,000 and 760,000" (*Birth of the Palestinian Refugee Problem*, p. 298). According to the *Palestinian Refugee Research Net*, "In 1949, the United Nations Conciliation Commission put the number at 726,000; the newly established United Nations Relief and Works Agency subsequently put the number at 957,000 in 1950," http://www.arts.mcgill.ca/MEPP/PRRN/proverview.html.

25. Quoted in Shavit, "Survival of the Fittest." In the interview, Morris said he had found evidence of twenty-four massacres, and that the total civilian Palestinian death toll as a result of massacres and executions numbered approximately eight hundred. Morris said he had uncovered evidence of "about a dozen" rapes, a number he further characterized as "not the whole story . . . the tip of the iceberg." He also cited a Jewish war toll approximating six thousand, but this would have included fighting forces as well as civilians, which he did not delineate.

26. "Progress Report of the United Nations Mediator on Palestine," UN Doc. A/648, September 16, 1948, p. 14.

27. Morris, *Birth of the Palestinian Refugee Problem*, p. 259.

28. Ibid., p. 295.

29. Ibid., p. 280.

30. Ibid., p. 282. The first two bracketed items are mine; the remaining three are Morris's.

31. See United Nations Web site: http://un.org/unrwa/refugees/index.html. The "Overview" page of the UNRWA section of the UN Web site says UNRWA was "originally envisaged as a temporary agency." Furthermore, it states that "in the absence of a solution to the Palestine refugee problem, the General Assembly has repeatedly renewed UNRWA's mandate, most recently extending it until 30 June 2008."

32. "U.N. Agency Marks 50 Years of Service to Palestinian Refugees," CNN/ *CNN World Report*, May 7, 2000.

33. Universal Declaration of Human Rights, UN General Assembly resolution 217 A (III), 10 December 1948; United Nations Web site: http://www.un.org/Overview/rights.html.

34. Convention Relating to the Status of Refugees, 28 July 1951; Human Rights Watch Web site: http://www.hrw.org/campaigns/israel/return/crsr-rtr.htm.

35. The International Covenant on Civil and Political Rights, 16 December 1966; Human Rights Watch Web site: http://www.hrw.org/campaigns/israel/return/iccpr-rtr.htm.

36. The Human Rights Committee General Comment on Article 12 of the International Covenant on Civil and Political Rights (November 1999), emphasis added; Human Rights Watch Web site: http://www.hrw.org/campaigns/israel/return/hrc-gen-cmt-rtr.htm.

37. UN General Assembly A/RES/194 (III), 11 December 1948.

38. UN General Assembly A/RES/2535 (XXIV) A–C, 10 December 1969.

39. UN General Assembly A/RES/3236 (XXIX), 22 November 1947.

40. Text of the "Law of Return, 5710–1950," Israel Foreign Ministry online archive, www.mfa.gov.il (in English).

41. Ibid.

42. According to Clyde Mark, U.S. aid to Israel for immigration assistance from 1949 through fiscal year 2006 totaled an estimated $1.48 billion ("Israel: U.S. Foreign Assistance," Congressional Research Service, Library of Congress, April 26,

2005, pp. 11–12). According to Carol Migdalovitz, $40 million for "migration and refugee assistance" was granted for fiscal 2007 ("Israel: Background and Relations with the United States," Congressional Research Service, Library of Congress, November 14, 2006, p. 18).

43. Israel Ministry of Immigrant Absorption, www.moia.gov.il.

44. Mark, "Israel: U.S. Foreign Assistance," pp. 12, 14.

45. Ibid., pp. 3–4. Congress authorized an original loan guarantee amount of $10 billion in October 1992. Reductions in the loan guarantees to censure Israeli settlement activity in the West Bank and Gaza between 1993 and 1997 totaled $1.35 billion, a figure offset by $585 million reinstated for security interests. Thus, the final aggregate figure available for the loan guarantees amounted to $9.2 billion (p. 4). The Congressional Research Service report noted that "no U.S. government funds go directly to . . . Israel, but a subsidy is appropriated to be set aside in a Treasury account, held against a possible default. . . . It was reported that the subsidy for he Israeli loan-guarantee program was about 4 percent of the [original] $10 billion" (p. 3).

46. Zev Stub, "Jews Make Up 81% of Israeli Population," *Jerusalem Post*, September 15, 2004.

47. Mark, "Israel: U.S. Foreign Assistance," pp. 11–12. More than one-third of all immigration grants—totaling nearly $1.4 billion from 1949 to 2004—were made from 1997 to 2004 (in the amount of $520 million), with Israel receiving $60 million in immigrant aid grants in FY2002 and FY2003 and $50 million in 2004. A further $50 million was requested for FY2005.

48. The $3.16 billion estimate of U.S. contributions to UNRWA from 1950 to 2007 is derived from State Department data presented in two Congressional Research Service Reports. The United States contributed an estimated $2.785 billion to UNRWA from 1950 to 2004 (Clyde Mark, "Palestinians and Middle East Peace: Issues for the United States," Congressional Research Service, April 26, 2005, p. 15), as well as an additional $375 million from 2005 to 2007: $108 million in FY05, $137 million in FY06, and $130 million in FY07 (Paul Morro, "The Palestinian Territories: Background and U.S. Relations," Congressional Research Service, July 5, 2007, p. 13).

The following information on U.S. contributions to UNRWA was provided by the agency's New York City office in October 2004: "According to figures provided by UNRWA's External Relations Department [in Gaza], the sum total of U.S. contributions to UNRWA since 1950 is $2.9 billion, of which $2.5 billion has taken the form of cash contributions to UNRWA's 'regular' or 'core' budget (basic education, health and community development/poverty alleviation programs). The remainder, approximately $400 million, has taken the form of contributions to current emergency appeals and other special appeals including ones for the Occupied Palestinian Territories (during the first intifada [1987–93]) as well as Lebanon, and also includes in-kind contributions (e.g. food)."

49. Statistics compiled from UNRWA Web site: www.unrwa.org.

50. Mark, "Palestinians and Middle East Peace," p. 15.

51. Moti Bassok, "On Eve of 5765, Population Stands at 6.8m," *Haaretz*, September 15, 2004.

52. Zeev Klein, "Israel's Population Up 1.6% in 5764 to 6.8 million," *Globes* online, September 14, 2004.

53. Bassok, "On Eve of 5765."

54. Jay Bushinsky, "Israel Asks U.S. to Clarify Position on Palestinians," *Chicago Sun-Times*, May 14, 1992.

55. Ibid.

56. The annual reaffirmation of UN General Assembly Resolution 194 was included in omnibus General Assembly resolutions concerning the Israeli-Palestinian conflict, which until 1995 was titled "Question of Palestine" and since 1996 has been titled "Peaceful settlement of the question of Palestine." Under either title, the specific language regarding reaffirmation of Resolution 194 stressed the need for "resolving the problem of the Palestine refugees in conformity with General Assembly Resolution 194 (III) of 11 December 1948."

The voting record on the omnibus resolutions from 1992 to 2004 is as follows: *1992* (UN General Assembly Resolution 47/64): against: United States, Israel, Marshall Islands, Micronesia (93 in favor, 60 abstained or absent); *1993* (UNGA Res. 48/158): against: United States, Dominican Republic, Israel, Marshall Islands, Micronesia (92 in favor, 51 abstained, 36 non-voting); *1994* (UNGA Res. 49/62): against: United States, Israel (136 in favor, 7 abstained, 39 non-voting); *1995* (UNGA Res. 50/84): against: United States, Israel, Micronesia (143 in favor, 3 abstained, 36 non-voting); *1996* (UNGA Res. 51/26): against: United States, Israel (152 in favor, 4 abstained, 27 non-voting); *1997* (UNGA Res. 52/52): against: United States, Israel (155 in favor, 3 abstained, 25 non-voting); *1998* (UNGA Res. 53/42): against: United States, Israel (154 in favor, 3 abstained, 26 non-voting); *1999* (UNGA Res. 54/42): against: United States, Israel, Marshall Islands (149 in favor, 2 abstained, 34 non-voting); *2000* (UNGA Res. 55/55): against: United States, Israel (149 in favor, 3 abstained, 35 non-voting); *2001* (UNGA Res. 56/36): against: United States, Israel, Marshall Islands, Micronesia, Nauru, Tuvalu (131 in favor, 20 abstained, 32 non-voting); *2002* (UNGA Res. 57/110): against: United States, Israel, Marshall Islands, Micronesia (160 in favor, 3 abstained, 24 non-voting); *2003* (UNGA Res. 58/21): against: United States, Israel, Marshall Islands, Micronesia, Palau, Uganda (160 in favor, 5 abstained, 20 non-voting); *2004* (UNGA Res. 59/31): against: United States, Israel, Australia, Grenada, Marshall Islands, Micronesia, Palau (161 in favor, 10 abstained, 13 non-voting); *2005* (UNGA Res. 60/39): against: United States, Israel, Australia, Marshall Islands, Micronesia, Palau (156 in favor, 9 abstained, 20 non-voting); *2006* (UNGA Res. 61/25): against: United States, Israel, Australia, Marshall Islands, Micronesia, Nauru, Palau (157 in favor, 10 abstained, 18 non-voting).

In addition to calling for reaffirmation of Resolution 194, all of these omnibus resolutions from 1992 to 2006 called for "the withdrawal of Israel from the Palestinian territory occupied since 1967" and from 1994 to 2006 referred to the "illegality of the

Israeli settlements in the territory occupied since 1967 and of Israeli actions aimed at changing the status of Jerusalem." (The 1992 resolution called for "dismantling the Israeli settlements in the territories occupied since 1967"; the 1993 resolution called for "resolving the problem of the Israeli settlements, which are illegal and an obstacle to peace.")

57. Madeleine K. Albright, representative of the United States of America to the United Nations, to the incoming president of the UN General Assembly (addressed in the letter as "Excellency"), August 8, 1994. Copy of letter acquired from United States Mission to the United Nations, Office of Press and Public Affairs, New York.

58. Aviva Carol, "Israel Is Just a Springboard to the Region" (in Hebrew), *Globes*, July 11, 1994.

59. Uri Ram, "The Promised Land of Business Opportunities: Liberal Post-Zionism in the Glocal Age," in Gershon Safir and Yoav Peled, eds., *The New Israel: Peacemaking and Liberalization* (Boulder, Colo.: Westview Press, 2000), p. 228.

60. William Orme Jr., "Israeli Business Flies Like a Dove," *New York Times*, October 18, 1998.

61. Sandro Contenta, "Barak Asks Prime Minister to Let in Thousands of Refugees," *Toronto Star*, April 13, 2000.

62. Nomi Morris, "Refugees' Placement Key Issue at Summit: Barak, Arafat Far Apart on Their 'Right of Return,'" *San Diego Union-Tribune*, July 14, 2000. Following Israeli-Palestinian negotiations in Taba, Egypt, in January 2001, the Associated Press reported: "A Palestinian official said on condition of anonymity that Israel had proposed accepting 150,000 Palestinian refugees over 20 years. The report could not be confirmed independently." See "Israel, Palestinians Focus on Refugee Issue," *St. Louis Post-Dispatch*, January 23, 2001.

63. Jay Hancock, "Summit Ends Without Accord," *Baltimore Sun*, July 26, 2000.

64. Mark Matthews, "Palestinians Seeking $40 Billion in Aid: Money Would Build State, Assist Refugees," *Baltimore Sun*, July 7, 2000.

65. Morris, "Refugees' Placement Key Issue at Summit."

66. John Kifner, "Talks Stir Memories but Not Much Hope for Refugees in Lebanon," *New York Times*, July 12, 2000. No further mention is made in the story of the massacre at Deir Yassin on April 9, 1948, in which renegade Zionist forces of the Irgun and Stern Gang attacked the village and massacred scores of inhabitants. Morris describes the village as having been "generally non-belligerent. . . . The attack loosely meshed with the objective of Operation Nahshon, which was to secure the western approaches to Jerusalem. After a prolonged firefight, in which Arab family after family were slaughtered, the dissidents rounded up many of the remaining villagers, who included militiamen and unarmed civilians of both sexes, and children, and murdered dozens of them. Altogether some 250 Arabs, mostly non-combatants, were murdered; there were also cases of mutilation and rape. The surviving inhabitants were expelled to Arab-held East Jerusalem" (*Birth of the Palestinian Refugee Problem*, p. 113). In recent years Arab scholars have revised the death toll downward to approximately 125. News

of the massacre, which the *New York Times* reported on April 10, 1948, is widely cited as having compelled many Palestinians to flee the country for fear of future massacres.

67. Kate Seelye, "Palestinians Living in Lebanese Refugee Camps Anxious for Camp David Summit to End to Discover Their Fate," NPR/*All Things Considered*, July 14, 2000. A similar theme was apparent in an *All Things Considered* piece broadcast on National Public Radio on September 11, 2000. Reported by Jennifer Ludden, the piece cast Palestinian refugees in Jordan as being more advantaged than their compatriots in Lebanon, but with a far from ideal status nonetheless. It cited a recent, anonymous leaflet that appeared on the streets of Amman "promoting Jordan for the Jordanians." Observed Ludden: "Any suggestion that Jordan must deal permanently with its Palestinians is perceived as blasphemous Zionist thinking, abandonment of the cherished goal of the refugees' return."

68. Hilary Andersson, "West Bank Palestinian Refugees Hoping Any Peace Deal to Be Signed at Camp David Would Give Them Their Lands Back," ABC News/ *World News This Morning*, July 14, 2000.

69. Tracy Wilkinson, "Palestinians Divided on Dreams for a Homeland," *Los Angeles Times*, July 18, 2000.

70. Mohalhel Fakih ("Future TV" correspondent), "Fate of Palestinian Refugees Remains Sticking Point in Israeli-Palestinian Negotiations," CNN/*World Report*, July 30, 2000.

71. Hugh Dellios, "Palestinian Exiles' Hopeless Life in Lebanon Fuels a Growing Rage," *Chicago Tribune*, April 26, 2000.

72. Christiane Amanpour, "Crisis in the Middle East: Cultivating Palestinian Rage at Qalandia Refugee Camp," CNN/*CNN Today*, October 11, 2000.

73. Rula Amin, "Palestinian Refugee Camp Outraged in Response to Mideast Summit," CNN/*CNN Saturday*, October 14, 2000.

74. Ben Wedeman, "Anger Mounts Among Palestinian Refugees in Jordan," CNN/*CNN WorldView*, October 30, 2000.

75. Susan Taylor Martin, "A Primer on the Question of Palestinian Refugees," *St. Petersburg Times*, November 5, 2000.

76. Mark Matthews, "Arafat Left to Consider Options: 'Right of Return' Issue Unresolved in Mideast Peace Plan; U.S. Allows More Time," *Baltimore Sun*, December 27, 2000.

77. Joel Greenberg, "Palestinians Outline Objections to Clinton Peace Plan," *New York Times*, January 3, 2001. In a "Web Exclusive" dated December 29, 2000, and headlined "Irreconcilable Differences?" *Newsweek* published—online but apparently not in its print issue for that week—the entire text of the Palestinian memorandum.

78. Akiva Eldar, "How to Solve the Palestinian Refugee Problem," *Haaretz*, May 29, 2001. Eldar's report was quoted extensively by American syndicated columnist William Pfaff, "Israeli and Palestinian Negotiators Can Agree When They Try, " *International Herald Tribune*, July 12, 2001.

79. Rula Amin, "Right of Return for Palestinian Refugees Emerges as Stumbling Block in Peace Negotiations," CNN/*CNN Saturday*, December 30, 2000.

80. Larry Kaplow, "Mideast Deal Could Mean Hard Choices for Refugees," *Atlanta Journal-Constitution*, January 3, 2001.

81. John Kifner, "Out of Place: The Price of Peace Will Be Paid in Dreams," *New York Times*, December 31, 2000.

82. David Hawkins, "Palestinian Refugees Still Hoping to Return to Israel," *CBS Evening News*, January 13, 2001.

83. Howard Schneider, "For Palestinian Refugees, Rhetoric Confronts Reality," *Washington Post*, January 12, 2001.

84. Jennifer Ludden, "Fate of Palestinian Refugees Remains Key Stumbling Block in Efforts to Forge a Final Peace Deal," NPR/*All Things Considered*, January 3, 2001.

85. Cameron Barr, "A Long Wait to the Point of No Return," *Christian Science Monitor*, January 5, 2001.

86. Dan Ephron, "Arafat's Choice," *Newsweek*, January 8, 2001.

87. Martin Fletcher, "Palestinian Refugees Carry High Hopes of Return to Home as Fighting Continues in Mideast," *NBC Nightly News*, January 14, 2001.

88. Matthew McAllester, "In Search of a Home: Many Palestinian Refugees Are Leaving the Middle East," *Newsday*, January 21, 2001.

89. Christiane Amanpour, "Palestinian Right to Return Crucial Issue in Israeli Election," CNN/*CNN Today*, February 1, 2001.

90. Keith Richburg, "For Refugees, Home Is Where the Dream Is: Displaced Palestinians' Hopes of Returning to Land in Israel May Be Dashed by Peace Terms," *Washington Post*, January 3, 2001.

91. Hugh Dellios, "Arab Refugees Fear Losing Their Dream," *Chicago Tribune*, January 4, 2001.

92. Lee Hockstader, "Palestinians Hail a Heroine: Israelis See Rising Threat; Suicide Bomber Elicits Pride and Fear," *Washington Post*, January 31, 2002.

93. James Bennet, "In Camps, Arabs Cling to Dream of Long Ago," *New York Times*, March 10, 2002.

94. Michael Slackman, "Displaced Palestinians Put Faith in Jihad," *Los Angeles Times*, March 29, 2002.

95. Neil MacFarquhar, "Grimly, Palestinians Stay Tuned to News," *New York Times*, March 31, 2002. The reference to the UN Security Council was in error. It was the UN General Assembly that passed Resolution 194 pertaining to the Palestinian refugees' right of return.

96. Neil MacFarquhar, "For Palestinian Refugees, Dream of Return Endures," *New York Times*, April 16, 2002.

97. Brent Sadler, "Palestinian Refugees Dealing with Harsh Realities of Israeli Occupation," CNN/*American Morning with Paula Zahn*, March 27, 2002.

98. Larry Kaplow, "Bitterness Deepens in Jenin Camp: Refugees Say Fight Will Go On," *Atlanta Journal-Constitution*, April 25, 2002.

99. Charles Radin, "Hard-line Refugees Won't Budge on Israel," *Boston Globe*, August 25, 2002.

100. Bennet, "In Camps, Arabs Cling to Dream of Long Ago."

101. See "State Department Archived Biographies—Phyllis E. Oakley."

102. Phyllis E. Oakley, "Act Now on Mideast Refugees," *Washington Post*, July 6, 2000.

103. Wilkinson, "Palestinians Divided on Dreams for a Homeland."

104. Johanna McGeary, "The Four Sticking Points: Peace Will Never Be Achieved Unless Israel and the Palestinians Compromise on Some Extremely Tough Issues," *Time*, April 22, 2002.

105. Michael Tarazi, PLO legal adviser, interview with author, Chicago, June 12, 2002.

106. Charles Sennott, "The Loss of Homes Marked at Rallies," *Boston Globe*, May 16, 2001.

107. Farnsworth did not correct Barchil's characterization that 1 million Palestinian Arabs "chose to stay" in the country in 1948. In fact, approximately 156,000 Palestinians remained in Israel at the time, and this population multiplied sevenfold over fifty years by virtue of natural increase to exceed 1 million.

108. Elizabeth Farnsworth, "Unsettled Lives," PBS/*The NewsHour with Jim Lehrer*, August 29, 2000.

109. Prusher, "Of War and Peace and a Family."

110. Slackman, "Displaced Palestinians Put Faith in Jihad"; Jonathan Curiel and Michael Young, "Among Refugees, Seething Anger," *San Francisco Chronicle*, December 9, 2001; Anthony Shadid, "Anger Inside Camps, and Out: Plight of Refugees a Point of Passion for Arabs, Muslims," *Boston Globe*, October 25, 2001; Judy Woodruff and Wedeman, "Anger Mounts Among Palestinian Refugees in Jordan"; Gene Randall and Amin, "Palestinian Refugee Camp Outraged in Response to Mideast Summit"; Amanpour, "Crisis in the Middle East"; Dellios, "Palestinian Exiles' Hopeless Life in Lebanon Fuels a Growing Rage," and "Arab Refugees Fear Losing Their Dream"; MacFarquhar, "For Palestinian Refugees, Dream of Return Endures"; Bennet, "In Camps, Arabs Cling to Dreams of Long Ago"; Richburg, "For Refugees, Home Is Where the Dream Is"; Kifner, "Out of Place"; Wilkinson, "Palestinians Divided on Dreams for a Homeland"; Radin, "Hard-line Refugees Won't Budge on Israel"; Ludden, "Fate of Palestinian Refugees Remains Key Stumbling Block in Efforts to Forge a Final Peace Deal"; Amin, "Right of Return for Palestinian Refugees Emerges as Stumbling Block in Peace Negotiations"; Ralph Wenge and Mohallel Fakih, "Fate of Palestinian Refugees Remains Sticking Point in Israeli-Palestinian Negotiations," CNN/*CNN World Report*, July 30, 2000.

111. MacFarquhar, "For Palestinian Refugees, Dream of Return Endures."

112. Christison, *Perceptions of Palestine*, p. 310.

113. Mark Lavie, "Israeli Prime Minister Sets Condition for Peace Negotiations," Associated Press, May 6, 2003.

114. Barry Schweid, "U.S. Stands Firm on Concessions to Sharon," Associated Press, April 27, 2004.

115. Text of a statement by UN Secretary-General Kofi Annan at a news conference following a meeting of the quartet in New York City, *Federal News Service*, May 4, 2004.

116. Barry Schweid, "Bush Steps Back from Concessions to Israel, Says It Should Withdraw from Land Gained in 1967 War," Associated Press, May 6, 2004.

117. Mohammed Daraghmeh, "Palestinian Survey Shows Few Refugees Would Return to What Is Now Israel," Associated Press, July 13, 2003.

118. James Bennet, "Palestinian Mob Attacks Pollster," *New York Times*, July 14, 2003.

119. Daniel Klaidman and Michael Hirsh, "The Price of Peace," *Newsweek*, July 31, 2001.

120. Finkel, "Playing War."

121. Fox News/*Fox Special Report with Brit Hume*, April 24, 29, and 30, 2002.

3. REPORTING ON ISRAELI SETTLEMENTS

Epigraph. R. Emmet Harrigan, Crystal Lake, Ill., letter to the editor, *Chicago Tribune*, May 23, 2001.

1. "Geneva Convention Relative to the Protection of Civilian Persons in Time of War," adopted on August 12, 1949, by the Diplomatic Conference for the Establishment of International Conventions for the Protection of Victims of War, held in Geneva from April 12 to August 12, 1949; entry into force October 21, 1950.

2. "The Number of New Settlements Each Year (chart)," in "The Price of the Settlements" (special report), *Haaretz*, September 26, 2003.

3. UN General Assembly Resolution 61/25, "Peaceful Settlement of the Question of Palestine," adopted December 1, 2006.

4. The estimate that by the end of 2006, 452,900 Israeli settlers were living in the West Bank and areas of Jerusalem annexed by Israel in 1967 is based on the following breakdown:

West Bank. According to a *Haaretz* report, Israel's Population Administration reported the population of West Bank Jewish settlements at 268,400 at the end of 2006 (Shahar Ilan, "Population Administration: West Bank Settlements Grew by 6 Percent Last Year," *Haaretz*, January 10, 2007). A slightly lower figure of 267,163 West Bank settlers was reported by the *Jerusalem Post*, quoting Interior Ministry statistics (Tovah Lazaroff, "Report: 12,400 New Settlers in 2006," *Jerusalem Post*, online edition, January 10, 2007).

Jerusalem. According to a report published online by the Jerusalem Institute for Israel Studies, "At the end of 2003, 403,300 Jerusalem residents (Jewish and Arab) lived in areas annexed to the city following its unification in 1967. . . . About 44% of the residents of these areas are Jewish [177,452], comprising 39% of the overall Jewish population of the city" (Maya Choshen, Michal Korach, and Avraham Diskin, "Jerusalem: Facts and Trends/Population," May 10, 2006, www.jiis.org.il). Based on the 1.3 percent annual growth rate for Jerusalem's Jewish population (also cited in the report), by the end of 2006 the number would have reached approximately 184,500.

Furthermore, by 2004 about 20,000 Israeli settlers populated the Golan Heights, which Israel occupied in 1967 and annexed on December 14, 1981. Three days later, on December 17, the UN Security Council adopted Resolution 497, which declared "the Israeli decision to impose its laws, jurisdiction and administration in the occupied Syrian Golan Heights" to be "null and void and without international legal effect."

5. Moshe Gorali, "Legality Is in the Eye of the Beholder," in "The Price of the Settlements," *Haaretz*, September 26, 2003.

6. "Israeli Spokesmen May Be Allowed to Say 'Occupation,' *Haaretz*, May 27, 2003.

7. Gidon Alon, "PM Redefines His Use of 'Occupation' After A-G Rebukes Him," *Haaretz*, May 27, 2003.

8. The exception was Israel's withdrawal from the major Palestinian towns in the West Bank and Gaza Strip in late 1993 until reoccupation in the spring of 2001. In the interim period, however, the Israeli military maintained control of the majority of lands outside Palestinian population centers.

9. Clyde Mark, "Israel: U.S. Foreign Assistance," Congressional Research Service, Library of Congress, April 26, 2005, p. 6.

10. "Jewish Settlements in Territories Up by 50 Percent Since 1993: Peace Now," Agence France-Presse, December 4, 2000.

11. According to the U.S. State Department's *Congressional Budget Justification for Foreign Operations, Fiscal Year 2001*, as of March 15, 2000, Israel was slated to receive $1.98 billion in regular military aid (Foreign Military Financing [FMF]) and $840 million in nonmilitary aid (Economic Support Funds [ESF]), excluding supplemental grants and loans.

12. "The Price of the Settlements," *Haaretz*, September 26, 2003: Moti Bassok and *Haaretz* staff, "The Extra Civilian Price Tag: At Least NIS [New Israel Shekel] 2.5 Billion a Year"; Amnon Barzilai, "Military Spending/An Extra Command and Several Brigades"; Ziv Maor and Moti Bassok , "Housing/NIS 11 Billion on Homes"; Anat Georgi and Moti Bassok, "Roads/Paved with Gold."

13. "Price of the Settlements."

14. Mark, "Israel: U.S. Foreign Assistance," pp. 6–7.

15. Corky Siemaszko, "Israeli Settlement Spike: Population and Costs Are Soaring," *Daily News*, September 24, 2003 (based on *Haaretz* preview of its "Price of the Settlements" report: Moti Bassok, "Settlements Cost NIS 2.5B a Year in Non-Military Outlays," September 23, 2003); "The Cost of Israeli Settlements" (editorial), *New York Times*, October 3, 2003; Sonni Efron and Henry Chu, "U.S. Criticizes Israeli Plan for Settlement Expansion," *Los Angeles Times*, October 3, 2003; "More Housing, More Trouble" (editorial), *Chicago Tribune*, October 4, 2003.

16. Mark Lavie, "Israel Tab for West Bank Settlements $14B," Associated Press, February 3, 2006.

17. Clyde Mark, "Palestinians and Middle East Peace: Issues for the United States," Congressional Research Service, Library of Congress, July 8, 2004, p. 10.

18. Kathleen Christison, *Perceptions of Palestine: Their Influence on U.S. Middle East Policy* (Berkeley: University of California Press, 1999), p. 169.

19. Ibid., p. 184.

20. Ibid., p. 193.

21. Ibid., pp. 193–94.

22. Ibid., pp. 201–2.

23. Ibid., p. 210.

24. Ibid., p. 211.

25. Ibid., pp. 240–41.

26. Ibid., pp. 261–62.

27. Ibid.

28. Ibid., pp. 261–62.

29. Ibid., pp. 271–72.

30. Ibid., p. 277.

31. Ibid., p. 278.

32. Ibid.

33. Ibid., p. 279.

34. Amir Oren, "American Spy Chiefs Want More Pressure on Settlements," *Haaretz*, November 3, 2003.

35. U.S. Embassy, Israel, "U.S. Assistance to Israel: 1949–2004 Total," July 2004, p. 6.

36. Lara Sukhtian, "Palestinians Say U.S. Deduction from Israel Loan Guarantees Insufficient to Stop Settlement, Wall Construction," Associated Press, November 26, 2003.

37. U.S. Embassy, Israel, "U.S. Assistance to Israel," p. 2.

38. Mark, "Israel: U.S. Foreign Assistance," p. 4.

39. Larry Derfner, "Unsettled Times," *U.S. News & World Report*, January 19, 2004.

40. Steven Erlanger, "Sharon Issues Bids for New Housing Units for Settlers," *New York Times*, August 18, 2004.

41. John Ward Anderson, "Israel to Build More Housing at Settlements," *Washington Post*, August 18, 2004.

42. Transcript of State Department regular briefing (excerpt), Federal News Service, Washington, D.C., August 17, 2004.

43. Danna Harman, "In Crisis, Israel Rallies Behind Settlers," *Christian Science Monitor*, April 26, 2002.

44. William Schneider, "Jewish Settlements One of Many Issues on West Bank," CNN/*CNN Live Today*, April 12, 2002.

45. Carol Lin, "Settlements Are Key Issue in Israeli-Palestinian Conflict," CNN/*American Morning with Paula Zahn*, May 16, 2002.

46. Mark Matthews, "Jewish Settlers Anticipate Being Casualties of Peace," *Bal-

timore Sun, July 19, 2000; Dan Ephron, "Jewish Settlers Lead Lives on the Front Line," *Boston Globe,* November 8, 2000; Uli Schmetzer, "Defiant Settlers at the Center of Mideast Turmoil," *Chicago Tribune,* November 2, 2000; Deborah Sontag, "For Israeli Settlers, Life Under Fire," *New York Times,* December 1, 2000; Susan Taylor Martin, "Settlers Ask: Why Would We Leave Our Homeland?" *St. Petersburg Times,* October 15, 2000; Keith Richburg, "Jewish Settlers Pose Hurdle to Peace with Palestinians," *Washington Post,* October 28, 2000.

47. Richard Boudreaux, "The Mideast Summit: Jewish Settlers Express Relief over Deadlock," *Los Angeles Times,* July 26, 2000; Tyler Marshall, "Clashes Drag Down Upscale Settlers," *Los Angeles Times,* November 12, 2000.

48. Hugh Dellios, "As Troops Die, Israelis Question Settlements," *Chicago Tribune,* December 1, 2000.

49. Deborah Sontag, "Three-Way Tensions over Issue of Settlements Rise in Israel," *New York Times,* May 1, 2000, and "Should Israel Sacrifice Its Hopes for Peace for Settlers?" *New York Times,* November 15, 2000.

50. See note 4.

51. Matt Rees, "Into the War Zone: Palestinians Are Now Directly Attacking Israeli Settlements," *Time,* December 4, 2000.

52. Mike Shuster, "Israel's Settlements in the West Bank and Gaza, One of the Major Reasons for Failure of the Camp David Peace Summit," NPR/*All Things Considered,* December 7, 2000.

53. Linda Gradstein, "Settlements at the Heart of the Palestinian-Israeli Violence," NPR/*Weekend Sunday Edition,* November 19, 2000.

54. Flore de Preneuf, "Settlers Are Reluctant Warriors for Sharon," *St. Petersburg Times,* February 2, 2001.

55. Keith Richburg, "Settlers See Sharon as Their Protector: Jewish Communities in West Bank and Gaza Are There to Stay, Many Believe," *Washington Post,* February 8, 2001.

56. "Jewish Settlers See Sharon's Victory as Peace of Mind," Associated Press, in *St. Louis Post-Dispatch,* February 11, 2001.

57. Jennifer Ludden, "Israel Continues to Construct Settlements Despite International Criticism," NPR/*All Things Considered,* April 10, 2001.

58. Cameron Barr, "A West Bank Rabbi Argues for Expanding Settlements," *Christian Science Monitor,* May 18, 2001.

59. Lee Hockstader, "Group Says Israel Added Settlements: Government Denies Report of Outposts," *Washington Post,* May 21, 2001. This story included three paragraphs on the previous day's shelling by Israeli tanks of the home of Jabril Rajoub, the Palestinian West Bank security chief, as well as three paragraphs on criticism of Israel's use of F-16 jet fighters the previous week to bomb Palestinian targets in response to a Palestinian suicide bombing of an Israeli shopping mall. However, the story's headline, lead paragraph, and two-thirds of its body copy focused on the Peace Now settlement update.

60. Sheila MacVicar, "Israeli Settlement Building Continues Despite Falling Demand," CNN/*CNN Tonight,* May 22, 2001.

61. Larry Kaplow, "Jewish Settlements Stand in Way Of Peace, Many Say," *Atlanta Journal-Constitution*, May 23, 2001.

62. Hugh Dellios, "Jewish Settlers Eye 'Natural' Growth," *Chicago Tribune*, May 24, 2001.

63. Joshua Hammer, "Inside the Wild East," *Newsweek*, July 6, 2001.

64. Mike Hanna, "Settlers Love Their Land and Call It Home," CNN/*CNN Live at Daybreak*, August 9, 2001.

65. James Bennet, "Settlers Find Solace in an Isolated Gaza Community," *New York Times*, November 25, 2001.

66. Jennifer Griffin, Fox News/*Fox Special Report with Brit Hume*, January 23, 2002.

67. Holger Jensen, "Settlements Take Toll on Rights," *Rocky Mountain News*, February 18, 2002.

68. "34 New West Bank Settlements Spotted," *New York Times*, March 19, 2002.

69. Deirdre Shesgreen, "In Shadow of War, Settlers Mark Israeli Independence," *St. Louis Post-Dispatch*, April 18, 2002.

70. James Bennet, "Despite Violence, Settlers Survive and Spread," *New York Times,* April 28, 2002.

71. Danna Harman, "In Crisis, Israel Rallies Behind Settlers," *Christian Science Monitor*, April 26, 2002.

72. Stephen Franklin and Christine Spolar, "Tied to the Land, Settlers Vow to Stay," *Chicago Tribune*, April 30, 2002.

73. Charles Radin, "The Seeds of Conflict Sown in Settlements," *Boston Globe*, April 21, 2002.

74. David Hawkins, "Jewish Settlers an Obstacle to Achieving Peace Between Israelis and Palestinians," *CBS Evening News*, July 24, 2002.

75. Anne Garrels, "Illegal Israeli Settlements Continue to Spring Up on Palestinian Lands," NPR/*All Things Considered*, August 28, 2002.

76. Tim Golden, "Dreams of Land Collide as Israeli Settlers Grow in Numbers," *New York Times*, July 3, 2002.

77. Dan Ephron and Joanna Chen, "Middle East: The Sky's the Limit," *Newsweek*, May 27, 2002.

78. Daniel Williams, "Settlements Expanding Under Sharon," *Washington Post*, May 31, 2002.

79. Golden, "Dreams of Land Collide as Israeli Settlers Grow in Numbers."

80. Peter Kenyon, "Continued Expansion of Israel's West Bank Settlements," NPR/*All Things Considered*, May 29, 2002.

81. Joel Greenberg, "Israel Begins Dismantling Outposts in West Bank," *Chicago Tribune*, June 10, 2003.

82. John Kifner, "The Bush Plan: Put the Toughest Hurdles First," *New York Times*, June 8, 2003.

83. Linda Gradstein, "Israel Begins Dismantling Illegal West Bank Settlement

Outposts," NPR/*All Things Considered*, June 9, 2003; Mike Lee, "Israel Destroying Uninhabited Outposts," ABC News/*World News Tonight*, June 9, 2003.

84. Ian Fisher, "In Israeli Gesture, Tower Is Removed Near Settlement," *New York Times*, June 10, 2003; Greenberg, "Israel Begins Dismantling Outposts in West Bank"; Solomon Moore and Laura King, "Israeli Army Pulls Up Settler Outposts' Stakes," *Los Angeles Times*, June 10, 2003.

85. Glenn Frankel, "Abbas Condemns Attacks on Soldiers: Israel Dismantles Several West Bank Outposts," *Washington Post*, June 10, 2003.

86. Larry Derfner and Thomas Omestad, "Balancing Act," *U.S. News & World Report*, June 16, 2003.

87. Peter Kenyon, "Prospect of Israeli Withdrawal Alarms Israeli Settlers in Gaza," NPR/*All Things Considered*, June 26, 2003.

88. Greta Van Susteren, "Interview with Former Presidential Adviser David Gergen," Fox News/*Fox on the Record with Greta Van Susteren*, June 19, 2003.

89. Joshua Hammer, "Good Fences Make . . . ," *Newsweek*, June 9, 2003.

90. Nichole Gaouette, "Mideast Road Map Hits Impasse," *Christian Science Monitor*, July 31, 2003.

91. "Israeli Army Confiscates Three Hectares in Gaza Strip," Agence France-Presse, August 2, 2003.

92. Peter Enav, "Israel to Encourage West Bank Settlement, Newspaper Reports," Associated Press, August 7, 2003.

93. Ravi Nessman, "Israel Announces Plans to Build Hundreds of New Houses in Settlements," Associated Press, October 2, 2003.

94. Ravi Nessman, "Israeli, Palestinian Security Officials Meet as U.S. Monitors Arrive in Region," Associated Press, June 14, 2003.

95. "Palestinians Need $250 Million and Three Years to Rebuild Destroyed Police Posts: Security Chief," Associated Press, August 9, 2003.

96. Greg Myre and Steven Weisman, "Israel to Build 600 Homes in 3 Settlements: U.S. Officials Are Critical," *New York Times*, October 3, 2003.

97. Salim Muwakkil, "Biased Coverage Prolongs Conflict," *Chicago Tribune*, April 23, 2001.

98. Edward Said, "American Zionism—The Real Problem (3)," *Al-Ahram Weekly Online*, November 2–8, 2000.

99. Ephron and Chen, "Middle East: The Sky's the Limit."

100. Samantha Shapiro, "The Unsettlers," *New York Times Magazine*, February 16, 2003.

101. Alex Fishman, "Kiryat Arba to Revert in the Future to Palestinian Sovereignty" (in Hebrew), *Yediot Aharonot*/ "Yom Shishi," May 19, 2000.

102. Zuhair Sabbagh, "The Impact of Israeli Settlement on the Permanent Status Negotiations" (paper presented at the international seminar "1991–2000: The Palestinian-Israeli Peace Process," sponsored by the Arab Cause Solidarity Committee, Madrid, Spain, September 2000).

103. Jeff Halper, "The 94 Percent Solution: A Matrix of Control," *Middle East Report*, no. 216 (fall 2000): 15.

104. Robert Malley, "Fictions About the Failure at Camp David," *New York Times*, July 8, 2001.

105. Hussein Agha and Robert Malley, "Camp David: The Tragedy of Errors," *New York Review of Books*, August 9, 2001.

106. Deborah Sontag, "Quest for Mideast Peace: How and Why It Failed," *New York Times*, July 26, 2001.

107. The Palestine National Council reaffirmed Palestinian recognition of Israel in December 1998 when, at a meeting in Gaza attended by President Clinton, it voted to nullify the section of the PLO Charter calling for the destruction of the State of Israel.

108. Agha and Malley, "Camp David: Tragedy of Errors."

109. Akiva Eldar, "What Went Wrong at Camp David—The Official PLO Version," *Haaretz*, July 24, 2001.

110. Negotiations Affairs Department of the PLO, "Israel's Pre-emption of a Viable Two State Solution," http://www.nad-plo.org (accessed October 19, 2002).

111. Ibid.

112. Molly Moore, "On Remote Hilltops, Israelis Broaden Settlements," *Washington Post*, December 8, 2002.

113. Shapiro, "Unsettlers."

114. "Powell Says Future Palestinian State Must Be 'Real State,' Not 'Diced' Up by Israeli Settlements," Associated Press, January 26, 2003; "Powell Presses Israel for a 'Real' Palestinian State," Reuters, January 26, 2003.

115. Derfner, "Unsettled Times."

116. Ilene Prusher, "A New Boost for Gaza Pullout," *Christian Science Monitor*, June 16, 2004.

117. Amiram Cohen, "Agriculture Minister Plans Jordan Valley Settlement Expansion," *Haaretz*, September 8, 2004.

118. Ari Shavit, "The Big Freeze," *Haaretz*, October 8, 2004.

119. Tom Raum, "Bush Calls for 'Contiguous' Palestinian State," Associated Press, February 21, 2005.

120. William Douglas, "Bush Promises $50 Million in Aid to Palestinian Authority," Associated Press, May 27, 2005.

121. Joel Brinkley and Steven R. Weisman, "Rice Urges Israel and Palestinians to Sustain Momentum," *New York Times*, August 18, 2005.

122. Arthur Max, "New Figures Show Jewish Population Is Expanding Rapidly in the West Bank," Associated Press, August 25, 2005.

123. Ibid.

124. Ratios are based on population estimates at the time of Israel's withdrawal from Gaza: Jewish population of Israel (including West Bank settlers and residents of areas of Jerusalem occupied by Israel since 1967), 5.3 million; Arab population

of Israel, 1.4 million; Palestinian population of West Bank, 2.2 million; Palestinian population of Gaza, 1.3 million.

125. Greg Myre, "The Suburban Lure of the West Bank," *New York Times*, June 20, 2004.

4. APEX OF THE SPIRAL

Epigraph. Quoted in *Jerusalem Post*, June 20, 2002.

1. Israel Ministry of Foreign Affairs, "Passover Suicide Bombing at Park Hotel in Netanya, March 27, 2002," http://www.mfa.gov.il.

2. "U.S. Envoy to Resume Truce Talks with Israelis, Palestinians," Agence France-Presse, March 24, 2002.

3. "Chronology of Suicide Bombings in Israel," *Haaretz*, October 6, 2002.

4. Ibid.

5. "European Donors Estimate Damage from Israeli Incursion at Dlrs 361 Million," Associated Press, May 15, 2002.

6. "Chronology of Suicide Bombings in Israel." The report also noted two other suicide bombings in the West Bank during this period in which only the suicide bombers were killed and no one was injured.

7. Keith Miller, "Worst Suicide Bombing Yet Takes Place at Jewish Dinner During Passover," *NBC Nightly News*, March 27, 2002.

8. "Mayor Miriam Fireberg of Netanya, Israel, Discusses the Suicide Bombing That Occurred in Her Town," CBS News/ *The Early Show*, March 28, 2002.

9. Larry Kaplow, "Victim: Passover Attack 'Like the 10 Plagues,'" *Atlanta Journal-Constitution*, March 29, 2002.

10. Martin Himel, "Living in Fear," PBS/ *The NewsHour with Jim Lehrer*, April 9, 2002.

11. Joel Brinkley, "Mideast Turmoil: The Bereaved; Israelis Mourn Their Dead in Long Search for Solace," *New York Times*, April 19, 2002.

12. Anna Badkhen, "Families Shattered by Bombs: Some Parents Seek Peace, Others Revenge After Children Killed, Maimed," *San Francisco Chronicle*, April 29, 2002.

13. A year earlier, on May 3, 2001, *Boston Globe* correspondent Charles Sennott reported that an estimated 13,000 Palestinians had been injured by Israeli forces in the seven months since the second intifada began in September 2000.

14. Uli Schmetzer, "Suicide Attack Survivors Maimed, Scarred, Fearful," *Chicago Tribune*, May 9, 2002.

15. Clyde Mark, "Palestinians and Middle East Peace: Issues for the United States," Congressional Research Service, Library of Congress, July 8, 2004, p. 12.

16. John Kifner, "In Israel, Press Kits Roll Out with Tanks," *New York Times*, March 30, 2002.

17. Joel Brinkley with Todd Purdum, "Palestinian Goal of Statehood vs. Israeli Aim of Cease-Fire," *New York Times*, March 31, 2002.

18. Herb Keinon and Gil Hoffman, "Sharon to Netanyahu: Be the Great Explainer," *Jerusalem Post*, April 2, 2002.

19. Gil Hoffman, "Netanyahu, Barak to Aid PR Effort," *Jerusalem Post*, April 5, 2002.

20. Mark Jurkowitz, "News Outlets Decry Israel's Coverage Limit," *Boston Globe*, April 3, 2002.

21. David Shaw, "From Jewish Outlook, Media Are Another Enemy," *Los Angeles Times*, April 28, 2002.

22. Serge Schmemann, "Palestinians Say Israeli Aim Was to Destroy Framework, from Archives to Hard Drives," *New York Times*, April 16, 2002.

23. Gillian Findlay, "Israel Destroys Palestinian Ministry of Education in Efforts to Root Out Terrorism," ABC News/*World News Tonight*, April 17, 2002.

24. Ibid.

25. Doug Struck, "A School System Without Memory: Palestinian Records, Computer Gear Seized in Israeli Raids," *Washington Post*, April 20, 2002.

26. Danna Harman, "Israel Assesses the Damage," *Christian Science Monitor*, April 19, 2002.

27. Edward A. Gargan, "West Bank Wasteland: Israeli Troops Leave Palestinians' Land Bereft of Services," *Newsday*, April 23, 2002

28. Christine Spolar, "Palestinian Officials Shake Heads over Ramallah Damage," *Chicago Tribune*, April 22, 2002.

29. Gargan, "West Bank Wasteland."

30. Doug Struck, "Israeli Troops Pull Out from 2 Major Cities: Soldiers Are Accused of Looting," *Washington Post*, April 22, 2002.

31. Bill Glauber, "Ramallah Emerges to Assess Damage: Israeli Soldiers Went Too Far, Palestinians Say as They Begin Cleanup," *Baltimore Sun*, April 22, 2002.

32. Christiane Amanpour, "U.N. Appoints Mission to Discover What Happened in Jenin . . ." CNN/*NewsNight with Aaron Brown*, April 22, 2002.

33. Glauber, "Ramallah Emerges to Assess Damage."

34. Linda Gradstein, "Destruction of Palestinian Property During Three-Week Israeli Incursion," NPR/*Morning Edition*, April 22, 2002.

35. David Rohde, "Palestinians Say They Are Too Angry to Celebrate the Israeli Withdrawal," *New York Times*, April 22, 2002.

36. Joel Greenberg, "In All Corners of Ramallah, Big Footprints of Israel Army," *New York Times*, April 23, 2002.

37. Glauber, "Ramallah Emerges to Assess Damage."

38. Struck, "Israeli Troops Pull Out from 2 Major Cities."

39. Ted Koppel, "The Holy Land: The Adversaries; Interviews with Yasser Arafat and Ariel Sharon," ABC News/*Nightline*, May 1, 2002.

40. Ted Koppel, "Images of War, War of Images: Israel and Palestine Strive to Show Positive Image [*sic*] to Outside World," ABC News/*Nightline*, May 2, 2002.

41. "Political Headlines," Fox News/*Fox Special Report with Brit Hume*, May 2, 2002.

42. Peter Kenyon, "What's Next for the Middle East," NPR/*Talk of the Nation*, May 2, 2002; John Yang, "Siege Continues at Church of Nativity in Bethlehem," ABC News/*World News Tonight*, May 2, 2002.

43. T. Christian Miller, "Palestinians Inside Church Torn Between Loyalty, Fear," *Los Angeles Times*, May 2, 2002; Walter Rodgers, "Interview with Charles Sennott of 'The Boston Globe,'" CNN/*CNN Live Today*, May 2, 2002.

44. Tracy Wilkinson and Mary Curtius, "Arafat Tours Ruins: Church Siege Goes On," *Los Angeles Times*, May 3, 2002; Robert Gee, "Free at Last, Arafat Cheered by Crowds," *Atlanta Journal-Constitution*, May 3, 2002.

45. C. J. Chivers, "A Death and a Breach by Activists as Bethlehem Siege Persists," *New York Times*, May 3, 2002.

46. Doug Struck, "Focus Turns to Bethlehem Shrine," *Washington Post*, May 3, 2002.

47. Scott Anderson, "An Impossible Occupation," *New York Times Magazine*, May 12, 2002.

48. Dan Harris, "Israeli Defense Forces Search for Terrorist in Bethlehem," ABC News/*World News Tonight*, June 2, 2002.

49. Joshua Hammer, "A Shark Hunt in the Night," *Newsweek*, July 15, 2002.

50. Anderson, "Impossible Occupation."

51. Amira Hass, "Someone Even Managed to Defecate into the Photocopier," *Haaretz*, May 6, 2004.

52. Laurie Copans, "Six Israeli Soldiers Indicted on Charges of Stealing Palestinian Property, Money," Associated Press, May 8, 2002.

53. "Five Israeli Soldiers Sent to Prison for Looting, Vandalizing Palestinian Property," Associated Press, May 27, 2002.

54. "Former IDF Soldier Says Army Lax on Looters," Reuters (carried on the English-language Web site of *Haaretz*), August 25, 2002.

55. Adam Gregerman of New York City, letter to the editor, *New York Times Magazine*, May 26, 2002.

56. Robby Ameen of New York City, letter to the editor, *New York Times Magazine*, May 26, 2002.

57. Daniel Williams, "Attacks Strip Away Foundation of Palestinian Rule," *Washington Post*, April 5, 2002.

58. Amanpour, "U.N. Appoints Mission to Discover What Happened in Jenin. . . ."

59. "PLO Legal Advisor Michael Tarazi and Israeli Consul General Alon Pinkas Discuss Documents Seized That Allegedly Link Yasser Arafat to Suicide Bombers," CNBC/*Hardball with Chris Matthews*, April 2, 2002.

60. "Text of Bush Remarks on Mideast," Associated Press, April 4, 2002.

61. Anne E. Kornblut, "Bush's Call on Mideast: 'Enough,'" *Boston Globe*, April 5, 2002.

62. Lee Hockstader, "Offensive Widens Despite U.S. Plea: Troops Battle in Hebron, Refugee Camp," *Washington Post*, April 5, 2002.

63. Douglas Frantz, "Israel Says Papers Prove Arafat Paid Terrorists," *New York Times*, April 5, 2002.

64. Hockstader, "Offensive Widens Despite U.S. Plea."

65. Don Melvin, "Crisis in the Middle East: No Turning Back Now, Israel Asserts," *Atlanta Journal-Constitution*, April 5, 2002.

66. Martin Fletcher, "Documents Captured by Israelis Show Arafat Connected to Suicide Bombings," *NBC Nightly News*, April 19, 2002.

67. Lee Hockstader, "Israel Sets Out Charges Arafat Supported Terror," *Washington Post*, May 6, 2002.

68. David Rhode, "Israelis Release More Documents Accusing Arafat of Terror," *New York Times*, May 6, 2002.

69. Deborah Blachor and Corky Siemaszko, "Sharon Offers Link of Arafat and Terror; Will Give Bush Notes of Correspondence," *Daily News*, May 6, 2002.

70. Hockstader, "Israel Sets Out Charges Arafat Supported Terror."

71. Steve Weizman, "Will Church of Nativity Door Open? Does Ariel Sharon Have Smoking Gun?" CNN/*Wolf Blitzer Reports*, May 6, 2002.

72. Gillian Findlay, "Ariel Sharon Brings Documents to Washington as Part of Campaign to Discredit Palestinian President Yasser Arafat," ABC News/*World News Tonight*, May 6, 2002.

73. "Israel Accuses Saudis of Helping in Palestinian Terror Attacks," Associated Press, May 6, 2002.

74. Weizman, "Will Church of Nativity Door Open?"

75. David Ensor, "Israel Trying to Convince Bush Arafat's Behind Suicide Bombings," CNN/*Daybreak*, May 8, 2002.

76. Ronen Bergman, "The Ra'is Will Sign and Give His Approval," *Yediot Aharonot*, July 12, 2002 (in Hebrew; English-language translation provided to journalists by the Israel Government Press Office on July 30, 2002).

77. Ensor, "Israel Trying to Convince Bush Arafat's Behind Suicide Bombings."

78. Daniel Sobelman, "The Lowdown on Israel's Lowdown on Arafat," *Haaretz*, May 7, 2002.

79. Bergman, "The Ra'is Will Sign and Give His Approval."

80. Todd Purdum, "State Dept. Report Investigating Arafat's Links to Terror Is at Odds with Israeli Claims," *New York Times*, May 17, 2002.

81. Bergman, "The Ra'is Will Sign and Give His Approval."

82. Greer Fay Cashman, "Army Intelligence Expert Warns of Nuclear-Equipped Iran," *Jerusalem Post*, June 20, 2002.

83. Barry Schweid, "Bush Calls for Arafat's Removal," Associated Press, June 24, 2002.

84. Cashman, "Army Intelligence Expert Warns of Nuclear-Equipped Iran."

85. Greer Fay Cashman, "Judy Shoots from the Hip Again/Grapevine," *Jerusalem Post*, June 21, 2002.

86. Lesley Stahl, "The Arafat Papers," CBS News/*60 Minutes*, September 29, 2002.

87. This characterization is based on an archival search of the Israeli dailies *Haaretz, Maariv, Yediot Aharonot,* and the *Jerusalem Post* from April through December 2002, as well as a LexisNexis search of U.S. print and broadcast outlets for the same time frame.

88. An interview with Fuad Shubaki quoted the Palestinian Authority's chief financial officer as saying: "I don't deny that I did visit Iraq, Libya and Yemen as part of my job to pay members of our armed forces and PLO workers who are still in these countries. We have many embassies all over the world" (Khaled Abu Toameh, "Shubaki to 'Post': Arafat Abandoned Me: 'Karine A' Paymaster Speaks from Jericho Jail for First Time," *Jerusalem Post*, August 28, 2002). However, the *Post* story went on to report: "Shubaki said the fact that he visited Iraq and Libya several times is not significant, because the two countries were never involved in sending weapons to the Palestinian areas."

A *Haaretz* news report stated: "Iraq has stepped up its attempts to move weapons and financial aid to the Palestinian Authority areas, in an effort to resume terror attacks against Israel. Baghdad's plan is to refocus international attention on the Israeli-Arab conflict and hope for a second front in case of a U.S. attack against Baghdad. The defense establishment has spotted new signs of attempted Iraqi weapons smuggling to the West Bank and Gaza, including from Jordan" (Oren Amir, "Iraq Steps Up Arms, Money Transfer to Palestinians," *Haaretz*, September 13, 2002). However, the declarative assertion and vague characterization carried no attribution, and such a second front never materialized after the start of the U.S. war in Iraq.

Palestinian-Iraqi ties also appeared to be predicated on common popular political sentiment. The *Haaretz* report continued: "The Iraqi-backed Arab Liberation Front yesterday held a rally in Gaza where financial grants from Saddam Hussein were handed out to 32 families of Palestinian dead. The rally included an appearance by Hamas spiritual leader Sheikh Ahmad Yassin, who called for 'unity in the ranks of the resistance,' and drew a connection between Palestinian resistance to the Israeli occupation and the U.S. threats to strike at Iraq."

A later *Haaretz* report identified the Arab Liberation Front as "pro-Iraqi," noting that "Iraq has in the past two years delivered $15 million to the territories, to compensate Palestinians injured during the intifada" (Amos Harel, "Saddam's $15 Million Intifada Handouts," *Haaretz*, October 9, 2002). With no specific reference to suicide bombers or perpetrators of terror attacks, the paper reported that families of killed Palestinians generally received $10,000 each from Iraq; badly injured persons received $1,000 each; and less severely injured Palestinians received $500 each. The report identified this information as having come from an interrogation by the Israeli domestic security agency Shin Bet of a local ALF leader in the West Bank, whom the report also identified as having met with Saddam Hussein and as being an adviser to Yasser Arafat. In a vaguely attributed and unsubstantiated characterization similar to those in the *60 Minutes* piece, the report stated: "The newly gathered information about the activities of pro-Iraq organizations in the territories [the *Haaretz* report mentioned only one such organization, the ALF] establishes that Saddam's regime has a clear intention to strengthen its support of Palestinian terror, Israeli officials contend."

An Associated Press advance story on the *60 Minutes* broadcast reported: "CBS said Israeli documents indicated that Arafat has supplied money to some members of [Mohammed] Abbas' Palestine Liberation Front in the West Bank, though it was not immediately clear if alleged recipients of the funds were involved in guerrilla activity. The group also was long involved in internal Palestinian politics" (Laurie Copans, "Iraq Accused of Palestinian Terror," Associated Press, September 28, 2002).

89. Copans, "Iraq Accused of Palestinian Terror." A *Jerusalem Post* column indicated that the arrests had taken place in August 2003 (Caroline Glick, "The Baghdad-Ramallah Axis," *Jerusalem Post*, October 11, 2002).

90. Daniel Sobelman, "The Lowdown on Israel's Lowdown on Arafat," *Haaretz*, May 7, 2002.

91. Miriam Fox and Hanan Shlein, "The Program '60 Minutes' Reveals the 'Axis of Evil' in the Middle East: Iraq and Iran in the Service of Arafat" (in Hebrew), *Maariv*, September 29, 2002.

92. This appears to be a reference to the State Department's annual report "Patterns of Global Terrorism."

93. Transcript of State Department briefing, September 30, 2002, Federal Information and News Dispatch, Inc.

94. This is indicated by a search of newspaper and newsmagazine reports and television transcripts in the LexisNexis database, which does not include transcripts of talk-radio broadcasts.

95. O'Reilly referred to the *60 Minutes* report twice on October 3, 2002, in the "Top Story" and "Impact" segments of *The O'Reilly Factor*; on October 7 in the "Impact" segment of the program; and on October 10 in the "FACTOR Follow-Up" segment.

96. Fox News/*The O'Reilly Factor*, December 6, 2002; January 23, 2002; March 18, 2003.

97. Greg Myre, "Israel's Case Against Arafat," *New York Times*, September 21, 2003.

98. Footage of Powell's remarks to the House International Relations Committee is included in an interview with Yasser Arafat by Mike Wallace, CBS News/*60 Minutes*, February 10, 2002.

99. "Battle for the Holy Land," PBS/*Frontline*, program no. 2015, originally aired April 4, 2002.

100. Steven Feuerstein of Chicago, "Watching Israel," letter to the editor, *Chicago Tribune*, May 2, 2002.

5. THE WAR AT HOME

1. Leonore R. Siegelman, "Did The Washington Post Tell It? An Analysis of the News Coverage of Lebanon / Summer, 1982," Louis D. Brandeis District, Zionist Organization of America, 1983, p. 70.

2. In 2002, Ahmed Bouzid, president of the pro-Palestinian Palestine Media Watch, told *Newsday*: "Most of the Arabs and Muslims are recent immigrants and they are not in the tradition of writing letters. They are smart, articulate and educated but not heard" (quoted in Rita Ciolli, "An Electronic Eye: Web Sites Evolve into Media Monitor," *Newsday*, May 29, 2002).

The *Boston Globe* reported that CAMERA, the leading pro-Israel media watchdog group in the United States, had annual revenues of $1.8 million from dues and contributions, employed about twenty staffers, served about forty thousand dues-paying members, and had recently hired a staffer to direct the "congressional dimension" of its activity (Mark Jurkowitz, "Blaming the Messenger: When the Pro-Israeli Group Camera Sees News from the Middle East That It Deems Unfair or Wrong, It Targets the Media—and Doesn't Let Go," *Boston Globe*, February 9, 2003).

The *American Journalism Review* reported that pro-Israel Web sites "are better staffed and funded" than their pro-Palestinian counterparts, and generate "about 10 times as much mail" in protest of media coverage of the conflict as do pro-Arab sites (Barbara Matusow, "Caught in the Crossfire," *American Journalism Review* 26, no. 3 [June–July 2004]).

3. David Shaw, "The Middle East: From Jewish Outlook, Media Are Another Enemy," *Los Angeles Times*, April 28, 2002.

4. Felicity Barringer, "Mideast Turmoil: The News Outlets; Some U.S. Backers of Israel Boycott Dailies over Mideast Coverage That They Deplore," *New York Times*, May 23, 2002.

5. Tim Jones, "Pro-Israel Groups Take Aim at U.S. News Media," *Chicago Tribune*, May 26, 2002.

6. Ciolli, "Electronic Eye."

7. Barringer, "Mideast Turmoil."

8. Terence Smith, "Pressure Points," PBS/ *The NewsHour with Jim Lehrer*, July 3, 2002.

9. Jones, "Pro-Israel Groups Take Aim at U.S. News Media."

10. Nathan Gutman, "Neutrality Isn't Enough for American Jews," *Haaretz*, August 18, 2002.

11. Nat Ives, "A TV Campaign Is Intended to Gain Support for Israel, But Not Everyone Likes It," *New York Times*, October 1, 2002.

12. "For the Record" (interview with Edward Said), *Palestine Report*, August 30, 2001.

13. Daniel Williams, "Conflict Deepens Despair for Palestinians in Gaza," *Washington Post*, August 20, 2001; Michael Slackman, "Israel Boosts Its Policy of Retaliation," *Los Angeles Times*, August 15, 2001; Tracy Wilkinson, "Another Kind of Intifada," *Los Angeles Times*, August 22, 2001; Clyde Haberman, "For Palestinians a Daily, Dirty Obstacle Course," *New York Times*, August 21, 2001; Cameron Barr, "Palestinian Morale Rises with Death Toll," *Christian Science Monitor*, August 27, 2001.

14. Lee Hockstader, "Reports of Torture by Israelis Emerge," *Washington Post*, August 18, 2001; "Israeli's Death Brings Grief to Palestinians," *Washington Post*, August 31, 2001; and "A Cycle of Death in West Bank Town," *Washington Post*, September 7, 2001.

15. Amira Hass, "Separate and Unequal on the West Bank," *New York Times*, September 2, 2001.

16. Lee Hockstader, "Palestinians Find Heroes in Hamas," *Washington Post*, August 11, 2001; Daniel Williams, "Where Palestinian Martyrs Are Groomed," *Washington Post*, August 15, 2001; Clyde Haberman, "City Israel Raided Is Oddly Jubilant," *New York Times*, August 15, 2001; Vivienne Walt, "Dying for a Cause," *Newsday*, August 20, 2001; E. A. Torriero, "No Room for Mistakes," *Chicago Tribune*, August 24, 2001; Mary Curtius, "Anguish, Not Pride, Fills Parents of Suicide Bomber," *Los Angeles Times*, August 26, 2001; Hugh Dellios, "His Father's Son: The Making of a Bomber," *Chicago Tribune*, August 27, 2001.

17. Lee Hockstader, "The Suicide Bomber Took Malki's Life, But Not Our Convictions," *Washington Post*, August 19, 2001.

18. Steuard Jensen of Chicago, "Failed Terror," letter to the editor, *Chicago Tribune*, August 30, 2001.

19. Ruth Abrams of Toronto, "Glamorizing Terror," letter to the editor, *Chicago Tribune*, September 1, 2001.

20. Harvey J. Barnett of Highland Park, Ill., "Tribune Bias," letter to the editor, *Chicago Tribune*, September 1, 2001.

21. Robert B. Footlik of Chicago, "All Are at Risk," letter to the editor, *Chicago Tribune*, September 11, 2001.

22. Joel Greenberg, "2 Girls, Divided by War, Joined in Carnage," *New York Times*, April 5, 2002.

23. Joshua Hammer, "How Two Lives Met in Death," *Newsweek*, April 15, 2002.

24. "Mail Call and Corrections," letters to the editor, *Newsweek*, April 29, 2002.

25. Lillian Swanson, "Word by Word and Story by Story, Mideast Coverage Is Under Scrutiny," *Philadelphia Inquirer*, July 15, 2002.

26. John F. Burns, "The Attacker: Bomber Left Her Family with a Smile and a Lie," *New York Times*, October 7, 2003.

27. John F. Burns, "Block by Block: A War-Weary People Reach Out in Pain—and Hope," *New York Times*, October 12, 2003.

28. Michael Getler (ombudsman's columns), "Middle East Coverage," *Washington Post*, July 29, 2001; "Readers and Reporters—Who's Biased?" *Washington Post*,

March 24, 2002; "The Shadow of the Bombers," *Washington Post*, April 7, 2002; "Caught in the Crossfire," *Washington Post*, May 5, 2002; "Unasked Questions," *Washington Post*, August 11, 2002; and "Plugging the Holes," *Washington Post*, July 6, 2003.

29. Mark Jurkowitz, "News Outlets Pressed on Bias in Mideast Coverage," *Boston Globe*, June 26, 2002.

30. Jim Rutenberg, "CNN Navigates Raw Emotions in Its Coverage from Israel," *New York Times*, July 1, 2002.

31. Oliver Burkeman, "Ted's Tears," *Guardian*, June 18, 2002.

32. Howard Kurtz, "Turner's Terrorism Comments Criticized," *Washington Post*, June 19, 2002.

33. Ibid.

34. "CNN News Chief in Israel on Damage-Control Visit," Reuters, June 21, 2002.

35. *CNN Wolf Blitzer Reports*, June 24, 2002; "An Intimate Look at the Victims of Mideast Terrorism," *CNN Live Today*, June 25, 2002; "Profile of Victims of Terror," *CNN Live Today*, June 26, 2002; "Netanya Has Been Hard Hit by Suicide Attacks," *CNN Live Today*, June. 27, 2002.

36. John Vause, "Israeli Bus Drivers Absorb Shock of Attacks," CNN.com, June 26, 2002; "Terror Takes Enormous Toll on Israel," CNN.com, June 28, 2002; John Vause, "Israeli Youth: 'I Don't Want to Die Today,'" CNN.com, June 28, 2002; John Vause, "Paramedic: 'It Is Very Hard to Work,'" CNN.com, June 28, 2002.

37. *CNN Wolf Blitzer Reports*, June 24, 2002.

38. Rutenberg, "CNN Navigates Raw Emotions in Its Coverage from Israel."

39. Robert Fisk, "CNN Caves In to Israel on Reports About Settlers," *Independent*, September 3, 2001.

40. Interviews with fifteen Jerusalem-based correspondents who had reported the Israeli-Palestinian story for thirteen major U.S. news organizations from 1985 to 2002 were conducted in 2003 and 2004; see chapter 6.

41. Barbie Zelizer, David Park, and David Gudelunas, "How Bias Shapes the News: Challenging *The New York Times'* Status as a Newspaper of Record on the Middle East," *Journalism: Theory, Practice and Criticism* 3, no. 3 (December 2002): 283–307.

42. Ibid., p. 290.

43. Ibid.

44. Ibid., pp. 295–96

45. Ibid., p. 297.

46. Ibid., pp. 299–300.

47. John McManus, "The Newsworthiness of Death: Why Did The Mercury News and Associated Press Give Israeli Deaths Greater Prominence than Palestinian in the Middle East Conflict?" *Grade the News*, Stanford University, www.stanford.edu/group/gradethenews/pages/middleeast.htm (December 18, 2003).

48. Denis H. Wu, Judith Sylvester, and John Maxwell Hamilton, "Newspaper

Provides Balance in Palestinian/Israeli Reports," *Newspaper Research Journal* 23, nos. 2–3 (spring–summer 2002): 6–17.

49. Ibid., p. 12.

50. Ibid.

51. Greg Philo and Mike Berry, *Bad News from Israel* (London: Pluto Press / Glasgow University Media Group, 2004).

52. Ibid., pp. 250–51.

53. Ibid., p. 259.

54. Ibid., pp. 251, 252.

55. Ibid., p. 250.

56. Ibid., p. 259.

57. Ibid., p. 258.

58. Ibid., pp. 258–59.

59. John J. Mearsheimer and Stephen M. Walt, "The Israel Lobby and U.S. Foreign Policy," March 2006, John F. Kennedy School of Government, Harvard University, p. 1, http://ksgnotes1.harvard.edu/Research/wpaper.nsf/rwp/RWP06–011.

60. Ibid., p. 14.

61. Ibid., p. 15.

62. Ibid., p. 5.

63. Ibid., p. 6.

64. Ibid., p. 18.

65. Ibid., pp. 20, 16–17.

66. Ibid., p. 21.

67. Ibid., p. 30.

68. Ibid., pp. 10, 11.

69. Ibid., p. 11.

70. Ibid, pp. 10, 13.

71. Ibid., p. 14.

72. Ibid., p. 16.

73. Ibid., p. 24.

74. Ibid., pp. 31–32.

75. Ibid., p. 42.

76. Noam Chomsky, "The Israel Lobby?" *Znet*, March 28, 2006, http://www.zmag.org.

77. Joseph Massad, "Blaming the Lobby," *Al-Ahram Weekly*, no. 787, March 23–29, 2006.

78. Glenn Frankel, "A Beautiful Friendship? In Search of the Truth About the Israel Lobby's Influence on Washington," *Washington Post*, July 16, 2006.

79. Charles A. Radin, "'Israel Lobby' Critique Roils Academe: Some Assail Paper by a Harvard Dean," *Boston Globe*, March 29, 2006; "Of Israel, Harvard and David Duke," *Outlook* section (no byline), *Washington Post*, March 26, 2006; Michael Powell, "Academic Paper Stirs Debate: Report on Effect of Israel Lobby

Distorts History, Critics Say," *Washington Post*, April 3, 2006; Richard Beeston, "Harvard Disowns Anti-Jew Report," *Weekend Australian*, March 31, 2006.

80. Searches of the LexisNexis and ProQuest databases and Google showed that the following newspapers published news or feature pieces (versus editorials and columns) on "The Israel Lobby" from mid-March through early April 2006: *Australian* (Australia); *Independent, Financial Times, Guardian,* and *Observer* (England); *South China Morning Post* (Hong Kong); *New Straits Times* (Malaysia); and *Haaretz* and *Jerusalem Post* (Israel).

81. Jay Lindsay, "Academics' Paper on 'Israel Lobby' Blasted," Associated Press, April 5, 2006.

82. CNN/*Lou Dobbs Tonight*, March 20, 2006.

83. John Mearsheimer and Stephen Walt, "The Israel Lobby," *London Review of Books*, March 23, 2006, www.lrb.co.uk/v28/no6/print/mear01_.html.

84. "America and Israel: Shutting Down Debate Is Bad for the U.S. and Bad for Israelis" (editorial), *Financial Times* (London), April 1, 2006.

85. Radin, "'Israel Lobby' Critique Roils Academe."

86. Powell, "Academic Paper Stirs Debate."

87. Ron Grossman, "2 Profs Spark Political Firestorm," *Chicago Tribune*, April 6, 2006.

88. Ori Nir, "Professor Says American Publisher Turned Him Down," *Forward*, March 24, 2006.

89. Fox News Network/*WSJ Editorial Report*, March 25, 2006.

90. Jeff Jacoby, "A Nation Like Ours," *Boston Globe*, March 29, 2006.

91. Geoffrey Wheatcroft, "Most Favored Nation," *Boston Globe*, April 2, 2006.

92. "'The Lobby': Post and Ripostes," *Boston Globe*, April 2, 2006.

93. "Of Israel, Harvard and David Duke."

94. Eliot A. Cohen, "Yes, It's Anti-Semitic," *Washington Post*, April 5, 2006.

95. Nicholas Goldberg, "Who's Afraid of the 'Israel Lobby'?" *Los Angeles Times*, March 26, 2006.

96. Max Boot, "Policy Analysis—Paranoid Style," *Los Angeles Times*, March 29, 2006.

97. Tom Regan, "Terrorism & Security: More Debate over Report on Israel's Influence in U.S.," CSMonitor.com, April 6, 2006. On March 30 the *Monitor* gave a nod to the Mearsheimer-Walt monograph, citing only a single paragraph from it in an editorial urging the Bush administration "to intervene boldly" with the Palestinians and Israel alike following their respective parliamentary elections ("Bush must now focus on the West Bank").

98. "Academic Israeli Path Goes Astray" (editorial), *Boston Herald*, March 26, 2006; "Claim That Jewish Cabal Runs U.S. Government Is Rubbish" (editorial), *Chicago Sun-Times*, March 27, 2006.

99. David Gergen, "An Unfair Attack," *U.S. News & World Report*, April 3, 2006.

100. James Klurfeld, "'Israeli Lobby' Didn't Con Bush into Invading Iraq," *Newsday*, April 7, 2006.

101. Ori Nir, "Scholars' Attack on Pro-Israel Lobby Met with Silence," *Forward*, March 24, 2006.

102. Ibid.

103. Mark Mazower, "When the Logic of Vigilance Undermines Freedom of Speech," *Financial Times* (London), April 4, 2006.

104. Julian Borger, "U.S. Professors Accused of Being Liars and Bigots over Essay on Pro-Israel Lobby," *Guardian*, March 31, 2006.

105. Ben Lynfield, "Israel's Doves and Hawks Have Plenty to Say About Paper's Motivation and Veracity," *South China Morning Post*, April 1, 2006.

106. Beeston, "Harvard Disowns Anti-Jew Report."

107. W. Scott Thompson, "Looking Anew at Israel Through Clear Lenses," *New Straits Times*, March 20, 2006.

108. Daniel Levy, "So Pro-Israel That It Hurts," *Haaretz*, March 23, 2006.

109. "America and Israel: Shutting Down Debate Is Bad for the U.S. and Bad for Israelis."

6. IN THE FIELD

1. The interviews were conducted as follows and denote the correspondents' news organizations at the time they reported the Israeli-Palestinian story: Robert Ruby, *Baltimore Sun*, telephone, November 20, 2003; George Moffett, *Christian Science Monitor*, Elsa, Ill., December 19, 2003; Tim Phelps, *Newsday*, Washington, D.C., December 12, 2003; Carol Morello, *Philadelphia Inquirer*, Washington, D.C., December 12, 2003; Clyde Haberman, *New York Times*, New York City, January 13, 2004; Ethan Bronner, *Boston Globe*, New York City, January 13, 2004; Storer Rowley, *Chicago Tribune*, Evanston, Ill., January 24, 2004; Barton Gellman, *Washington Post*, New York City, January 13, 2004; Ann LoLordo, *Baltimore Sun*, Baltimore, Md., December 11, 2003; Deborah Horan, *Houston Chronicle*, Chicago, Ill., February 1, 2004; Dan Klaidman, *Newsweek*, telephone, February 12, 2004; Gillian Findlay, ABC News, telephone, February 16, 2004; Chris Hedges, *New York Times* and *Dallas Morning News*, Princeton, N.J., January 14, 2004; Dean Reynolds, ABC News, Chicago, Ill., March 16, 2004; Lisa Beyer, *Time*, New York City, January 14, 2004.

2. Findlay is Canadian. At the time of this interview, she had returned to work at the Canadian Broadcasting Corporation, where she had worked before joining ABC News.

3. Findlay's report, broadcast on January 27, 2001, was introduced by anchor Aaron Brown: "Back overseas in the Middle East, peace talks ended today with rare encouraging words. The two sides say they are closer to a deal than ever, and higher-level talks may begin as soon as next week. One of the issues they must resolve is the so-called right of return, a right of tens of thousands of Palestinians to return to land that was theirs or their family's before there was a modern state of Israel. This

story is a look at one side of that issue, one family, one home, one village. Consider it that way." At the end of Findlay's report, Brown added: "Again, that is one side of a complicated story. Keep in mind that in many cases these villages are now occupied by people whose families were also refugees in the aftermath of World War II."

4. Edward Said, a professor of comparative literature at Columbia University and advocate for the Palestinian cause, died in 2003.

7. TOWARD A NEW WAY OF REPORTING THE ISRAELI-PALESTINIAN CONFLICT

1. Kathleen Christison, *Perceptions of Palestine: Their Influence on U.S. Middle East Policy* (Berkeley: University of California Press, 1999), p. 15.

2. Edith Lederer, "Israel Vows to Continue Building Barrier Despite U.N. Call to Tear It Down," Associated Press, July 21, 2004.

3. Ramit Plushnick-Masti, "Israeli [*sic*] Continues Building West Bank Barrier Despite U.N. Resolution Calling for Tearing It Down," Associated Press, July 21, 2004.

4. Ramit Plushnick-Masti, "Israeli Cabinet OKs Withdrawal from Gaza," Associated Press, February 20, 2005.

5. Aluf Benn, Mazal Mualem, and Amos Harel, "Cabinet Votes 17–5 in Favor of Evacuating Settlements," *Haaretz*, February 20, 2005.

6. Ethan Bronner, interview with author, New York City, January 13, 2004.

7. Barton Gellman, interview with author, New York City, January 13, 2004.

8. Stephen Zunes, "United Nations Security Council Resolutions Currently Being Violated by Countries Other than Iraq," *Foreign Policy in Focus*, October 2, 2002, www.fpif.org.

9. Five newspapers noted Zunes's findings: *Newsday* published a story on October 8 by reporter Mohamad Bazzi that was picked up the same day by the *Seattle Times*; the *Pittsburgh Post-Gazette* ran Bazzi's report on October 9. On October 20, 2002, the *Chicago Tribune* ran a *Los Angeles Times* report by Maggie Farley that referenced the Zunes study. A search of the LexisNexis database turned up no other newspaper or broadcast coverage of the study, although on October 24 the NPR program *Talk of the Nation* featured an interview with Zunes that covered similar ground.

10. "Poll Reveals Arab Views Toward U.S. Policy," United Press International, July 23, 2004.

11. Ami Eden, "9/11 Commission Finds Anger at Israel Fueling Islamic Terrorism Wave," *Forward*, July 30, 2004.

12. Rami Khouri, "Colin, Smell the Arghileh, Read the Polls," *Daily Star* (Beirut), July 29, 2004.

13. "President's Press Conference" (transcript), Federal Information and News Dispatch, Inc., March 16, 2005.

14. Salah Nasrawi, "Jordan's King Proposes Arab Summit Relations with Israel Before It Returns Arab Land Seized in 1967 Mideast War," Associated Press, March 18, 2005.

15. Salah Nasrawi, "Arab Ministers Rework Jordanian Proposal, Reaffirming Strategy of Exchanging Land for Normalization with Israel," Associated Press, March 19, 2005.

16. Salah Nasrawi, "Arab League Chief Says Arab Summit Will Not Accept Jordan's Proposal for Normalizing Relations with Israel," Associated Press, March 20, 2005.

17. Steve Weizman, "Report: Israeli Defense Minister Approves Construction of 3,500 Settler Homes in West Bank," Associated Press, March 20, 2005.

18. Gavin Rabinowitz, "U.S. Envoys Press Sharon on West Bank Settlement Construction," Associated Press, March 23, 2005.

19. Paul Richter and Tyler Marshall, "Israeli Settlement Plan 'at Odds' with U.S.," *Los Angeles Times*, March 25, 2005.

20. Salah Nasrawi, "Arab League Demands Israeli Concessions," Associated Press, March 22, 2005.

21. Barry Schweid, "Arab League Envoy Rejects U.S. Call for Relations with Israel," Associated Press, March 24, 2005.

22. David Remnick, "Checkpoint," *New Yorker*, February 7, 2005.

23. James Bennet, "The Interregnum," *New York Times Magazine*, March 13, 2005.

24. Ted Koppel and Hillary Brown, "Standing Up," ABC News/*Nightline*, December 2, 2003.

25. Steven Erlanger, "Israeli Critic of Settlements Says Financing Was Illegal," *New York Times*, March 10, 2005.

26. Bob Simon, "The Fence," CBS News/*60 Minutes*, December 21, 2003.

27. Dean Reynolds, "Complex Friendship: Espionage Between U.S. and Israel Not New," ABC News/*World News Tonight*, August 28, 2004.

28. Peter Jennings, "A Closer Look: One on One with Pervez Musharraf," ABC News/*World News Tonight*, September 20, 2004.

29. Douglas Frantz et al., "The New Face of al-Qaeda," *Los Angeles Times*, September 26, 2004.

30. Deborah Amos, "Kuwait's Culture and Support of U.S.-Led War Against Iraq," NPR/*All Things Considered*, October 20, 2004.

31. Tarek al-Issawi, "Tape Purportedly by bin Laden Deputy Calls for Attacks Against U.S., British Interests," Associated Press, October 1, 2004.

32. "Excerpts of Osama bin Laden's Video Statement," Associated Press, October 29, 2004.

33. Gillian Findlay, ABC News, telephone interview with author, February 16, 2004. For a complete text of the interview, see chapter 6.

34. Henry Siegman, "Sharon and the Future of Palestine," *New York Review of Books*, December 2, 2004. A NYRB Web link to the piece identifies Siegman as a

senior fellow on the Middle East at the Council on Foreign Relations and a former executive head of the American Jewish Congress and the Synagogue Council of America, and as having served as general secretary of the American Association for Middle East Studies.

35. "Bin Laden's Helpful Reminder," *Chicago Tribune*, October 30, 2004.

36. "From Osama Video, Unity?" *Christian Science Monitor*, November 1, 2004.

37. "Bin Laden's Message," *USA Today*, November 1, 2004.

38. Chicago Council on Foreign Relations, "Global Views 2004: American Public Opinion and Foreign Policy," October 2004, pp. 50–51.

39. Stefanija Prasnjak Harris of Mount Horeb, Wis., "U.S. Policy Sending Wrong Message," letter to the editor, *Milwaukee Journal Sentinel*, April 14, 2002.

40. Tapio Tulisaari of Park Falls, Wis., "It Seems Israelis Have Turned the Tables," letter to the editor, *Milwaukee Journal Sentinel*, April 14, 2002.

41. Jenny E. Alexander of Largo, Fla., "Holding Israel to a Different Standard," letter to the editor, *St. Petersburg Times*, April 16 2002.

42. Michelle D. Smith of Port Richey, Fla., "Unanswered Questions," letter to the editor, *St. Petersburg Times*, April 16, 2002.

43. Transcript of "Peter Jennings: Reporter," ABC News/*Primetime Live*, August 10, 2005.

44. Brent Cunningham, "Re-thinking Objectivity," *Columbia Journalism Review* 42, no. 4 (July–August 2003): 24–28.

45. Scott C. Althaus, "When News Norms Collide, Follow the Lead: New Evidence for Press Independence," *Political Communication* 20, no. 4 (October 2003): 382.

46. W. Lance Bennett, "Toward a Theory of Press-State Relations in the United States," *Journal of Communication* 40, no. 2 (spring 1990): 105.

47. Edward S. Herman and Noam Chomsky, *Manufacturing Consent: The Political Economy of the Mass Media* (New York: Pantheon Books, 2002), p. 305.

48. Robert Cox, "Social Forces, States and World Orders: Beyond International Relations Theory," *Millennium: Journal of International Studies* 10, no. 2 (1981): 129, 130.

49. Society of Professional Journalists, Code of Ethics, http://www.spj.org/ethics_code.asp.

50. Cunningham, "Re-thinking Objectivity."

51. Daniel Okrent, "Is the *New York Times* a Liberal Newspaper?" *New York Times*, July 25, 2004.

52. George Hishmeh, "Out with American Self-Censorship," gulfnews.com, August 26, 2004.

53. James Bennet, "Children Fill Ledger of Death, No Matter How, or How Many," *New York Times*, May 21, 2004.

INDEX